Victims and the Labour of Justice at the International Criminal Court

CLARENDON STUDIES IN CRIMINOLOGY

Published under the auspices of the Institute of Criminology, University of Cambridge; the Mannheim Centre, London School of Economics; and the Centre for Criminology, University of Oxford.

Recent titles in this series:

Security and Policing of Sports Mega-Events: Security, Spectacle, and Camouflage in Rio de Janeiro
Pauschinger

Character, Circumstances, and Criminal Careers: Towards a Dynamic Developmental and Life-Course Criminology
Wikstrom, Treiber, and Roman

Children in Police Custody: Adversity and Adversariality Behind Closed Doors
Bevan

Victims and Criminal Justice: A History
Cox, Shoemaker, and Shore

Rethinking Drug Laws: Theory, History, Politics
Seddon

A Precarious Life: Community and Conflict in a Deindustrialized Town
Willis

From Conflict to Modern Slavery: The Drivers and the Deterrents
Heys

Exporting the UK Policing Brand 1989–2021
Sinclair

Penality in the Underground: The IRA's Pursuit of Informers
Dudai

Assessing the Harms of Crime: A New Framework for Criminal Policy
Greenfield and Paoli

Victims and the Labour of Justice at the International Criminal Court

The Blame Cascade

Leila Ullrich

Associate Professor of Criminology, Faculty of Law, University of Oxford, St. Cross Rd, Oxford OX1 3UL, UK

OXFORD
UNIVERSITY PRESS

OXFORD
UNIVERSITY PRESS

Great Clarendon Street, Oxford, OX2 6DP,
United Kingdom

Oxford University Press is a department of the University of Oxford.
It furthers the University's objective of excellence in research, scholarship,
and education by publishing worldwide. Oxford is a registered trade mark of
Oxford University Press in the UK and in certain other countries

Published in the United States of America by Oxford University Press
198 Madison Avenue, New York, NY 10016, United States of America

British Library Cataloguing in Publication Data

Data available

Library of Congress Control Number: 2024930856

ISBN 9780198870258

DOI: 10.1093/9780191915048.001.0001

Printed and bound by
CPI Group (UK) Ltd, Croydon, CR0 4YY

Series Editor's preface

The *Clarendon Studies in Criminology series* aims to provide a forum for outstanding theoretical and empirical work in all aspects of criminology and criminal justice, broadly understood. The Editors welcome submissions from established scholars, as well as manuscripts based on excellent PhD dissertations. The Series was inaugurated in 1994, with Roger Hood as its first General Editor, following discussions between Oxford University Press and Oxford's then Centre for Criminological Research. It is edited under the auspices of three centres: The Centre for Criminology at the University of Oxford, the Institute of Criminology at the University of Cambridge, and the Mannheim Centre for Criminology at the London School of Economics. Each supplies members of the Editorial Board and, in turn, the Series General Editor or Editors.

Victims and the Labour of Justice at the International Criminal Court: The Blame Cascade by Leila Ullrich is a lively, engaged, and wide-ranging contribution to the literature on transitional justice and international criminal justice. Drawing on rich empirical material gathered between 2013 and 2019 in a range of sites, Ullrich offers an original and critical account of the international criminal court (ICC) in Kenya and Uganda with a specific focus on victim engagement. She explores how justice is conceived, how victims are defined, and who gets to decide. She also explores the form and effect of legal interventions, and their ties to wider, economic structures.

As the book's title suggests, much of this important study is concerned with the experiences of victims. But this is not typical victimology. Instead, Ullrich is interested in the symbolic, ideological and above all the material relationship between victims, courts, and justice. Victims, in her view are the product and the driving force behind the ICC. The court identifies them and thus, to some extent defines them, but the victims are not abject. Instead, in small ways and large, they sometimes challenge or disrupt the court's logic, demanding more or different treatment and outcomes.

The story Ullrich tells is a complicated one in which neither the ICC nor the nature of the justice it metes out is at all straightforward. Some victims are excluded from consideration by rules about the duration of the original atrocity, others simply find it hard to access legal hearings due to their geographical location. While the ICC engages in considerable local outreach, not everyone's case can be heard. And perhaps the court would not want to do so anyway. For, as Ullrich argues, the kinds of legal and humanitarian interventions by the ICC effectively create victims as capitalist subjects. Not only does their labour contribute to the court's legitimacy and funding, not to mention the work of surrounding NGOs, but once designated as victims by the court people are encouraged to access reparations in the Trust Fund for Victims. These reparations, Ullrich points out, no matter how welcome, maintain their victim status, rather than economic independence. They are not, in other words, supported in their claims and demands for money or land.

Through carefully selected vignettes, and an appealing and energetic writing style, Ullrich takes us to multiple sites and introduces us to a range of local people and legal practitioners, with whom we explore some of the most complicated questions facing courts and societies which are created by mass atrocities. It hardly needs to be said, that such matters seem to remain, with depressing regularity, questions that need to be aired and understood, yet rarely are. This book focuses specifically on events and sites in Kenya and Uganda, but its lessons are fare wider. We are thrilled to include in the Clarendon Studies in Criminology.

Mary Bosworth and Carolyn Hoyle
General Editors
Centre for Criminology, University of Oxford
November 2023

Preface

This book emerged from an unloved dissertation on the ICC's victim engagement that I was eager to leave behind. I realized before too long that this was not really an option in today's academia: a book is a must to get and retain your job, and I couldn't write one from scratch, but neither could I bring myself to publish *that* dissertation. I therefore decided to return to Northern Uganda in summer 2019 for further fieldwork, which gave me a different perspective on the Court's victim engagement. Partly this was because the Court's processes changed since I had completed my PhD fieldwork there in 2014. The ICC was much more active on the ground, mobilizing victims and affected communities to attend outreach and victims' meetings, watch the trial, and tell their stories. As I talked to the Court's field staff and intermediaries and observed victims, I was struck by how exhausting justice was; how much it looked like work, hard work, in fact, both for the Court's staff and for intermediaries and victims.

It is not a coincidence that I started to see justice differently. It has a great deal to do with my own political formation in the changing world I have inhabited since I started to think about international criminal justice as an undergraduate student. I became much more aware of all the labour we do in the justice industry: paid and unpaid, visible and invisible, valued and devalued. In some ways, that thinking started when I worked as an intern at the Court in 2013 and 2014: every evening I cycled home from the Court's premises in Voorburg and collapsed into my bed, slurping Chinese noodles from a take-away box, and nibbling and crumbling Marzipan chocolate on my sheets while absorbing one TV series after the other. I was unable to think or read. I wondered what it was about the job that made it so exhausting: the working hours were long but reasonable, my tasks mundane and predictable. I realized that it was something about the emotional labour of the job, the everyday management of relationships and egos, the smiling, the listening and understanding, trying to find a way of being at the Court as an intern and researcher, being seen and not seen, and making others comfortable with my presence. That work never stops and is not paid.

While I was never a gooey-eyed international criminal justice enthusiast, I was still mesmerized by the Court: I wanted to be 'there' in The Hague, at the seat of justice. Every morning I underwent the ritual of entering 'justice': waiting in the queue in front of the Court's high-rise building, passing security checks, squeezing myself through the revolving door, travelling up the elevator to the Registry's offices, where I worked. I became intrigued both with my work *for* justice and justice's work *on* me. Marxist-Feminism and Marxist ideology theory equipped me with the tools to interrogate that dual labour of justice: the former helped me understand the work we do *for* justice, the latter the work justice does *on* us.

Rethinking justice as labour then raised new questions. What are the different forms of labour involved, how are they valued and divided, who does the labour of justice, and what is its product? I increasingly came to see that victims in the Global South are both the producers and the products of that labour: they labour to receive justice and, in doing so, gradually become sucked into the precarious rhythm and logic of global capitalist relations: up and down, included and excluded, forwards and backwards, attracted and repelled.

Then the pandemic hit in March 2020, and made all that labour politically visible in a new and visceral way: the essential work that continued to be done in hospitals and nursing homes, the well-paid office work that suddenly looked redundant, and the caring labour at home that became even more intense. The theory came alive for me, and this book is not only a product of that time, but also itself congeals a tremendous amount of unpaid labour, as the acknowledgements will show.

Acknowledgements

My biggest debt is to so many justice workers without whom this book would simply not have been possible. They generously gave me their time and ideas (unpaid labour!) in The Hague, Kenya, and Uganda. My biggest guilt is that the book is quite critical, and I sincerely hope that it will not be read as a critique of justice workers but as a critique of the conditions and relations of justice production.

I also want to acknowledge the labour of colleagues and friends who, despite the stress and workload of neoliberal academia, generously gave their time to review my work and whose comments and ideas tremendously improved the book.

Isobel Roele gave immensely valuable feedback on Chapter 1 (check out her new book on *Articulating Security*!). Richard Clements very deeply and thoroughly engaged with Chapter 2 (check out his forthcoming book on the *Justice Factory*!). Christine Schwöbel-Patel gave me brilliant comments on Chapter 3 (her book on *Marketing Global Justice* is obviously a trailblazer for critical scholarship on international criminal justice). Nicola Palmer generously reviewed the introduction and Chapter 5. Nikki's excellent work on international criminal justice and the intellectual and caring labour she, Phil Clark, and Miles Jackson did, running Oxford Transitional Justice Research (OTJR) as an exciting and inclusive research group, was hugely formative for me and I owe them greatly. Eva Nanopoulos pushed me to improve not only the introduction and conclusion of this book but also to deepen my theoretical engagement with Marxist-Feminism. I am super grateful for her friendship and excited to continue working together! Many thanks also to those who have engaged with my work including at conferences and workshops: Mark Drumbl, Immi Tallgren, Sara Kendall, Holly Porter, Luis Eslava, Vanja Hamzić, Vasuki Nesiah, Lucia Zedner, Arushi Garg, Elena Butti, and many others.

I also want to thank my colleagues at Queen Mary who have greatly inspired me with their critical thinking and activism, and warmly supported me in my first job: Eva Nanopoulos, Isobel Roele, Ruth Fletcher,

Neve Gordon, Tanzil Chowdhury, Jeffrey Kennedy, Roxana Banu, Thomas MacManus, Shazia Choudhry, Penny Green, and many others.

My PhD supervisor, Carolyn Hoyle, gave me the confidence that I could be a scholar. She made being an academic look deceptively easy and fun, while nurturing my skills and confidence generously, without making a fuss about it.

I also wholeheartedly thank my colleagues and mentors at the Centre for Criminology at Oxford for creating such a wonderful and stimulating working environment: Mary Bosworth, Lucia Zedner, Carolyn Hoyle, Ian Loader, Rachel Condry, Katrin Mueller-Johnson, and Samuel Singler.

I received funding through a 1+3 ESRC scholarship and a British Academy Postdoctoral Fellowship, which created the material conditions for the production of this book. One chapter (Chapter 4), although in a very different form and connected to a different argument, has been previously published as a journal article (see Leila Ullrich, 'Beyond the "Global-Local Divide": Victims, Local Intermediaries and the Justice Politics of the International Criminal Court' (2016) 14(3) Journal of International Criminal Justice 543). There are also some material overlaps with a journal article I published with Carolyn Hoyle (see Carolyn Hoyle and Leila Ullrich, 'New Court, New Justice? The Evolution of "Justice for Victims" at Domestic Courts and at the International Criminal Court' (2014) 12(4) Journal of International Criminal Justice 681).

Many thanks also to my PhD examiners, Kieran McEvoy and Rachel Condry, and my editors at OUP, especially Kate Plunkett, and two anonymous reviewers who provided very valuable feedback.

Thank you so much to my friends who made sure I also had a bit of fun and were kind and caring when I couldn't stop moaning about the book: Arushi, Hanna, Eva, Caroline, Finn, Molly, Tom, Rozzie, Sandra, Dan, Roxana, Maayan, Claire, Clara, Elena, Sara, Francesca, Ruth, Jenny, Zarah, Marie, Julian, and many others!

I would also like to thank Ilya Afanasyev, who not only endured my never-ending crises of confidence and bouts of exhaustion and exasperation but also read the full manuscript twice! He will likely remain the only person (apart from myself) who will ever do that to themselves, and for his intellectual inspiration, generosity, and care, I remain grateful.

This book would not exist without the labour of my mother, Scheherezade, and my sister, Vanessa. Mama, you are an incredible woman! If I have only half your strength and spirit, I'll count myself very lucky! I am because you are.

Vani, you are brilliant and beautiful. You will kick ass!

Contents

List of Abbreviations

ARLPI	Acholi Religious Leaders Peace Initiative
ASP	Assembly of States Parties
BLM	Black Lives Matter
CAR	Central African Republic
CLR	common legal representative
DRC	Democratic Republic of the Congo
ECCC	Extraordinary Chambers in the Courts of Cambodia
ESRA	early social reproduction analyses
FGD	focus group discussion
FIDH	International Federation for Human Rights
ICTR	International Criminal Tribunal for Rwanda
ICTY	International Criminal Tribunal for the former Yugoslavia
IDPs	internally displaced persons
ILOAT	Administrative Tribunal of the International Labour Organisation
LRA	Lord's Resistance Army
OPCV	Office of the Public Counsel for Victims
OTJR	Oxford Transitional Justice Research
OTP	Office of the Prosecutor
PMC	professional–managerial class
SGBV	sexual and gender-based violence
SRT	social reproduction theory
TFV	Trust Fund for Victims
TJ	Transitional Justice
TWAIL	Third World Approaches to International Law
UWA	Ugandan Wildlife Authority
VPRS	Victims Participation and Reparations Section
VWU	Victims and Witnesses Unit

1
Introduction

International Criminal Court (ICC) Premises, Voorburg, The Hague, November 2013

'Our statute is clear . . . I can read it for you in the preamble', the prosecuting counsel says as he leafs through the pages of the Rome Statute.[1] I had come to the Court as a PhD researcher to explore what its ubiquitous promise to deliver 'justice for victims' meant. Widely celebrated as a 'victims' court', the ICC provides victims with 'innovative' rights to participate in the trials and to receive assistance and reparations.[2] But when I asked the Court's practitioners what 'justice for victims' meant, their responses were ambiguous and conflicting. On the one hand, many officials emphasized that the ICC's core justice mission is to try alleged perpetrators.[3] On the other hand, they linked the Court to broader concepts of justice,

[1] Interview with Counsel, Office of the Prosecutor (OTP), The Hague (13 November 2013).

[2] These rights are enshrined in the Rome Statute (1998), especially in art 68(3), art 75, and art 79. For an excellent analysis of the ICC's victims' rights provisions see Brianne McGonigle Leyh, *Procedural Justice? Victim Participation in International Criminal Proceedings* (Intersentia 2011). For a more recent analysis of jurisprudential and institutional developments see Rudina Jasini and Gregory Townsend (eds), *Advancing the Impact of Victim Participation at the International Criminal Court: Bridging the Gap Between Research and Practice* (ESRC, OUP 2020) https://www.law.ox.ac.uk/sites/files/oxlaw/iccba_-_oxford_publication_30_november_2020_.pdf (accessed 11 March 2022). On the innovative, victim-centred character of these provisions see Human Rights Center, UC Berkeley School of Law, 'The Victims' Court? A Study of 622 Victim Participants at the International Criminal Court' (2015) 1 https://humanrights.berkeley.edu/sites/default/files/publications/vp_report_2015_full_rev_b-4.pdf (accessed 9 March 2022); OTP, 'Policy Paper on Victims' Participation' (2010) 5 https://www.icc-cpi.int/iccdocs/otp/Policy_Paper_on_Victims_Participation_April_2010.pdf (accessed 4 March 2022); Judge Sang-Hyun Song, 'Speech: From Punishment to Prevention on the Future of International Criminal Justice' (2012) 8 https://www.icc-cpi.int/Pages/item.aspx?name=14022012lecture (accessed 4 March 2022); ICC, 'Independent Expert Review of the International Criminal Court and the Rome Statute System: Final Report' (2020) § 856 ('the Rome Statute innovated when it decided to put victims at the heart of the Court. With that aim, the rights of victims were woven directly into the fabric of the Rome Statute').

[3] Adrian Fulford, 'The Reflections of a Trial Judge' (2011) 22 Criminal Law Forum 215, 216; ICC, 'Understanding the International Criminal Court' 1 https://www.icc-cpi.int/resource-library/documents/uicceng.pdf (accessed 4 March 2022); International Criminal Court, 'Strategic Plan 2019–2021' (2019) 5 https://www.icc-cpi.int/sites/default/files/itemsDocuments/20190717-icc-strategic-plan-eng.pdf (accessed 17 December 2022).

Victims and the Labour of Justice at the International Criminal Court. Leila Ullrich, Oxford University Press.
 DOI: 10.1093/9780191915048.003.0001

including 'restorative justice', 'transformative justice' and 'gender justice'. Even more curiously, many ICC lawyers did not have a ready-made answer to my question and instead referred me back to the ICC's core legal text, the Rome Statute. Some of them then literally started to fumble for their copy on their desks to find the relevant provisions. That reach for legal clarification was, however, often in vain. The Rome Statute's provisions on victims and justice are very vague, leaving it to the Court's practitioners to give shape to the ICC's victim engagement. Yet, how do their conflicting justice ideas relate to the Court's victim practices in the field?

ICC Community Outreach Event at St Monica Vocational School for Girls, Gulu, Northern Uganda, 17 July 2019

'Happy Justice Day to all of us, to all of you—the champions of justice, the champions of accountability, the champions of the protection of human rights. You deserve that', the ICC's outreach officer greets the crowd, 'so please respond, "Happy Justice Day"'. 'Happy Justice Day', the audience echoes back. 'Thank you. Today is the 21st anniversary of the Court. The Court is now fully functional.'[4]

A big blue banner hangs over a podium in the hall. Colourful figures dance on the white wallpaper behind it. The banner reads, 'Public Dialogue in Commemoration of International Justice Day, Theme: "Humanity against Crimes" at St. Monica, Gulu. In solidarity with victims and affected communities. #humanityagainstcrime. #justicematters.'[5] The hall was first filling up slowly but is now packed. The public has come to the dialogue. Some people are chatting to each other, others reprimand their children, many are glued to their phones, some listen attentively, and a few elderly people are nodding off.

The ICC's outreach officer announces from the podium: 'We bring the Court closer to victims. The ICC now has field offices in all situation countries.' She points to the banner, explaining, 'the theme of the anniversary is humanity against crimes . . . To achieve global peace and justice, humanity needs to be united. By now, we all know that without justice there can be

[4] Fieldwork Diary, Gulu (17 July 2019).

[5] See also the ICC's website, 'Humanity against Crimes' https://www.icc-cpi.int/humanity-against-crimes and 'Justice Matters' https://www.icc-cpi.int/get-involved (both accessed 4 March 2022).

no sustainable peace'. The purpose of the public dialogue is to increase the knowledge of the victims: 'We are transforming lives through knowledge and information. We know that knowledge is power.'

She then explains victim participation in the *Ongwen* case: 'It was just a handful of victims who came to The Hague—only seven—but it was a good representation of victims. The Court does not have the capacity to bring 4000 victims to The Hague.' This, she contends, may be a relief for victims: 'the victims are very vulnerable. We don't expect them to come to The Hague'. She continues: 'It's a handful of victims who will benefit. We need to manage expectations. If you were harmed on 31 January rather than 30 January, you might fall outside the scope of the charges. It is the law.' Victims who cannot participate in the *Ongwen* trial can, however, 'still participate in traditional justice, amnesty, reconciliation and nation-building [in Uganda]. Ultimately, the greatest responsibility for justice lies with the government of Uganda'.[6]

Then, there is time for questions. One woman jumps up. She is a victim, and this is the first time she is attending an outreach meeting. She complains: 'The perpetrators are walking free. They are being protected by the government while the victims must fend for themselves.' She returned from rebel captivity with children and then married, but her marriage did not last because of her troubled past. Her intervention is followed by a priest from Kitgum, who demands that the Court 'should change the law so that the suspect has to carry the burden of proof'. The ICC's outreach officer retorts calmly but assertively: 'Ongwen is innocent until proven guilty. He who accuses must prove. Unfortunately, the law is like that. You are neither the judge nor the policeman. There are institutions to enforce law and order so that we don't take the law into our own hands.'

Finally, there is a panel of victims and victims' representatives. In fact, there is only one victim on the panel, Betty, from Lukodi. The ICC's outreach officer admonishes her: 'We know the terrible things. Don't talk about them. It would take a whole day.' And so, Betty, simultaneously instructed to speak and not to speak, does not talk about her experiences as a victim. Instead, she talks about the impact of the Court on her community: 'Crimes have gone down in our community because people now fear accountability. Justice is an aspect of the future. We show the screenings of the ICC's trial to our children and tell them, "if you misbehave, you will be held to account. You will be sent to the ICC." Our children will have a better

[6] Fieldwork Diary, Gulu (17 June 2019).

future.' Awkward laughter fills the room as she makes that pronouncement. A victims' representative, who speaks after Betty, asserts that 'they look after the suspect better than the victims. To be represented as a victim does not convey the pain. Pain cannot be represented'.[7]

1.1 The Justice Paradox

Returning from my fieldwork in The Hague, Kenya, and Uganda, I mulled over two paradoxes. The first paradox was the concept of justice itself. I was struck by how versatile my interviewees' justice discourses were, how they absorbed many different and conflicting ideas and practices: punishment, fair trials, reparation, reconciliation, truth, law and order, parental control, social transformation, freedom, and love—justice meant everything and nothing.[8] How can justice be so contradictory? How can it be so central to the Court's mission and simultaneously so ill-defined?

The second paradox was people's engagement with justice. In Kenya, even as the ICC's cases against the President and the Deputy President were on the brink of collapse, victims would still come forward to participate in the trials.[9] In fact, the enthusiastic reception of the Court when it launched its cases in 2011 was rather curious: many Kenyans celebrated the Court's intervention and watched the trials in Nairobi's shopping malls.[10]

[7] ibid.

[8] The Assembly of States Parties (ASP) also puts the ICC in the context of a rather expansive vision of justice: 'Convinced that the International Criminal Court ("the Court") is an essential means of promoting respect for international humanitarian law and human rights, thus contributing to freedom, security, justice and the rule of law, as well as to the prevention of armed conflicts, the preservation of peace and the strengthening of international security and the advancement of post-conflict peacebuilding and reconciliation with a view to achieving sustainable peace, in accordance with the purposes and principles of the Charter of the United Nations.' ASP, Resolution ICC-ASP/20/Res.5, 'Strengthening the International Criminal Court and the Assembly of States Parties', adopted at the 8th plenary meeting on 9 December 2021, by consensus, at 1.

[9] Sehmi reports that even after the collapse of the *Kenyatta* case, 'the views of victims regarding their participation were, perhaps surprisingly, positive'. Anushka Sehmi, '"Now that we have no voice, what will happen to us?" Experiences of Victim Participation in the Kenyatta Case' (2018) 16(3) Journal of International Criminal Justice 571, 583, n 62.

[10] Interview with Judge, The Hague (19 December 2013); Interview with Legal Officer, Registry, The Hague (12 November 2013). Overall support of the ICC among Kenyans remained relatively high and stable between 2010 and 2014, hovering between 67 per cent and 61 per cent, although varying, of course, by ethnicity, and dropped only when the ICC threatened to withdraw the charges. Support among victims was generally higher. See Rorisang Lekalake and Stephen Buchanan-Clarke, 'Support for the International Criminal Court in Africa Evidence from Kenya' (2015) 23 Afrobarometer Policy Paper 1, 4–6 https://www.afrobarometer.org/wp-content/uploads/migrated/files/publications/Policy papers/ab_

Some even named their newborns after the ICC's judges.[11] Ugandans, by contrast, initially gave the Court a cold reception. The ICC's indictments of five commanders of the Lord's Resistance Army (LRA) in 2005 threatened ongoing peace talks between the government and the LRA.[12] Today, as the guns have been silent for more than a decade, affected communities are much more receptive to the ICC. Northern Ugandans come to the Court's outreach meetings in great numbers and participate in the *Ongwen* trial as victims. No one has received any reparations yet and few people have received tangible assistance. Why do people in Kenya and Uganda engage in justice processes that offer so little, so late? Why and how do they become the Court's 'victims' and 'intermediaries'? What work do those labels perform on them?

My starting point was the concepts and questions of two distinct bodies of scholarship: transitional justice and victimology. Transitional justice explores how societies address past or ongoing atrocities: can international criminal trials, truth commissions, domestic trials, local justice rituals, or a combination thereof achieve justice and reconciliation?[13] Victimology, an offshoot of criminology, examines victimhood: who is recognized as a victim and who is not? What type of justice do victims want and how do

r6_policypaperno23_kenya_anti_corruption.pdf (accessed 1 April 2023); Lionel Nichols, *The International Criminal Court and the End of Impunity in Kenya* (Springer 2015) 14. See also the popular slogan first aired in the Kenyan parliament in 2009: 'Don't be vague. Let's go to the Hague.' Samuel M Makinda, 'Kenya, Uhuru Kenyatta and politicising the International Criminal Court' *The Conversation* (30 May 2013) https://theconversation.com/kenya-uhuru-kenyatta-and-politicising-the-international-criminal-court-14583 (accessed 1 April 2023).

[11] Interview with Judge, The Hague (13 February 2014). This initial enthusiasm soon turned sour in the context of Kenya's election politics. Sara Kendall, '"UhuRuto" and Other Leviathans: The International Criminal Court and the Kenyan Political Order' (2014) 7(3) African Journal of Legal Studies 399; Gabrielle Lynch, 'Electing the 'alliance of the accused': The success of the Jubilee Alliance in Kenya's Rift Valley' (2014) 8(1) Journal of Eastern African Studies 93.

[12] Barney Afako, 'Reconciliation and Justice: "Mato Oput" and the Amnesty Act' (2002) 11 Accord 64; Kasaija Phillip Apuuli, 'Peace over Justice: The Acholi Religious Leaders Peace Initiative (ARLPI) vs. the International Criminal Court (ICC) in Northern Uganda' (2011) 11(1) Studies in Ethnicity and Nationalism 116.

[13] See eg Ruti Teitel, *Transitional Justice* (OUP 2000); Paige Arthur, 'How "Transitions" Reshaped Human Rights: A Conceptual History of Transitional Justice' (2009) 11 Human Rights Quarterly 321; Phil Clark and Nicola Palmer, 'Challenging Transitional Justice' in Nicola Palmer, Phil Clark, and Danielle Granville (eds), *Critical Perspectives in Transitional Justice* (Intersentia 2012); Dustin N Sharp, 'What Would Satisfy Us? Taking Stock of Critical Approaches to Transitional Justice' (2019) 13(3) International Journal of Transitional Justice 570; Mohamed Sesay, 'Decolonization of Postcolonial Africa: A Structural Justice Project More Radical than Transitional Justice' (2022) 16(2) International Journal of Transitional Justice 254.

they perceive criminal justice processes? How is the victim label used politically?[14] These questions were initially helpful, but they missed a bigger story. While I had set out to understand what justice means and how it is practised by the Court's different stakeholders, I became more interested in what justice does: its effects both on the legal professionals and intermediaries, who interpret and implement victims' rights, and on the victims and affected communities subjected to it through outreach, victim participation, reparation, and assistance. How does 'justice' create new types of subjects that assume certain roles and duties in the world?

The literature has largely neglected these questions.[15] Legal scholarship has examined the Court's victim engagement mainly as a procedural problem.[16] While some legal scholars see victim participation and reparation as empowering for victims[17] and advocate for more extensive

[14] Ezzat Fattah, 'Victimology: Past, Present and Future' (2000) 33 Criminologie 17; Carolyn Hoyle and Richard Young (eds), *New Visions of Crime Victims* (Hart Publishing 2004); Paul Rock, *Constructing Victims' Rights: The Home Office, New Labour, and Victims* (OUP 2004); Sandra Walklate, *Imagining the Victim of Crime* (McGraw-Hill Education 2006); Paul Rock, 'Theoretical Perspectives on Victimisation' in Sandra Walklate (ed), *Handbook of Victims and Victimology* (1st edn, Routledge 2007); Ezzah Fattah, 'The evolution of a young and promising discipline: sixty years of victimology, a retrospective and prospective look' in Shlomo Giora Shoham, Paul Knepper, and Martin Kett (eds), *International Handbook of Victimology* (1st edn, CRC Press 2010) 43; Rianne Letschert and others (eds), *Victimological Approaches to International Crimes: Africa* (Intersentia 2011); Luke Moffett, *Justice for Victims before the International Criminal Court* (Routledge 2014); Joris van Wijk, 'Who is the "little old lady" of international crimes? Nils Christie's concept of the ideal victim reinterpreted' (2013) 19(2) International Review of Victimology 159; Antony Pemberton and others, 'Coherence in International Criminal Justice: A Victimological Perspective' (2015) 15(2) International Criminal Law Review 339; Lisa Long, 'The ideal victim: A critical race theory (CRT) approach' (2021) 27(3) International Review of Victimology 344.

[15] Although see Maria Elander's excellent work on the Extraordinary Chambers in the Courts of Cambodia (ECCC). Elander also examines the production of victim subjects, what she calls 'victiming', but looks at this process discursively rather than through a political economy perspective. She also uses the concept of interpellation but through Butler's rather than Althusser's reading. Maria Elander, *Figuring Victims in International Criminal Justice* (Routledge 2018) 9–13, 32. See also Christine Schwöbel-Patel, 'Figuring Victims in International Criminal Justice: The Case of the Khmer Rouge Tribunal' (2020) 31(4) European Journal of International Law 1597. For another excellent recent book that also complicates victimhood by reinscribing the agency and resistance of recaptive slaves into the history of international criminal justice see Emily Haslam, *The Slave Trade, Abolition and the Long History of International Criminal Law: The Recaptive and the Victim* (Routledge 2019).

[16] Mugambi Jouet, 'Reconciling the Conflicting Rights of Victims and Defendants at the International Criminal Court' (2007) 26 Saint Louis University Public Law Review 249; Salvatore Zappalà, 'The Rights of Victims v the Rights of the Accused' (2010) 8(1) Journal of International Criminal Justice 137.

[17] For 'mildly empowering' see Tom M Antkowiak, 'An Emerging Mandate for International Courts: Victim-Centered Remedies and Restorative Justice' (2011) 47 Stanford Journal of International Law 279; Luke Moffett, *Justice for Victims before the International Criminal Court* (Routledge 2014); Luke Moffett, 'Elaborating Justice for Victims at the International Criminal

victims' rights,[18] others fear that they undermine the Court's due process.[19] Procedural rights are rarely meaningful for victims, they point out, while they lengthen the proceedings and threaten to erode the defendant's rights to a fair trial.[20] Critical scholars, by contrast, tend to argue that the Court merely uses and commodifies victims to raise money, build legitimacy, and reassure audiences in the Global North that something is being done about egregious violence in the Global South.[21] The victim, they argue, functions as an 'imaginary', 'idealized', 'disembodied', 'hapless', and 'passive' figure, which positions international criminal justice as the saviour of 'innocent victims' while erasing more complex, structural causes of international crimes.[22] The victims' discursive centrality, however, has little to do with

Court: Beyond Rhetoric and The Hague' (2015) 13 Journal of International Criminal Justice 281, 286.

[18] Mariana Pena and Gaelle Carayon, 'Is the ICC Making the Most of Victim Participation?' (2013) 7(3) International Journal of Transitional Justice 518; Gaelle Carayon and Jonathan O'Donohue, 'The International Criminal Court's Strategies in Relation to Victims' (2017) 15(3) Journal of International Criminal Justice 567, 588; Carla Ferstman and Merryl Lawry-White, 'Participation, Reparation, and Redress: Draft Article 12 of the ILC's Draft Articles on Crimes Against Humanity at the Intersection of International Criminal Law and Human Rights Law' (2018) 16(4) Journal of International Criminal Justice 813; Liesbeth Zegveld, 'Victims as a Third Party: Empowerment of Victims?' (2019) 19(2) International Criminal Law Review 321.

[19] For more critical assessments of victim participation see Charles P Trumbull, 'The Victims of Victim Participation in International Criminal Proceedings' (2007) 29 Michigan Journal of International Law 777; McGonigle Leyh (n 2) 782.

[20] Christine H Chung, 'Victims' Participation at the International Criminal Court: Are Concessions of the Court Clouding the Promise?' (2008) 6 Northwestern Journal of International Human Rights 459; Christine Van den Wyngaert, 'Victims Before International Criminal Courts: Some Views and Concerns of an ICC Trial Judge' (2012) 44 Case Western Reserve Journal of International Law 475.

[21] Sara Kendall and Sarah Nouwen, 'Representational Practices at the International Criminal Court: The Gap between Juridified and Abstract Victimhood' (2014) 76 Law and Contemporary Problems 235; Kjersi Lohne, *Advocates of Humanity: Human Rights NGOs in International Criminal Justice* (OUP 2019) 145; Immi Tallgren, 'The Voice of the International: Who is Speaking?' (2015) 13(1) Journal of International Criminal Justice 135; Christine Schwöbel-Patel, *Marketing Global Justice: The Political Economy of International Criminal Law* (CUP 2021).

[22] Makau Mutua, 'Savages, Victims and Saviors: The Metaphor of Human Rights' (2001) 42 Harvard International Law Journal 201; Kamari Maxine Clarke, *Fictions of Justice: The International Criminal Court and the challenge of legal pluralism in Sub-Saharan Africa* (CUP 2009) 4; Tshepo Madlingozi, 'On Transitional Justice Entrepreneurs and the Production of Victims' (2010) 2(2) Journal of Human Rights Practice 208, 213; Mark Drumbl, *Reimagining Child Soldiers in International Law and Policy* (OUP 2012); Kieran McEvoy and Kirsten McConnachie, 'Victims and Transitional Justice: Voice, Agency and Blame' (2013) 22(4) Social & Legal Studies 489, 502; Laurel E Fletcher, 'Refracted Justice: The Imagined Victim and the International Criminal Court' in Christian de Vos, Sara Kendall, and Carsten Stahn (eds), *Contested Justice: The Politics and Practice of International Criminal Court Interventions* (CUP 2015); Rachel Killean, *Victims, Atrocity and International Criminal Justice: Lessons from Cambodia* (Routledge 2018); Christine Schwöbel-Patel, 'The "Ideal" Victim of International

their actual role in the criminal proceedings, which is reduced to mass participation mediated through a handful of victims' lawyers.[23] Thus, both perspectives, despite promoting very different visions of justice, tend to see 'justice for victims' at the ICC as an 'empty promise': it doesn't do much for victims.

This book's provocation is that 'justice for victims' is not merely symbolic, expressive, distracting, or instrumental.[24] It is also productive: it both produces the Court as a relevant institution and turns victims into productive and reproductive capitalist subjects. The Court needs and creates victims to reproduce itself but in so doing also plays a broader role in the material and moral reproduction of global capitalism. Indeed, the increasing drive to integrate victims as participants in legal processes has transformed them from idealized tropes into 'active' racialized and gendered labourers, who produce and reproduce international criminal justice cheaply precisely because their labour is concealed as 'participation'. In the process, victims are called upon to become the Court's 'champions'[25] and to serve global

Criminal Law' (2018) 29(3) The European Journal of International Law 703; Kamari Maxine Clarke, 'Affective Justice: The Racialized Imaginaries of International Justice' (2019) 42(2) PoLAR: Political and Legal Anthropological Review 244, 246; Kamari Maxine Clarke, *Affective Justice: The International Criminal Court and the Pan-Africanist Pushback* (Duke UP 2022).

[23] Kendall and Nouwen (n 21) 254; Emily Haslam and Rod Edmunds, 'Whose Number Is it Anyway? Common Legal Representation, Consultations and the 'Statistical Victim' 2017 15(5) *Journal of International Criminal Justice* 931.

[24] On symbolic victims' inclusion see eg Emily Haslam and Rod Edmunds, 'Common Legal Representation at the International Criminal Court: More Symbolic than Real?' (2012) 12(5) International Criminal Law Review 871; McGonigle Leyh (n 2) 10, 234; Moffett (n 17) 290; Juan-Pablo Perez-Leon-Acevedo, 'Victims and appeals at the International Criminal Court (ICC): evaluation under international human rights standards' (2021) 25(9) The International Journal of Human Rights 1598, 1607. On the expressive function of international criminal justice see Tim Meijers and Marlies Glasius, 'Trials as Messages of Justice: What Should Be Expected of International Criminal Courts?' (2016) 30(4) Ethics and International Affairs 429; Carsten Stahn, *Justice as Message: Expressivist Foundations of International Criminal Justice* (OUP 2020). On the instrumental use of victims as fictions or commodities and its distracting function from global structural injustice see Clarke, *Fictions of Justice* (n 22) 4; Schwöbel-Patel (n 21) 98.

[25] At a field visit to the Central African Republic (CAR), the TFV Executive Director said: 'The beneficiaries we heard are indeed *walombe*—champions, as they refer to themselves. Together with the TFV partners, they have demonstrated what transformative reparations are and the processes, staff and time required to achieve such transformation. We will take the beneficiaries' calls for an increased engagement by the TFV to the donors and plead for funds to continue and extend the programme in CAR.' ICC Press Release, 'ICC President and Acting Executive Director of the Trust Fund for Victims visit Central African Republic to witness Court's work on the ground' (28 November 2022) https://www.icc-cpi.int/news/icc-president-and-acting-executive-director-trust-fund-victims-visit-central-african-republic (accessed 9 December 2022).

capitalism as wives, mothers, workers, debtors, and micro-entrepreneurs.[26] Far from empowering victims, the institutionalization of victims' rights in international criminal justice, I argue, reflects and reinforces a shift in the victim's role from passive, suffering victims in Africa that legitimated international interventions in the 1990s to active, blameworthy 'victim-workers' in the Global South who reproduce the global capitalist order and its institutions.[27]

1.2 Justice as Ideology

To make sense of this process of victim subject production, I have relied on ideology theory.[28] Ideology theory is certainly not in fashion in transitional justice, international criminal justice, victimology, or criminology more generally.[29] Scholars have taken flight from it not only because of its links with Marxism, but also in a critical rejection of the patronizing quality of 'false consciousness', a concept that is heavily associated with ideology theory.[30] The latter may seem remote even to critical scholars who work with feminist,[31] critical race, post-colonial,[32] and TWAIL (Third World

[26] *Prosecutor v Lubanga* (Annex A: Collective Reparations projects in relation to the conviction of Thomas Lubanga Dyilo before the International Criminal Court) [2017] ICC-01/04-01/06-3273-AnxA, 17 ('The development of savings and loans initiatives is one way to enable young entrepreneurs to make investments and benefit from loans and access to credit in return').

[27] For an excellent chapter on how international criminal justice developed in the 1990s see ch 3, 'A Brand New Justice' in Christine Schwöbel-Patel, *Marketing Global Justice: The Political Economy of International Criminal Law* (CUP 2021).

[28] Jan Rehmann, *Theories of Ideology: The Powers of Alienation and Subjection* (Brill 2013); Himani Bannerji, *The Ideological Condition: Selected Essays on History, Race and Gender* (Brill 2020).

[29] Although see Ian Loader and Richard Sparks, 'Ideologies and crime: political ideas and the dynamics of crime control' (2016) 17(3) Global Crime 314.

[30] Terry Eagleton, *Ideology: An Introduction* (Verso 1991) 11–17; Susan Marks, 'Big Brother Is Bleeping Us: With the Message that Ideology Doesn't Matter' (2001) 12(1) European Journal of International Law 109, 109; Rehmann (n 28) 6.

[31] Janet Halley, 'Rape in Berlin: Reconsidering the Criminalisation of Rape in the International Law of Armed Conflict' (2008) 9 Melbourne Journal of International Law 78; Doris Buss, 'Performing Legal Order: Some Feminist Thoughts on International Criminal Law' (2011) 11 ICLR 409.

[32] Ratna Kapur, 'The Tragedy of Victimization Rhetoric: Resurrecting the "Native" Subject in International/Post-Colonial Feminist Legal Politics' (2002) 15 Harvard Human Rights Journal 1; Vasuki Nesiah, 'The Ground beneath her Feet: "Third World" Feminisms' (2003) 4(3) Journal of International Women's Studies 30; Ratna Kapur, *Erotic Justice: Law and the New Politics of Postcolonialism* (Routledge 2005); Ratna Kapur, '"The First Feminist War in All of History": Epistemic Shifts and Relinquishing the Mission to Rescue the "Other Woman"' (2022) 116 AJIL Unbound 270.

Approaches to International Law) paradigms.[33] Curiously, however, this link was cut off rather recently. For example, Spivak's canonical text 'Can the Subaltern Speak?' begins with a critique of 'the disavowal of ideology' in post-structuralist scholarship.[34] Spivak uses a rather chummy conversation between Foucault and Deleuze to make her point. When Deleuze asks 'how is it that people whose interests are not being served can strictly support the existing power structure by demanding a piece of the action?', his answer is not 'ideology' but 'desire'.[35] Instead of practising 'ideology critique', Foucault and Deleuze substitute it with an analysis of power, desire, and interest.[36]

The disavowal of ideology, Spivak tells us, idealizes the oppressed as a knowing subject who does not need representation.[37] Yet, by the same sleight of hand by which the intellectual removes himself from the picture, he also reinserts himself. In fact, he becomes bigger and bigger and no longer needs to justify his de facto representation of the subaltern. Rather than the 'nonrepresenting intellectual making space for her [the subaltern] to speak', Foucault and Deleuze restore her as an essentialized subject, Europe's 'Other', rendered transparent and unified through the intellectual.[38] 'False consciousness' has been swept away, alongside the epistemic violence that tethers the intellectual to the subaltern under global capitalism. In their place, a 'speaking subaltern' and a 'listening intellectual' have ostensibly entered the stage. 'Neither Deleuze nor Foucault seems aware', Spivak observes, 'that the intellectual within socialized capital, brandishing

[33] Makau Mutua and Antony Anghie, 'What is TWAIL?' (2000) 94 Proceedings of the Annual Meeting (American Society of International Law) 31; BS Chimni, 'Third World Approaches to International Law: A Manifesto' (2006) 8 International Community Law Review 3; Michelle Burgis-Kasthala, 'Scholarship as Dialogue? TWAIL and the Politics of Methodology' (2016) 14(4) Journal of International Criminal Justice 921; John Reynolds and Sujith Xavier, '"The Dark Corners of the World": TWAIL and International Criminal Justice' (2016) 14(4) Journal of International Criminal Justice 959; Luis Eslava, 'TWAIL Coordinates' *Critical Legal Thinking* (2 April 2019) https://criticallegalthinking.com/2019/04/02/twail-coordinates/ (accessed 29 June 2022).

[34] Gayatri Chakravorty Spivak, 'Can the subaltern speak?' in Patrick Williams and Laura Chrisman (eds), *Colonial Discourse and Postcolonial Theory: A Reader* (Columbia UP 1994) 66.

[35] Michel Foucault and Gilles Deleuze, 'Intellectuals and power: A conversation between Michel Foucault and Gilles Deleuze' Transcript from 1972 https://libcom.org/library/intellectuals-power-a-conversation-between-michel-foucault-and-gilles-deleuze (accessed 15 February 2022).

[36] ibid. See also Terry Eagleton's critique of how postmodernism has disavowed ideology. Eagleton (n 30) xi–xii.

[37] Spivak (n 34) 69.

[38] ibid 84.

concrete experience, can help consolidate the international division of labor'—a division, which relegates the subaltern to the bottom rung.[39]

While critical scholarship on international criminal justice has, for the most part, not heeded Spivak's warning about the disavowal of ideology, there is a small but significant strand of Marxist scholarship in international law that has engaged in ideology critique.[40] Citing John Thompson, Susan Marks defines ideology as 'the ways in which meaning serves to establish and sustain relations of domination'.[41] She deploys ideology critique to show how international law naturalizes and rationalizes capitalism and the unjust property and power relationships that underpin it.[42] In a similar vein, Tor Krever uses ideology critique to argue that the politics of international criminal law does not only unfold through the strategic manoeuvres of powerful states but also plays out 'in the generalized discourse and rhetorical patterns produced and reproduced by legal scholarship'.[43] International criminal law scholarship operates ideologically, he argues, by eclipsing the capitalist and colonial background conditions of international crimes as well as concrete international interventions such as imperial wars and neoisl structural adjustment programmes that 'shape or even help establish the environment from which such conflicts and violence emanate'.[44]

While ideology critique illuminates the discursive strategies of ideology—how ideology normalizes, naturalizes, and rationalizes injustice[45]—it tells us less about how ideology operates as an institutional *practice*. To capture the latter, this book moves from ideology critique to critical ideology theory, building on the work of Jan Rehmann and Louis Althusser.[46] Rehmann distinguishes three approaches to ideology in the

[39] ibid 69.
[40] Marks (n 30); Susan Marks, *The Riddle of All Constitutions: International Law, Democracy, and the Critique of Ideology* (OUP 2003); Tor Krever, 'International Criminal Law: An Ideology Critique' (2013) 26 Leiden Journal of International Law 701; Robert Knox, 'Marxist approaches to international law' in Anne Orford and Florian Hoffman (eds), *The Oxford Handbook of the Theory of International Law* (OUP 2018). For Marxist scholarship on international law generally see China Miéville, *Between Equal Rights: A Marxist Theory of International Law* (Brill 2005); Ntina Tzouvala, *Capitalism as Civilisation: A History of International Law* (CUP 2020); Eva Nanopoulos, *The Juridification of Individual Sanctions and the Politics of EU Law* (Hart Publishing 2021). For international criminal law see Grietje Baars, *The Corporation, Law and Capitalism* (Brill 2019).
[41] Marks (n 30) 110.
[42] ibid. See also Eagleton on 'ideological strategies': Eagleton (n 30) 45.
[43] Krever (n 40) 703.
[44] ibid 720.
[45] Marks (n 30) 110.
[46] Louis Althusser, *On Ideology* (Verso 2020); Louis Althusser, *For Marx* (Verso 2005).

Marxist tradition: Following Lenin, the first is an ideology-neutral approach, which interprets ideology as a class-specific conception of the world. Within this neutral approach, Marxism figures as much as an ideology as liberalism.[47] The second approach, often called 'ideology critique', developed by György Lukács and the Frankfurt School, by contrast, reveals the inversions, elisions, and distortions of dominant capitalist and liberal arguments and discourses.[48] Finally, the third approach, ideology theory, which centres on the work of Louis Althusser, Antonio Gramsci, and Stuart Hall, brings into view the materiality of 'the ideological':[49] 'the ideological as the ensemble of apparatuses and forms of praxis that organise the relation of individuals to the self and to the world'.[50] Rather than asking what is 'false' about ideology, ideology theory explores what makes it effective, examining how ideology filters into people's common sense and unconscious practice.[51] This book combines the critical perspective of the second and the material and practice orientation of the third approach to further develop what Rehmann calls critical ideology-theory.[52]

Critical ideology theory shifts our focus in several ways compared to ideology critique: first, it moves our attention from international criminal *law* to international criminal justice *institutions*. It is institutions, Althusser thought, like schools, churches, families, and the media—what he called 'ideological state apparatuses'—that produce and reproduce ideology. He did not consider courts as ideological state apparatuses because he thought that they work through 'repression' rather than 'ideology'.[53] International criminal courts, however, do not only discipline and punish 'criminals', they also court affected communities to become their champions and enlist

[47] Rehmann (n 28) 21.
[48] ibid 21, 42.
[49] Nicos Poulantzas: 'To understand this, of course, it is necessary to break with a whole conception of ideology as a "system of ideas" or as a coherent "discourse", and to understand it as an ensemble of material practices.' Nicos Poulantzas, *Classes in Contemporary Capitalism* (Verso 1978) 17. See also Stuart Hall, 'Gramsci's Relevance for the Study of Race and Ethnicity' (1986) 10(4) Journal of Communication Inquiry 5, 21.
[50] Rehmann (n 28) 22.
[51] ibid 5–6, 130–31; Stuart Hall, *Cultural Studies 1983: A Theoretical History* (Jennifer Daryl Slack and Lawrence Grossberg eds, Duke UP 2016) 137.
[52] Rehmann (n 28) 8. Rob Knox observes that Althusserian and Gramscian debates about ideology 'did not have a huge impact upon the international legal field. Here the most important theories of ideology have been those of ideology critique drawn from the Frankfurt School, exemplified in the work of Susan Marks'. Knox (n 40) 320, although see Rose Parfitt, *The Process of International Legal Reproduction: Inequality, Historiography, Resistance* (CUP 2019).
[53] Althusser, *On Ideology* (n 46) 17.

victims and intermediaries in their processes. To understand how institutions work we need to further redirect our attention from legal *scholars* to *practitioners* and from legal *texts* to the everyday *labour* of the Court's judges, bureaucrats, victims' lawyers, non-governmental organizations (NGOs), intermediaries, and victims both inside and outside the courtroom. Indeed, while critical legal scholars tend to centre 'the trial' as the key site of ideological production,[54] I argue that 'the field', 'in Africa', where the Court engages victims, rather than the courtroom, is the primary site where ideological subjects are produced.

These shifts in analytical focus, then, support an argument which differs in important respects from the existing ideology critique. Rather than merely masking global structural injustice through the dichotomous representation of the 'innocent victim' versus the 'evil perpetrator', international criminal justice, I contend, is a key medium through which victim subjects are created and integrated into the unequal and precarious logic of global capitalist social relations.

Indeed, our justice paradox—why do people engage with justice processes that offer not only little material gain but also an ill-defined notion of justice—can be resolved once we consider 'justice for victims' as an effective mode of ideological subject production. We usually assume that a concept has to be clear and coherent to be effective. Muddled thinking persuades no one. So how do contradictory justice ideas and practices still enthral people?

First, victims are interpellated by the Court more than they are persuaded. Althusser showed how ideology works by creating its own subjects. He chose an everyday scene to make his point: a police officer hailing, 'hey, you there!'—and in turning your head, you have become interpellated—you recognized that the call was addressed to you, and you responded—you have become a subject.[55] As Althusser put it, 'you and I are always already subjects, and as such constantly practice the rituals of ideological recognition'.[56] Interpellation entails two moves: it creates subjects, for example, 'believers' for religion or 'citizens' for the state, and it calls on them to subject themselves to a higher being or idea—the Subject ('God', 'the

[54] Christine Schwöbel-Patel, 'Spectacle in international criminal law: the fundraising image of victimhood' (2016) 4(2) London Review of International Law 247; Kate Leader, 'The trial's the thing: Performance and legitimacy in international criminal trials' (2020) 24(2) Theoretical Criminology 241.

[55] Althusser, *On Ideology* (n 46) 48.

[56] ibid 46.

nation'). Althusser gives the example of Christianity, which 'hails' individuals as subjects of God: 'and the Lord cried to Moses, "Moses!" And Moses replied "It is (really) I! I am Moses thy servant, speak and I shall listen!" '[57] In other words, ideology first creates 'free subjects' so that they can then voluntarily submit to ideology 'all by themselves'.[58]

Ideology, therefore, does not work so much through persuasion or force but by calling people names ('victims', 'intermediaries'). The outreach officer in Gulu does not really explain why Ugandans need international criminal justice, how the Court fights impunity, or what evidence there is that deterrence works. She is not supposed to persuade people as outreach is 'neutral, independent and non-political'.[59] Instead, she designates the audience as the Court's natural supporters ('you are the champions of justice'). Rather than being persuaded, they are being celebrated. They know that they celebrate ('Happy Justice Day') before they know why they celebrate. They learn that this is a happy day, a day to celebrate 'us' ('humanity against crimes') and that they 'deserve' that day. This is established in the first seconds of the outreach officer's speech. Rather than explaining, the outreach officer is naming people and allocating roles ('you are the victims', 'this is the law').

Secondly, ideology operates through practices as much as ideas. People's beliefs are often complex and ambiguous. As Eagleton puts it, 'can't people be in some way more critical, even more sceptical, of those values and beliefs, and nevertheless continue to conform to them?'[60] Kenyans and Ugandans attend the ICC's meetings not because they necessarily believe that the Court is beneficial or will deliver meaningful justice (in fact, many attendees criticized the Court vociferously during the meeting), but because they have been interpellated as 'victims' or 'affected communities'. They may be sceptical about the court, but they still *practise* their victim roles. They come to the meeting and congratulate each other: 'happy justice day!'. The audience confirms, 'yes, we are what you call us. We are the victims', thus acknowledging the court's authority to assign roles to them.

Thirdly, contradictions make ideologies more, not less, effective.[61] A muddled idea may not work well for persuasion, but it works well for

[57] ibid 53.
[58] ibid 56.
[59] International Criminal Court, 'Interacting with Communities' (2014) 2 https://iccforum.com/media/background/outreach/2014-07-08_Interacting_with_Communities-ICC-PIDS.pdf (accessed 16 February 2022).
[60] Pierre Bourdieu and Terry Eagleton, 'Doxa and Common Life' (1992) 191(1) New Left Review 111, 113.
[61] See also Hall (n 49) 22.

interpellation. It allows for change. One crucial question that Althusser's interpellation theory dodges is how subjects can be reinvented as global capitalism evolves.[62] How do subjects transition from 'factory workers' to 'gig workers' or from 'housewives' to 'working moms'? How do Ugandans and Kenyans transition from 'victims' to 'survivors'? Even more importantly, how do people resist dominant ideologies?[63] When and how do we respond to subversive interpellation like 'we are the 99%' or #metoo?[64] Ideologies are malleable because they entail conflicting ideas. They form ideological terrains rather than discreet 'worldviews'; they blur into and borrow from each other.[65] Effective ideologies rant against 'benefit scroungers' as well as 'the elite', they call for 'order' and 'justice', 'freedom', and 'discipline'.[66] When Donald Trump cheered on protesters who flouted the Covid-19 lockdown that he himself, as President of the United States, had signed into law, the contradictory quality of ideology was in plain sight.[67] It was possible for Trump both to embody the state and the opposition to the state, the lockdown and its critique, the establishment and the anti-establishment.

Fourthly, ideology is a form of labour, which ropes its subjects into labouring relationships. Rehmann's definition of ideology 'as an ensemble of apparatuses and praxis-forms' shifts our analytical focus from institutional ideologies (eg legalism, managerialism)[68] to everyday ideological practice, but it does not further dissect the forms of labour this practice consists of.[69] On one level, it is evident that the Court's victim engagement requires a great deal of labour, legal labour in the courtroom, bureaucratic labour in the institution, and plenty of labour in the field (identifying victims, meeting them, helping them fill out application forms, listening to

[62] Rehmann (n 28) 188.

[63] See also Göran Therborn, *The Ideology of Power and the Power of Ideology* (Verso 1980) 9.

[64] See eg Cinzia Arruzza, Tithi Bhattacharya, and Nancy Fraser, *Feminism for the 99%: A Manifesto* (Verso 2019).

[65] Hall (n 51) 137.

[66] Rehmann (n 28) 3.

[67] 'Coronavirus: President Trump defends tweets against US states' lockdowns' *BBC News* (17 April 2020) https://www.bbc.co.uk/news/world-us-canada-52330531 (accessed 12 March 2022).

[68] Judith N Shklar, *Legalism* (Harvard UP 1964); Kieran McEvoy, 'Beyond Legalism: Towards a Thicker Understanding of Transitional Justice' (2007) 34 Journal of Law and Society 411.

[69] Rehmann (n 28) 83. While there has been a turn to 'practice', there has not been much analysis of the labouring relationships of international criminal justice. Jens Meierhenrich, 'Foreword: The Practices of the International Criminal Court' (2013) 76(3–4) Law and Contemporary Problems i, i–x; Jens Meierhenrich, 'The Practice of International Law: A Theoretical Analysis' (2014) 76 Law and Contemporary Problems 1; Christian Sperfeldt, *Practices of Reparations in International Criminal Justice* (CUP 2022).

their stories). On a deeper level, ideology is a form of production that creates victims as labouring subjects. As Therborn argues, ideology does not only *subject* (ie subjugate), it also *qualifies* its subjects to take up their roles in the social order.[70] This double function of ideology is already implied in the double meaning of the term subject, which connotes both a 'subject of the existing order' (subjugated, passive) and a 'subject of history' (qualified, active).[71] The Court recruits ideological labourers in The Hague and in the field—victims' lawyers, field assistants, intermediaries, etc.—who both subject and qualify victims as legal subjects for the Court and as capitalist subjects for the broader global order.

In making this ideological labour visible, I draw on the insights of social reproduction theory.[72] Social reproduction theory is a diverse body of Marxist–Feminist thinking. Like Marx, social reproduction theorists begin their analysis of the capitalist system with the commodity, but they reveal that the commodity does not only hide productive labour and the surplus value it creates for capital, but also socially reproductive labour, all the birthing, nursing, feeding, educating, and caring that is required to reproduce the worker and her labour power, which, of course, is capitalism's special commodity.[73] As such, they uncovered that domestic labour, which mostly women do either as unpaid wives and mothers or as underpaid care workers, is essential for reproducing the capitalist system.

Social reproduction theory helps us refine our understanding of ideological labour in at least two ways. First, it reveals that ideological labour is a form of social reproduction labour; it does not produce commodities but labouring subjects ready for capitalist exploitation.[74] Secondly, it suggests that labour is always double use. It can be used both for producing commodities and for producing people and communities, both for replenishing

[70] Therborn (n 63) 17.
[71] ibid vii.
[72] I use the term social reproduction theory loosely to encompass both early social reproduction analyses (ESRA) by scholars such as Mariarosa Dalla Costa and Silvia Federici and the more recent body of social reproduction theory (SRT) by Tithi Bhattacharya, Nancy Fraser, and Susan Ferguson, amongst others, which builds on the work of Lise Vogel. See Alessandra Mezzadri, 'A Value Theory of Inclusion: Informal Labour, the Homeworker, and the Social Reproduction of Value' (2021) 53(4) Antipode 1186; Tithi Bhattacharya (ed), *Social Reproduction Theory: Remapping Class, Recentering Oppression* (Pluto Press 2017).
[73] Lise Vogel, *Marxism and the Oppression of Women: Toward a Unitary Theory* (2nd edn, Brill 2013); Silvia Federici, *Revolution at Point Zero: Housework, Reproduction, and Feminist Struggle* (PM Press 2021); Mariarosa Dalla Costa, 'Women and the Subversion of the Community' (1971) https://la.utexas.edu/users/hcleaver/357k/357kDallaCostaSubversionTable.pdf (accessed 17 February 2022).
[74] I explain this more in ch 4.

the Court's victim engagement and for disrupting it, both for reproducing capitalist social relations and for challenging them.[75] The more labour is withdrawn from commodity and ideology production and poured into community production, the more people prioritize life-making over profit-making, the more resistive this labour becomes.

1.3 Becoming the Court's Victims

How then does ideological labour operate with regard to victims? The Court calls and lures people to become its subjects—'Happy Justice Day! You are the champions of justice—we are united as humanity against crimes'. The concept of justice is wide open: it promises unity, peace, and prosperity. But once you declare yourself a subject of the Court, a victim, or an intermediary, once you have made yourself comfortable in your chair, prepared to sit through the meeting and engage with the Court, the discourse shifts as lofty justice promises are filtered through legal procedure. You can know the law, but you cannot change it. You can speak, but please do not tell us about the horrible things—we already know them and will only select your story if it is relevant. You can participate, but you are not the judge: 'there are institutions to enforce law and order'.[76] What the Court gives with one hand, it takes away with the other. The Court's officers do not even deceive affected communities; they are very honest, 'it's a handful of victims who will benefit'. But no one leaves the room. How is that done?

This book argues that 'justice for victims' is an effective ideological form that works by luring, disciplining, and blaming victims. Victims are first lured to become the Court's subjects, they are then disciplined as the Court's subjects and, eventually, they carry the blame for being the Court's subjects. The ICC disciplines victims by regulating victimhood. It defines who can participate in the proceedings and who deserves what kind of reparations, when, and under what conditions.[77] The first regulatory move is to divide affected communities into those who are eligible to participate in

[75] Susan Ferguson, *Women and Work Feminism, Labour, and Social Reproduction* (Pluto Press 2019) 2; Federici (n 73) 99; Susan Ferguson, 'Social Reproduction: What's the Big Idea?' https://www.plutobooks.com/blog/social-reproduction-theory-ferguson/ (accessed 28 January 2022).

[76] Fieldwork Diary, Gulu (17 June 2019).

[77] These forms of regulation have been examined in the existing literature. See eg Valentina Spiga, 'Indirect Victims' Participation in the *Lubanga* Trial' (2010) 8(1) Journal of International Criminal Justice 183; Kendall and Nouwen (n 21).

the Court's processes and those who are not, creating a 'privileged' victim category that is simultaneously arbitrary, precarious, and highly regulated. As a victims' lawyer in Kenya told me:

> One of my field staff was talking to this woman; she had been raped six times, house burnt down—extremely egregious crimes—and then my field staff said: 'what day was that?', and the woman said 'it was on 6 January 2008', and my field assistant said, 'Oh my God, I wished she would just say 26 [January].' Because the 26th is within the temporal scope of the charges but the 6th is outside. And, on the same day, I spoke to a man, and I said: 'Did you lose any family?' 'No, no', 'was your house burnt down?' 'No, no' . . . then he said, 'but they did take a hundred loaves of bread from me' . . . Now, this falls within the scope of the charges. So, this man was not particularly complaining about his condition in life, but he becomes a victim, and the lady who was raped six times on the wrong day is not a victim.[78]

Who is included in the Court's victim category ultimately depends on the Prosecutor's case selection, the time period the judges set for victims to apply to participate in the proceedings, the ability of the Court's field teams to reach affected communities in rural areas in Kenya and Uganda, and the legal skills of intermediaries in helping victims fill out application forms.[79] The Court then fuses its arbitrary categories with moral implications. Victims have to undergo a vetting procedure to establish whether they are 'really' victims according to the Court's changing definitions, and travel for hours to be interrogated by the ICC's lawyers. Could they really have run all the way from the place of attack to the hospital where they were treated?[80] Did they actually lose five cows? Are they lying to the Court?

Once the victim label is bestowed, victims risk losing that recognition at every turn of the trial. The scope of the charges may narrow, they may be exposed as 'fake victims', they may die as the proceedings drag on for years, and the accused may be acquitted either for all charges or those they have been victimized by. What the Court gives, it regulates and can withdraw any time. Victims are in constant danger of having their status stripped off

[78] Interview with Victims' Lawyer, The Hague (24 November 2013).
[79] See ICC (n 2) § 862.
[80] Fieldwork Diary, Victims' Registration Mission, Western and Nyanza Provinces, Kenya (21 August 2014).

them again. This also breeds divisions among victims. In Northern Uganda, people often told me, 'we are the real victims', or 'the court engages the wrong victims'.[81] They used very different criteria than the Court in making this determination, distinguishing, for example, between people who were locally displaced ('home people') and those who were abducted and forced to live in LRA captivity ('bush people'), and between those who lost loved ones and those who suffered sexual- and gender-based violence (with the former often seen as 'real victims'[82]). The Court's selectivity thus fosters allegations of 'fraudulent victims' not only by the court's practitioners but also by victims themselves, keeping the very category of 'victims' suspicious. Meanwhile, the benefits of participation dwindle as the Court's lawyers manage victims' expectations ('the chances of receiving reparations are minimal').[83]

In addition to policing the victim category, disciplining victims also works by inculcating a sense of duty into them. This ideological labour is shared between the Court's local staff, victims' lawyers, and intermediaries. One field assistant described to me how they inaugurated people into their role of victims in the Court's proceedings:

> When we came in, at the beginning, it was very, very difficult to have a civil relationship, an amicable discussion with some members of the community, because they had so many expectations. I give you an example: the first meeting we had in Lukodi. We had gone there to give them updates as is expected from us about how the trial is going, analysing what the witnesses were saying etc. And they didn't seem so much interested . . . I remember this gentleman getting up and he had a lot of questions that were not exactly friendly, and they were not intended to get a response, but to trigger the community . . . You know that the

[81] Focus Group Discussion, Lukodi (25 July 2019); Interview with Local Women's Advocate, Gulu (19 July 2019); Interview with Formerly Abducted Survivor, Gulu (27 July 2019); Interview with Local Teacher and Religious Leader, Gulu (30 July 2019); Interview with Victims and Women's Advocate, Gulu (19 July 2019). Those, who were abducted by the LRA, often felt they were the real victims, while their communities tend to see them as perpetrators, often harassing them by calling them 'bush people'.

[82] One victims' lawyer told me that the victims they represent believe that losing a loved one is the worst form of victimization and that they sometimes neglect the harms suffered by those who were abducted, raped, and/or forcibly married. Interview with Victim's Lawyer Assistant, Kampala (9 July 2019).

[83] 'Expectation management' has become a buzzword as well as a strategy promoted by civil society, academics, and the Court's practitioners to improve the ICC's victim engagement. See ICC (n 2) § 917.

> Court gives us transport costs to give to people when we call them for a meeting. It's supposed to be 5000 Shillings [1 Pound] per person regardless of where they are coming from . . . He asked, 'the 5000 Shillings [we receive], are we supposed to treat it as reparations?' But the tone he was using was not that he was confused about that, and that he genuinely wanted to know, but he was trying to get people to underestimate what we do, and I remember there was a lot of cheering and no one was willing to listen to our response, and it took a lot for us to get them to a point where they were willing to listen and have a proper discussion with us about what our role is and what their expectations are.[84]

Once victims listen, once they participate in the trial, the discourse shifts. Victim participation becomes their duty. The same field assistant explained:

> They still don't understand fully how it works and even what is expected of them. At the beginning, we had clients who were telling us that they are tired of attending meetings, but one would expect that this is something that someone who has chosen to participate would understand, this is the expectation: this is their duty. So, this is something we had to go through over and over again and tell them, step by step: 'Do you remember when you came in to apply? This is what participation means. This is what is expected of you, to share your views. The trial cannot go on without you giving us your views. It becomes pointless if we are to work without you. We only work with what you have told us.' It took time.[85]

Even if people initially resist or mock the Court, participation disciplines them: you have agreed to participate, now you must share your views. As victims are roped into the process, victim participation morphs from a democratic form—'have your say'—to a labour form—'work with us'. Victims' demands for reparations have been disciplined, too. They are 'unrealistic expectations' of which the Court needs to disabuse them.

These regulatory moves of simultaneous inclusion and exclusion of victims in the Court's trials map onto capitalist pressures for the simultaneous inclusion and exclusion of subjects in the Global South as both workers and surplus populations. As such, they express deeper contradictions in the

[84] Interview with Victims' Lawyer Assistant, Kampala (9 July 2019).
[85] ibid.

capitalist mode of production, which both needs to turn all living humans into capitalist subjects, and, at the same time, renders them surplus. The forms and terms of victims' inclusion at the Court, moreover, are not only arbitrary from the perspective of victims' lived experience, they also continue to be procedurally uncertain and unsettled, revealing another striking parallel between the precarity of victim participation and the precarity of labour participation.[86] This parallel suggests that the hope expressed by NGO advocates that 'over time, further decisions of different chambers may lead to greater consistency and predictability regarding the Court's approach to participation and reparation' may be in vain.[87] The lack of consistency and predictability is not a temporal anomaly but a key lever to manage victims as capitalist subjects.[88] Indeed, I argue that the tendency to simultaneously include and exclude victims in the Court's legal processes not only mirrors but also creates their simultaneous inclusion/exclusion in global capitalist relations. By engaging in the Court's processes, people not only become victims; they also become capitalist subjects, a metamorphosis that becomes more evident, once we examine the Court's outreach, assistance, and reparation work in the field.

[86] See also ICC Prosecutor Karim Khan's speech for the opening of the judicial year 2022 https://www.youtube.com/watch?v=lyTRSzYhUk4 (accessed 26 November 2022) ('One request I perhaps make is that after 20 years of evolution we are now a mature institution. I think defense, legal representatives for victims and prosecution really do increasingly ask for greater predictability in procedural decisions'). Megan Hirst and Sandra Sahyouni argue that three key procedural uncertainties remain with regard to victim participation: (1) whether victims need to apply to participate 'in proceedings which are not related to an active case'; (2) uncertainty regarding how broadly or narrowly Chambers will interpret victims' 'personal interests' which will determine the scope and modalities of participation; and (3) 'it remains unclear if and when victims are entitled to appeal decisions'. Megan Hirst and Sandra Sahyouni, 'Effective legal representation for participating victims: principles, challenges and some solutions' in Rudina Jasini and Gregory Townsend (eds), *Advancing the Impact of Victim Participation at the International Criminal Court: Bridging the Gap Between Research and Practice* (ESRC, OUP 2020) 4, 11–12 https://www.law.ox.ac.uk/sites/files/oxlaw/iccba_-_oxford_publication_30_november_2020_.pdf. Regarding reparation, Luc Walleyn argues that 'as a result of conflicting legal interpretations and decisions, the present picture of reparations before the ICC is quite chaotic. Victims and their counsel do not know what to expect.' Luc Walleyn, 'The Participation of Victims in the Process of Collective Reparations at the ICC' in Jasini and Townsend ibid 77, 89.

[87] Gaelle Carayon and Jonathan O'Donohue, 'The International Criminal Court's Strategies in Relation to Victims' (2017) 15(3) Journal of International Criminal Justice 567, 588; Mariana Pena and Gaelle Carayon, 'Is the ICC Making the Most of Victim Participation?' (2013) 7(3) International Journal of Transitional Justice 518.

[88] Such inconsistency and unpredictability are partly due to adversarial legal procedure, which determines which charges are confirmed and which crimes, if any, the defendant will be convicted of, and partly a peculiarity of the ICC as its judges have, by and large, failed to agree on principles and modalities of victim participation and reparation that would be applied across cases.

1.4 Creating Capitalist Subjects in the Global South

To understand how victims are created as capitalist subjects, we need to look beyond courtroom proceedings to what the Court does 'in the field'. The ICC has 'gone local' in recent years, both institutionally and ideologically, as the principle that courts should keep distance from affected communities to be objective and neutral is unravelling.[89] The Court has very few trials, only one in Uganda, but it engages millions of people through its interactive outreach programmes including victims, affected communities, and local stakeholders, as well as lawyers, academics, and journalists.[90]

[89] I believe that there has been a gradual shift away from the principle of 'distant justice', which Phil Clark documents in his book as a product of ongoing justice contestations at the Court. See Phil Clark, *Distant Justice: The Impact of the International Criminal Court on African Politics* (CUP 2018). I will develop this point more fully in chs 2 and 3. Just to give a few examples, in his swearing-in speech, the ICC's new Prosecutor Karim Khan said: 'The Hague itself should be a city of last resort. Whenever possible, we should have trials in the country or in the region, wherever possible. It is easier for survivors and victims. It can save costs, reduce the carbon footprint, but also importantly, it shows we are not in the export business.' IntlCriminalCourt, 'Swearing-in ceremony: Speech of new ICC Prosecutor Karim Asad Ahmad Khan QC, 16 June 2021' https://www.youtube.com/watch?v=tDldr2ma1S0 (accessed 2 August 2022). See also the Prosecutor's speech at the Assembly of States Parties in December 2022: '"In 2022 my Office has implemented significant changes to make us more agile, field-focused & increase our capacity to partner effectively with survivors & impacted communities" #ICC Prosecutor #KarimAAKhanKC at #ASP21' ICC Twitter account (5 December 2022) https://twitter.com/IntlCrimCourt/status/1599754055341199361 (accessed 9 December 2022); OTP, 'Strategic Plan 2023–2025' (Strategic Goal 4) https://www.icc-cpi.int/sites/default/files/2023-06/OTP-Strategic-Plan_2023-2025.pdf (accessed 10 July 2023). Vasuki Nesiah, likewise, argues that 'today the discourse of local ownership and democratic legitimacy is front and centre in contemporary discussions of the ICC'. Vasuki Nesiah, 'Local Ownership of Global Governance' (2016) 14(4) Journal of International Criminal Justice 985, 986. A shift towards localization and decentralization has informed development interventions for some time but is more recent in international criminal justice. See Luis Eslava and Sundhya Pahuja, 'The State and International Law: A Reading from the Global South' (2020) 11(1) Humanity: An International Journal of Human Rights, Humanitarianism, and Development 118. See also the following ASP resolution: 'Conscious of the vital role of field operations in the Court's work in situation countries and the importance of stakeholders working together to create suitable conditions for field operations' and 'emphasizing the importance of effective outreach to victims and affected communities in order to give effect to the unique mandate of the Court towards victims and determined to ensure the effective implementation of victims' rights, which constitute a cornerstone of the Rome Statute system'. Resolution ICC-ASP/20/Res.5 (n 8) 3. The Chambers likewise have confirmed the importance of outreach. See eg *Situation in the People's Republic of Bangladesh/Republic of the Union of Myanmar* (Order on Information and Outreach for the Victims of the Situation) [2020] ICC-01/19-28, § 7 ('The Chamber considers that a meaningful exercise of this obligation is premised on the victims having access to complete and accurate information about their role at the Court during the various stages of the proceedings. Outreach facilitates and enables victims to enjoy and exercise their rights and the Court to fulfil its duties').

[90] ICC, 'Outreach Report' (2010) 1 https://www.icc-cpi.int/iccdocs/PIDS/publications/OUR2010Eng.pdf (accessed 4 March 2022); ICC, 'ICC Outreach: Building bonds every

'For the process to become really meaningful to the communities', the ICC's outreach section claims, 'messages shall be repeated and holding frequent meetings with the same groups are needed'.[91] Even during the pandemic year 2020, as outreach shifted online, 17,089 Northern Ugandans attended town-hall style meetings, radio listening clubs, and trial screenings, while the Court's interactive radio programmes and quizzes reached 14 million Ugandans.[92] In 2020 alone, the ICC reportedly engaged 253 million affected community members across its situation countries, while also distributing facemasks with the ICC's logo and advertising 'justice-related messages on billboards and stickers'.[93]

This move towards localizing international criminal justice means that victims, rather than perpetrators, are its pivot. In Northern Uganda, the Court organized monthly trial screenings in twenty-five locations, which, according to the ICC's former Registrar, 'bring the ICC courtrooms to every single member of the affected community'.[94] Indeed, more people watched the *Ongwen* trial in rural Uganda than in the cramped public gallery in The Hague.[95] Some victims were puzzled by the ICC's decision also to screen the trial in Dominic Ongwen's village:

day' https://www.icc-cpi.int/sites/default/files/Publications/outreachENG.pdf (accessed 23 July 2023).

[91] *Prosecutor v Ongwen* (Public redacted version of 'Report of the Registry on the outreach mission (9 April 2015) ICC-02/04-01/15-218-Conf-Exp) [2015] ICC-02/04-01/15-218-Red 18-12-2015, § 26.

[92] International Criminal Court, 'Report on activities and programme performance of the International Criminal Court for the year 2020' (2021) Assembly of States Parties (ICC-ASP/20/7) §§ 208, 209.

[93] ibid 91, §§ 195, 196. See also 30 billboards in #CentralAfricanRepublic announce the #ICC #Said trial opening on 26/9 https://twitter.com/IntlCrimCourt/status/1572585259564421122 (accessed 23 July 2023).

[94] At the launch of the 'Access to Justice' programme in Northern Uganda, the ICC Registrar said: 'It is our purpose, to transform these local interests into popular participation and ownership of the processes, and to strengthen local confidence in the Court's work and in justice and accountability in general. It is our profound confidence, that this project will help us to bring the ICC courtrooms to every single member of the affected community.' ICC Press Release, 'Danish Ambassador and ICC Registrar Launch "Access to Justice" Project in Uganda and mark International Criminal Justice Day' (17 July 2017) https://www.icc-cpi.int/news/danish-ambassador-and-icc-registrar-launch-access-justice-project-uganda-and-mark (accessed 9 December 2022); Maria Mabinty Kamara, 'An Insider Look at Outreach efforts in bringing the proceedings closer to the Victims and Affected Populations in Northern Uganda' *Justice in Conflict* (3 February 2021) https://justiceinconflict.org/2021/02/03/an-insider-look-at-outreach-efforts-in-bringing-the-proceedings-closer-to-the-victims-and-affected-populations-in-northern-uganda/ (accessed 4 March 2022).

[95] In all, 13,000 Ugandans attended the opening of the *Ongwen* trial in the ICC's viewing centres alone. See Lino Owor Ogora, 'Ongwen trial screenings in Uganda: Lessons in making

> I have heard that the screening is also going on at Coorom where Dominic Ongwen comes from. In my view, there would be no need to have another screening center there because the LRA did not attack Coorom. The ICC is wasting money there, which should be used to pay the school fees of orphans whose parents were killed during the Lukodi attack by LRA.[96]

This statement reflects a new common sense that international criminal trials are about victims, rendering Hannah Arendt's observation that 'a trial resembles a play in that both begin and end with the doer, not with the victim' arguably outdated.[97] Indeed, the discursive and institutional move towards 'justice for victims' at the ICC—often pushed along by NGO pressure as well as internal contradictions—has been consequential.[98] To attract state funding and public support, it is no longer sufficient for the Court to pay lip service to victims. Instead, the ICC actively manufactures and intimately engineers victim subjects who come to outreach meetings, watch the trial, participate in the proceedings, meet the Court's lawyers, and mobilize other community members.[99] 'The work also involves putting a human face on the Court so that this institution is not seen as an abstract entity but an institution that . . . [consists of] human beings and cares for the concerns of human beings', Maria Kamara, the court's outreach coordinator in Kenya and Uganda, herself from Sierra Leone, tells viewers in an

justice visible?' (2017) http://www.coalitionfortheicc.org/news/20170119/ongwen-trial-screenings-uganda-lessons-making-justice-visible (accessed 9 March 2022).

96 Cited in Owor Ogora (n 95).

97 Hannah Arendt, *Eichmann in Jerusalem: A Report on the Banality of Evil* (Penguin 2006) 27. 'I assure you that victims are at the heart of the ICC's mandate', ICC President Hofmański said on a recent field trip to the Central African Republic. ICC Press Release, 'ICC President and Acting Executive Director of the Trust Fund for Victims visit Central African Republic to witness Court's work on the ground' (28 November 2022) https://www.icc-cpi.int/news/icc-president-and-acting-executive-director-trust-fund-victims-visit-central-african-republic (accessed 9 December 2022).

98 NGOs would often claim that 'the court, after all, belongs to them [the victims]' and would insist that local knowledge and proximity to victims is more important than legal expertise on the ICC when appointing victims' lawyers at the ICC. These arguments are often made to counter attempts to 'internalise' legal representation of victims through the Office of the Public Counsel of Victims (OPCV). See FIDH, 'Whose Court is it? Judicial handbook on victims' rights at the International Criminal Court' (2021) 6–7, 25–27 https://www.fidh.org/IMG/pdf/fidh_whose_court_is_it_en.pdf (accessed 6 April 2023).

99 More than 15,000 victims had participated in the Court's proceedings by 2018 and 11,024 new applications were received between 2015 and 2020. See International Criminal Court, 'Report on activities and programme performance of the International Criminal Court for the year 2020' (2021) Assembly of States Parties (ICC-ASP/20/7) 92.

ICC video, entitled 'See, Understand and Relate', as the camera zooms in on African women feeding their babies at an outreach meeting.[100] Indeed, to produce and reproduce a more 'caring' international criminal justice, the Court needs the manifold labour of victims, victims' practitioners, and intermediaries both inside and outside the court's premises.

But the Court's victim engagement does not only create victims as legal subjects. It also creates capitalist 'survivors', and here we encounter another incarnation of the Court, the Trust Fund for Victims (TFV), which epitomizes the humanitarian and developmental ambitions of international criminal justice.[101] Endowed with two mandates, reparations and assistance, the TFV not only implements Court-ordered reparations but also 'provide[s] physical, psychological, and material support to victims and their families' in the Court's situation countries, even when there are no judicial proceedings.[102] Having assisted more than 104,000 people directly, and 350,000 family and community members indirectly, with reconstructive surgery, provision of prosthetic limbs, trauma-based counselling, educational support, income-generating activities, conflict mediation, and reconciliation,[103] the TFV 'assist[s] victims to return to a dignified and contributory life within their communities', and thereby 'contributes to realizing sustainable and long-lasting peace by promoting restorative justice and reconciliation'.[104]

[100] ibid. ICC Website, 'Making justice happen: Stories from ICC staff' https://www.icc-cpi.int/get-involved/staff-stories (accessed 21 January 2032).

[101] While some scholars and the Court's practitioners insist that the Court is not a 'development organization', ch 5 will show that the Trust Fund uses development methodology and partners for both its reparation and assistance mandates. See also Frédéric Mégret, 'Justifying Compensation by the International Criminal Court's Victims Trust Fund: Lessons From Domestic Compensation Schemes' (2010–2011) 36 Brooklyn Journal of International Law 124; Carolyn Hoyle and Leila Ullrich, 'New Court, New Justice? The Evolution of "Justice for Victims" at Domestic Courts and at the International Criminal Court' (2014) 12(4) Journal of International Criminal Justice 681, 696–97, 699; Peter Dixon, 'Reparations, Assistance and the Experience of Justice: Lessons from Colombia and the Democratic Republic of Congo (DRC)' (2016) 10 International Journal of Transitional Justice 88; Sara Kendall and Sarah MH Nouwen, 'International criminal justice and humanitarianism' in Kevin Heller and others (eds), *The Oxford Handbook of International Criminal Law* (OUP 2020) 719.

[102] TFV Website https://www.icc-cpi.int/tfv (accessed 13 March 2022); Rome Statute, arts 75, 79.

[103] ICC, 'Report to the Assembly of States Parties on the projects and the activities of the Board of Directors of the Trust Fund for Victims for the period 1 July 2017 to 30 June 2018' (23 July 2018) ICC-ASP/17/14, 3; *Prosecutor v Ongwen* (Trust Fund for Victims' Final Observations on Reparations) [2022] ICC-02/04-01/15-1992, § 34. This includes 60,000 victims in Northern Uganda since 2008.

[104] TFV Website (n 102).

The Trust Fund has introduced the term 'victim–survivor' to conform both to the Court's legal texts, which tie it to the terminology of victims, and to accepted discourse among feminist academics and social workers who insist on calling victims 'survivors'.[105] An evaluator of the Trust Fund's programmes applauded this creativity. 'My training is in public health so I always would say "survivor"', she told me, 'to see particularly women who suffered from sexual violence as victims goes against my approach to that work . . . "I'm a victim"; it is such a passive state'.[106] Victims are celebrated as survivors, yet a closer analysis of the Trust Fund's programmes reveals that survival, as much as victimhood, is entangled with preconditions. Victims can only survive if they transform themselves into productive and reproductive capitalist subjects. To 'start a new life', victim–survivors, often women, receive microloans, vocational training, and business training.[107] They learn hairdressing and tailoring, rearing poultry, and growing cash crops. They also learn how to manage their budgets and sell their products on local markets and, ideally, for export.[108] Expressing her gratitude about this assistance, one victim of sexual and gender-based violence said:

> The microcredit was the biggest benefit I received. It gave me dignity and made me respectable. I can even afford to make myself beautiful. Without that, I couldn't have found a husband. Nobody wants to marry a woman who was raped, but he finds me beautiful because I can take care of myself.[109]

[105] TFV Strategic Plan 2014–2017 (n 786) 7 (footnote 4). The 2020–2021 Strategic Plan uses 'victims' and the TFV website uses a combination of victims and survivors https://www.trustfundforvictims.org/ (accessed 17 February 2022). For the shift in feminist discourse from 'victims' to 'survivors' see Jennifer L Dunn, '"Victims" and "Survivors": Emerging Vocabularies of Motive for "Battered Women Who Stay"' (2005) 75 Sociological Inquiry 1. See also Norma Jean Profitt, '"Battered Women" as "Victims" and "Survivors": Creating Space for Resistance' (1996) 13(1) Canadian Social Work Review/Revue Canadienne de Service Social 23; Brianna C Delker, Rowan Salton, and Kate C McLean, 'Giving Voice to Silence: Empowerment and Disempowerment in the Developmental Shift from Trauma "Victim" to "Survivor-Advocate"' (2020) 21(2) Journal of Trauma & Dissociation 242.

[106] Telephone interview with TFV's Evaluator (3 January 2014).

[107] Edda Kristjánsdóttir, 'International mass claims processes and the ICC Trust Fund for Victims' in Carla Ferstman, Mariana Goetz, and Alan Stephens (eds), *Reparations for Victims of Genocide, War Crimes and Crimes Against Humanity: Systems in Place and Systems in the Making* (Martinus Nijhoff 2009) 167.

[108] TFV, 'Material Support' https://www.trustfundforvictims.org/en/what-we-do/assistance-programmes/material-support (accessed 13 March 2022); Interview with Victim-Intermediary, Gulu (24 July 2019).

[109] International Center for Research on Women, 'External Evaluation of the Trust Fund for Victims Programmes in Northern Uganda and the Democratic Republic of Congo: Towards a

Using these 'victim–survivor stories' to illustrate its success, the TFV portrays victim–survivors as 'resourceful',[110] 'motivated to improve',[111] 'actively involved in economically productive activities',[112] 'making savings',[113] getting married, avoiding divorce, and producing children.[114] The Court's staff often recount these stories when asked about the Trust Fund:

> If someone tells you, 'as a result of that rape, I have developed a fistula for so many years; I lost my marriage, my relationships; I've been abandoned and ostracized in my community. But thanks to the Trust Fund, I got married [again]. I have confidence; my dignity has been restored . . . and I have even been able to have a baby. Because of the damages that I suffered, it looked impossible but the Trust Fund's project, the surgery that I went through helped me to overcome my fear and now I feel normal again'. Those are powerful statements coming from victims who themselves have benefited from the Trust Fund.[115]

Victims' survival is thus premised on good capitalist subjecthood. By undergoing physical and psychological rehabilitation, attending peace schools, taking out debt and doing casual labour, victims 'resume their roles as productive and contributing members of their societies'.[116] There is, however, no question of them going to university or getting an office job. With the help of the Trust Fund, victims, effectively, become better wives and better workers.[117]

Perspective of Upcoming Interventions' (2013) 34 https://www.icrw.org/wp-content/uploads/2016/10/ICRW-TFV--Evaluation-Report.pdf (accessed 4 March 2022).

[110] TFV, 'Victims Voices' https://www.trustfundforvictims.org/en/victims-voices (accessed 30 March 2022); TFV, 'Mary (Northern Uganda)' https://www.trustfundforvictims.org/en/stories/mary-northern-uganda (accessed 30 March 2022).

[111] ibid.

[112] ibid.

[113] TFV, 'Marie (Democratic Republic of Congo)' https://www.trustfundforvictims.org/en/stories/marie-democratic-republic-of-congo (accessed 30 March 2022).

[114] TFV, 'Salima (Democratic Republic of Congo)' https://www.trustfundforvictims.org/en/stories/salima-democratic-republic-of-congo (accessed 30 March 2022); TFV, 'Cissy (Democratic Republic of Congo)' https://www.trustfundforvictims.org/en/stories/cissy-democratic-republic-of-congo (accessed 30 March 2022).

[115] Interview with Registry Officer, Kampala (2 August 2019).

[116] TFV, 'A Road to Recovery: Healing, Empowerment and Reconciliation' (2014) vii https://www.trustfundforvictims.org/sites/default/files/reports/TFV%20Programme%20Progress%20Report%20%20-%20Winter%202014.pdf (accessed 13 March 2020).

[117] Kendall also argues that the TFV produces productive subjects, but she interprets this process through a Foucauldian lens of legal humanitarian governance rather than a Marxian lens of the creation of capitalist subjects and relations. Sara Kendall, 'Beyond the restorative

This returns us to a key question: who is international criminal justice for? While critical scholars have argued that international criminal trials are spectacles which are mainly created for audiences in the Global North,[118] this book suggests that they are also about people in the Global South. Global capitalism, after all, needs their work and acquiescence. Most of the Court's cases are in Africa, which forms the periphery of the global system. If we look at the African continent from the perspective of commodity production or geopolitics, its role may not look decisive. Most of its people appear as 'surplus population'; value, seemingly, is not generated by their labouring bodies but hides in their land and raw materials. In Northern Uganda, for example, it appears, as Branch and Yen have argued, as if psycho-pharmaceutical forms of governance have drugged local communities into passivity to rob their land and resources.[119]

Such a perspective, however, neglects the centrality of 'surplus populations' to the capitalist mode of production. The surplus population, Marx argued, 'forms a disposable industrial reserve army, which belongs to capital just as absolutely as if the latter had bred it at its own cost . . . it creates a mass of human material always ready for exploitation by capital in the interests of capital's own changing valorization requirememts'.[120] Surplus people may be individually or even collectively disposable, but the reserve army of labour is not. It holds the key to capitalist expansion: 'there must be the possibility of suddenly throwing great masses of men into the decisive areas without doing any damage to the scale of production in other spheres'.[121] Surplus subjects, consequently, have to be 'always ready' for new forms of capitalist exploitation and ideology is the process that makes and keeps them ready.[122] While traditional forms of industrial wage labour have receded, human labour remains the animating force of global capitalism,

turn: The limits of legal humanitarianism' in Christian de Vos, Sara Kendall, and Carsten Stahn (eds), *Contested Justice: The Politics and Practice of International Criminal Court Interventions* (CUP 2015) 352, 369–74.

[118] Clarke, *Fictions of Justice* (n 22) 4; Tallgren (n 21); Lohne (n 21) 145; Schwöbel-Patel (n 22).

[119] Adam Branch and Adrian Yen, 'Neoliberal discipline and violence in Northern Uganda' in Jörg Wiegratz, Giuliano Martiniello, and Elisa Greco (eds), *The Dynamics of Neoliberal Transformation* (Zed Books 2018).

[120] Karl Marx, *Capital Volume I: A Critique of Political Economy* (Penguin Books 1990) 784.

[121] ibid 785.

[122] See ch 3 for how debt makes surplus populations productive. See also Susanne Soederberg, *Debtfare States and the Poverty Industry Money, Discipline and the Surplus Population* (Routledge 2014).

'mediat[ing] the metabolism between men and nature, and therefore human life itself'.[123] Even capitalist forms that look 'immaterial' such as the digital world ultimately consist of natural resources (eg rare earth metals) mixed with human labour. What is sold and bought, in the final analysis, is human creativity, social activity, relations and attention, forms of labour, which, like social reproduction work, have been invisibilized and thus cheapened by global capitalism.[124]

Once we look at the world from a social reproduction perspective, we see how it is held together by human labour. The Court's victim engagement both consists of different forms of labour—legal and emotional, professional and manual, productive and reproductive—and operates as a mechanism of creating labourers. Through outreach, victim participation, reparation, and assistance, the Court both creates and disciplines highly gendered and racialized capitalist subjects in the Global South who are supposed to 'stop crying', 'work hard', 'be peaceful', 'get married', 'repay debt', and accept their place at the bottom of the global division of labour.[125] These labourers, moreover, need to be reproduced without a wage and that is what women do through their subsistence and social reproduction work. If we look at 'Africa' from the perspective of social reproduction, we see how women in the Global South both sustain and can potentially disrupt the global capitalist order.[126]

[123] Marx (n 120) 133.

[124] See Christian Fuchs and Sebastian Sevignani, 'What Is Digital Labour? What Is Digital Work? What's their Difference? And Why Do These Questions Matter for Understanding Social Media?' (2013) 11(2) tripleC 237, 237 ('Online activity creates content, social networks and relations, location data, browsing data, data about likes and preferences, etc. This online activity is fun and work at the same time—play labour').

[125] See also Stephen Gill, 'Globalisation, Market Civilisation, and Disciplinary Neoliberalism' (1995) 24(3) Millennium 399.

[126] Silvia Federici, *Re-enchanting the World: Feminism and the Politics of the Commons* (PM Press 2018); Lyn Ossome, 'Land in transition: from social reproduction of labour power to social reproduction of power' (2021) 39(4) Journal of Contemporary African Studies 550. Alessandra Mezzadri points out that 'the majority of people on this planet labour in the informal economy.' Alessandra Mezzadri, 'On the value of social reproduction: Informal labour, the majority world and the need for inclusive theories and politics' (2019) 2.04 Radical Philosophy 33, 37.

1.5 The Blame Cascade: The Materiality of Victim Blaming

The production of victims as labouring subjects occurs through a broader institutional mechanism, what I call the blame cascade, which integrates the moral and material economy of international criminal justice. More specifically, I use the blame cascade as a metaphor to make visible three key dynamics. First, the blame cascade unveils how the visible legal process of attributing and apportioning blame to the defendant in the courtroom is accompanied by an invisible institutional process, whereby blame cascades down through the mundane, everyday racialized and gendered devaluation of labour. Secondly, the blame cascade counters the idealist reading of the justice cascade, which claims that powerful leaders are increasingly brought to justice in international relations, through a materialist reading of global capitalist relations. Such a reading reveals that in order to reproduce the existing capitalist order morally —to create the semblance of its justice—blame needs to be channelled to those at the bottom. Thirdly, the blame cascade unearths how it is ultimately victims, and not only perpetrators, who are blamed in the process: the judges in The Hague blame the victims' lawyers in Kenya and Uganda, the metropolitan victims' lawyers—the intermediaries 'in the field', and the 'entrepreneurial' intermediaries—the 'lazy' victims. White men in suits in The Hague pass blame on to black men in suits in the Court's situation countries, who pass it on to women's lawyers and NGO workers, who further pass it on to feminized victims and affected communities in rural Uganda and Kenya.[127] In this way, the blame cascade brings into view the interplay between race, gender, labour, and blame in a new way.

The question of race and racism has, of course, been a long-standing concern for an institution which has mainly focused on Africa. In fact, in early 2017, the African Union threatened with a mass exodus from the ICC, arguing that the Court was unfairly targeting Africa.[128] This was not a new allegation. Some African heads of states had long argued that the ICC is a

[127] On the feminized and racialized segmentation of the international division of labour see Maria Mies, *Patriarchy and Accumulation on a World Scale: Women in the International Division of Labour* (Zed Books 1999) 142–43.

[128] 'African Union backs mass withdrawal from ICC' *BBC News* (1 February 2017) https://www.bbc.co.uk/news/world-africa-38826073 (accessed 24 July 2023); ICC Forum, 'Africa Question: Is the International Criminal Court (ICC) targeting Africa inappropriately?' https://iccforum.com/africa (accessed 30 September 2022).

neo-colonial tool of powerful states.[129] All of the Court's thirty-one cases to date have been against African and Arab nationals, while permanent members of the Security Council like the United States, China, France, and the United Kingdom have not only systematically evaded the Court's legal scrutiny but have also enjoyed the privilege to refer other countries and conflicts to the Court's jurisdiction.[130] This does not mean, however, that African heads of states are necessarily 'victims' of the Court's interventions.[131] To the contrary, they have often been quite shrewd at using the Court against their domestic opponents, and, so far, only Burundi (and the Philippines) have acted on their threats to leave the Court.[132]

Beyond these political contestations, critical race and TWAIL scholars have more subtly analysed how international criminal justice perpetuates a racialized global order not least through the construction of the evil black perpetrator.[133] Both the ICC's jurisdictional regime and substantive law,

[129] Geoffrey Lugano, 'Counter-Shaming the International Criminal Court's Intervention as Neocolonial: Lessons from Kenya' (2017) 11 International Journal of Transitional Justice 9. Vice News, 'Is the International Criminal Court Racist? System Error' *YouTube* (15 March 2021) https://www.youtube.com/watch?v=2RaraCu8zXg (accessed 24 July 2023); Oumar Ba, 'A Truly International Criminal Court: Why the New Prosecutor should look beyond Africa' *Foreign Affairs* (18 June 2021) https://www.foreignaffairs.com/articles/africa/2021-06-18/truly-international-criminal-court (accessed 24 July 2023).

[130] ICC, 'Cases' https://www.icc-cpi.int/Pages/cases.aspx (accessed 29 March 2022). See Rome Statute, art 13. The situations in Darfur and Libya were referred to the ICC by the Security Council. The situation is different for Russian nationals since its military intervention in Ukraine. See ICC, 'Situation in Ukraine' https://www.icc-cpi.int/situations/ukraine (accessed 7 August 2023).

[131] Former ICC defendant and current president of Kenya, William Ruto, for example claimed that he was a victim of the ICC. See Kamari Maxine Clarke, '"We ask for justice, you give us law": The rule of law, economic markets and the International Criminal Court' in Christian de Vos, Sara Kendall, and Carsten Stahn (eds), *Contested Justice: The Politics and Practice of International Criminal Court Interventions* (CUP 2015) 272–73; Kendall (n 11).

[132] Clark (n 89); Oumar Ba, *States of Justice: The Politics of the International Criminal Court* (CUP 2020); 'Burundi leaves International Criminal Court amid row' *BBC News* (27 October 2017) https://www.bbc.co.uk/news/world-africa-41775951 (accessed 30 September 2022); ICC, 'Republic of the Philippines' https://www.icc-cpi.int/philippines#:~:text=While%20the%20Philippines'%20withdrawal%20from,and%20including%2016%20March%202019 (accessed 30 September 2022).

[133] Obiora Chinedu Okafor and Uchechukwu Ngwaba, 'The International Criminal Court as a "Transitional Justice" Mechanism in Africa: Some Critical Reflections' (2015) 9(1) International Journal of Transitional Justice 90; Asad Kiyani, John Reynolds, and Sujith Xavier, 'Foreword' (2016) 14(4) Journal of International Criminal Justice 915; John Reynolds and Sujith Xavier, 'The Dark Corners of the World': TWAIL and International Criminal Justice' (2016) 14(4) Journal of International Criminal Justice 959; Kamari M Clarke, Abel S Knottnerus, and Eefje de Volder (eds), *Africa and the ICC: Perceptions of Justice* (CUP 2016); Christopher Gevers, 'Africa and international criminal law' in Kevin Heller and others (eds), *The Oxford Handbook of International Criminal Law* (OUP 2020); Souheir Edelbi, 'Making Race Speakable in International Criminal Law: Review of Lingaas' *The Concept of Race in International Criminal Law*' (2020) TWAILR: Reflections #16/2020 1, 4.

López argues, spotlight black guilt while eclipsing white guilt.[134] Clarke has further shown how the African perpetrator 'often stands for a figure of [irrational] violence', thus obfuscating not only the collective perpetration of atrocity crimes but also longer histories of colonial violence without which such crimes become unintelligible.[135] Apart from the racialization of perpetrators, Mégret and Falco have highlighted how structural racism suffuses the Court's practices without necessarily 'relying on racist actors'.[136] 'The devil of structural racism', they argue, 'is in the details, the distance between theory and practice and the many cracks through which prejudice, be it conscious or unconscious, slips in rather than in some grand overall racist conspiracy'.[137]

Yet, both accounts of racialization—the narrow legal blaming of individual black perpetrators and the broad structural racism and subtle prejudices—miss how materially and openly racialization works through the Court's social relations. Indeed, the focus on the Court's legal regime (its jurisdiction, referral mechanisms, and cases), and on its criminal justice functions (criminalization, sentencing, and imprisonment) has obscured how integral racialization and feminization are to the Court's political economy. After all, without the free and underpaid labour of 'local' lawyers, investigators, field assistants, interpreters, intermediaries, and victims in the Global South, the ICC could not simultaneously undertake investigations, outreach, and victim engagement in seventeen different countries while facing the prospect of 'zero budget growth'.[138] The Court itself admits that 'what you see in the Courtroom is the tip of the iceberg. For just one day of Court hearings, hundreds of people are working behind the scenes

[134] Rachel López, 'Black guilt, white guilt at the International Criminal Court' in Matiangai Sirleaf (ed), *Race and National Security* (OUP 2023).

[135] Kamari Maxine Clarke, 'Refiguring the perpetrator: culpability, history and international criminal law's impunity gap' (2015) 19(5) The International Journal of Human Rights 592, 594.

[136] Randle C DeFalco and Frédéric Mégret, 'The invisibility of race at the ICC: lessons from the US criminal justice system' (2019) 7(1) London Review of International Law 55, 64.

[137] ibid 70.

[138] NGOs often argue that the ICC is a 'sound investment for peace' and rather cheap compared to 'the conflicts that make it necessary', but they rarely explain what makes it cheap. Their critique of states' attempts to impose a 'zero-nominal growth' budget policy on the ICC is less about labour exploitation of intermediaries and volunteers, and more about its impairment of the Court's ability to work independently and impartially. See Coalition for the International Criminal Court (CICC), 'Victims could lose out with states' double-standard on International Criminal Court resources' (2022) https://www.coalitionfortheicc.org/news/20220330/OpenLetter_ICCresources (accessed 15 July 2022); CICC, 'A sufficient budget' https://www.coalitionfortheicc.org/fight/state-support/sufficient-budget (accessed 15 July 2022).

to make it happen'.[139] African lawyers can be hired cheaply as field assistants or interpreters, and intermediaries, often victims themselves, do most of the work of engaging communities as unpaid 'volunteers' or 'friends' of the Court.[140] In other words, racialized and feminized labour devaluation is what makes the Court's work possible in the first place. Materially, the Court works because feminization and racialization makes labour invisible and thus cheap. Morally, recruiting people from affected communities to work for the Court makes it easier to blame them as 'unreliable', 'opportunistic', or 'lazy' when things go wrong, as they often do.[141] The Court's 'racism problem', therefore, does not only lie in the selectivity of its jurisdiction and case selection, but also in the materiality of its everyday operations.

These everyday operations unfold gradually through different actors and levels, like a cascade, which is already a popular metaphor to describe international justice processes. Most prominently, Kathryn Sikkink's book, *Justice Cascade: How Human Rights Ideas Change World Politics*, published in 2011, documented a 'dramatic new trend in world politics toward holding individual state officials, including heads of state, criminally accountable for human rights violations'.[142] Sikkink particularly highlighted the work of human rights activists in turning 'a small stream'—the norm of individual criminal accountability—into a sweeping 'cascade'.[143] My interest here lies less in discussing Sikkink's claims and more in appropriating her metaphor. Only where Sikkink sees a global diffusion of justice norms, I see a cascade of blame flowing from the powerful to the powerless. And where Sikkink sees eager human rights activists passionately promoting justice norms, I see neocolonial intermediaries who are simultaneously formed by and pass on a justice ideology that situates them awkwardly as somewhat privileged but also always blameworthy justice compradors.

[139] ICC, 'Justice at Work https://www.icc-cpi.int/get-involved/justice-at-work (accessed 11 November 2022).

[140] Interview with Victims' Lawyer, London (10 September 2018). The ICC regards intermediaries as volunteers and only pays them for activities explicitly requested by the Court and Counsel. See ICC, 'Guidelines Governing the Relations between the Court and Intermediaries for the Organs and Units of the Court and Counsel working with intermediaries' (2014) 12–13 https://www.icc-cpi.int/iccdocs/lt/GRCI-eng.pdf (accessed 16 November 2021). A Registry officer in Kampala told me that they pay 'volunteers' who organize the screenings of the *Ongwen* trial 150,000 Ugandan Shillings [£32] per screening. Interview with Registry Officer, Kampala (2 August 2019).

[141] I will demonstrate this particularly in chs 3 and 4.

[142] Katherine Sikkink, *The Justice Cascade: How Human Rights Prosecutions are Changing World Politics* (WW Norton & Co 2011) 5.

[143] ibid 5, 11.

At each level of the cascade, the main accusation is that the people 'below' don't work enough or lack competence and integrity. Victims' lawyers have particularly tried the patience of the Court's judges. One judge described them to me as 'a new caste of lawyers who make big money out of the suffering of the people'.[144] Intermediaries, likewise, have been a popular target of complaints. They are diverse actors, ranging from victims and community leaders to grassroots organizations and national NGOs, who help the Court with evidence collection and victim engagement on the ground, usually for very little or no compensation. The Court's staff regularly accuse them of 'gatekeeping', 'incompetence', 'unreliability',[145] and 'corruption', worrying that they will compromise the Court's judicial integrity.[146] But

[144] Interview with Judge, The Hague (19 December 2013). Elisa Hoven's interviews with practitioners at the ECCC also revealed that they blamed the problems of victim participation to a considerable extent on the victims' lawyers or the failure of the judges to better manage them. See Elisa Hoven, 'Civil Party Participation in Trials of Mass Crimes: A Qualitative Study at the Extraordinary Chambers in the Courts of Cambodia' (2014) 12 Journal of International Criminal Justice 81.

[145] Concerns about the unreliability of intermediaries have not only been expressed by the Defence but also by the Prosecution, the Chambers, and the Registry. *Prosecutor v Lubanga* (Redacted Decision on the 'Defence Application Seeking a Permanent Stay of the Proceedings') [2011] ICC-01/04-01/06-2690-Red2, §§ 75–87, 198; *Prosecutor v Lubanga* (Judgment pursuant to Article 74 of the Statute) [2012] ICC-01/04-01/06-2842, § 184. *Prosecutor v Lubanga* (Redacted Decision on Intermediaries) ICC-01/04-01/06-2434-Red2) [2010], §§ 135–49 ('the prosecution suggests for that for those intermediaries whom the Chamber has deemed "sufficiently tainted" by specific allegations, they should be brought to The Hague to appear before the Chamber as court witnesses, to be questioned by the Chamber alone (in the absence of both parties) without revealing their identities to the defence'). On the OTP's use of intermediaries see *Prosecutor v Lubanga* (Judgment pursuant to Article 74 of the Statute) [2012] ICC-01/04-01/06-2842, §§ 183–205, 188 ('P-0582 explained that it was considered necessary to avoid intermediaries who were not serious in their offer to help the Court, and the investigators did not use intermediaries who were trying to gain publicity or money by introducing witnesses to the OTP').

[146] The Registry has, for example, argued that 'it is vital to assess, select, train and monitor intermediaries properly' and for Registry staff to be present in the field when intermediaries assist victims in filling out victim applications to 'also help to guard against abuse and the need for the Court to return later to verify applications'. *Prosecutor v Ntaganda* (Registry Observations in compliance with the Decision ICC-01/04-02/06-54-Conf) [2013] ICC-01/04-02/06-57, § 13. In my interviews, Registry staff and victims' lawyers often mentioned gatekeeping, corruption, and unreliability of intermediaries as key challenges although they also acknowledged their difficult position: 'And we have had instances where we hear later that victims say, "but I was promised that I would get reparations". It is so hard. Because we understand why intermediaries also don't want to convey bad news. They want to please people; they want people to engage in the process . . . What we do informally sometimes we say [to other ICC offices] "be careful of this one [intermediary]". Sometimes we have decided not to use, not to work with certain intermediaries because they don't seem trustworthy or not have the victims' interests at their heart etc.' Interview with Senior Registry Official, The Hague (16 December 2013); Interview with Legal Officer, Registry, The Hague (12 November 2013). I present more evidence in ch 4 on intermediaries.

intermediaries are also the ones who have to listen to the victims, see them break down, tell them that they are no longer recognized as victims by the Court, that the accused has been acquitted, that there will not be any reparations. The darker you are, the closer you are to victims, the more emotional labour you do, the less valuable your work is. Intermediaries justify the Court's 'legal limitations' and 'manage' victims' expectations. Even more, they have staked their legitimacy on the Court and will bear the brunt on the ground when the Court fails to deliver.[147]

Intermediaries, however, try to pass the buck. They want to mobilize the victims enough to squeeze resources out of the 'international community' to maintain their professional labour as NGO officers, cultural, or religious leaders, but not so much that victims start making political demands that unravel the local order, and, more specifically, the division between professional and manual labour.[148] Affected communities in Uganda and Kenya, intermediaries complain, have become lazy and difficult. The victims have to 'stop crying' and go back to toil in the fields.[149] Effectively, intermediaries are pulling themselves up while pushing others down. They discipline victims into 'their role' as farmers and menial labourers while anxiously protecting their precarious privileges as professional and intellectual labourers.[150]

The dynamics of the blame cascade are also something I experienced myself working as an unpaid intern at the Court. A key part of our work at the Registry's cooperation section was to coordinate between the different organs of the Court (Registry, Office of the Prosecutor (OTP), Presidency, and Chambers). When something went wrong with the joint scheduling of a cooperation seminar with Latin American states, I—as an unpaid intern—was blamed not because it was actually my fault, but because it was the easiest way to soothe fractured relations between the Court's organs and their staff. Blame goes down, praise goes up, and having a large

[147] 'The fact that the Court's own outreach is so limited means that the "intermediaries" receive the brunt of the society's complaints about the functioning of the Court. "Intermediaries" are also at the receiving end of the complaints from victims when the victims see that their cases have not advanced or have not been recognised by the Court.' Victims' Rights Working Group, 'Comments on the Role and Relationship of 'Intermediaries' with the International Criminal Court' (2009) 3 https://www.fidh.org/IMG/pdf/VRWG_Role_of_intermediaries_ICC_-_February_2009_En_.pdf (accessed 12 December 2022).

[148] Interview with NGO Representative, Gulu (18 July 2019); Interview with Cultural Leader, Gulu (20 July 2019); Interview with Women's Rights Lawyer, Gulu (24 July 2019).

[149] Interview with ICC Field Assistant, Gulu (17 July 2019).

[150] Interview with NGO Representative, Gulu (18 July 2019).

pool of precarious, unpaid, and temporary staff makes it easy to externalize blame.[151] The Court manages these relations by inculcating a sense of duty into its working subjects. When I tried to leave my internship before the end of my contract, my boss admonished me: 'you have agreed to work for the Court, and you cannot simply leave. The Court needs you' (just not enough to pay me).[152] She was constructing this as a moral duty to the Court and my team rather than a legal obligation (as an unpaid intern, I could leave any time, as long as I gave two weeks of notice).[153]

Eventually, victims also bear blame for the Court's processes. The judges do not blame victims directly; that would not only be tasteless but also impractical as the victims are far away. Instead, blame cascades downwards through multiple layers of intermediation and informal labour. Rather than being merely discursive, victim blaming becomes entrenched through material relationships, as this book will show, especially by incorporating victims and intermediaries into labour and debt relations. Ultimately, victims are blamed not for the crimes they suffered, but for failing to become successful capitalist survivors.[154]

[151] Labour rights and pay have become more prominent issues at the Court in recent years. In December 2022, the burgundy ribbon campaign by external defence team members culminated in an 'historic' labour strike, illuminating the precarious labour conditions of defence support staff, 'having no contract, no job termination period, no sick leave, no vacation pay, and no parental pay', and being paid on average 30 per cent less than the prosecution team. See Ciara Dinneny, 'EU dispatch: ICC legal defence staff launching historic strike over labour rights, pay disparity' *Jurist* (2 December 2022) https://www.jurist.org/news/2022/12/eu-dispatch-icc-legal-defence-staff-launching-historic-strike-over-labor-rights-pay-disparity/ (accessed 10 December 2022). See also the Twitter posts by defence counsel: https://twitter.com/MlissaBeaulieu1/status/1599676504413130753; https://twitter.com/itsmececileL/status/1595443104018235392 (both accessed 24 July 2023). In light of the findings of the ICC Independent Expert Review, there has been more focus on gender equality, inclusion, ethics, and well-being in the workplace at the ICC, although not on fair pay. ICC, Registry Strategic Plan 2023–2025, §§ 50, 61–64. See also Angela Mudukuti, 'Gender imbalance at the ICC: The continued hegemonic entrenchment of male privilege' in Florian Jeßberger, Leonie Steinl, and Kalika Mehta (eds), *International Criminal Law: A Counter-Hegemonic Project?* (TMC Asser Press 2023).

[152] Fieldwork Diary, The Hague (7 February 2014).

[153] Labour relations are structured not only through law (the contract) but also through other informal sets of obligations, benefits, forms of coercion, inducement, or co-operation. See eg Stewart Macaulay, 'Non-Contractual Relations in Business: A Preliminary Study' (1963) 28(1) American Sociological Review 55; Sally Falk Moore, 'Law and Social Change: The Semi-Autonomous Social Field as an Appropriate Subject of Study' (1973) 7 Law & Society Review 719. I thank Nicola Palmer for her observation here and the references.

[154] In advancing this argument, my book also connects to critical literature on peacebuilding, development, humanitarianism, and human rights, like the scholarship of Adam Branch, which has shed light on how international interventions like the ICC have not only depoliticized the causes of violence and poverty but have also disciplined war-affected people into neoliberal forms of individual self-management through 'local ownership' and participation. My book differs from this scholarship in that it looks at these processes not only through the

In this way, the blame cascade discloses a much broader material process of victim blaming, which has been overlooked in existing critical scholarship on international criminal law. Critical scholars have, of course, long argued that individual criminal responsibility creates an impunity gap as international crimes are too deeply entangled with structural injustices.[155] In reality, however, international criminal law does not rely on the production of black, evil perpetrators alone. This book suggests that blaming the perpetrator is only one side of the story, the official, legal story. A dual mechanism—blaming the perpetrator and blaming the victims—plays out through international criminal justice: one stream of blame flows towards the perpetrator in the courtroom and another stream flows towards the victims in the field; one operates through law, the other through everyday material relations of labour and debt. Indeed, the very mechanisms that create injustice, relationships of exploitation, and expropriation also shift blame down. The justice cascade becomes the blame cascade.

What, then, is the relationship between justice, blame and ideology? Justice is a central concept of any ideology because all ideologies, in one way or another, claim to be just. They therefore need to explain away any signs of injustice which contradict their official portrayal.[156] Ideologies usually justify a deficit in justice by blaming those who most flagrantly violate their expectations—the wretched of the earth (you, too, can move from rags to riches and, if you fail, you only have yourself to blame). Blame, in short, is the logical counterpart to justice; the two operate in tandem as part of an ideological metabolism in which blame plugs the justice deficit. International criminal justice throws this relationship between justice and blame into particularly sharp relief. People come to the Court because they want justice, they are then recruited to work for justice, they become trapped in the contradictions of justice, and they end up as blameworthy capitalist subjects whose work is neither recognized nor valued.

lens of 'discipline' but through 'ideology', and not only at the point of intervention, but through a close study of the entire institution, revealing contradictions, contestations, and traces of resistance at all levels of the Court's victim engagement. See Adam Branch, *Displacing Human Rights: War and Intervention in Northern Uganda* (OUP 2011); Branch and Yen (n 119); Nesiah (n 89); Pádraig McAuliffe and Christine Schwöbel-Patel, 'Disciplinary Matchmaking: Critics of International Criminal Law Meet Critics of Liberal Peacebuilding' (2018) 16(5) Journal of International Criminal Justice 985; Kendall and Nouwen (n 101).

155 Clarke (n 135).
156 Therborn (n 63) 18.

1.6 Resisting Justice

'People are too busy to care, but there is no resistance.' That is what I often heard about victims' attitudes to international criminal justice in Northern Uganda. But 'too busy to care' may itself offer clues about resistance. What is symptomatic about the Court's victim engagement, but rarely registered as resistance, is that victims come late to the Court's meetings, they bring along their children and people who were not invited by the Court, they forget what they were taught last time by the Court's lawyers, and they haggle about transport reimbursement. This happened at all meetings I attended, and victims' lawyers regularly complain about it. Reflecting on the challenges of victim engagement, one field assistant told me:

> But the community is a crazy one, because look at the poverty rate . . . the time that they should sit and update themselves [about the trial] might not be there—from [mornings in] the garden until the evening somebody's still in the kitchen cooking and the following morning you're back in the garden and it's crazy. And so, by the time the team comes back next month, you would have forgotten totally, everything. There are people that you ask, and they have forgotten—not that they had not mastered—but they would need a click or something like that.[157]

Why do people forget? Because they are busy with caring, cooking, cultivating, and cleaning. Why do people come late? Because they have to look after their subsistence crops in the morning. Their lives centre around subsistence and social reproduction and that shapes their engagement with international criminal justice.

Many victims, whether supportive or critical, come to the ICC's meetings, but they bring their social reproduction and subsistence roles along with them, and this creates tensions between ideology-making and life-making. Whereas the Court designates the meeting as a space for invited victims only; it is a space to deliberate law and justice, victims immediately reinvent the space. Explaining the legal developments of the *Ongwen* trial, the victims' lawyers are often drowned out by crying babies, chatting neighbours, clanking dishes, chewing, slurping and the snoring of a few elderly men and women. As people's social reproduction practices disrupt the

[157] Interview with Field Assistant, Gulu (17 July 2019).

Court's ideology-making, they also shift what justice is about. Justice becomes about social reproduction and subsistence.

If ideology works by constituting its subjects and their practices, resistance works through alternative subjectivities and practices. Different ways of creating value—both economically and in life—might nurture these alternative subjectivities, a relationship that E.P. Thompson and James Scott captured through the concept of 'moral economy'. The latter posits that moral expectations emanate from the social and economic practices of the subalterns rather than from abstract principles, whether due process, retribution, or reconciliation. The term, in E.P. Thompson's words, describes:

> A popular consensus as to what were the legitimate and what were the illegitimate practices in marketing, milling, baking etc. This in its turn was grounded upon a consistent traditional view of social norms and obligations, of the proper economic functions of several parties within the community, which, taken together, can be said to constitute the moral economy of the poor.[158]

This moral economy informed peasants' views on which dues were tolerable and which were intolerable, how much to drudge and endure, and when to revolt.[159] On this reading, food riots in eighteenth-century England were not a spasmodic reaction to hunger and deprivation, but a highly complex form of direct popular action against a violation of social norms.[160] 'The fear of food shortages', James Scott points out, 'has in most precapitalist peasant societies, given rise to what might appropriately be termed a "subsistence ethic" which sits at the heart of peasant politics'.[161]

Such a subsistence ethics can also be observed in affected communities in Northern Uganda, which live at the crossroads of a subsistence economy that secures their survival and a burgeoning capitalist economy that threatens it.[162] In this context, victims of war crimes might even judge

[158] EP Thompson, 'The Moral Economy of the English Crowd in the Eighteenth Century' (1971) 50 Past & Present 76, 79.

[159] James Scott, *The Moral Economy of the Peasant: Rebellion and Subsistence in Southeast Asia* (Yale UP 1976) 3.

[160] ibid 78.

[161] ibid 2.

[162] For an analysis of the moral restructuring of Ugandan society in the wake of neoliberal capitalism since 1986 when President Museveni seized power see Jörg Wiegratz, 'Fake capitalism? The dynamics of neoliberal moral restructuring and pseudo-development: the case of Uganda' (2010) 37(124) Review of African Political Economy

their current life unfavourably compared to their life in LRA captivity. 'Due to the enormous challenges they face in their post-abduction life', Lino Owor Ogora observes, 'it is not surprising that some of the women believe they had a better life while in captivity where they did not have to struggle with the day to day realities of struggling to meet the basic needs of their children'.[163]

As one woman, who lived in LRA captivity, explained:

> I have faced a lot of hardship that I should say is more than that we faced while in captivity. I say this without fear that if Kony came back today to abduct people again, I would personally join him back. I know many of my fellow sisters would do the same because life is so hard here. I have two children, but I cannot take them to school. Here everything needs money, and I cannot find that money which is enough to pay school fees and provide all the basic requirements. Sometimes my children and I even sleep hungry without any food to eat. I thought the government cared but it seems the government does not.[164]

A violent past can thus seem more just than the negative peace of living in an uncaring capitalist economy without money, shattering the ICC's straightforward progress narrative of the victim–survivor, who underwent great suffering and trauma, and now wants formal accountability for past evil.[165]

Moral economy, however, does not capture the full picture of people's multi-faceted and interconnected forms of resistance to international criminal justice and its imbrication with global capitalism. First, the concept's purview is somewhat limited by its orientation towards the past. Both Thompson and Scott were interested in traditional practices that survived in the interstices of capitalist and state systems. Moral economy, in other words, is what happens either in the past or at the periphery of world

123; Jörg Wiegratz, Giuliano Martiniello, and Elisa Greco (eds), *Uganda: The Dynamics of Neoliberal Transformation* (Zed Books 2018).

[163] Lino Owor Ogora, 'Victims of Sexual and Gender Based Violence Crimes Need Special Reparations' *International Justice Monitor* (3 July 2017) https://www.ijmonitor.org/2017/07/victims-of-sexual-and-gender-based-violence-crimes-need-special-reparations/ (accessed 10 March 2022).

[164] ibid.

[165] Johan Galtung, 'Violence, Peace and Peace Research' (1969) 6(3) Journal of Peace Research 167.

systems. Such a reading dovetails with how the Court's practitioners make sense of the reproductive interruptions and disruptions of victim engagement. They interpret them as 'challenges' rather than 'resistance', challenges that are external to international criminal justice and have to do with people's material circumstances, their poverty, which make it hard to concentrate on 'higher order' needs such as legal justice. Such challenges, in their eyes, will be overcome through modernization and development.

But what if these reproductive symptoms are not challenges to be overcome but feminized alternatives in the making? This points to a second problem with the concept of moral economy, namely that it does not sufficiently unpack the gender division of labour in global capitalist patriarchy.[166] Specifically, it neglects the social reproduction labour of women, which is key not only because it shapes moral expectations, but also because capitalism depends on it as free or underpaid labour. A social reproduction perspective, by contrast, brings into view all the feminized work that reproduces relationships and communities but also larger political and economic orders. When women withdraw or repurpose that labour, they are tugging at the very threads that hold the capitalist order together. Their work is essential rather than peripheral. It is the work of the many, not the few. It is about the future, not the past.

We should, however, be cautious not to idealize social reproduction work. It, too, is exploited labour that (mostly) women do under conditions they did not choose. Its resistive potential arises from the fact that it is essential work—it will have to be done under any mode of production—and that women do it, not for capital, but to replenish their families and communities. As such, a simmering tension between life-making and profit-making characterizes this work, which can give rise to resistance, but only if that work is turned upside down; if people do it differently from how capitalist patriarchy wants them to do it: after work, behind closed doors, by subordinated women, in isolation, using up as little space, time, and resources as possible. By moving socially reproductive labour from the private to the public, by reconfiguring it from individual into collective, political work, Northern Ugandans threaten the capitalist order precisely because it depends on the hidden, naturalized, and feminized condition of this work.

[166] Mies (n 127) 4, 115 ('This implies the splitting up of the economy and the labour market into a so-called formal, modern sector, in which mainly men work, and into an informal sector, where the masses of women work who are not considered to be real wage-workers, but housewives').

Social reproduction labour is thus both a form of exploitation and, potentially, a form of resistance; it both reproduces existing institutions and creates alternatives to them.[167] In this way, a social reproduction perspective makes us see resistance not only in (male-dominated) political revolts and workers' struggles, but also in the everyday life-making practices of women in the Global South.[168]

'The concern of [ideology critique]', Susan Marks writes, 'is to investigate not just the realities of ideology, but the alternative possibilities too that can be shown to dwell in its shadows'.[169] What is dwelling in the shadows of people's engagement with the Court is an alternative world in which life-making is more important than profit-making, in which land is held in common rather than privately, in which resources are used ecologically rather than destructively, in which people take care of each other. Social reproduction and subsistence are thus not a pre-capitalist residual, but potentially prefigurative in a warming world in which we must find new ways of relating to the environment and the land. This is an alternative world which women are creating every day.

1.7 Contributions, Methods, and Fieldwork

This book provides an in-depth socio-legal analysis of a key international justice institution, illuminating its interplay with global capitalist relationships, while engaging with a rich variety of criminological, legal anthropological, international law, and international relations scholarship. Through a close reading of the institutional, embodied, mundane and intimate workings of capitalist subject formation through international criminal justice, the book aims to address a gap in the existing literature. The latter tends to either offer sophisticated critical, theoretical, historical, and doctrinal work on international law or rich empirical studies of transitional justice institutions in the Global South but few attempts to marry the two. In attempting

[167] In black feminist thought, there is a long tradition of seeing the work that black women do to nurture their families and communities as a form of resistance against the devaluation of black people and their work by racial capitalism. See eg bell hooks, 'Homeplace: A Site of Resistance' in bell hooks, *Yearning: Race, Gender, and Cultural Politics* (South End Press 1990); Patricia Hill Collins, *Black Feminist Thought Knowledge, Consciousness, and the Politics of Empowerment* (2nd edn, Routledge 2000) 46.

[168] See also Kathi Weeks, *Constituting Feminist Subjects* (Verso 2018); Stefano Harney and Fred Moten, *The Undercommons: Fugitive Planning & Black Study* (Minor Compositions 2013).

[169] Marks (n 30) 119.

such a synthesis, the book moves from an external, 'big picture' analysis which risks providing an overly homogenous, static account of the ICC as ideological superstructure, which distracts from and legitimates its economic base, to a more immanent, empirically grounded study of 'justice for victims' as a contested and contingent form of victim production in the Global South.

Methodologically, I create this synthesis through a symptomatic reading of the Court's victim engagement, starting with an empirical analysis of the everyday life of international criminal justice and then using the tools of Marxist theory to unearth the underlying material relations and contradictions as well as the possibilities of resistance that emerge in the interstices of the Court's relation with victims.[170] If Marxist theory brings into view relations of production and reproduction, which humans enter to meet their needs and to reproduce themselves,[171] a symptomatic reading makes these relationships visible in the legal realm by 'actively produc[ing] meanings based on symptoms in the text'.[172] It reveals the 'forbidden vision' of the text, what the text represses or dismisses because of its ideological commitments.[173] 'The text', in this book, is understood broadly, encompassing qualitative interviews, ethnographic observations, legal filings, policy documents, promotional videos, and social media posts, amongst others.[174]

Inspired by Marcus's multi-sited ethnography, the book traces the material relationships and ideological forms of 'justice for victims' as they enmesh manifold actors and institutions across the Court's different sites.[175] More specifically, the book draws on ethnographic observations of the

[170] Louis Althusser and others, *Reading Capital: The Complete Edition* (Verso 2016) 27. I elaborate on this approach in ch 5.

[171] See Karl Marx and Friedrich Engels, *The German Ideology* (Lawrence & Wishart 2007) 42–52; Marx (n 120) 166–67, 273, 716. At its most basic level, capitalist relations of production are relations between those who own the means of production (capitalists) and those who own only their labour power (workers).

[172] Warren Buckland, 'Symptomatic reading in Althusser, Cahiers du cinéma, and Zizek' (2013) 55 Jump Cut: A Review of Contemporary Media Jump Cut https://www.ejumpcut.org/archive/jc55.2013/Buckland-Lincoln/text.html (accessed 3 December 2022).

[173] Althusser and others (n 170) 25.

[174] For symptomatic readings that focus on legal texts see Tzouvala(n 40) 11–14; I Bennett Capers, 'Reading Back, Reading Black' (2006) 35(1) Hofstra Law Review 9.

[175] George E Marcus, 'Ethnography in/of the World System: The Emergence of Multi-Sited Ethnography' (1995) 24 Annual Review of Anthropology 95. See also Gregory Feldman, 'If ethnography is more than participant-observation, then relations are more than connections: The case for nonlocal ethnography in a world of apparatuses' (2011) 11 Anthropological Theory 375; Gregory Feldman, 'Illuminating the apparatus: Steps toward a nonlocal ethnography of global governance' in Chris Shore, Susan Wright, and Davide Peró (eds), *Policy Worlds: Anthropology and the Analysis of Contemporary Power* (Berghahn 2011).

Court's work in The Hague, Kenya, and Uganda and 134 semi-structured interviews with the Court's lawyers, judges, bureaucrats, victim's lawyers, NGOs, local intermediaries, and victim activists. Working as an intern at the ICC's Registry between October 2013 and February 2014, I immersed myself in the Court's working practices and institutional culture, and interviewed the Court's staff. Overall, I interviewed five ICC judges, twelve Registry staff members, three employees of the Office of the Prosecutor (OTP), one of the Presidency, two of the Chambers, two defence counsel, six victims' lawyers, and seven civil society representatives in addition to many informal conversations. I then spent three months in Kenya and Uganda interviewing fifty local ICC staff members, field assistants, translators, intermediaries, and NGO officers between June and September 2014. I also accompanied a victims' lawyer on a registration mission in Western Kenya from 18 to 22 August 2014, observing first-hand how victim participation works on the ground. I took detailed field notes of the trip and interviewed the intermediaries who organized the meetings. Returning to The Hague in June 2018, I attended an ICC workshop on victim participation and conducted a few follow-up interviews with the Court's practitioners. I then spent another month in Northern Uganda in July and August 2019, conducting thirty-five interviews as well as one focus group discussion (FGD) with affected communities, and observing several of the Court's outreach events in Gulu, and in Lukodi, one of the four locations, where Dominic Ongwen has been convicted of committing war crimes and crimes against humanity.

Such 'mobile' ethnography comes at a price. It is impossible to achieve the depth and rigour of a single-sited ethnography in each location.[176] Besides, there is also a political concern that 'multi-sited ethnography' decentres the subaltern—the traditional subject of ethnography—while foregrounding the voices of metropolitan elites.[177] This book is a case in point. While 'justice for victims' is its focus, victims' perspectives are not at the core of the research. Yet, 'elite' is a relative term and while many local NGOs and victim-intermediaries I interviewed were more powerful than most of the Court's victims, they did not belong to the elite globally or nationally speaking.

I have struggled with a certain reflexivity discourse common for socio-legal and criminological research in the Global South that obligingly

[176] Marcus (n 175) 100.
[177] ibid 101–102.

confesses the researcher's positionality as privileged, white, fe(male), cis, hetero, able-bodied, and Global North-based academic who does research with vulnerable people in post-/neo-colonial Africa.[178] While important, methodological and epistemological 'fixes'—participatory action research, knowledge co-production, capacity training for local researchers—and token material and social gestures—donating royalties, returning to the community with the published book, linking communities to development and assistance programmes—do not ameliorate the inequality of global knowledge production.[179] A critical ideology approach requires an acknowledgement that my research subjects, as manual labourers, and I, as professional labourer, are not necessarily on the same side. Spivak tells her students in the villages in India, where she teaches: 'I'm your enemy . . . Just don't forget I'm rich and you're poor. So we are not in the same group at all.'[180]

Reflexivity is, of course, still important to reveal the partial, situated, and inter-subjective nature of the knowledge created.[181] Throughout the book, I use ethnographic vignettes to locate the different knowledges my research participants and I produced in concrete sites and social encounters. Decolonizing knowledge production is important, but so is the admission that global knowledge production under conditions of global capitalism

[178] Kerry Carrington, Russell Hogg, Máximo Sozzo, 'Southern Criminology' (2016) 56(1) The British Journal of Criminology 1; Leon Moosavi, 'A Friendly Critique of "Asian Criminology" and "Southern Criminology"' (2019) 59(2) The British Journal of Criminology 257; Claire Lockard, 'Unhappy confessions: The temptation of admitting to white privilege' (2016) 2(2) Feminist Philosophy Quarterly 1. For more reflections on my research approach and positionality see ch 2 of my thesis: Leila Ullrich, 'Schizophrenic Justice: Exploring "Justice for Victims" at the International Criminal Court (ICC)' University of Oxford (2016) https://ora.ox.ac.uk/objects/uuid:8d73d52b-9cd6-4d06-b613-69b0827aa03e (accessed 16 July 2022).

[179] Some researchers build more sustainable relationships with affected communities and local researchers: Philipp Schulz, 'Research, relationships and reciprocity in Northern Uganda' *Open Democracy* (25 June 2019) https://www.opendemocracy.net/en/beyond-trafficking-and-slavery/research-relationships-and-reciprocity-northern-uganda/ (accessed 16 July 2022); Felix Mukwiza Ndahinda and others, 'Rwandan researchers are finally being centred in scholarship about their own country' *The Conversation* (25 May 2022) https://theconversation.com/rwandan-researchers-are-finally-being-centred-in-scholarship-about-their-own-country-183142 (accessed 3 December 2022).

[180] Steve Paulson, 'Critical Intimacy: An Interview with Gayatri Chakravorty Spivak' *Los Angeles Review of Books* (29 June 2016) https://www.lareviewofbooks.org/article/critical-intimacy-interview-gayatri-chakravorty-spivak/ (accessed 15 July 2022).

[181] Donna Haraway, 'Situated Knowledges: The Science Question in Feminism and the Privilege of Partial Perspective' (1998) 14(3) Feminist Studies 575. For a good example see Sarah Nouwen, '"*As You Set out for Ithaka*": Practical, Epistemological, Ethical, and Existential Questions about Socio-Legal Research in Conflict' (2014) 27 Leiden Journal of International Law 227, 257.

is always exploitative and extractive.[182] Legally, I own this knowledge and I'm the only one who can transform it into material gain (for example, an academic salary).[183] I compensated the community members who participated in the FGD and interviews with £2 per person for one hour of work (which was double the going rate).[184] This is not only far below the minimum wage in the UK, where I earn my salary, but it is also less than the amount Dominic Ongwen makes 'light cleaning' the communal areas in the detention facility in The Hague (he earns €25 a week part-time).[185] The fact that Ongwen was making money in detention caused considerable consternation among affected communities in Northern Uganda: 'We were told that Ongwen is working and on a monthly basis, sending money to his children. And a person who is suffering might not have anything to send their child to school.'[186] Building non-exploitative relationships and solidarity between intellectual, manual, and socially reproductive workers globally is hard work and something that I am still grappling with and have, so far, admittedly, not furthered through my research practice.

1.8 Structure and Chapter Outline

All chapters examine the Court's victim engagement but from different angles. Chapter 2 situates the Court's promise to deliver 'justice for victims' in the context of the reproduction of a *sui generis* legal institution and its social

[182] Eve Tuck and K Wayne Yang, 'Decolonization is not a metaphor' (2012) 1(1) Decolonization: Indigeneity, Education & Society 1; Linda Tuhiwai Smith, *Decolonizing Methodologies: Research and Indigenous Peoples* (Zed Books 2012); Raewyn Connell, 'Using Southern Theory: Decolonizing Social Thought in Theory, Research and Application' (2014) 13(2) Planning Theory 210; Vivetha Thambinathan and Elizabeth Anne Kinsella, 'Decolonizing Methodologies in Qualitative Research: Creating Spaces for Transformative Praxis' (2021) 20 International Journal of Qualitative Methods 1.

[183] On exploitation in UK academia, particularly the practices of hiring local research assistants in the Global South see Mayssoun Sukarieh and Stuart Tannock, 'Subcontracting Academia: Alienation, Exploitation and Disillusionment in the UK Overseas Syrian Refugee Research Industry' (2019) 51(2) Antipode 664.

[184] Transport costs for victims in Uganda were reimbursed by the ICC with 5,000 Ugandan Shillings (£1) at the time of research though some victims' lawyers paid 10,000 (£2). Daniel Hammett and Deborah Sporton, 'Paying for interviews? Negotiating ethics, power and expectation' (2012) 44(4) Area 496.

[185] Tom Maliti, 'Away from courtroom, Ongwen plays football, does light cleaning at detention center' *International Justice Monitor* (12 August 2019) https://www.ijmonitor.org/2019/08/away-from-courtroom-ongwen-plays-football-does-light-cleaning-at-detention-center/ (accessed 16 July 2022).

[186] Interview with Parish Chief, Lukodi (25 July 2019).

relationships. Designed as a retributive justice institution in Rome in 1998 with vague provisions for victim participation and reparation, the ICC has increasingly incorporated its restorative justice alternatives, both institutionally and ideologically. This incorporation, however, is not 'mere co-optation', as critical scholars often presume, because the Court is not fully in control of the ideological contestations that have ensued. Mapping these contestations between including victims and safeguarding legal procedure, the chapter shows how they have set in motion a conceptual and practical shift from victim *participation* in the courtroom to victim *engagement* in the field.

Chapter 3 investigates what exactly happens when the Court engages victims in the field. What does 'inclusion' do to them? I show how victims are spotlighted, lured, schooled, and disciplined in their encounters with the Court's field officers and victims' lawyers, and in the process become not only the Court's ideological subjects, its 'champions', but also active capitalist subjects. The chapter further illuminates how the Court's assistance and reparation programmes suture victims into material relationships of labour and debt, which transform them from innocent victims into indebted subjects. This metamorphosis of victims is underwritten by the blame cascade, which gradually and subtly carries blame downwards through the Court's multi-layered labouring relations. Chapter 4 disentangles those relationships. Who does the labour of justice and why? What does that labour consist of and how is it valued? I will answer these questions by zeroing in on a particular set of actors, the Court's local intermediaries, but rather than merely looking at the Court's designated 'intermediaries', the chapter identifies intermediation as a key mechanism of the blame cascade. Instead of bridging the cultural divide between the 'global' and the 'local', intermediaries ideologically manage victims both for the Court and the global economy, and their ideological labour, like all labour, is classed, gendered, and racialized.

Chapter 5 explores the Court's attempts to resolve its own justice contradictions by promising 'transformative reparations'. As the Court's victim engagement deepens, and the tensions between retributive and restorative justice crystallize, 'transformative justice' emerges as a necessary if utopian solution. Examining the Trust Fund's assistance programmes in Northern Uganda, I will, however, demonstrate that it is precisely the promise of transformative justice that reproduces the status quo. Far from tackling the structural causes of international crimes and their gendered manifestations, the concept ends up shifting the responsibility of 'transformation' to the individual victim–survivor. Chapter 6, finally, explores victims' resistance to these processes of subject creation. While Chapter 3 relates the Court's victim engagement to debt relations and Chapter 4 to labour relations, Chapter 6 relates it to land struggles in Northern Uganda. The conclusion situates the argument within the critical literature on international criminal justice and further theorizes the blame cascade for future research.

2
What Is Justice and Does It Matter? The Rome Statute and Its Disciples

2.1 Introduction

> Before the law sits a gatekeeper. To this gatekeeper comes a man from the country who asks to gain entry into the law. But the gatekeeper says that he cannot grant him entry at the moment. The man thinks about it and then asks if he will be allowed to come in later on.
>
> 'It is possible', says the gatekeeper, 'but not now'.[1]

Kafka's parable 'Before the Law' is a popular entry point for investigating the force of law. Dezalay uses it to illustrate the distance between the law and those it allegedly serves in international criminal justice. Like the man from the country, the victims of the International Criminal Court (ICC) are far away from the Court's seat in The Hague.[2] Even if they travelled all the way to the Netherlands, they would end up in front of highly securitized doors.[3] 'International Criminal Law promises justice', Schwöbel-Patel writes, 'but the gatekeepers stand in the way—they might come in the form of barriers of race, class, gender, ableism; linguistic barriers, [and] cultural barriers'.[4] 'Inclusion in the law', Ypi asserts, 'also requires fighting its

[1] Franz Kafka, 'Before the Law' (Franz Kafka Online, Ian Johnston tr) https://www.kafka-online.info/before-the-law.html (accessed 4 January 2024).
[2] Sara Dezalay, 'Book Review: Distant Justice: The Impact of the International Criminal Court on African Politics by Phil Clark (Cambridge University Press 2018, 379 pp., £26.99 (pbk))' (2020) 47 Journal of Law & Society 175.
[3] Jacques Derrida, 'Before the Law' in Derek Attridge (ed), *Acts of Literature* (Routledge 1992) 181.
[4] Christine Schwöbel-Patel, 'Symposium on "Marketing Global Justice": A Letter on Kafka, Coca-Cola, and Vergès' *OpinioJuris* (11 May 2023) http://opiniojuris.org/2023/05/11/symposium-on-marketing-global-justice-a-letter-on-kafka-coca-cola-and-verges/ (accessed 24 July 2023).

Victims and the Labour of Justice at the International Criminal Court. Leila Ullrich, Oxford University Press.
 DOI: 10.1093/9780191915048.003.0002

gatekeepers'.[5] Judith Butler even developed their idea of gender performativity from Derrida's reading of 'Before the Law':

> There [is] the one who waits for the law, sits before the door of the law, attributes a certain force to the law for which one waits. The anticipation of an authoritative disclosure of meaning is the means by which that authority is attributed and installed: the anticipation conjures its object. I wondered whether we do not labor under a similar expectation concerning gender, that it operates as an interior essence that might be disclosed, an expectation that ends up producing the very phenomenon that it anticipates.[6]

For Butler, the law works not through the power of the gatekeeper but through the anticipation of the law's authority. The gatekeeper almost disappears from the story.

Kafka himself considered 'Before the Law' the only part of his novel *The Trial* that was worth publishing. He published it during his lifetime, while the novel itself was published ten years after his death. In the novel, a prison chaplain tells the protagonist, Joseph K., 'Before the Law' not as a story per se but as 'the opening paragraphs to the law', the preamble, effectively.[7] 'So the doorkeeper cheated the man', Joseph K. blurts out as the chaplain finishes the story.[8] 'Don't be too quick', the chaplain replies. He then recounts different interpretations of the preamble. One is that it is the gatekeeper who is 'deluded in a way that's far worse [than the man from the country], a way that's to do with his service'.[9] The man from the country is free; 'there's nothing in the story to say he was forced' to wait all his life before the law.[10] The gatekeeper, by contrast, 'is kept to his post by his employment'.[11] In fact, the relationship may be the reverse: the gatekeeper is effectively 'in the service of this one man who the door's intended for'.[12]

[5] Lea Ypi, 'Why the right's new strongmen are winning everywhere' *The Guardian* (16 March 2020) https://www.theguardian.com/commentisfree/2020/mar/16/right-new-strongmen-winning-everywhere-brazil-hungary-rightwing (accessed 23 October 2021).
[6] Judith Butler, *Gender Trouble* (Routledge 2007) xv.
[7] Franz Kafka, *The Trial* (David Wyllie tr, Dover Publications 2012) 154.
[8] ibid 155.
[9] ibid 158.
[10] ibid 157.
[11] ibid.
[12] ibid 158.

This chapter is about the gatekeepers or guardians who sit closest to 'the law', the lawyers, judges, and bureaucrats in The Hague. Kafka's 'Before the Law' raises several questions that this chapter will explore: first, how do 'we' become the kind of subjects that seek entry to, wait for, or guard the law? Secondly, how does ideology work through these legal subjects? Who is more in ideology: the gatekeeper or the man from the country, the lawyer, or the victim? Finally, the parable raises the question of deception. Is ideology mainly about deception and, if so, who deceives whom? Did the gatekeeper deceive the man from the country, as Joseph K. suspects, or was he himself duped by the logic of legal relations?

Law and its promise of justice, this book will show, not only create 'victims' and 'lawyers' but also relations between them. Arguably, the key insight of 'Before the Law' is that law already works through the relationship between the gatekeeper and the man from the country, between the lawyer and the victim. The deception, then, lies in the very idea that law is somewhere else, 'behind the gate', when, in reality, it already works through them, through the one who waits, and the one who keeps him waiting. This relationship, as the next chapters will show, is ultimately a labour and class relationship, which, as E.P. Thompson reminds us, 'must always be embodied in real people and in a real context'.[13]

This chapter traces the contradictory impulses of opening and closing the Court's processes to victims, which is also reflected in the tensions that characterize practitioners' justice discourses: justice cannot be purely procedural (fair trials), and it cannot be purely subjective or substantive (victims' needs and wants); it constantly moves between the two and, in doing so, negotiates the precarious terms of victims' inclusion. While victims' inclusion is often read as a 'democratic move' towards more deliberative justice,[14] the Court's legal procedures are not open for bottom-up change;[15]

[13] EP Thompson, *The Making of the English Working Class* (Pelican Books 1968) 9.

[14] As Braithwaite put it: 'Restorative justice is deliberative justice; it is about people deliberating over the consequences of crimes, and how to deal with them and prevent their recurrence. This contrasts with the professional justice of lawyers deciding which rules to apply to a case and then constraining their deliberation within a technical discourse about that rule application.' John Braithwaite, 'Restorative Justice and a Better Future' (1996) 76(1) Dalhousie Law Review 9, 16. On the deliberative potential of international criminal justice see Marlies Glasius, 'Do International Criminal Courts Require Democratic Legitimacy' (2012) 23 The European Journal of International Law 43, 61; Pablo de Greiff, 'Deliberative Democracy and Punishment' (2002) 5 Buffalo Criminal Law Review 373, 403; Mark Findlay and Ralph Henham, *Transforming International Criminal Justice: Retributive and Restorative Justice in the Trial Process* (Routledge 2012).

[15] Jo-Anne Wemmers' interviews with ICC practitioners found no support for involving victims more directly in decision-making: 'The Rome Statute as well as the Rules of Procedure

victims are included not as citizen subjects but as capitalist subjects.[16] There are two dimensions to the victims' role: the first is that the Court needs to reproduce itself and victims are a necessary part of that reproduction both ideologically (the Court needs to be seen to be doing 'justice for victims') and materially (the victims need to labour for the Court). Secondly, the Court's reproduction as an ideological institution is part and parcel of the broader reproduction of capitalist relations. Here, the precarious inclusion of victims in the court's processes both reflects and anticipates the precarious inclusion of people in the Global South in global capitalist processes.

This will be shown in three parts. The first part teases out the ambivalent role of the Court's practitioners as both subjects and producers of the justice ideology. While lawyers treat justice as secondary to the Court's legal processes, they always return to it to justify the Court's existence. Justice is both conceived as something outside of law, and something that is ultimately essential for the Court's reproduction. After establishing this broader relationship between law and justice, the second part examines how 'justice for victims' became part of the Court's justice promise and was institutionalized through victims' rights to participation and reparation in the Rome Statute. Victims' inclusion in international criminal justice, however, sat uneasily with the rigidity of legal procedure causing tensions between retributive and restorative justice, deliberative and judicial decision-making, and procedure and substance. The third part then moves from concepts to practices of justice, charting how these tensions play out in the relationships between the judges, the new victims' stakeholders, and the victims. While the literature has focused on how victims' rights have been narrowed in the courtroom, I show how these judicial forms of exclusion are accompanied by and partly offset by non-judicial forms of inclusion: courtroom participation has been superseded by victim engagement in the field, and individual legal reparations have been complemented with and partially

and Evidence clearly place decision-making power with the judges, and all the respondents felt that decision-making power should remain in the hands of criminal justice authorities.' Jo-Anne Wemmers, 'Victims' Rights and the International Criminal Court: Perceptions within the Court Regarding the Victims' Right to Participate' (2010) 23(3) Leiden Journal of International Law 629, 637.

16 Edwards argues that the concept of participation is 'intimately tied up with the idea of *citizenship*—of an individual being able to make decisions about his own life, and to have a say in those social and political structures forming the basis of community and state organization'. Ian Edwards, 'An Ambiguous Participant: The Crime Victim and Criminal Justice Decision-Making' (2004) 44 British Journal of Criminology 867, 972.

eclipsed by collective reparation and assistance programmes in the Court's situation countries. Every form of exclusion, I argue, creates new forms of inclusion, which means that the Court's victims' rights regime is in constant movement.

2.2 Justice and Law

What is the relationship between law, justice, and ideology? This section first considers how international criminal law lawyers relate to the justice ideology before asking what role, if any, justice plays amidst the bureaucratic struggles of a relatively new legal institution scrambling to run its day-to-day operations. I then analyse how lawyers think about justice and the extent to which their ideas are beholden to the legal text, the Rome Statute. I conclude that, while the Court's lawyers find questions about justice rather tedious, justice holds the key to the Court's reproduction.

2.2.1 Lawyers and Ideology

If international criminal justice is ideology, what does that mean for the people staffing its institutions? Are they simply cynical ideologists who deceive others, be they victims or the general public? Althusser cautioned against such an instrumental view of ideology: '[T]he men who would use an ideology purely . . . as a tool, find that they have been caught by it, implicated by it, just when they are using it and believe themselves to be the absolute masters of it.'[17] While the existing ideology critique uncovers the discursive mechanisms of legal ideology—how international criminal law naturalizes, rationalizes, and obfuscates relationships of domination—it does not flesh out how ideology relates to people and their relationships.[18]

Writing shortly after the creation of the ICC, Mégret marvelled at the enthusiasm that drove lawyers into international criminal justice: '[W]hy would international lawyers, whom one might expect to be trained to demonstrate a certain caution, seem so eager to overthrow some of the

[17] Louis Althusser, *For Marx* (Verso 2005) 234.

[18] Susan Marks, 'Big Brother Is Bleeping Us: With the Message that Ideology Doesn't Matter' (2001) 12(1) European Journal of International Law 109, 109. Tor Krever, 'International Criminal Law: An Ideology Critique' (2013) 26 Leiden Journal of International Law 701.

founding canons of their discipline in an apparent effort to leap upon the bandwagon of the new prophets of the international criminal order?'[19] Of course, as lawyers generally benefit from the proliferation of legal institutions, it cannot be said that they suffer from 'false consciousness'. Their faith in international criminal law, however, seems to go beyond professional self-interest and borders on religious devotion.[20] In Tallgren's words, 'everybody knows that prevention does not work, even if we hope it might one day. Everybody knows, but the knowledge has no consequences. Prevention is cited simply because of the void of alternatives, the rational ones . . . International criminal justice comes close to a religious exercise of hope and perhaps of deception'.[21] How do lawyers become believers in international criminal law, and how faithful are they? What explains the double role of Mégret's 'expert in horror'—both a cunning strategist who knows how to play the game of the juridical field, and a faithful liberal, who believes in international criminal justice?[22]

Long before Althusser developed the concept, Kafka had already described how law works through interpellation.[23] When Joseph K. is trying to leave the church, a priest suddenly calls out his name:

> [h]is cry was quite unambiguous and there was no escape from it, he called 'Josef K.!' K. stood still and looked down at the floor. In theory he was still free, he could have carried on walking, through one of three dark little wooden doors not far in front of him and away from there. It would simply mean he had not understood, or that he had understood but chose not to pay attention to it. But if he once turned round he would be trapped, then he would have acknowledged that he had understood perfectly well, that he really was the Josef K. the priest had called to and that he was willing to follow.[24]

[19] Frédéric Mégret, 'Three Dangers for the International Criminal Court: A Critical Look at a Consensual Project' (2001) 7 Finnish Yearbook of International Law 193, 194.

[20] David S Koller, 'The Faith of the International Criminal Lawyer' (2008) 40 International Law and Politics 1019; Carsten Stahn, 'Between "Faith" and "Facts": By What Standards Should We Assess International Criminal Justice?' (2012) 25(2) Leiden Journal of International Law 251.

[21] Immi Tallgren, 'The Sensibility and Sense of International Criminal Law' (2002) 13 European Journal of International Law 561, 561.

[22] Mégret (n 19) 243; Pierre Bourdieu, 'The Force of Law: Toward a Sociology of the Juridical Field' (1987) 38 The Hastings Law Journal 814.

[23] Louis Althusser, *On Ideology* (Verso 2020) 17.

[24] Kafka (n 7) 151.

Once we turn our head, we accept that we really are what we are called and that we are willing to perform the expectations associated with that role. But that does not mean that we are true believers. Note the ambivalence of Joseph K: he wants to follow, and he wants to flee; he is both free and unfree. The law mysteriously traps him. Both the gatekeeper and the man from the country are in thrall to the law, which produces them as legal subjects. Both are waiting; neither can enter. Yet their positionality towards the law differs. The gatekeeper is both the subject and the producer of the justice ideology. The man from the country is just a subject.

For Butler, the key to interpellation is the anticipation of an authoritative disclosure of meaning. At the ICC, however, the source of authority is contested. Is it the legal text, the bureaucratic superiors, or the states that created the Court? And how much attention do the Court's practitioners really pay to those authoritative sources? How do they produce not only the law but its mesmerizing effect, which stops people in their tracks and makes them wait, even for a lifetime. Interpellation is a useful metaphor that captures how we are created as legal subjects, but it does not explain what follows that initial call. For that, we need to understand the institutional context in which our subjects operate.

2.2.2 Bureaucracy and Justice

> I don't think that there is room for us, employees here, to think lofty thoughts about what our personal definition of justice for this institution is, because we have operational tasks to perform. And I really want to boil this down to what we are: we are nothing else but a court, and in a court, people do what they are supposed to be doing according to specific tasks that are assigned to them. The great thoughts that I think, once I leave this place, I will have regarding my definitions of justice, which may differ from yours, which is completely legitimate, normal and inevitable, but this is nothing that will have an effect on the every-day working structure of the Court.[25]

My interviewee is an adviser of the Court's president. The bright LED light of the ICC's cafeteria accentuates his raised eyebrows as he reads through

[25] Interview with Legal Adviser, Presidency, The Hague (8 January 2014).

my interview questions, most of which are preoccupied with the concept of justice: what does 'justice for victims' mean? How does it shape the ICC's work? Does rendering justice to the accused mean the same as providing justice to victims? As I observe him reading the questions, I almost wished that they were not my questions.

At the time of the interview in early 2014, I had been working as an intern at the Registry's Cooperation Unit for three months, drafting, filing, and dispatching the ICC's cooperation requests to states. Most filings concerned Sudan's then president, Omar Al Bashir. My team followed Bashir's travel schedule very closely (by reading newspapers), and whenever he set a foot outside Sudan, participating in a conference in South Africa or a meeting of African Union heads of states in Ethiopia, we would send a request for arrest and surrender of Bashir to the host state.[26] None of those states ever arrested Bashir, and more often than not, he had already left the state in question by the time the cooperation request arrived at the embassy. It seemed pointless. Nonetheless, I was running up and down the Court's corridors, collecting signatures, printing, scanning, and filing paper like there was no tomorrow. One day, my boss burst into my office, dishevelled and distraught: 'IT services just disconnected my email account without telling me in advance. Can you believe it? What if a state emails me?'[27]

In that context, my questions about justice seemed somewhat ridiculous, out of place, not only to my interviewees, but increasingly to myself, as I became immersed in the Court's legal bureaucracy. Those questions were not born out of working at the Court. They came from another place, 'academia' or 'philosophy'. My interviewees felt that it was somewhat futile to talk about justice and that I should instead learn from the Court's practices. When I asked how comfortable the Court's staff are with notions of 'retributive justice', a senior official pondered: 'You don't really hear that type of discussion around here. People are trying to apply [the Statute] . . . [Questions about justice] are not necessarily relevant on a day-to-day basis.'[28] The President's adviser was blunter; he may have great thoughts about justice once he leaves the Court, but they do not shape the Court's daily work. Justice was relegated to the background; it is something that happens outside the Court; I will think about it 'once I leave this place'.

[26] For a more recent example see *The Prosecutor v Omar Hassan Ahmad Al Bashir* (Request to the Republic of Belarus for Cooperation in the Arrest and Surrender of Omar Hassan Ahmad Al-Bashir') [2018] ICC-02/05-01/09-395.

[27] Field notes, The Hague (2013).

[28] Interview with Senior Official, The Hague (16 December 2013).

He was not alone in seeing justice as empty rhetoric. As most bureaucracies, the ICC, many of my interviewees believed, is really about power, money, and turf wars. 'You have to be rather Machiavellian to operate within the Court', a Registry officer advised me. He added, 'if you ask anyone in the Court about anything, ask at least ten other people'.[29] The ICC, some felt, was a particularly nasty institution:

> When you come to an international organization, especially one where there is this fight for power and influence, at one point you need to realize that there are things that you cannot do, otherwise, you will be beaten severely, or you will have to leave. At some point, you will have to choose between 'I leave' or 'I stay but accept the logic'.[30]

And still, I was not prepared to let go of the concept of justice,[31] not least because it did pop up in unexpected places. One of the first events I attended at the Court was the farewell drinks for the Deputy Registrar. As far as I could tell, this was an internal event, and still the Prosecutor and the Registrar talked about fighting impunity, and that the ICC was a 'Court for Africans' rather than a 'Court against Africans'. I glanced around the room; there were no journalists, no cameras, so why bore staff members with that empty rhetoric?

When I asked a seasoned ICC bureaucrat why the Court's senior managers would talk about justice at an internal meeting, he replied: 'It is like in Soviet Russia, where politicians both internally and externally paid lip service to the ideas of communism. It is difficult to tell who the real believers are and who belongs to the silent majority.'[32] A key insight of critical ideology theory, however, is that we do not need to distinguish the 'true believers' from those who use justice strategically. As long as we practise our justice roles, speak the language, and perform the rituals, we are 'in ideology': we are both the subjects and the producers of the justice ideology. After all, ideology is not just ideas but also practices. Even if there are no 'true believers' in justice that does not mean that justice is empty rhetoric.

[29] Field notes (n 27).

[30] Interview with Senior Official, Chambers, The Hague (8 January 2014). For the pathologies of international organizations see Michael Barnett and Martha Finnemore, 'The Politics, Power, and Pathologies of International Organizations' (1999) 53(4) International Organization 699.

[31] Nobody stands outside of ideology, including, of course, the Oxford student who decides to write her thesis on 'justice for victims' at the ICC.

[32] Field notes (n 27).

Besides, the question of authority was not as clear-cut as the president's adviser suggested, when he said that 'in a court, people do what they are supposed to be doing according to specific tasks that are assigned to them'. Bureaucratic authorities, after all, are not set in stone. While I was interning at the Court, the Registry's *Re*-vision project was underway.[33] I remember awkwardly sipping wine on Friday afternoons (wine o'clock) with the *Re*-vision team, a team of external consultants, who enthusiastically showed us on flip charts how they will 'streamline' the Registry's structure, while my wine-sipping colleagues looked rather gloomy, fearing, as they did, for their jobs. One victim's lawyer quipped:

> You can read this draft [of the Revision project] as a Shakespearean drama with an open end . . . We have a new young king [the Registrar] and we have barons, earls or ladies, governing big parts of his country for more than 10 years, the heads of OPCD [Office of the Public Counsel for the Defence], OPCV [Office of Public Counsel for Victims], VPRS [Victims Participation and Reparation Section] and CSS [Court Support Section]. They have been there for more than 10 years, and they know how to run the Court without Mr Hebel [the Registrar]. So, what does a new king do to get authority? He destroys the old system and builds up new loyalties.[34]

Authority, in other words, is rarely a given when a new institution starts to define and reproduce itself.

Besides, heads of offices and line managers are not the only source of authority at the Court. In my interviews, the Court's staff more often invoked another authority, the legal text, the Rome Statute. Most of them began their 'search' for the meaning of justice in the preamble, as it is 'the place where the kind of values behind the Statute are supposed to come through'.[35] When I asked whether the Court pursues 'retributive justice', a prosecuting counsel replied:

> I think . . . that retribution cannot be the basis of punishment for international crimes . . . I don't think that this is really the objective. Our

[33] For an analysis of the *Re*vision project see Richard Clements, '*Re*Visiting the ICC Registry's *Re*Vision Project' (2019) 17 Journal of International Criminal Justice 259.

[34] Jens Dieckmann, 'The Participation of Victims in Proceedings of the International Criminal Court: Observations from a Counsel's Perspective' Speech at the University of Oxford (2 March 2015).

[35] Interview with Senior Official, Registry, The Hague (16 December 2013).

> preamble says that the Court, through its investigations and prosecutions, contributes to preventing crimes in the future. And I think that goes to the core of the vision that states had when setting up the ICC. What is the basis of punishment? It is deterrence . . . Our statute is clear . . . I can read it for you in the preamble.[36]

But when actually reading the preamble, it turned out that this was much less clear than expected. The preamble 'affirm[s] that the most serious crimes of concern to the international community as a whole must not go unpunished and that their effective prosecution must be ensured by taking measures at the national level and by enhancing international cooperation'.[37] It is also 'determined to put an end to impunity for the perpetrators of these crimes and thus to contribute to the prevention of such crimes'.[38] The Chamber in the *Bemba* sentencing decision concluded, on the basis of these two sentences, 'that the Preamble establishes retribution and deterrence as the primary objectives of punishment at the ICC'.[39] Another judge, whom I interviewed, unsuccessfully tried to find clues on why the Court punishes in the sentencing and penalties section of the Statute.[40]

Reading aloud the preamble punctuates the higher purpose of the Court's work, while supporting the particular reading of the orator. A legal adviser, for example, explained the role of the Trust Fund for Victims (TFV) as follows:

> [w]e are dealing, to my mind, with the preamble of the Statute and I can read it if you want: 'United by common bonds, their cultures pieced together in a shared heritage, and concerned that this delicate mosaic may be shattered at any time' . . . so if it's shattered, we don't only need justice, but we also need to repair harm, and the repairing aspect is with the Trust Fund.[41]

[36] Interview with Counsel, OTP, The Hague (13 November 2013).
[37] Rome Statute, preamble.
[38] ibid.
[39] *Prosecutor v Bemba* (Decision on Sentence pursuant to Article 76 of the Statute) [2016] ICC-01/05-01/08-3399, § 10.
[40] The question of 'why punish' persists in international criminal justice. See Florian Jeßberger and Julia Geneuss (eds), *Why Punish Perpetrators of Mass Atrocities?* (CUP 2020).
[41] Redress, 'Webinar: Victim Participation and Reparations at the ICC: Assessing the Impact of the IER' *YouTube* (8 December 2020) at 55:30 minutes https://www.youtube.com/watch?v=kcbYcmMe-T4 (accessed 25 October 2021).

She read the preamble to a large audience of floating Zoom heads at an event on victim participation and reparation, even though the preamble does not say anything about the Trust Fund or even about repairing harm. In a similar vein, ICC Prosecutor Karim Khan opened his remarks for the judicial year 2022:

> [f]riends in the cause of international justice . . . here we are: judges, diplomats, prosecution . . . legal representatives of victims, the defence, the registrar and all court staff united by a common purpose which is the Rome Statute . . . by acting independently and impartially and with fidelity to something much more important and much more lasting than our transient existence, which is the law. The law remains an anchor that will stabilize the ships of states in inclement weather ... all of this shows that we are united. No people are left behind. We look at the laws in the Talmud, in the Bible, in the *Quran*, the teachings of Confucius, and Krishna and Buddha. This is important because the Rome Statute that we have the honour to serve incorporates aspects that are the shared inheritance of every man, woman and child alive, whether they are Rome Statute nationals or not.[42]

The religious solemnity of these readings makes the listener almost forget that the text of the Rome Statute was negotiated by diplomats in 1998. The preamble sits before the first legal article of the Statute, like Kafka's parable, which also serves as the preamble of the law that Joseph K. must answer to. The preamble is simultaneously part of the Statute and outside of it ('before it' or 'behind it'), just as justice is part of law and outside of it, or like the Trust Fund is part of the Court and outside of it.[43]

These consultations of the Rome Statute suggest that its text is at the same time authoritative and obscure for the Court's practitioners. Their efforts to find definite legal answers to questions about justice in the Statute were almost comical—an habitual reach for the text and an almost religious belief that the text should be able to answer all questions. This reaction is curious given that it is widely acknowledged that the Statute's provisions are vague and require substantive interpretation by the Chambers. 'When they see the Statute', an ICC judge observed, 'lawyers ask, "but where is the criminal code?"'[44] The Statute's 'constructive ambiguity' was the product

[42] ICC, 'ICC marks opening of the Judicial Year 2022' https://www.youtube.com/watch?v=lyTRSzYhUk4 (accessed 4 December 2022).

[43] I will explain the relationship between the Court and the Trust Fund in ch 5.

[44] Interview with Judge, The Hague (17 December 2013).

of a diplomatic strategy in the Rome negotiations.[45] As states could not overcome substantive disagreements, diplomats forged consensus around vague wording, thus 'plac[ing] a high burden on the shoulders of the judges' to ascertain what the text means.[46]

The bewilderment at the lack of statutory guidance reflects how practitioners both pretend that abstractions such as justice do not matter and still operate as if they do. While 'thinking about justice' is not part of their jobs, they assume that 'justice', as the ICC's core concept, is surely defined somewhere in the Statute or in the Court's jurisprudence. The 'anticipation of an authoritative disclosure of meaning', however, fails since the text is vague. Even those who desire to be faithful interpreters inevitably end up being 'unfaithful' to a text which requires them to fill in the gaps. But when they fill in the gaps, they often put concepts and ideas into the 'ICC's mandate' that either are not in the Statute or are only expressed in rudimentary form. For example, practitioners routinely refer to the ICC's 'retributive' and 'restorative justice' mandate, even though neither of these concepts is entailed in the Statute.[47] In a report to the Assembly of States Parties (ASP), the Court, for instance, explained the Rome Statute's vision as a 'vision of justice in the broadest sense, an end to impunity for the perpetrators of mass atrocities, and the notion that justice is not just punitive but restorative—and hopefully preventative'.[48]

Beneath the surface, the Court's practitioners negotiate what type of justice mandate the Rome Statute bestows. Asked to what extent the Court has a role beyond conducting trials, a legal adviser of the Chambers replied:

> I would say this is unclear, for instance: does the Rome Statute propagate a democratic organization of politics? I don't know. It is not in the text. And if you look at the States Parties, it is not necessarily a priority for each and every one of them. If you say that this Court is essentially

[45] Christine Van den Wyngaert, 'Victims Before International Criminal Courts: Some Views and Concerns of an ICC Trial Judge' (2012) 44 Case Western Reserve Journal of International Law 475, 478, 486.

[46] ibid 486.

[47] See eg Anushka Sehmi, '"Now That We Have No Voice, What Will Happen to Us?" Experiences of Victim Participation in the Kenyatta Case' (2018) 16(3) Journal of International Criminal Justice 571, 590.

[48] Assembly of States Parties, 'Report of the Court on the Revised strategy in relation to Victims' [2012] ICC-ASP/11/40 § 14, n 15; Assembly of States Parties, 'Report of the Court on the Strategy in Relation to Victims' [2006] ICC-ASP/8/45, § 3. See also Claire Garbett, 'The International Criminal Court and Restorative Justice: Victims, Participation and the Processes of Justice' (2017) 5(2) Restorative Justice 198.

> a common denominator but a relatively low common denominator, where people say: 'well, these are just outrageous crimes *where irrespective of your political ideology* your organization of society or whatever, pretty much every human being in the world can agree that you must not rape, you must not kill innocent civilians in times of war, but then most of the people here probably think that this is not enough, but it is the lowest standard on which everybody could agree and that also needs to be respected. But sometimes, you obviously feel you want to do a little bit more'.[49]

Here, ideology enters the Court's discourse. What is written in the Statute is something every human being in the world can agree you must not do. It is irrespective of ideology.[50] For the Court's staff, criminal law exists outside of ideology, but the same is not true of democracy or, as we shall see later, of victims. The text reflects the lowest common denominator, and that needs to be respected, but 'most of the people here'—the Court's staff—want to do 'a little bit more'.

Some even want to do a great deal more, or rather, they think that what you do or do not do is a political choice. Another legal adviser working in the Chambers observed:

> I have been disagreeing with members of the Presidency in meetings in front of NGOs. They say that we have to concentrate on criminal law; we have to concentrate on our trials. And I said that this is not the only mandate of the ICC. And it is not that we have to. It is a choice. Basically, if you choose that you only have to convict people or to acquit them, then this is your choice. But don't tell me that this is the Statute. It is just your choice. You can do more than that. But there is no political will, for the moment, to do more than that.[51]

What is part of the ICC's 'mandate', and what is not? The ambiguity of the text is simultaneously confusing and empowering for lawyers. Interpretation is always a creative act and sheepish adherence, even if desired, is impossible. The subjects become the producers. The preamble is

[49] Interview with Legal Adviser, Chambers, The Hague (10 January 2014) (emphasis added).
[50] This is, of course, a core tenet of liberal legal ideology. Judith N Shklar, *Legalism* (Harvard UP 1964).
[51] Interview with Legal Adviser, Chambers, The Hague (8 January 2014)..

read aloud, more than it is read, and justice is invoked more than it is defined. Definition may work against its symbolic invocation. 'I have noticed in my years of experience', an OTP lawyer told me, 'that judges often say, "it's in the interest of justice to do one thing or the other", and I also, more and more, got the impression that they do that when there is no other legal basis to do so . . . It's very difficult to define it [justice]'.[52] It may not be opportune either.

2.2.3 Lawyers' Justice?

One way of making sense of this interpretive process is through Bourdieu's concept of the 'juridical field', which he identified as a particularly powerful social field in terms of the influence it exerts both on its members and on society at large.[53] 'Organized around a body of internal protocols and assumptions, characteristic behaviours and self-sustaining values—what we might informally term a "legal culture"', the juridical field shapes lawyers' beliefs and conduct.[54] In my interviews, I often heard the phrase, 'as a lawyer, my understanding of justice is x', or 'as a criminal court, the Court's justice mandate is y'.

Justice, many ICC practitioners agreed, means fair legal procedure or procedural justice. As a victim's lawyer and defence counsel explained to me:

> The procedure itself must contain several elements and, finally, if these elements are respected, we have a chance to get a decision that is accepted as a just decision by . . . all parties of the proceedings . . . In an open society with a high level of tolerance [regarding] different concepts of life, values and religion, these basic values like dignity and justice must be understood not in a material way but rather in a procedural way . . . this is my understanding being a lawyer and a criminal counsel in this system.[55]

[52] Interview with Counsel, OTP, The Hague (13 November 2013).
[53] Bourdieu (n 22). See also Frédéric Mégret, 'International Criminal Justice as a Juridical Field' (2016) 8 Champ pénal/Penal field 1.
[54] Richard Terdiman, 'Translator's Introduction' in Pierre Bourdieu, 'The Force of Law: Toward a Sociology of the Juridical Field' (1987) 38 The Hastings Law Journal 805, 806.
[55] Telephone interview with Legal Representative for Victims (4 November 2013).

'The same goes for justice to victims', I was told by the legal adviser in the cafeteria, 'because it is not a flowery concept that is in our head, it is a down-to-earth concept that is foreseen in the Statute, that there is a possibility of victim participation in the proceedings and that there is a possibility of reparations'.[56] 'Justice for victims', in other words, *is* victim participation and reparation.

'I think, what you will find, the more you dig into this topic', a legal officer advised me, 'is that there is a huge divide between lawyers and everyone else on what is meaningful for victims . . . Especially in-house lawyers like the OPCV would claim "my client cares about procedural rights . . . they want access to the confidential case file, that is what justice means for my victims or my clients". It is very legal. I don't think anyone cares whether their lawyers have access to the confidential case file'.[57] Lawyers project their procedural concept of justice onto 'their victims', something the legal officer disavows. In reality, only lawyers care about accessing 'the confidential case file', presumably because it increases their power in the juridical field. Victims, on the other hand, do not care.

Contrary to his expectations, what I found, digging into this topic, is that lawyers often express rather different ideas about justice. Reflecting upon my interviews with ICC practitioners, it is helpful to make an initial distinction between a purely subjective and substantive justice concept ('What is justice? It is so many things. It is like love', one interviewee suggested[58]), and an institutionally defined, procedural concept (justice means investigating and prosecuting international crimes in accordance with due process norms). The views of my interviewees fell on a continuum between these two positions. Most of them felt that the concept of justice cannot simply be derived from the Court's practices, but neither did they think that justice is a purely relativistic concept contingent on culture, personal beliefs, or politics.[59]

While Bourdieu acknowledges interpretive struggles over legal texts within the legal profession, he argues that 'divergences between "authorized interpreters" are necessarily limited, and the coexistence of a multitude of juridical norms in competition with each other is by definition excluded from the juridical order'.[60] This, however, neglects the diversity and tensions

[56] Interview with Adviser, Presidency, The Hague (8 January 2014).
[57] Interview with Legal Officer, Registry, The Hague (12 November 2013).
[58] Interview with Defence Counsel, The Hague (4 December 2013).
[59] Interview with Legal Adviser, Chambers, The Hague (10 January 2014); Interview with Legal Coordinator, Registry, The Hague (4 February 2014).
[60] Bourdieu (n 22) 818.

among the 'experts in horror'.[61] Most obviously, the ICC's lawyers have rather different backgrounds. They were trained in different jurisdictions and have practised different types of law in domestic courts, international organizations, and non-governmental organizations (NGOs). These diverse legal experiences can translate into different justice conceptions. One interviewee, for example, observed that 'generally, there might be a difference between the human rights lawyer that talks about justice, and the hard-core criminal lawyer that talks about justice'.[62]

This diversity of perspectives at the ICC, when it is acknowledged at all, is almost exclusively attributed to the two legal traditions that the Court's law combines: the common and the civil law traditions.[63] These legal traditions supposedly have an enormous hold on the imagination of lawyers, sparking tensions when practitioners continue to evaluate the Court's practices in terms of 'how things are done at home'.[64] To give an example, many common law lawyers felt uncomfortable with the ICC's slogan—'10 Years of Fighting Impunity'—to celebrate the Court's tenth anniversary.[65] As a senior Registry official expressed:

> And I have to say, as a common law lawyer, I don't feel that comfortable with this sort of language of 'fighting against impunity' . . . for me, it is more, you are looking for justice. Because, otherwise, that makes it sound as if you already decided that people are guilty . . . I think this could be a legal cultural thing, because I have had other common law lawyers who agree with me. Somehow it offends my sense of [pause], but, of course, in civil law cultures you also have the concept of 'innocent until proven guilty', so I don't know why. But somehow, for me, I prefer to talk about the importance of accountability, the importance of justice.[66]

[61] Mégret (n 19) 194.

[62] Interview with Adviser, Presidency, The Hague (8 January 2014). See also Darryl Robinson, 'The Identity Crisis of International Criminal Law' (2008) 21 Leiden Journal of International Law 925; Christian Sperfeldt, *Practices of Reparations in International Criminal Justice* (CUP 2022) 305.

[63] Brianne McGonigle Leyh, *Procedural Justice? Victim Participation in International Criminal Proceedings* (Intersentia 2011) 10, 234; Luke Moffett, 'Elaborating Justice for Victims at the International Criminal Court: Beyond Rhetoric and The Hague' (2015) 13 Journal of International Criminal Justice 281, 286.

[64] McGonigle Leyh (n 63) 226.

[65] ICC Weekly Update No 135 (9 July 2012) https://www.icc-cpi.int/sites/default/files/NR/rdonlyres/E6D289BC-9672-4304-BC32-79BD024D1E07/284716/ED135_ENG.pdf (accessed 28 January 2023).

[66] Interview with Senior Official, Registry, The Hague (16 December 2013).

Almost in the same breath in which she invokes the 'legal cultural thing', she revokes it. It is not simply a question of common law versus civil law. What seems to matter, to her and to many ICC lawyers, is what justice is not. It is not retributive; punishment is not its purpose.

By reducing the Court's staff to lawyers operating in the juridical field, we miss how tenuously their justice ideas relate to law. Their justice ideas, in fact, were quite ordinary, commonsensical even, not least because law already inflects common sense in many societies. You do not need to be a lawyer to think or talk like my interviewees. Here, Gramsci's observation that ideology consists of two distinct floors, philosophy, and common sense, is useful.[67] The organic historical role of ideology, Hall argues, 'can only be found when and where philosophical currents enter into, modify, and transform the practical everyday consciousness of the masses. The latter is what [Gramsci] calls "common sense"'.[68] The power of ideology neither lies in its persuasiveness nor its coherence as a philosophy—that is why it seems a little futile to disprove the rationality or coherence of international criminal law, like many critical scholars do—ideology is fought out, not in philosophy classes or publications, but on the fragmentary, disjointed, and contradictory terrain of common sense.[69]

While philosophy requires careful definition and justification of premises, justice is rarely openly discussed at the Court or deliberated in the courtroom. Many ICC lawyers are not even aware that their colleagues have rather different ideas about justice. One senior Registry official, for example, told me,

> [f]or me, there are no different meanings of justice. Justice is justice. Justice means conformity to the moralities and the law. The meaning of justice per se is always the same and it cannot be changed . . . If you are a practitioner, the notion of justice is quite clear; what is right and what is fair . . . to be simple.[70]

However, as soon as we introduce the idea that justice does not only mean conformity to the law but also to morality, the practitioners I interviewed

[67] Stuart Hall, *Cultural Studies 1983: A Theoretical History* (Jennifer Daryl Slack and Lawrence Grossberg eds, Duke UP 2016) 165.

[68] ibid. See also Stuart Hall, 'Gramsci's Relevance for the Study of Race and Ethnicity' (1986) 10(4) Journal of Communication Inquiry 5, 20.

[69] ibid.

[70] Interview with Senior Official, ICC Registry, The Hague (10 January 2014).

did not find it that 'simple' to settle what is 'right and fair' in international criminal justice. In fact, another senior Registry official presented exactly the opposite idea of how the concept of justice functions at the Court: 'It does not mean one thing. It means different things to different people . . . Talking about justice for victims is soft if you like, it is how different people see it, but it does not say that in the Statute. In a way, it does not mean anything.'[71]

This brings me back to the insinuation that my questions are very 'philosophical' and not relevant to everyday legal practice. One defence counsel even asked his colleague from the same office to participate in the interview to 'help' him with my 'difficult' questions. This is an excerpt from our interview:

ME: But, in a sense, justice is not a legal concept. It is a concept that the judges have not defined. So, there may be some room for different interpretations?

HIM: But the ICC is a court. Justice means something. If somebody has to face justice because something occurred against global law and ICC text, justice is having a whole process with all the actors respecting the highest standards. Justice, for me, is not 'fighting against impunity'. It's only a part. The ICC was celebrating 10 years of ICC, saying '10 years of fighting against impunity' whereas for me, I'm not fighting against impunity.

ME: What are you fighting for?

HIM: Justice.

ME: And what do you mean by that?

HIM: Justice is a global process. It's a whole structure and 'fighting against impunity' is just a part. I think it's the role of the prosecutor. But the judges' role is not to fight against impunity. Their role is to say, 'this is justice; he or she is innocent'.[72]

This excerpt is rather typical of my interviews. Initially, my interviewees insist that 'justice does not really matter' and that they do not spend their time thinking about what it means. Between the lines, there is a palpable sense of frustration of spending precious time on useless questions with a researcher/intern. But when I probed further, they would usually defend the idea that the 'ICC does justice' and that 'justice means something'.

[71] Interview with Senior Official, ICC Registry, The Hague (16 December 2013).
[72] Interview with Defence Counsel, The Hague (4 December 2013).

Justice is treated as a footnote of the international criminal process. The footnote seems supplementary, but it is also the basis of the text, the feet it stands on. Without its feet, the text cannot move. The footnote becomes essential, perhaps even more important than the text. Law needs justice, but justice does not need law. As Salmon puts it, paraphrasing Derrida:

> Our system of law is predicated on the existence of justice, as our systems of theology are predicated on the existence of God, and yet neither justice nor God occur within the systems, nor can their existence be guaranteed. They are both, argues Derrida 'to come'. But this does not refute the system, rather it is the engine of both its survival and its need to adapt. Law will cease to have a function on the arrival of justice, as theology will be made redundant by the arrival of God, and philosophy on the arrival of Truth.[73]

Rather than law colonizing justice, it is justice that haunts law. It is no surprise, then, that the Court's practitioners are unwilling to abdicate the ICC's claim to 'do' or deliver 'justice'. But justice needs to remain secondary. There is a risk, however, that this relationship turns: law is only one among many approaches to achieve justice, and the ICC is only one particular legal and organizational form among many. A notoriously slow and expensive court, the ICC perennially fears substitution either by special tribunals or other transitional justice mechanisms. The Court was a fragile achievement to begin with, as one judge recalled from the Rome negotiations: 'Everything seemed possible at the end of the Cold War. [Then] we realized that we had to go for the good rather than the perfect. It all took very long, and we already thought that it might be an imaginary exercise.'[74]

When I asked the legal adviser who had frowned upon my questions in the cafeteria whether there is a difference between domestic courts and international criminal courts, he replied:

> It is exactly the same when it comes to the tools you apply on the operational side, but different philosophically . . . where the [ICC's] President often has to talk about these issues: Does it make sense? Do we need an international justice mechanism? Can we do it nationally? Does transitional justice make sense? Is it helpful? Was it good that the ICC indicted

[73] Peter Salmon, *An Event Perhaps: A Biography of Jacques Derrida* (Verso 2020) 14–15.
[74] Interview with Judge, The Hague (17 December 2013).

> Bashir? . . . In the national system, you don't ask yourself the question why it is there. While at the international justice level, in any institution I have worked in, the ICC, ICTR, ICTY, you always have to ask the question: why should the institution exist in the first place?[75]

As much as the Court's practitioners prefer focusing on legal matters, they nonetheless have to wrestle with irksome philosophical questions: '[W]hy should the institution exist in the first place?' Questions of justice, in short, are essential for the Court's existence and reproduction. The next section examines how 'justice for victims' became a key rationale for the Court and how it has shaped its institutional development and reproduction.

2.3 Justice for Victims: Combining Retributive and Restorative Justice

Justice is the reason the institution exists and so it matters for the Court's institutional reproduction. The Court cannot simply operate as a regular criminal court, much as the Court's staff would like that.[76] Domestic criminal courts arguably operate more as repressive than as ideological state apparatuses. They are more about order than justice.[77] The ICC, by contrast, is often regarded as a 'global civil society achievement' as NGOs advocated vociferously for its establishment. What drove them was the pursuit of 'justice for victims'.[78] As one NGO representative declared during the Rome negotiations:

[75] Interview with Legal Adviser, Presidency, The Hague (8 January 2014).

[76] In my interviews, ICC practitioners often treated 'their' domestic criminal justice systems as the bar that the Court should strive to meet.

[77] Some of my ICC interviewees expressed the idea that justice is less of a topic in established domestic criminal justice systems (in Europe). One judge said that 'in a very orderly society, justice means small matters . . . In countries like Germany justice is looked through a magnifying glass . . . In countries like the DRC, justice concerns much bigger issues, war and murder and it also involves different countries'. Interview with Judge, The Hague (17 December 2013); Interview with Legal Adviser, Registry, The Hague (23 October 2013). Glasius points out that the idea 'that international criminal courts have a responsibility to explain themselves to affected communities . . . is not necessarily taken for granted in the pursuit of 'normal' domestic criminal justice'. Glasius (n 14) 46, 49; Carolyn Hoyle and Leila Ullrich, 'New Court, New Justice? The Evolution of "Justice for Victims" at Domestic Courts and at the International Criminal Court' (2014) 12(4) Journal of International Criminal Justice 681, 700. That said, domestic courts have also begun doing more outreach work. See eg UK Supreme Court, 'Moving Education and Outreach Online' https://www.supremecourt.uk/news/moving-education-and-outreach-online.html (accessed 2 January 2023).

[78] Marlies Glasius, *The International Criminal Court: A Global Civil Society Achievement* (Routledge 2007).

> Punishing criminals is not enough. There will be no justice without justice for victims. And in order to do justice for victims, the ICC must be empowered to address their rights and needs.[79]

Here we can already sense a tension between 'victims' rights', which can be determined legally, and 'victims' needs', which may well exceed their legal rights. Although initially many state delegations in Rome insisted that victims' rights were already recognized through the Court's 'retributive and deterring functions', they gradually came to accept that victims' interests in restorative justice are distinct. These victims' interests were eventually integrated into the Statute as victims' rights to participation and reparation, especially through Article 68 and Article 75.[80] Article 68(3) stipulates:

> [w]here the personal interests of the victims are affected, the Court shall permit their views and concerns to be presented and considered at stages of the proceedings determined to be appropriate by the Court and in a manner which is not prejudicial to or inconsistent with the rights of the accused and a fair and impartial trial.[81]

Article 75, meanwhile, provides that 'the Court shall establish principles relating to reparations to, or in respect of, victims, including restitution, compensation and rehabilitation', while Article 79 establishes the TFV, which is mandated to provide reparation and assistance to victims and their families.

The much vaunted 'ground-breaking' nature of these victims' rights becomes clearer when contextualized in the historical trajectory of international criminal justice.[82] Emerging after the end of the Second World War, international criminal justice institutions initially ignored the victim,

[79] Victims' Rights Working Group, 'Speech by Fiona McKay on behalf of the Victims' Rights Working Group' (17 June 1998) https://www.legal-tools.org/doc/46e5ed/pdf/ (accessed 2 August 2023).

[80] Christopher Muttukumaru, 'Reparations to Victims' in Roy S Lee (ed), *The International Criminal Court: The Making of the Rome Statute: Issues, Negotiations, Results* (Kluwer Law International 1999) 264.

[81] Rome Statute (1998)https://www.icc-cpi.int/sites/default/files/RS-Eng.pdf> (accessed 4 January 2024).

[82] Silvana Arbia, 'Justice for all? The International Criminal Court: 10 year review of the ICC' Speech by the ICC Registrar at the Conference (14 February 2012) 4 https://www.icc-cpi.int/NR/rdonlyres/8C6B4B5B-D854-4F18-BA76-E0F687F2D60C/284274/Speech_10anniversary_Australia.pdf (accessed 5 December 2022). I should note that this account is based on a

recognizing him or her only in the role of the witness.[83] The Statute of the Nuremberg Tribunal, for example, did not include any reference to victims, not to mention their rights or interests in international criminal proceedings.[84] Indeed, 'the very concept of a "victim" in the sense of a private individual with a legal status under international law by virtue of having suffered injury or harm in consequence of a violation of its rules' had been alien to international criminal law for much of the twentieth century.[85]

The gradual move of the victim from the margin to the centre of international criminal justice unfolded in the context of three overlapping developments. Most fundamentally, the 1960s witnessed the emergence of victims' rights movements in many common law countries whose advocates decried the 'secondary victimization' victims experienced at the hands of the criminal justice system not only due to their marginalization but also due to the traumatic experiences of cross-examination in court.[86] Drawing inspiration from civil law countries' extensive victims' rights to participation and reparation as *partie civile*, they demanded a greater role for victims in the criminal justice process. Their advocacy also gained traction at the international level, culminating in two UN General Assembly resolutions that enshrine the rights of victims to access justice and reparation.[87] The shift towards victims' needs and interests can also be attributed

Eurocentric historiography of international criminal justice and that more recent, critical histories chart richer global genealogies connecting international criminal justice to the abolition of the slave trade and to the Africa Blue Books, among others. Emily Haslam, *The Slave Trade, Abolition and the Long History of International Criminal Law: The Recaptive and the Victim* (Routledge 2019); Christopher Gevers, 'The "Africa Blue Books" at Versailles: The First World War, Narrative, and Unthinkable Histories of International Criminal Law' in Immi Tallgren and Thomas Skouteris (eds), *The New Histories of International Criminal Law: Retrials* (OUP 2019) 145.

[83] Claude Jorda and Jérôme de Hemptinne, 'The status and role of the victim' in Antonio Cassese, Paola Gaeta, and John Jones (eds), *The Rome Statute of the International Criminal Court: A Commentary* (OUP 2002).

[84] Sam Garkawe, 'Victims and the International Criminal Court: Three Major Issues' (2013) 3 International Criminal Law Review 345, 347.

[85] Conor McCarthy, 'Victim Redress and International Criminal Justice: Competing Paradigms, or Compatible Forms of Justice?' (2012) 10 Journal of International Criminal Justice 351, 354; Conor McCarthy, *Reparations and Victim Support in the International Criminal Court* (CUP 2012).

[86] Mina Rauschenbach and Damien Scalia, 'Victims and International Criminal Justice: A Vexed Question?' (2008) 90 International Review of the Red Cross 441, 442; Charles Trumbull, 'The Victims of Victim Participation in International Criminal Proceedings' (2007) 29 Michigan Journal of International Law 777, 782.

[87] 'Declaration of Basic Principles of Justice for Victims of Crime and Abuse of Power' UN Doc A/Res/40/34 (29 November 1985); 'Basic Principles and Guidelines on the Right

to the ascent of restorative justice institutions such as truth and reconciliation commissions in Transitional Justice (TJ) in the 1980s and 1990s.[88] Unlike retributive justice, restorative justice makes the recognition of, consultation with, and redress of victims the centrepiece of TJ processes.[89] Finally, the idea of 'justice for victims' became salient in the wake of the legitimacy crisis of international criminal justice in the 1990s as the societal impact of the International Criminal Tribunal for the former Yugoslavia (ICTY) and the International Criminal Tribunal for Rwanda (ICTR) was increasingly found wanting, especially because they failed to resonate with the needs and interests of victims and affected communities.[90] Against this backdrop, the ICC's victims' rights provisions were heralded as a way of overcoming the alienation and marginalization experienced by victims at previous tribunals.[91]

Reflecting on how the victims' articles entered the Statute, first with brackets[92] and later without, the Court's practitioners often invoke the influence of civil law countries, especially France, alongside the influence of NGOs.[93] There were, however, deeper reasons why these victims' provisions lingered on in the text, as this judge indicates:

to a Remedy and Reparation for Victims of Gross Violations of International Human Rights Law and Serious Violations of International Humanitarian Law' UN Doc A/RES/60/147 (21 March 2006).

[88] Ruti Teitel, 'Transitional Justice Genealogy' (2003) 16 Harvard Humanitarian Rights Journal 69, 78.

[89] Carolyn Hoyle, 'Can international justice be restorative justice? The role of reparations' in Nicola Palmer, Phil Clark, and Danielle Granville (eds), *Critical Perspectives in Transitional Justice* (Intersentia 2012) 189, 194–95; Heather Strang and Lawrence Sherman, 'Repairing the Harm: Victims and Restorative Justice' (2003) 15 Utah Law Review 15.

[90] Mariana Goetz, 'The International Criminal Court and its Relevance to Affected communities' in Phil Clark and Nicholas Waddell (eds), *Courting Conflict? Justice, Peace and the ICC in Africa* (Royal African Society 2008) 65, 65, 71; Emily Haslam, 'Law, Civil society and contested justice at the International Criminal Tribunal for Rwanda' in Marie-Bénédicte Dembour and Tobias Kelly (eds), *Paths to International Justice* (CUP 2007) 68–69; Mirko Klarin, 'The Impact of the ICTY Trials on Public Opinion in the Former Yugoslavia' (2009) 7 JICJ 89; Janine Clark, 'The Impact Question: The ICTY and the restoration and maintenance of peace' in Bert Swart, Alexander Zahar, and Göran Sluiter (eds), *The Legacy of the International Criminal Tribunal for the Former Yugoslavia* (OUP 2011).

[91] Fiona McKay, 'Victim Participation in Proceedings before the International Criminal Court' (2008) 15 Human Rights Brief 2, 2; Mariana Pena, 'Victim Participation at the International Criminal Court: Achievements Made and Challenges Lying Ahead' (2009) 16 ILSA Journal of International and Comparative Law 497, 499.

[92] Christine Evans, *The Right to Reparation in International Law for Victims of Armed Conflict* (CUP 2012) 99, 100.

[93] Interview with Adviser, Chamber, The Hague (8 January 2014); Gilbert Bitti and Hakan Friman, 'Participation of Victims in the Proceedings' in Roy S. Lee and others (eds),

> Well, of course, for those who have *partie civile*, it is easier for them to understand how victims can be part of the process. But the system that we created, well, it was very much pushed by the French, but of course the system we have is not necessarily the French system at all. I think it was more based on this idea that this court needed to be more accessible to victims than the other tribunals. *So, it is more based on ideology, I would say* than based on any system, with this idea that making them more visible would also give more impact to the work of the Court.[94]

While criminal law exists outside or irrespective of ideology, the same is not true for victims, who are recognized as an ideological element. The ICC needed to be more accessible than preceding tribunals; 'the law should always be accessible for everyone', as Kafka's man from the country put it.[95] Accessibility makes victims more *visible*, and it is their visibility that makes the Court impactful. What matters to the law is not that victims 'enter' but that they 'come'. They should be visible at the gate of the law.

Many of the Court's first-generation judges, some of whom were diplomats at the Rome conference, had reservations about this victims' mandate. 'Why does it not really work?', one former diplomat turned ICC judge explained to me:

> If you have a murder case in the UK, France whatever, and if one, two people are murdered, it is possible to see justice being done. Their lawyer is with them [the victims]; they are part of the process of justice. I will now sit again in confirmation of charges proceedings in the Gbagbo and the Ntaganda case. The number of victims is already abstract.[96]

In addition to the large number of victims of international crimes, ICC practitioners and scholars are concerned that the *justice experiment* of combining 'retributive' and 'restorative' justice hollows out the key norms of international criminal justice: impartiality, due process, and the equality of

The International Criminal Court: Elements of Crimes and Rules of Procedure and Evidence (Transnational Publishers 2001) 457.

[94] Interview with Judge, The Hague (30 January 2014) (emphasis added).
[95] Kafka (n 1).
[96] Interview with Judge, The Hague (19 December 2013).

arms.[97] By pursuing both retributive and restorative justice with scarce resources, the ICC, moreover, risks failing in its 'core mandate' of conducting expeditious trials. Recalling the 'countless hours spent on determining the victim status of hundreds and in the future perhaps thousands of applicants', former ICC Judge Christine Van den Wyngaert has claimed that the Court's victims' engagement has considerably lengthened its judicial proceedings.[98] On this basis, she and other critics have argued that 'justice for victims' should be channelled through separate restorative justice institutions, such as truth and reparations commissions.[99]

What role victims should play at the ICC remains contested. Once during my internship I tried to arrange an interview with an ICC judge through 'his' intern. In her confirmation email to me, she copied not only the judge but also other senior officials of his division, adding: 'Judge x also would like to refer you to the award-winning manuscript by Brianne McGonigle Leyh with the title "Procedural Justice? Victim Participation in International Criminal Proceedings" with the hope that it will be useful for your research.'[100] Before I had the chance to reply, one of the senior officials copied in had replied to all of us:

> Maybe you [the judge's intern] should underline that this is a study made by a common law lawyer who received an award by common law lawyers who generally are not very favourable to victims' participation, because they do not know it in their system, and common law lawyers tend

[97] Lucia Zedner, 'Reparation and Retribution: Are They Reconcilable?' (1994) 57 The Modern Law Review 228; Mugambi Jouet, 'Reconciling the Conflicting Rights of Victims and Defendants at the International Criminal Court' (2007) 26 Saint Louis University Public Law Review 249; Salvatore Zappalà, 'The Rights of Victims v. the Rights of the Accused' (2010) 8(1) Journal of International Criminal Justice 137. For an overview of the procedural role of victims see Tatiana Bachvarova, *The Standing of Victims in the Procedural Design of the International Criminal Court* (Brill 2017).

[98] Van den Wyngaert (n 45) 493. Judge Fulford, by contrast, has argued that victim participation did not significantly extend the length of the proceedings in the Lubanga case. Adrian Fulford, 'The Reflections of a Trial Judge' (2011) 22 Criminal Law Forum 222.

[99] Van den Wyngaert (n 45) 493; Brianne McGonigle Leyh, 'Victim-Oriented Measures at International Criminal Institutions: Participation and its Pitfalls' (2012) 12 International Criminal Law Review 375, 407; Christine H Chung, 'Victims' Participation at the International Criminal Court: Are Concessions of the Court Clouding the Promise?' (2008) 6 Northwestern Journal of International Human Rights 459, 542; Mirjan Damaska, 'What Is the Point of International Criminal Justice?' (2008) 83 Chicago-Kent Law Review 329, 342–43. See also more recent proposals of creating a separate reparation chamber: Luke Moffett, 'Reparations for Victims at the International Criminal Court: A New Way Forward?' (2017) 21(9) The International Journal of Human Rights 1204.

[100] Email communication, 'Research Request' (4 December 2013).

> to not like, and very often not to understand, what is not in their national system. This is particularly true for lawyers from the USA (the award was given by the American branch of the AIDP, which is not a good sign). By referring this student to such a book, you obviously do not want to give the impression that Judge x is sharing the partial view of a common law lawyer on victims' participation.[101]

This reaction is instructive for several reasons. First, the positions of the Court's senior officials, especially the judges, on victim participation are well known at the Court.[102] The judge I had contacted was known to be critical of victim participation. One of his colleagues had told me earlier: 'Judge x is concerned that it will destroy the Court.'[103] The senior official who replied so promptly, on the other hand, was well known as a 'victims' supporter'. Secondly, it shows how blame for the Court's ideological struggles is projected on its weakest members, a theme that I will further tease out below. In this case, an unpaid intern was blamed as the judge himself could not be attacked. During my internship, a senior staff member lectured me: 'you need to understand the hierarchies. I'm a P5 and you are a P0'.[104] Finally, the exchange also reveals that victim participation is not a trivial issue for the judges:

> 'Victims' is a very touchy issue because you touch the balance of power and where this institution could go. You don't joke with that, and the judges know very well that you don't joke with it. They say, 'this is where we want to go' and your legal influence [as a legal adviser] may become zero [if you try to go against their ideas].[105]

You are a P0; your influence becomes zero. Zeros have no influence. The judges hold ultimate interpretive power, but they do not always pull in the same direction, not least because the Court's victims' rights regime is marked by several contradictions.

101 ibid.

102 Some sitting judges have even published their concerns in academic articles. Van den Wyngaert (n 45); Hans-Peter Kaul, 'Victims' rights and peace' in Thorsten Bonacker and Christoph Safferling (eds), *Victims of International Crimes: An Interdisciplinary Discourse* (TMC Asser Press 2013).

103 Interview with Judge, The Hague (17 December 2013).

104 Field notes (n 27).

105 Interview with Senior Official, Chambers, The Hague (8 January 2014).

At least three contradictions are worth noting here.[106] First, what characterizes international crimes and makes the Court necessary is mass victimization, but the latter is also what makes victims' meaningful inclusion difficult as legal procedures and courtrooms are not designed to accommodate thousands of victims.[107] Secondly, and relatedly, there is an obvious tension between victim participation and a notion of due process that excludes them.[108] It is ultimately the contradiction between wanting change and wanting things to remain the same. Victims' perspectives should be heard, but only where the Court deems them relevant, and without influencing either the Court's legal framework or institutional operations.[109] There are, thirdly, tensions between conceiving victims as a burden and an asset for international criminal justice. Victims are inconvenient from the perspective of legal procedure (the risks their inclusion poses to a fair trial), but they are convenient, even necessary, as a legitimating narrative for international criminal justice.[110]

On the face of it, these contradictions have been resolved by diluting victims' rights. Through their legal representatives, victims can make opening and closing statements, access the case file, examine witnesses, challenge the admissibility of evidence, and submit evidence.[111] These rights, however, are subject to the discretion of the respective Chamber and have differed between cases.[112] Over the years, there has been a trend in Chambers' decisions to limit victim participation.[113] The Appeals Chamber in *Lubanga* decided, early on, that victims could not participate at the investigation stage, which is arguably the most important stage for those victims who want to

[106] Carsten Stahn, 'Reparative Justice after the Lubanga Appeal Judgment: New Prospects for Expressivism and Participatory Justice or 'Juridified Victimhood' by Other Means?' (2015) 13(4) Journal of International Criminal Justice 801, 802–803.

[107] Luke Moffett, *Justice for Victims before the International Criminal Court* (Routledge 2014) 10; Antony Pemberton and others, 'Coherence in International Criminal Justice: A Victimological Perspective' (2015) 15(2) International Criminal Law Review 339, 349.

[108] Victims are recognized as participants but not parties in the proceedings. Liesbeth Zegveld, 'Victims as a Third Party: Empowerment of Victims?' (2019) 19(2) International Criminal Law Review 321, 330–31.

[109] See also Rome Statute, art 68.3.

[110] Stahn (n 106) 803.

[111] ICC Rules of Procedure and Evidence, rr 91–92.

[112] Hoyle and Ullrich (n 77) 689; Luke Moffett, 'Meaningful and Effective? Considering Victims' Interests Through Participation at the International Criminal Court' (2015) 26 Criminal Law Forum 255, 266.

[113] Mariana Pena and Gaelle Carayon, 'Is the ICC Making the Most of Victim Participation?' (2013) 7(3) International Journal of Transitional Justice 518; Gaelle Carayon and Jonathan O'Donohue, 'The International Criminal Court's Strategies in Relation to Victims' (2017) 15(3) Journal of International Criminal Justice 567, 590; Megan Hirst and Sandra Sahyouni, 'Effective legal representation for participating victims: principles, challenges and some

see their perpetrators prosecuted.[114] Victim participation has become more collective—with hundreds and even thousands of victims being grouped together and represented by one or two Court-appointed lawyers.[115] At the same time, the judges have failed to develop a common approach to victims. Every Chamber develops a different model of victim participation for every case, which has caused much confusion, while some participatory rights like the victims' role in appeals proceedings remain contested.[116] While the overall trend has been to water down victims' rights, even those judges who are adamant that victims have no place in the courtroom had to tread carefully. There is a limit to which the Court can frame its *raison d'être* around 'doing justice for victims', while erasing them from the process, not least because of pressure by NGOs and victims' advocates.

In the remainder of this chapter, I will trace the Court's attempts to resolve these contradictions by gradually shifting victims from judicial to non-judicial and field-based processes overseen by administrative bodies such as the registry and the TFV. The starting point for this process, however, was institutional necessity: to implement victims' rights, a whole

solutions' in Rudina Jasini and Gregory Townsend, *Advancing the Impact of Victim Participation at the International Criminal Court: Bridging the Gap Between Research and Practice* UK Economic and Social Research Council (ESRC) (30 November 2020) https://www.law.ox.ac.uk/sites/files/oxlaw/iccba_-_oxford_publication_30_november_2020_.pdf (accessed 11 March 2022).

[114] *Prosecutor v Lubanga* (Judgment on victim participation in the investigation stage of the proceedings in the appeal of the OPCD against the decision of Pre-Trial Chamber I of 7 December 2007 and in the appeals of the OPCD and the Prosecutor against the decision of Pre-Trial Chamber I of 24 December 2007) [2008] ICC-01/04-556, § 45.

[115] Emily Haslam and Rod Edmunds, 'Common Legal Representation at the International Criminal Court: More Symbolic than Real?' (2012) 12(5) International Criminal Law Review 871; Moffett (n 63) 291.

[116] The Independent Expert Review, for example, noted in 2020 that 'the right to victim participation has yet to crystallise into a consolidated and clear practice'. It further observes that 'some points were made about the inconsistencies in procedure adopted by different Chambers creating confusion and uncertainty'. Different chambers provide victims' counsel with different leeway in questioning witnesses, for example, and they have differently interpreted victims' rights to choose counsel. See Independent Expert Review of the International Criminal Court and the Rome Statute System: Final Report' (30 September 2020) § 863, §§ 865–69. See also FIDH, 'Whose Court is it? Judicial handbook on victims' rights at the International Criminal Court' (April 2021) 8 https://www.fidh.org/IMG/pdf/fidh_whose_court_is_it_en.pdf (accessed 2 August 2023). On victims' role in appeals see eg *Situation in Afghanistan* (Dissenting Opinion of Judge Luz del Carmen Ibáñez Carranza to the Majority's decision dismissing as inadmissible the victims' appeals against the decision rejecting the authorisation of an investigation into the situation in Afghanistan) [2020] ICC-02/17-137-Anx; Juan-Pablo Perez-Leon-Acevedo, 'Victims and Appeals at the International Criminal Court (ICC): Evaluation under International Human Rights Standards' (2021) 25(9) The International Journal of Human Rights 1598.

victims' apparatus had to be created, which produced new victims' stakeholders, not only victims' bureaucrats and victims' lawyers, but also intermediaries and victims, who work for the Court. In the process, something much more useful emerged than empty rhetoric. As the next chapter will show, the victim changed from a legitimating narrative into flesh-and-blood ideological subjects. But first, I illustrate how the contradictions inherent in the victims' rights regime translated into conflicts in the Court's relationships, resulting both in tendencies to compromise with and discipline the new victims' stakeholders.

2.4 New Victims' Stakeholders and Blame Subjects

The ICC is much more than a normal court. It 'is a jurisdiction on its own', the Court's former Registrar elaborated, 'in a national legal system, you have a police department, you have the justice department, you have the judiciary, you have the detention facilities, and these types of things. Over here [at the ICC], everything is part of one organization'.[117] The Court engages not only in a much broader range of activities than its domestic counterparts including community outreach, witness protection, victim participation, reparation, and assistance, but also operates in far-away countries, mainly in the Global South, which are often scarred by ongoing conflict. Owing to its focus on the Court's jurisprudence, however, the ICC literature tends to neglect the institutional life of the Court's victims' provisions.[118] The latter have opened international criminal justice to a plethora of new victims' stakeholders such as the TFV, the Victims Participation and

[117] Taegin Reisman, 'Q & A with International Criminal Court Registrar Herman von Hebel: Part I' *International Justice Monitor* (21 August 2013) https://www.ijmonitor.org/2013/08/q-a-with-international-criminal-court-registrar-herman-von-hebel-part-i/ (accessed 30 March 2023).

[118] Although see Mikkel Jarle Christensen and Richard Clements for institutional and sociological analysis of the ICC more generally. For example, Mikkel Jarle Christensen, 'Celebrating International Criminal Justice: A Sociology of the Twentieth Anniversary of the International Criminal Court' (2021) 9(3) London Review of International Law 351; Mikkel Jarle Christensen and Nabil M Orina, 'The International Criminal Court as a Law Laboratory: Professional Battles of Control and the "Control of the Crime" Theory' (2022) 20(3) Journal of International Criminal Justice 699; Richard Clements, 'From Bureaucracy to Management: The International Criminal Court's Internal Progress Narrative' (2019) 32(1) Leiden Journal of International Law 149. See also Peter Dixon and Chris Tenove, 'International Criminal Justice as a Transnational Field: Rules, Authority and Victims' (2013) 7(3) International Journal of Transitional Justice 393; Mégret (n 53); and more recently Christian Sperfeldt, *Practices of Reparations in International Criminal Justice* (CUP

Reparations Section (VPRS), the Office of the Public Counsel for Victims (OPCV), the Victims and Witnesses Unit (VWU), the outreach unit, victims' lawyers, and local intermediaries, which also means that lawyers are not the only professionals at the Court.[119] In a recent series called 'justice at work', the Court proudly displayed on its website the 'hundreds of people . . . working behind the scenes to make it [justice] happen'.[120] The series includes, amongst others, the profile of a 'trauma expert', who concludes her reflections on working at the Court as follows: 'In my view, we are very focused on the perpetrators, and of course the ICC has an important role there: it's retributive justice. But, still, I think what we do as psychologists is a little part of making the entire process more victim-centred. This is what drives me, every day.'[121]

The new victims' stakeholders engage in different justice practices from judges or prosecutors. 'We have a bit of a mixed role', a victims' officer explained to me, 'because the issue of victim participation cannot be only legal; it also has to be linked to the beneficiaries and the beneficiaries are in the field'.[122] His work includes regular trips to the Court's situation countries where he engages with community leaders, victims' lawyers, local intermediaries, NGOs, and victims. Lawyers become victims' officers and victims' lawyers and develop new practices appropriate to their role. Many worked as defence counsel or prosecutors before and only became more interested in victims' issues as they engaged with them. One victims' lawyer told me:

> It is also very important that the person should feel like they have been listened to. That is why I think victim participation is such a great idea. I was personally involved in making decisions at the prosecution of the

2022); Nicola Palmer and Tomas Hamilton, 'Legal Humility and Perceptions of Power in International Criminal Justice' (2022) 23(3) International Criminal Law Review 416.

[119] Not all of these institutions were envisaged in the Rome Statute. Neither outreach nor intermediaries were mentioned in the Rome Statute or the ICC's Rules of Procedure and Evidence, and the judges only set up OPCV (reg 81) and the VPRS (reg 86.9) in 2004 through the Regulations of the Court.

[120] ICC, 'Justice at Work' https://www.icc-cpi.int/get-involved/justice-at-work (accessed 10 April 2023).

[121] ICC, 'The Trauma Expert' https://www.icc-cpi.int/get-involved/justice-at-work/story/the-trauma-expert (accessed 10 April 2023). See also 'The Taskmaster', 'The Courtroom Pianist', 'The Judges' Legal Officers', 'The Litigator', 'The Protector' https://www.icc-cpi.int/get-involved/justice-at-work (accessed 25 July 2023).

[122] Interview with Legal Officer, Registry, The Hague (21 January 2014).

> ICTY to not prosecute entire municipalities in certain cases without ever picking up the phone to speak to a single victim.[123]

When asked what 'justice for victims' means, another victims' officer reflected:

> To make the Court closer, to reduce the gap, having a respectful interaction . . . making the Court closer to them, explaining the realities of the Court on the one hand, and also to the Court and the Chamber to explain the realities of victims on the other hand.[124]

Another victims' lawyer at the OPCV professed:

> To go to the field, to speak to people that are struggling to survive after having suffered the attacks, and the first thing they tell you is, 'OK, thank you for the information about the proceedings. But when are we getting financial assistance? Because I have this disease that needs treatment, because I don't have enough food for my family, my five children, because I don't have a roof for me to sleep under, and everyone is cold', so the idea of justice changed very much depending on whether I was at the OTP, where my main concern of justice was retribution and punishment to where I am now, where my main concern of justice is to eventually provide for the restoration of the rights of victims.[125]

As lawyers engage with victims, tensions arise between a purely procedural concept of justice (victim participation) and more substantive justice ideas (getting financial assistance, food on the table, a roof over the head). The relationship between the gatekeeper and the man from the country shifts the further they are away from the seat of the law. Victims put pressure on their advocates to stand up for their interests beyond the technicalities of the trial and that in turn creates more conflicts between judges and victims' lawyers.

Once the promise of 'justice for victims' was made, a certain accommodation had to be found between the judges' procedural preferences for expeditious trials and victims' substantive demands. The judges have balanced

[123] Interview with LRV, The Hague (24 November 2013).
[124] Interview with Legal Officer, Registry, The Hague (21 January 2014).
[125] Interview with Legal Officer, Registry, The Hague (4 February 2014).

these competing pressures by gradually shifting victim participation from courtroom to field-based and administrative processes. The Chambers' adoption of the A–B–C approach in 2014 to streamline victim applications is a case in point. The A–B–C approach gives a greater role to the Registry in deciding on victim applications. In determining whether a person is eligible to participate in a legal case before the Court, the Registry classifies the applicants into three categories: (i) applicants who clearly qualify as victims (Group A); (ii) applicants who clearly do not qualify as victims (Group B); and (iii) applicants for whom the Registry could not make a clear determination for any reason (Group C).[126] Only Group C will be transmitted to the judges and the legal parties for their deliberation.[127] This procedure allows a greater number of victims to participate 'in the field' without extensive litigation of their applications, thus limiting judicial time spent on victims, while putting more pressure on Registry staff and intermediaries to facilitate the victim application process in the field.[128] As victim *representation* became more collective and distant in The Hague, victim *engagement* became more intimate and deeper in the Court's situation countries. This solution speaks to the way judges value their time differently from victims' time and the time administrative and field staff spend engaging them 'in Africa'. But it also speaks to a shift in the conception of victim participation from victims having 'their day in court' to victims being mobilized and active 'in the field'.

Indeed, many court practitioners no longer imagine victim participation as something that happens primarily in the courtroom.[129] The ICC's YouTube video (2013) on victim participation is instructive in this regard. It starts with an ICC officer, pictured in the courtroom in The Hague, explaining to the audience:

[126] *Chambers Practice Manual* (5th edn, 2021) § 96 iv.

[127] For a recent articulation of the 'procedure for admission of victims to participate in the proceedings' see *The Prosecutor v Maxime Jeoffroy Eli Mokom Gawake* (Order on the conduct of the confirmation of charges proceedings) [2022] ICC-01/14-01/22-62, § 40. The Chamber, however, specifies that 'while the Registry's conclusions may be of assistance, it is for the Chamber to ultimately authorise or reject an applicant to participate in the proceedings' (§ 40x).

[128] For an overview of this shift from judicial to administrative decisions on victim applications see Karen Lønne Ring's recent article, which argues that this development is in conflict with the Court's legal framework. Karen Lønne Ring, 'The Evolution of the Procedure for Reviewing Victim Applications at the International Criminal Court' (2023) 21(1) Journal of International Criminal Justice 29.

[129] 'Each meeting was of great importance to the victims, and arguably constituted the most meaningful part of victim representation.' Sehmi (n 47) 582. NGOs such as the International Federation for Human Rights (FIDH) have been debunking the myth that 'victim participation is a matter solely for the Court and for the courtroom' for some time and have particularly

> For the first time in the history of international criminal justice systems, the Rome Statue . . . is putting victims at the centre of its proceedings . . . In the courtroom, victims are represented by lawyers, who ensure that their views and concerns are heard by the judges, but the process of victims' participation starts on the ground, in the situation-related countries, in the affected communities, in the towns and villages where the victims reside.[130]

The setting changes. We are suddenly riding in a white jeep through a lush green landscape in the Central African Republic, seated next to an ICC field officer. The image switches again and we see black men and women in colourful dresses sitting on white plastic chairs under mango trees. They are already waiting for us. Victim participation, the message seems to be, 'really' happens by engaging victims 'in the field'. As one Registry officer put it:

> I do not think, for victims, in my experience, the legal process in and of itself is what's meaningful. I think it's really about engagement with a legal representative and consistently, not one off, and the concept of being treated [respectfully] is important. For the first time perhaps ever, someone is listening to you . . . And if we don't have structures in place, like a legal representative with a complementary team to facilitate consistent interaction, we don't have participation.[131]

One early example of how that shift unfolded in the Court's jurisprudence was Trial Chamber V's decision on victims' representation and participation in the Kenyan cases on 3 October 2012. That decision was widely interpreted as a setback for victims' rights as it marked a shift from individual to collective forms of victim participation.[132] James Gondi, for example,

highlighted the importance of meeting with victims on the ground. FIDH, 'Five Myths about Victim Participation in ICC Proceedings' (2014) 23–25 https://www.fidh.org/IMG/pdf/cpi649a.pdf (accessed 12 December 2022).

[130] ICC, 'Victims' participation before the International Criminal Court' *YouTube* (23 April 2013) https://www.youtube.com/watch?v=chymGL8teX4 (accessed 21 April 2022).

[131] Interview with Registry Officer, The Hague (12 November 2013).

[132] See eg former Judge Fulford's critique in Samuel Linehan, 'International criminal courts: progress made, progress needed' *iLawyer* (1 November 2014) http://ilawyerblog.com/international-criminal-courts-progress-made-progress-needed/ (accessed 30 March 2022). The critique has also focused on how the Chamber's decision split the role of legal

described it as 'the least victim-friendly decision that the ICC Chambers have ever issued'.[133] Yet, less attention has been paid to the fact that the decision also required the victims' lawyers to be based in Kenya with a team of in-country assistants.[134] In this way, the decision gave the victims' lawyers more room to engage with victims. A field assistant in Kenya, for example, claimed that she had conducted twice as many missions to meet victims since the changes brought about by the decision:

> Of course, victim participation has become more involving. We can feel more of an effect, and I can't help but have the feeling that this is because the Chamber made the decision to have the common legal representative based in the field. This makes him more accessible to the victims; it makes him more accessible to the assistants.[135]

Accessibility is no longer about victims coming to the court, but about lawyers coming to the victims.

Being 'in the field', some victims' lawyers have expanded their role to advocate for victims' interests beyond criminal proceedings. The same field assistant in Kenya explained:

> You know the mandate as defined by the Court is extremely legalistic. Of course, they are going to put [victims' engagement] into legal limits because they have to cover their ass . . . [Yet] after interacting with the victims you literally have to push the boundaries of your mandate. You

representation between the common legal representative (CLR) based in Kenya (the lead counsel) and the OPCV in The Hague. The concern is that much nuance of victims' views is lost because it is OPCV rather than the CLR which represents victims in the courtroom on a daily basis. Sara Kendall and Sarah Nouwen, 'Representational Practices at the International Criminal Court: The Gap between Juridified and Abstract Victimhood' (2014) 76 Law and Contemporary Problems 235; *Prosecutor v Ruto and Sang* (Amicus Curiae Observations of Kituo Cha Sheria pursuant to Rule 103 of the Rules of Procedure and Evidence) [2012] ICC-01/09-01/11-478, §§ 22–23, § 27.

[133] James Gondi, 'Victim participation in ICC case is crucial' *The Star* (15 October 2012) https://allafrica.com/stories/201210161157.html (accessed 30 March 2023).

[134] *Prosecutor v Ruto and Sang* (Decision on victims' representation and participation) [2012] ICC-01/09-01/11-460 § 60; *Prosecutor v Muthaura and Kenyatta* (Decision on victims' representation and participation) [2012] ICC-01/09-02/11-498, § 59 ('The Chamber believes that greater geographic proximity between victims and the Common Legal Representative is important to ensure that victims can communicate easily and personally with their representative and thus ensure meaningful representation').

[135] Interview with CLR field assistant, Nairobi (30 June 2014).

> have to, because the expectations of these victims are really high. We try to manage them, but it is something that you could do. It is strictly not within your mandate to look for assistance for these victims; it is not. But every time you go and meet them that is a demand. And when you look at their impoverished circumstances; they live lives which you would not even wish on your worst enemies.[136]

While 'justice for victims' is used strategically at the Court, its introduction has also created cracks and leaks that can foster broader and more political justice practices. The victims' lawyer in the *Kenyatta* case, for example, actively lobbied for his client's demands for reparation and resettlement in Kenya, harnessing the spotlight created around the ICC in local and international media.[137] He also wrote a letter to the UN Special Rapporteur on the human rights of internally displaced persons (IDPs), calling on him to put more pressure on the Kenyan government to end discrimination in victim compensation, while also petitioning the Security Council to express the victims' opposition to the suspension of the case.[138] He was not the first victims' lawyer to petition the Security Council. The victims' lawyers in the *Al Bashir* case also wrote to the latter, urging it not to defer the prosecution of the President of Sudan.[139] Some ICC practitioners even think that 'beyond the courtroom' activism is the whole point of having external victims' lawyers, 'because they can say things we cannot say'.[140]

There have, admittedly, also been backlashes against victim engagement in the field. Having the lead counsel based in the field did not become the norm in subsequent cases, and the Chambers have, in fact, often preferred in-house representation of victims by the OPCV to external counsel.[141] In the *Ongwen* case, for instance, the single judge decided that victims in Northern Uganda who had chosen their own representation did not qualify

[136] Interview with Intermediary, Nairobi (30 June 2014).
[137] See also Sehmi (n 47) 589.
[138] Fergal Gaynor, Letter to the Special Rapporteur on the Human Rights of IDPs Dr. Chaloka Beyani (22 May 2014) (on file with the author); Fergal Gaynor, Letter to the Security Council (3 November 2013) (on file with the author).
[139] Legal Representatives for Darfur Victims Division, 'Legal Representatives for Darfur Victims, Attorneys Raymond M Brown and Wanda M Akin, Urge United Nations Security Council Not to Defer Indictment of Omar Hassan Ahmad al-Bashir' https://brownakin.com/wpbrownakin/wp-content/themes/brownakin/pdf/IJP-DVP_Press_Release_Bashir_Indictment.pdf (accessed 31 March 2023).
[140] Interview with Legal Officer, Registry, The Hague (12 November 2013).
[141] FIDH (n 116) 7 ('The role of OPCV requires clarification, as it seems to have become increasingly the go-to option for common legal representation, even though it was not initially intended to replace external counsel').

for legal aid from the Court.[142] Either they could choose 'free' representation by the OPCV or they would have to pay for their own lawyer, a decision which caused consternation among victims' advocates as it effectively stripped victims of their right to choose a lawyer, enshrined in Rule 90 of the Court's Rules of Evidence and Procedure.[143] Given that more than 2,000 victims had chosen the same two victims' lawyers, there was also no practical justification for the denial of legal aid. The judge, nonetheless, rejected their claim as the victims' lawyers had 'not been selected pursuant to a transparent and competitive procedure organized by the Registry'.[144] Despite this decision, the external victims' lawyers started representing victims by fundraising through NGOs.[145] Eventually, the Registry granted them legal aid under the Regulations of the Court, thus effectively superseding the judge.[146] Notwithstanding the Court's efforts to internalize victims' representation, it has become difficult to exclude external counsel.[147]

This also reflects a broader tendency at the ICC to localize and personalize its victim engagement.[148] Victims' lawyers organize regular meetings at local venues to update victims on the trial, discuss their views and concerns, and report them back to the Court. Some lawyers wonder whether it is their therapeutic or their legal labour that creates value for victims.[149] One victims' lawyer told me:

[142] *Prosecutor v Ongwen* (Decision on contested victims' applications for participation, legal representation of victims and their procedural rights) [2015] ICC-02/04-01/15-350, § 18.

[143] Human Rights Watch, 'Who Will Stand for Us? Victims' Legal Representation at the ICC in the Ongwen Case and Beyond' (2017) 37, 40–41 https://www.hrw.org/sites/default/files/report_pdf/ijongwen0817_web.pdf (accessed 31 October 2021).

[144] *Prosecutor v Ongwen* (Decision on contested victims' applications for participation, legal representation of victims and their procedural rights) [2015] ICC-02/04-01/15-350, § 20.

[145] Interview with Victims' Lawyer, London (10 September 2018).

[146] Human Rights Watch (n 143) 40–41.

[147] FIDH claimed that virtually all of the ICC practitioners they interviewed, apart from representatives of OPCV, said that the common legal representative should be an external lawyer although they disagreed on whether or not they should be based in the situation country. They also quote ICC Judge Bruno Cotte: 'I think it is necessary to have lawyers in the courtroom who have an external view, who are not an organ of the Court and who will not feel, even unwittingly, too involved in its operation, its habits and its constraints.' FIDH (n 116) 26–27.

[148] There is also increasing pressure by victims to hold local hearings which is a possibility under the Rules of Procedure and Evidence and has been considered in many cases before the Court but has, so far, not been granted. See eg *Situation in the People's Republic of Bangladesh/ Republic of the Union of Myanmar* (Victims' joint request concerning hearings outside the host State) [2020] ICC-01/19-34, § 11.

[149] Edna Erez, Michael Kilchling, and Jo-Anne Wemmers (eds), *Therapeutic Jurisprudence and Victim Participation in Justice. International Perspectives* (Carolina Academic Press 2011). Some victims' lawyers emphasize the therapeutic value of their work. See eg Joseph A Manoba

> We also found that out of these engagements with people, who have been victimized, I think a number of people got healing. This is something that the court, in my view, doesn't see, doesn't understand, perhaps is not interested in. But from my experience, in giving these individuals the opportunity to tell their stories, let them break down, emotions . . . we found many were speaking about these things for the very first time since they came back . . . We were not prepared for this. We're not trained counsellors.[150]

Even the OPCV's lawyers feel they cannot rely exclusively on their legal expertise in representing victims. At an ICC workshop on victim participation, Paolina Massidda, the head of the OPCV, insisted that her relationship to the victims she represents is like a family relationship.[151] The victims would call her if they got married or pregnant as you would do with a close family member. These claims speak to a new caring sensibility, where lawyers should be close to victims, know them and their circumstances, listen to their stories, and help them access assistance.[152] The OPCV also contracts local counsel, who regularly meet victims in their villages, even though there is much contestation on whether they are doing as much as external counsel.[153]

Another example of how the Court has compensated its judicial narrowing of victims' rights by broadening non-judicial forms of victims' inclusion is the relationship between reparation and assistance.[154] While

and Francisco Cox, 'Victims' participation in the Ongwen case: strengths, weaknesses and lessons learned' in FIDH, 'Victims at the Center of Justice: From 1998 to 2018: Reflections on the Promises and the Reality of Victim Participation at the ICC' (2018) 48, 52 https://www.fidh.org/IMG/pdf/droitsdesvictimes730a_final.pdf (accessed 10 December 2022).

150 Interview with Victims' Lawyer, Kampala (10 July 2019).

151 ICCBA and Oxford Workshop on Victim Participation (31 May–1 June 2018) https://www.law.ox.ac.uk/centres-institutes/centre-criminology/advancing-impact-victim-participation-international-criminal (accessed 31 March 2023).

152 As the single judge affirmed, victims' lawyers should have knowledge both of the Court's procedures and of the local context and culture to provide the best possible victims' representation. *Prosecutor v Ongwen* (Decision on contested victims' applications for participation, legal representation of victims and their procedural rights) [2015] ICC-02/04-01/15-350, § 24. NGOs have often argued that the latter is more important than the former. FIDH (n 116) 7.

153 Human Rights Watch (n 143) 28–29. This was also a recurrent theme in my interviews.

154 To ease the pressure on the Court to provide victims with reparations, which is predicated on a conviction of the perpetrator, the Court's practitioners often rely on the trust fund's assistance mandate. In the *Ntaganda* case, the single judge expressed that she was 'mindful that the usual length and complexity of the proceedings before the Court, as well as the ensuing fact that a significant amount of time can elapse between the opening of a case and the time when victims may be awarded reparations, might in some instances result in their disappointment

reparation is determined through a judicial process, assistance is decided and distributed administratively by the TFV.[155] An early example of plugging the reparation gap with assistance was the Court's approach in the *Lubanga* case, where the Prosecutor only presented one charge (enlisting and conscripting of child soldiers), thus significantly limiting the number and type of victims eligible for participation and reparation.[156] In fact, the Prosecutor was widely criticized for not including sexual and gender-based violent (SGBV) crimes in the charges against Lubanga despite evidence that Lubanga's troops had committed such crimes, including against child soldiers.[157] Spiga, for example, has argued that:

> the Court should be alert to the risks of granting access to justice only to a limited group of victims, while leaving without standing a large number of persons who cannot meet the strict requirements set by the Trial

and frustration. Access to immediate and meaningful assistance would often be beneficial to them. In light of this, the single judge believes that the unique role of the TFV should also be adequately illustrated during the outreach missions. In particular, it should be highlighted that projects for the benefit of victims of crimes within the jurisdiction of the Court (i.e., within the scope of the DRC situation) have already been put in place in the country'. *Prosecutor v Bosco Ntaganda* (Decision Establishing Principles on the Victims' Application Process) [2013] ICC-01/04-02/06-67, § 15. An outreach assistant in Uganda whom I interviewed in 2014 told me: '[w]hen we go to do outreach, we explain, "even if there is no guilty verdict, there is no trial, there is nothing . . . there is something being done in Northern Uganda. The Trust Fund is already implementing 18 projects in Northern Uganda"'. Interview with ICC Field Staff, Kampala (22 July 2014).

[155] Assistance programmes still have to be linked to harm created by crimes that fall under the Court's jurisdiction. See also Liesbeth Zegveld, 'Victims as a Third Party: Empowerment of Victims?' (2019) 19(2) International Criminal Law Review 321, 323, 340 ('the ICC has a tendency to address victims' damage as a humanitarian problem that can be solved through humanitarian assistance'). See also Sara Kendall, 'Beyond the restorative turn: The limits of legal humanitarianism' in Christian de Vos, Sara Kendall, and Carsten Stahn (eds), *Contested Justice: The Politics and Practice of International Criminal Court Interventions* (CUP 2015) 352; Sara Kendall and Sarah Nouwen, 'International criminal justice and humanitarianism' in Kevin Heller and others (eds), *The Oxford Handbook of International Criminal Law* (OUP 2020) 583.

[156] Lucia Catani, 'Victims at the International Criminal Court: Some Lessons Learned from the *Lubanga* Case' (2012) 10(4) Journal of International Criminal Justice 905.

[157] Louise Chappell, 'The Gender Injustice Cascade: 'Transformative' Reparations for Victims of Sexual and Gender-based Crimes in the Lubanga Case at the International Criminal Court' (2017) 21(9) The International Journal of Human Rights 1223, 1224; ICC Women, 'ICC Judges uphold conviction of Lubanga: *The Prosecutor v Thomas Lubanga Dyilo*' (2014) http://www.iccwomen.org/documents/First-conviction-and-sentence-upheld-on-appeal-at-the-ICC-REVISED-April-2015.pdf (accessed 31 March 2023).

> Chamber. This is especially true when the charges against the accused may not reflect the complexity of the crimes actually committed.[158]

But the Court appears to be sensitive to these risks.[159] In its reparation decision of 7 August 2012, Trial Chamber I included a much broader category of victims as beneficiaries of reparations, holding that 'the Court should formulate and implement reparation awards for victims of sexual and gender-based violence', even though Lubanga was not convicted for these crimes.[160] It further determined that not only victims and their families but also 'broader communities' can benefit from collective reparations.[161] While the Appeals Chamber reversed this broad inclusion of SGBV victims and communities in the reparation order against Lubanga, it also felt the need 'to give them something', namely TFV assistance and referrals to other NGOs.[162] As an adviser to the Chambers reasoned:

> And I think this is perhaps an explanation for what we have seen so far . . . this thought, 'ok, we need to broaden this slightly because otherwise it is just not understandable that these victims that were 'lucky' enough to be selected by the prosecutor for her case get reparations while others don't' . . . You would then rely on the Trust Fund. The victim doesn't really care whether she gets money or access to health care because of reparations or assistance.[163]

A similar dynamic also played out in the *Bemba* case. After Bemba was acquitted on 8 June 2018, abruptly ending the hopes of reparation for more than 5,000 victims participating in the case, the trust fund decided to

[158] Valentina Spiga, 'Indirect Victims' Participation in the Lubanga Trial' (2010) 8 JICJ 183, 198.
[159] In its reparation decision, the Chamber recognized that the selectivity of its charges and the limited categories of victims recognized 'could give rise to a risk of resentment on the part of other victims and the re-stigmatisation of former child soldiers within their communities'. *Prosecutor v Lubanga* (Decision establishing the principles and procedures to be applied to reparations) [2012] ICC-01/04-01/06-2904, § 193, n 383.
[160] ibid § 207.
[161] ibid § 206. Redress, 'At Long Last: Reparations for Victims can now proceed in the ICC's first case' (2015) http://www.redress.org/downloads/pr-lubanga-reparations-appeals-decision030315.pdf (accessed 31 March 2023).
[162] *Prosecutor v Lubanga* (Judgment on the appeals against the "Decision establishing the principles and procedures to be applied to reparations" of 7 August 2012 with AMENDED order for reparations (Annex A) and public annexes 1 and 2) [2015] ICC-01/04-01/06-3129 § 199.
[163] Interview with Adviser, Chambers, The Hague (10 January 2014).

accelerate the launch of its assistance programmes in the Central African Republic (CAR), especially for victims of SGBV: 'The Trust Fund for Victims wishes to assure the victims in the *Bemba* case and other victims who have suffered harm in the CAR I situation: You are not forgotten. The harms you have suffered are recognized and urgently call for a meaningful response.'[164] As one legal adviser put it, 'justice may require correcting the one-sidedness of reparations with assistance'.[165] In other words, both in the realm of victim participation and reparation, there has been a shift from judicial to administrative processes, the latter of which require extensive victim engagement in the field.[166]

In his book, *Distant Justice*, Phil Clark quotes a senior judge at the ICTR whom he interviewed in 2003:

> I have never been to Rwanda and I have no desire to visit. Going there and seeing the effect we are having would only make my work more difficult. How can I do my job—judging these cases fairly—with pictures in my mind of what is happening over there? This task is already complicated enough.[167]

It would be difficult for an ICC judge to say something like this now. On the contrary, in an interview in March 2021 ICC Judge Bruno Cotte asserted that 'field visits are essential. They enabled us to see the places and their topography, to meet the local community, victims and witnesses, and therefore to make the ICC closer and more visible than through video recordings of the proceedings'.[168] This 'move to the field' is also reflected

[164] ICC press release, 'Following Mr Bemba's acquittal, Trust Fund for Victims at the ICC decides to accelerate launch of assistance programme in Central African Republic' (13 June 2018) https://www.icc-cpi.int/news/following-mr-bembas-acquittal-trust-fund-victims-icc-decides-accelerate-launch-assistance (accessed 27 November 2022). See also Miriam Cohen, *Realizing Reparative Justice for International Crimes: From Theory to Practice* (CUP 2020) 145.

[165] Interview with TFV adviser, The Hague (1 June 2018). See also Independent Expert Review of the International Criminal Court and the Rome Statute System: Final Report' (30 September 2020) § 926 ('Of recent, the acquittal of Mr. Bemba on 8 June 2018 prompted the initiation of assistance in the CAR, as a way to aid vulnerable victims, but also to mitigate the victim community's negative reactions to the verdict. This may also have created a precedent for future cases of acquittal').

[166] Regina Rauxloh, 'Good Intentions and Bad Consequences: The General Assistance Mandate of the Trust Fund for Victims of the ICC' (2021) 34(1) Leiden Journal of International Law 203.

[167] Phil Clark, *Distant Justice: The Impact of the International Criminal Court on African Politics* (CUP 2018) 43.

[168] FIDH (n 116) 18; ICC press release, 'ICC judges in Ongwen case visit northern Uganda' (11 June 2018) https://www.icc-cpi.int/news/icc-judges-ongwen-case-visit-northern-uganda (accessed 3 December 2022).

in the ICC's 2023 budget, which includes resources for an increased field presence in Bangladesh, Sudan, Venezuela, and Ukraine 'in line with the Prosecutor's vision of . . . bringing our work closer to the communities impacted by Rome Statute crimes'.[169] The Court's 'move to the field' is thus by no means restricted to its victim engagement, although this is where it is arguably most developed. Spending time in the field, knowing and caring about victims, going beyond black letter law is part and parcel of the role of the new victims' stakeholder. Promoting the local—which is their site of legitimacy and expertise—the victims' stakeholders are also themselves a product of the local turn in international criminal justice.[170]

The opposite of this development is that the new victims' stakeholders can also be blamed for the manifold challenges of the Court's victim engagement.[171] In the Kenyan cases, for example, the lawyers who began submitting victims' applications to the Court were accused of being the 'first ones to have their foot in the door'.[172] While they claimed to have received their mandate from the victims, some of them were allegedly associated with the accused, using their platform as victims' lawyers to promote 'the narrative of the accused', namely that victims want reconciliation, not trials.[173] Besides, they were accused of incompetence. A Registry officer recalled:

[169] ICC, 'Proposed Programme Budget for 2023 of the International Criminal Court: Executive Summary' Assembly of States Parties (ICC-ASP/21/INF.2) (21 July 2022), § 42; Stuart Ford, 'Funding the ICC for its third decade' in Carsten Stahn (ed), *The International Criminal Court in Its Third Decade: Reflecting on Law and Practice* (Brill 2023). The OTP's new strategic plan (2023–2025) elevated 'bring[ing] justice closer to communities and deepen[ing] engagement with civil society' to a key strategic goal. OTP, 'Strategic Plan 2023-2025' https://www.icc-cpi.int/sites/default/files/2023-06/OTP-Strategic-Plan_2023-2025.pdf (accessed 10 July 2023).

[170] Not least due to NGO demands that the Court extend its field presence and outreach efforts. See Human Rights Watch (n 143) 12. On a putative 'local turn' in international criminal justice see Christian de Vos, Sara Kendall, and Carsten Stahn, 'Introduction' in Christian de Vos, Sara Kendall, and Carsten Stahn (eds), *Contested Justice: The Politics and Practice of International Criminal Court Interventions* (CUP 2015) 7. In the same volume see also Carsten Stahn, 'Justice Civilisatrice? The ICC, Post-colonial Theory, and Faces of "the Local"' 46; Vasuki Nesiah, 'Local Ownership of Global Governance' (2016) 14(4) Journal of International Criminal Justice 985. See also Patryk I Labuda, *International Criminal Tribunals and Domestic Accountability: In the Court's Shadow* (OUP 2023).

[171] See ch 3 for an elaboration of the role of victims' lawyers in the blame cascade.

[172] Interview with Legal Officer, Registry, The Hague (4 February 2014).

[173] ibid. In the *Ruto and Sang* case, ninety-three victim participants sent a letter to the Court through an intermediary 'withdrawing' their participation from the case to engage in Kenya's peace process instead. *Prosecutor v Ruto and Sang* (Common Legal Representative for Victims' Comprehensive Report on the Withdrawal of Victims from the Turbo area by Letter dated 5 June 2013) [2013] ICC-01/09-01/11-896-Corr-Red, §§ 12–13. In the *Banda and Jerbo* case, victim participation was allegedly used to promote the political agenda of the Sudanese government. Emily Haslam and Rod Edmunds, 'Victim Participation, Politics and

> These lawyers also started filling out application forms before they have ever been trained . . . and they were a disaster. One of these lawyers organized a meeting with 1800 people, promised them the world and then submitted to us 1800 incomplete applications. We spent a full year trying to track these people down and complete their forms.[174]

Local lawyers are seen as fishing for clients to land prestigious and well-paid freelance work with the Court. Other local actors, too, may seize an opportunity to make a quick buck by associating themselves with the Court. The same registry officer told me that he kept a sign in his office drawn up by an intermediary, who sold reparation awards to victims, impersonating a court official.[175]

Considering these challenges and abuses, cynicism about victim participation was running high when I was an intern at the Court in 2013 and 2014. As one victims' officer put it:

> So, if you want to know how the Court uses victim participation, this is precisely how it does it . . . I think if you did a survey—and surveys have been done—about what the Court thinks internally about victim participation, you would get a resoundingly negative opinion. But they still love the window-dressing of victim participation. They still love to say, 'we do it for the victims' . . . while, internally, they try to strangle it and put it in a box.[176]

A legal adviser even speculated that the victims' provisions of the Rome Statute were a ruse to begin with:

> All the hopes of Rome are failures. But those who were against the victims did not want to be too clear . . . Don't be too clear and then we can delete that in a few years demonstrating that it does not work. Of course,

the Construction of Victims at the International Criminal Court: Reflections on Proceedings in Banda and Jerbo' (2014) 14 Melbourne Journal of International Law 727.

[174] Interview with Legal Officer (n 172).
[175] Interview with Adviser, Chambers, The Hague (12 November 2013).
[176] ibid.

> with the usual hypocrisy you make everything complex so that it does not work in order to prove that it does not work in order to take it out.[177]

The 'designed to fail' argument retables the question of deception. Is there a cunning plan to use victims and then get rid of them? Such speculations arguably overestimate the power of the 'designer' in controlling the interpretation and implementation of 'justice for victims' over many years. Even placing the 'right people' at the top of a complex and diverse institution does not guarantee ideological continuity over time. The 'designed to fail' perspective also exaggerates the 'inconvenience' or 'burden' that victims represent for the Court. Victims, I argue, are much less burdensome to the Court than often assumed. As the next chapter will show, the Court creates its own victim subjects; it wants them active and involved in its processes, if not necessarily in the courtroom.

What we see at work here is a complex ideological metabolism. By promising 'justice for victims', international criminal law incorporated its alternative, restorative justice, and in the process changed into a more field-based, administrative, and caring justice hybrid.[178] While critical scholars have argued that the ICC occupies the space of global justice by sidelining alternatives and remaking other justice institutions in its own image, less attention has been paid to how the Court absorbs its alternatives.[179] This is not merely cooptation, as critical scholars suggest, as the ICC is not in full control of these alternatives. Neither does it mean that 'justice matters', as constructivists argue, because it shapes state norms and practices.[180] Rather, I argue that 'justice for victims' matters as an ideological metabolism which swallows up alternatives and sets in motion a whole digestive system with unpredictable consequences.

While victims' rights promised the redemption of international criminal law, they have, instead, punctuated its contradictions. While not set up to fail, the victims' regime has stirred tensions that call for practical and moral resolution. Blame is a key mechanism of managing these tensions. The

[177] Interview with Adviser, Chamber, The Hague (8 January 2014). See also Redress, 'The Participation of Victims in International Criminal Court Proceedings' (2012) 8 https://redress.org/wp-content/uploads/2017/12/121030participation_report.pdf (accessed 9 April 2023).

[178] Garbett (n 48).

[179] Sarah Nouwen and Wouter Werner, 'Monopolizing Global Justice: International Criminal Law as Challenge to Human Diversity' (2015) 13 JICJ 157. As we shall see in ch 5, the Court has also absorbed more radical alternatives especially transformative justice.

[180] Katherine Sikkink, *The Justice Cascade: How Human Rights Prosecutions are Changing World Politics* (WW Norton & Co 2011).

victims' apparatus produced convenient scapegoats that could be blamed when things went wrong, as they often do. It is victims' lawyers, rather than the Court, who are incompetent and self-serving. It is intermediaries, who are 'deceiving' victims. It is the intern who 'misrepresented' the judge's position. Ideological struggles are externalized through blame subjects, who are sufficiently internal to absorb blame, but sufficiently external to carry it away from the Court.

2.5 Conclusion

Granting victims rights to participation and reparation was a compromise at Rome, which supplemented the Court's 'core mandate' of prosecuting those responsible for international crimes. The Court's victims' mandate, however, was contested from the start, and the judges quickly moved to restrict victims' role in the courtroom. Instead, they created more avenues for victim engagement and assistance in the field, where it was less harmful to legal procedure. It seemed like a good compromise. Yet, when I returned to Northern Uganda in July 2019, the ICC's victim machinery had grown and it is increasingly questionable whether its only purpose is to provide good photo-ops for judges and the Prosecutor.[181] As victim engagement moves outside the courtroom, it moves into a broader ideological realm, less regulated by law, but mediated through different disciplines including development, humanitarianism, and psychology as Chapter 5 will show. The practical resolution—moving victims into field and non-judicial processes—also became a moral resolution as it localizes blame. Indeed, the

[181] See eg ICC Press Release, 'ICC judges in Ongwen case visit northern Uganda' (11 June 2018) https://www.icc-cpi.int/news/icc-judges-ongwen-case-visit-northern-uganda (accessed 6 August 2022); ICC press release, 'The Embassy of Ireland and the Trust Fund for Victims conclude a joint monitoring visit to northern Uganda between 13–17 September 2022' https://www.icc-cpi.int/news/embassy-ireland-and-trust-fund-victims-conclude-joint-monitoring-visit-northern-uganda-between (accessed 30 September 2022). The ICC has a very active Twitter account that regularly produces images of ICC officials meeting victim-survivors in the field. See eg https://twitter.com/IntlCrimCourt/status/1575145171519508485 https://twitter.com/IntlCrimCourt/status/1574466607916748812 https://twitter.com/IntlCrimCourt/status/1574350772715851780 https://twitter.com/IntlCrimCourt/status/1677016332947320834 (all accessed 3 August 2023). Isabella Banks, however, has argued that the Court's Twitter communication has been state-centred and has failed genuinely to engage with local stakeholders. Isabella Banks, 'Facilitating #dialogue or #buildingsupport? An Exploration of the International Criminal Court's Use of 280 Characters' (2022) 20(1) Journal of International Criminal Justice 55.

veneration of the local also responsibilizes those who embody it, thus allowing blame to cascade downwards.

Both law and justice form part of the ideological terrain; they interpellate subjects and are reproduced through common sense and everyday practices.[182] In the process of operationalizing the Statute's victims' provisions, new institutions had to be created and new subjects interpellated. If we perceive ideology as systems of ideas, we notice that lawyers express conflicting and even contradictory justice ideas, but if we study it more as a practice of subject production, we see that both lawyers and victims are interpellated and reproduce ideology through their relationships. The ambivalence of the justice producers, their justice contestations, the authoritative yet confusing role of the legal text—all of this is highly productive for the reproduction and rejuvenation of ideology. But this fluidity also constitutes a threat: ideological systems need to incorporate alternatives, but they cannot fully master them. Indeed, ideology works through a complex metabolism, inhaling and digesting new ideas and practices, which need to be recuperated or excreted or they may transfigure the body beyond recognition. There is constantly a risk of slippage such as the production of maverick lawyers or resistive victim subjects in the Global South.

In *The Trial*, the prison chaplain tells Joseph K., 'the court doesn't want anything from you. It accepts you when you come, and it lets you go when you leave'.[183] This is an astonishing thing to tell an accused who has been summoned by a court, and who is eventually executed. It may be more accurate for victims as they do not have to participate in the Court's processes.[184] But this elides the hegemony of the juridical framework which addresses suffering by creating legal subjects—victims. The success of such legal interpellation can be glimpsed from interviews with victims in Northern Uganda: 'Ongwen as the accused has a lawyer, we who suffered should have a lawyer. It is important for us to also have a lawyer who will stand for us', one victim insisted.[185] Those who suffer need a lawyer as law becomes the solution to suffering, as the next chapter will show.

Like the man from the country in Kafka's parable, victims at the ICC wait for many years for a judgment in their case or even to hear back on

[182] Hall (n 67) 165.
[183] Kafka (n 7) 160.
[184] 'Such participation is voluntary.' ICC, 'Victims' https://www.icc-cpi.int/about/victims (accessed 31 March 2023).
[185] Human Rights Watch (n 143) 1.

the outcome of their application.[186] Many die before the judgment is pronounced and reparations are awarded.[187] The point of 'Before the Law', however, is not that people obey the law, but that they seek it out. They hasten to define their struggles and aspirations in its terms so that eventually there is nothing outside the law. When I asked a victim of post-election violence in Kenya why he was working for free for the Court, riding his bicycle from village to village to persuade victims to come to a meeting with the ICC's lawyers, he said, 'because I want justice to prevail'.[188] And then victims have to wait. But waiting is an active process; it is an integral part of both the Court's processes and global capitalism. Surplus populations have to be 'ready' for the day of entry, when the gates of the Court and the gates of the factory open. Justice for victims is not just a façade—it does ideological work of creating people in the Global South both as the Court's and as global capitalist subjects.

[186] Waiting for the Court's determination of victims' status in the proceedings was particularly a problem in the early years of the Court's victim engagement including in Northern Uganda where the VPRS initially engaged victims across the region, who applied to participate, but were later found not to be eligible for participation given the much narrower scope of the *Ongwen* case ('The engagement that we had with the victims at the time was not that tailored. We had the arrest warrants—they were vague about the locations and the potential crimes against the indictees. And the VPRS unfortunately went out to the communities without knowing the specifics—which locations and what crimes we are looking at—and assisted as many victims as possible especially in the Lango, West Nile and Teso area . . . But from January 2015 when Ongwen was surrendered everything changed both positively and negatively. I would say negatively because the case locations are not in the areas where the VPRS had been working so there was a lot of disappointment from some of those areas'). Interview with Victims' Officer, Kampala (4 July 2019). For victims waiting for an outcome of their application see also Sara Kendall, 'Beyond the restorative turn: The limits of legal humanitarianism' in Christian de Vos, Sara Kendall, and Carsten Stahn (eds), *Contested Justice: The Politics and Practice of International Criminal Court Interventions* (CUP 2015) 352, 367; Karen Lønne Ring, 'The Evolution of the Procedure for Reviewing Victim Applications at the International Criminal Court' (2023) 21(1) Journal of International Criminal Justice 29.

[187] There have been extreme delays especially in the award and implementation of reparation and assistance. See eg ICC, 'Independent Expert Review of the International Criminal Court and the Rome Statute System: Final Report' (30 September 2020) § 879 ('Overall, profound delays exhibit the whole process. Victims, it was asserted to the Experts, wait a lifetime').

[188] Interview with Victim-Intermediary, Western Kenya (19 August 2014).

3
Creating the Victim: From Innocent Victims to Indebted Subjects

3.1 Introduction

The debate about the Court's victim engagement often polarizes around two positions: 'not enough' versus 'too much'. On the one hand, non-governmental organizations (NGOs) and many scholars deplore that the Court is not doing enough for victims. It should do more and better outreach, more and better victim participation, more and better reparation.[1] Legal scholars, on the other hand, often lament that the Court is doing too much and therefore is not doing anything well.[2] The Court should become 'more realistic' and stick to its 'core' mandate, investigating and trying perpetrators of international crimes.[3] As Vasiliev argues: '[T]he scaling down of the grand restorative ambitions in developing the participatory scheme is the most affordable of the sacrifices for the Court; this is a key lesson that

[1] Gaelle Carayon and Jonathan O'Donohue, 'The International Criminal Court's Strategies in Relation to Victims' (2017) 15(3) Journal of International Criminal Justice 567; Jennifer Easterday, 'Transforming Outreach and Engagement with Local Stakeholders' *International Justice Monitor* (15 July 2020) https://www.ijmonitor.org/2020/07/transforming-outreach-and-engagement-with-local-stakeholders/ (accessed 12 April 2022); FIDH, 'Whose Court is it? Judicial handbook on victims' rights at the International Criminal Court' (2021) 6–7, 31–32 https://www.fidh.org/IMG/pdf/fidh_whose_court_is_it_en.pdf (accessed 26 July 2023). For a more general articulation of the 'not enough' position see Amnesty International, 'The ICC must become a champion of justice over abuse of power' (2018) https://www.amnesty.org/en/latest/news/2018/02/the-icc-must-become-a-champion-of-justice-over-abuse-of-power/ (accessed 1 April 2023).

[2] Sergey Vasiliev, 'Victim participation revisited: What the ICC is learning about itself, in Carsten Stahn (ed), *The Law and Practice of the International Criminal Court* (OUP 2016).

[3] Mirjan Damaska, 'What Is the Point of International Criminal Justice?' (2008) 83 Chicago-Kent Law Review 329, 342–43; Carsten Stahn, 'Between "Faith" and "Facts": By What Standards Should We Assess International Criminal Justice?' (2012) 25(2) Leiden Journal of International Law 251; Florian Jessberger and Julia Geneuss, 'Down the Drain or Down to Earth? International Criminal Justice under Pressure' (2013) 11 JICJ 501; Mark Kersten, 'Whither the Aspirational ICC, Welcome the "Practical" Court?' *EJIL Talk!* (22 May 2019) https://www.ejiltalk.org/whither-the-aspirational-icc-welcome-the-practical-court/ (accessed 1 April 2023).

Victims and the Labour of Justice at the International Criminal Court. Leila Ullrich, Oxford University Press.
 DOI: 10.1093/9780191915048.003.0003

the ICC must have learnt after the protracted journey of rediscovering itself as a primarily retributive justice institution.'[4] Both perspectives ring true not least because the Court's work is uneven. Its outreach programmes are a case in point. In some situation countries, they are developed and active; in others, they are practically non-existent.[5] Northern Uganda has witnessed the whole spectrum from a slow outreach start to early hibernation to belated reanimation when Dominic Ongwen, rather surreptitiously, landed in the Court's dock in 2015. Yet, the 'not enough' versus 'too much' polarization has thwarted a more careful investigation of what the Court actually does when it engages victims and affected communities.

In studying the relationship between institutions and the people they govern, socio-legal scholars and criminologists usually consider three mechanisms: force, interests and norms.[6] Institutions may force people to comply with their rules, people may benefit from observing their rules or they may be persuaded by the merits of those rules. While courts work through force with regard to defendants: they summon, detain, convict and punish them, the same cannot be said about victims. Affected communities in Kenya and Uganda are not forced to attend outreach meetings or to participate in the trial as victims. Is it in their interest to do so? There are some material inducements to come to the Court's meetings, and victim participants, of course, hope to receive reparations. Given the destitution of many victims, material incentives may be sufficient to explain victims' willingness to engage with the Court. But the thrust of the Court's victim engagement is to manage victims' expectations and to refrain from making any promises to them. Trials drag on for years and the vast majority of victims will not benefit from these processes, something the Court tells them very directly.[7]

[4] Vasiliev (n 2) 1137.

[5] Easterday (n 1).

[6] See eg Ian Hurd, 'Legitimacy and Authority in International Politics' (1999) 53(2) International Organization 379; Marlies Glasius, '"We ourselves, we are part of the functioning": The ICC, victims, and civil society in the Central African Republic' (2009) 108(430) African Affairs 49; Philipp Schulz, 'Discussing community-based outreach activities by the International Criminal Tribunal for Rwanda' (2017) 11(2) Journal of Eastern African Studies 347.

[7] This happened both at the outreach meeting I observed in Gulu on 17 July 2019 and on the victims' registration mission in Western Kenya I observed in 2014, where the victims' lawyers told victims: 'forget about reparations, the case is too weak'. Field notes, Registration Mission, Western Kenya (18–22 August 2014).

Finally, the Court might persuade victims of its legitimacy. The Court's supporters and its critics often argue about how legitimate the ICC is.[8] 'Legitimacy is very important in the world today', former ICC Prosecutor Moreno-Ocampo explained, 'legitimacy is our power'.[9] Legitimacy, Vasiliev writes, 'is a plant that needs to be watered regularly. It is not a fixed state but a continuous exercise in persuasion'.[10] While socio-legal scholars disagree on how legitimate international criminal courts are, they do increasingly agree that these courts can enhance their legitimacy by engaging with, educating and listening to affected communities.[11] 'The Court's ideal relation to the demos', Glasius argues, is 'not democratic in the classic sense, but communicative and cognitive instead. In other words, international criminal courts should expand on the small strides made in explaining themselves,

[8] Janine Clark, 'International Criminal Courts and Normative Legitimacy: An Achievable Goal?' (2015) 15(4) International Criminal Law Review 763; Harlan Grant Cohen and others, 'Legitimacy and International Courts: A Framework' (2017) 17(3) PluriCourts Research Paper; Kieran McEvoy and Kirsten McConnachie, 'Victims and Transitional Justice: Voice, Agency and Blame' (2013) 22(4) Social & Legal Studies 489, 490. See also Nicola Palmer, *Courts in Conflict: Interpreting the Layers of Justice in Post-Genocide Rwanda* (OUP 2015) 160; Tonny Raymond Kirabira, 'NGOs and the legitimacy of international criminal justice: The case of Uganda, in Florian Jeßberger, Leonie Steinl, and Kalika Mehta (eds), *International Criminal Law: A Counter-Hegemonic Project?* (TMC Asser Press 2023) 153. I have myself used the concept of legitimacy in the past. See Carolyn Hoyle and Leila Ullrich, 'New Court, New Justice? The Evolution of "Justice for Victims" at Domestic Courts and at the International Criminal Court' (2014) 12(4) Journal of International Criminal Justice 681, 700.

[9] Barry Stevens, *The Prosecutor* (Film) (2011). Former ICC President and current President of the Assembly of States Parties (ASP) Silvia Fernández de Gurmendi also regularly uses the concept of legitimacy in her speeches: 'Promoting the universal participation in the Rome Statute is of fundamental importance in order to enhance the effectiveness and the legitimacy of the institution and its capacity to contribute to the rule of law, justice, and sustainable peace and development.' Judge Silvia Fernández de Gurmendi, 'Remarks to the United Nations General Assembly delivering the Court's annual report' (30 October 2017) 9.

[10] Sergey Vasiliev, 'The crises and critiques of international criminal justice' in Kevin Heller and others (eds), *The Oxford Handbook of International Criminal Law* (OUP 2020) 626, 651; David Luban, 'After the Honeymoon: Reflections on the Current State of International Criminal Justice' (2013) 11 Journal of International Criminal Justice 505, 509 ('My point is that ICJ will always be an extraordinary institution that perpetually needs to persuade the world of its own legitimacy').

[11] Victor Peskin, 'Courting Rwanda: The Promises and Pitfalls of the ICTR Outreach Programme' (2005) 3 Journal of International Criminal Justice 950; Marlies Glasius, 'Do International Criminal Courts Require Democratic Legitimacy' (2012) 23 European Journal of International Law 43, 46; Tim Meijers and Marlies Glasius, 'Trials as Messages of Justice: What Should Be Expected of International Criminal Courts?' (2016) 30(4) Ethics and International Affairs 429; Phil Clark, *Distant Justice: The Impact of the International Criminal Court on African Politics* (CUP 2018) 149 ('while some sections of the Court enjoy a certain degree of popular legitimacy, the ICC broadly has failed to establish constructive working relations with local actors. In particular, it has failed to communicate its aims and modalities effectively'); Isabella Banks, 'Facilitating #dialogue or #buildingsupport? An Exploration of the International Criminal Court's Use of 280 Characters' (2022) 20(1) Journal of International Criminal Justice 55.

but also open themselves up to social learning'.[12] The Court, likewise, acknowledges that 'lack of understanding and misperceptions of the Court's purpose and activities among affected communities can undermine the ICC's legitimacy', and attempts to overcome these obstacles through community outreach.[13]

This chapter, on the other hand, argues that we learn more about the Court's victim engagement if we examine it through theories of ideology rather than legitimacy. Drawing on Althusser, I argue that victims are interpellated as the Court's ideological subjects rather than persuaded by its legal method or justice objectives. While liberal scholars have studied victim participation as a form of inclusion, critical scholars have exposed the exclusionary mechanisms of juridical victimhood, which filters 'real' victims out of the legal process through juridical criteria.[14] Only those victims who meet the Court's ever-changing legal definitions and overcome bureaucratic and material hurdles are eventually recognized as the Court's victims.[15]

A critical ideology approach, by contrast, unveils a more complex inclusion/exclusion dynamic. Victims are never fully in or out. Even if they do not make the final cut as 'case victims' or 'reparation awardees', they are still engaged as 'affected communities', 'situation victims' or 'assistance beneficiaries' through multi-layered modalities on a continuum from judicial to non-judicial interventions. The Court's precarious inclusion of victims (everyone can be engaged but not everyone can participate in the trial) not only reflects but also prepares them for their precarious integration into

[12] Glasius (on Weber) (n 11) 64. See also Mark C Suchman, 'Managing Legitimacy: Strategic and Institutional Approaches' (1995) 20 The Academy of Management Review 571, 574; Daniel Bodansky, 'The Legitimacy of International Governance: A Coming Challenge for International Environmental Law?' (1999) 93(3) The American Journal of International Law 596, 601; Allen Buchanan and Robert O Keohane, 'The Legitimacy of Global Governance Institutions' (2006) 20 Ethics and International Affairs 405; Aaron Fichtelberg, 'Democratic Legitimacy and the International Criminal Court: A Liberal Defence' (2006) 4(4) Journal of International Criminal Justice 765.

[13] ICC, 'Report of the Court on the Public Information Strategy 2011–2013' ICC-ASP/9/29 (22 November 2010) § 8c; ICC, 'Integrated Strategy for External Relations, Public Information and Outreach'. See also Matias Hellman, 'Challenges and limitations of outreach' in Christian De Vos, Sara Kendall, and Carsten Stahn (eds), *Contested Justice: The Politics and Practice of International Criminal Court Interventions* (CUP 2015) 251, 254 ('outreach is one of the key measures for attaining such support, or perceived legitimacy. While outreach alone cannot secure the legitimacy of an international court or tribunal, it is a necessary companion of prosecutorial and judicial activities, and serves as the institution's interface with local populations. In this sense, outreach forms an integral part of court operations and a vital element for the achievement of policy goals').

[14] Sara Kendall and Sarah Nouwen, 'Representational Practices at the International Criminal Court: The Gap between Juridified and Abstract Victimhood' (2014) 76 Law and Contemporary Problems 235.

[15] ibid.

capitalist social relations (everyone should be productive but not everyone will find work). Legal and capitalist processes are intrinsically linked as the former creates ideological subjects 'ready' for 'their role' in the latter. In other words, the puzzle of victim participation, why it exists, what forms it assumes, what functions it fulfils, can be resolved once we see the legal process as part of wider social processes. As people are interpellated as victims, they are also inaugurated as capitalist subjects whose undervalued and surplus labour forms an integral part of capitalist reproduction.

This argument will be developed through three parts. The first part looks at the encounter between the Court's officers and victims, elucidating the effects of legal interpellation in Northern Uganda and dissecting four mechanisms of subject creation—spotlighting, luring, schooling and blaming. The second part sheds light on the process that lies behind ideological subject creation, changing register from victim creation in 'the field' to the relationships and actors that give shape to the Court's victim engagement. I call this process the blame cascade, because blame, seemingly, articulates these relationships through different layers: judges pass blame on to victims' lawyers and officers, who pass it on to intermediaries, who pass it on to victims. In the process, responsibility is displaced to the lower level. The third part, then, materializes the blame cascade. What animates the blame cascade, I argue, are labour and debt relationships. Indeed, what crystallizes when we trace the blaming discourse from the judges to victims is that it is really about work ('people below don't do their job'), which ultimately reproduces the global division of labour. While the next chapter will disentangle the labour relations of international criminal justice, this chapter analyses the Court's relationship with victims as a creditor–debtor relationship, which becomes evident when we examine the Trust Fund's microcredit programmes in the field.

3.2 Creating the Victim Subject

ICC Community outreach event, Update by the Defence Lawyer, Lukodi, Northern Uganda (23 July 2019)

The defence lawyer is an agitator. He shouts rousingly: 'If Ongwen was your child, wouldn't you want him to come back?' The response is not as clear-cut as he had hoped. An elderly man rises and replies fiercely: 'I would not want him to come back even if he was my child.' Others are more ambiguous: 'It is the responsibility of the community to correct the child so that they are happy to receive him back. It should not be a foreign agency.' The defence lawyer then explains why the Prosecutor erred, charging Ongwen with the crime of 'forced marriage': 'You couldn't refuse to take a wife. You didn't have a choice. It was also not a marriage according to our culture as no bride price was paid.'[16] Finally, he reassures victims that 'the government should pay reparations regardless of whether or not Ongwen is convicted'. Then it is time for community members to ask questions:

> You said that Ongwen did not attack in any of the four locations. Where did he attack then?; wasn't he promoted so quickly through the ranks of the LRA because he was working so hard killing people?; how far away from Lukodi is that mountain [where Ongwen allegedly was at the time of the attack]?; were you with him on that mountain [sarcastically]? How do you know he was there?; you told us that Ongwen had no position of authority within the LRA, but you also said he persuaded Kony not to kill. How could he persuade Kony if he had no authority?; can you give us an assurance on reparations?

The defence lawyer is taken aback by the hostility: 'You have given me the knife from the sharp end', he laments. But why would he be surprised at a less than enthusiastic reception by the communities affected by the crimes that Ongwen allegedly committed? Did he simply assume that the ICC was so unpopular that the defence is, by definition, the hero?

The agitator and his audience are mismatched. His passionate appeals and sweeping claims collide with specific questions about evidence and coherence of argumentation. 'They seemed to be quite well informed?', I quizzed him on the way back. 'They were informed', he replied, 'but they had the wrong information'.

From a critical ideology perspective, the defence lawyer's intervention is an example of failed interpellation. He interpellates victims in Lukodi as members of a shared cultural community. Ongwen is also a member of that community. He could be your child. He could be you. But the defence

[16] For a discussion on 'forced marriage' practices in the LRA see Erin Baines, 'Forced marriage as a political project: Sexual rules and relations in the Lord's Resistance Army' (2014) 51(3) Journal of Peace Research 405. For a discussion of the dilemmas of the *Ongwen* trial see Adam Branch, 'Dominic Ongwen on Trial: The ICC's African Dilemmas' (2017) 11(1) International Journal of Transitional Justice 30.

lawyer comes late; his impassioned pleas fall on deaf ears. The Court's outreach officers and victims' lawyers have been there before him, and they come on a monthly basis. Victims in Lukodi speak the language of law, evidence and logic. This, however, does not necessarily mean that legal interpellation has overwritten cultural interpellation. Victims are ambivalent about the ICC, and their roles as the 'Court's victims' are not set in stone, as this chapter will illustrate. But the 'us versus them' appeal, the cultural community against the Western court, did not exert any automatic pull.

3.2.1 The Power of Legal Interpellation

The concept of legitimacy presumes that people are independent of the institutions that govern them, and whose legitimacy they evaluate. Fully formed through local culture or other domestic forms of socialization, these subjects are portrayed as relatively static and passive in their relationship with the Court. The Court may be able to shape their values and beliefs but not their subjecthood. I challenge this notion of fixed and essentialized subjects underpinning the legitimacy concept by showing how powerful institutions like the ICC continuously create and recreate their subjects. In other words, an institution will produce the subjects that regard it as legitimate. Rather than enhancing its legitimacy in the eyes of victims, I will illustrate how the ICC works by 'hailing' its subjects ('victims', 'intermediaries'). Yet, what makes that call so powerful?

Part of it is that we learnt to react to our names before we even learnt to speak. Butler refers to this as 'corporeal vulnerability': 'an unwilled receptivity, susceptibility and vulnerability, a way of being exposed to language prior to any possibility of forming or enacting a speech act'.[17] But this should not obscure that responding to a name is still a learnt process and as such can be unlearnt as new names supersede old names. Keeping people named as 'victims'—keeping people in ideology—requires constant repetition and re-enactment, as this chapter will show. In this process, the practice or the role precedes the subject. In Butler's words, 'the act that one does, the act that one performs, is, in a sense, an act that has been going on before one arrived on the scene'.[18]

[17] Judith Butler, 'When gesture becomes event' in Anna Street and others (eds), *Inter Views in Performance Philosophy: Crossings and Conversations* (Palgrave Macmillan 2017) 171, 178.

[18] Judith Butler, 'Performative Acts and Gender Constitution: An Essay in Phenomenology and Feminist Theory' (1988) 40(4) Theatre Journal 519, 526.

The act has been going on before the victims arrived on the scene even though the victims are supposedly the rationale for the Court. Why would there be a court if there are no victims? But it works exactly the other way around: the Court, and its professionals, are there first, and they produce 'their victims' in designated 'atrocity spaces'.[19] Althusser's ideology theory helps us reshuffle the norm persuasion model, which informs the legitimacy concept.[20] The norm persuasion model assumes that the subject is there first, that this subject has a consciousness, that this consciousness produces beliefs and norms, which then guide decisions and actions ('supporting the Court'). For Althusser, by contrast, the institution comes first (the church, the school or the court), that institution produces a subject through its practices or rituals, and those practices then produce a consciousness ('I'm a believer', 'I'm a citizen', 'I'm a victim', 'I'm a woman'). So, while in the norm persuasion model, the Court's intervention comes rather late at the level of beliefs and norms, as Figure 3.1 shows, in the ideological subject model the Court already enters the process at the level of subject creation. Having said this, it is important to clarify that institutions such as the ICC, what Althusser calls 'ideological state apparatuses', do not exist in a vacuum, but are both the product of and the mediator of capitalist social relations.[21]

To understand how the Court creates its victims, our starting point is its outreach programme which ensures 'public dissemination of appropriate, *neutral* and timely information concerning the activities of the Court' but also 'aims at fostering public understanding and support for the work of

[19] I thank Richard Clements for his brilliant comments on this chapter. Please also see his forthcoming book, *The Justice Factory*, on the uses and effects of managerial expertise in international criminal justice. This is not to deny that there are people who have been victimized by atrocities in these spaces but only to highlight that this does not automatically make them victims engaged in the Court's processes.

[20] There is a significant constructivist International Relations literature on how institutions and actors can change norms through communication and persuasion. See eg Thomas Risse, '"Let's Argue!": Communicative Action in World Politics' (2000) 54(1) International Organization 1. Expressivist theories also interpret international criminal justice as a mechanism of norm persuasion or norm expression. See Carsten Stahn, *Justice as Message: Expressivist Foundations of International Criminal Justice* (OUP 2020).

[21] Louis Althusser, 'Ideology and ideological state apparatuses (notes towards an investigation)' in Louis Althusser, *Lenin and Philosophy and Other Essays* (NLB 1977) 121, 140 ('the Ideological State Apparatuses may be not only the *stake*, but also the *site* of class struggle, and often of bitter forms of class struggle'); Nicos Poulantzas, *Classes in Contemporary Capitalism* (Verso 1978) 25 ('The apparatuses are never anything other than the materialization and condensation of class relations').

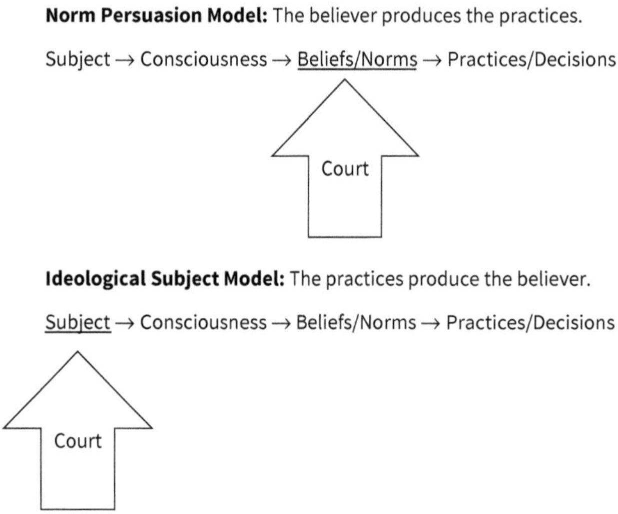

Figure 3.1 The Norm Persuasion and the Ideological Subject Model

the Court'.[22] This tension between 'neutrality' and 'creating support' permeates the Court's victim engagement more generally.[23] 'We always say we are not trying to persuade individual victims to apply for participation or reparations', a senior Registry official elaborated, 'our role is to explain and facilitate'.[24] Indeed, the court officers I observed did not try to persuade affected communities of the Court's merits. Instead, they were doing something much more effective: they celebrated them as 'champions of justice'[25] and interpellated them as 'victims'. Creating 'champions' is a key rationale of the Court's victim engagement as the head of VPRS made clear:

[22] ICC, 'Regulations of the Registry' (2018) ICC-BD/03-03-13, Regulation 5 bis 1 and 2. See also ICC, 'Strategic Plan for Outreach of the International Criminal Court' (2006) ICC-ASP/5/12, § 13; Registry Strategic Plan 2023–2025, § 43.

[23] ICC Head of the Outreach Unit, Email (1 May 2012) ('outreach is strictly neutral'). Pre-Trial Chamber I in the Situation of Palestine, on the other hand, stipulated that 'outreach and public information activities in situation countries are quintessential to *foster support*, public understanding and confidence in the work of the Court' (emphasis added). *Situation in the State of Palestine* (Decision on Information and Outreach for the Victims of the Situation) [2018] ICC-01/18-2, § 7.

[24] Interview with Senior Official, Registry, The Hague (16 December 2013).

[25] See also ICC Press Release, 'ICC President and Acting Executive Director of the Trust Fund for Victims visit Central African Republic to witness Court's work on the ground' (28 November 2022) https://www.icc-cpi.int/news/icc-president-and-acting-executive-director-trust-fund-victims-visit-central-african-republic (accessed 9 December 2022).

> We try to get our foot on the ground as quickly as possible. We are not only doing one training; we do multiple trainings. You have individuals in front of you who have very different concepts of justice. You have to start from scratch to make people understand what we represent and do . . . we make these people become champions of what we do.[26]

'Champion', of course, is a much more active role than 'victim'. Champions do not passively accept institutions; they champion them.

Creating champions requires continuous, local presence. Engaging with affected communities in their villages, the Court 'bridges the gap' and promotes 'local ownership'. 'The idea is ownership', a Registry officer explained to me, 'in each community in which you go, you involve the local actors to be part in the process, this is the only way they will own what you are bringing, they will own the message, they will own the programme'.[27] It is curious that a property relationship is projected onto justice messages and norms. Why do people accept 'ownership' of the Court?

Initially, they did not. The ICC had a rough start when it began working in Northern Uganda in 2005, particularly in Acholi sub-region. Its arrest warrants against five commanders of the Lord's Resistance Army (LRA) were seen as threatening ongoing peace negotiations between the Ugandan government and the LRA.[28] But the situation is rather different now, first, because the LRA has not attacked Northern Uganda for more than a decade and, secondly, because after a dormant presence for many years, the Court ramped up its community engagement with the start of the *Ongwen* trial in 2016.[29] In 2019, when I returned to Northern Uganda, ICC outreach and

[26] Redress, 'Webinar: Victim Participation and Reparations at the ICC: Assessing the Impact of the Independent Expert Review' *YouTube* (3 December 2020) https://www.youtube.com/watch?v=kcbYcmMe-T4 (accessed 20 April 2023).

[27] Interview with Registry Officer, Nairobi (23 June 2014). Redress (n 26). See also the introduction and chs 4 and 6 of this book. For a discussion on the distance and proximity of international criminal law based on recently published books in the field see Richard Clements, 'Near, Far, Wherever You Are: Distance and Proximity in International Criminal Law' (2021) 32(1) European Journal of International Law 327.

[28] For a discussion on the LRA and the ICC's intervention in Uganda more generally see Phil Clark, 'Law, Politics and Pragmatism: The ICC and Case Selection in Uganda and the Democratic Republic of Congo, in Nicholas Waddell and Phil Clark (eds), *Courting Conflict: Justice, Peace and the ICC in Africa* (Royal African Society 2008) 37; Clark (n 11); Tim Allen and Koen Vlassenroot, *The Lord's Resistance Army: Myth and Reality* (Zed Books 2010); Branch (n 16) 38; Mareike Schomerus, *The Lord's Resistance Army: Violence and Peacemaking in Africa* (CUP 2021).

[29] Clark (n 11) 139–40.

victims' activities were buzzing, and I had the chance to observe several outreach events and talk to the victims' lawyers in the *Ongwen* case.

What I noticed in the process is that those whom the Court engages through regular outreach and victim participation have become legal subjects. When I asked victims in Lukodi, 'what would be the impact on the community if Dominic Ongwen was acquitted?', the response was prompt: 'We will appeal and then we will sue the government for damages in the courts of law due to their negligence as they have failed to protect the people in the camps'.[30] The Court's victims are legalistic and litigious. 'Those who have interacted with the ICC outreach team over a long time, and some who have registered to participate as victims in the case of *Ongwen*, are fully in support of the charges and get agitated with the slightest possibility of acquittal', the Refugee Law Project noted about its consultations with affected communities.[31] In short, victims have been successfully interpellated ('we will appeal').

The Court's advocates see this as evidence of victims' support for procedural justice.[32] This is true in the sense that victims reframe their demands in legal terms, but it does not necessarily mean they believe in the legal method.[33] Victims in Lukodi support the ICC, because they believe that it is less corrupt than Ugandan courts.[34] Yet, this support was conditional on them 'winning their case': 'if we are defeated, we only look at the Court. The ICC can also be corrupted very fast, like the courts in Uganda', they told me.[35] What Ongwen did speaks for itself, they insisted, 'there's no need for somebody to come and testify'.[36] The right outcome is clear, but those in power are corruptible.[37]

[30] Focus Group Discussion, Lukodi (25 July 2019).
[31] Refugee Law Project, 'Ongwen's Justice Dilemma Part II' (2016) 12 https://www.refugeelawproject.org/files/others/Ongwen_Justice_Dilemma_II.pdf (accessed 20 April 2023).
[32] The Office of Public Counsel for Victims, 'Representing Victims before the International Criminal Court: A Manual for legal representatives' (2nd edn, 2012) 8.
[33] '[The legal method is] not based on the truth', a cultural leader observed; instead, 'it's based on who presents the best argument, whether it is the truth or not'. Interview with Cultural Leader, Gulu (22 July 2019).
[34] Focus Group Discussion (n 30).
[35] ibid.
[36] ibid.
[37] Refugee Law Project (n 31) 12.

3.2.2 Four Mechanisms of Subject Creation

How does the Court create its victim subjects? Studying the Court's victim engagement in Northern Uganda and Kenya, I have identified four mechanisms of subject creation: 1) Spotlighting, 2) Luring, 3) Schooling, and 4) Blaming. Shining the global spotlight on affected communities, the Court lures a subset of them to become its victims and intermediaries. It then schools them on 'their' roles, manages their expectations, and disciplines and blames them as the Court's subjects.

My starting point was an interview with a cultural leader in Northern Uganda. He was the only person I talked to who explicitly saw the ICC as an ideological tool that works by creating its own victims. He explained:

> Their [the community's] investment, their attention is brought on more by external interest in the matter. I mean, if Ongwen had come back like the rest [of the LRA commanders] came back, by now, there would be nothing going on; it would be sorted. But because of external forces, external interest... now, all what is happening is happening in the interest of those external. To make sure to link that external interest to our local context, they have to create a local interest, and now they have created the victims.[38]

His point was that without the ICC, the distribution of perpetrator and victim labels among communities suffering from twenty years of war and mass displacement would by now have faded. After all, more than 20,000 former LRA combatants (including commanders) have been re-integrated in Northern Uganda since the war ended.[39]

[38] Interview with Cultural Leader, Gulu (22 July 2019).

[39] Interview with CSO Representative, Kampala, 7 August 2014). The distribution of 'victim' and 'perpetrator' labels is in any case highly contested in Northern Uganda as those the Court recognizes as victims, for example, the forced wives of Ongwen are often seen as perpetrators by those who were not abducted, who see themselves as real victims of the LRA, while victims of other ethnic communities such as Langi and Teso sometimes see all Acholis as associated with the LRA and thus as 'perpetrators'. For a discussion of the reintegration efforts of LRA ex-combatants and their challenges see Grace Akello, 'Reintegration of Amnestied LRA Ex-Combatants and Survivors' Resistance Acts in Acholiland, Northern Uganda' (2019) 13(2) International Journal of Transitional Justice 249; Tim Allen, Jackline Atingo, and Melissa Parker, 'Rejection and Resilience: Returning from the Lord's Resistance Army in Northern Uganda' (2022) 24(2–3) Civil Wars 357.

Spotlighting

Spotlighting is key for creating victim subjects. It can be dizzying, which is why it is used as a hunting method for nocturnal animals. The latter do not recognize the light as a source of danger as they would recognize a human being. They are dazzled by the light, and unable to move. The *Ongwen* trial was important, the Refugee Law Project concluded, 'because it once again draws attention back to northern Uganda and highlights the plight of victims and survivors of a horrendous and protracted conflict'.[40] As the Court's website explains:

> The people of northern Uganda live in the aftermath of over two decades of violence. Whenever they are gathered, it is very easy to see the heavy burden of the conflict on the collective soul of the community. The people of Acholi are generally a jolly lot, but even in their smiles, one can easily see the individual suffering and the community pain just a layer beneath. Things that atrocities of war can do to a people![41]

Casting the global spotlight on Northern Uganda, the Court exalts people's suffering, and that matters, because it radiates from a place of power, and promises recognition.

The ICC creates this 'spotlighting' effect through its outreach programme especially through the monthly screenings of the Ongwen trial, which were 'jam-packed'.[42] In my focus group discussion in Lukodi, participants complained that the Court's staff had recently shown them pre-recorded trial sequences rather than 'live' screenings. Having sat 'live' through some ICC trial sessions myself, I found that demand for 'live' viewings curious. Even the 'highlights' of court room proceedings such as witness interrogations

[40] Refugee Law Project (n 31) 13.

[41] ICC, 'Trauma, healing and hope in northern Uganda' https://www.icc-cpi.int/get-involved/pages/aj-story/trauma-healing-and-hope-in-northern-uganda (accessed 21 April 2022).

[42] Lino Owor Ogora, 'Ongwen trial screenings in Uganda: Lessons in making justice visible?' (2017) http://www.coalitionfortheicc.org/news/20170119/ongwen-trial-screenings-uganda-lessons-making-justice-visible (accessed 9 March 2022). Interview with Registry Officer, Kampala (2 August 2019). See the Court's 'Access to Justice' project funded by the Danish government. ICC, 'Access to justice: watching the ICC Ongwen trial' https://www.icc-cpi.int/get-involved/pages/aj-story/from-courtroom-to-communities (accessed 21 April 2022); Maria Mabinty Kamara, 'An Insider Look at Outreach efforts in bringing the proceedings closer to the Victims and Affected Populations in Northern Uganda' *Justice in Conflict* (3 February 2021) https://justiceinconflict.org/2021/02/03/an-insider-look-at-outreach-efforts-in-bringing-the-proceedings-closer-to-the-victims-and-affected-populations-in-northern-uganda/ (accessed 30 July 2022).

and judicial decisions are a far cry from a decisive football match that is better watched in real time. Yet, the immediacy of a live screening was important because it made both the trial and the audience special. Only important happenings are projected live, only important people can watch them live. The more glamorous the Court is, the more desirable its ownership becomes.

More generally, I was struck by the external orientation of the people I spoke to. The 'West', the 'world', 'European people', 'American youth' were frequent reference points in my interviews with Northern Ugandans. Stuck at the periphery of a world system, which habitually drowns out their suffering, many people welcomed global attention. The trial screening, one viewer told the ICC's outreach team, 'is the writing of history; the writing of history about us'.[43] As one victim from Lukodi put it:

> I want the community to be heard. I'm not looking to the government but for outside help . . . the outside friends, the civil society organizations have a wider net that is bigger than that of the Ugandan government; they should combine resources. They can make that payment fast and then the government will come in later . . . but the world should first help us because—where we are—things are not okay in the community.[44]

This, of course, also suggests that the hope for material support from 'outside friends' is part of the reason why people engage with the Court.

Luring

Spotlighting is not exclusive; everyone is celebrated as a 'champion' of justice; everyone is recognized as a victim of the war in Northern Uganda. From this larger audience, a subset is invited to engage more exclusively with the Court as designated 'victims' and 'intermediaries'. As the cultural leader, whom I quoted at the beginning, pointed out, 'many organizations come, almost, I don't want to say they're bribing [chuckles], but they use a lot of inducements to get their way and people are responding to these inducements or potential inducements'.[45] As most international organizations, the Court offers different levels of inducements for different types

[43] ICC, 'Ugandans say: "This is the writing of history . . . about us" ' https://www.icc-cpi.int/get-involved/pages/aj-story/this-is-the-writing-of-history (accessed 24 April 2022).
[44] Female Participant, Focus Group Discussion (n 30).
[45] Interview with Cultural Leader, Gulu (22 July 2019).

of engagement. Town hall meetings come with limited benefits. They provide some food and soft drinks but usually no money. Local stakeholder meetings are more exclusive: they take place at a hotel or conference venue, offer decent catering and reimburse transport costs. They also offer the prospect of becoming a mobilizer or intermediary for Court-organized events, which comes with more significant side payments.[46]

Victims' meetings with their lawyers also provide food and reimburse transport. 'Victims come to get reimbursement, tea and lunch and see some friends', one field assistant in Kenya remarked.[47] Of course, victims also hope to receive reparations for the harm they suffered.[48] Money plays a role, but the Court also uses that to furnish the notion of a deserving victim who does not want money. As one victims' lawyer told me:

> And so, they [the victims] have also internalized this idea that if they say they want money . . . that will cheapen their suffering somehow, because people will say they're only in it for the money, where I think, frankly, your entire life has been ruined. Like, you can't even begin to quantify that. And if you actually did want some money to make up for the fact that you haven't had the education you would have had, you're living in inadequate housing, you've got massive mental health issues, which you can't afford to pay a psychologist for. What would be wrong asking for money for that? If someone smashes into my car, it's thought to be normal that I would ask for money for that. And yet, if someone smashes into your life, you're not meant to ask for money?! It's so strange. But I see that at the court all the time. And I really have a lot of respect for the clients who stand up and say, 'No'. In Uganda, the clients are really clear that they want material, individual compensation.[49]

In the moral calculation of international criminal justice, the worse the harm you suffered, the more inappropriate a demand for monetary compensation becomes. Real victims don't want money.[50] In fact, the Court

[46] 150,000 Ugandan Shillings [32 Pounds] per meeting. Interview with Registry Officer (n 42).

[47] Interview with Field Assistant, Nairobi (30 June 2014).

[48] Avocats sans Frontières, 'A Beggar has no Choice: Victims' Perspectives on a Reparations Framework for Uganda' (2017) 19 https://www.asf.be/wp content/uploads/2017/07/ASF_UG_ABeggarhasnoChoice_EN_201704.pdf (accessed 12 January 2022).

[49] Interview with Victims' Lawyer, London (10 September 2018.

[50] One senior Registry official insisted: 'We have since 2005 assisted a little bit more than 15,000 people, out of them not even 10% have requested reparations. I would say in our

strangely overregulates the most basic provisions for victims. It has cut transport reimbursement and one victims' lawyer told me with outrage that the Counsel Support Section had proposed that victims should only receive lunch and tea at the meeting if they have travelled from far.[51] Money is a double-edged sword. It lures victims to engage with the Court, but it also tarnishes their victimhood.

Schooling

Victims do not have to respond to the Court's overtures, but a power relationship is nonetheless staged in the ICC's victim engagement. Observing a victims' registration mission in Kenya in 2014, I was surprised by how much meetings between lawyers and victims resemble a school class. The lawyer speaks, the victims listen and learn. The Court produces knowledge, the victim produces experience.[52] The victim then trades her experience for the Court's knowledge. The Court's insistence that outreach is 'two-way communication' does not mean it is an equal exchange.[53] 'Knowledge is power', the motto of ICC outreach, and it always trumps experience.[54]

In each class, the teacher begins by repeating the lessons learnt in the previous class and asks pupils to feed the knowledge back in their own words. The first thing that victims had to learn was not to expect reparations:

> we have to discuss that [reparations] every time, and it's funny now, because if you have a new person who has not attended the rest of the meeting, and they ask a question about that, someone within the meeting who has been attending can get up and respond. They do that especially for the things we discuss often. We give them the opportunity to respond on behalf of the community and they've come to appreciate it now, but we feel like it's something we have to say anytime we're discussing reparations, we have to make sure there is a clear explanation before we discuss it so that there's no, you know, expectation.[55]

experience that they attach the concept of justice to participation rather than reparations.' Interview with Senior Official, Registry, The Hague (10 January 2014).

[51] Field notes, Western Kenya (Migori, Kolweny, Ahero, Vihiga) (18–22 August 2014).
[52] Linda Alcoff and Laura Gray, 'Survivor Discourse: Transgression or Recuperation?' (1993) 18(2) Signs 260, 264.
[53] ICC, 'Strategic Plan for Outreach' (n 22) § 3.
[54] ICC, 'Promoting Access to Justice' https://www.icc-cpi.int/get-involved/access-to-justice (accessed 21 April 2022).
[55] Interview with Field Assistant, Gulu (17 July 2019).

The mature students rid the newcomers of 'unrealistic expectations'. They begin to 'own' the message. It is now a fact of the community that people are not entitled to reparations merely because they suffered harm.[56]

Even more, the lawyers debunk victims' expectations as unreasonable:

> But we've tried to challenge them in many respects . . . for example, when people say they want reparations, we have asked, 'what kind of reparations?', and they say, 'we want a school.' We say, 'okay, a school. So, if the school is built and put for your community, are you ready to buy school uniforms? Are you ready to pay the teachers?'. . . And so the question of responsibility has opened their minds . . . And, of course, it has gotten people thinking twice, saying, 'okay, maybe it's not a good idea'. So yes, you have to really think about these things. And you must remember, of course, that [reparations] can only come if there's a conviction. Without a conviction, there isn't much the court can do.[57]

Lawyers exorcize victims of expectations and responsibilize them for reparations. How can you ask for a school if you cannot pay the teachers? Their expectations are not only constructed as 'unrealistic', but also as ill-conceived—they did not think it through.

Victims' lawyers also share the teacher's frustration about their students' inability to remember. Even good students keep asking the same questions. They fail to do their homework. After the same questions were asked time and again, the lawyers decided to role play the Court with the victims:

> And so, we had to act, as in role-play the court—the judges sit here, you sit here, you are the victims' counsel. Now you are OTP, now you are defence, and your client is here. Now the three of you are the judges. So, this is our answer. This is their role. This is their role. This is their role.[58]

Court simulations are a popular teaching method: law students, for example, argue imaginary cases in 'moot courts'. Victims' lawyers pass that method on, but its purpose changes in the process. Victims don't argue cases, they play roles. The 'role-play model' is officially part of the ICC's

[56] Their right to reparation depends on several factors: the conviction of the accused for the crimes they suffered, the recognition of their victimhood by the court and the willingness of the international community to pay if the perpetrator is indigent (as in Ongwen's case).

[57] Interview with Victim's Lawyer, Kampala (10 July 2019).

[58] Interview with Field Assistant (n 55).

outreach programme for children, and the Court has already enacted it in 40 secondary schools in Northern Uganda.[59] But the victims' lawyers felt it was necessary for adults, too:

> At the end of the day, I work with communities. I know human nature. I know that I've started meetings with people, and I've said ABC and they repeated BCB immediately after, so I wouldn't want to put the blame on outreach's failure . . . Last time, I was telling them that maybe we should do simulations, to have a demonstration. We have reached a point where we have to do that, so that people can actually see, kind of like a mini play.[60]

Simulating the court gives victims the illusion of being in the courtroom. It both reduces the physical distance between the court and affected communities, and the difference between those who watch, and those who conduct the trial: you could be sitting in the courtroom. But it also reifies their role as victims and puts them in their place. Ultimately, you are not the judge; you are the victim. This is your role.

Disciplining and Blaming

Once people have been schooled in their role as victims, the question is how they remain engaged over many years. This is when disciplining and, ultimately, blaming enter the picture. Blaming is not a mechanism of subject creation per se, but a way of tying people to victimhood, of reproducing them as victims. To understand how it operates we first have to explore the disciplinary effects of the inclusion/exclusion dynamics of victim participation. While 'victims', according to the Court's Rules of Procedure and Evidence, means any persons 'who have suffered harm as a result of the commission of any crime within the jurisdiction of the Court', only victims of designated cases before the Court have rights to participate in the legal proceedings and to receive reparations.[61] This is known as the distinction between

[59] ICC, 'Outreach Report' (2010) 14 https://www.icc-cpi.int/sites/default/files/OUR2010Eng.pdf (accessed 20 April 2023). On the role of judicial theatre and legal performance see Stahn (n 20) 250–52.

[60] Interview with Victim's Lawyer Assistant, Kampala (9 July 2019).

[61] Rules of Procedure and Evidence, r 85a: 'Definition of victims'. Victims can also 'include organizations or institutions that have sustained direct harm to any of their property which is dedicated to religion, education, art or science or charitable purposes, and to their historic monuments, hospitals and other places and objects for humanitarian purposes'. See r 85b.

'situation victims' and 'case victims'.[62] The judges, ultimately, decide who can participate and in what forms.[63] There are two dynamics at play in this inclusion/exclusion dialectic: those who are excluded but claim victimhood are blamed as 'fraudulent' victims or cheaters; those who are included are disciplined through the precarious terms of inclusion; they are expected to perform their victimhood as champions, who are eager to participate, rather than as passive victims, who are tired of attending meetings.[64]

While in the Ugandan case, the VPRS on the ground, relying on local intermediaries such as law students, helped victims fill out application forms to determine whether they qualify as 'case victims', in the Kenyan cases, this was the task of the victims' lawyers.[65] For the registration mission I observed in Western Kenya in 2014, the victims' lawyers and his assistants determined whether victims were eligible to participate in their case. The case only covered attacks perpetrated by the Mungiki gangs against people perceived as 'non-Kikuyu' in Nakuru and Naivashsa from 24 to 28 January 2008, which is publicly available information. Because the Court's criteria for victimhood are so narrow and arbitrary in the context of ongoing atrocities—only particular types of victimization on particular days and in particular localities can be considered—victims may modify the parameters of their victimhood to fit within the parameters of the case. One victims' lawyer told me that, in his experience, victims sometimes fitted too neatly with the case's delimitation.[66] He had encountered situations where one victim after the other began their story with, 'it happened on the' and then said the same date, making him suspect that the intermediary who had mobilized victims for the meeting had also coached them in advance on what they should tell the lawyers. Some of the lawyer's field assistants tested victims' stories: 'you said that you came from this area, can you tell

[62] 'The differentiation between "situation" and "case" level, although not explicitly mentioned in the ICC's constitutive documents, emanates from the structure of the Statute.' Elisabeth Baumgartner, 'Aspects of victim participation in the proceedings of the International Criminal Court' (2008) 90(870) International Review of the Red Cross, 409, 414; Amnesty International, 'Crying for Justice: Victims' Perspectives on Justice for the Post-Election Violence in Kenya' (2014) 9 https://www.amnesty.org/en/documents/afr32/001/2014/en/ (accessed 1 April 2023).

[63] Rome Statute, art 68(3); Rules of Procedure and Evidence, r 89(1).

[64] Interview with Victims' Lawyer Assistant (n 60).

[65] In the *Ongwen* case, law students of Gulu University helped VPRS with the process. *Prosecutor v Ongwen* (First Report on Applications to Participate in the Proceedings ICC) [2015] ICC-02/04-01/15-303, §§ 4–5. Human Rights Watch, 'Who will stand for us?: Victims' Legal Representation at the ICC in the Ongwen Case and Beyond' (2017) 26 https://www.hrw.org/sites/default/files/report_pdf/ijongwen0817_web.pdf (accessed 31 October 2021).

[66] Interview with Victims' Lawyer, Nairobi (1 July 2014).

me the name of the local hospital?' 'How far was the place of attack from the local police station?'[67] Those who lie or whose stories are muddled will not qualify as victims. Their victimhood is no longer a fact of life but a question of law; it has become juridified.[68] The victims' lawyer himself did not interrogate victims' stories too closely. He thought it was better to include ten 'fraudulent' victims in the proceedings than to exclude one 'genuine' victim.[69] Besides, the chances of victims receiving anything substantive out of these proceedings such as reparations were slim in that case. There was no point in poking holes into their stories. Those victims who did not fall within the case's parameters were told so immediately after the interview.

Even though unintentional, there was something disturbing about this procedure: victims are turned into 'cheaters' because they do not fit the narrow and ultimately arbitrary delimitation of the case. It was not clear whether victims fully understood the process or the criteria for inclusion. One interview I observed was between the victims' lawyer and a young man.[70] When asked about his age, the man stated that he was 27. The lawyer pointed out that his ID said that he was 17. The man explained that there was a mistake with his ID. Later during the interview, he claimed that he was 37. This left the lawyer rather confused. There are many possible explanations for this story and perhaps the language barrier is the most obvious. But I could not help feeling that the young man had understood that there was an exclusionary mechanism but wrongly assumed that it was age rather than the date and place of the attack. He seemed quite anxious in his attempts to persuade the victims' lawyer that he was older than he looked and than his documents claimed. Perhaps he thought that one had to be above the age of 18 to participate in the case.

There is a tendency at the ICC to create moral panics about 'fraudulent' or 'fake victims' accessing the Court, which keeps the victim category exclusive and well policed.[71] 'Fraudulent' victims are those who claim

[67] Field notes (n 51).
[68] Kendall and Nouwen (n 14).
[69] Field notes (n 51).
[70] I should clarify that the lawyers ensured that I was never present when victims relayed their names or other personal information.
[71] At a workshop on victim participation in The Hague, some victims' lawyers expressed concern about 'fraudulent victims', while others insisted that victims' lawyers should not 'interrogate' victims as they would interrogate witnesses. ICCBA and Oxford Workshop on Victim Participation (31 May–1 June 2018) https://www.law.ox.ac.uk/centres-institutes/centre-criminology/advancing-impact-victim-participation-international-criminal (accessed 31 March 2023).

victimhood without meeting the Court's criteria. In the Ugandan case, VPRS only had six months to file applications for victim participation and they were able to reach 4,095 victims out of up to 50,000 potential victims of the case.[72] Fear of fraud and concerns about judicial economy made the judges reluctant to extend the deadline for victim registration. The judges believe that any 'real victims' should have come forward by now, one victims' officer reckoned.[73]

Yet it is not only exclusion but also inclusion that has disciplinary effects on victims. For those included, the privileged category of 'victim participant' creates expectations. If you are among 4000 victims granted the right to participate out of 50,000 potential victims, if you agreed to participate, if the Court pays for your lawyer, you have a duty to participate. As one victims' lawyer put it, 'if we [the judges] have allowed you to participate in the proceedings, then that's your job. That's the role. That's what we want to know about'.[74] From duty, however, there is only a small step to blame.

Victimologists have long argued that criminal justice operates through the binary of 'innocent victims' versus 'evil perpetrators': the law saves and revenges innocent victims by blaming and punishing evil perpetrators.[75] The compulsion to blame, McEvoy and McConnachie argue, may even be stronger in transitional justice contexts where 'crimes are often egregious and accompanied by a lack of effective legal redress through corrupt or inept justice systems'.[76] As they put it, 'in such places, blame offers sharper distinctions between the wicked and the righteous'.[77]

This debate has also been at the heart of the *Ongwen* trial, as Ongwen himself was abducted as a child, and then indoctrinated and brutalized by the LRA.[78] He was thus a victim of the same crimes he later perpetrated. 'One of the complexities of Ongwen's case', Sander observes, 'is that

[72] *Prosecutor v Ongwen* (Annex I Public Registry Report on the Mapping Exercise) [2012] ICC-02/04-01/15-1919-AnxI, §§ 30–31.

[73] Interview with Registry Officer, The Hague (1 June 2018).

[74] Interview with Victims' Lawyer, Kampala (10 July 2019).

[75] Nils Christie, 'The ideal victim' in Ezzat A Fattah (ed), *From Crime Policy to Victim Policy* (Palgrave Macmillan 1986); Christine Schwöbel-Patel, 'The "Ideal" Victim of International Criminal Law' (2018) 29(3) The European Journal of International Law 703.

[76] Kieran McEvoy and Kirsten McConnachie, 'Victims and Transitional Justice: Voice, Agency and Blame' (2013) 22(4) Social & Legal Studies 489, 502.

[77] ibid.

[78] Branch (n 16) 38; Mark Drumbl, '"Getting" an Unforgettable Gettable: The Trial of Dominic Ongwen' (*Justice in Conflict* (5 February 2021) https://justiceinconflict.org/2021/02/05/getting-an-unforgettable-gettable-the-trial-of-dominic-ongwen/ (accessed 30 July 2022). On the complexity of victimhood in Northern Uganda more generally see Erin Baines, *Buried in the Heart: Women, Complex Victimhood and the War in Northern Uganda* (CUP 2017).

his victim-perpetrator status challenges the binary coding of international criminal law, which . . . derives its energy from, and in turn disseminates polarities of guilt/or innocence, capacity/or incapacity, adult/or child, and victim/or perpetrator'.[79] I would argue, however, that the blurry victim-perpetrator is a convenient rather than troublesome figure for ICL as it depoliticizes violence by reinforcing the image of the always already blameworthy victim. In this depiction, the Global South appears as a cauldron of violent and unpredictable people—victims as well as perpetrators—endowing the Court with the mission to regulate and discipline them. This imagery also propels the Trust Fund for Victims' (TFV) assistance programmes. For example, the TFV funds 'peace schools' that teach 'communities, amongst themselves, to try find solutions for the root causes of conflict in a way that is non-violent'.[80] But 'peace schools' for victims only make sense if victims are part of why the violence happened in the first place. Victims are judged as much as perpetrators. The victim-perpetrator cements the status of victims as inherently suspicious and helps to justify their unceremonious abandonment by the Court if charges are not confirmed or defendants not convicted.

3.3 The Blame Cascade

Blaming matters in the Court's victim engagement, but it does not operate through the binary of innocent victims versus evil perpetrators. Instead, I argue, it works through a cascade. White, cosmopolitan judges in The Hague blame 'African' victim lawyers and officers, victim lawyers in Nairobi or Kampala blame the intermediaries 'in the field', and 'professional' intermediaries in Gulu or Lukodi blame 'peasant' victims. Blaming does not only happen at the point of victim creation; it features in the Court's relationships more broadly, at all levels. It is not a direct but an indirect relationship which is mediated through different layers of the justice process.

[79] Barrie Sander (citing Mark Drumbl), 'We Need to Talk About Ongwen: The Plight of Victim-Perpetrators at the ICC' (*Justice in Conflict* (19 April 2016) https://justiceinconflict.org/2016/04/19/we-need-to-talk-about-ongwen-the-plight-of-victim-perpetrators-at-the-icc/ (accessed 20 April 2023); Mark Drumbl, 'Victims who victimise' (2016) 4(2) London Review of International Law 217, 240. See also Mark Drumbl, *Reimagining Child Soldiers in International Law and Policy* (OUP 2012).

[80] Pieter de Baan cited in ICC, 'Victims' participation before the International Criminal Court' *YouTube* (23 April 2013) https://www.youtube.com/watch?v=chymGL8teX4 (accessed 21 April 2022). I will explain this dynamic in ch 5.

The judges do not blame victims directly. That would not only contradict their impartiality but also be difficult as the victims are far away. The Court wants people to 'own' its processes. To achieve that, it recruits new blame subjects at every level of victim engagement which greases the blame cascade. Blame eventually accumulates at the bottom, where the victims are.

In the first instance, the ICC recruits victims' lawyers to bring the Court closer to victims, but in doing so, it also outsources responsibility for the difficulties of making victim participation meaningful. One judge told me with indignation:

> It [victim participation] has led to the emergence of a new caste of lawyers who make big money out of the suffering of the people . . . To be a legal representative of victims is a relatively easy job. It is not the same as being a defence counsel of an accused, because the Prosecutor does all the work . . . They get a mandate of the victims and otherwise they don't care about them. It's just a piece of paper they care about. I have a mandate of 100 victims in the DRC or in Ivory Coast and this allows me to sit in the courtroom to earn 30,000 or 20,000 Euros a month for this 'work'. They do not even report back. There is no dialogue and no ongoing communication with the victims, which, in my view, is a disaster.[81]

Both the rather condescending attitude by the judges towards lower-ranking staff and the accusations against victims' practitioners are well documented in the Independent Expert Review of the Court, which was published in 2020. 'There appears to be an approach of self-perceived aristocracy from some Judges', the Reviewers observe, 'treating staff as "commoners" '. It further notes that 'criticism was levelled at staff mandated to work with and for victims as lacking the basic skills required'.[82] The Court's judges act like 'kings', one Registry lawyer quipped. They protested, he told

[81] Interview with Judge, The Hague (19 December 2013). See eg Hans-Peter Kaul, 'Victims' rights and peace, in Thorsten Bonacker and Christoph Safferling (eds), *Victims of International Crimes: An Interdisciplinary Discourse* (TMC Asser Press 2013) 226 ('After receiving the mandate to appear before the ICC, some lawyers did not find it necessary to maintain contact with the victims and to seek their views; they seemed to be primarily interested in representing their own interests'). See also Elisa Hoven, 'Civil Party Participation in Trials of Mass Crimes: A Qualitative Study at the Extraordinary Chambers in the Courts of Cambodia' (2014) 12 JICJ 81.

[82] ICC, 'Independent Expert Review of the International Criminal Court and the Rome Statute System: Final Report' (2020) § 74; § 853.

me, when their big portraits in the lobby to the courtrooms were replaced by slightly smaller ones.[83]

The symbolic violence of these hierarchies also transpires in the courtroom. One female victims' lawyer reflected:

> I can't even believe that every time I stand up in Court I'm still called 'Mrs' . . . and when I tell the legal officer, 'I don't want to be referred to as "Mrs". My marital status, my incorrect marital status is not a matter for public consumption or the Chamber', it's kind of laughed off as if it's not a thing. I mean it's a small thing, but it's 2018. And then I look around the courtroom: three male judges, one male lead prosecutor, the two defence counsel are men. As always, the only counsel level woman in the court room is [name of female victims' lawyer] . . . when she is there . . . and it's the victims' thing. The victims are like women fuzzy . . . And yeah . . . if they are happy to demean women staff members, it's not surprising that when they are dealing with witnesses, they have the same prejudices.[84]

Victims' work is gendered and racialized as white, brown, and black women do most of this work. Victims are 'women fuzzy'.

One level down, the Court's victims' officers and victims' lawyers further outsource blame to local intermediaries, who are recruited to assist with outreach and victim engagement on the ground. As 'volunteers' or 'friends', they are barely compensated for their work. Intermediaries are the perfect blame subjects; they are a bit more powerful than victims, so it is less dubious to blame them, but not powerful enough to strike back. As one victims' lawyer explained:

> Because we are asking too much of intermediaries and it is true that a lot of these issues are caused by intermediaries. And the judges constantly say, 'these forms are so badly filled in'. We [the victims' lawyers] were not there and it's probably not their fault either because they were asked to fill in 4000 forms in the space of a month . . . Who set that deadline? And intermediaries probably think: 'Why are we taking the blame for errors in the form when we have been asked to play the role of lawyer, interpreter and scribe basically for free' . . . That's a fundamental flaw in the process

[83] Field Notes, The Hague (December 2013).
[84] Interview with Victims' Lawyer, London (10 September 2018).

> as we've designed it. Not a thing to put blame on the individuals who are giving their time to try and help people access the Court.[85]

Apart from complaints about their legal competency, intermediaries are often accused of gatekeeping. As one victims' officer put it:

> As long as it doesn't result in this kind of gatekeeper mentality that we don't want to create in the wake of our intervention, you know, this infrastructure of like, 'human rights people', when they might otherwise have been something else. That always really worried me about this, you know, people who were farmers or were businessmen or whatever, are seeing an opportunity to just get involved on the development train and become this kind of 'pseudo-helping' muzungu [foreigners or white people] reach their little village, as if that's an actual career.[86]

Of course, in each case, the accusation could be levelled back. Is the ICC judge who makes US$200,000 a year tax-free and sues the Court for a higher salary so different from the victims' lawyer idling in the courtroom?[87] Are we not all making a career out of 'pseudo-helping' victims (including, of course, the writer of this book)? Isn't the difference simply that the accuser benefits from this more than the accused because he is higher up and better paid?

Local lawyers and intermediaries push blame further down. They complain that affected communities in Northern Uganda have become lazy.[88] The victims have to 'stop crying' and go back to toil on the fields.[89] I was struck by how uniformly intermediaries, including NGO officers, local businessmen, religious and cultural leaders, teachers and social workers, expressed that idea. The war had derailed the Acholi youth, they claimed. During the war, the government forcibly displaced 90% of the population

[85] ibid.
[86] Interview with Registry Officer, The Hague (1 June 2018).
[87] Marlise Simons, 'In The Hague's Lofty Judicial Halls, Judges Wrangle Over Pay' *The New York Times* (20 January 2019) https://www.nytimes.com/2019/01/20/world/europe/hague-judges-pay.html (accessed 21 April 2022).
[88] Interview with Local Healer, Gulu (29 July 2019) ('[W]hen people stayed in the camp and they went back home, people have become very lazy. People no longer do the kind of work these people used to do. Respect is lost . . . People have lost the value of culture').
[89] Interview with Field Assistant (n 55).

in Northern Uganda from their homes into concentration camps[90] ostensibly to protect them from attacks by the LRA, but also to cut the latter off any local resources.[91] Two decades of war and mass displacement destroyed both the material and cultural fabric of Acholi society. Living in confinement, Northern Ugandans could not till their fields and depended on hand-outs from the World Food Programme for their survival. Mass displacement, moreover, interrupted socialization in the hard graft of agriculture: 'if you look at the current generation, they are very lazy because they were born in that type of environment', one women's rights lawyer observed.[92] 'Now, especially the youth are not willing to go and dig', a parish chief complained, 'they want to eat freely because they used to eat freely in the camp'.[93] Life in the camps made it difficult for the elders to instil Acholi beliefs and values, and to teach economic practices, to the new generation. The youth did not learn how to till the land or guard the animals, nor did they witness cultural rituals or celebrations.

Of course, few of the people I interviewed were eager to do farming themselves. They either had professional jobs or cultural, religious, or governmental positions. Even if they did farm on the side or as a business, few were swinging the hoe day in day out. When I asked a cultural leader what his priority was, he replied:

> My priority is that I cannot just lament that these things happened and now we have an excuse . . . I try to do community outreach—they [the youth] begin to understand. 'Come easy' is not possible. You have to work hard. And our socio-economic system is based on the land. People who grew up in camps don't know how to till the land. They have to go back to the basics.[94]

Acholi youth, my interviewees claimed, want Western lifestyles but without any of the hard work.[95] They want to consume but not produce. 'The young people love pleasure', one NGO worker pointed out:

[90] Some of my interviewees in Northern Uganda described them as concentration camps. See also Adam Branch, 'Humanitarianism, Violence and the Camp in Northern Uganda' (2009) 11 Civil Wars 477.

[91] Adam Branch, *Displacing Human Rights: War and Intervention in Northern Uganda* (OUP 2011).

[92] Interview with Women's Rights Lawyer, Gulu (24 July 2019).

[93] Interview with Parish Leader, Lukodi (25 July 2019).

[94] Interview with Cultural Leader, Gulu (20 July 2019).

[95] ibid.

> And the world of music is a world of pleasure. You see how these people compose themselves and you want to start living that life, the music stars, they want to dress like that . . . They think these people are not working . . . so for them rather than to concentrate to get money or to go to school, they just want to jump into those lifestyles.[96]

'Ugandans are rich', President Museveni declared on his 'wealth creation' tour in 2019: 'Look at all of you, you're all dressed in clothes and shoes which are imported. They're paid for, moreover in dollars! . . . The campaign I'm on is to tell you we can produce all those things here. Those who are not doing agriculture, with my support go into the industries and produce the sweaters, handbags, shoes using our leather, clothes and many others.'[97] 'Ugandans should start appreciating hard work, discipline, time management and patriotism', the government's 'Uganda 2040 vision' demands.[98]

But blaming was not restricted to Northern Ugandans' failure to engage in 'productive' work, it also targeted their reproductive roles. Women were blamed for failing in 'their role' of caring for and educating their children: 'Mothers don't know how to bring up their children . . . The girls are into prostitution, they are jumping from one nightlife place to another', one cultural leader lamented.[99] A woman I met at an ICC outreach meeting in Gulu, likewise, deplored: 'We have lost our culture. It has been destroyed. It's all due to lives in the camp—now she [the young woman] doesn't listen. She leaves the baby at home and goes dancing'.[100] 'Young people are dancing like the act of having sexual intercourse', a local teacher opined, 'they put naked photos of themselves on facebook'.[101] I wondered whether this anxiety only concerned women's refusal or failure at reproductive work or whether it expressed deeper fears about gender expressions that flout the binary.[102] Spending time in Gulu, I saw 'men' painting their toenails pink

[96] Interview with NGO representative, Gulu (18 July 2019). See also Julia Vorhölter, 'Youth as "identity entrepreneurs": emerging neoliberal subjectivities in Uganda, in Jörg Wiegratz, Giuliano Martiniello, and Elisa Greco (eds), *Uganda: The Dynamics of Neoliberal Transformation* (Zed Books 2018).

[97] NBS Television, 'Museveni's Wealth Creation Tour' (18 July 2019)https://www.facebook.com/nbstelevision/photos/president-museveni-ugandans-are-rich-look-at-all-of-you-youre-all-dressed-in-clo/2404837896273828/ (accessed 22 December 2022).

[98] Government of Uganda, 'Uganda Vision 2040' 12 http://www.npa.go.ug/wp-content/uploads/2021/02/VISION-2040.pdf (accessed 24 December 2022).

[99] ibid.

[100] Informal conversation with Cultural Leader Assistant, Gulu (17 July 2019).

[101] Interview with Teacher, Gulu (30 July 2019).

[102] See eg Stella Nyanzi, 'Dismantling Reified African Culture through Localised Homosexualities in Uganda' (2013) 15(7–8) Culture, Health & Sexuality 952; Rahul Rao,

and wearing flamboyant clothes. For the first time in my life, I was the only 'woman' at a yoga class, my clumsy yoga movements put to shame by sleek 'male' bodies moving elegantly in colourful tights. For the first time, too, I saw female construction workers in significant numbers, paving Gulu's dusty roads. Such challenges to gender roles, in other words, may erode the reproduction of a conservative social order.[103]

Blame is a way of tying people into obligations; it is a mechanism of disciplining them in labour relationships, revealing that victims are part of these relationships; they work for the Court. Indeed, if blame works through a binary, it is not between 'innocent victims' and 'wicked perpetrators' but between intellectual and manual labourers. The division between manual and intellectual labour, Marx and Engels claimed, sits at the heart of the formation of ideology.[104] 'What explains the emergence of religion as an ideology out of the magic and natural mysticism of pre-state societies is not an "inverted consciousness"', Rehmann observes, 'but rather the formation of a specialised priesthood that is set free from manual labour'.[105] Priests were the first ideologists; they justified why they should pray, think, and write, while others should drudge on the field, prepare food, and bear children.[106] As Marx and Engels put it, 'the division of labour implies the possibility, nay the fact that intellectual and material activity—enjoyment and labour, production and consumption—devolve on different individuals'.[107] As the next chapter will show, policing the division between manual and professional labour is a key function of local intermediaries.

Our initial focus on the relationship between ideology producer and ideological subject gradually lays bare a cascade. Ideological producers are also ideological subjects as this process unfolds at different levels at the same time. The victims' lawyers do not only interpellate the victims; they are themselves interpellated at an earlier stage in the process. The judges

'Global homocapitalism' (2015) 194 Radical Philosophy 38, 47. See also Uganda's new law on homosexuality; a more severe version of its previously struck down the 2014 Anti-Homosexuality Act, criminalizing LGBTQ+ minorities. Human Rights Watch, 'Uganda's Parliament Threatens to Criminalize Homosexuality Protect, Don't Punish Vulnerable Minorities' (2023) https://www.hrw.org/news/2023/03/06/ugandas-parliament-threatens-criminalize-homosexuality (accessed 30 March 2023).

[103] See also Adam Branch, 'The Violence of Peace: Ethnojustice in Northern Uganda' (2014) 45 Development and Change 608.
[104] Karl Marx and Friedrich Engels, *The German Ideology* (Lawrence & Wishart 2007) 51.
[105] Jan Rehmann, *Theories of Ideology* (2013) 30.
[106] Marx and Engels (n 104) 51.
[107] ibid 52.

'hail' the victims' lawyers and officers, the victims' lawyers and officers 'hail' the intermediaries, and the intermediaries 'hail' the victims.

3.4 Materializing the Blame Cascade: Blame, Work, and Debt

Looking at the process empirically, blaming ties different subjects at different levels into the justice process. At the higher levels, blame revolves around legal competency, integrity, industriousness and pay, at the lower levels, it centres on the division between manual and mental labour, and productive and reproductive labour.[108] In between, it boils down to the question of who 'sits' in the courtroom and who 'gets their hands dirty' in the field. Blaming, however, is the surface dynamic which is ultimately driven by material relations of labour and debt, into which victims and intermediaries are gradually integrated. Victims are not blamed as victims but as lazy workers and unreliable debtors. By participating in the Court's trials, they are also incorporated into productive processes, yet in ways that deny or devalue their labour. As one victims' lawyer put it:

> And so we treat them [victims] as if their time is not valuable, because their time is not monetized. Because all they would be doing with their time—'all they would be doing with their time' like it's nothing—is ploughing their field and doing subsistence work that is not remunerated, then we feel we can ask them to attend a meeting whenever we want. And I'm quite worried about that. Yes, we organize it on working days to suit our own schedules. It's also expensive to send so many people *down*. But that might not be convenient for them. It might be a day when they want to go to church or to sell their stuff at the market and we are like 'No, you need to come to our meeting today or you miss out'.[109]

The Court's victim engagement reproduces a hierarchy of labour wherein the labour and time of lawyers trump the labour and time of victims.

[108] I will unpack this further in the next chapter.

[109] Interview with Victims' Lawyer, London (10 September 2018. Also note the spatial metaphor in the quote: the victims' lawyers are sent 'down' there 'to Africa' where labour does not count.

Victims' subsistence and social reproduction work is not valued. But why would victims accept that devalorisation of their labour time?

Because they don't want to 'miss out'. The subtle threat of 'missing out' offers clues about the relationship between victim participation and capitalist integration. Victim participation in the Court's legal processes not only mirrors but anticipates the logic of capitalist social relations. The Court wants as many victims as possible to participate in its processes but on its own terms. Victims play pre-assigned roles at the periphery of the legal process. On the one hand, the Court's practitioners blazon rising numbers of victim applications and people attending the ICC's outreach meetings.[110] On the other hand, they restrict and regulate the terms of victim inclusion. In a speech on outreach, the Registrar, for example, enumerated:

> Field outreach teams directly targeted 46,499 people, of which 11,605 were women. Through 375 audio and video programs produced by the Court—153 more than during the previous year—local audiences were informed about the developments at the Court. In addition, estimated audience of nearly 70 million people was regularly exposed to the Court's information through radio and television programs. I hope you will agree that this is an impressive achievement considering the limited resources granted to the Outreach Unit.[111]

Yet, a few lines later, the Registrar stressed that the main role of outreach is expectation management: 'I hope we can agree that unrealistic expectations could negatively affect the way victims perceive the Court and international criminal justice in general.'[112] In a nutshell, the Court wants victims but not their expectations.

Integration into global capitalist relations operates analogously. Subjects in the Global South join global value chains at the bottom not the top or the

[110] The Court often measures its achievements in terms of numbers of victims it engaged with. See ICC, 'Report on activities and programme performance of the International Criminal Court for the year 2020' (2021), Assembly of States Parties (ICC-ASP/20/7) 92, 96. See also more recently: ICC, 'Rome Statute: 25 years' https://www.youtube.com/watch?v=URKsOqo0GYE (accessed 10 August 2023) (10,900 victims who participated in court proceedings, ,2500 victims who received court-ordered reparations, over 130,000 survivors supported by the Trust Fund for Victims Programmes).

[111] See eg 'The speech of the Registrar on the launching of the 4th Outreach Report' New York (7 December 2010) 1 https://www.icc-cpi.int/sites/default/files/NR/rdonlyres/F3BAEC29-4029-4829-8637-3A2314D59F36/0/RegSpeech.pdf (accessed 22 April 2022).

[112] ibid 3.

middle. They occupy a pre-assigned role as precarious, low-paid labour. To ensure that integration happens on the terms of capitalists not workers it has to remain precarious and partial. Not everyone can be integrated and not all the time. There is always a risk of 'missing out'.

The Court's need to create its victim subjects for its own reproduction, therefore, feeds into the wider need to create working subjects for capitalist reproduction. Legal relations are social relations which are simultaneously relations of production and reproduction, cutting through any neat division between legal, economic, and political spheres. Moral and material relations are inextricably intertwined in the capitalist social formation. Capitalism needs to extract surplus value through labour exploitation, financialization and dispossession, and the Court produces blameworthy victims who are 'ready' for their social roles.

3.4.1 From Victim to Debtor

While labour is a key dynamic of the blame cascade, debt increasingly penetrates the lives of victims at the periphery of the Global South, especially in Uganda, where 95 percent of the population works in the informal sector, engaging in subsistence agriculture and small-scale trade.[113] Excluded from the formal wage relation, but included through debt relations, they belong to the surplus population, which forms an integral part of the capitalist mode of production. Capitalist accumulation, argues Marx, 'constantly produces . . . a relatively redundant working population, i.e. a population which is superfluous to capital's average requirements for its own valorization, and is therefore a surplus population.'[114] In fact, it is workers themselves who produce 'both the accumulation of capital and the means by which . . . [they are] made relatively superfluous' as the employment of machinery (constant capital) reduces the relative need for labour (variable capital).[115] This puts workers in a contradictory position: by working, they produce the very lever, the surplus population, that threatens to make them redundant, and is deployed to whittle away their rights and wages. We see a complex inclusion/exclusion dynamic in motion: by being

[113] William Odinga Balikuddembe, 'Access to loans for the poor: Microfinance in northern Uganda' (5 July 2022) https://ddrn.dk/3367/ (accessed 24 December 2022).
[114] Karl Marx, *Capital Volume I: A Critique of Political Economy* (Penguin Books 1990) 782.
[115] ibid 781, 783.

included in capitalist production, workers create the exclusion of others (as surplus) while also rendering the conditions of their own inclusion ever more precarious. Yet, this does not mean that the surplus population is external or superfluous to capitalism. On the contrary, it is an essential wheel for capitalist movement: when capitalism expands it needs to recruit the surplus population which 'become[s] one of the most energetic agencies for its reproduction.'[116]

This resembles the constant motion between inclusion and exclusion in the Court's victim engagement: victim participation produces 'surplus victims' who are neither eligible to participate in the Court's trials nor to receive reparations, but who can, nonetheless, come to the Court's outreach meetings and benefit from the Trust Fund's assistance mandate. As I demonstrated in Chapter 2, reparation and assistance dovetail in a dialectical relationship. As one closes the other opens; as one excludes the other includes. Under its assistance mandate, the Trust Fund can provide victims with 'urgent interim relief' as soon as an investigation is underway and independently of whether victims participate in any specific case.[117] 'As a practical matter, not much will turn on the nomenclature of "reparation" in contrast to "assistance", Judge Eboe-Osuji observed, 'where all value for such repair is placed on a stylised idea of "reparation", as following conviction, one questions whether many victims will really value such an idea of "reparation" that follows the conviction of an indigent convict, as opposed to substantive "assistance" such as the TFV is able to give in the circumstances regardless of the question of conviction.'[118]

As part of its assistance and reparation programmes, the TFV has extended microloans to victims and affected communities. This type of 'financial inclusion', I argue, fosters a metamorphosis from victim to debtor that needs to be read in the broader context of microfinance's reproduction of the surplus population in the Global South. The same inclusion/exclusion dynamic that we witnessed in the Court's victim engagement also plays out in the relationship between labour and debt, finance and microfinance. Those who are excluded from formal work and finance, the unemployed and unbanked, those at the periphery, are picked up by the development and humanitarian sector through softer structures such as Village Savings and Loans Associations (VSLA) which mark the first step into 'financial

[116] ibid 785.
[117] FIDH (n 1) 70.
[118] ibid.

inclusion'. The Trust Fund funds such VSLA groups, describing them as follows:

> VSLA members receive small loans that enable them to mobilize capital to engage in income generating activities. The VSLA groups receive regular supervision and guidance on book keeping as well as governance support. Beneficiaries may also be engaged in agri-business where they are able to grow, for example, soya beans, green beans, sun flower, cotton, and cereal crops for sale in area markets to supplement their income and saving.[119]

The TFV aims to integrate as many victims as possible into these groups: 'VSLA is spreading like wild fire', a district leader from Gulu remarked, 'it is the best initiative that has been established in the entire region of northern Uganda'.[120] Care International, one of the TFV's early implementing partners in Uganda, developed the VSLA method, integrating more than 600,000 Ugandans into 22,000 loan and saving groups since 1998.[121] These village groups meet regularly to decide how to allocate microloans among its members. The victims learn fast: 'They gave me $10 and I bought a bag of coal', one female victim described: 'I put my training to use, sold the coal and earned $18 on my $10 purchase. The next time, I borrowed $30, then $50, and now up to $100. I have my own business and I learned how to manage it here.'[122]

Once the groups 'mature'—meaning they have successfully managed and invested their savings—Care International links them up with banks such as Barclays to unleash more financial opportunities.[123] 'Banking on

[119] TFV, 'Material Support' https://www.trustfundforvictims.org/en/what-we-do/assistance-programmes/material-support (accessed 23 April 2022). TFV, 'Promoting income generating activities' https://www.trustfundforvictims.org/en/about/our-impact/income-generating-activities (accessed 23 April 2022). See also *Prosecutor v Lubanga* (Annex A: Collective Reparations projects in relation to the conviction of Thomas Lubanga Dyilo before the International Criminal Court) ICC-01/04-01/06-3273-AnxA [2017], 17–18.

[120] International Center for Research on Women (ICRW), 'External Evaluation of the Trust Fund for Victims Programmes in Northern Uganda and the Democratic Republic of Congo: Towards a Perspective of Upcoming Interventions' (2013) 33 https://www.icrw.org/wp-content/uploads/2016/10/ICRW-TFV--Evaluation-Report.pdf (accessed 4 March 2022).

[121] ibid 31, 55–57. Other former TFV partners such as the Northeast Chili Producers Association (NECPA) and the Anglican Diocese of Northern Uganda have also set up VSLA groups. Care Uganda, 'Village Saving and Loans Association' (2014) https://www.care.org.au/wp-content/uploads/2014/12/CARE-VSLA-Report-Uganda-Eco-Devel.pdf (accessed 2 May 2022).

[122] ICRW (n 120) 35.

[123] Care Uganda (n 121).

change', Care calls this programme, thus exposing the connections between rural development, international criminal law and finance, as well as the interplay between non-profit and for-profit lending as the former creates debtors who are 'ready' for the latter.[124] Uganda has one of the most developed microfinance sectors in Africa, providing an important source of finance for households in Northern Uganda, even though high interest rates have effectively limited the uptake of loans.[125] Microfinance also forms a key tenet of the Ugandan government's development strategy especially for rural areas.[126]

Such savings and loans groups teach capitalist fledglings to honour the debt relation. When I asked a female survivor of SGBV in Gulu what happens if women fail to repay the loan, she retorted: 'You have to pay because people make like a law. They sign for it.'[127] VSLAs do not tolerate 'arrears': 'All arrears should be announced at the weekly meetings', Care Uganda instructs, 'members should not tolerate fund losses caused by members' failure to repay loans'.[128] 'Make money, be strong, this is how we do it', a local healer and VSLA member explained to me as we sat in her grass-thatched hut on the outskirts of Gulu.[129] Repayment rates are very high. If women fail to repay, they will lose access to other support and training channelled through the group: 'I normally tell them', the local healer said, 'why do you block your way from getting money? . . . Why don't you concentrate on working for something that comes your way?'[130] Rather than formal employment, the expectation is to work on 'something

[124] ibid.

[125] Andy Carlton, Hannes Manndorff, Andrew Obara, Walter Reiter, Elisabeth Rhyne 'Microfinance in Uganda', L und R Social Research (December 2001) 10 https://www.oecd.org/countries/uganda/35481055.pdf (accessed 24 December 2022); USAID, 'Microfinance, Youth and Conflict: Central Uganda Case Study' (February 2006) 10 https://www.marketlinks.org/sites/default/files/resource/files/ML3488_mr_38_mf__youth___conflict_central_uganda_case_study.pdf (accessed 24 December 2022); Balikuddembe (n 113). 'Speaker urges finance minister to resolve challenges slowing saving groups' *The Independent* (1 December 2022) https://www.independent.co.ug/speaker-urges-finance-minister-to-resolve-challenges-slowing-saving-groups/ (accessed 24 December 2022).

[126] Republic of Uganda, 'National Financial Inclusion Strategy 2017–2022' (October 2017) 6, 19 https://www.bou.or.ug/bou/bouwebsite/bouwebsitecontent/publications/special_pubs/2017/National-Financial-Inclusion-Strategy.pdf (accessed 24 December 2022); National Planning Authority, 'Third National Development Plan (NDPIII) 2020/21–2024/25' (July 2020) 113 http://www.npa.go.ug/wp-content/uploads/2020/08/NDPIII-Finale_Compressed.pdf (accessed 24 December 2022); Republic of Uganda, 'The Peace Recovery Development Plan 3 for Northern Uganda July 2015–June 2021' (August 2015) 21, 23.

[127] Interview with Survivor Advocate, Gulu (27 July 2019).

[128] Care Uganda (n 121) 6.

[129] Interview with Local Healer (n 88).

[130] ibid.

that comes their way' like casual agricultural labour. The loan 'helps' focus their minds on work.[131] VSLA has created 'a new economic culture', Care Uganda boasts: 'The VSLA methodology has moved people from being idle to being very productive and busy. Many participants have adopted better work ethics and habits; people work harder, keep time better and deliver on their word.'[132]

Two key features characterize the relationship between debt and surplus populations. First, debt makes surplus populations productive.[133] 'Up until now', Verónica Gago explains, 'a system of debt for which the wage was the horizon reinforced the obligation and commitment to one's job and to the successive conditions of precarization that it may have imposed: It is something else entirely to go into debt without having a job.'[134] Finance increasingly extracts value from household economies in the Global South, 'those economies historically considered not to be productive', forcing people to do any type of money-generating activity (legal or illegal, safe or unsafe, formal or informal) to repay the loan.[135] No longer distinguishing between workers and the unemployed, producers and consumers, men and women, debt includes everyone: 'everyone is a "debtor" accountable to and guilty before capital'.[136]

Second, debt helps reproduce surplus populations. As Soederberg argues, 'the debt relation, which lies at the heart of the poverty industry . . . facilitates the social reproduction of the surplus population as a category of labour power'.[137] Since social reproduction is gendered as the role of women, microfinance institutions have predominantly targeted women as their grantees.[138] Financial inclusion supposedly empowers women,

[131] ibid.

[132] Care Uganda (n 121) 8.

[133] This applies both to subjects in the Global North and the Global South. See eg Susanne Soederberg, *Debtfare States and the Poverty Industry Money, Discipline and the Surplus Population* (Routledge 2014).

[134] Verónica Gago, *Feminist International: How to change everything* (Verso 2020) 140.

[135] Lucí Cavallero and Verónica Gago, *A Feminist Reading of Debt* (Liz Mason-Deese tr, Pluto Books 2021) 7.

[136] Maurizio Lazzarato, *The Making of the Indebted Man* (Semiotext(e) 2012) 7.

[137] Soederberg (n 133) 4.

[138] For a book-length study of the relationship between microcredit and gender see Lamia Karim, *Microfinance and its Discontents: Women in Debt in Bangladesh* (University of Minnesota Press 2011). See also Vasuki Nesiah, 'Indebted: The Cruel Optimism of Leaning into Empowerment' in Janet Halley, Prabha Kotiswaran Rachel Rebouché Hila Shamir (eds), *Governance Feminism: Notes from the Field* (Minnesota UP 2019). For a recent special issue on gender and microfinance see Supriya Garikipati and others, 'Microfinance and Gender: Issues, Challenges and The Road Ahead' (2017) 53 (5) The Journal of Development Studies 641; Marcella Corsi and Marina De Angelis, 'Gender Discrimination in Microfinance? Some Evidence from Uganda' (2017) 53 (5) The Journal of Development Studies 723.

celebrating them as 'responsible householders' and 'creative entrepreneurs'.[139] A feminist reading of debt, however, reveals that finance's interest in women has more to do with their socially reproductive labour than with their entrepreneurial potential.[140] Recruiting social reproducers (those who grow subsistence crops and care for children), extractive finance valorizes the reproduction of life.[141] While microloans are ostensibly designed for investment in 'productive activities', many women in rural Uganda, predictably, use them for reproduction especially paying school fees and buying necessities.[142] Food security often declines following the uptake of microcredit because women have less time to do subsistence farming and may skip meals to repay the loan.[143] Women's gendered commitment to feeding their children makes them both good social reproducers and reliable debtors.

Even more insidiously, the debt relation feasts on the social bonds nurtured by reproductive labour. Indeed, those bonds furnish the social collateral that underwrites the debt. In the absence of physical collaterals, the group itself guarantees the repayment of the loan.[144] 'At the group level', the Trust Fund asserts, 'VSLA is laudable for its contribution towards strengthening of social cohesion and facilitating the building of social capital for the majority of the members'.[145] While these groups can provide social and psychological support for women survivors of SGBV,[146] they can also be a

[139] TFV, 'Promoting income generating activities', https://www.trustfundforvictims.org/en/about/our-impact/income-generating-activities (accessed 23 April 2022); *Prosecutor v Lubanga* (Annex A: Collective Reparations projects in relation to the conviction of Thomas Lubanga Dyilo before the International Criminal Court) ICC-01/04-01/06-3273-AnxA [2017] 17. See also Carlton and others (n 125) 19.

[140] Cavallero and Gago (n 135).

[141] ibid 7.

[142] Faith Namayengo, Johan van Ophem, and Gerrit Antonides, 'Women and microcredit in rural agrarian households of Uganda: Match or mismatch between lender and borrower?' (2016) 10(2–3) Applied Studies in Agribusiness and Commerce 77, 84.

[143] Faith Namayengo, Gerrit Antonides, and Francesco Cecchi, 'Microcredit and Food Security: Evidence from Rural Households in Uganda' (2018) 27(4) Journal of African Economies 457.

[144] See also George Okello Candiya Bongomin, Atsede Woldie and Aziz Wakibi, 'Microfinance accessibility, social cohesion and survival of women MSMEs in postwar communities in sub-Saharan Africa: Lessons from Northern Uganda' (2020) 27(5) Journal of Small Business and Enterprise Development 749.

[145] *Prosecutor v Lubanga* (Draft Implementation Plan for collective reparations to victims Submitted to the Amended Reparations Order of 3 March 2015 in the case against Thomas Lubanga Dyilo) [2015] ICC-01/04-01/06-3177-AnxA, § 164.

[146] ibid; TFV, 'Mobilising Resources and Supporting the Most Vulnerable Victims through Earmarked Funding, Programme Progress Report Winter' (2012) 9 https://www.trustfundforvictims.org/sites/default/files/reports/TFV%20Programme%20Progress%20Report%20-%20Winter%202012.pdf (accessed 11 April 2023). Adam Branch, in his research on Northern

site of conflict and collective policing especially when women fail to repay the loan.[147] Karim calls this 'the economy of shame'.[148] The women themselves become debt collectors forcing their peers to sell property like furniture (tables, radios and even mattresses) to repay the loan and interest.[149] They also have to navigate the gendered power dynamics of kin relationships as male family members often demand the money for their own use, while the women are stuck with the responsibility of repayment.[150] This social entanglement of loan repayment unveils how capitalism colonizes the reproduction of life; relationships that women build to nourish people and communities are repurposed to service the debt relation.[151] Rather than merely extracting wealth from the poor, finance ideologically reshapes communities and their relationships. By recruiting women victims both as debtors and as debt collectors, debt not only 'includes' them but commits them to a capitalist future.

In addition to enduring the stress of loan and interest payments, women are also blamed for lacking innovation in their pursuits. Women [in rural Uganda], one academic study noted, 'usually start low-return activities that have little potential to lift them out of poverty . . . and reflect little innovativeness and ambition'.[152] Women fail to embody the neoliberal vision of the 'entrepreneurial poor' who just need a little training and start-up capital to create innovative businesses for global value chains. The indebted woman is always already guilty.

It may seem counter-intuitive that victims should incur debt as reparation for mass atrocities. It has nonetheless become a regular form as reparation programmes have turned to microfinance. 'The microfinance

Uganda, also emphasized the empowering effects of these women's groups. Adam Branch, *Displacing Human Rights: War and Intervention in Northern Uganda* (OUP 2011) 138–39.

[147] Silvia Federici, 'From Commoning to Debt: Financialization, Microcredit, and the Changing Architecture of Capital Accumulation' (2014) 113(2) The South Atlantic Quarterly 231, 237.

[148] Lamia Karim, *Microfinance and its Discontents: Women in Debt in Bangladesh* (University of Minnesota Press 2011) xviii.

[149] ibid.

[150] ibid xvi. One NGO representative told me that women's support groups in Teso, Northern Uganda made the consent of the husband the precondition for a woman's participation in loan and trade groups. They had experienced problems in the past with loan repayment as husbands simply took the money from their wives: 'Getting permission from the husband means that he knows she has to pay back the loan.' Interview with Women's Rights NGO Officer, Kampala (30 July 2014).

[151] Cavallero and Gago (n 135) 7; Federici (n 147) 232.

[152] Namayengo, van Ophem, and Antonides (n 142) 85.

revolution', Seibel and Armstrong argue in the *Oxford Handbook of Reparations*, 'open[s] up a new world of new options for agencies providing reparation payments to victims of human rights abuses'.[153] Microfinance addresses concerns that 'reparation payments which are not invested profitably may be wasted'.[154] There at least two reasons why it seems unremarkable for reparation programmes to turn victims into both creditors and debtors. First, debt relations are not immediately recognized as forms of extraction because they supposedly offer 'opportunities' to the 'underbanked'. Second, and more pertinent to a study on the ICC, there is a peculiar affinity between criminal law and debt which has been rearticulated through international criminal law.

In fact, the concept of debt has deep roots in criminal law.[155] Early medieval law, for example, fixed precise monetary compensations for bodily mutilation: 'If anyone knocks out a man's eye, he shall give him 66 shillings, 6 pence and the third part of a penny as compensation', one such code demanded.[156] Nietzsche already pondered 'how debt and restitution became the primary framework for conceptualising criminality and punishment'[157], while Derrida mused that 'the origin of the legal subject, and notably of penal law, is commercial law; it is the law of commerce, debt, the market, the exchange between things, bodies and monetary signs, with their general equivalent and their surplus value, their interest'.[158] The logic of debt repayment, in short, imbues criminal law.

Of course, in this conception, the perpetrator is the debtor. Initially, they owed the debt to their victims, but as crimes morphed from offences against victims to offences against law, it became less clear whom the debt is owed to.[159] This question is even more complicated at the ICC, because, so far, the only defendants the Court has successfully convicted have been penniless

[153] Hans Dieter Seibel with Andrea Armstrong, 'Reparations and Microfinance Schemes' in Pablo de Greiff (ed), *The Handbook of Reparations* (OUP 2006) 681.

[154] ibid 678.

[155] David Graeber, *Debt: The First 5000 Years* (Melvin House Publishing 2011); James Whitman, 'At the Origins of Law and the State: Monopolization of Violence, Mutilation of Bodies, or Fixing of Prices?' (1996) 71 Chicago-Kent Law Review 41.

[156] Whitman (n 155) 50.

[157] Judith Butler, 'On Cruelty' (2014) 36(14) London Review of Books 1 https://www.lrb.co.uk/the-paper/v36/n14/judith-butler/on-cruelty (accessed 23 April 2022).

[158] ibid.

[159] Tony Kearon and Barry S. Godfrey, 'Setting the scene: a question of history, in Sandra Walklate (ed), *Handbook of Victims and Victimology* (Routledge 2007); Marie Manikis, 'Conceptualising the Victim in England and Wales and the United States within a Spectrum of Public and Private Interests' (2021) 41 (1) Oxford Journal of Legal Studies 219.

African rebels and warlords, who could not pay for their own defence let alone for reparations.[160] This means that the Trust Fund had to step in, complementing the reparation liability of the defendant through voluntary contributions it receives from states. Victims and defendants thus resemble each other in that both need legal aid to participate in the Court's processes, making them both a financial burden to the ICC.

The simultaneous integration of victims into international criminal justice and capitalist social relations, paradoxically, renders them closer to the perpetrator. The TFV turns the debt of the indigent perpetrator into a loan to the victim, which simultaneously transforms victims into debtors (like the perpetrator) and entrepreneurs and investors (like the capitalists). In reality, though, victims become more like perpetrators. They sink down with the rest of the poor, entrapped in debt, while producing interest for capital. No amount of 'innovation' will generate investment and demand in rural Uganda where the poor sell to the poor. The gap between the reality of debt and the potential of profitable investment becomes the victims' fault. They lack in creativity; they are not industrious. 'Many [words for debt] are synonyms for "fault", "sin", or "guilt", Graeber notes, 'just as a criminal owes a debt to society, a debtor is always a sort of criminal'.[161] In German, the concept of blame ('Schuld') is derived from the concept of debt ('Schulden'), which, Nietzsche argued, shows how moral notions ('keeping your word', 'being on time') evolved out of the quintessential relation between creditor and debtor.[162] As victims become embroiled in the Court's processes, they, like the perpetrator, become guilty capitalist subjects.

The main critique of the Trust Fund, expressed by the court's practitioners, NGOs and expert reviewers, however, is not that it turns victims into capitalist subjects but that it is not doing enough of it.[163] In Northern Uganda, the TFV has phased out material assistance 'in light of the difficulty of proving that the primarily economic harms being remedied were

[160] Those defendants with assets, such as Kenya's former president, Uhuru Kenyatta, Kenya's former deputy president and current president, William Ruto, and Congolese politician, Jean-Pierre Bemba Gombo, were acquitted (or their charges were voided).

[161] Graeber (n 155) 121.

[162] Lazzarato (n 136) 30.

[163] Anne Dutton and Fionnuala Ní Aoláin, 'Between Reparations and Repair: Assessing the Work of the ICC Trust Fund for Victims Under Its Assistance Mandate' (2019) 19(2) Chicago Journal of International Law 490, 493. Phil Clark observes that material support, especially the loans, have been perceived positively by Northern Ugandans. Clark (n 11) 141–42.

traceable to the conflict after so many years'.[164] Its most recent programme cycle in Northern Uganda (April 2019–April 2024) focuses on psychosocial support and group counselling though microfinance and income-generating activities remain part of its assistance and collective reparation programmes in the Democratic Republic of Congo (DRC) and the Central African Republic (CAR).[165] They will also likely be part of the collective, socio-economic measures that the TFV proposes for reparation in the *Ongwen* case.[166] One day there are loans, the next day there are none, and the day after they are back. People need to remain flexible and ready but without expectations, seizing opportunities when they arise, while striving to self-improve.

The Court is no longer the saviour of 'innocent victims'; it is a creditor and investor, but this does not change the morality of the Court's relationship with victims.[167] The Court shifts blame to victims through an underlying material relation that is ultimately a debt relation. 'There's no better way to justify relations founded on violence', Graeber asserts, 'to make such relations seem moral, than by reframing them in the language of debt—above all, because it immediately makes it seem that it's the victim who's doing something wrong'.[168] Victims are debtors because of development infrastructures (microcredits, rural credit markets) that convert them into indebted subjects and by virtue of being citizens of indebted states (through structural adjustment programmes). The debt relation enables a silent moral reversal which creates proximity between the criminal and the victim (the victim is guilty). It is no longer the Court that ought to pay victims for participation and reparation, it is the victims who have to repay the loan.

[164] Anne Dutton and Fionnuala Ní Aoláin, 'Between Reparations and Repair: Assessing the Work of the ICC Trust Fund for Victims Under Its Assistance Mandate' (2019) 19(2) Chicago Journal of International Law 490, 542–43.

[165] TFV Management Brief Q3/2021 (1 July–30 September 2021) 2, 17–18.

[166] *Prosecutor v Ongwen* (Trust Fund for Victims' Final Observations on Reparations) [2022] ICC-02/04-01/15-1992, § 76; *Prosecutor v Ongwen* (Trust Fund for Victims' Observations relevant to Reparations) [2021] ICC-02/04-01/15-1920, § 164.

[167] Makau Mutua, 'Savages, Victims and Saviors: The Metaphor of Human Rights' (2001) 42 Harvard International Law Journal, 201. As Baars put it, 'the "humanitarian" school of law on ICL . . . [has] by far the strongest appeal'. Grietje Baars, 'The making of an international criminal law' in Christine Schwöbel (ed), *Critical Approaches to International Criminal Law* (Routledge 2014) 196.

[168] Graeber (n 155). On the role of debt in creating imperialist relations that enable capitalist accumulation see Robert Knox, 'Haiti at the League of Nations: Racialisation, Accumulation and Representation' (2020) 21 Melbourne Journal of International Law 4.

3.5 Conclusion

What exactly is the relationship between victim production in international criminal justice and their assimilation into global capitalist relations? Critical scholars have focused on how the legal process gradually sifts victims out of 'juridical victimhood'.[169] As 'the situation of Uganda' is first translated into a selected number of cases, and then into a selected number of charges in selected localities, tied to limited temporalities, most victims drop out of the legal process. Meanwhile, the participation of the 'lucky' selected ones is so heavily mediated through legal representation as to become meaningless.[170] Victims, the argument implies, are used as ideological prop to justify legal interventionism and global market expansion, but they are not themselves important subjects in the process.[171]

Rather than reading the Court's victim engagement as a juridical process of exclusion, we can, instead, interpret it as a social process of inclusion. Far from excluded, victims are precariously included through multi-layered forms of judicial and non-judicial interventions which mutually condition each other. In a similar vein, everyone can and should be included as a capitalist subject. Victims' precarious and partial integration into international criminal justice, this chapter suggested, prepares them for their precarious and partial integration into global capitalist relations. The Court, ultimately, creates ideological subjects for future value extraction.

Nietzsche saw the origins of human society rooted in credit rather than exchange (e.g., barter).[172] For him, the creditor–debtor relation is the first social relation, distinguishing humans from animals, which in turn supplied the key terms of our moral apparatus.[173] Drawing on Nietzsche, Graeber and Lazzarato have argued that the unequal creditor–debtor relation rather than the formally equal market relation (consumer–producer, buyer–seller) is the key relationship under neoliberal capitalism.[174] In market exchange, producer and consumer are formally equal subjects who exchange something of equal value (commodity against money). Meeting

[169] Kendall and Nouwen (n 14).
[170] ibid.
[171] Christine Schwöbel-Patel, *Marketing Global Justice: The Political Economy of International Criminal Law* (CUP 2021) 78; Kamari Maxine Clarke, *Affective Justice: The International Criminal Court and the Pan-Africanist Pushback* (Duke UP 2019).
[172] Gilles Deleuze, *Nietzsche and Philosophy* (Hugh Tomlinson tr, Continuum 2002) 155 cited in Maurizio Lazzarato, *The Making of the Indebted Man* (Semiotext(e) 2012) 33.
[173] Lazzarato (n 136) 39–42.
[174] Graeber (n 155); Lazzarato (n 136) 32.

in the marketplace, they both have something the other wants, goods and money change hands, and their relationship ends.[175] It is a fleeting relationship that only exists in the moment of exchange.

The creditor–debtor relation differs markedly from the buyer–seller relation as there is no equal exchange. One party has something the other party does not have (capital), and the latter has to pay for it more than its value (debt plus interest). The temporality of the relationship concerns the future more than the present. Creditor and debtor do not part ways after the transaction. Rather, the creditor owns the future labour time of the debtor and if the debtor fails to honour the terms of debt repayment, the creditor may own their property, their body, their children or their bondage depending on the power relationship between creditor and debtor as mediated by the state and its laws.[176] The Court creates debt subjects and relations more than market subjects and relations or, rather, it creates the latter through the former. The creditor–debtor relationship is prior. As such, the 'market metaphor' of international criminal justice can be misleading if it assumes that the most important function of capitalism is to create markets and market exchange.[177] The ICC does turn victims into consumers and workers, but it does so through their role as debtors.

The Court's primary role is not exclusion—punishing perpetrators—but inclusion, integrating victim subjects at the periphery into global capitalist social relations. Both the Court's supporters and critics agree that the triumph of liberal capitalism in the early 1990s formed the conditions of possibility for the ICC.[178] Indeed, many African states signed up to the Court and other global governance institutions to unlock credit from the Global North.[179] Yet, the Court not only intervenes in and disciplines states in the Global South; it also socializes their citizens as capitalist subjects. Targeting those at the margins, those who have been unproductive because of war

[175] Graeber (n 155) 104.

[176] Lazzarato (n 136) 46.

[177] Schwöbel-Patel (n 171) 8; Mikkel Jarle Christensen, 'The Professional Market of International Criminal Justice: Divisions of Labour and Patterns of Elite Reproduction' (2021) 19(4) Journal of International Criminal Justice 783, 785.

[178] Schwöbel-Patel (n 171) 86.

[179] Peter Brett and Line Engbo Gissel, 'Explaining African Participation in International Courts' (2018) 117 (467) African Affairs 195; Kamari Maxine Clarke, 'Why Africa?, in Richard H. Steinberg (ed), *Contemporary Issues Facing the International Criminal Court* (Brill Nijhoff 2016) 326, 332; See also Kamari Maxine Clarke "'We Ask for Justice, You Give Us Law': The Rule of Law, Economic Markets and the Reconfiguration of Victimhood" in Christian de Vos, Sara Kendall, and Carsten Stahn (eds), *Contested Justice: The Politics and Practice of International Criminal Court Interventions* (CUP 2015).

and displacement, such as women survivors of SGBV and former child soldiers, the Court creates the ideological terms on which they are included; it creates 'victim-perpetrators'. Not guilty of the crimes they suffered, victim-perpetrators are nonetheless blameworthy for their persisting condition of destitution. Victims are integrated into international legal relations, which are distinct articulations of global capitalist relations, but on precarious terms.[180]

In this process of integration, ideology not only influences beliefs but constitutes its subjects. The subject is continuously constructed and reconstructed in its encounter with powerful institutions and their agents at different levels. This also means there is no prior, authentic, innocent, true victim subject with values and beliefs that we can fall back on to measure the legitimacy of transitional justice institutions.[181] While transitional justice scholarship has been preoccupied with the question of whether international legal mechanisms are more or less legitimate than their local or domestic alternatives, it has paid less attention to their similarities as relatively top-down institutions which create their own ideological subjects.[182] Watching both the ICC's video on victim participation and a documentary on mato oput, commissioned by Ker Kwaro Acholi, the Acholi cultural institution, I was struck by how similar their optics were.[183] In both videos, experts teach victims how to play their roles. As such, the question, which one is more legitimate or true to people's beliefs, may be beside the point. Indeed, the problem of legitimacy is that it forecloses a material reading of the Court's relationship with victims, instead locking the analysis into a circular logic, where legal governance is the self-evident function of these institutions. Once we shift our analysis from victim participation and reparation as a legal or democratic form to a material form, we see that

[180] Rob Hunter, 'Critical Legal Studies and Marx's Critique: A Reappraisal' (2021) 31(2) Yale Journal of Law & the Humanities 389.

[181] Linda Alcoff and Laura Gray, 'Survivor Discourse: Transgression or Recuperation?' (1993) 18(2) Signs 260, 264.

[182] See also Maria Elander, *Figuring Victims in International Criminal Justice* (Routledge 2018) 32. Unlike Elander, my interest lies not in forms of representation but in the material production of victims as subjects ready for capitalism. In doing so, I'm using the slippage of the victim category; the victim being not only a victim of crime but a victim/loser of the global capitalist order. In Chapter 6, I will use the concept of 'capitalist complementarity' to make the point that all transitional justice institutions are compatible with capitalist relations.

[183] IntlCriminalCourt, 'Victims' participation before the International Criminal Court (ICC)' *YouTube* (23 April 2013) https://www.youtube.com/watch?v=chymGL8teX4 (accessed 11 January 2022); weinformers1, 'Mato Oput Acholi Traditional Justice System' *YouTube* (17 April 2010) https://www.youtube.com/watch?v=eb2hnrkvRXA (accessed 30 July 2023) (all three parts). See also Branch (n 103).

transitional justice institutions, not only the ICC, play important roles in the capitalist transformation of peripheries in the Global South.

On an institutional level, critical ideology theory, moreover, helps us grasp the ideological effects of the Court's everyday victim practices. Whether or not the Court is a good thing, it is 'there', 'on the ground', engaging victims, not as abstraction, but as flesh- and-blood subjects. While legitimacy assumes the existence of passive subjects that accept governance institutions as long as they adhere to certain principles (e.g., legal, traditional or charismatic),[184] ideology creates active subjects who come to the Court's meetings and participate in its trials. By 'going local', the Court creates and includes these victims, and in the process also shifts blame for its failures onto its subjects.

In the shadows of the Court's intervention, as the next chapters will show, victims and intermediaries, nonetheless, have their own dealings and meaning-making processes. While legal interpellation has been quite effective in Northern Uganda, the attraction of the law lies less in its method than in its promise of recognition, discipline and, ultimately, material wealth. Indeed, many Northern Ugandans embrace the ICC as a disciplinary method in a community grappling with staggering change. A local healer I interviewed was very clear when I asked her how they deal with rape: 'We call the police. The law is important . . . they should go to prison. We need to teach them a lesson.'[185] Invoking the symbolic role of the Court in Northern Uganda, an ICC outreach officer observed:

> ICC has become a household theme in the communities, and that is very important in maintaining peace and stability. Because people know that if something happened, even if it's not a major crime, I can go to the local authority for it to be addressed. So that alone, it is a step forward in fighting impunity, not very big crime, but a law-and-order framework and sending a clear message that impunity has no place.[186]

The law promises a better future by projecting the lives of the 'Subject', the ideology producer and former colonizer. If we do things like the

[184] Max Weber, *Law in Economy and Society* (Simon and Schuster 1954 (1967)) 336; Martin E Spencer, 'Weber on Legitimate Norms and Authority' (1970) 21(2) The British Journal of Sociology 123, 123–25.

[185] Interview with Healer, Gulu (29 July 2019).

[186] Interview with Registry Assistant, Gulu (17 July 2019).

colonizers (through law), one day we will live like them (living off other people's labour).[187]

More mundanely, the Court, for many victims, has become part of their everyday social reproduction and subsistence strategies. The latter, however, always override the former which means that the Court can easily fall into oblivion or disrepute. The fragility of legal interpellation also explained the nervousness of victims' stakeholders about the global pandemic. When the Covid-19 lockdown halted outreach and victims' meetings in 2020, the Court's victim staff were anxious to maintain victims' commitment. As the head of VPRS lamented: 'To organize meetings virtually is very difficult outside of capitals. At the moment, we have a scarce footprint on the ground because of Covid-19, which is a huge challenge for victim participation.'[188] Without regular outreach and victims' meetings, the Court risks being forgotten: 'Actually, we are thinking little about the trial because we cannot come together, we cannot interact, and we are preoccupied with thinking about how to survive during this lockdown', Stella, a community member from Barlonyo, told the International Justice Monitor.[189] Pamela from Abok agreed, 'for me I think people are more focused on survival for now, but of course we cannot forget that the ruling is coming soon'.[190] People forget because they are preoccupied with subsistence and reproductive work even though that work is rarely acknowledged much less remunerated. In fact, talking to the victims' lawyers, their concern was less to overcome victims' resistance to the Court, or even to make them understand how the ICC works, but to make them remember. As one field assistant put it: 'they [the victims] come for the meeting, they understand, the next day they've forgotten'.[191] The Court fights forgetting more than resistance. Or rather, forgetting is a form of resistance, as Chapter 6 will show, a typical 'weapon of the weak' that erodes power without openly challenging it.[192] The Court constantly needs to overwrite people's other roles and concerns.

[187] On how colonialism worked through mimicry see Homi Bhabha, 'Of Mimicry and Man: The Ambivalence of Colonial Discourse' (1984) 28 Discipleship: A Special Issue on Psychoanalysis 125.

[188] Redress (n 26).

[189] Lino Owor Ogora, 'Communities in Northern Uganda Optimistic for a Timely Judgment in Ongwen's Case' *International Justice Monitor* (16 June 2020) https://www.ijmonitor.org/2020/06/communities-in-northern-uganda-optimistic-for-a-timely-judgment-in-ongwens-case/ (accessed 21 April 2022).

[190] ibid.

[191] Interview with Field Assistant (n 55).

[192] James Scott, *Weapons of the Weak: Everyday Forms of Peasant Resistance* (Yale UP 1985).

4

Translators, Compradors, or Ideological Labourers? The Role of the ICC's Intermediaries

ICC Local Stakeholder Outreach Meeting, Update by the Defence Lawyer, Churchill Courts Hotel, Gulu (Uganda), 23 July 2019

Ongwen's defence lawyer is in town to update 'local stakeholders' on the ICC's case. The setting is different from the Court's community outreach event that I described in Chapter 3. Rather than orating to village residents under mango trees, he is speaking to NGO professionals, religious and cultural leaders in an air-conditioned hotel room. Churchill Courts is a decent hotel frequented by international visitors. As he speaks, a photographer whizzes around, snapping shots of the attendees, who can later buy their pictures in a pretty frame, branding their role as a 'local ICC stakeholder'.

The defence lawyer opens the meeting by asking his wife to share her impressions from visiting Dominic Ongwen in the ICC's detention centre. His wife tells the audience:

> Dominic Ongwen is very charming and intelligent. He is a man whom everyone who has interacted with him would love to spend more time with. He was captured when he was nine years old, to live in the forests with the monkeys. How do you think this child would turn out? Would he still adapt like the humans live or like the monkeys live? He would definitely be like the monkeys. Ongwen needs help. It wasn't his fault that he was taken where he went. He is actually a victim. Because when you are under the leadership of someone who is making orders, it's like when you have a boss. You don't have a right when your boss says 'go and do this'; would you refuse? You cannot refuse because you are afraid of losing your job. You are afraid of losing what you have. So, for me, Ongwen is a victim. We should pray that he gets out of that situation. He is a very happy and charming young

Victims and the Labour of Justice at the International Criminal Court. Leila Ullrich, Oxford University Press.
 DOI: 10.1093/9780191915048.003.0004

> man. And if he comes back to this community, he can bring so much to this community.[1]
>
> After she finishes her remarks, the defence lawyer observes: 'We have laid the basic foundation of what I'm going to say . . . it's not much.'[2]

It was true. That was the gist of the verbose lecture that followed. The defence lawyer did not say much about the ongoing legal proceedings or his legal strategy; the key purpose of his speech was to make Ongwen relatable and sympathetic. Presumably, that is why he asked his wife to perform this emotional rather than legal labour. Of course, there is a tension in his wife's portrayal of Ongwen as both 'one of us' ('charming and intelligent'; 'he can bring so much to this community') and 'like a monkey' who blindly followed orders. Curiously, she likened the relationship between a child and their violent abductor to the relationship between an employee and their boss. 'Would you refuse?', she asked the professional audience before concluding herself: 'You cannot refuse because you are afraid of losing your job.' It is a striking analogy. It both unmasks the coercive obedience hidden behind the veil of professional work and creates commonalties between Ongwen, 'the monkey', and the 'business casual' audience. Contradictory or not, the defence lawyer and his wife project an imagery of Ongwen that local stakeholders can identify with. Ongwen could be you. He is one of us. Of course, the 'us' is a different 'us' from the one the defence lawyer constructed for victims in the previous chapter. It is the 'us' of a local elite defined through professional rather than manual work.

This chapter is about the Court's intermediaries who attend such 'local stakeholder' meetings.[3] Intermediaries are actors ranging from individuals such as victims, family members of victims, and community leaders to grassroots organizations and national NGOs in the Court's situation countries. They help the Court with evidence collection, community outreach, victim identification, victim participation, reparation, and assistance on the ground. The Court defines an intermediary as 'someone who comes between one person and another; who facilitates contact or provides a link

1 Field notes, Gulu, Uganda (23 July 2019).

2 ibid.

3 The chapter builds on Leila Ullrich, 'Beyond the 'Global–Local Divide': Local Intermediaries, Victims and the Justice Contestations of the International Criminal Court' (2016) 14(3) Journal of International Criminal Justice 543.

between one of the organs or units of the Court or Counsel on the one hand, and victims, witnesses, beneficiaries of reparations and/or affected communities more broadly on the other'.[4]

The Office of the Prosecutor (OTP) has admitted that 'it is not an exaggeration to say that the prosecutions themselves are impossible without the assistance of intermediaries'.[5] In situation countries such as Kenya and Sudan where the government is hostile to the ICC's intervention and state cooperation is often wanting, the Court heavily depends on the help of in-country actors for nearly all of its operations.[6] However, the Court needs intermediaries in all situation countries, hostile to the ICC or not, particularly when the security situation is volatile.[7] As a Registry official told me:

> We have a new situation or case somewhere, we have to immediately, sometimes very quickly for us . . . but even quicker, of course, for the prosecutor, we have to be able to work there. We can't just walk into the places, where we think that the victims are, and say, 'hi, here we are'. We have to rely on local people to lead us to the victims and especially local people who potentially have the trust of and the knowledge of the victims.[8]

But how can we make sense of the role of intermediaries in the broader enterprise of international criminal justice?

In this chapter, I will illuminate the role of intermediaries through theories of ideology, social reproduction, and racial capitalism. To do so,

[4] ICC, 'Guidelines Governing the Relations between the Court and Intermediaries for the Organs and Units of the Court and Counsel working with intermediaries' (March 2014) 5 https://www.icc-cpi.int/sites/default/files/GRCI-Eng.pdf (accessed 7 August 2023).

[5] *Prosecutor v Lubanga* (Prosecution's Submissions in Response to Trial Chamber's Oral Request of 10 February 2010) [2010] ICC-01/04-01/06-2310-Red) § 12.

[6] The Sudanese government became more cooperative after mass protests led to the ousting of Sudanese president and ICC indictee, Omar al Bashir, in 2019, but the situation is very uncertain especially since fighting between the Sudanese military and the paramilitary Rapid Support Forces (RSF) broke out in 2023. Omar al Bashir remains in custody in Sudan. See Zeinab Mohammed Salih and Oliver Holmes, 'Sudan's ex-leader Omar al-Bashir being held in military hospital, says army' *The Guardian* (26 April 2023) https://www.theguardian.com/world/2023/apr/26/sudan-former-president-accused-of-genocide-may-be-free-after-prison-attack (accessed 6 August 2023). For Kenya see Janet Anderson and Benjamin Duerr, 'In a Storm of Lies and Half-truths: The Role of Media Professionals in Spreading and Combatting Misinformation about the International Criminal Court' (2022) 20(1) JICJ 191.

[7] In the *Lubanga* case, the volatile security in Ituri province in the DRC was cited as the main reason for using intermediaries. *Prosecutor v Lubanga* (Judgment pursuant to Article 74 of the Statute) [2012] ICC-01/04-01/06-2842, § 167 ('the only solution to the security problem was to use intermediaries, who enabled the team to contact witnesses').

[8] Interview with Senior Official, Registry, The Hague (16 December 2013).

I will first turn to the different interpretive frames that define the role of those who 'go in between'. Liberal scholars and NGO practitioners, on the one hand, tend to see intermediaries through the prism of a 'global-local divide', where they act as cultural translators who either promote or erode the Court's local legitimacy.[9] Critical scholars, by contrast, claim that global justice is better understood as a commodity rather than a cultural form.[10] From a critical perspective, it is the figure of the comprador rather than the translator that leaps to the eye. Comprador is the Portuguese term for 'buyer' and describes 'a person who acts as an agent for foreign organizations engaged in investment, trade, or economic or political exploitation'.[11] The term developed in the nineteenth and twentieth centuries to capture the role of Chinese merchants in the European colonization of East Asia.[12] Intermediaries, in this reading, buy and sell justice and victims as commodities and take a cut as compradors. They work for the Court but also put the victims to work. Yet, is justice best understood as a commodity? If so, who creates its value and who buys it? What are the markets on which this commodity is sold? Are states, the Court's 'shareholders', also the consumers of international criminal justice?[13]

This chapter argues that what intermediaries do for the Court is better understood as socially reproductive rather than commodified labour; it is closer to the unpaid domestic labour women perform in the home. I call this 'ideological labour'. Ideological labour reproduces capitalist relations

[9] Open Society Justice Initiative (OSJI), 'Intermediaries and the International Criminal Court: A Role for the Assembly of States Parties' (2011) http://www.opensocietyfoundations.org/sites/default/files/intermediaries-20111212.pdf (accessed 10 April 2023); Holly Dranginis, 'The Middle Man: Intermediaries of International Criminal Justice' *Justice in Conflict* (21 August 2011) http://justiceinconflict.org/2011/08/21/the-middle-man-the-intermediaries-of-international-criminal-justice/ (accessed 10 April 2023); FIDH, 'Five Myths about Victim Participation in ICC Proceedings' (December 2014) 19 https://www.fidh.org/IMG/pdf/cpi649a.pdf (accessed 10 April 2023). See also Mariana Pena, 'The role of intermediaries and third parties in victim participation' in Kinga Tibori-Szabo and Megan Hirst (eds), *Victim Participation in International Criminal Justice: Practitioners' Guide* (TMC Asser Press 2017) 95.

[10] Sara Kendall, 'Commodifying Global Justice: Economies of Accountability at the International Criminal Court' (2015) 13 Journal of International Criminal Justice 113; Christine Schwöbel-Patel, *Marketing Global Justice: The Political Economy of International Criminal Law* (CUP 2021).

[11] Lexico Dictionary https://www.lexico.com/definition/comprador (accessed 27 November 2021).

[12] As Hui Po-Keung observes, 'in the case of Hong Kong, we can clearly see that the Chinese middlemen, that is the compradors, were indispensable actors making possible colonial domination'. Hui Po-Keung, 'Comprador politics and middleman capitalism' in Tak-Wing Ngo (ed), *Hong Kong's History: State and Society under Colonial Rule* (Routledge 1999) 30, 42.

[13] Kendall (n 10) 113.

not only by interpellating people as workers in the public sphere, but also by managing them at the public/private intersection where lawyers and victims, workers and homemakers, NGO professionals and subsistence farmers, law and justice, and society and nature meet. The public, in the capitalist imaginary, is where labour is visible and paid, whereas the private is where labour is invisible and not paid or barely paid.[14] Ideological labour is thus also a form of border management that regulates people's movement between productive and reproductive, market and non-market, public and private spheres. But why do intermediaries do ideological labour for the Court?

Here the ICC's own terminology is revealing. The Court recruits intermediaries as 'local stakeholders'.[15] They have a stake in the Court because they have a stake in the division between manual and mental labour.[16] The key role of the ICC's intermediaries, I contend, is not to bridge cultural gaps but to maintain and manage divisions of labour. Both the cultural translator and the comprador image obscure the role of intermediaries in postcolonial economies and their historical connections to what Mamdani calls the 'decentralized despotism' of colonial rule. Here, the colonial intermediary, the customary chief, is an important predecessor.[17] Unlike their colonial forerunners, intermediaries no longer extract forced labour or collect taxes for colonial regimes, but they ideologically form and discipline productive and reproductive workers in the Global South.

The ideological role of intermediaries is, however, not a simple matter. It is often contradictory as it lies in policing classed, gendered and racialized divisions of labour that intermediaries themselves partake in. The complexity lies in how the intermediary exploits and is exploited at the same time and often along the very same lines. I have tried to capture this relationship through the notion of a blame cascade which I have already outlined in Chapter 3. What ties the different actors in the blame cascade together is

[14] I use 'public' and 'private' in inverted commas because the distinction is itself a capitalist fiction. See eg Louis Althusser, 'Ideology and ideological state apparatuses (Notes towards an investigation)' in Louis Althusser, *Lenin and Philosophy and Other Essays* (NLB 1977) 121, 137 ('The distinction between the public and the private is a distinction internal to bourgeois law, and valid in the (subordinate) domains in which bourgeois law exercises its 'authority').

[15] Amnesty International and TMC Asser Instituut, 'The Rome Statute at 40' (May 2021) 13 https://www.asser.nl/media/794895/report-rome-statute-at-40-final.pdf (accessed 1 April 2023).

[16] I use mental labour here to refer to intellectual, professional, and creative labour.

[17] Mahmood Mamdani, *Citizen and Subject: Contemporary Africa and the Legacy of Late Colonialism* (2nd edn, Princeton UP 2018).

labour rather than norms. The blame cascade extracts work by devaluing it, and thus rewrites the story of Sikkink's justice cascade.[18] Rather than justice norms flowing from the global to the local, the blame cascade carries both work and blame from the powerful to the powerless. If we read the relationship between the Court and victims through a 'labour' rather than a 'culture' lens, the key divide is no longer between the 'global' and the 'local' but between different forms of labour.[19] Who works what for what money? Whose labour is valued and how? Differentiating and devaluing labour not only cuts costs, but also shifts blame down. Intermediaries can be blamed for the Court's shortcomings, and they can be relied upon to blame and discipline victims. Those whose labour is not recognized can be blamed for 'not working', and those whose labour is recognized can be blamed for not working hard enough or not being competent enough. Legal expertise trumps other expertise; professional labour trumps manual labour.

The structure of this chapter mirrors the book's twofold argument. The book first shows how 'justice for victims' not only serves as an institutional justification, but also reproduces the Court by generating working subjects such as victims' lawyers, intermediaries, and victims. The book subsequently elucidates how 'justice for victims' also provides an entry point for the Court's broader ideological role of creating and managing capitalist subjects in the Global South. What makes the Court's ideological role so effective is precisely that its institutional definitions and legal functions conceal it. To grasp the Court's role as an intermediary of global capitalism, we cannot study it on its own terms, but need to work with and through the tensions that it ferments, as can be seen in its relationship with local intermediaries.

The chapter unfolds through six sections. Section 4.1 situates intermediaries in the Court's legal texts and discourse as well as in the wider literature. Section 4.2 analyses their role through a social reproduction lens, shifting our gaze from exchange to production and reproduction. It ponders what exactly intermediaries do in the production of international criminal justice and whether the latter is best understood as a commodity. Teasing

[18] Katherine Sikkink, *The Justice Cascade: How Human Rights Prosecutions are Changing World Politics* (WW Norton & Co 2011).

[19] It is noteworthy that while international NGOs have advocated for the Court to provide better protection for intermediaries, they have been less vocal on the question of their labour compensation. International Refugee Rights Initiative and Open Society Initiative, 'Commentary on the ICC Draft Guidelines on Intermediaries' (18 August 2011) 6 https://www.justiceinitiative.org/uploads/020e3651-cbf2-4fe7-8ab4-a9ef4e64a5ed/icc-intermediaries-commentary-20110818.pdf (accessed 17 December 2022).

out both the insights and the limitations of a commodity analysis, I eventually argue that intermediaries are better understood as ideology rather than commodity producers. Section 4.3, then, sheds light on the Court's contradictory approach to intermediaries and victims through a critical ideology analysis. Revisiting the blame cascade, the section unveils how the Court uses intermediaries not only to devalue labour but also to manage its own ideological contradictions. The section, finally, returns to the local stakeholder meeting in Gulu to ask why intermediaries accept their role with the Court, and how they in turn engage with victims in Northern Uganda.

Section 4.4 develops the notion of 'ideological labour' to specify what exactly intermediaries do for the Court and how victims relate to that labour. Section 4.5 departs from the ICC context to ask how we can move beyond the figures of both the 'cultural translator' and the 'market comprador' to make sense of the role of intermediaries in colonial capitalist relations. To answer that question, the section draws out the analogy between the ICC's intermediaries and colonial customary chiefs under British 'indirect rule' in Africa. Section 4.6 then illuminates how intermediaries manage ideological borders, especially between professional and manual, productive and reproductive, market and subsistence, legal and emotional labour. Intermediaries are border guards, and the most intense social struggles happen at the border. The border is key to understanding both capitalist reproduction and rupture.

4.1 Going between What? Situating the ICC's Intermediaries

Although intermediaries are essential for the Court's work on the ground, there is no legal framework or basis for using them in the Court's core texts.[20] In March 2014, the Court, therefore, adopted *Guidelines on Intermediaries* as a post-facto rationalization of a widespread practice.[21] 'That was one of the difficulties', one OTP official explained to me, 'to draft one protocol on intermediaries whereby everyone understands something completely different'.[22] The Guidelines are not only vague on the question

[20] ICC (n 4) 2. The exception are the Regulations of the Trust Fund for Victims (TFV) which state that the TFV can use intermediaries 'to facilitate the disbursement of reparations awards'. See Regulations of the Trust Fund for Victims, Resolution, r 67, ICC-ASP/4/Res.3 (3 December 2005).

[21] ICC (n 4).

[22] Interview with Counsel, OTP, The Hague (13 November 2013); ICC (n 4) 2–3.

of their implementation, but also leave the relationship between the Court and many of its intermediaries unclear. They only apply to intermediaries working under a contractual relationship with an organ or unit of the Court or counsel.[23] Their application to intermediaries without contract, including the significant number of intermediaries that are 'self-appointed' or chosen by victims or witnesses, will be determined on a case-by-case basis.[24] It is noteworthy that none of the intermediaries interviewed for this research in Kenya and Uganda indicated that they had a contract with the Court.

The guidelines do not appear to have changed much for how the Court uses intermediaries. Four years after their adoption, a Registry officer reflected:

> Nobody can do anything without intermediaries. So, we just came right back to where we were before. Everyone has their own relationship with intermediaries. It's not clear, whether the intermediary guidelines—that don't say anything—are being applied in any kind of uniform way. Who is the overseer of those things? Nobody knows. And I think, frankly, it's probably for the best, because I think that the relationship that each section or organ has with intermediaries is so different. To think that we could have a universal principle or guideline for all of us. It's just not practical.[25]

The guidelines represent, if not a fiction, at least a narrowing of who intermediaries are and what they do. While the guidelines insist that intermediaries should not perform 'core functions' of the Court, they also concede that what precisely those 'core functions' are is far from clear:

> The nature of the Court itself, with its many different organs and units, significantly complicates the relationship between the Court and intermediaries. While intermediaries may assist and support, they should

[23] ICC (n 4) 5–6, 10.

[24] ibid. In their recommendations to the ASP in November 2015, the Victims' Rights Working Group also asked the Court to address unresolved questions such as how the guidelines are used and how many intermediaries actually benefit from a contract. See Victims' Rights Working Group, 'Recommendations to the 14th Session of the Assembly of States Parties' (November 2015) 3 https://redress.org/wp-content/uploads/2017/12/November-Victims-Rights-Working-Group-Recommendations-to-the-14th-Session-of-the-Assembly-of-States-Parties.pdf (accessed 6 August 2023).

[25] Interview with Legal Officer, Registry, The Hague (1 June 2018).

> not be called upon to undertake core functions of the Court. However, this seemingly clear restriction is blurred by the fact that core functions may differ from one organ or unit of the Court to another.[26]

How exactly a diverse and divided Court should 'use' intermediaries thus remains contested.[27]

Even though the ICC actively solicits their help, usually without remuneration,[28] intermediaries are portrayed as a liability for the Court.[29] This perception partly stems from the events surrounding the ICC's first trial, the *Lubanga* trial. As a drove of journalists descended on The Hague to report on this shiny new court, the first prosecution witness suddenly retracted his testimony: he told the judges that he was not a child soldier and that intermediaries had coached him to lie to the Court.[30] Since then,

[26] ICC (n 4) 2.

[27] Indeed, what constitute the Court's core functions remains contested. Outreach, for example, has been both considered an 'important' and even 'essential' function of the Court and a 'non-core mandate' which could be funded through voluntary contributions. See Coalition for the International Criminal Court, 'Comments and Recommendations to the 11th Session of the Assembly of States Parties' (9 November 2012) 7 https://iccforum.com/media/background/outreach/2012-11-09_CICC_Communications_Team_Comments_and_Recommendations_to_the_Eleventh_Session_of_the_ASP.pdf (accessed 6 August 2023). For an affirmation of outreach see Assembly of States Parties, Resolution ICC-ASP/21/Res.2 'Strengthening the International Criminal Court and the Assembly of States Parties' (adopted at the 9th plenary meeting on 9 December 2022) 3, § 74.

[28] According to the OTP's investigation team leader in Lubanga, 'the majority of the intermediaries were not paid and did not request payment. However, if they travelled as part of their activities, their expenses for transport and communication were reimbursed. "Up to a certain point" it had not been proposed to pay intermediaries for their work, because it was undertaken on a voluntary basis. P-0582 suggested the investigators were very stringent when reimbursing costs'. *Prosecutor v Lubanga* (Judgment pursuant to Article 74 of the Statute) [2012] ICC-01/04-01/06-2842, § 198. More evidence on the Court's remuneration of intermediaries is provided below.

[29] This is particularly evident in the defence's allegations against intermediaries, but it also reflects a broader discourse at the Court. It is also evident from the 'Code of Conduct for Intermediaries', which stipulates that intermediaries shall not participate in 'corrupt practices' or misuse or abuse their relationship with the Court. ICC, 'Code of Conduct for Intermediaries' (March 2014) § 3.3, § 3.4 https://www.icc-cpi.int/sites/default/files/CCI-Eng.pdf (accessed 6 August 2023). See also Déirdre Clancy, '"They told us we would be part of history": reflections on the civil society intermediary experience in the Great Lakes region' in Christian de Vos, Sara Kendall, and Carsten Stahn (eds), *Contested Justice: The Politics and Practice of International Criminal Court Interventions* (CUP 2015) 219, 221 ('When the conduct of intermediaries was placed under judicial scrutiny in the ICC's first trial of Thomas Lubanga, intermediaries also found themselves portrayed as betrayers of trust, both of local communities and of the cause of international justice itself').

[30] *Prosecutor v Lubanga* (Transcript) [2010] ICC-01/04-01/06-T-236-Red2-ENG, 20/21. See also, 'Lubanga witness says he was paid US$200 to tell lies' *International Justice Monitor* (8 February 2010) https://www.ijmonitor.org/2010/02/lubanga-witness-says-he-was-paid-us200-to-tell-lies/ (accessed 17 December 2022).

defence counsel have, on numerous occasions, challenged the Court's use of intermediaries and demanded the disclosure of their identities, alleging that they have tampered with witnesses and unduly influenced victims.[31] In its 'Decision on Intermediaries' of 31 May 2010, Trial Chamber I noted that 'the precise role of the intermediaries (together with the manner in which they discharged their functions) has become an issue of major importance in this trial'.[32] When asked about intermediaries, my interviewees at the OTP became reticent: 'Intermediaries is a very crucial and sensitive thing for us, so I would not like to go into detail', one said.[33]

Unlike the Court's practitioners,[34] scholars and civil society often view intermediaries more positively, interpreting their role through the prism of a 'global-local divide'. The latter highlights the distance and even mismatch between the ICC's far-away international justice bureaucracy and the local justice ideas and rituals of affected communities in the Court's situation countries.[35] This distance is often visualized by contrasting sterile images of the Court's building in The Hague with colourful pictures of communities gathering under tropical trees 'in Africa'.[36] Invoking the global–local divide,

[31] *Prosecutor v Banda and Jerbo* (Defence Application to restrain legal representatives for the victims a/1646/10 & a/1647/10 from acting in proceedings and for an order excluding the involvement of specified intermediaries) [2010] ICC-02/05-03/09-113, §§ 14–20; *Prosecutor v Lubanga* (Judgment pursuant to Article 74 of the Statute) [2012] ICC-01/04-01/06-2842, §§ 178–82; *Prosecutor v Ruto and Sang* (Public redacted version of 'Ruto defence request to appoint an amicus prosecutor') [2016] ICC-01/09-01/11-2028-Red), §§ 1–4. Institute for War & Peace Reporting, 'ICC Intermediaries Allegedly Concocted Evidence' (12 February 2010) https://iwpr.net/global-voices/icc-intermediaries-allegedly-concocted-evidence (accessed 10 April 2023). On the role of witness proofing see Wayne Jordash, 'The Practice of "Witness Proofing" in International Criminal Tribunals: Why the International Criminal Court Should Prohibit the Practice' (2009) 22(3) Leiden Journal of International Law 501.

[32] *Prosecutor v Lubanga* (Redacted Decision on Intermediaries) [2010] ICC-01/04-01/06-2434-Red2, § 135. Intermediaries allegedly also played a role in witness tampering in the Kenyan cases. Human Rights Watch, 'Kenya: ICC Defendant Found Dead Tried on Alleged Witness Tampering in Case Involving Kenyan President Ruto' (2 November 2022) https://www.hrw.org/news/2022/11/02/kenya-icc-defendant-found-dead (accessed 11 March 2023).

[33] Interview with Attorney, OTP, The Hague (29 November 2013).

[34] Given my focus on the ICC's victim engagement, I mainly interviewed the ICC's judges, the Registry's staff, and victims' lawyers.

[35] Luke Moffett, 'Elaborating Justice for Victims at the International Criminal Court' (2015) 13 Journal of International Criminal Justice 281, 286; Justice Hub, 'My Justice: Mariana Pena' (27 February 2015) https://ciccglobaljustice.wordpress.com/2015/03/03/mariana-pena-justice-is-a-human-value/ (accessed 18 February 2024). See also ICC, 'Integrated Strategy for External Relations, Public Information and Outreach' http://www.icc-cpi.int/NR/rdonlyres/425E80BA-1EBC-4423-85C6-D4F2B93C7506/185049/ICCPIDSWBOR0307070402_IS_En.pdf (accessed 10 April 2023).

[36] See eg the book covers of Kamari Clarke, *Fictions of Justice: The International Criminal Court and the Challenge of Legal Pluralism* (CUP 2009); Rosalind Shaw, Lars Waldorf, and Pierre Hazan (eds), *Localizing transitional justice: interventions and priorities after mass violence* (Stanford UP 2010). See also Kieran McEvoy and Lorna McGregor, *Transitional Justice*

Human Rights NGOs such as FIDH and Amnesty International have urged the Court to improve its local engagement.[37] From this perspective, intermediaries can be part of the solution to the Court's foreignness. They can help to bridge the linguistic, cultural, and knowledge gaps between the ICC and local communities.[38]

Ostensibly, then, intermediaries appear in two different guises: either as a solution to the Court's local legitimacy problem or as a liability: potential cheaters and spoilers who threaten the Court's judicial integrity. Both images, however, form part of the global–local divide, which is the dominant interpretive frame in the socio-legal literature.[39] This frame construes intermediaries as 'norm translators' who vernacularize Western norms like human rights or international criminal accountability to make them intelligible to 'local cultures'.[40] Foregrounding their role as activists, some scholars express concern that the Court's training of intermediaries makes them closer to the Court's professionals. Haslam and Edmunds, for example, have argued that the Court's adoption of guidelines reflects and reinforces a broader move towards 'professionalizing' intermediaries, which 'is problematic to the extent to which it creates obstacles for the involvement of counter-hegemonic voices in international criminal law'.[41]

from Below: Grassroots Activism and the Struggle for Change (Hart Publishing 2008); Tim Kelsall, *Culture under Cross-Examination: International Justice and the Special Court for Sierra Leone* (CUP 2009).

[37] FIDH (n 9) 19; Amnesty International and TMC Asser Instituut, 'The Rome Statute at 40' (May 2021) 5,7 https://www.asser.nl/media/794895/report-rome-statute-at-40-final.pdf (accessed 6 August 2023) ('In fleshing out "where" engagement takes place, a distinction can be made between the "local" and the "global" . . . Serious consideration should be given by the ICC and all stakeholders as to how more local stakeholders can engage with the ICC in The Hague').

[38] OSJI (n 9); Dranginis (n 9); Pena (n 9) 95.

[39] See eg Kristina Simion, *Rule of Law Intermediaries: Building Influence in Myanmar* (CUP 2021); Clancy (n 29). The pervasiveness of the global–local divide in human rights studies has been analysed and criticized by Mark Goodale, 'Locating Rights, Envisioning Law between the Global and the Local' in Mark Goodale and Sally Engle Merry (eds), *The Practice of Human Rights: Tracking Law between the Global and the Local* (CUP 2007).

[40] Aaron Boesenecker and Leslie Vinjamuri, 'Lost in Translation? Civil Society, Faith-Based Organizations and the Negotiation of International Norms' (2011) 5(3) The International Journal of Transitional Justice 345, 345; Sally Engle Merry, 'Transnational Human Rights and Local Activism: Mapping the Middle' (2006) 108(1) American Anthropologist 38; Amitav Acharya, 'How Ideas Spread: Whose Norms Matter? Norm Localization and Institutional Change in Asian Regionalism' (2004) 58(2) International Organization 239, 241.

[41] Emily Haslam and Rod Edmunds, 'Managing a New Partnership: Professionalization, Intermediaries and the International Criminal Court' (2013) 24 Criminal Law Forum 49, 49.

Yet, 'professionalizing' intermediaries is not necessarily in the Court's interest. As 'activists'[42] and 'carers', the ethical standards expected of them are impossibly high. They can be accused of abusing the Court's and victims' trust by gatekeeping or lying. The intermediary as 'gatekeeper' is the logical pendant to the intermediary as 'translator'. There is always the possibility of them being unfaithful translators, of taking advantage of their role.[43] Both images hide the ideological work that the global–local divide itself does for the Court; it obscures what intermediaries actually do: they work for the Court, often for free. It is easier to exploit them if their labour is hidden, denied, and deprofessionalized. Yet, what exactly is the nature of that labour and what does it produce?

Marx elevated the production of commodities to the centre stage of the capitalist system, challenging classical political economists' focus on commodity exchange. Profit does not emerge through exchange but through production, Marx argued. The commodity harboured a secret, the secret of surplus value, which is the value that the worker creates for capital but is not compensated for through the wage.[44] The driving force of capitalism is the appropriation and accumulation of surplus value as profit. But by centring the commodity and the relentless commodification of life, we miss the background conditions of capitalism, which make the production of the commodity possible in the first place, namely labour relations, and the reproduction of society and nature.[45]

Social reproduction theorists have highlighted that much of society's reproduction happens outside of what would traditionally be thought of as 'the market', namely in the home, in schools, in hospitals, and in nature.[46]

[42] The team leader of the OTP's investigation in the *Lubanga* case referred to intermediaries as activists ('They met activists, including certain "militant activists", during their initial mission who wanted to provide information, and this led them to identify the first intermediaries'). *Prosecutor v Lubanga* (Judgment pursuant to Article 74 of the Statute) [2012] ICC-01/04-01/06-2842, § 143, § 167 ('human rights activists') § 184 ('in reality, the intermediaries were activists').

[43] *Prosecutor v Lubanga* (Judgment pursuant to Article 74 of the Statute) [2012] ICC-01/04-01/06-2842, § 205 ('P-0582 was aware of the risk that the intermediaries might manipulate the investigators they dealt with').

[44] Karl Marx, *Capital Volume I: A Critique of Political Economy* (Penguin Books 1990) 280.

[45] Nancy Fraser, 'Behind Marx's Hidden Abode: For an Expanded Conception of Capitalism' (2014) 86 New Left Review 1; Nancy Fraser, 'Crisis of care? On the social reproductive contradictions of contemporary capitalism' in Tithi Bhattacharya (ed), *Social Reproduction Theory: Remapping Class, Recentering Oppression* (Pluto Press 2017) 21.

[46] Tithi Bhattacharya, 'Introduction: Mapping social reproduction theory' in Tithi Bhattacharya (ed), *Social Reproduction Theory: Remapping Class, Recentering Oppression* (Pluto Press 2017) 1–2.

Capitalism needs these non-market spheres, relationships and values to exist, replenish and expand.[47] Hidden behind the equality of market relations (buyer-seller) is the inequality of production relations (capitalist-worker), and hidden behind the gender equality of productive relations (male worker-female worker) is the gender inequality of reproductive relations (husband-wife, parent-child).[48] Social reproduction theory thus

> reveals the essence-category of capitalism, its animating force, to be human labor and not commodities. In doing so, it exposes to critical scrutiny the superficiality of what we commonly understand to be 'economic' processes and restores to the economic process its messy, sensuous, gendered, raced, and unruly component: living human beings, capable of following orders as well as flouting them.[49]

This chapter argues that ideology, too, is a form of social reproduction labour. Social reproduction entails both ideology-making and people-making and it is precisely the tensions between the two that creates 'human beings, capable of following orders as well as flouting them'.[50] But what does ideological labour add to our understanding of the role of intermediaries?

4.2 The Role of Intermediaries: Selling Justice Commodities or Creating Justice Ideologies?

Intermediaries (like victims) is both a highly sought after and a precarious status. Not everyone can be an intermediary. There are different notions of who should be an intermediary and thus reap the meagre financial benefits associated with the position. Victims in Uganda often insist that those among them who lost loved ones are the most deserving and should thus become the Court's intermediaries.[51] But the Court does not want the most vulnerable victims to be intermediaries. They want the most useful, those who speak the Court's language and have the capacity to mobilize others.

47 David Harvey, 'The New Imperialism: Accumulation By Dispossession' (2004) 40 Socialist Register 63; Fraser, 'Crisis of care?' (n 45).

48 Lise Vogel, *Marxism and the Oppression of Women: Toward a Unitary Theory* (2nd edn, Brill 2013); Silvia Federici, *Revolution at Point Zero: Housework, Reproduction, and Feminist Struggle* (PM Press 2021).

49 Bhattacharya (n 46) 19.

50 ibid.

51 Interview with Assistant of Victim's Lawyer, Kampala (9 July 2019).

The Court's criteria for selecting intermediaries include: (i) adherence to confidentiality and respect for dignity, (ii) credibility and reliability, and (iii) capacity, knowledge and experience including 'cultural, social and linguistic proximity to affected communities'.[52] The Court interpellates the local elite as 'ICC stakeholders' and then recruits intermediaries among them. Every intermediary is a local stakeholder but not every local stakeholder can become an intermediary. The Court keeps intermediaries on their toes, playing them off against each other and substituting them if they disappoint.[53] Intermediaries, like victims, need to remain a suspicious and contested category.

The Court's problem is that it depends on intermediaries including for core functions such as investigations, evidence collection and victim participation. This dependence is structural as the Court cannot operate effectively in seventeen countries across four continents without cheap or free local labour. Using intermediaries is, therefore, primarily a cost-saving measure for the Court.[54] As one Registry officer told me,

> You know, there was this really stupid thing that the court did where they were like, 'intermediaries—they are risky; let's stop using them; let's do things ourselves', and that happened to coincide with the same moment where the states were like, 'oh, zero growth-budget'. So, we don't have resources and we're not using intermediaries. Oh wait, we can't do anything.[55]

This dependence is masked by hiding intermediaries' labour. 'The services provided by an intermediary are generally provided on a voluntary basis', the Guidelines on Intermediaries stipulate.[56] Indeed, the Court

[52] ICC (n 4) 8–10.

[53] Clancy identifies three phases in the Court's relationship with intermediaries: 'The first phase was generally characterised by enthusiasm and energy, the second by disappointment and retreat, and the third by mutual wariness and efforts to corral intermediaries through regulation'. Clancy (n 29) 228.

[54] ICC, 'Second Report of the Court on the financial implications of the draft Guidelines governing the relations between the Court and Intermediaries' Assembly of States Parties (30 October 2013) (ICC-ASP/12/53) § 19 ('it is important to reiterate that the use of intermediaries is ultimately cost effective for the Court. Intermediaries undertake work that would be extremely costly for the Court to perform, such as communicating with victims and witnesses in remote and sometime insecure locations').

[55] Interview with Legal Officer, Registry, The Hague (1 June 2018).

[56] ICC (n 4) 6.

insists that 'the function of an intermediary to the ICC is in principle unpaid'.[57] There is no question of paying wages or even paying for services. The Court can only 'reimburse' intermediaries for eligible expenses such as transport or telephone air time incurred for activities explicitly requested by the Court or Counsel.[58] The Court's staff often point out that intermediaries are local people 'who have their foot in the door'[59] and/or 'have the trust of the victims'.[60] Their asset is not professional (legal) expertise but their cultural and personal proximity to victims (not least because they are often victims themselves), or their role and networks as community leaders or activists.[61]

By reinventing intermediaries as 'carers' or 'activists', by associating them with the reproductive sphere, their labour is hidden while moral expectations are heightened.[62] Victim engagement demands a lot of emotional

[57] ICC, 'Questions and Answers: The Court's Engagement with Intermediaries', 2 https://www.icc-cpi.int/sites/default/files/QA-ICC-intermediariesEng.pdf (accessed 6 August 2023).

[58] ICC (n 4) 12–13.

[59] Interview with Legal Officer, Registry, The Hague (12 November 2013).

[60] Interview with Senior Official, Registry, The Hague (16 December 2013). The single judge in the *Ntaganda* case gave the following instructions to the Victims Participation and Reparations Section (VPRS) on the use of intermediaries: 'Such individuals should be identified and selected from amongst those vested with leading roles in the affected communities and who, by the nature of their positions, *are trusted by the population*. Such individuals may include, for example, the following: community leaders, chefs de village, or staff members of local NGOs. *The VPRS is instructed to make the most extensive use of the assistance provided by intermediaries* in the field pursuant to their developed best practices' (emphasis added). *Prosecutor v Ntaganda* (Decision Establishing Principles on the Victims' Application Process) [2013] ICC-01/04-02/06-67, § 27.

[61] ICC, 'Strategic Plan for Outreach of the International Criminal Court' (2006) ICC-ASP/5/12, § 66 ('The development of partnerships is important for reaching the broader local population through culturally appropriate intermediaries, particularly where ICC staff is unable to contact the general public due to lack of resources, logistical or other constraints or security concerns'); Interview with Senior Official, Registry, The Hague (16 December 2013); Interview with Legal Officer, The Hague (21 January 2014) ('You also have individuals, maybe like religious leaders, human rights activists that took the role to assist the communities and because they are more literate or for different reasons they have the trust of the people . . . And we also have people who assist on the basis of the feeling of home, for example because it is a member of the family but you may not have formal relationship with them'). The Independent Expert Review also notes that the VPRS relies heavily of 'local activists' for identifying victims ('Similar criticisms of the time-scale and reliance on local activists were made about the position in Georgia, where it was only possible to submit 69 representations on behalf of 6,335 victims in the 30 days allowed. It is said that the total number of victims there is in the region of 28,000'). ICC, 'Independent Expert Review of the International Criminal Court and the Rome Statute System: Final Report' (30 September 2020) § 857.

[62] As Clancy notes in her research on ICC intermediaries: 'the idea that local interlocutors should function as mere volunteers of the Court divested of their own politics or interests is prevalent', and remarks further in a footnote, 'it is interesting that the political, ego or careerist ambitions of others in the international justice constituency do not appear to attract the same degree of suspicion and scrutiny [as those of intermediaries]'. See Clancy (n 29) 227 (n 21).

labour. Note, for example, how a victims' officer in Uganda described her work of facilitating victims' applications to participate in the Court's proceedings:

> They gave us six months to file applications after the confirmation of charges . . . One thing that struck me is that many victims, and I met with all of the 4100 victims, for all or most of them, it was the first time that they ever sat down with someone to listen to them, to take down their story, from their perspective, for them to understand what actually happened to them. They felt it was one of the best things that could ever happen to them . . . Doing this was, personally, and I come from Northern Uganda, so it was an interesting thing, but it was also sad, because I didn't see how we were able to close the wounds that we were opening through the application process . . . It was emotionally draining. In fact, I got sick after the application process, like, it was manic; it was very fast; it was emotional. For me, there was just too much that I had to deal with.[63]

The quote illustrates the thick emotional texture of the legal process and the quantity and intensity of the socially reproductive labour it exerts. It begins with how judicial temporalities force field staff to work 'manically', reaching as many victims as possible within a short time window, and then fleshes out the ideological effects of that process: people become victims; it is the first time someone sits down with them and listens to their story; it's 'one of the best things that could ever happen to them', which gives validation to the victim officer's work, but also stirs unease as they know the Court is unlikely to deliver ('close the wounds it opened'). Another field assistant confessed:

> [w]orking with victims is emotionally very hard. I had to seek therapy last year because I got panic attacks. The only way you can deal with it is by building walls, but then I started building these walls with everyone. I would sit next to my best friend and feel she was a stranger.[64]

[63] Interview with Victims' Officer, Kampala (9 July 2019). It is noteworthy that the Registry relied on intermediaries/volunteers, especially law students, to facilitate victim applications.

[64] Interview with Assistant of Victim's Lawyer, Kampala (9 July 2019).

Intermediaries listen to victims' stories, see them break down, and offer them comfort. They are often from the same community as the victims and lived through the same atrocities, which makes their work potentially retraumatizing. They are expected to care selflessly for their kin and, if they fail to do so, are vilified as gatekeepers and cheaters.

Love, in fact, often creates stronger obligations than law. 'What is justice?', one defence counsel mused; 'it is so many things. It is like love.'[65] It is easier to blame people if they fail in love, not law. Think, for example, of society's relentless blaming of 'the uncaring mother', that unpaid essential worker, who becomes the ultimate scapegoat 'for everything that is wrong with the world'.[66] The more people are recognized as 'productive/professional workers', on the other hand, the harder it is to ask them to work for free. In medieval England, love could even trump law: 'Agreement prevails over law and love over judgment', a source from early twelfth-century England tells us.[67] There was nothing sentimental about it. Love 'was a bond of affection, established by public undertakings before witnesses and upheld by social pressure'.[68] Such bonds of affection were steeped in power relationships like the one between lords and vassals: 'we offer love only to those whom we cannot do without'.[69] As such, love became a way of demanding free work: 'on the estates of St Albans abbey to make love meant to do an extra piece of work for the lord', Clanchy observes.[70]

Even if less literally, the Court's sections also rely on love rather than law in their dealings with intermediaries. As a Registry officer observed, 'we can have contracts. The thing is, you have to be careful, because we don't offer much. Normally, in Kenya, we do not offer anything, which has been a problem. It is hard to say, "we don't offer you anything, but this is what you are going to do for us, and then sign here" '.[71] Intermediaries are nonetheless

[65] Interview with Defence Counsel, The Hague (4 December 2013).

[66] Jacqueline Rose, *Mothers: An Essay on Love and Cruelty* (Faber & Faber 2018) 1. In German, there is even a special term for a bad mother, *Rabenmutter* (mother of ravens).

[67] Michael Clanchy, 'Law and love in the Middle Ages' in John Bossy (ed), *Disputes and Settlements: Law and Human Relations in the West* (CUP 2003) 47.

[68] ibid.

[69] ibid 48.

[70] ibid.

[71] Interview with Legal Officer, Registry, The Hague (12 November 2013). The OTP is more likely to use contracts in its dealings with intermediaries. See *Prosecutor v Lubanga* (Judgment pursuant to Article 74 of the Statute) [2012] ICC-01/04-01/06-2842, § 203 ('With time it became apparent that certain intermediaries were so indispensable that they had to be provided with some form of more appropriate compensation. A special contract was devised that spelt out the duties of the intermediary, including the protection of the witnesses').

expected to sign a special code of conduct that obliges them to 'observe the highest standards of integrity and conduct in discharging' their functions, and to 'act fairly, in good faith and with respect and courtesy' in their relationships with the Court's staff, counsel, and victims.[72] One NGO intermediary from Nairobi fumed,

> The intermediary question is one of those which make me extremely angry. With the Court, we have had discussions since 2011, and what do they come up with? Some bloody guidelines which intermediaries are supposed to sign . . . What for? You don't offer us security . . . Literally, nothing of that [their work] is compensated by the Court.[73]

Many victims' lawyers prefer using victims rather than civil society organizations as intermediaries. 'Rule number one is to kill gate keeping as much as possible', one field assistant in Nairobi explained to me, 'so that the people you identify to play a role . . . they have to be our clients; they are victims; so you do not have an outsider engage in affairs of participation'.[74] Of course, with victims, it is even easier to argue that what they do for the Court is their pursuit of justice ('love') rather than labour.

Even where labour is clearly professional, racialization and feminization devalue intermediaries' work. Many intermediaries are professional workers; they have university degrees, and many are trained as lawyers, but few are recognized as such by the court. For example, the function of the common legal representative of victims is usually split between white lawyers who represent victims in the court room in The Hague, one black lawyer who is the 'intermediary' between the white lawyers and the victims, and his team on the ground, who are often lawyers, too, but are employed as 'field assistants' or 'translators'.[75] Professional labour does not have a uniform value but works through racialized and gendered differentiation.[76] The darker you are, the closer you are to victims, the more emotional labour you do, the less valuable your work is.

[72] ICC (n 29) § 3.1, § 6.2.
[73] Interview with former Intermediary, Nairobi (30 June 2014).
[74] Interview with Legal Assistant, Nairobi (25 June 2014).
[75] The field assistants interviewed for this research in Kenya and Uganda were often established lawyers and even translators had often graduated from law school.
[76] Robert Knox, 'Valuing race? Stretched Marxism and the logic of imperialism' (2016) 4(1) London Review of International Law 81, 125.

Why does labour need to be devalued and exploited? One possible answer is because international criminal justice is a commodity. Kendall, for example, argues that 'the field is deeply imbricated with a stakeholder economy that narrows and commodifies a particular conception of 'global justice' as individual criminal accountability'.[77] Schwöbel-Patel observes that 'selling a particular cause is more important than the cause itself'.[78] Her new book explores how international criminal justice is commodified and marketed in a competitive donor economy in which market values increasingly trump social values.[79] Both focus on what happens to the commodity in the Global North: how it is marketed and sold. But the secret of the commodity lies in its production, and the question of who creates value.

The answer to that question is far from straightforward and reveals contradictory perceptions of victims by the court's practitioners. Anxious to cut the production costs of international criminal justice, many of the Court's practitioners not only hide or undervalue the labour of intermediaries, but also treat victims as a 'cost' that needs to be slashed. 'When we talk about victims we talk about costs', one intermediary from Kenya observed, 'we don't talk about costs when it comes to prosecution'.[80] One victims' lawyer told me:

> [f]rom my perspective, it looks very much like, we have two competing things here. We have victims' voices, and we have judicial economy, and judicial economy must prevail. And for me that kind of also sums up where we are at the court today. Like in our case, it feels like that every time you want to say something for the victims, the answer is 'judicial economy'. No, shut up, we need to get on with things.[81]

Once, in the courtroom, she was examining a victim-witness who needed a bit more time 'to get into the flow of his evidence', but the judge insisted she should 'wrap it up'. She sighed:

> [w]hen you think about the amount of court resources which have gone into bringing this person here. You know, they go down to Kampala for several days, like weeks in advance, so that they can get their health

[77] Kendall (n 10) 114.
[78] Schwöbel-Patel (n 10) 6.
[79] ibid 1, 8.
[80] Interview with Intermediary, Kisumu (26 August 2014).
[81] Interview with Victims' Lawyer, London (10 September 2018).

> checked and their psyche checked and everything else and be prepared, you know, and then they go back up to their community. And then they come back down, and they spend some more time in Kampala; they've their clothes purchased for them. They're put on a plane, they are brought to The Hague, they spend two days in The Hague sitting around; they have familiarization with everybody. They go to the courtroom; someone walks them there, like all of that. And then, once all of this time and money has been spent, you couldn't have them in the courtroom for another hour?[82]

Of course, this focuses on the Court's resources and time rather than that of witnesses and victims who take time out of their lives and labour to become the Court's subjects. Neither does 'judicial economy' necessarily strike where most money is spent. Indeed, the judges' eagerness to save money is somewhat ironic given that several of them have launched a lawsuit against the court, demanding a pay rise of 26.7 per cent because US$200,000 annual salary, tax-free, is, according to them, no adequate compensation for their labour.[83]

That demand, however, makes sense in light of a widespread belief that it is them and the prosecutor, rather than the victims or their lawyers, who create value. The real purpose of the Court is to 'fight impunity', and that is more effectively done without victims.[84] As the Independent Expert Review of the Court notes about victim participation:

[82] ibid.

[83] See Marlise Simons, 'In The Hague's lofty judicial halls, judges wrangle over pay' *New York Times* (20 January 2019) https://www.nytimes.com/2019/01/20/world/europe/hague-judges-pay.html (accessed 29 November 2021). For an analysis of the judges' complaint before the Administrative Tribunal of the International Labour Organisation (ILOAT) see Owiso Owiso, 'Remuneration Debacle at the International Criminal Court: Should ICC Judges Get a Pay Rise?' *OpinioJuris* (23 November 2020) http://opiniojuris.org/2020/12/23/remuneration-debacle-at-the-international-criminal-court-should-icc-judges-get-a-pay-rise-part-i/ (accessed 29 November 2021).

[84] In the words of former ICC Judge, Christine Van den Wyngaert: '[I]f victims' participation slows down proceedings, fewer trials can be held. Seen from that perspective, victims' participation may be in conflict with the basic purpose of the ICC, which is to fight impunity.' Christine Van den Wyngaert, 'Victims Before International Criminal Courts: Some Views and Concerns of an ICC Trial Judge' (2012) 44 Case Western Reserve Journal of International Law 475, 495. The late Judge Hans-Peter Kaul has argued that the best way to achieve justice for victims is through criminalizing and prosecuting the crime of aggression rather than victim participation. Hans-Peter Kaul, 'Victims' rights and peace' in Thorsten Bonacker and Christoph Safferling (eds), *Victims of International Crimes: An Interdisciplinary Discourse* (TMC Asser Press 2013) 226.

The most fundamental concern relates to the overall cost of the system when compared to the benefits realised. There is also some concern that the way in which it has evolved may have resulted in the diversion of resources from the prosecution of accused. Some have shared with the Experts that a proper audit may be advisable to assess the real cost of victim participation and its contribution to the pursuit of justice. A cost/benefit analysis has also been proposed.[85]

'Imagine for a moment', one judge told me, 'if we had no system of victim participation, the Court would run much more smoothly. There would be less filings, less delays, less complications. The machinery would function better.'[86] Victim participation, from this perspective, does not create value but throws a spanner into the machinery of international criminal justice.[87]

But would anyone still 'buy' international criminal justice if victims refused to participate? Doesn't their participation create value without which international criminal justice becomes less 'marketable'? After all, the Court itself acknowledges that the failure to ensure victims are able to participate in the proceedings 'place[s] the credibility of the entire Rome Statute system and the Court's work at risk'.[88] When victims complain that they are tired of attending the Court's meetings,[89] they perhaps also express the idea that victim participation is work and should be remunerated.[90] This idea, however, is rather implicit. In a world centred on commodity production, the commodity form itself manipulates the worker into thinking that it is

[85] ICC (n 61) § 856.
[86] Interview with Judge, The Hague (19 December 2013).
[87] FIDH, 'Whose Court is it? Judicial handbook on victims' rights at the International Criminal Court' (April 2021) 12 https://www.fidh.org/IMG/pdf/fidh_whose_court_is_it_en.pdf (accessed 3 December 2022) ('the various practitioners and experts interviewed for this report unanimously drew attention to the need for judges to genuinely recognise that victims bring added value to the ICC, that victims can help judges to fulfil their mandate').
[88] ICC, 'Report of the Bureau on Victims and Affected Communities and the Trust Fund for Victims and Reparations', ICC-ASP/11/32 (23 October 2012) § 24. See also Gilbert Bitti, 'A court for victims?' in FIDH, 'Victims at the Center of Justice: From 1998 to 2018: Reflections on the Promises and the Reality of Victim Participation at the ICC' (2018) 5 https://www.fidh.org/IMG/pdf/droitsdesvictimes730a_final.pdf (accessed 10 December 2022) ('Victims represent for the Court a very powerful means of legitimising its actions').
[89] Interview with Victims' Lawyer Assistant, Kampala (9 July 2019).
[90] The Court insists that victim participation should not be compensated. See VPRS, 'Victim's Booklet: Victims before the International Criminal Court: A guide for the participation of victims in the proceedings of the ICC', 21 https://www.icc-cpi.int/sites/default/files/itemsDocuments/vprs/abd-al-rahman/VPRS-Victims-booklet_ENG.pdf (accessed 17 December 2022) ('Victims who participate in proceedings are given the opportunity to present their views and concerns to the Court, but will not receive any form of compensation or payment for this participation').

the machines (eg the court) rather than herself who creates surplus value.[91] Victims, in fact, rarely perceive themselves, and are rarely perceived by others, as labourers who produce the justice commodity. Rhetorically, they appear either as 'cost', 'consumers' or as 'commodities' themselves. Indeed, under capitalism, if something is free for you, it usually means that you are the product. Tech commentators use that phrase to explain how free social media apps such as WhatsApp and Facebook work, but it may also explain victim participation, which is 'free' as the Court usually pays for victims' lawyers through its legal aid budget. Does that mean that victims are a commodity that intermediaries sell?

While working well as a metaphor, the notion of 'justice' or 'victims' as a commodity loses its analytical purchase as soon as we scratch the surface. The commodity, after all, hides the centrality of both productive and reproductive labour. It is labour power, not humans, which is congealed in the commodity. Victims cannot be bought and sold. What can be bought and sold is their participation time.[92] When we say that justice is a commodity, then there must be a commodity owner (the court? states?) who sells the commodity (trials? judgments? victims?) to a consumer (states? the public?). While a cause can be 'sold' to donors, that does not automatically make it a commodity. Warning against a widespread view wherein 'capitalism propels the ever-increasing commodification of life as such', Nancy Fraser reminds us that not every realm is directly subsumed under capitalist production.[93] Justice is not produced or sold capitalistically. Just as the reproduction of people has often been cheaper outside of the market, so too is ideological reproduction, including the ICC, which is publicly rather than privately funded. Similarly, the role of intermediaries, as this chapter will show, is not to sell justice commodities in the Global North but to ideologically manage victims in the Global South.

[91] George Lukács, *History and Class Consciousness: Studies in Marxist Dialectics* (The Merlin Press 2010) 86.

[92] 'For his relation to continue, the proprietor of labour-power must always sell it for a limited period only, for if he were to sell it in a lump, once and for all, he would be selling himself, converting himself from a free man into a slave, from an owner of a commodity into a commodity.' Marx (n 44) 271.

[93] Fraser (n 45).

4.3 The Blame Cascade Revisited: Outsourcing Contradictions and Managing Labour Divides

A 'commodity analysis', moreover, flattens out the Court's ambiguous victim engagement. Does the Court want victims or not? Some ICC organs and actors want as many victims as possible, others as few as they can get away with. The OTP, for example, has often given victims short shrift.[94] The Independent Expert Review notes that while 'support from local CSOs and media is key to acquiring cooperation from the affected populations and victims' groups . . . the OTP focuses on meeting with high level government representatives, to the exclusion of civil society and victims groups'.[95] In outreach meetings, the OTP's absence means that intermediaries often have to fill the gap.[96] An intermediary in Uganda observed:

> In all these outreach sessions where people raise questions about the Office of the Prosecutor, the PIDS [outreach] people would not respond . . . So, many times, it is us from the civil society who would respond to the questions from our own understanding of how the Prosecutor's office works . . . All these different sections and departments operate like this. They look at themselves as independent of each other, notwithstanding that they sit in the same building, share the same office space . . . For heaven's sake, if you are going to do an outreach session, perhaps, they need to sit down and agree. And say, 'for purposes of field outreach, this should be our strategy'. So that you don't leave people's minds lingering about whether this is the same Court or not.[97]

[94] Jennifer Easterday, 'It's Complicated: The ICC Prosecutor's Office and the Need for Reform' (18 May 2020) https://www.ijmonitor.org/2020/05/its-complicated-the-icc-prosecutors-office-and-the-need-for-reform/ (accessed 31 March 2023).

[95] ICC (n 61) § 380, § 384.

[96] ibid § 395.

[97] Interview with CSO Representative, Kampala (28 July 2014). See also Matias Hellman, 'Challenges and limitations of outreach' in in Christian De Vos, Sara Kendall and Carsten Stahn (eds), *Contested Justice: The Politics and Practice of International Criminal Court Interventions* (CUP 2015) 251, 262 ('Indeed, when working for ICTY outreach, I was often caught in the dilemma of whether to try to explain the OTP's policies with the information available from public statements, or whether to simply state that I was not able to answer the question, and that it should be put to the OTP'). The Independent Expert Review also documents 'an impression of confusion within the Registry about the point at which outreach is appropriate and which of PIOS, VPRS and OPCV is responsible for what in light of "mixed signals" coming from each'. ICC (n 61) § 857.

Indeed, the Court uses intermediaries not only to outsource its work but also to hide its own ideological contradictions.[98] To give an example, the VPRS, which 'in many ways has required the most from 'intermediaries', [and] has provided the least in terms of protection, support and assistance'[99] has justified its stingy approach, in two ways: '(i) it has no money; (ii) it does not want to be seen as encouraging victim participation'.[100] Some victims' lawyers, however, had a rather different impression of the Registry's approach to victims,

> for the Court, if only 20 victims show up [to a meeting], they feel it is a failure. I think the organization of the Court, of the Registry and so on and a lot of NGOs feel that there is a problem, if only a small group of victims comes to the Court. They think it is a success, if 5000 victims sign a statement that they want to participate . . .[101]

In this context, intermediaries might feel they need to 'deliver' victims for the Court's meetings. When I tried to arrange an interview with an intermediary in Kisumu (Western Kenya), he mistook me for an ICC outreach officer or victim's lawyer, and immediately promised to mobilize a large number of people for a meeting. It is thus not surprising that intermediaries sometimes ' "make a little gesture"—meaning providing gifts—to encourage victims to participate'.[102] Both the Court's practitioners and international NGOs balk at this; it is like 'buying off' victims and thus undermines the idea that victim participation is a right rather than a manipulative tool to engineer consent.[103] And yet, in doing so, intermediaries effectively fill in the logical gaps in the Court's practice. The Court can 'neutrally' inform victims because intermediaries have already done the job of

[98] For the confusion created in the field about the roles and relationships of the ICC's different actors and offices see also Phil Clark, *Distant Justice: The Impact of the International Criminal Court on African Politics* (CUP 2018) 143.

[99] Victims' Rights Working Group, 'Comments on the Role and Relationship of 'Intermediaries' with the International Criminal Court' (6 February 2009) 5 https://www.fidh.org/IMG/pdf/VRWG_Role_of_intermediaries_ICC_-_February_2009_En_.pdf (accessed 12 December 2022).

[100] ibid.

[101] Telephone Interview with Legal Representative of Victims (15 January 2014).

[102] Human Rights Watch, 'Courting History: The Landmark International Criminal Court's First Years' (2008) 200 https://www.hrw.org/reports/2008/icc0708/icc0708web.pdf (accessed 29 November 2021).

[103] ibid.

recruiting them. As the ICC's handmaiden, intermediaries have to second-guess what the Court 'really' wants and can later be blamed for it.

The Court thus resolves the tension between outreach and advocacy, victim engagement and client acquisition, victims' rights and victim commodities, law and politics by outsourcing the latter to intermediaries, which then further feeds into the 'intermediaries as liability' discourse. Intermediaries, some Registry staff members pointed out, have made unwarranted promises of assistance and reparations to victims and some have even tricked the latter out of money.[104] 'And we also have to worry', a Registry officer contended, 'that by kind of legitimating the work of a grassroots intermediary, they may take that document and wave it around in their hometown or village and become gatekeepers and little emperors, which we have also seen happening'.[105] In reality, the Court's practitioners create a convenient scapegoat. They outsource the Court's mandatory responsibilities of evidence collection and victim engagement to intermediaries, for which they do not provide adequate compensation much less security. They confuse intermediaries with different agendas emanating from the ICC's different sections, and then blame them for failing to achieve the impossible: 'managing the expectations' of a victim population that often has no other avenue to seek redress.[106]

[104] These risks of using intermediaries were also highlighted more broadly in interviews with Registry staff and with victims' lawyers. Interview with Legal Officer, Registry, The Hague (21 January 2014) ('you also have categories of the opportunists'); Interview with Legal Coordinator, Registry, The Hague (6 February 2014) ('Because we have had some issues with intermediaries, some intermediaries that asked [for] money, we learnt that they had asked money from victims, to be given our applications which is not normal, it should be given freely, some intermediaries that have had some behaviour that was not acceptable, things like that. Then, when we learn that, we stop working with them, but it would be better to have a pre-assessment of their reliability before we start working with them, which is not what we are able to do currently'). The Registry has argued that 'it is vital to assess, select, train and monitor intermediaries properly' and for Registry staff to be present in the field when intermediaries assist victims in filling out victim applications also to 'help to guard against abuse and the need for the Court to return later to verify applications'. *Prosecutor v Ntaganda* (Registry Observations in compliance with the Decision ICC-01/04-02/06-54-Conf) [2013] ICC-01/04-02/06-57, § 13.

[105] Interview with Legal Officer, Registry, The Hague (12 November 2013).

[106] 'Expectation management' has become a buzzword among civil society, academics, and the Court's practitioners as the way to improve the ICC's victims' engagement. Redress, 'Independent Panel of experts report on victim participation at the International Criminal Court' (2013) § 60, § 73 https://redress.org/wp-content/uploads/2017/12/July-Independent-Panel-of-experts-report-on-victim-participation-at-the.pdf (accessed 11 April 2023); *Prosecutor v Katanga* (Queen's University Belfast's Human Rights Centre (HRC) and University of Ulster's Transitional Justice Institute (TJI) Submission on Reparations Issues pursuant to Article 75 of the Statute) [2015] ICC-01/04-01/07-3551, §§ 2–3; ICC, 'Integrated Strategy for External Relations, Public Information and Outreach' http://www.icc-cpi.int/NR/

The Court can also abandon intermediaries at any point. One Ugandan intermediary told me how the Court moved its field staff from Uganda to Kenya due to lack of judicial developments in the Ugandan cases before Ongwen's surrender:

> In 2014, we remained a lead intermediary organization. The Court was simply closing its field office and moved to Nairobi. [We told them], 'we are shocked with your decision without consulting us. That you decide to close the field office. You put us to be the image of the Court in the community. We are the ones challenged with accountability—victims ask us, "what's going on?", and then you close without engaging us. You left us without feedback. We are the ones that support the victims. If you ask us, "out of those who applied [to participate], how many are still alive?" You don't know. We know who has died and who is alive'.[107]

Another intermediary in Kenya complained, 'when you are reading the newspaper, the cases are not going well . . . I feel that if anything happens to that case, let the prosecutor come herself to the victims and tell them. I'm done with being the bearer of bad news'.[108] The case she referred to, the Kenyatta case, indeed collapsed a few months after the interview, in December 2014. It is hard to escape the impression that intermediaries are set up to fail and serve as a convenient buffer for the Court which itself has contested visions of whether, how and for what purpose to engage with victims.[109]

Thus, intermediaries' labour is denied or devalued both for material reasons (it makes it easier to extract unpaid or barely paid labour) and for ideological reasons (it makes it easier to blame them for the Court's own contradictions). Why do intermediaries accept the poisoned chalice? Because they have a stake in the division between professional and manual

rdonlyres/425E80BA-1EBC-4423-85C6-D4F2B93C7506/185049/ICCPIDSWBOR0307070402_IS_En.pdf (accessed 10 April 2023).

[107] Interview with Former Intermediary, Kampala (11 July 2019).

[108] Interview with Intermediary, Nairobi (2 July 2014). The Victims' Rights Working Group's consultations with intermediaries similarly found that 'the general sense of 'intermediaries' consulted on their role and relationship with the Court is that of frustration'. Victims' Rights Working Group, 'Comments on the Role and Relationship of "Intermediaries" with the International Criminal Court' (6 February 2009) 5 https://www.fidh.org/IMG/pdf/VRWG_Role_of_intermediaries_ICC_-_February_2009_En_.pdf (accessed 30 March 2023).

[109] Ullrich (n 3).

labour. The blame cascade is a cascade rather than a simple relationship of exploitation because intermediaries reproduce exactly the same dynamic with victims. Once we look beyond the actors that the Court designates as intermediaries, we discover that intermediation is a broader working mechanism of both international criminal justice and global capitalism. While the *Guidelines on Intermediaries* restricts the term to 'local actors', international NGOs arguably also fulfil intermediary functions for the Court.[110] In fact, some Court practitioners have used the intermediary concept more broadly, describing, for example, victims' lawyers as 'intermediaries' that go between the Court and victims.[111] At the highest level, the Court itself appears as an intermediary of global capitalism and the state system.

Indeed, far from creating a single relationship between the Court and an intermediary, intermediation creates multiple, hierarchical relationships, like Russian dolls, which are ultimately chains of differently valued labour. Beth Lyons argues that the Guidelines,

> [r]aises the spectre of a two-tiered system: a more formalized quasi-staff structure of contracted intermediaries (with certain benefits and privileges), and a secondary, more local and informal structure of uncontracted/free agent intermediaries (whose support is decided on a case-by-case basis and who are likely to be at a greater risk, because they may have less or no access to resources provided by the UN). A parallel to this is the unequal situation of ICTR employees in Arusha, where "foreign" nationals are paid at a higher rate than "local" staff, although the positions and tasks of each may be similar or even identical.[112]

Here, intermediation emerges as a method of differentiating labour performing 'similar or identical' tasks. But rather than merely two tiers, a multi-tiered system of labour relations takes shape: International organizations subcontract to national NGOs, who subcontract to local organizations, who subcontract to grassroots organizations, who then operate through local leaders or victim intermediaries. Moving to the 'second tier', the next section

[110] ICC (n 4) 6; Nicole De Silva, 'Intermediary Complexity in Regulatory Governance: The International Criminal Court's Use of NGOs in Regulating International Crimes' (2017) 670(1) The ANNALS of the American Academy of Political and Social Science 170; International Refugee Rights Initiative and Open Society Initiative (n 19) 9.

[111] Kaul (n 684) 225.

[112] Beth Lyons, 'The Intermediary Industry and the ICC' *INTLAWGRRLS* (6 June 2014) https://ilg2.org/2014/06/06/the-intermediary-industry-and-the-icc/ (accessed 17 December 2022).

will shed light on the role of local stakeholders in Northern Uganda, who act as intermediaries for multiple national and international organizations. There is a dual exploitation at play: intermediaries are exploited by the Court as precarious workers and they, in turn, exploit the victims.

ICC Local Stakeholder Outreach, Update by the Defence Lawyer, Churchill Courts Hotel, Gulu, 23 July 2019

Back at the ICC's local stakeholders' meeting, it is time for a break. The defence lawyer has been spouting stories of Ongwen's brutalizing childhood in the LRA for several hours, and the audience is a bit worn out. A lavish lunch is served in the courtyard of the hotel and immediately lightens the mood. As I finish lunch, I observe a group of men at the next table. They are passionately arguing in the local dialect—loud speeches, forceful gestures and derisive laughter underline the polemic. I ask Steve,[113] a local NGO worker, who sits next to me in the conference room, what the argument was about. It was about voting rights in Uganda, he told me, and whether people should have the same or differential voting rights. He and most of the other men agreed that people who contribute more to GDP and are better educated should have higher weighted voting rights. 'The poor only vote the regime back into power because they give them T-shirts and a thousand shillings [21 pence] even though they suffer so much under the regime', Steve explained to me; 'if it wasn't for the poor, the regime would not be in power anymore.'

Later we argue about Donald Trump. 'I don't think that Donald Trump is bad', Steve insists, 'he puts the interests of his people first, not like in Uganda where the government implements foreign interests. It is good for us, too, that he restricts migration. We should solve our problems here. Many people who leave are professionals. They should stay here. Instead of taking the money to get a US visa and travel there, invest in a business. Africa has the potential and the resources to be prosperous'.[114]

Local stakeholders are not a passive audience that simply accepts the Court's interpellation. Rather, they are active ideology producers in their

[113] Not his real name.
[114] Field notes (n 1).

own right. Many intermediaries/stakeholders[115] I met in Northern Uganda were corporatist more than liberal: everyone in society should fulfil their designated role to create social harmony, they believed. An overriding principle of Acholi culture, social harmony is also the ideology of the status quo in many peasant communities, what Laura Nader has called 'harmony ideology'.[116] While most people toil as farmers, a tiny minority has the privilege of spiritual, intellectual, creative or professional labour.

***

Intermediaries regulate this division between manual and professional labour, a division they benefit from. Indeed, from women's rights lawyers and NGO workers to cultural leaders, teachers and social workers, my interviewees insisted that 'the problem' in Northern Uganda is that people have become lazy and unwilling to dig. This was curious not only because I hadn't asked any questions about work (my questions focused on 'justice'), but also because neither I nor most of my interviewees were grafting in the field. 'Those who were born in the camps, they were not used to work', a local teacher told me, 'because, there, they would only sit, especially the youth, so when they came back home, they just find working something tedious, hectic and fairly difficult.'[117] Intermediaries were particularly incensed by 'the spirit of getting free things inculcated by the war in northern Uganda'.[118] Displaced from their fields, 'people lost their ability to eat from their sweat', a peacebuilding worker in Gulu claimed.[119] Even though Northern Ugandans have long since returned to their homesteads, NGOs have continued to nurture this 'dependency syndrome'. The same peacebuilding officer asserted:

115 While not all 'local stakeholders' will become 'ICC intermediaries', there is a slippage between the two categories which provides an entry point into rethinking their role.

116 Holly Porter, *After Rape: Violence, Justice and Social Harmony in Uganda* (CUP 2016); Interview with Cultural Leader, Gulu (22 July 2019); Laura Nader, *Harmony Ideology: Justice and Control in a Zapotec Mountain Village* (Stanford UP 1990).

117 Teacher, Focus Group Discussion, Lukodi (25 July 2019).

118 Willy Akena, 'From State of Hopelessness to Joy and Celebration' Diocese of Northern Uganda (former partner of the Trust Fund) (29 June 2014) http://dioceseofnorthernuganda.blogspot.com/2014/06/normal-0-false-false-false-en-us-x-none.html (accessed 29 November 2021).

119 Interview with NGO representative, Gulu (18 July 2019).

> When it's an emergency, it is an emergency, but that should not become a lifestyle. Emergencies should be limited to things that will allow you to be able to resurrect and maybe find something to do. Even the NGOs after the conflict, there are still a lot of handouts. Sometimes people go to the community to provide training, 'I have come to give you knowledge. You want me to pay you for the knowledge I'm giving you?' And in the community, if you're not going to pay them 'transport reimbursement', if you're not going to pay them 'sitting allowance', they will not come for your training . . . And if all program implementers could avoid this type of payment that makes people feel like I should be paid for any kind of meeting or training. It's going to help them with easing the dependency syndrome.[120]

He even went further, insisting that people 'should be forced to work . . . [the principle] "nothing for nothing" should be introduced'.[121] The message is clear: victim participation is not work and thus should not be paid. Nothing for nothing.

4.4 The Secret of Ideological Labour

Transitional justice and development practitioners often call the people they work with 'beneficiaries', but that arguably misconstrues the relationship. Who really benefits from these processes? NGOs, after all, need 'beneficiaries' to raise donor money to pay their professional salaries. If no one comes to the training, the NGO has lost its main asset—its ability to mobilize the community. Thus, it is not 'nothing for nothing' when people demand money to attend trainings. 'Beneficiaries' understand that their participation is something NGOs can monetize, and they thus demand their share. Human rights training or victim participation 'doesn't bring them food on the table'.[122] But that is not how the NGOs like to see it. They forcefully insist on the morality of work because what they do (sitting in the office) is recognized as work while what the community members do

[120] ibid.
[121] ibid.
[122] Interview with Intermediary, Nairobi (2 July 2014); Interview with Intermediary, Kisumu (25 August 2014).

(sitting in trainings) is not. But that is purely a matter of social convention. Who is to say what work is more productive?

Neither is 'productive' in the capitalist sense because neither directly produces surplus value.[123] 'Sitting in the office' and 'sitting in the training' is reproductive work; it is a specific form of reproductive labour, what I call ideological labour, which reproduces capitalist social relations. A key aspect of reproducing labour is to divide it. Those who sit in the office are reproduced as 'benefactors' and those who sit in the training as 'beneficiaries'. What helps to distinguish their ideological labour is the division between professional and manual labour, which explains the NGOs' efforts to discipline victims ('they should be forced to work'). Squeezed in a sector that depends on foreign money and offers salaried positions for very few people, intermediaries are simultaneously pulling up and pushing down. Even 'transport reimbursement' for victims threatens to unravel the distinction between work and participation, benefactor and beneficiary, professional and manual labour.

In short, ideological labour creates and manages social divisions of labour. Where does ideological labour happen in the capitalist production process? 'The division of labour', Marx writes in Capital Volume 1, 'is an organization of production which has grown up naturally, a web which has been, and continues to be, woven behind the backs of the producers of commodities'.[124] To the producers, he writes in an earlier passage, the division of labour appears to 'have been handed down by tradition'.[125] When the worker enters the production process, he is already a certain type of labourer: both the division of labour and his position within it have already been determined. Ideological labour reproduces class relations, first, by creating structural class places and, secondly, by allocating people to those places.[126] While this labour also happens in production and circulation, most of it unfolds in institutions of social reproduction as a Marxist–Feminist perspective reveals. As Tithi Bhattacharya describes:

> The production of labor power then takes place outside the immediate circuit of capital but remains essential for it. Within *capital's circuit*, labor

[123] See Nicos Poulantzas, *Classes in Contemporary Capitalism* (Verso 1978) 211 ('In the capitalist mode of production, productive labour is that which directly produces surplus-value, which valorizes capital and is exchanged against capital').

[124] Marx (n 44) 201.

[125] ibid 135.

[126] See Poulantzas (n 123) 28.

> power is a means of production for capital's reproduction, or valorization. But within *wage labor's circuit*, the worker consumes commodities as use values (food, clothing, housing, education) in order to reproduce herself. The second circuit is a *process of production of self for the worker or a process of self-transformation*. The goal of this process is not the valorization of capital, but the self-development of the worker.[127]

Ideological labour mostly falls within the second circuit, but it does not seem entirely accurate to describe the work of ideological state apparatuses like NGOs, courts, churches, schools, hospitals and families as a 'process of production of self for the worker or a process of self-transformation'.[128] While these apparatuses are not fully under the control of capital or states, they are even less under the control of the workers.[129] All are structured hierarchically as relationships between benefactors and beneficiaries, lawyers and victims, priests and believers, teachers and pupils, doctors and patients, parents and children. It is also perhaps misleading to say that 'the goal of this process is not the valorization of capital, but the self-development of the worker'. Rather, the goal is both to produce capitalist subjects and to birth people and communities,[130] and the tension between these two objectives offers a vantage point for resistance (as I will explore in Chapter 6). But for now, it is sufficient to note that people-making and ideology-making unfold in one and the same process of social reproduction, and form part of the same relationships of love, care and discipline.

Now that we have established 'where' ideological labour happens, the question is 'who' does it. One possible answer is the professional–managerial class (PMC). Barbara and John Ehrenreich developed the concept of the PMC to describe a class which emerged in the early twentieth century in the Global North under conditions of monopoly capitalism, and which differed both from the working class and the capitalist class. Like the working class, the PMC does not own the means of production and therefore must work for a wage. Unlike the working class, the main function of the PMC is not to produce commodities but to reproduce capitalist social

[127] Tithi Bhattacharya, 'How Not to Skip Class: Social Reproduction of Labor and the Global Working Class' in Tithi Bhattacharya (ed), *Social Reproduction Theory: Remapping Class, Recentering Oppression* (Pluto Press 2017) 81 (original emphasis); see also Marx (n 44).

[128] Bhattacharya (n 128) 81.

[129] Poulantzas emphasizes that it is ultimately the class struggle, which is materialized through the state apparatuses, rather than the apparatuses themselves that reproduce social classes. Poulantzas (n 123) 27, 29.

[130] Federici (n 48) 99.

relations.[131] Effectively, the PMC is the intermediary class between the capitalist and the working class; it recruits and manages labour for capital. From this perspective, local intermediaries appear as the lowest stratum of the global PMC.

When Bhattacharya writes that the working class 'must be perceived as everyone in the producing class who has in their lifetime participated in the totality of reproduction of society – irrespective of whether that labor has been paid for by capital or remained unpaid',[132] she usefully extends the category of the working class beyond direct commodity producers. Social reproducers, according to her definition, are part of the working class, whether their labour is paid or unpaid. But she also erases ideological labour, how it serves capitalism, and the divisions it creates within the global workforce. In her definition, the PMC dissolves as part of the working class. If, by contrast, we take Shivji's definition of 'working people' in the Global South—'peasants and pastoralists, proletarians and semi-proletarians, street hawkers selling consumer goods and peddlers selling cooked food, operators and repairers in backyard workshops'—whose material condition is 'minimizing . . . their necessary consumption and maximizing their labour',[133] the PMC fragments. Its lowest stratum consists of precarious 'working people'; its higher stratum is composed of well-paid professionals. Capitalism cuts into the necessary consumption of the former but not necessarily of the latter.

Yet, the difficulty of conceiving intermediaries as part of the PMC is twofold. First, the logic of intermediation fragments the capital-labour relationship beyond a three-class structure. Intermediaries soften hierarchies at every stage in the process: it is not the diplomat or the judge who tells victims to toil on the field. It is a local intermediary, often a victim herself, who does the 'dirty' ideological labour. Local intermediaries often occupy contradictory class positions. It is difficult to establish whether they are closer to the Court or the victims, to the capitalist or the worker. Second, ideological labour is not only performed by one class. Instead, it cuts across

[131] Barbara Ehrenreich and John Ehrenreich, 'Professional-Managerial Class' (1977) 11(2) Radical America 7, 13. The Ehrenreichs build on Nicos Poulantzas' 'distinction between labour necessary for production of commodities and labour necessary for the reproduction of capitalist social relationships'. See Poulantzas (n 123) 27–35.

[132] Bhattacharya (n 127) 89. This goes against Poulantzas' restrictive definition of the working class as those who engage in 'productive' labour.

[133] Issa G Shivji, 'The Concept of "Working People"' (2017) 6(1) Agrarian South: Journal of Political Economy 1, 11.

classes. Shared between the ideological producer and the ideological subject, this labour happens *through* their relationship. Intermediaries do ideological labour, but they are also themselves the products of the latter, just as the victims are. If ideology works through interpellation, if people are hailed as 'victims' by the court, if they are called to play 'their roles' as farmers in the capitalist order by intermediaries, and if they respond, 'yes, it's me. I'm a victim. I'm a farmer', then ideology-making does not really happen 'behind their backs', as Marx suggests, but through their active participation.

Ideological labour is a secret because we neither recognize it as 'ideological' nor as 'labour'. Instead, we see it as love and care, education and socialization, discipline and punishment. We also don't recognize our own participation in that labour which creates the illusion that it happens behind our backs. Explaining how he mobilizes victims for ICC meetings, one intermediary in Western Kenya said:

> I have a bicycle that helps me to go to the communities. I tell them about the ICC, some are eager to cooperate, others are not. They have different opinions about the ICC. Then, they come to the meeting, even those who were not that eager on the ICC . . . When they go back, they spread the information about the ICC. Then more people come.[134]

People have different views on the Court, but they still come to the meeting. The meeting is a key site of ideological subject formation. We can see, here, the similarities between commodity and ideology production. 'A commodity is therefore a mysterious thing', Marx writes, 'simply because in it the social character of men's labour appears to them as an objective character stamped upon the product of that labour'.[135] Much like commodity production is alienated cooperative labour, so too is ideological production, except that the latter is less alienated as it feeds off personal and even intimate relationships.[136] People attend the ICC's meetings because they receive a little money, want to see some friends, and are perhaps curious but, in doing so, they also work for the ideological reproduction of the system. Even more, victims participate in their own subjection. Intermediaries and victims share this ideological labour, but the former benefits from it more

[134] Interview with Intermediary, Western Kenya (19 August 2014).
[135] Cited in Lukács (n 91) 86: Marx (n 44) 164–65.
[136] See also Alva Gotby, *They Call It Love: The Politics of Emotional Life* (Verso 2023).

clearly than the latter. Eventually, they both lose as they reproduce their place at the bottom of the global division of labour.

People are actively interpellated as victim-survivors, they are recognized as 'victims' and a few moments later celebrated as 'survivors', who need to get on with life. Getting on with life means working, usually as farmers, who produce both for subsistence and the market.[137] 'If you live without earning money then that is a recipe for poverty', President Museveni chided subsistence farmers in Uganda; 'the people in the villages are only producing for eating. Yes, you get food for eating but what about all the other needs?'[138] The solution is to skill up, work hard, and invest in agribusiness. It's not only the Court that needs intermediaries; capitalism needs intermediaries, too. The ICC's intermediaries, and the Court as intermediary, participate in a much broader ideological regulation of relations of production and reproduction. The next section will tease out their role by reconstructing it through the colonial analogy. Rather than cultural translators or capitalist compradors, intermediaries resemble the customary chiefs of colonial rule in Africa.

4.5 Colonial Intermediaries and the Management of Labour

If the 'comprador' defined mercantile capitalism in the European colonization of East Asia, the 'customary chief' defined British colonialism in Africa. While, initially, the colonies were simply plundered (primitive accumulation), 'with the birth of imperialism', Knox observes, 'it became necessary to transform fundamentally peripheral territories. Natives needed to be forcibly transformed into "labourers" and capitalist social relations had to be implanted and intensified'.[139] The only way to achieve such radical transformation, Fanon believed, was through 'the destruction of cultural values' and their replacement by Western values.[140] Drawing on Mamdani, I will,

[137] Lyn Ossome, 'The care economy and the state in Africa's Covid-19 responses' (2021) 42(1) Canadian Journal of Development Studies/Revue canadienne d'études du développement 68, 76.

[138] Umaro Kashaka, 'Everybody should wake up now, says Museveni' *New Vision* (20 July 2019) https://www.newvision.co.ug/new_vision/news/1503892/wake-museveni (accessed 29 November 2021).

[139] Knox (n 76) 106.

[140] Frantz Fanon, *Toward the African Revolution: Political Essays* (Grove Press 1988) 39, cited in Knox (n 76) 106.

however, first complicate the idea that colonial capitalism required the wholesale destruction of 'local culture', and secondly, problematize the assumption that colonial capitalism expressed itself exclusively through marketization, commodification, and the privatization of land.[141] This is important to grasp both the role of colonial and of contemporary intermediaries.

By presenting what is always a complex amalgam of different practices and institutions as a 'pristine' pre-colonial monolith, the notion of 'the destruction of local culture' is misleading. 'The local' has always been in the grips of foreign conquest and internal change even before the onset of colonialism proper on the African continent in the 19th century. As Mamdani observes: 'The fact that these [conquest] states hardly exemplified a deeply rooted African tradition or that the colonial powers built on that nineteenth-century tradition of administratively appointed chiefs keeping in place a regime of force is hardly reason enough to remain silent about it.'[142] Tapping into multiple 'local' traditions and conflicting institutions, the British state cemented colonial rule. In highly centralized Buganda—the biggest kingdom in central Uganda—the British colonizers exploited the uneasy co-existence between traditional and administrative chiefs. The king of Buganda had previously imposed 'administrative chiefs' to secure his rule, but the latter were kept in check by 'traditional chiefs' who inherited their role through the clan structure.[143] While ostensibly propelled by a 'civilizing mission', the British quickly abandoned the promotion of 'Western values' and settled for a law-and-order administration whose central pillar was the enforcement of customary law. Rather than destroying local culture, 'Britain creatively sculpted tradition and custom as and when the need arose'.[144] Customary law, crucially, was a compromise formation between colonial law and local customs, between the colonizers and local power holders, which illustrates how colonial capitalism always operated through and on 'local culture'.[145]

The customary chiefs were the key intermediaries between the colonizers and the local population, and their role was to manage, not the 'cultural

[141] Mamdani (n 17) 38–48.
[142] ibid 40.
[143] ibid 42.
[144] ibid 49.
[145] I took the concept of 'compromise formation' from Projekt Ideolologietheorie. See Jan Rehmann, *Theories of Ideology: The Powers of Alienation and Subjection* (Brill 2013) 256. Martin Chanock makes this argument with regard to customary law in Malawi. See also Martin Chanock, 'Neo-Traditionalism and the Customary Law in Malawi' (1978) 16 African Legal Studies 80.

divide', but the divide between market and non-market relations. British colonial policy in Africa designated much land as customary rather than private land, administered by local chiefs.[146] Retaining access to the means of production through customary land, even if its legal status was precarious, peasants reproduced themselves outside of a waged labour relation.[147] As capitalism did not directly control the labour process, it relied on intermediaries, the customary chiefs, to manage peasant labour, forcing peasants to work on plantations for the market and do 'public work' for the colonial regime.[148] The chief thus regulated peasants' movement between subsistence and market economies and relations. Rather than a temporary anomaly, this was the quintessence of what has been called 'racial capitalism'.

As a term, 'racial capitalism' was used by South African Marxists in the anti-apartheid struggle to argue that modern capitalism thrived on 'the preservation of non-capitalist economies, not their destruction'.[149] In Cedric Robinson's words, 'capitalism had never been – any more than Europe—a "closed system"'; different modes of production often coexisted.[150] Rather than 'different modes of production', I prefer, following Banaji, to call them different forms of exploitation that form part of the capitalist totality.[151]

[146] Mamdani (n 17) 50. For the role of local chiefs in colonial Northern Uganda see Sverker Finnström, *Living with Bad Surroundings: War, History, and Everyday Moments in Northern Uganda* (Duke UP 2008) 41–46; Elizabeth Laruni, 'From the Village to Entebbe: The Acholi of Northern Uganda and the Politics of Identity, 1950–1985' PhD thesis, University of Exeter (2014) 69–72 https://core.ac.uk/reader/43093940 (accessed 13 August 2023).

[147] Shivji (n 133) 4. ('The control is rarely direct. "It is often mediated through intermediaries, those classes and social groups in the dominated social formation who play the role of compradores"').

[148] ibid 6–8.

[149] Arun Kundani, 'What is racial capitalism?' (23 October 2020) https://www.kundnani.org/what-is-racial-capitalism/ (accessed 1 December 2021); Andy Clarno and Salim Vally, 'The context of struggle: racial capitalism and political praxis in South Africa' (2023) 46 Ethnic and Racial Studies 3425; Catherine Hall, 'Racial Capitalism: What's in a Name?' (2022) 94 History Workshop Journal 5.

[150] Cedric J Robinson, *Black Marxism: The Making of the Black Radical Tradition* (Penguin 2020) 4.

[151] Once we pay attention to the racializing and feminizing dynamics of capitalism, it becomes clear that exploitation does not only work through the commodity and the wage form. '*Capitalist* relations of production', Banaji argues, 'can be based on forms of exploitation that are typically *precapitalist*' leading to different configurations of capital rather than one uniform model. Banaji developed his notion of 'forms of exploitation' to characterize the mixed economies of formerly colonized societies in the Global South in the 1970s. Jairus Banaji, *Theory as History: Essays on Modes of Production and Exploitation* (Brill 2020) 9 (original emphasis); Liam Campling, 'Debating Modes of Production and Forms of Exploitation: Introduction to the Symposium on Jahns Banaji's Theory as History' (2013) 21(4) Historical Materialism 3, 4; Alessandra Mezzadri, 'A Value Theory of Inclusion: Informal Labour, the Homeworker, and the Social Reproduction of Value' (2021) 53(4) Antipode 1186.

Capitalism erodes subsistence economies by taking land, labour, and time, while simultaneously depending on them for the reproduction of a low-waged or unwaged labour force and surplus population. Racialization plays a key role in managing the co-existence between these different forms of exploitation.[152] In South Africa, racialization facilitated the 'co-existence of an urban industrial capitalist economy, centered upon white society, and a black-centered rural, non-capitalist economy'.[153] Absorbing temporary black migrant labour from 'their homelands' as needed, urban industries did not have to pay for their reproduction as subsistence economies kept the costs of the reproduction of black labour far below the 'white wage'. 'Racism', Kudani observes, 'is a means by which the relationship between these two modes of production, and the associated differentiated forms of labour, are coded, managed and legitimated'.[154]

It was feminist, black Marxist and anti-colonial activists and theorists who unearthed the importance of capitalism's 'Others' to its reproduction.[155] Racialization, however, was insufficient for managing labour particularly in non-white settler colonies such as Uganda. 'Tribe' was a better tool as it fragmented the racialized majority into so many conflicting minorities.[156] In Uganda, for example, different regions and tribes became the source of different types of labour: large-scale agriculture and cash crop production was concentrated in the South whereas 'subsistence farming was the norm [in the North]'. The North became a 'labor reserve area' and, tellingly, also the site of the ICC's intervention.[157]

152 See also Stuart Hall, 'Gramsci's Relevance for the Study of Race and Ethnicity' (1986) 10(4) Journal of Communication Inquiry 5, 24.

153 Kundani (n 149).

154 ibid.

155 Rosa Luxemburg famously argued that 'the existence and development of capitalism requires an environment of non-capitalist forms of production'. In other words, for expanded reproduction, capitalism needs to create new markets for its products, access raw materials and recruit fresh labour, something it achieves through imperialism, which is a mode of penetrating into and capitalizing non-capitalist societies. 'Its predominant methods', she specifies, 'are colonial policy, an international loan system—a policy of spheres of interest—and war. Force, fraud, oppression, looting are openly displayed without any attempt at concealment'. Rosa Luxemburg, *The Accumulation of Capital* (1913) (chs 27 and 31) https://www.marxists.org/archive/luxemburg/1913/accumulation-capital/ch31.htm (accessed 1 December 2021). See also Santosh Anand, 'Foreclosed Temporalities: Imperialism and International Criminal Law' *Critical Legal Thinking* (18 November 2022) https://criticallegalthinking.com/2022/11/18/foreclosed-temporalities-imperialism-and-international-criminal-law/ (accessed 20 July 2023).

156 Mamdani (n 17) 90.

157 Anne L Bartlett and James T Dhizaala, 'Post-Conflict Capitalism in Northern Uganda' (2018) 30(2) Peace Review 168.

The division of labour was not only racialized and tribalized but also gendered. Men were naturalized as productive and women as reproductive workers. 'Under customary law in the Gold Coast', Ossome observes, '[al]though cash crops, such as cocoa, were gender neutral prior to colonialism, they became defined as male crops, while crops used primarily for domestic consumption became coded female'.[158] Men became part of the boom-and-bust capitalist economy, while women remained in the subsistence economy. Men also became the intermediaries between productive and reproductive labour as capitalism delegated to them the role of controlling the reproductive sphere, the family, and the clan, through the wage and the land. Women's access to land in Uganda depends on their fathers and husbands as land belongs to the clan and is transmitted through the patrilineal line. And yet, despite these separations, productive and reproductive labour relations are fundamentally interdependent.[159] What stabilizes peasant communities, Ossome argues, is gendered subsistence and social reproduction labour, which ensures their survival in the absence of wages and income from the formal sector.[160]

Capitalism does not always raze everything that pre-existed to the ground or, as Marx put it, melts all that is solid into air.[161] It is often cheaper and more effective to work through local structures—by reinventing customary law rather than imposing colonial law, and by marketing some areas and subjects but not others (e.g., men but not women, urban areas but not rural areas)—not least because it drains and fragments resistance.[162] This is why the notion of intermediaries as 'cultural translators' is misleading. There is no such clear-cut gap between global governance and local culture.[163] Just as colonial capitalism worked through the conflation of the global and the local, so does its neo-colonial iteration. While hiring local staff or working through local NGOs is often seen as 'overcoming' neo-colonialism in development interventions, it actually reproduces neo-colonial logics.[164]

[158] Lyn Ossome, 'Can the Law Secure Women's Rights to Land in Africa? Revisiting Tensions Between Culture and Land Commercialization' (2018) 20(1) Feminist Economics 155, 157.

[159] Alessandra Mezzadri, Susan Newman, and Sara Stevano, 'Feminist global political economies of work and social reproduction' (2022) 29(6) Review of International Political Economy 1783.

[160] Ossome (n 137) 76.

[161] Karl Marx and Friedrich Engels, *The Communist Manifesto* (OUP 2008) 6.

[162] See Terence Ranger, 'The invention of tradition in colonial Africa' in Eric Hobsbawm and Terence Ranger, *The Invention of Tradition* (CUP 1983) 211.

[163] Ullrich (n 3).

[164] Dutton and Ní Aoláin, for example, suggest that the Trust Fund's choice of implementing partners, whose staff are, by majority, themselves Ugandans from the northern region is 'to avoid the insidious manifestation of neo-colonial power-relationships in humanitarian

It is against this backdrop that we need to read the role of the ICC's intermediaries in Uganda. This is not to say that today's intermediaries play the same role as the customary chiefs. Unlike the colonial chiefs, their economic position is much more precarious. Whereas some are employed by NGOs or the state and receive decent salaries, many intermediaries are self-entrepreneurs relying on precarious side-payments. They cannot tax, bribe, or force local populations to work. Their role is often ideological rather than directly coercive.[165] Federici alludes to this when she points out that NGOs have replaced the weakened role of husbands as intermediaries in the Global South:

> These are the new supervisors and exploiters of women's reproductive work, and this new patriarchy relies on the collaboration of European and North American women who, like missionaries, are recruited to train women in the 'colonies' to develop the attitudes necessary to become integrated in the global economy.[166]

In other words, the NGO sector is an ideological sector that creates productive and reproductive capitalist subjects and relations in the Global South. No longer confined to training the worker in designated institutions like schools, ideology creates particular types of subjects—micro-entrepreneurs—who are responsible for their own reproduction by precariously navigating productive, reproductive, and subsistence spheres and functions.[167] These spheres and their relationships need to be managed ideologically, which is the role of intermediaries.

intervention settings'. Anne Dutton and Fionnuala Ní Aoláin, 'Between Reparations and Repair: Assessing the Work of the ICC Trust Fund for Victims Under Its Assistance Mandate' (2019) 19(2) Chicago Journal of International Law 490, 526–27.

[165] Social reproduction has changed, too. Cuts to public services and the intensification of land privatization under the World Bank's and the IMF's structural adjustment programmes has made social reproduction both harder and even more private. Federici (n 48) 68–69. For the role of social reproduction under conditions of global neoliberalism see Isabella Bakker and Stephen Gill, *Power, Production and Social Reproduction: Human In/security in the Global Political Economy* (Springer 2003); Isabella Bakker and Stephen Gill, 'Rethinking power, production, and social reproduction: Toward variegated social reproduction' (2019) 43(4) Capital & Class 503.

[166] Federici (n 48) 75.

[167] ibid 101.

4.6 Boundary Struggles and Border Guards

Like colonial intermediaries, contemporary intermediaries regulate boundaries, which coalesce around the division of labour. The division between professional and manual labour that we started with is bound up with the division between market and subsistence economies, productive and reproductive, and employed and surplus labour. Capitalist societies first install and naturalize these boundaries and subsequently regulate people's migration across them. Border guards sort between those subjects who have a right to cross (and when), and those who don't. These boundaries, Fraser argues, 'often become foci of conflict, as actors mobilize to challenge or defend the established boundaries separating economy from polity, production from reproduction, human from non-human nature'.[168] She calls these conflicts 'boundary struggles'.[169] Far from happening only at the point of production where capitalists and workers confront each other, conflicts in capitalist societies also transpire at the boundary where lawyers and victims, NGO workers and subsistence farmers, border guards and refugees, law and justice, and society and nature collide.

Like border guards, intermediaries both cement these divisions and manage people's temporary migration. As we already saw, they push communities in Northern Uganda to strive beyond subsistence. Cultural leaders (*rwodis*) admonish the youth: 'You must go and emulate what your fathers do. You gotta dig. You have to plant something. Plant two hectares of rice and see if you don't make money instead of sitting at these centers and drinking and betting the whole day.'[170] But that crossing cannot become a demand or a right to waged work in the capitalist economy. Northern Ugandans need to be able to fall back on their subsistence roles and accept the failure as theirs ('you didn't try hard enough'). The possibility of self-inflicted failure is always already built into the discourse of intermediaries. In his rallying cry to the Acholi youth ('plant something', 'make money'), the *Rwodi* already foreshadows their likely failure ('drinking and betting the whole day').

This type of anticipatory blame is very common in intermediaries' rhetoric and constitutes a key border management strategy. Note how

168 Fraser (n 45).
169 ibid.
170 Interview with Cultural Leader, Gulu (20 July 2019).

one women's rights lawyer described the 'main problem' in Northern Uganda to me:

> People are too lazy to work. There's lots of drinking alcohol. We have land; Acholi region is blessed with a lot of land. If only people could dig—apart from the land wrangles; the land disputes prevent people from utilizing the land—if people could really utilize the land, but people are lazy to dig. I would also say the skilling . . . because we need some entrepreneurial skills to do meaningful investments.[171]

In addition to people's individual failings ('laziness', 'alcohol', 'lack of skills'), the possibility of success ('really utilize the land') is thwarted through communal failings, what she referred to as 'land wrangles'. Families and communities fight about land (where are the boundaries?; who has the right to use land and who has the right to sell it?) which prevents its proper utilization. Although the region is 'blessed' with good land, the Acholi are not fit to put it to proper use. Most people will not succeed in shedding their role as subsistence farmers. They may be lucky for a day or a season but will probably go back to living from hand to mouth. The transition remains transitory.

Intermediaries similarly regulate the productive and reproductive labour divide. On the one hand, men are naturalized as capitalist subjects associated with cash crops, on the other hand, they are persistently blamed for failing in their role. And thus, women have to step up. They should become entrepreneurs by taking out microloans. Yet, even in the unlikely event of success, they are never released from their reproductive roles. Domestic violence regulates their 'migration' between home and market, and makes women internalize failure. Indeed, international NGO programmes often extend women's rights training, entrepreneurial skills and microloans to women only, and domestic violence is the predictable backlash.[172] In the words of one NGO worker: 'These humanitarian agencies came and said, "if you give food to a woman, she will cater to the whole family. If you give it to a man, he will probably sell it and get alcohol". So, women were empowered'.[173] 'They don't have that respect that they had

[171] Interview with Women's Rights Lawyer, Gulu (24 July 2019).

[172] See Adam Branch, *Displacing Human Rights: War and Intervention in Northern Uganda* (OUP 2011); Porter (n 116).

[173] Interview with NGO Representative, Kampala (23 July 2014).

before', another women's rights advocate told me, 'because for a woman, why should she respect you if you do not provide for her . . . She could even tell you, "you are a useless man", and this brings out domestic violence'.[174] Women can and should cross between production and reproduction but at a price that ties them back to the family. Making money does not mean independence as women are beaten back to their roles as wives and mothers. Although NGOs tackle domestic violence through family mediation and psycho-social support, their programmes are ultimately geared towards the protection of marriage and family life, as market and home represent complementary dynamics in the capitalist totality.

To protect such porous borders, intermediaries organize the conflict landscape away from boundary struggles. As Rwodi Frank told me:

> Now, there is a lot of land conflicts. Brothers are fighting brothers and all sorts of things. In fact, we don't hear much now about the atrocities of the LRA. We hear more about these contemporary problems, people are facing land disputes and gender-based violence. Mostly those two elements but also family neglect. There is a lot of deviant population, especially young people who are resorting to drug abuse.[175]

These conflicts are portrayed as 'our' community problems. Rather than the increasing privatization of land, which makes land sellable and erodes subsistence, the problem is conflicts within communities and families about who can sell the land. Rather than fighting the state or corporations, which take land and resources, Northern Ugandans fight their family members and neighbours, and women their husbands, what an NGO worker called the 'silent war in the communities'.[176] Intermediaries depoliticize these conflicts by focusing their interventions on 'land wrangles' and 'domestic violence'. But, of course, as we shall see in the last chapter, there is always a risk of these conflicts spilling over, of being redirected against the state and market relations. Capitalism's tendency to fight proxy wars in the reproductive sphere away from immediate sites of accumulation is unsustainable as it needs these family and community structures to stabilize the co-existence between different forms of exploitation.[177]

[174] Interview with Women's Rights Activist, Kampala (30 July 2014).
[175] Interview with Cultural Leader, Gulu (20 July 2019) (not his real name).
[176] Interview with TFV's Local Partner, Gulu (10 July 2014).
[177] Melinda Cooper, *Family Values: Between Neoliberalism and the New Social Conservatism* (Princeton UP 2017).

4.7 Conclusion

From a 'global–local divide' perspective, the Court, victims' lawyers, intermediaries, and victims can bridge cultural and knowledge divides. They learn to translate and understand each other's perspective; they share the same interest of bringing 'justice to victims'. Different justice initiatives can complement each other, and any problems that arise are 'misunderstandings' or 'mistranslations' between the 'global' and the 'local'. This looks very different from a labour perspective: here, the white prosecuting counsel earns €12,330 per month (tax-free) and the victims' lawyer €6,544 (after tax), which, counsel complain, is 'unreasonably low' given what other international courts pay.[178] The Court's field staff in Uganda receive what is a 'fair and reasonable' fee rate 'that represents the best prevailing conditions found locally', thus making them part of the local, professional elite.[179] Intermediaries in Northern Uganda, by contrast, receive 150,000 Ugandan Shillings [32 Pounds] for every meeting they organize whereas victims receive one to three Pounds of 'transport reimbursement' for every meeting they attend, while people who come to outreach events receive a soft drink and some snacks.[180] These inequalities are well understood and stir tensions. 'Even lawyers are sometimes insulted and aggressed', one victims' lawyer confessed, 'because [victims say] "you did nothing for us. We spend our energy every time you come here. We have to travel, spend money on it, take the risk to cross police barriers, pay bribes just to see you, and you are very well paid by the court and after 10 years, you just give us nothing." '[181] It requires plenty of ideological work to naturalize this division of labour; ideological labour that is shared by the court's staff, field assistants, victims' lawyers, intermediaries and victims. By accepting their role as 'victims', people also forfeit their claims for labour compensation.

This chapter has illuminated the role of intermediaries through a series of reconceptualizations: from seeing justice as a cultural form that underpins the legitimacy of legal institutions like the ICC, to interpreting it as a commodity exchanged on an international donor market, to theorizing

[178] Richard J Rogers, 'Assessment of the ICC's Legal Aid System' *Global Diligence* (5 January 2017) 49. For the income 'Illustrative Example: Net Income of Lead Counsel vs. P5 Prosecutor' see p 54. The ICTY, for example, pays counsel €16,710 plus €5,156 expenses monthly during trials.

[179] ibid 61.

[180] Interview with ICC Outreach Staff, Kampala (2 August 2019).

[181] Interview with Victims' Lawyer, The Hague (1 June 2018).

it as ideological labour collaboratively performed in the Global South. Conceptualizing justice as a commodity makes sense from the perspective of exchange: different international organizations have to 'sell' their causes to donors and compete for audiences in the volatile 'attention economy' of the Global North.[182] It makes less sense from the perspective of production: who creates the value of the 'justice commodity'—is it the victims, the judges, the prosecutor, the victims' lawyers, the outreach unit, or all of them? The ICC cannot simply buy victims. Rather, it needs to recruit them as victim participants. Intermediaries, similarly, must justify their role as professional labour in an economy, which forces most people to do manual, subsistence and reproductive work. They differentiate labour along racial, tribal and gendered lines but also manage boundaries not just within the postcolony but also between the Global North and the Global South. Rather than identifying an ideological class, the PMC, it is more helpful to identify a form of labour, ideological labour, and then trace how it operates and is divided at different levels of the capital-labour relationship.

More generally, critical ideology theory helps us peel the different layers of social appearances: Behind 'equal' market exchange, there is 'unequal' production, behind culture, there is differentiation of labour, behind productive labour, there is reproductive labour. What is behind law? This brings us back to Kafka's doorkeeper, who guards the door before the law, making the man from the country wait all his life without revealing its secret. While some believe that behind the door of law lies politics at best and naked domination at worst, others hope that, if they continue to hone the instruments of law, it is justice that awaits them. Nothing lies behind that door, Derrida, on the other hand, claims, and that is precisely the secret the doorkeeper is guarding: The essence of the law is that 'the latter has no essence', 'guarded by a doorkeeper who guards nothing, the door remaining open – and open on nothing'. 'That is the whole story of this non-story', Derrida concludes.[183] Yet, despite lacking an essence, law does articulate social relations which are, ultimately, relations of production and reproduction. In this context, the ideological role of intermediaries is not only to

[182] Christine Schwöbel-Patel, 'The "Ideal" Victim of International Criminal Law' (2018) 29(3) The European Journal of International Law 703.

[183] Jacques Derrida, 'Before the Law' in Derek Attridge (ed), *Acts of Literature* (Routledge 1992) 206.

mediate labour relations but to keep a secret, a secret even more troubling than surplus labour or capitalism's preservation of its Others.

That secret is capitalism's structural dependence on its Others and the resistive potential that arises from that dependency.[184] Capitalism needs labour power even though it immiserates its human bearers. Law needs justice even though it disavows its importance,[185] and the ICC needs intermediaries even though it designates them as volunteers.[186] Capitalism's Others, however, can and have existed in other social formations. Without essentializing labouring practices, which are historically and socially contingent, it is likely that people will always do necessary social labour (although in very different forms): make children, grow food, create communities, and resolve conflicts whether capitalism exists or not.[187] 'It seems to be a social law that the value of labor is proven and perhaps even created by its refusal', Federici observes.[188] Ideology makes such a refusal seem both impossible and undesirable, although it does not always succeed, as we will see in Chapter 6. Creating borders both devalues essential labour and the people who do it, blaming those who do not perform their role or who cross illicitly, thus locking labour and labourers in relations of cascading

[184] Of course, capitalist laws of motion make it in practice difficult to opt out of capitalist relations as we depend on them for our survival though the situation is somewhat different for those who still have access to the means of production and reproduction. See Rob Knox, 'Taking Capital's Laws of Motion Seriously: Marxism, Law and Capitalism' (2023) https://www.youtube.com/watch?v=3CtlnO1pvhk&t=3156s (accessed 13 March 2023).

[185] Martti Koskenniemi, *From Apology to Utopia: The Structure of International Legal Argument* (CUP 2006).

[186] These tensions go to the heart of capitalist contradictions. While capitalist accumulation depends on labour power both for surplus value creation and commodity consumption, it immiserates its human bearers to maximize profit, thus both generating crises of overproduction in the short term and threatening the reproduction of labour power in the long term. Despite depending on reproductive relations and products (ie humans, care, trust and nature), capitalism simultaneously drains them off resources (money, time, space, and community) while dumping its emotional and material waste on them, thus threatening not only its own reproduction but also the reproduction of planetary and human life. Its non-capitalist Others, however, can (in theory) live without capitalism. See Nancy Fraser, 'Contradictions of Capital and Care' (2016) 100 New Left Review 99; James O'Connor, 'On the two contradictions of capitalism' (1991) 2(3) Capitalism Nature Socialism 107; David Harvey, *Seventeen Contradictions and the End of Capitalism* (Profile Books 2014).

[187] Kathi Weeks, *Constituting Feminist Subjects* (Verso 2018) 121–22; Karl Marx and Friedrich Engels, *The German Ideology* (Lawrence & Wishart 2007) 48.

[188] Federici (n 48) 96.

blame.[189] Paradoxically, it is easier to blame those who fail in love, not law, those who are expected to do things 'voluntarily', those who do not have a contract that defines their labour. Intermediaries become blameworthy if they do not live up to expectations of care and love, if they are deemed unfaithful or disloyal, if they refuse to play their allocated roles, or do not play them well enough.

[189] See also Sara Farris' analysis of migrant women as a 'regular army of labour', where the sexual and the racial contract intertwine to cheapen and invisibilize their labour. Sara Farris, 'Femonationalism and the "Regular" Army of Labor Called Migrant Women' (2012) 2(2) History of the Present 184, 194; Sara Farris, *In the Name of Women's Rights: The Rise of Femonationalism* (Duke UP 2017).

5
Reparations, Abolitionist Imaginaries, and Self-transforming Victims: Transformative Justice at the ICC

5.1 Introduction

Early into my doctorate I discovered a concept in the Court's texts that I did not expect there: the concept of transformative justice.[1] The latter aims to use the reparation and assistance mandate of the International Criminal Court (ICC) not only to redress victims but also to rectify the structural conditions that made them particularly vulnerable to victimization. I found it curious that this concept, which is premised on a much broader understanding of harm and redress, would appear in the documents of an international criminal court. What was it doing there? Of course, there is an easy answer. We are used to hegemonic institutions incorporating radical vocabulary. It may be one of countless examples of how private and public marketing have appropriated feminism, 'black lives matter' or decolonization to rebrand commodities and institutions.[2] It may serve the window-dressing of these institutions: empty talk to lure donors and lull the wider public.[3] Except, the concept appeared in a reparation decision: a serious legal text that did not attract much publicity. And it left a scattered trail linking the reparation decision to international women's rights advocacy,

[1] Carolyn Hoyle and Leila Ullrich, 'New Court, New Justice? The Evolution of "Justice for Victims" at Domestic Courts and at the International Criminal Court' (2014) 12(4) Journal of International Criminal Justice 681, 684, 690, 692–99.

[2] See eg Christine Schwöbel-Patel, *Marketing Global Justice: The Political Economy of International Criminal Law* (CUP 2021).

[3] Some of the ICC practitioners I interviewed suspected that this was 'donor-friendly' language. More on this below.

Victims and the Labour of Justice at the International Criminal Court. Leila Ullrich, Oxford University Press.
 DOI: 10.1093/9780191915048.003.0005

the Trust Fund for Victims' (TFV) assistance programmes in Northern Uganda, as well as black feminist grassroots organizing in the United States.

This chapter charts how the promise of transformative justice plays out at an institution which, by design, is not only carceral but anti-structural. While the first three chapters examined how the concept of 'justice for victims' translates into material practices on the ground, especially victim participation, this chapter traces the use of 'transformative justice' both in the Court's reparation documents and in practitioners' discourses in The Hague, Kenya, and Uganda. Whereas ICC pundits have debated whether the Court can and should deliver 'transformative reparations', I will explore its ideological forms and functions.[4] Why did this concept emerge in such an unlikely place? What explains its lingering presence in the Court's discourse and practice? Such an analysis reveals that transformative justice assumes very different forms depending on where it sediments: it assumes a legal form in the deliberations about the ICC's reparation mandate; it assumes a developmental form in the Trust Fund's assistance programmes in Northern Uganda, and it takes on an altogether different form in black feminist and activist circles, where the concept originated, both as a concrete method of addressing sexual and gender-based violence (SGBV) and as an abolitionist imaginary. But what are the ideological functions of 'transformative reparations'?

In her ideology critique of the invocation of 'root causes' in human rights discourse, Susan Marks writes that 'human rights institutions and officials have grappled only partially and rather problematically with the question of why abuses occur, how vulnerabilities arise, and what it will take to bring about change'.[5] Rather than offering a deeper analysis of human rights abuses in a capitalist world order, 'root causes', Marks contends, act as another set of blinders that render human rights violations inexplicable and unsolvable.[6] This problem, however, is not confined to how human rights organizations *use* the language of root causes, structural violence, or

[4] See eg Margaret Urban Walker, 'Transformative Reparations? A Critical Look at a Current Trend in Thinking about Gender-Just Reparations' (2016) 10 IJTJ108, 108; Louise Chappell, 'The gender injustice cascade: "transformative" reparations for victims of sexual and gender-based crimes in the Lubanga case at the International Criminal Court' (2017) 21(9) The International Journal of Human Rights 1223, 1224; Luke Moffett, 'Reparations for victims at the International Criminal Court: a new way forward?' (2017) 21(9) The International Journal of Human Rights 1204, 1209; Brianne McGonigle Leyh and Julie Fraser, 'Transformative Reparations: Changing the Game or More of the Same' (2019) 8(1) Cambridge International Law Journal 39, 41.

[5] Susan Marks, 'Human Rights and Root Causes' (2011) 74 The Modern Law Review 57, 70.

[6] ibid 75.

structural inequality, it also inheres in the concepts themselves.[7] Reading the Court's grappling with transformative justice symptomatically, I argue that the very terms in which the problem of transformation is couched—'transforming structures', 'addressing root causes'—make transformation seem impossible not only for the ICC. After all, 'structures' and 'root causes' are abstractions and metaphors. We don't know how to change 'structures' or how to 'pull out' the problem 'at the root'. What transformative justice conceals is that structures consist of social relations and social relations can be challenged and changed. In doing so, transformative justice at the ICC, ultimately, rejuvenates and reproduces the justice status quo.

This chapter proceeds in four sections. The first section traces how transformative reparations became part of the Court's reparation principles, and how the Court's practitioners make sense of that promise of transformation. The second section delves into alternative genealogies of the concept, especially its roots in black feminist and abolitionist thinking, to understand its particular career at the Court. The third section offers a symptomatic reading of the Court's transformative justice discourse drawing on Marx, Althusser, and Jameson. The fourth section asks what really happens on the ground when the Court 'does' transformative justice by exploring the Trust Fund's assistance programmes in Northern Uganda. While the critique of transformative reparations has focused on the ICC's limited capacity, and the question of whether 'transforming societies' is or should be part of the Court's mandate, I argue that more fundamental problems characterize its practice on the ground. Although the ambitions of transformative reparations are seemingly watered down in the contestation between the Court's liberal and traditional stakeholders in its African situations, I will show, instead, that it is precisely the promise of transformation that reproduces the status quo. Far from addressing structural causes, the concept ends up shifting the responsibility for 'transformation' to victim–survivors. In the final analysis, it is the victim and not the state, the local community,

[7] With regard to Galtung's concept of structural violence, Graeber has argued that the problem 'is that it views "structures" as abstract, free-floating entities; when what we are really referring to here are material processes, in which violence, and the threat of violence, play a crucial, constitutive role'. David Graeber, 'Dead zones of the imagination: On violence, bureaucracy, and interpretive labor' (2012) 2(2) Journal of Ethnographic Theory 105, 113; Catia Confortini, 'Galtung, Violence, and Gender: The Case for a Peace Studies/Feminism Alliance' (2006) 31 Peace & Change 333; Vickie Cooper and David Whyte, 'Grenfell, Austerity, and Institutional Violence' (2022) 27(1) Sociological Research Online 207, 211.

the global economy, or the international community that has to do the transformation.

5.2 Transformative Justice at the ICC

> You can't take people back to where they were in 1984 and say that's sufficient and that's it. And everybody starts from that socio-economic situation and the governing relationship between the North and the South . . . That won't work . . . If you proceed on that basis, things will repeat themselves, problems will re-emerge . . . You have to have a transformative approach.[8]

I'm talking to the Trust Fund's officer in Kampala. For him, transformative justice follows logically from well-established reparation principles in international law, especially 'guarantees of non-repetition' and 'satisfaction for victims'. When I asked him whether a transformative approach might politicize the Court, he laughed: 'The Court is in that situation already. This is nothing it can avoid.'[9] After all, states established the Court, refer its cases, fund its budget, and facilitate its operations: 'You can't put your head into the sand and say, "it doesn't affect us, it doesn't affect us".'[10]

Nonetheless, transformative justice is still a rather new and daring concept. In fact, it poses a challenge to the conventional understanding of reparations in international law: full restitution. Restitution is the idea—as the Chorzow Factory case established in 1928—that 'reparation must, as far as possible, wipe out all the consequences of the illegal act and re-establish the situation which would, in all probability, have existed if that act had not been committed.'[11] Since then, the concept of reparation has developed further particularly through the UN General Assembly's adoption of the Basic Principles and Guidelines on the Right to a Remedy and Reparation for Victims of Gross Violations of International Human Rights Law and Serious Violations of International Humanitarian Law in 2005. The Guidelines list restitution, compensation, rehabilitation, satisfaction, and

[8] Interview with TFV Officer, Kampala (7 July 2014).
[9] ibid.
[10] ibid.
[11] *Factory at Chorzów (Germany v Poland)* (Judgment) (1928) PCIJ Series A No 1 (September 1928) § 125.

guarantees of non-repetition as 'full and effective' forms of reparations.[12] Parallel to these developments, Article 75 of the Rome Statute tasked the ICC with establishing reparation principles that include but are not limited to restitution, compensation, and rehabilitation.

On 16 March 2011, Trial Chamber I asked the Trust Fund for Victims (TFV) and the Registry to write a joint report on reparations to help the Chamber create the principles and procedures of reparations in the *Lubanga* case. Yet, after a period of consultations, the Registry and the TFV decided to submit separate reports due to differences in their views.[13] A closer reading of the two documents suggests that they embrace somewhat different ideas of reparations. Citing a report by UN Women, the TFV notes in its submission that 'reparations that support women's economic empowerment can contribute to transformative justice by placing them in a better position to break with historic patterns of subordination and social exclusion.'[14] In a subsequent report to the Chamber, the TFV elaborated on why 'transformative justice' should be part of the Court's reparation principles:

> [i]n the aftermath of war crimes, crimes against humanity and genocide, it will often not be appropriate to restore the *status quo ante* that gave rise to such crimes, in particular because the majority of victims of such crimes will likely have been the powerless and dispossessed at the time the conflict erupted.[15]

'Transformative reparations' should thus be adopted 'with a view to eliminating the pre-existing structural inequalities that have led to or encouraged the violence.'[16]

[12] UN General Assembly, 'Basic Principles and Guidelines on the Right to a Remedy and Reparation for Victims of Gross Violations of International Human Rights Law and Serious Violations of International Humanitarian Law' UN Doc A/RES/60/147 (21 March 2006), also known as the Bassiouni Principles, 7–8 (principles 19–23).

[13] They especially differed on whether the TFV is obliged to complement reparation awards with the voluntary contributions it receives. See *Prosecutor v. Lubanga* (Second Report of the Registry on Reparations) [2011] ICC-01/04-01/06-2806, § 2.

[14] *Prosecutor v Lubanga* (Trust Fund for Victims' First Report on Reparations) [2011] ICC-01/04-01/06-2803-Red, § 34; UN Women, 'Progress of the World's Women: In Pursuit of Justice' (2011) 98 https://www.unwomen.org/en/digital-library/publications/2011/7/progress-of-the-world-s-women-in-pursuit-of-justice (accessed 14 April 2023).

[15] *Prosecutor v Lubanga* (Observations on Reparations in Response to the Scheduling Order of 14 March 2012) [2012] ICC-01/04-01/06-2872, § 73.

[16] ibid § 77.

Transformative reparations are, however, contentious. In its separate report to the Trial Chamber, the Registry makes no mention of the idea. While the Registry's staff members I interviewed agreed that reparations should not reinforce pre-existing patterns of discrimination, especially gender discrimination, they were more cautious about using reparations to achieve broader societal transformations. As a senior Registry official put it:

> We are not trying to come in and transform a society as such. We are trying to come in and see what the impact of these crimes was and what we can do about them and then the transformation element would be relevant when we are looking at how we can do that . . . and, I suppose, the Trust Fund, because they have their broader assistance mandate, may be inclined to take a broader view.[17]

In its report, the Registry distinguishes between societal ills predating the crimes and those caused by the crimes and argues that reparations should only address the latter.[18]

Yet, far from existing in a vacuum, the TFV's concept of transformative reparations draws heavily on reparation principles developed by civil society, the jurisprudence of the Inter-American Court of Human Rights, and UN documents.[19] Most importantly, the TFV refers to the Nairobi Declaration on Women's and Girls' Right to a Remedy and Reparation, a civil society document drafted by women's rights advocates in 2007.[20] The Nairobi Declaration argues 'that reparation must drive post-conflict transformation of socio-cultural injustices, and political and structural inequalities that

[17] Interview with Senior Official, Registry (16 December 2013).

[18] *Prosecutor v Lubanga* (n 13) § 42.

[19] *Prosecutor v Lubanga* (n 15) §§ 10–11.

[20] Valerie Couillard, 'The Nairobi Declaration: Redefining Reparation for Women Victims of Sexual Violence' (2007) 1 IJTJ 444. There are many contestations regarding the meaning and modalities of reparations at the ICC. See eg Alina Balta, Manon Bax, and Rianne Letschert, 'Trial and (Potential) Error: Conflicting Visions on Reparations Within the ICC System' (2019) 29(3) International Criminal Justice Review 221, 222 ('Each of the chambers within the ICC seems to have conflicting ideas on what reparations should entail and how they should be implemented. Moreover, the Trust Fund for Victims (TFV) and the Court define and apply reparations differently. This incoherent approach appears to be mainly generated by the different interpretations, meanings, and priorities attached to the reparations regime, by both the TFV and the chambers within the ICC'). See also ICC, 'Independent Expert Review of the International Criminal Court and the Rome Statute System: Final Report' (30 September 2020) § 879 ('The Court's conceptual and procedural processes for reparations are laden with complexity and uncertainty, which gravely affects the victims' rights to meaningful participation and reparations').

shape the lives of women and girls'.[21] In the *Cotton Field* case, in 2009, the Inter-American Court of Human Rights stated that 'bearing in mind the context of structural discrimination in which the facts of this case occurred . . . the reparations must be designed to change this situation, so that their effect is not only of restitution, but also of rectification'.[22] Similarly, the UN Special Rapporteur on violence against women, Rashida Manjoo, stressed in 2010 that 'since violence perpetrated against individual women generally feeds into patterns of pre-existing and often cross-cutting structural subordination and systemic marginalization, measures of redress need to link individual reparation and structural transformation'.[23] The UN even submitted an *amicus curiae* in the *Katanga* case in 2015, advising the Chamber to adopt reparations that have transformative potential.[24]

In light of this broader advocacy, transformative reparations have gained traction in the Court's reparation decisions and the TFV's strategic plans.[25] In its reparation decision of 7 August 2012 in *Lubanga*, Trial Chamber I observed that reparations with transformative objectives may be appropriate and 'can help prevent future victimization'.[26] While amending the Trial Chamber's reparation order, the Appeals Chamber confirmed that

[21] 'Nairobi Declaration on Women's and Girls' Right to a Remedy and Reparation' (2007) 2 http://www.fidh.org/IMG/pdf/NAIROBI_DECLARATIONeng.pdf (accessed 22 January 2023).

[22] See *Gonzalez and Others ('Cotton Field') v Mexico*, Inter-American Court of Human Rights (series C) No 205 (16 November 2009) § 450. See also Ruth Rubio-Marín and Clara Sandoval, 'Engendering the Reparations Jurisprudence of the Inter-American Court of Human Rights: The Promise of the Cotton Field Judgment' (2011) 33 Human Rights Quarterly 1062; *Prosecutor v Lubanga* (Consultant's report on reparations in the Inter-American Human Rights System, Annex to the Second Report of the Registry on Reparations) [2012] ICC-01/04-01/06-2806-Anx) § 11. On transformative reparations in Colombia see Elena Butti and Brianne McGonigle Leyh, 'Intersectionality and Transformative Reparations: The Case of Colombian Marginal Youths' (2019) 19(5) International Criminal Law Review 753.

[23] 'Report of the Special Rapporteur on Violence against Women, its Causes and Consequences, Rashida Manjoo' A/HRC/14/22 (19 April 2010) § 24. See also Fionnuala Ní Aoláin, Catherine O'Rourke, and Aisling Swaine, 'Transforming Reparations for Conflict-Related Sexual Violence: Principles and Practice' (2015) 28 Harvard Human Rights Journal 97; Rashida Manjoo, 'Introduction: reflections on the concept and implementation of transformative reparations' (2017) 21(9) The International Journal of Human Rights 1193; Simeon Gready, 'The Case for Transformative Reparations: In Pursuit of Structural Socio-Economic Reform in Post-Conflict Societies' (2022) 16(2) Journal of Intervention and Statebuilding 182.

[24] *Prosecutor v Katanga* (United Nations Joint Submission on Reparations) [2015] ICC-01/04-01/07-3550, § § 33–37.

[25] *Prosecutor v Lubanga* (Observations of the Women's Initiatives for Gender Justice on Reparations) [2012] ICC-01/04-01/06-2876, §§ 12, 13, 17.

[26] *Prosecutor v Lubanga* (Decision establishing the principles and procedures to be applied to reparations) [2012] ICC-01/04-01/06-2904, § 222, § 236.

reparations with symbolic, transformative and preventative value are part of the Court's reparation modalities.[27] Transformative reparations were further elaborated in the Court's reparation order in the *Ntaganda* case on 8 March 2021. Known as the '*Ntaganda* reparation principles', the order explains that 'the transformative purpose of reparations aims at producing both a restorative and a corrective effect and to promote structural changes, dismantling discriminations, stereotypes, and practices that may have contributed to create the conditions for the crime to occur'.[28] In the reparation proceedings in the *Ongwen* case, the legal representatives of victims have also endorsed the principle of 'transformative reparations'.[29] Recognized as a key goal in the TFV's Strategic Plan (2014–2017), while disappearing from its Strategic Plan 2020–2021, transformative reparations are front and centre in the Trust Fund's new draft Strategic Plan (2023–2025), which proclaims that 'in the context of a surge of conflicts throughout the World, increasing economic inequality, and under the pressure of climate change, more than ever transformative reparations for victims of Rome Statute crimes need to be high on the international agenda'.[30]

Neither is the goal of transformative justice merely rhetorical. On the contrary, it shapes how the TFV interprets its reparation and assistance

[27] *Prosecutor v Lubanga* (Judgment on the appeals against the 'Decision establishing the principles and procedures to be applied to reparations' of 7 August 2012 with AMENDED order for reparations (Annex A) and public annexes 1 and 2) [2015], ICC-01/04-01/06-3129, § 202 (also known as the '*Lubanga* reparation principles').

[28] See *Prosecutor v Bosco Ntaganda* (Reparations Order) [2021] ICC-01/04-02/06-2659 § 94. See also Marina Lostal, 'The Ntaganda Reparations Order: a marked step towards a victims-centred reparations legal framework at the ICC' *EJIL:Talk!* (24 May 2021) https://www.ejiltalk.org/the-ntaganda-reparations-order-a-marked-step-towards-a-victim-centred-reparations-legal-framework-at-the-icc/ (accessed 22 January 2023). While the Appeals Chamber partially reversed the Ntaganda reparation decision and directed the Trial Chamber to issue a new reparation order, it found no error with its reparation modalities (including transformative reparations). See *Prosecutor v Bosco Ntaganda* (Judgment on the appeals against the decision of Trial Chamber VI of 8 March 2021 entitled 'Reparations Order') [2022] ICC-01/04-02/06-2782, §§ 397–401.

[29] *Prosecutor v Ongwen* (Victims' Preliminary Submissions on Reparations) [2021] ICC-02/04-01/15-1921, §§ 25–27.

[30] TFV Strategic Plan 2014–2017, 25 https://www.trustfundforvictims.org/sites/default/files/imce/1408%20TFV%20Strategic%20Plan%202014-2017%20Final%20ENG.pdf (accessed 16 April 2023); TFV, Strategic Plan 2020–2021 https://www.trustfundforvictims.org/sites/default/files/reports/TFV%20Strategic%20Plan%202020-2021.pdf (accessed 15 March 2023); TFV Draft Strategic Plan 2023–2025, 7 https://www.trustfundforvictims.org/sites/default/files/reports/Draft%20TFV%20Strategic%20Plan%202023-2025.pdf (accessed 15 March 2023).

mandates.[31] So far, the Trust Fund has fully implemented Court-ordered reparations in only one case, the *Katanga* case, where it paid out individual reparation awards of US$250 to 297 victims. It belatedly launched collective reparation programmes in the *Lubanga* case in 2021, nine years after Lubanga was convicted, and more recently began administering individual and collective reparations in the *Al Mahdi* case.[32] The TFV's assistance programmes have a somewhat better record. Having implemented such programmes in Northern Uganda and the DRC since 2008, the TFV launched a pilot programme in the Central African Republic in September 2020, while new assistance programmes are planned for Ivory Coast, Kenya, Georgia, and Mali.[33] Under its assistance mandate, the Trust Fund has supported initiatives such as the 'peace caravans' and the 'system of mutual solidarity' that may not have been traditionally understood as part of the 'necessary' victim assistance the TFV was mandated to provide.[34] The peace caravans are platforms for community dialogue and reconciliation, while the system of mutual solidarity, a village savings and loan scheme, is designed 'to creat[e] strong social ties among the members, as well as, rebuild

[31] *Prosecutor v Lubanga* (n 15) § 73; *Prosecutor v Lubanga* (Annex A: Collective Reparations projects in relation to the conviction of Thomas Lubanga Dyilo before the International Criminal Court) [2017] ICC-01/04-01/06-3273-AnxA, 5 ('Reparations, as a general principle, need to address any underlying injustices and should avoid replicating discriminatory practices or structures that predated the commission of the crimes'). See ICC press release, 'The Embassy of Ireland and the Trust Fund for Victims conclude a joint monitoring visit to northern Uganda between 13–17 September 2022' https://www.icc-cpi.int/news/embassy-ireland-and-trust-fund-victims-conclude-joint-monitoring-visit-northern-uganda-between (accessed 30 September 2022) ('The objective of the monitoring visit was to provide delegates with the opportunity to witness first-hand the transformative work of the TFV in northern Uganda').

[32] TFV Management Brief Q2/2021 (1 April–30 June 2021) https://www.trustfundforvictims.org/sites/default/files/reports/TFV%20Management%20Brief%20Q2%202021_0.pdf (accessed 15 March 2023). See also Marina Lostal, 'Implementing Reparations in the Al Mahdi Case: A Story of Monumental Challenges in Timbuktu' (2021) 19(4) Journal of International Criminal Justice 831.

[33] TFV, 'Decisions taken by the Board of Directors of the Trust Fund for Victims, January to July 2021' https://www.trustfundforvictims.org/en/news/decisions-taken-board-directors-trust-fund-victims-january-july-2021 (accessed 12 November 2021); TFV Management Brief Q2/2021 (1 April–30 June 2021) https://www.trustfundforvictims.org/sites/default/files/reports/TFV%20Management%20Brief%20Q2%202021_0.pdf (accessed 12 November 2021).

[34] TFV, 'Empowering Victims and Communities towards Social Change' (2012) 6, 23–27 http://www.trustfundforvictims.org/sites/default/files/imce/TFV%20PPR%20Summer%202012%20ENG%20Final_.pdf (accessed 16 April 2023); Article 50 (a)(i) of the TFV Regulations states 'that the Trust Fund shall be considered to be seized when the Board of Directors

trust.'[35] 'By assisting victims to return to a dignified and contributory life within their communities, [the TFV] contributes to the realization of sustainable and long-lasting peace through the promotion of restorative justice and reconciliation.'[36] As such, the TFV's understanding of reparative justice goes beyond what criminal justice institutions would usually consider their 'business'. It has even been criticized by non-governmental organizations (NGOs), which usually advocate for more victim support rather than less. Redress, for example, has argued that the Trust Fund's adoption of 'reconciliation' and 'peace building' as part of its goals exceeds its mandate.[37]

Even though the TFV's reparation and assistance mandates are different, with some describing the former as the TFV's 'justice component' and the latter as its 'humanitarian component',[38] both are informed by a transformative approach. Moreover, that difference between reparation and assistance will often disappear in the broader development efforts of the TFV's implementing partners, especially for collective reparation awards,

considers it *necessary* to provide physical or psychological rehabilitation or material support for the benefit of victims and their families' (emphasis added).

[35] TFV, 'Mobilising Resources and Supporting the Most Vulnerable Victims through Earmarked Funding, Programme Progress Report Winter' (2012) 9 https://www.trustfundforvictims.org/sites/default/files/reports/TFV%20Programme%20Progress%20Report%20-%20Winter%202012.pdf (accessed 11 April 2023). Phil Clark had a more positive impression of the peace caravans in the DRC. Phil Clark, *Distant Justice: The Impact of the International Criminal Court on African Politics* (CUP 2018) 147.

[36] TFV Website http://www.trustfundforvictims.org/ (accessed 16 April 2023).

[37] Redress, 'Comments to the Trust Fund for Victims on its Draft Strategic Plan 2014-17' (2014) https://redress.org/wp-content/uploads/2017/12/May-14-REDRESS-Comments-on-the-draft-strategic-plan-of-the-ICC-Trust-Fund-for-Victims.pdf (accessed 16 April 2023). In its first Strategic Plan, the TFV framed its work as akin to local, restorative justice mechanisms such as traditional justice rituals, cleansing and healing ceremonies that aim at community reconciliation and social reintegration. See TFV, 'Global Strategic Plan 2009–2012' (2008) 23. In the Lubanga case, the Chamber stated that 'reparations should secure, whenever possible, reconciliation between the convicted person, the victims of the crimes and the affected communities'. *Prosecutor v Lubanga* (Order for Reparations amended) [2015] ICC-01/04-01/06-3129-AnxA, § 72. For a critical analysis of the contribution of criminal trials to reconciliation see Janine Clark, *International Trials and Reconciliation: Assessing the Impact of the International Criminal Tribunal for the Former Yugoslavia* (Routledge 2014). For a critique of the TFV's assistance mandate see Regina Rauxloh, 'Good intentions and bad consequences: The general assistance mandate of the Trust Fund for Victims of the ICC' (2021) 34(1) Leiden Journal of International Law 203.

[38] Edda Kristjánsdóttir, 'International mass claims processes and the ICC Trust Fund For Victims' in Carla Ferstman, Mariana Goetz, and Alan Stephens (eds), *Reparations for Victims of Genocide, War Crimes and Crimes Against Humanity: Systems in Place and Systems in the Making* (Martinus Nijhoff 2009) 168, 174–75. Peter Dixon has argued for the merits of 'intentionally and carefully blur[ring] the distinction' between assistance and reparations. See Peter Dixon, 'Reparations, Assistance and the Experience of Justice: Lessons from Colombia and the Democratic Republic of Congo (DRC)' (2016) 10 IJTJ 88, 88.

which are the TFV's preferred modality. Contracting local and international NGOs, which have been running similar development and humanitarian programmes for many years, the TFV is 'adding some additional funding' to 'a train that is already moving'.[39] While in theory an independent institution within the Rome Statute system, the TFV, in practice, is part of the ICC.[40] It can only operate in situations in which the Court is active and only for the benefit of victims of crimes that fall within the ICC's jurisdiction.[41] In ICC documents, the TFV is often referred to as part of the Court or the ICC system.[42] More importantly, victims on the ground usually perceive the Court and the TFV as part of one institution. As one former TFV partner observed, 'they use the same cars, the same drivers, the same translators. It is difficult to tell them apart'.[43] Now that we have established the legal and programmatic relevance of transformative justice, the question is how the Court's practitioners make sense of the concept.

5.2.1 No Money, No Mandate, No Reparation Rationale

Many ICC practitioners and NGO officers in The Hague, Kenya, and Uganda whom I interviewed in 2013 and 2014, and in 2018 and 2019, were not familiar with the concept of 'transformative justice' not to mention the Court's and the TFV's ambition to contribute to it through reparations and assistance. Once I explained the concept, many interviewees were sceptical. Their critique centred around three 'No's': 'no money for transformation', 'no mandate for transformation', and 'no reparation rationale for transformation'.

[39] Telephone Interview with TFV evaluator (3 January 2014).

[40] *Prosecutor v Kenyatta* (Dissenting Opinion of Judge Eboe-Osuji) [2016] ICC-01/09-01/11-2038-Anx, §§ 31–33.

[41] See Rome Statute, art 79; TFV Regulations.

[42] ICC, 'Guidelines Governing the Relations between the Court and Intermediaries for the Organs and Units of the Court and Counsel working with intermediaries' (March 2014) 2 footnote 1 https://www.icc-cpi.int/sites/default/files/GRCI-Eng.pdf (accessed 7 August 2023); Assembly of States Parties, 'Report of the Court on the Revised strategy in relation to Victims' (2012) ICC-ASP/11/40, § 2, n 6.

[43] Telephone Interview with former TFV partner (26 April 2013).

No money

Transformation requires money. In 2022, the TFV was engaged at the reparation phase in five cases (*Lubanga*, *Katanga*, *Al Mahdi*, *Ntaganda*, and *Ongwen*) at a value of over €5 million and operated twenty assistance programmes at a value of €3 million.[44] These sums pale into insignificance in the face of the mammoth task of transforming societies emerging from decades of conflict. As a former TFV local partner in Northern Uganda reckoned:

> The war was here for 20 years, and when you come and say you are transforming our people and you are working for 5 years and the war was here for 20 years, do you think you will succeed? There is already a generational gap . . . If it is a long-term thing, like 30 years . . . I can assure you that you can transform the people.[45]

An NGO worker in Kampala was equally dismissive: 'What came out of that [the TFV's assistance programmes] was a few €20,000, €60,000, €80,000 projects that never had any substantive impact on the number of victims we are talking about.'[46] The TFV has struggled to attract donor money. Scathingly criticizing the Trust Fund's fundraising efforts, the Independent Expert Review noted that 'the Court's reparations and assistance scheme can hardly succeed without adequate financial resources and stability of its reserves. Court orders for reparations cannot just be numbers on paper'.[47]

No mandate

Apart from lack of resources, many interviewees in The Hague felt that the Court had no mandate to 'transform societies'. The late ICC Judge Hans-Peter Kaul observed:

> I am not sure whether I entirely understand this idea of transformative reparations. The task to make our societies fairer, more just and less discriminatory is an eternal task which has to be addressed by the

[44] Assembly of States Parties, 'Report of the Board of Directors of the Trust Fund for Victims to the Assembly of States Parties on the activities of the Trust Fund for the period 1 July 2021 to 30 June 2022' (2022) ICC-ASP/21/14, § 5.

[45] Interview with Priest, Gulu (10 July 2014).

[46] Interview with CSO Representative, Kampala (7 August 2014).

[47] ICC, 'Independent Expert Review of the International Criminal Court and the Rome Statute System: Final Report' (30 September 2020) §§ 891, 939, 942.

> communities and the political systems of the world. To expect that a society can be transformed through the necessarily limited reparations system of the International Criminal Court is, in my view, just a little bit too much.[48]

As a judicial institution, many practitioners argued, the ICC should not engage in what looks like a political agenda. 'I have not been aware of the concept of transformative justice', one judge said, 'I am not sure about it. It seems to turn reparations into a political process'.[49] 'What do I think of this concept?', a legal adviser at the Registry told me, 'I'm not opposed to it by any means. But to be blunt, I don't think that's a conceptual framework that actually falls within reparations'.[50]

Yet, the focus on the ICC's lack of money and mandate sidelines the question of whether an international criminal court *should* be 'transforming structures' at all in its situation countries. Some interviewees felt that this smacks of the neo-colonialism and interventionism that the Court has been accused of in its 'African situations'. As a Registry lawyer observed:

> And [transformative justice] may change one or two mindsets, but I can also see it being very donor-report friendly. I certainly would not use the word 'transformative' for a society, because it is, one, very arrogant and, second, because they will never be there long enough to do anything that is substantive.[51]

'Transformative justice is a very problematic concept', a legal adviser of the President added: 'It reminds me of Rumsfeld's rhetoric before the Afghanistan invasion. Transformation from outside does not work and even transformation from within is very problematic.'[52]

No reparation rationale

Furthermore, the rationale of reparations conflicts with the goal of societal change. Reparations at the Court are ordered against individual

[48] Interview with Judge, The Hague (19 December 2013).
[49] Interview with Judge, The Hague (16 January 2014) (quote based on my notes).
[50] Interview with Legal Adviser, Registry, The Hague (1 June 2018).
[51] Interview with Legal Officer, Registry, The Hague (12 November 2013).
[52] Informal conversation with Legal Adviser, Presidency (31 January 2014) (quote based on my notes).

perpetrators, not states or corporations.[53] 'You can talk to defence counsel', a Registry lawyer told me, 'but I am pretty sure that they would tell you: "I don't see why my client, who was convicted for enlisting children in this part of Ituri, has to pay to transform the whole region of Ituri, because my client is not responsible for that".'[54] 'Reparations are unlikely to contribute to broader goals of reconciliation or transformation where only one or a handful of perpetrator(s), from one-side or at a particular point in time of a conflict, are found responsible', Moffett and Sandoval point out, 'the ICC is necessarily selective and exemplary'.[55] A transformative agenda may not only be unfair to defendants but to victims too. Indeed, blurring the boundaries between reparations and societal transformation arguably deprives victims of recognition as it fails to acknowledge that they have been wronged as individuals and thus deserve reparations.[56] Pablo De Greiff, for example, contends that 'development programs have a very low reparative capacity, for they do not target victims specifically' and that reparations should not be turned 'into the means of solving structural problems of poverty and inequality'.[57] Urban Walker specifically criticizes the concept of 'transformative reparations' because 'it threatens to bypass or aims to displace reparative justice as a distinct and distinctly victim-centred imperative'.[58]

Some of the Court's practitioners went further in their critique, suspecting that the Trust Fund deliberately immerses itself in a big, 'utopian' concept to mask its failure to deliver on its narrower mandate of meaningful assistance and reparations for victims. As one legal coordinator observed,

> Instead of focusing on what we can do now, what is really the core mandate of the Court, we are going to forget that, accept that this is not fulfilled, and try to fight for something that we know we will never achieve, to say that we are doing something, but we are not doing anything that is meaningful. It has to be meaningful for victims.[59]

[53] Rome Statute, art 75(2).
[54] Interview with Legal Officer, Registry, The Hague (4 February 2014).
[55] Luke Moffett and Clara Sandoval, 'Tilting at windmills: Reparations and the International Criminal Court' (2021) 34(3) Leiden Journal of International Law 749, 752.
[56] See Moffett (n 4) 1209.
[57] Pablo de Greiff, 'Justice and Reparations' in Pablo de Greiff (ed), *The Handbook of Reparations* (OUP 2006) 451, 470.
[58] Urban Walker (n 4) 108.
[59] Interview with Legal Coordinator, Registry, The Hague (6 February 2014).

Many practitioners in Kenya and Uganda shared this suspicion. One NGO worker in Kisumu put it in no uncertain terms:

> First of all, they are joking, they have absolutely no power or influence—certainly not the Trust Fund. You cannot start assuming . . . that by looking at the structural causes you therefore have transformed the victims in your work . . . The original intention of the Trust Fund was very clear. They need to go back to that . . . and not talk about changing systems . . . they don't even have the resources. It is political and entrenched and they don't understand that and will never understand that.[60]

There seems to be a tacit agreement among many practitioners and legal academics that structural change lies beyond the court's capacity and purpose, especially its reparation mandate. In their submission on the ICC's reparation principles, academics of Queen's University Belfast and Ulster University challenged the Court's transformative justice ambitions, pointing out that 'the state has the mandate, responsibility and legitimacy to engage in national reparations that promote reconciliation, tackle underlying causes of victimisation, prevent further violence, and are transformative'.[61] Likewise, Luke Moffett concludes that 'if the ICC is an ineffectual or inappropriate locus in delivering transformative reparations, then the state in which the crime occurs is the primary actor to ensure the rights of victims'.[62]

Curiously, then, both practitioners and academics reaffirm the state as the legitimate, responsible, and capable agent of structural change. Only states can bring about structural transformation as it requires the power to change laws and enforce them. Gender equality, for example, can hardly be achieved without changing legislation on matters such as equal pay, inheritance, divorce, and domestic violence. Yet, there is a tension between the insistence that states are the only effective agents of structural change and the admission that states usually are not very keen on the latter. A legal officer at the Registry sighed:

[60] Interview with NGO Worker, Kisumu (26 August 2014).

[61] *Prosecutor v Katanga* (Queen's University Belfast's Human Rights Centre (HRC) and University of Ulster's Transitional Justice Institute (TJI) Submission on Reparations Issues pursuant to Article 75 of the Statute) [2015] ICC-01/04-01/07-3551, § 6. See also Anne Dutton and Fionnuala Ní Aoláin, 'Between Reparations and Repair: Assessing the Work of the ICC Trust Fund for Victims Under Its Assistance Mandate' (2019) 19(2) Chicago Journal of International Law 509.

[62] Moffett (n 4) 1214.

> Of course, I would love this. The concept of transformative justice, it is a beautiful concept. But thinking with a legal mind, I don't know to what extent this concept falls squarely within the scope of the Court's mandate . . . I don't know to what extent States Parties would be willing to go along with it. Because everything that is transformative, states are normally reluctant about.[63]

On the surface, the critique is that transformative reparations are unrealistic. They are neither part of the Court's mandate nor beneficial to victims. Yet, as practitioners and scholars grapple with the concept, a very particular reading of 'transformative justice' emerges that centres the post-colonial state as the responsible agent of transformation. Such a reading not only erases the possibility of revolutionary or bottom-up change but also the structural entanglement between the Global North and the Global South. While structures such as patriarchy and capitalism inhere in the state form, they also transcend it and cannot be abolished by any single state, especially not in the Global South. By centring the state, scholars as much as the ICC's staff both disavow and reaffirm the Court's role, which is a particular institutional expression of the state system, while, at the same time, abdicating the ICC's responsibility for structural change.

5.3 Genealogies of Transformative Justice

Interestingly, whereas the Court's staff and the surrounding literature conclude that 'transformative justice' is the responsibility of the state, the concept itself has deep roots in state-critical and abolitionist thinking. Many scholars, writing on transformative reparations, trace the concept back to the Nairobi conference in 2007, where the Coalition for Women's Rights, a civil society coalition, advocated for a transformative approach to reparations eying the recent establishment of the ICC and its Trust Fund.[64] Yet, a few years earlier, in April 2000, another conference took place in Santa Cruz, entitled the 'Colour of Violence', which proposed a very different conception of transformative justice. The conference was urgently called,

[63] Interview with Legal Officer, Registry, The Hague (4 February 2014).
[64] Couillard (n 20) 451.

> to address violence against women of color in all its forms, including: attacks on immigrants' rights and Indian treaty rights, the proliferation of prisons, militarism, attacks on the reproductive rights of women of color, medical experimentation on communities of color, homophobia/heterosexism, and hate crimes against lesbians of color, economic neo-colonialism, and institutional racism.[65]

The conference took place against the backdrop of the adoption of carceral solutions to domestic violence and rape by the Violence against Women movement.[66] 'The turn towards carceralism', Amia Srinivasan observes, '[was] part of a broader shift in emphasis within feminism since the 1970s, away from the transformation of socio-economic life towards securing women's equality in the pre-existing structures of capitalism'.[67] The conference participants, including prominent activist-scholars like Angela Davis and Kimberlé Crenshaw, by contrast, resolved to develop political strategies 'that place women of color at the center' and 'encourage the anti-violence movement to reinsert political organizing into its plan of action'.[68] While the conference was initially planned for only a couple of hundred scholars and activists, it was scaled up after the organizers received more than 2000 inquiries.[69]

One key theme that transpired was 'the importance of organizing against personal forms of violence in a way that is mindful of the larger structures of institutional violence'.[70] Black and brown women suffering sexual violence at the hands of intimate partners, relatives or strangers were looking for ways to be safe without further brutalizing and depleting their communities, which were already suffering from mass incarceration and police violence at the hands of the state.[71] Transformative justice was a key concept that emerged in that context, acquiring a double meaning: it 'involves

[65] Andrea Smith, 'The Color of Violence: Violence against Women of Color' (2001) 1(2) Meridians 65, 67.

[66] Elizabeth Bernstein, 'Militarized humanitarianism meets carceral feminism: The politics of sex, rights, and freedom in contemporary antitrafficking campaigns' (2010) 36(1) Signs 45, 47; Anna Terwiel, 'What Is Carceral Feminism?' (2020) 48(4) Political Theory 421.

[67] Amia Srinivasan, *The Right to Sex* (Bloomsbury Publishing PLC 2021) 163. See also Beth E. Richie, *Arrested Justice: Black Women, Violence, and America's Prison Nation* (New York UP 2012) 94–98.

[68] Smith (n 65) 67.

[69] ibid 70.

[70] ibid 67–68.

[71] Clarissa Rojas, Mimi Kim, and Alisa Bierria, 'Community Accountability: Emerging Movements to Transform Violence' (2012) 37(4) Social Justice 1, 3.

a willingness to deeply question the status quo, and asks for imagination beyond [the] current system'.[72] But it also describes a concrete method for responding to harm, different from both retributive and restorative justice, and emanating from 'a long lineage of BIPOC (Black, Indigenous, and People of Colour) folks practicing alternative systems of accountability and community safety in cases of sexual violence'.[73]

The earliest usage of 'transformative justice' I have found was by Ruth Morris, a Canadian Quaker and prison abolitionist, who herself was inspired by Native Canadian Healing Circles and New Zealand's Community Group Conferences.[74] While transformative justice shares that indigenous lineage with restorative justice, it differs from the latter in its critical stance towards the state and law enforcement.[75] Unlike restorative justice, which is implemented, funded, initiated or sanctioned by state institutions, transformative justice is often practiced within marginalized communities and social movements. As a form of community accountability, its processes are 'informal, decentralized, and largely undocumented'.[76] Whereas restorative justice seeks to *restore* relationships between victims, offenders and their communities, which have been broken or ruptured by 'crime', transformative justice aims to *transform* these relationships, seeing 'crime' as a symptom rather than a cause of much deeper structural inequality and systemic violence.[77] Explicitly abolitionist, transformative justice 'understands the criminal justice system as one that serves to maintain conditions

[72] Anti-Oppression Resource and Training Alliance, 'Aorta Destabilizing Rape Culture Handout', 2 https://www.nasco.coop/sites/default/files/srl/AORTA%20Destabilizing%20Rape%20Culture%20Handout.pdf (accessed 12 November 2021).

[73] Sexual Assault Centre of Edmonton (SACE), 'Understanding Transformative Justice and Restorative Justice' https://www.sace.ca/learn/transformative-restorative-justice/ (accessed 12 November 2021).

[74] Ruth Morris, *Stories of Transformative Justice* (Canadian Scholars Press 2000) 3; Anthony J. Nocella II, 'An Overview of the History and Theory of Transformative Justice' (2011) 6(1) Peace & Conflict Review 1, 4.

[75] Mimi E Kim, 'Transformative justice and restorative justice: Gender-based violence and alternative visions of justice in the United States' (2021) 27(2) International Review of Victimology 162, 169–70.

[76] Mimi E Kim, 'From carceral feminism to transformative justice: Women-of-color feminism and alternatives to incarceration' (2018) 27(3) Journal of Ethnic & Cultural Diversity in Social Work 219, 227.

[77] As Ruth Morris put it, 'but even restorative justice does not go far enough. It still accepts the idea that one event now defined all that matters of right and wrong—it leaves out the past, and the social causes of all events' See Morris (n 74) 4. See also Donna Coker, 'Transformative Justice: Anti-Subordination Processes in Cases of Domestic Violence' in Heather Strang and John Braithwaite (eds), *Restorative Justice and Family Violence* (CUP 2002) 128, 129–30.

of structural violence', and instead strives 'to respond to violence without creating more violence'.[78]

Given that carceral violence was the foil against which the concept materialized in its black and brown feminist lineage in the United States, it is curious that the state re-emerges as an agent of transformative justice in international criminal justice discourse. The latter recuperates two notions of the state: first, 'states', generically, as legitimate representatives of their people, and, secondly, 'the post-colonial state', as a legitimate and responsible representative of the people in the Court's African situation countries. Legitimacy and responsibility are tethered together here; a state is a legitimate representative of its people in international law, independently of its form of government, and is responsible for whatever violence happens within its borders, independently of the broader imperialist and capitalist context.[79]

Of course, the US criminal justice context differs markedly from the ICC's interventions in post-colonial states. As the most powerful imperial state, which has not ratified the Rome Statute, the US can subject black and brown communities to mass incarceration and police violence without fearing external intervention. The ICC, by contrast, can only intervene when the state, which has jurisdiction, is a member state of the Court and is 'unwilling or unable genuinely to carry out the investigation or prosecution' itself.[80] The decision on whether states are unwilling or unable, however, lies with the Court's judges. It is thus not surprising that the post-colonial state emerges as a compromise formation[81] that both ICC supporters, and those who criticize the institution as a tool of Western hegemony, can agree on as a legitimate locus of structural change. Recognized by 'the family of nations', the post-colonial state also serves as a bulwark against external interventions.[82] Haunted by the threat of recolonization, the post-colonial

[78] Kim (n 76), 227.

[79] Luis Eslava and Sundhya Pahuja, 'The State and International Law: A Reading from the Global South' (2020) 11(1) Humanity: An International Journal of Human Rights, Humanitarianism and Development 118.

[80] Rome Statute art 17.

[81] Jan Rehmann, *Theories of Ideology: The Powers of Alienation and Subjection* (Brill 2013) 255.

[82] See eg 'Judge Richard Goldstone: The International Criminal Court deserves the continued support of South Africa and all other peace-loving nations' *Wayamo Foundation* (19 August 2020) https://www.wayamo.com/archives/goldstoneiccoped (accessed 5 January 2023).

state, many believe, is an insurance policy against Western interventionism rather than the product of the latter.[83]

Transformative justice is thus a concept haunted by a colonial world order. Is it, perhaps, a new edition of the civilizing mission? Some of my Kenyan interviewees insisted that while transformative justice may be appropriate for 'failed states', it is beside the point in Kenya. One Kenyan lawyer exclaimed:

> The Kenyan situation is not anywhere near what was happening in Northern Uganda, in the DRC, or Sudan. There is absolutely no relationship. These are communities [in Kenya] who led absolutely normal lives at the time the violence happened. These were not people who were living in the jungle; they were not destitute. We are talking about people who were economically empowered . . . It should be approached differently. All the Kenyan victims ask for is 'take us back to where we were before'.[84]

The civilizational subtext is evident. Communities in Kenya led 'normal lives'; they were not 'living in the jungle'. Such discourse retools and internalizes the civilizing mission by dividing the African continent into 'civilized' and 'uncivilized' societies: Northern Uganda, the DRC and Sudan, unlike 'civilized' and 'modern' states such as Kenya, Nigeria, and South Africa, are ripe for transformation.[85] 'We', in Kenya, do not need that.

Another genealogy of the concept of transformative justice that is closer to the ICC can be traced back in the transitional justice, conflict transformation, and peacebuilding literature. Writing about the Truth and Reconciliation Commission in South Africa in 2002, Erin Daly claims that 'the two principal goals of transformative justice are the related aims of reconciliation and deterrence'.[86] Daly does not disavow a state-based and

[83] B.S. Chimni, 'Third World Approaches to International Law: A Manifesto' (2006) 8(3) International Community Law 3.

[84] Interview with Kenyan Lawyer, The Hague (28 October 2013).

[85] Antony Anghie, *Imperialism, Sovereignty and the Making of International Law* (CUP 2005); Ntina Tzouvala, *Capitalism as Civilisation: A History of International Law* (CUP 2020) 11–14.

[86] Erin Daly, 'Transformative Justice: Charting a Path to Reconciliation' (2002) 12(1&2) International Legal Perspectives 73, 84. For scholarship looking at the nexus between transitional justice, development, and social justice see Rama Mani, 'Dilemmas of Expanding Transitional Justice, or Forging the Nexus between Transitional Justice and Development' (2008) 2(3) International Journal of Transitional Justice 253; Mahmood Mamdani, 'Beyond Nuremberg: The Historical Significance of the Post-apartheid Transition in South Africa' (2015) 43(1) Politics & Society 61.

institutional approach to transformative justice, but argues that it needs to be 'deeply rooted in the culture it seeks to transform'.[87] Wendy Lambourne uses the concept to develop a more holistic approach to transitional justice that 'not only deals with the past but also establishes conditions and structures in order to achieve justice in the present and the future'.[88] Similar to Lambourne, Gready and Robins pick up the concept in 2014 to address the limitations of top-down, state-based approaches to transitional justice by foregrounding community approaches that they hope to 'scale up' to achieve broader structural change.[89] The transitional justice literature thus birthed its own concept of transformative justice, which is no longer tied to abolitionist, feminist, and anti-racist agendas. In this reading, legal and state-based justice are part of a transformative agenda, but they are not enough.[90]

Thus, by the time I started discussing the concept with the Court's staff and NGO advocates in 2013 and 2014, it had itself undergone several transformations. It still demands structural change but no longer ties structural violence to state violence, thus allowing the state to re-emerge as the solution to the problem. It still focuses on violence against women but no longer considers 'the colour of violence'. As international criminal law produces black perpetrators, black victims, and black intermediaries, the whiteness of the institution and its laws is not further interrogated.[91] The concept, moreover, is no longer oriented towards abolition of criminal justice but recognizes that retributive justice, while important, is not sufficient. It has even forfeited its community roots. Instead, it has become embedded in particular legal and developmental modalities, namely reparations and assistance.

[87] Daly (n 86) 94.

[88] Wendy Lambourne, 'Transitional Justice and Peacebuilding after Mass Violence' (2009) 3 The International Journal of Transitional Justice 28, 45.

[89] Paul Gready and Simon Robins, 'From Transitional to Transformative Justice: A New Agenda for Practice' (2014) 8(3) IJTJ 339, 360. Their concept is critical of liberal state- and institution-building but not abolitionist: '[A] transformative approach will need to balance pursuing wrongdoers with whatever best institutionalizes peace and effective service delivery, and as such it is likely that principle and pragmatism will cohabit in approaches to institutions.' See ibid 345.

[90] For more recent studies of transformative justice in the realm of transitional justice see Matthew Evans, 'Structural Violence, Socioeconomic Rights, and Transformative Justice' (2016) 15(1) Journal of Human Rights 1; Matthew Evans (ed), *Beyond Transitional Justice: Transformative Justice and the State of the Field (or Non-field)—Directions and Developments in Criminal Justice and Law* (Routledge 2022).

[91] Randle C DeFalco and Frédéric Mégret, 'The invisibility of race at the ICC: lessons from the US criminal justice system' (2019) 7(1) London Review of International Law 55, 64.

5.4 Transformative Justice, Ideology, and Political Unconscious

In international criminal law, transformative justice has become 'transformative reparations', which have been either dismissed as 'unrealistic'[92] or as mere co-optation and window-dressing. The Court's practitioners were the first to express their scepticism. But something prefaced their disavowal that offers a glimpse into the ideological function of the concept. Many of them quite literally sighed as they uttered the word. Recall, for example, the legal officer, who sighed: 'Of course, I would love this. The concept of transformative justice, it is a beautiful concept', before he cautioned, 'but thinking with a legal mind, I don't know to what extent this concept falls squarely within the scope of the Court's mandate'.[93] 'I think that is extremely useful', one judge admitted, before venturing: 'I think, of course, this exceeds the powers of the Court. The Court is not a human rights court. And I don't think we could be involved in ordering measures of these types of things to the states.'[94] One legal adviser went further:

> If at one point you really want, as they always say all the time, we are going to prevent crimes against humanity. We are instruments of prevention. This is where you have to act. If you want to be serious. At least you need to say that the root cause is that, actually, in Colombia, the state has been taking the land from the farmers and that the farmers have tried to resist and that they [the state] have created specific paramilitary units in order to crush the revolt, basically, by the farmers. You know, it's very simple. The situation is complex, but that's the root. So, if you don't change that, you don't prevent anything. But, of course, you need to restructure the country. Can an international criminal court do such a thing? Many people are going to smile, if you say that, but I don't think you have to give up.[95]

The sigh disrupts the text and prevents a purely cynical reading, echoing a famous quote by Marx:

[92] Chappell (n 4) 1224.
[93] Interview with Legal Officer, Registry, The Hague (4 February 2014).
[94] Interview with Judge, The Hague (30 January 2014).
[95] Interview with Adviser, Chamber, The Hague (8 January 2014).

> *Religious* distress is at the same time the *expression* of real distress and also the *protest* against real distress. Religion is the sigh of the oppressed creature, the heart of a heartless world, just as it is the spirit of the spiritless condition. It is the *opium* of the people.[96]

The sigh signals an admission, a yearning even: structural change is necessary 'if you really want to prevent crimes against humanity'. Perhaps we can contribute to it, some of my interviewees suggested cautiously. The sigh may also express the real distress of working under the weight of the Court's contradictions. Of course, the lawyers in The Hague are not really 'oppressed creatures', but the sigh may offer a slightly different reading of why transformative justice, despite all disavowals, has lingered on in the Court's texts and practices.

By noticing the sigh, we are listening to the symptoms of the text; we include what is often omitted in interview transcripts, and thus engage in a symptomatic form of reading. In *Reading Capital*, Althusser explains how Marx, by reading classical political economy *symptomatically*, was able to revolutionize its foundational concepts, moving from the static notion of *labour* as a thing that has a price to the dynamic notion of *labour power* as the animating force of capitalism and the social producer of surplus value.[97] The curious aspect here is that the 'correct' answer was produced by classical political economy (not Marx), but it was not an answer to any question it had itself posed.[98] As Althusser explains:

> [w]hat political economy does not see is what it *does*: its production of a new answer without a question, and simultaneously the production of a new latent question contained in relief in this new answer. Through the lacunary terms of its new answer political economy produced a new question, but 'unconsciously'. It made '*a complete change in the terms*

[96] Karl Marx, 'The Introduction to Contribution to the Critique of Hegel's Philosophy of Right' (1844) Marx/Engels Internet Archive (2000) https://www.marxists.org/archive/marx/works/1844/df-jahrbucher/law-abs.htm (accessed 14 November 2021).

[97] Louis Althusser and others, *Reading Capital: The Complete Edition* (Verso 2016) 20–21.

[98] The question that classical political economists, especially Adam Smith, posed was 'what is the value of *labour*?' (at 20), which led to the answer: 'the value of labour is equal to the value of the subsistence goods necessary for the maintenance and reproduction of the labourer' (at 21). But in that answer lies an unexplained shift from labour, as a thing, to the labourer, as a living being, which Marx bridged through the concept of 'labour power'. Althusser and others (n 97) 20–21.

> *of the (original) problem*', and thereby produced a new problem, but without knowing it.[99]

Similarly, 'transformative justice' emerges as an answer to a question that has not been posed in the idiom of international criminal justice. In fact, we can reformulate Althusser's sentence as follows: 'What international criminal justice does not see is what it *does*: its production of a new answer (transformative reparations) without a question, and simultaneously the production of a new latent question contained in relief in this new answer: how can we (really) prevent mass atrocity violence?

While borrowed from other texts, transformative justice is a production of international criminal law, taking shape as 'transformative reparations', as the Court's practitioners wrestle with existing concepts of reparations and their limitations in the context of mass atrocity violence. But posed in this form, as 'transformative reparations', the problem becomes unsolvable. The Court can only order reparations against individual perpetrators, but the latter cannot redress structural violence and inequality. So how can we make sense of the concept's presence at the Court?

Althusser writes:

> [T]hese new objects and problems are necessarily *invisible* in the field of the existing theory, because they are not objects of this theory, because they are *forbidden* by it—they are objects and problems necessarily without any necessary relations with the field of the visible as defined by its problematic. They are invisible because they are rejected in principle, repressed from the field of the visible: and that is why their fleeting presence in the field when it does occur (in very peculiar and symptomatic circumstances) *goes unperceived*, and becomes literally an undivulgeable absence—since the whole function of the field is not to see them, to forbid any sighting of them.[100]

This is literally true of transformative justice. It is not *seen* or *heard* even though it is *there*. It is the forbidden version of the text. And, in that sense, the idea of recuperation or co-optation of radical vocabulary is misleading. The concept is not plastered all over the Court. It is not 'donor-friendly'. Instead, it drifts in and out of the Court's texts, appears, and disappears. It is

[99] ibid 22 (emphasis added).
[100] ibid 24.

both self-evident and unthinkable, which also explains how the concept is simultaneously embraced and disavowed, how practitioners use it and may not even be aware of it.

Indeed, even though 'transformative reparations' are mentioned in the Court's reparation decisions, few ICC practitioners seem to be familiar with the concept, and even if they are dimly aware of it, they often forget about it. In fact, when I re-interviewed the Trust Fund's officer in Kampala, with whom the chapter started, in 2019, he seemed, five years later, to have no recollection of the concept, and I had to explain it again. His answer was more circumspect than the first time:

> Transformation? I mean, I think, in many cases that we are working in, for many cases that the court is likely to be engaged in, the situation requires transformation. However, I mean, I think, we are mindful that, we are, you know, we are the Trust Fund slash ICC; we're not the only actor in those environments. We may be one of many. And it is, first and foremost, the responsibility of the government to fulfill its obligations, to fulfill the rights of the victims. And so, our ability to be transformative, I think, needs to be realistic with regards to the context, with regards to our own mandates, as well. We can do what we can, but it's not possible for us alone, you know, to transform the environment.[101]

'Together we can work to put in place transformative reparations for and with victims', the TFV's Chair of the Board of Directors hailed at the Assembly of States Parties in 2022; 'together we can mitigate the negative effects of #RomeStatute crimes for the next generations. Together we can work for peace and stability'.[102] The word 'transformative' was mentioned thirteen times in the TFV's draft Strategic Plan (2023–2025) but

[101] Interview with TFV Officer, Kampala, Kampala (9 July 2019).

[102] Chair of @TFV_FPV Board of Directors at #ASP21. ICC Twitter Account (5 December 2022) https://twitter.com/IntlCrimCourt/status/1599756626373726208 (accessed 7 August 2023); See also the statement by Franziska Eckelmans, TFV Acting Executive Director in ICC, 'Trust Fund for Victims calls for contributions to provide reparations to victims of conflict-related sexual violence' (Press Release 13 March 2023) ('through the Trust Fund for Victims . . . victims of conflict-related sexual violence, including children born out of rape, can have access to holistic and transformative reparations and regain hope and dignity') https://www.icc-cpi.int/news/trust-fund-victims-calls-contributions-provide-reparations-victims-conflict-related-sexual> accessed 19 March 2023.

completely disappeared from the version that was eventually adopted.[103] Transformative justice is both present and absent, inside and outside, visible and invisible.

While restorative justice was consciously embraced, transformative justice is the 'political unconscious' of the Court, a symbolic solution to a real but unconsciously felt social and political problem.[104] It reflects a dim premonition that justice requires 'giving back the land', that it demands the societal transformations that the Court simultaneously invokes ('international community', 'common bonds') and represses. In developing the concept of the political unconscious, Fredric Jameson drew on Lévi-Strauss' interpretation of the body paintings of the Caduveo women.[105] An indigenous Brazilian tribe, the Caduveo used elaborate body paintings to mark their distinction from, and superiority to, their natural 'naked' environment.[106] But the combination of asymmetrical and symmetrical patterns in their facial paintings, also represented, Lévi-Strauss believed, a symbolic resolution of a real social contradiction.[107] Regimented through a strict class hierarchy, the problem of the Caduveo, according to Lévi-Strauss, was their 'aristocratic arrogance'.[108] Despite depending on the lower classes for their reproduction, the higher classes feared that any softening of class boundaries would scupper their privileges: 'they were paralysed by the fear of losing face, of not living up to their rank and, most important of all, of marrying below their station'.[109] As such, 'each caste tended to shut itself in upon itself, thus impairing the cohesion of the social body as a whole'.[110] While exhibiting a similar class structure as the Caduveo, related tribes partially resolved this problem of social reproduction by creating a cross-cutting symmetric structure (like the one indicated in the paintings) which facilitated inter-marriages. Even as they faced the threat of extinction, the

103 Compare TFV Draft Strategic Plan 2023–2025 (n 30) with TFV Strategic Plan 2023–2025 https://www.trustfundforvictims.org/sites/default/files/reports/TFV%20Strategic%20Plan%202023-2025%20ENG.pdf (accessed 16 July 2023).

104 Fredric Jameson, *The Political Unconscious: Narrative as a Socially Symbolic Act* (Cornell UP 1981) 62–64. See also Oxford References, 'Political Unconscious' https://www.oxfordreference.com/display/10.1093/oi/authority.20110803100334787;jsessionid=41AE0DA5E0EB98A308E220BE30FC2FDD (accessed 2 April 2023).

105 Jameson (n 104) 62–64; Claude Lévi-Strauss, *Tristes Tropiques* (Penguin Classics 2011).

106 Lévi-Strauss (n 105) 188, 195.

107 ibid 196.

108 ibid.

109 ibid 195.

110 ibid.

Caduveo could not bring themselves to adopt such social solutions, but they did project them in their bodily art 'as the phantasm of a society ardently and insatiably seeking a means of expressing symbolically the institutions it might have, if its interests and superstitions did not stand in the way'.[111]

Similar to the Caduveo, our societies face the threat of extinction through the climate catastrophe and, like them, we struggle to find the necessary social solutions—ecologically sustainable life forms—and thus express them symbolically ranging from advertisements that see 'men' reunited with nature through the use of a commodity (often, ironically, a car) to the private politics of household recycling and eco-friendly consumption, to the repeated attempts and failures to introduce 'ecocide' as a crime under the Rome Statute.[112] Much like the Caduveo, we suffer from the failed attempt to escape our condition of mutual dependency, firstly, by creating a separation between humans and nature which facilitated the subjugation of the latter, and secondly, by forging social hierarchies among people which enabled the exploitation of those designated as 'lower' (women, racialized people, working classes, migrants), ultimately making life miserable and dangerous both for the oppressed and the oppressors.

Law, like the bodily art of the Caduveo, represents a symmetrical structure ('everyone is equal before the law', 'every legal subject has the same human rights') that both reproduces and softens the boundaries of class society. Projekt Ideologietheorie therefore described law as a 'compromise formation': it was 'pressure from below which forced class-domination into . . . the juridical form', which is an operative mode from above.[113] The first written constitution of Athens from seventh century BC, for example, also 'contained some demands for the protection of the people against arbitrary and violent attacks from the aristocracy'.[114] Pressured for by the lower classes, law was written by the middle classes (e.g., lawyers) and reluctantly conceded to by the nobility.[115]

[111] ibid 197.

[112] For recent efforts see the 'Stop Ecocide Campaign' https://www.stopecocide.earth (accessed 2 April 2023). Donna Minha, 'The Proposed Definition of the Crime of Ecocide: An Important Step Forward, but Can Our Planet Wait?' *EJIL:Talk!* (1 July 2021) https://www.ejiltalk.org/the-proposed-definition-of-the-crime-of-ecocide-an-important-step-forward-but-can-our-planet-wait/ (accessed 14 November 2021). Given the difficulty of adding ecocide as a crime under the Rome Statute, other scholars suggest 'greening reparations'. See Rachel Killean, 'From ecocide to eco-sensitivity: "greening" reparations at the International Criminal Court' (2021) 25(2) The International Journal of Human Rights 323.

[113] Rehmann (n 81) 255–56.

[114] ibid.

[115] ibid 256.

Curiously, just like the 'political unconscious' borrows from Freud, so does the compromise formation. Freud used the term 'compromise formation' to capture how two opposing forces, the superego and the repressed Id 'meet once again in the symptom and are reconciled, as it were, by the compromise of the symptom', which, according to Freud, also explains why the neurotic symptom is so resistant: 'it is supported by both sides'.[116] The initial title of my PhD thesis (on which this book is based) was 'schizophrenic justice', a title my examiners did not like and perhaps 'neurotic justice' would have been better. Tellingly, Jung describes his neurotic patients as socially well-integrated but troubled by existential questions, and as consisting 'not of believers but of those who had lost their faith', descriptions that would also fit many lawyers and academics working in and on international criminal justice.[117]

Transformative justice is not only the political unconscious of the Court. It speaks to a larger problem that we don't know how 'to do' structural change. Many agree it is necessary, but nobody really knows how it is done. Structural change, is, as the legal adviser put it, both very simple and very complex. 'Give back the land', 'redistribute income'—doing that on a mass scale would be a form of structural change, but it cannot be done within the existing capitalist structure. The problem is not only the existing institutional set-up (e.g., that the Court cannot transform societies), but also that we cannot quite imagine what structural change would look like. Indeed, framed in that way—'transforming structures', 'addressing root causes'[118]—the problem becomes unsolvable, but the non-solution is still appealing. We can all agree that transformative justice is necessary precisely because it does not offer any clear course of action. Transformative justice, moreover, changes its meaning not only in different institutional contexts and across time but also once we shift settings in international criminal justice. What role, if any, does transformative justice play in 'the field'? How is it interpreted and implemented? The next section will investigate these questions by examining the Trust Fund's assistance programmes in Northern Uganda.

[116] ibid.
[117] Carl G Jung and Aniela Jaffé, *Memories, Dreams, Reflections* (Vantage Books 1989) 140.
[118] Marks (n 5) 70.

5.5 What Transformation and of Whom?

On the ground, the Trust Fund relies on local and international NGOs for implementing its assistance and reparation programmes. Selected and trained as 'local partners', these organizations go into the communities to identify 'victim-beneficiaries' for the TFV's programme, meaning those victims of crimes that fall within the Court's jurisdiction.[119] The TFV strives 'to build the capacity of community-based change agents—including traditional and faith leaders, women's grassroots organizations, educators, local government authorities and the media'.[120] Yet, while many of the TFV's 'change agents' want change, a closer analysis of their discourse reveals conflicting and even contradictory ideas of what a changed society should look like.[121]

Before we dive into that analysis, it is noteworthy that the Court's practitioners in The Hague were interested in a rather specific meaning of 'transformative justice' as addressing gender discrimination, inequality, and violence.[122] They were less comfortable with tackling broader socio-economic injustices that drive conflicts. It is probably no coincidence that the key documents that developed and invoked the concept have been preoccupied with the prevention of SGBV.[123] In Northern Uganda, however, a rather different picture presented itself. While supportive of the economic reading of transformative justice as redressing poverty, my interviewees were more ambivalent about gender justice and expressed rather different ideas of what it means.[124]

Indeed, there is little agreement in Northern Uganda on the direction in which society should be changed not least because its social fabric has

[119] Interview with TFV Officer, Kampala (7 July 2014). See also TFV, 'Assistance & Reparations Achievements, Lessons Learned, and Transitioning' (2015) 13–14 https://www.trustfundforvictims.org/sites/default/files/reports/TFV%20Programme%20Progress%20Report%202015.pdf (accessed 16 April 2023).

[120] TFV Strategic Plan 2014–2017 (n 30) 25.

[121] Part of this section, although in modified form, has been published in Leila Ullrich, 'Doing gender justice in northern Uganda' *Open Democracy* (23 July 2015) https://www.opendemocracy.net/en/author/leila-ullrich/ (accessed 16 March 2023).

[122] See also *Prosecutor v Ongwen* (Victims' Preliminary Submissions on Reparations) [2021] ICC-02/04-01/15-1921, § 27.

[123] See Couillard (n 20); *Prosecutor v Katanga* (United Nations Joint Submission on Reparations) [2015] ICC-01/04-01/07-3550, §§ 35–36.

[124] Like my interviewees in The Hague, most ICC staff, intermediaries, and TVF local partners I interviewed in Uganda were not familiar with the concepts of 'transformative justice' or 'transformative reparations'.

eroded over twenty years of war. In addition to horrific crimes perpetrated by the LRA and government soldiers, most of the population was displaced by the government's military strategy and dwelled for years in squalid displacement camps.[125] Alienating Northern Ugandans from their communal forms of life, the social conditions of the camps also unleashed new gender dynamics.[126] As one women's rights officer in Kampala put it:

> During the war, gender roles shifted. Women were more active within the camps. Even if it was only a small garden, they would plant something. Men were just there to wait for people to bring food and they got used to it. And now, they are back and are still waiting for food. Women have taken up this strong role of providing food for the family, but now the men are starting to question this power that the women have.[127]

'Post-conflict situations' often generate contradictory consequences especially for women. On the one hand, war allegedly creates 'a gender dividend' as women take on more responsibilities as providers for their families, workers and even warriors, thereby destabilizing traditional gender roles.[128] On the other hand, research suggests that women's experiences of SGBV are frequently continuous: while violence against women peaks during times of conflict, it persists after conflict, especially in the form of domestic violence.[129] In a study on female survivors of conflict-related sexual violence in Northern Uganda, ninety out of the ninety-seven SGBV survivors interviewed said that they still face the same threats of sexual violence as in the past.[130] The literature refers to this phenomenon as the 'post-war backlash' as men return home after the war and try to reassert

[125] See Adam Branch, *Displacing Human Rights: War and Intervention in Northern Uganda* (OUP 2011).

[126] See Refugee Law Project, 'Gender against men' (2009) https://www.youtube.com/watch?v=mJSl99HQYXc (accessed 16 April 2023).

[127] Interview with NGO Officer, Kampala (30 July 2014).

[128] Colleen Duggan and Adila Abusharaf, 'Reparation of sexual violence in democratic transitions: The search for gender justice' in Pablo de Greiff (ed), *The Handbook of Reparations* (OUP 2006) 629.

[129] Cynthia Cockburn, 'Don't talk to me about war. My life's a battlefield' *Open Democracy* (25 November 2012) https://www.opendemocracy.net/5050/cynthia-cockburn/%E2%80%9Cdon%E2%80%99t-talk-to-me-about-war-my-life%E2%80%99s-battlefield%E2%80%9D (accessed 16 April 2023).

[130] Justice and Reconciliation Project, 'Establishing the Extent of SGBV Revictimisation among Female Survivors of Conflict SGBV in Northern Uganda' (2014) http://justiceandreconciliation.com/wp-content/uploads/2014/11/SGBV-Baseline-Report-Summary-WEB.pdf (accessed 16 April 2023).

their power.[131] Domestic violence is rampant in today's Northern Uganda possibly due to these changing gender dynamics and what has been dubbed the 'identity crisis' of men.[132]

Many Northern Ugandans, however, see the high rate of violence against women as part of a bigger social order problem.[133] They blame the erosion of cultural cohesion during the war and the weakening of traditional authority for violence against women and the rise in land conflicts. A priest of the Diocese of Northern Uganda, a former TFV implementing partner, told me that one of the main challenges for the community is that young people do not respect their elders anymore.[134] Before the war, elders knew the boundaries of the land, but many died in the IDP camps and those who returned after years of displacement either did not know the boundaries or could not find them anymore due to changes in the natural topography.[135] Many young people, who suffer from unemployment and failed reintegration, see the land as a commercial source and sell it to start a *boda-boda* (motorbike) business often without consulting the elders.[136] Communities have been arming themselves in the face of ongoing land disputes, for example, in the Adjumani and Amuri districts.[137] Women have particularly lost out amidst rising family disputes about land as their property rights are the least secure.[138]

After our interview, the priest confided in me, with some distress, that he was not even sure the young women trained at his church in vocations such as tailoring would still kneel down in his presence. He then waved a

[131] Donna Pankhurst, 'Introduction: Gendered war and peace' in Donna Pankhurst (ed), *Gendered Peace: Women's Struggles for Reconciliation and Justice* (Routledge 2008) 4.

[132] Moses Chrispus Okello and Lucy Hovil, 'Confronting the Reality of Gender-Based Violence in Northern Uganda' (2007) 1 IJTJ 433.

[133] For the importance of social harmony in Northern Uganda see Holly Porter, 'Justice and Rape on the Periphery: The Supremacy of Social Harmony in the Space between Local Solutions and Formal Judicial Systems in Northern Uganda' (2012) 6 Journal of Eastern African Studies 81; Holly Porter, *After Rape: Violence, Justice and Social Harmony in Uganda* (CUP 2016).

[134] Interview with Priest, Gulu (10 July 2014).

[135] IRIN, 'Uganda: Land Disputes threaten Northern Peace' (19 April 2012) https://www.refworld.org/docid/4f990e032.html (accessed 7 August 2023).

[136] Saferworld, 'Promoting Conflict-Sensitive Approaches in Amuru District, Northern Uganda' (2015) https://www.saferworld.org.uk/resources/publications/896-promoting-conflict-sensitive-development-in-northern-uganda (accessed 16 April 2023).

[137] Refugee Law Project, 'Shoot us all Down: The Lakang & Apaa Land Conflict' https://www.youtube.com/watch?v=2IJUP4xuHp8 (accessed 16 April 2023).

[138] Christopher Burke and Doreen Nancy Kobusingye, 'Women's Land Rights in Northern Uganda' (2014) https://mokoro.co.uk/wp-content/uploads/SecuringWomenLandRightsNorthernUganda_Oxfam.pdf (accessed 2 April 2023).

young woman over to demonstrate this 'degeneration of morals', but, to my embarrassment, the young woman immediately fell down on her knees.[139] The booklet of his church made for uncomfortable reading. It tells the story of Esther, an orphan, whose uncle offered to pay for her education in return for sexual services. The booklet comments:

> The good news is that Esther is a Born Anglican Christian. Her love for the Lord has made her determined to live a sexually pure life—even when it meant being uneducated. She could not trade the Temple of the Holy Spirit for a mere 500,000 shillings for school fees.[140]

The 'good news' is not that Esther will be protected from her uncle or that she is provided with free schooling, but that she managed to preserve her sexual purity in difficult circumstances.

Indeed, some of the TFV's 'change agents' long for the old order that supposedly afforded more protection for women. A representative of the Acholi Religious Leaders Peace Initiative (ARLPI), an organization that seeks to 'mainstream the empowerment of women' in all of its activities, complained that, nowadays, women who return to their father's house after a failed marriage or their husband's death are often chased away with their children.[141] This was very different 'in the good old days': '[I]f you are my sister and you went to your home but your marriage did not work, and then you came back home, my father would say, "you are also our daughter . . . we, as your brothers, will construct a hut for you. This is where you will stay; this is where your death will find you".'[142] From this perspective, a 'transformative' Northern Uganda has to go backwards in order to go forward.

Here, my analysis intersects with another debate in the transitional justice literature which has been particularly polarizing in Northern Uganda: the role of 'traditional justice' rituals in dealing with the past. On the one hand, there are those who celebrate 'traditional justice' as a more authentic and often more humane alternative to the 'Western' model of

[139] Field notes, Gulu (10 July 2014).
[140] ibid.
[141] Acholi Religious Leaders Peace Initiative, 'Women Empowerment' https://sites.google.com/a/arlpi.org/www/women-empowerment (accessed 16 April 2023); Interview with Officer of a Faith-based NGO, Gulu (13 July 2014).
[142] Interview with Officer of a Faith-based NGO, Gulu (13 July 2014).

retributive justice.[143] Some, although by no means all, justice practices in Northern Uganda are 'restorative'; rather than punishing the perpetrator, a ritual is performed and compensation is paid to reconcile clans and community members.[144] On the other hand, there are those who decry 'traditional justice' either as a sham or as falling short of both victims' rights to justice and the defendant's right to a fair trial.[145]

Yet, what role, if any, can traditional justice play in achieving transformative justice? For some of my interviewees, this was a no-brainer. A civil society representative exclaimed:

> Transformative justice? . . . You cannot do it without engaging the traditional justice systems . . . Only 33% of all Ugandans have ever engaged with any of the justice, law and order sectors, ministries or departments, courts, police, prison . . . That means that about 70% are in the alternative justice system and many of them in the traditional justice system.[146]

For many people in rural areas, the formal criminal justice system is simply not accessible. Besides, the court and police system are seen as expensive and corrupt: 'When I have money, the case is gone. So, money speaks really much louder', one woman told me.[147] Traditional practices are seen as legitimate to the extent that they resolve local conflicts.[148] They also epitomize Northern Ugandans' suspicions of any claims by state institutions and powerful foreigners of doing justice in their name.[149] In fact, it is precisely communal forms of justice such as Acholi justice rituals which have inspired transformative justice practices in marginalized communities and activist spaces in the Global North.

[143] Barney Afako, 'Reconciliation and Justice: "Mato Oput" and the Amnesty Act' (2002) 11 Accord 64; Erin Baines, 'Spirits and Social Reconstruction: Rethinking Transitional Justice' (2010) 109 African Affairs 409.

[144] For a good overview of the debate on traditional justice see Anna Macdonald and Tim Allen, 'Post-Conflict Traditional Justice: A Critical Overview'(2013) 3 Justice and Security Research Programme Working Paper 1 https://assets.publishing.service.gov.uk/media/57a08a34ed915d3cfd000642/JSRP3-AllenMacdonald.pdf (accessed 16 April 2023). For a critical perspective see Adam Branch, 'The Violence of Peace: Ethnojustice in Northern Uganda' (2014) 45 Development and Change 608.

[145] Human Rights Watch, 'The Lack of Accountability' (2005) http://www.hrw.org/reports/2005/uganda0905/6.htm (accessed 16 April 2023).

[146] Interview with CSO Representative, Kampala (7 August 2014).

[147] Interview with TFV Local Partner, Lira (18 July 2014).

[148] Phil Clark, 'Bringing the Peasants back in, again: State Power and Local Agency in Rwanda's Gacaca Courts' (2014) 8 Journal of Eastern African Studies 193.

[149] Porter, *After Rape* (n 133).

Yet, other local and international actors want none of that. They see 'culture' and 'tradition' rather than the war and its consequences as the biggest problem for women. In their eyes, traditional justice rituals look more like mechanisms of reproducing local patriarchy rather than providing justice for women. They criticize the way these traditional justice mechanisms deal with rape as a 'pollution of the spirits' rather than a crime. Perpetrators are 'cleansed' in a public ritual rather than punished. Male elders usually conduct the rituals with women performing 'highly valued' but nonetheless supplementary roles such as preparing ceremony requirements and food.[150] Working with victims of the conflict in Northern Uganda, a psychologist insisted:

> From my point of view, there is no justice for women [in Northern Uganda]. The lack of justice is not because of the war but because of the culture. Culturally, when you marry, you go to the clan of the husband, where you count [for] nothing. Justice you can only have if you have the capacity to bribe the police . . . It is not a war issue.[151]

But even the women themselves may have different priorities. Some women's rights advocates told me that their work of 'empowering women' is difficult because many survivors of SGBV primarily want communal acceptance and reintegration. 'Most women will be reluctant for that [transformative] approach', a women's rights officer observed, 'they tell you: "what do you want from me? I'm already a pariah. Now you want to add another burden?"'[152] A young woman, who volunteered for one of the TFV's former partners in Lira, explained to me:

> We feel that the most we can do here is to enable women to play their traditional roles again because they have lost community standing due to their physical injuries. We know it is not much, but if we rehabilitate them physically, we can help them perform their traditional roles again and this gives them community acceptance. We don't quite see how we can transform societies. Obviously, we talk to men, and we try to

[150] Justice and Reconciliation Project, 'Gender and Generation in Acholi Traditional Justice Mechanisms' (2012) 6–7 http://justiceandreconciliation.com/wp-content/uploads/2012/11/Gender-and-Generations-in-Acholi-Traditional-Mechanisms-Web.pdf (accessed 16 April 2023).
[151] Interview with Psychologist, Gulu (9 July 2014).
[152] Interview with NGO Officer, Kampala (30 July 2014).

> sensitize them to women's rights but, essentially, we help women become the types of women that are accepted by their communities.[153]

Others try to do a little bit more. 'We want to change the attitudes of our community members so that they look at women differently, so that they look at violence in our community differently', one women's rights officer in Kampala explained to me, 'you know, violence [against women] in an African context, it's kind of a normal thing'.[154] She continued: 'Personally, I was married using 10 cows and I'm like, oh my god, I'm just worth ten cows. So now it's like you've bought me and you can do anything with me . . . and in most cultures once a woman is married, you're not supposed to go back home.'[155] Her organization uses the SASA[156] approach, which mobilizes influential community members like cultural and religious leaders to create social norm change.[157]

Let's pause here to reflect how the transformative justice discourse changes once we move sites in international criminal justice. What we see unfolding in Northern Uganda is a contestation between liberal progress and the traditional order which culminates in the conflict between women's rights and women's roles—this, at least, is the reading of the NGO practitioners on the ground. The vocabulary of structural change has also shifted as the state and its laws are discursively less prominent than they were in The Hague. Instead, local change agents, awareness-raising, changing community norms, attitudes and behaviours form the language of social transformation. Structural change cannot happen from above; it needs to be inserted in the norms and practices of ordinary people.[158]

On the face of it, transformative ambitions like dismantling patriarchy are pulverized on the ground in the tug war between liberal and traditional stakeholders. Asked about transformative justice, my interviewees in Uganda, like in The Hague, sighed: we are trying, but we need to work with the stakeholders of the old order and also take seriously what the women themselves want. The TFV's 'local change agents' do not share the

153 I am paraphrasing here an informal conversation held on 19 July 2014 in Lira, Northern Uganda.

154 Interview with NGO worker, Kampala (12 July 2019).

155 ibid.

156 'SASA! means "now" in Kiswahili and is an acronym for approach's four phases: start, awareness, support and action.' See 'Raising Voices: Preventing Violence against Women & Children' https://raisingvoices.org/women/sasa-approach/ (accessed 14 November 2021).

157 ibid.

158 Interview with CSO Representative, Kampala (7 August 2014).

same vision of change. Indeed, transformative justice, by definition, challenges the power of many traditional stakeholders such as religious leaders. By enlisting them as 'change agents', the TFV runs the risk of making their assistance programmes part of a more conservative agenda that pushes for the return to a pre-war order in which women often had even fewer rights.

5.5.1 Transforming People versus Transforming Structures

Of course, 'transformative justice' is a tall order for an organization that has an annual budget of a few million Euros, spread across the Court's situation countries. Transforming societal structures is painstaking. It requires a lot of time and money. It is also difficult to deal with 'traditional stakeholders' in that pursuit. Yet, the TFV has never claimed that it can 'transform societies' on its own. Rather, it wants to use its programmes to move towards that goal. It also does not work alone but through local partners and governmental structures, where possible. So, perhaps, we should evaluate the TFV's programmes in light of a more modest aim: are they pushing in the direction of structural transformation?

This is far from clear at this point. Listening to my interviews, I noticed an almost seamless shift from the idea of transformative justice as 'transforming structures' to the idea of transformative justice as 'transforming people'. I explained the concept in terms of the former, but my interviewees talked about it in terms of the latter: it is the people who need to be 'transformed'. One local partner in Lira elaborated:

> The most important thing the Trust Fund has ever tried to support is 'transforming somebody', so that he or she cannot reflect back to the other situation he or she went through or the situation that she was in before the war. For example, the Trust Fund has been trying to provide artificial limbs to people who were amputated during the war . . . now he or she has an artificial limb, he or she can walk, can work, and participate in economic activities.[159]

[159] Interview with TFV's Local Partner, Lira (21 July 2014).

At first, I thought the local partners had misunderstood the concept. Yet, a closer reading of the TFV's activities suggest that, in practice, it does aim at transforming people rather than structures.[160]

The TFV combines physical and psychological rehabilitation with material support to create 'reparative value for victims and survivors'.[161] Psycho-social support features prominently in the Trust Fund's activities in Northern Uganda. The TFV has, for example, supported 'Healing of Memories' workshops facilitated by the Anglican Diocese of Northern Uganda that aim at 'spiritual healing, reconciliation, and peace-building'.[162] The purpose of these sessions is individual transformation through forgetting and accepting.[163] Many organizations in Northern Uganda which claim to do 'counselling', a psychologist told me, really give 'advice according to the cultural manner, "stop crying, be strong and forget it"'.[164] Even more collective activities such as community therapy and drama are designed to make people function better within existing structures rather than changing them.[165] Indeed, the therapeutic approach is restorative but not transformative; it treats suffering as an inherently personal or communal experience rather than the product of violent structures.

The TFV's victim survivor stories also reveal that it ultimately aims at individual transformation and a rather limited one for that matter.[166] On its website, the TFV tells the story of Mary, an LRA abductee and former 'wife' of Kony who was abused and tortured by the LRA and then later

[160] Some scholars see transformative reparations as encompassing both the transformation of people and structures ('The desire to transform the lives of victims as well as the power structures that sustain unequal relationships and promote victimisation is compelling'). McGonigle Leyh and Fraser (n 4) 49.

[161] In its 2020–2021 Strategic Plan, the TFV claimed that 'the reparative value of international criminal justice, as an international public good, is ultimately defined by the appreciation of its beneficiaries'. TFV Strategic Plan (2020–2021) 7 https://www.trustfundforvictims.org/sites/default/files/reports/TFV%20Strategic%20Plan%202020-2021.pdf (accessed 10 August 2023).

[162] TFV, 'Programme Progress Report Summer' (2014) 29 https://www.trustfundforvictims.org/sites/default/files/reports/TFV%20Programme%20Progress%20Report%20-%20Summer%202014.pdf (accessed 16 April 2023).

[163] ibid.

[164] Interview with Psychologist, Gulu (9 July 2014).

[165] As Alcoff and Gray put it, the therapeutic establishment 'tends to promote a solution of private therapy geared toward social functioning rather than political action geared toward change'. Linda Alcoff and Laura Gray, 'Survivor Discourse: Transgression or Recuperation?' (1993) 18(2) Signs 260, 283.

[166] TFV, 'Victims Voices' https://www.trustfundforvictims.org/en/victims-voices (accessed 30 March 2022).

raped by the Uganda People's Defence Force.[167] Mary's history made her 'unmarriageable'.[168] She tried to report the rape to the police but was not given a hearing. After only five sessions of counselling by the TFV's partner, Mary's symptoms of fear and anger improved.[169] 'Over time she learned to express her anger and sadness in a healthy way . . . and her relationships with others also improved.'[170] Mary, moreover, became 'actively involved in economically-productive activities', tailoring and selling clothes.[171] She even began teaching tailoring and hopes to run her own tailoring school in the future.[172] The TFV's partners also helped Salima from the DRC by training her to run a small business: 'Now, I have two plots of land, and I have a husband!', Salima exclaimed.[173] Cissy, another LRA abductee from the DRC, suffered stigma and violence by her husband and her community who accused her of having 'the character of bush people'.[174] After the TFV's partner counselled both Cissy and her husband, her husband agreed that Cissy could live with his mother but was no longer allowed to call herself his wife. 'For this I really do say thanks to COOPI because they have saved my children and me', Cissy said.[175] Far from tampering with the structural conditions that constrain Mary's, Salima's and Cissy's lives such as patriarchy, marriage customs, and institutional indifference, the TFV helps women put up with them while turning them into productive and reproductive capitalist subjects.

Of course, it could be said that 'transforming people' is 'good enough' and perhaps more realistic.[176] There are, however, at least two problems with this approach. First, it implies that there is something wrong with people who are caught up in conflicts. One of the initiatives that the TFV

[167] TFV, 'Mary (Northern Uganda)' https://www.trustfundforvictims.org/en/stories/mary-northern-uganda (accessed 30 March 2022).
[168] ibid.
[169] ibid.
[170] ibid.
[171] ibid.
[172] ibid.
[173] TFV, 'Salima (Democratic Republic of Congo)' https://www.trustfundforvictims.org/en/stories/salima-democratic-republic-of-congo (accessed 30 March 2022).
[174] TFV, 'Cissy (Democratic Republic of Congo)' https://www.trustfundforvictims.org/en/stories/cissy-democratic-republic-of-congo (accessed 30 March 2022).
[175] ibid.
[176] https://www.qeh.ox.ac.uk/events/making-do-"good-enough"-transitional-justice-rethinking-concept; Paul Gready and Simon Robins, 'Transitional Justice and Theories of Change: Towards Evaluation as Understanding' (2020) 14(2) International Journal of Transitional Justice 280; Mariam Salehi, 'Trying Just Enough or Promising Too Much? The Problem-Capacity-Nexus in Tunisia's Transitional Justice Process' (2022) 16(1) Journal of Intervention and Statebuilding 98.

has supported in the DRC is the 'peace school' whose rationale it explains as follows:

> 'L'école de la Paix' implemented by the Missionnaires d'Afrique is a good example of *shifting the mindset of young people*. Actually, formal and non-formal education remains a cornerstone for empowerment and *behaviour change*. Through their activities outside and inside the formal education system, thousands of teenagers have received training dealing with everyday matters regarding peace, passive cohabitation, social cohesion, accepting differences and diversities. *Transforming the culture of those young people could have a long term positive effect.*[177]

By focusing on the behavioural change of young people, the TFV may unwittingly contribute to an understanding of conflicts as caused by 'violent youngsters', thereby glossing over legitimate grievances and the structural causes of war. In Uganda, such a discourse plays into widespread stereotypes that portray the Acholi as 'innately violent and primitive'. It also erases the economic and political marginalization of Northern Uganda and the repression of its people, which have been major drivers of successive rebellions and civil war.[178]

Another problem is that 'transforming people' often becomes the demand on victims essentially to transform themselves as soon as possible and with very little in terms of assistance.[179] To grasp how the demand to self-transform materializes, the TFV's activities need to be contextualized within two prevailing paradigms: the 'survivor paradigm' that celebrates victims' resilience and agency by calling them 'survivors' rather than 'victims', and the 'development paradigm' which is predicated on the philosophy

[177] TFV, 'Empowering Victims' (2012) 24 (emphasis added).

[178] Tim Allen, 'Ritual (ab)use? Problems with traditional justice in Northern Uganda' in Phil Clark and Nicholas Waddell (eds), *Courting Conflict? Justice, Peace and the ICC in Africa* (Royal African Society 2008) 47. See also Sverker Finnström, *Living with Bad Surroundings: War, History, and Everyday Moments in Northern Uganda* (Duke UP 2008).

[179] The TFV, for example, defines its physical rehabilitation work as 'supporting victims who have suffered physical injury in order to recover and resume their roles as productive and contributing members of their societies'. TFV, 'A Road to Recovery: Healing, Empowerment and Reconciliation' (2014) vii https://www.trustfundforvictims.org/sites/default/files/reports/TFV%20Programme%20Progress%20Report%20%20-%20Winter%202014.pdf accessed 13 March 2020.

of self-help.[180] Steeped in both paradigms, the Trust Fund introduced the term 'victim–survivor' to conform both with the Court's legal terminology of 'victims' and accepted gender and development discourse that calls them 'survivors'.[181] When I asked a TFV evaluator how people who had received TFV assistance would identify, she replied:

> We have an issue of translation. A lot of the beneficiaries would refer to themselves as victims, and I don't know whether this is how they view themselves with everything this implies in English: "I'm a victim"; it is such a passive state or whether it does not carry the same weight in their language or because they know the programme that they are benefiting from calls them victims.[182]

Another possibility is that it may be difficult for people to see themselves as survivors when they struggle to meet their basic needs. In his research with victims' focus groups in Kenya and Uganda, Tenove found that all participants 'agreed that the term "victim" was appropriate for them . . . [linking] victim status to a moral and social claim for redress'.[183] In a survey in Northern Uganda in 2010, 97 per cent of respondents considered themselves victims of the conflict.[184] In fact, the term 'survivor' may be problematic as it carries normative expectations: you are expected to stop crying, move on, build a new life, be a compliant citizen and a self-sufficient

[180] TFV, 'Background Summary'(2008) 1 https://www.icc-cpi.int/sites/default/files/NR/rdonlyres/E582AE21-D718-4798-97ED-C6C9F0D9B42D/0/TFV_Background_Summary_Eng.pdf (accessed 2 January 2023) ('The TFV helps in this process by supporting sustainable self- help projects designed to rebuild lives, and insure that the victims and their families work side-by-side'). See also TFV press release, 'On International Women's Day 2021 the TFV calls for renewed commitment to the most vulnerable women and girls' ('The TFV knows the strength and resilience of women, however. In our programmes women's voices and opinions are integrated across the design and evaluation of our activities') https://www.trustfundforvictims.org/en/news/international-women%E2%80%99s-day-2021-tfv-calls-renewed-commitment-most-vulnerable-women-and-girls (accessed 2 January 2023).

[181] TFV Strategic Plan 2014–2017 (n 30) 7 (n 4).

[182] ibid.

[183] Chris Tenove, 'International Justice for Victims? Assessing the International Criminal Court from the Perspective of Victims in Kenya and Uganda' Africa Portal (September 2013) 11 https://www.researchgate.net/publication/320386086_International_Justice_for_Victims_Assessing_the_International_Criminal_Court_from_Victims%27_Perspectives_in_Kenya_and_Uganda (accessed 16 April 2023).

[184] Patrick Vinck and Phuong N Pham, 'Transitioning to Peace: A Population-Based Survey on Attitudes about Social Reconstruction and Justice in Northern Uganda' (December 2010) 44 https://www.law.berkeley.edu/files/HRC/Publications_Transitioning-to-Peace_12-2010.pdf (accessed 22 January 2023).

economic actor. The concept 'survivor', Gupta argues, 'underplay[s] the oppressive power of the system' and thereby decreases the pressure on the state to provide its citizens with the support they need to 'build a new life'.[185]

Furthermore, the TFV's assistance programmes are shaped by development methodology and its emphasis on self-help, as reflected in its vocational training and microloan initiatives.[186] In its reparation implementation plan in the *Lubanga* case, the TFV noted that former child soldiers are often 'perceived to be of limited value to the community' because they missed out on educational opportunities.[187] By teaching them 'marketable skills', improved agricultural techniques and vocations that fit with local market needs, 'victims experience a significant improvement and transformation of their ability to undertake economic activities' and 'are able to provide for their families in a sustainable way'.[188] Some of them are then selected as 'positive deviants', people who made it against the odds, a former child soldier, for instance, who now runs a successful business, to serve as role models for the TFV's programmes.[189] Thus, instead of trying to change the odds, victims learn from 'exceptional examples' of those who made it nonetheless.

Logically, this emphasis on 'exceptional individuals' and self-help fuels frustration with those victims who don't make it against the odds, who are the 'norm' if you want. Describing her experiences with female victims who had received vocational training in sewing, a Ugandan women's rights officer noted:

> It takes them so long to learn how to sew. They end up not being able to produce anything so fantastic apart from bags, and then the production is not so huge . . . how do we enlarge the production and push them

[185] Rahila Gupta, '"Victim" vs "survivor": Feminism and language' *Open Democracy* (16 June 2014) https://www.opendemocracy.net/en/5050/victim-vs-survivor-feminism-and-language/ (accessed 22 January 2023).

[186] Through access to credit, people can become entrepreneurs and set up their own businesses, as described in ch 3.

[187] *Prosecutor v Lubanga* (Annex A: Collective Reparations projects in relation to the conviction of Thomas Lubanga Dyilo before the International Criminal Court) ICC-01/04-01/06-3273-AnxA [2017], 13.

[188] ibid 14–15.

[189] International Center for Research on Women, 'External Evaluation of the Trust Fund for Victims Programmes in Northern Uganda and the Democratic Republic of Congo: Towards a Perspective of Upcoming Interventions' (November 2013) 45 https://www.icrw.org/wp-content/uploads/2016/10/ICRW-TFV--Evaluation-Report.pdf (accessed 7 August 2023); Telephone interview with TFV Evaluator (3 January 2014).

> away from the present so that they can produce for export? But honestly, they are very happy to sew two dresses, hang it in front of their shops and then go to their garden (she laughs) . . . Women are usually tailors and hairdressers. And then you want to tell them: 'Why can't you be a designer? Why can't you think about producing?'[190]

Thus, the expectation is that after a few months of vocational training the victim should be a designer producing for global export. In practice, transformative justice shifts the responsibility of transformation to the individual 'victim survivor'. It comes down to assisting people in better performing the societal and economic roles assigned to them by the existing system, the same system in which terrible crimes were committed against them. The quote also illustrates how subsistence work is not only ignored but suppressed in local stakeholder discourse. 'The garden' is dismissed as a form of leisure activity when it is the garden, where women grow subsistence crops, rather than the shop, that will secure the survival of the family and community as the next chapter will show.

Through this focus on survivors' agency and self-help, the TFV's assistance programmes contribute to normative expectations of 'individual betterment' while undermining the case for structural change and comprehensive victims' support from the state and the international community. Victims are supported to become better wives and better workers. Ultimately, it is the victim who has to do the transformation and not the state, the community, the world system, or the global economy.[191] A slippage between 'transforming structures' and 'transforming people' suits both traditional and liberal stakeholders. Both try to transform people after mass violence to refit them into existing structures. Both are aligned with a neoliberal vision of society, even though traditional stakeholders are routinely blamed by their liberal counterparts for the failure to achieve more ambitious social change. Once we probe transformative justice practices on the ground, the contestation fades. Indeed, structural transformation had already slipped out of the discourse before any contestation between liberal and traditional values occurred.

[190] Interview with Women's Rights Officer, Kampala (30 July 2014).

[191] See also Eslava and Pahuja (n 79) 127 ('Subjects [in the Global South] are expected to acquire that sovereignty—the ability to stand on their own feet—with minimal amounts of state support. Examples include micro-credit schemes, cash-transfer, "entrepreneurship" training, land titling programs, and neighborhood legalization schemes as well as the move to formalize informal vendors').

5.6 Conclusion

Transformative justice takes on different forms in different institutional and social contexts. From a critical ideology perspective, it is curious that the promise of transformative justice emerged at an international criminal court. What explains its stealthy presence in the Court's discourse and practice? By invoking transformative justice, the Court unconsciously produces a solution to a problem that cannot be posed and solved on the theoretical terrain of international criminal justice. It thus manifests in a rather truncated form as 'transformative reparations', a solution to the problem of repairing harm after mass atrocity and gendered violence. The Court's production of an answer without a question symptomatically reflects the broader problematic of the social and political context in which it operates. It expresses a disillusionment with liberal institutions and a concomitant shift from the institutional to the structural level: building good institutions is no longer seen as sufficient to solve societal problems. We also need structural change.[192] But once put in those terms ('transforming structures', 'addressing root causes'), the problem becomes intractable not only for the Court but also for social movements and community activists.

Whereas transformative justice at the ICC ultimately recuperates the state as the key agent of social change, it functions both as an abolitionist imaginary and a concrete practice of community accountability in black and brown feminist communities. In both settings, however, it also expresses a deeper desire for structural change that transcends the institutional context in which the concept washes up. Transformative justice invokes the change that is both necessary and inconceivable: it is not only that we don't know how 'to do' structural change, but that we cannot quite imagine what it might look like. The 'top-down' solution, the 'reimagining from above' fails.

If we pose the problem from a Marxist perspective, it becomes solvable albeit in a different manner; the solution is world revolution: overthrowing state institutions and seizing the means of production. But even that is rather abstract, and it is not entirely clear how revolutionary change will come about in the current conjuncture. Yet, as I will show in the next chapter, if we pose the problem in a different form, if we study structures as social

[192] See eg recent books which express the need to 'change everything'. See Verónica Gago, *Feminist International: How to change everything* (Verso 2020); Ruth Wilson Gilmore, *Change Everything: Racial Capitalism and the Case for Abolition* (Haymarket Books 2023).

relations, 'embodied in real people and in a real context', they can be subverted and resisted. Apart from revolutionary agitation, or in a more liberal vein, reforming institutions or changing structures, resistance also takes shape in the everyday undoing of capitalist relations and the defence of the means of social reproduction.

At the ICC, transformative justice ultimately rejuvenates and reproduces the justice ideology as a compromise formation between traditional and liberal stakeholders. In black feminist activist circles, it leads to a search for future alternatives, which seems quite utopian to the extent that it is premised on the same analysis of root causes and structural inequality. While transformative justice emerged as an antidote to carceral feminism, it has been recuperated as its tool, rectifying the limitations of punishment through reparations. The substitute became a supplement. The alternative an add-on. As the concept moved through international fora and legal documents its radical roots were cut off, but it did not fizzle out as empty rhetoric. The urgency of transformation remained but the responsibility for it was first shifted onto the post-colonial state, then onto the stakeholders of the traditional order and, finally, onto feminized and racialized victim–survivors. Blaming traditional powerholders for the failure of gender justice obscures the compromise formation of 'transforming people' rather than structures that both liberalism and traditionalism neurotically sustain. Ultimately, transformative justice comes down to assisting people in better performing the societal and economic roles assigned to them by the existing capitalist system.

And thus, the Court's attempt to resolve its contradictions fails. The sigh that transformative justice elicits, despite signalling real distress, does not pave the way to structural change. But that does not mean that nothing changes. Recuperation negotiates rather than voids change. Interpellation into racialized and gendered hierarchies is crucial in cementing global capitalism but it also creates a doubled subject: an active victim who needs to become a survivor; a loser who needs to become a winner. While victims become active subjects, they do not necessarily become active in the way capitalism wants them to be, revealing the subversive potential of the contradictory interpellation of victim–survivors, which the next chapter will further explore.

6
Money and Land: Resistance in Times of Capitalist Complementarity

6.1 Resistance in International Criminal Justice

In *The Wretched of the Earth*, Frantz Fanon argues that metropolitan states work through ideology, while colonies work through violence:

> In the capitalist countries, a multitude of moral teachers, counsellors, and 'bewilderers' separate the exploited from those in power. In the colonial countries, on the contrary, the policeman and the soldier, by their immediate presence and their frequent and direct action maintain contact with the native and advise him by means of a rifle-butts and napalm not to budge.[1]

This dichotomy, however, may be too stark for the post-colony. The post-colony boasts a multitude of ideological institutions and the International Criminal Court (ICC) and the United Nations (UN) play important roles here, precisely because they are formally separate from the state and the market. The ICC cannot force affected communities to participate in its proceedings, but it can ideologically form them as 'its victims'. Yet, what does resistance to ideology look like and how does it connect to broader struggles against colonial capitalism?

This chapter explores how, when, and why victims in Northern Uganda (and Kenya) resist international criminal justice.[2] In studying resistance, transitional justice scholars often scrutinize the tensions or frictions between global and local, retributive, and restorative, and legal and cultural

[1] Frantz Fanon, *The Wretched of the Earth* (Penguin Classics 2001) 29.
[2] The focus will be on Northern Uganda.

Victims and the Labour of Justice at the International Criminal Court. Leila Ullrich, Oxford University Press.
 DOI: 10.1093/9780191915048.003.0006

justice institutions and practices.[3] Uganda has been a focal point of this debate. When the ICC began working in Northern Uganda in 2005, many Acholi cultural and religious leaders, and their Western NGO supporters, argued that the ICC was not only threatening a fragile peace, but also interfered with traditional justice mechanisms.[4] The traditional chiefs, *rwodi*, mediate these reconciliation ceremonies, known as *mato oput*, 'which many Acholi believe can bring true healing in a way that the formal justice system cannot'.[5] Northern Ugandans, it was argued, did not need international criminal justice. Some local leaders even called on Acholis to attack the ICC's vehicles.[6]

In light of such tensions between justice and peace, and law and culture, some scholars have explored whether international criminal law (ICL) can accommodate local justice processes through the concept of complementarity.[7] Complementarity has different meanings in ICL.[8] Most prominent

[3] Nicola Palmer, 'Re-examining resistance in post-genocide Rwanda' (2014) 8(2) Journal of Eastern African Studies 231; Briony Jones and Thomas Brudholm, 'Introduction: Rethinking Resistance to Transitional Justice' (2016) 2 Conflict and Society 68.

[4] Adam Branch, 'Uganda's Civil War and the Politics of ICC Intervention' (2007) 21(2) Ethics and International Affairs 179; Kasaija Phillip Apuuli, 'Peace over Justice: The Acholi Religious Leaders Peace Initiative (ARLPI) vs the International Criminal Court (ICC) in Northern Uganda' (2011) 11(1) Studies in Ethnicity and Nationalism 116.

[5] Barney Afako, 'Reconciliation and Justice: 'Mato Oput' and the Amnesty Act' (2002) 11 Accord 64, 67. Bishop Ochola II MB, 'Where is Justice in the case of Dominic Ongwen, who is being tried by the ICC in The Hague' (28 March 2016) (on file with the author). For a more critical perspective on Mato Oput see Tim Allen, 'Ritual (ab)use? Problems with traditional justice in Northern Uganda' (2008) in Phil Clark and Nicholas Waddell (eds), *Courting Conflict? Justice, Peace and the ICC in Africa* (Royal African Society 2008) 47.

[6] In 2007, a local elected government official (local council), Chairman Mao, allegedly went on MEGA FM, a popular radio station in the North, and called on the people to resist the ICC: 'If you see those people with this licence [and he gives the number plates of the ICC's cars], don't help them, keep them away.' In another version of the same story, Chairman Mao even called on people to burn the ICC's vehicles down, which 'indirectly meant killing those in the car'. Interview with TFV Officer, Kampala (7 July 2014); Interview with former TFV Partner, Kampala (7 July 2014). See also Adam Branch, 'Dominic Ongwen on Trial: The ICC's African Dilemmas' (2017) 11(1) International Journal of Transitional Justice 49.

[7] Tim Kelsall, *Culture under Cross-Examination: International Justice and the Special Court for Sierra Leone* (CUP 2009); Martha Minow, 'Do alternative justice mechanisms deserve recognition in international criminal law: Truth commissions, amnesties, and complementarity at the international criminal court'(2019) 60(1) Harvard International Law Journal 1; Nicola Palmer, *Courts in Conflict: Interpreting the Layers of Justice in Post-Genocide Rwanda* (OUP 2015); Adina-Loredana Nistor, Andrew Merrylees, and Barbora Holá, 'Spellbound at the International Criminal Court: The intersection of spiritualism & international criminal law' in Julie Fraser and Brianne McGonigle Leyh (eds), *Intersections of Law and Culture at the International Criminal Court* (Edward Elgar Publishing 2020).

[8] Sarah Nouwen, *Complementarity in the Line of Fire: The Catalysing Effect of the International Criminal Court in Uganda and Sudan* (CUP 2013); Christian de Vos, *Complementarity, Catalysts, Compliance: The International Criminal Court in Uganda, Kenya, and the Democratic Republic of Congo* (CUP 2020).

is the principle, stipulated in Article 17 of the Rome Statute, that the ICC is a 'court of last resort', which only steps in if domestic jurisdictions fail to investigate and prosecute international crimes genuinely. While some construe the principle of complementarity narrowly as an admissibility rule, others see it as an opening for the coexistence between the ICC and alternative justice mechanisms.[9] This is an old debate, but it resurfaced following the ICC's sentencing of Dominic Ongwen to twenty-five years in prison in May 2021, as some scholars and practitioners lamented that the Court had failed to use complementarity more creatively to carve out a role for Acholi traditional justice.[10] As Ongwen's defence team put it in their appeal of his conviction, 'in 2021, the issue is no longer *should* international criminal justice address cultural issues but, *how* will judges manage the intersection of cultural and legal issues'.[11]

International criminal justice and cultural institutions can, however, also perfectly well work together and that was the context I encountered when I returned to Northern Uganda for fieldwork in summer 2019 (before the *Ongwen* verdict).[12] The contestation between global and local justice, criminal law and traditional justice no longer seemed to be the most important issue. I was struck when the ICC's officer reassured victims at an outreach meeting in Gulu that those who fall outside the scope of the Court's cases can still participate in traditional justice, amnesty, reconciliation, and nation-building in Uganda.[13] Amnesties, I had thought, were anathema to

[9] Darryl Robinson, 'Serving the Interests of Justice: Amnesties, Truth Commissions and the International Criminal Court' (2003) 14 European Journal of International Law 481.

[10] Ayodele Akenroye and Beth Lyons made that argument at the online panel discussion, 'After the Verdict: Dominic Ongwen & the Many Sides of Justice' hosted by the Justice and Reconciliation Project (JRP) and the University of British Columbia on 7 May 2021 https://sppga.ubc.ca/events/event/after-the-verdict-dominic-ongwen-the-many-sides-of-justice/ (accessed 14 June 2022). See also Wui Ling Cheah, 'International criminal law and culture' in Kevin Heller and others (eds), *The Oxford Handbook of International Criminal Law* (OUP 2020) 748.

[11] *The Prosecutor v Ongwen* (Public Redacted Version of 'Defence Appeal Brief Against the Convictions in the Judgment of 4 February 2021', filed on 21 July 2021 as ICC-02/04-01/15-1866-Conf) [2021] ICC-02/04-01/15-1866-Red, § 430 (original emphasis).

[12] This chapter focuses on 35 semi-structured interviews, one focus group discussion, and ethnographic observations of the Court's victim engagement I conducted in Kampala, Gulu and Lukodi in July and August 2019.

[13] Field notes, ICC Public Dialogue, Gulu (17 July 2019). See also the ASP 2021 resolution: 'Recalling the full range of justice and reconciliation mechanisms with restorative measures that are complementary to criminal justice processes, including truth and reconciliation commissions, national reparations programmes and institutional and legal reforms, including guarantees of non-recurrence.' Resolution ICC-ASP/20/Res.5, 'Strengthening the International Criminal Court and the Assembly of States Parties', adopted at the 8th plenary meeting on 9 December 2021, by consensus, 2.

the Court.[14] I was also surprised to meet a number of cultural and religious leaders at the Court's outreach meetings, some of whom even did outreach work for the Court. They did not seem troubled by the ICC's intervention.

What they worried about was the Acholi youth who 'grew up without proper guidance' either in the camps or in Lord's Resistance Army (LRA) captivity.[15] They are lazy, want quick money, and refuse to engage in farming.[16] This is where the ICC can play a useful role, some local leaders believe. It can teach people that there is a price to pay for what you do. It works not only as a deterrent against egregious crimes but as a disciplinary tool and thus fits into their agenda of getting the youth to toil in commercial agriculture. Far from threatening the local order, the ICC can shore up the power of local leaders, which has been eroded by twenty years of war, mass displacement, and contradictory governmental policies.[17] Rather than a problem or a solution, complementarity has become a reality on the ground. Different justice institutions complement each other in pursuing law and order. The ICC has become useful in compelling Acholis towards 'productive' work. I call this capitalist complementarity. From the perspective of capitalist complementarity, any justice institution that secures capitalist accumulation is acceptable. It matters less whether the mechanism is retributive or restorative, whether it works through the 'global' or the 'local'.[18]

But resistance, of course, cannot be reduced to the agendas and practices of local leaders. A key question is what victims want. Victims, it is often argued, are divided on the *Ongwen* trial and verdict.[19] They disagree on whether Ongwen is a victim or a perpetrator, whether he should have received a lighter sentence, and whether he should have been tried in Uganda rather than in The Hague. Ongwen, many feel, has been unfairly singled out

[14] Kjersti Lohne, *Advocates of Humanity: Human Rights NGOs in International Criminal Justice* (OUP 2019) 133. See also Josepha Close, 'The ICC refrains from affirming a general ban on amnesties in the Gaddafi admissibility appeal decision' (*International Law Blog* (20 April 2020) https://internationallaw.blog/2020/04/20/the-icc-refrains-from-affirming-a-general-ban-on-amnesties-in-the-gaddafi-admissibility-appeal-decision/ (accessed 14 June 2022).

[15] Interview with Cultural Leader, Gulu (20 July 2019). This was a common theme across my interviews with a wide variety of local stakeholders.

[16] See chs 3 and 4.

[17] Mahmood Mamdani, *Citizen and Subject: Contemporary Africa and the Legacy of Late Colonialism* (2nd edn, Princeton UP 2018).

[18] Adam Branch, 'The Violence of Peace: Ethnojustice in Northern Uganda' (2014) 45 Development and Change 608.

[19] Lino Owor Ogora, 'Mixed reactions from Northern Uganda as ICC delivers judgment in Ongwen's case: Community members call for light sentence' *International Justice Monitor* (5 February 2021) https://www.ijmonitor.org/2021/02/mixed-reactions-from-northern-uga

for punishment, while the majority of former LRA commanders have received amnesties, and the Ugandan government has so far enjoyed blanket impunity for its war crimes.[20] In their analysis of the only domestic war crimes trial in Uganda, the trial of Thomas Kwoyelo, Anna Macdonald and Holly Porter argue that what type of justice victims want depends on the social relationship they have with the perpetrator.[21] That explains why some of Ongwen's 'wives' (women who were forcibly married to Ongwen in LRA captivity) want him to be released so that he can support their children.[22] Victims who do not have continuing social bonds with Ongwen, by contrast, often want to see him punished, while Northern Ugandans, who were not directly affected by his crimes, subsume the *Ongwen* case into their broader perspectives on the war, displacement, and the region's contested relationship with the central government.[23]

But this focus on divisions has overshadowed important commonalities among victims, above all, that the vast majority of them demand reparations, especially money and land. It has also neglected an important fact: people, whether supportive or critical, still come to the Court's meetings.[24] They criticize the Court, but they still engage with it. Both local leaders and affected communities do. They enter into relationships with the Court's field staff, victims' lawyers, and intermediaries. The same journalists who report on 'divided opinions' in Northern Uganda also observe that the Court's meetings

nda-as-icc-delivers-judgment-in-ongwens-case-community-members-call-for-light-sentence/ (accessed 13 August 2023); Jazzmin Jiwa, 'Trial of LRA commander Ongwen still divides northern Uganda' *The New Humanitarian* (30 June 2021) https://www.thenewhumanitarian.org/news-feature/2021/6/30/trial-of-LRA-commander-ongwen-still-divides-northern-uganda (accessed 8 August 2023).

[20] Adam Branch, 'Dominic Ongwen on Trial: The ICC's African Dilemmas' (2017) 11(1) International Journal of Transitional Justice 30.

[21] Anna Macdonald and Holly Porter, 'The Trial of Thomas Kwoyelo: Opportunity or Spectre? Reflections from the ground on the first LRA prosecution' (2016) 86 Africa 698. See also Holly Porter, *After Rape: Violence, Justice, and Social Harmony in Uganda* (CUP 2017).

[22] Jiwa (n 19).

[23] Macdonald and Porter (n 21).

[24] Other scholars, following James Scott, have argued that everyday resistance to state-orchestrated, top-down transitional justice processes is often expressed through strategies of avoiding participation. See eg Susan Thomson, 'Whispering truth to power: The everyday resistance of Rwandan peasants to post-genocide reconciliation' (2011) 110(40) African Affairs 439.

are 'packed'.[25] It is thus important to study what people do and not only what they say.[26]

This chapter proposes a methodology of studying resistance that takes the relationships that form in and through international criminal justice seriously. Such a methodology posits that victims' social relationships to the Court, and not only to the perpetrator, matter for reading resistance. We need to look more closely at what happens when the Court engages victims to unravel the different layers of resistance. The chapter begins with the conflicts on the surface: between victims' demands for money and land and the Court's insistence on its legal boundaries and functions. My contention is that people resist not the Court per se but the Court's terms of the relationship.[27] They want to redefine what the Court's intervention is about. Victims resist by making the ICC about land and money rather than punishment, and by making justice about subsistence and social reproduction rather than law.

While the Court's practitioners tend to dismiss victims' demands for money and land as 'economic' rather than 'legal' demands, the Court's legal forms are themselves mired in economic assumptions. Even more, they obscure the ICC's prior ideological interventions which are not only confined to courtroom proceedings but also take place in the field. The chapter shows how the ICC's various stakeholders not only produce victims but also capitalist subjects by reforming and co-opting victims' subjectivities and demands. Indeed, 'the field' rather than the courtroom emerges as the key 'production site' of justice. This is where the Court's staff and victims' lawyers regularly meet victims, this is where evidence is collected and cases are built, this is where much legal and emotional labour is expended and exploited, this is where 'justice for victims' happens.

The chapter then reads the Court's meetings with victims 'in the field' symptomatically, revealing that the contestation between victims' demands and the Court's legal mandate is not the only conflict that transpires at the meeting. As the Court reaches into people's lives, frictions emerge between

[25] Jiwa (n 19).

[26] Following Malinowski, this is, of course, a central credo of ethnography. See also Holly Porter, 'Justice and rape on the periphery: the supremacy of social harmony in the space between local solutions and formal judicial systems in northern Uganda' (2012) 6(1) Journal of Eastern African Studies 81.

[27] For complex and varied forms of resistance in the context of criminal justice institutions see eg Mary Bosworth and Eamonn Carrabine, 'Reassessing Resistance: Gender, Race and Sexuality in Prison' (2001) 3(4) Punishment and Society 501.

life-making and ideology-making. By coming late, by bringing their friends, by nursing their children and chatting to neighbours, victims drown out the Court's ideology-making with people- and community-making. Victims, in other words, immediately repurpose the Court's meetings as sites of social reproduction and subsistence. Does that matter? Can life-making be a form of resistance? And how does such resistance relate to other struggles in Northern Uganda?

To answer these questions, the chapter then turns to social reproduction theory. To understand how social reproduction can become a site of resistance we need to appreciate how the relationship between production, social reproduction and capitalist accumulation differs in Northern Uganda. In Euro-America, the main site of Marxist-Feminist theory production, unwaged domestic labourers, often middle-class housewives, were 'doubly separated' from the means of production.[28] In Northern Uganda, by contrast, many women still have access to customary and communal land. Rather than a double separation, there is a direct struggle between the social reproducers (often women) and the capitalist accumulators (corporations, states), and that struggle centres on the land.[29] In Northern Uganda, women have been at the forefront of the fight against land expropriation.

Effectively, then, the chapter connects three levels of resistance: the level of discourse, where victims' justice conceptions clash with the Court's legal categories, the level of practice, where victims disrupt the Court's meetings with their life-making practices, and the level of material struggle, where capitalism's reluctant preservation of its alternatives gestates resistive subjects, values and practices that can challenge its pursuit of accumulation. The chapter weaves these threads together by following the contestations between the Court and victims from the courtroom in The Hague, to the meeting venue in Gulu, to the struggle for land that simmers in the backdrop of the Court's intervention. It thus proceeds analogously to Marx's excavation of the logic of capitalism by moving from the visible marketplace to the hidden abode of production, and to the latter's roots in regimes of primitive accumulation. Just as resistance to international criminal justice

[28] Lise Vogel, *Marxism and the Oppression of Women: Toward a Unitary Theory* (2nd edn, Brill 2013) 159 n 3.

[29] Lyn Ossome, 'Pedagogies of Feminist Resistance: Agrarian Movements in Africa' (2021) 10(1) Agrarian South: Journal of Political Economy 41, 51–52.

emanates from within the Court's relationships with victims, so too does resistance to colonial capitalism emanate from its 'internal exteriors.'[30]

Resistance occurs when people prioritize social reproduction over production, exactly the opposite of what ideology tells them to do. It happens at the point of contradiction when justice means that the perpetrator will be fed but the victims won't be, when it is 'unrealistic' for victims to demand as reparation, for losing family members, the same amount that lawyers charge for two weeks of victims' representation, when victims are interpellated as 'survivors' who should become productive entrepreneurs, but survival depends on the village and subsistence production more than on the market or the state, when values nurtured by social reproduction labour (right to subsistence and reciprocity) come into conflict with those of production (protecting property, working hard, repaying debt), when conflict arises between using land as a means of subsistence or as a means of accumulation. By overwriting the Court's justice processes with subsistence and social reproduction practices, the Court's victims not only challenge its capitalist progress narrative but also undo their legal interpellation.

6.2 Justice Contestations: What Do Victims Want?

What does justice mean? And what type of justice do victims want? These questions are contested even at the Court.[31] Some of the Court's staff insist that justice for victims means holding the perpetrator accountable. Others believe that international criminal trials will end impunity and thereby prevent future crimes.[32] Still others highlight how trials establish the truth of what happened, reaffirm moral values and provide victims with a voice and emotional closure.[33] In victimology, a key debate centres on whether

[30] Santosh Anand, 'Foreclosed temporalities: Imperialism and international criminal law' *Critical Legal Thinking* (18 November 2022) https://criticallegalthinking.com/2022/11/18/foreclosed-temporalities-imperialism-and-international-criminal-law/ (accessed 20 July 2023).

[31] These observations are based on interviews I conducted at the ICC in The Hague between October 2013 and February 2014. For more detail see Carolyn Hoyle and Leila Ullrich, 'New Court, New Justice? The Evolution of "Justice for Victims" at Domestic Courts and at the International Criminal Court' (2014) 12(4) Journal of International Criminal Justice 681; Leila Ullrich, 'Beyond the 'Global–Local Divide': Local Intermediaries, Victims and the Justice Contestations of the International Criminal Court' (2016) 14(3) Journal of International Criminal Justice 543.

[32] See ch 2.

[33] ibid.

victims want procedural or distributive justice.[34] Procedural justice posits that victims do not only care about the outcome of trials, the conviction and punishment of the perpetrator and reparations ('distributive justice').[35] They also care about the process. They want a voice in the proceedings and be treated respectfully.[36] The Court's victim practitioners tend to emphasize the importance of procedural justice. The OPCV's 2012 manual for legal representatives of victims, for example, states that 'the right to receive information regarding their case', respectful treatment and having a voice in the proceedings are 'among the most important interests of victims'.[37]

Moving beyond the procedural versus distributive justice debate, NGOs, academics, and victims' rights advocates often claim that 'justice for victims' is very complex.[38] 'We get all these divided opinions', one practitioner expressed; 'I'm not in that school of thought that tries to prescribe: "this is what people want". People want a whole lot of things.'[39] 'There can't really be a single definition', another NGO officer told me, 'because justice for victims will depend on the individual victim: on his or her cultural background, gender, what he or she has been a victim of, the when, the how, where the victim is at the moment, what his or her expectations are'.[40] Many NGO practitioners therefore insist that justice has to be 'holistic' to be meaningful.[41] As one women's rights advocate in Kenya observed:

[34] Ben Bradford, 'Voice, Neutrality and Respect: Use of Victim Support Services, Procedural Fairness and Confidence in the Criminal Justice System' (2011) 11 Criminology & Criminal Justice 345; Tinneke Van Camp and Jo-Anne Wemmers, 'Victim satisfaction with Restorative Justice: More than Simply Procedural Justice' (2013) 19 International Review of Victimology 117.

[35] Tom R Tyler, 'Social Justice: Outcome and Procedure' (2000) 35 International Journal of Psychology 117.

[36] Jo-Anne Wemmers, Rien Van der Leeden, and Herman Steensma, 'What is Procedural Justice: Criteria used by Dutch Victims to Assess the Fairness of Criminal Justice Procedures' (1995) 8 Social Justice Research 329.

[37] The Office of Public Counsel for Victims, 'Representing Victims before the International Criminal Court: A Manual for legal representatives' (2nd edn, 2012) 8.

[38] Alina Balta, Manon Bax, and Rianne Letschert, 'Trial and (Potential) Error: Conflicting Visions on Reparations Within the ICC System' (2019) 29(3) International Criminal Justice Review 221, 224–25.

[39] Interview with CSO Representative, Kampala (7 August 2014).

[40] Telephone interview with NGO representative (3 July 2013).

[41] Anne Dutton and Fionnuala Ní Aoláin, 'Between Reparations and Repair: Assessing the Work of the ICC Trust Fund for Victims Under Its Assistance Mandate' (2019) 19(2) Chicago Journal of International Law 490, 493. *Prosecutor v Ongwen* (Amicus Curiae brief pursuant to article 75 of the Statute and Rule 103 of the Rules of Procedure and Evidence) [2022] ICC-02/04-01/15-1971, § 7.

> Even if we do legal representation for rape victims, it's not that we just work for the prosecution of the perpetrators, we go through medical treatment, we do psycho-social support, we try to put them through economic empowerment programmes, we try to resettle them . . . It's very simple. And without all these other parts of justice, they couldn't care less about punitive justice.[42]

Of course, victims want to be treated respectfully and no one objects to 'holistic' justice. Yet, focusing on the differences between victims and the complexity of justice is problematic for two reasons. First, it conceals that victims share many common demands, especially to receive money and land. Secondly, it obfuscates the divisions between victims and those who claim to represent them, whether the Court, NGOs, academics, or local leaders, most obviously, the division between professional and manual labour, and more fundamentally, contestations between capitalist and non-capitalist life forms.[43]

'Our animals were taken, and our properties were looted and destroyed', Lukodi victims asserted in our focus group discussion. They demanded that 'every woman, every man and every child should receive their own reparation award . . . money in the hand'.[44] As Redress puts it, 'most victims have indicated a preference for individual reparations and some have strongly rejected the notion of collective reparations'.[45] After consulting victims in the DRC, one ICC officer reached a similar conclusion:

[42] Interview with Intermediary, Nairobi (30 June 2014).

[43] Tshepo Madlingozi, 'On Transitional Justice Entrepreneurs and the Production of Victims' (2010) 2(2) Journal of Human Rights Practice 208.

[44] Focus Group Discussion, Lukodi (25 July 2019). In the Registry's mapping of victims' reparation demands, land and livestock were the highest priority, especially for sexual and gender-based violence (SGBV) victims and for former child soldiers. See *Prosecutor v Ongwen* (Registry Submission on Reparations in the *Ongwen* Case) [2021] ICC-02/04-01/15-1919-AnxII, § 44, 47: 'Many of the individuals consulted highlighted the special importance that land has in all the different cultures in Northern Uganda and that modern tools and technical assistance with farming should be awarded as a reparations measure'.

[45] Redress, 'No Time to Wait: Realising Reparations for Victims before the International Criminal Court' (2019) 54 https://redress.org/publication/no-time-to-wait-realising-reparations-for-victims-before-the-international-criminal-court/#:~:text=Landmarks%20Half%20Marathon-,No%20Time%20to%20Wait%3A%20Realising%20Reparations%20for%20Victims%20before%20the,enshrined%20in%20its%20legal%20texts (accessed 12 January 2022). See also FIDH, 'Whose Court is it? Judicial handbook on victims' rights at the International Criminal Court' (2021) 9 ('While the Court has a tendency to favour collective reparations, often victims show a preference for individual reparations, and sometimes even reject the notion of collective reparations') https://www.fidh.org/IMG/pdf/fidh_whose_court_is_it_en.pdf. See also Balta, Bax, and Letschert (n 38) 232–33. The Chamber in the

> We filed a very comprehensive report on what had been tried on these people, like lab rats, for the last 10 years in terms of development. And what they really really wanted, and what they thought would be meaningful, even understanding very clearly and firmly the limited resources... they did say this over and over again, 'give me one Euro before you give me a collective award'.[46]

Fearing that NGOs and intermediaries will absorb or appropriate collective reparations, victims demand money and land.[47] 'There are those who have gone to school', one victim noted, 'those ones will oppress us. They will take everything and leave those of us who have not been to school'.[48] And how do they feel about building a school for them? Many victims are sceptical. Not all of them have school-aged children. 'How will the old benefit from a school?', one asked.[49] These voices became louder after the *Ongwen* verdict: 'If our mothers could be given land so that they don't have to rent', one formerly abducted child expressed.[50] 'All they [the survivors] wanted', one writer reported, 'was to be able to buy a plot of land to help them make a fresh start'.[51] 'The only way to make us feel better is to pay us something', Evelyn from Lukodi told journalists in no uncertain terms.[52] Victims' demands are complex but they are also simple: they want money and land.

Katanga Reparation Order recognized the victims' explicit demand for individual reparations. See *Prosecutor v Katanga* (Order for Reparations pursuant to Article 75 of the Statute) [2017] ICC-01/04-01/07-3728-tENG, § 339.

[46] Interview with Legal Officer, Registry, The Hague (1 June 2018).

[47] A study on reparation demands in Haiti found the same strong preference for individual material reparations. Nicolas Lemay-Hébert and Rosa Freedman, 'Appraising the Socio-Economic Turn in Reparations: Transitional Justice for Cholera Victims in Haiti' (2021) 15(3) International Journal of Transitional Justice 533. However, some scholars see redistributive potential in collective reparations as they move away from ICL's bias towards individualism. For a more general study of reparation programmes across the world, see Luke Moffett, *Reparations and War: Finding Balance in Repairing the Past* (OUP 2022).

[48] Avocats sans Frontières, 'A Beggar has no Choice: Victims' Perspectives on a Reparations Framework for Uganda' (2017) 19 https://www.asf.be/wp-content/uploads/2017/07/ASF_UG_ABeggarhasnoChoice_EN_201704.pdf (accessed 12 January 2022).

[49] ibid 27.

[50] Transnational Justice Project, 'After the verdict: Dominic Ongwen & the many sides of justice' *YouTube* (8 June 2021) https://www.youtube.com/watch?v=y9biRu5YHCs (accessed 12 January 2022).

[51] Jiwa (n 19).

[52] Sally Hayden, 'Lukodi massacre: "They should pay us because we lost so many people"' *The Irish Times* (5 February 2021) https://www.irishtimes.com/news/world/africa/lukodi-massacre-they-should-pay-us-because-we-lost-so-many-people-1.4477432. (accessed 12 January 2022).

6.2.1 Reforming Victims' Demands: Ideological Labour, Legal Translation, and Subject Production

How does the Court react to victims' demands? This section will analyse the Court's reaction in terms of different types of ideological labour which silence, modify or reform victims' demands.[53] Legal translation is the most subtle form. As victims' demands for money and land are translated into reparation filings, their meaning is altered. We don't yet know that there is a conflict.

Legal translations in reparation proceedings

Recognizing that reparations are a 'key feature' of the ICC, the judges have claimed that 'the success of the Court is, to some extent, linked to the success of its system of reparations'.[54] They, however, only accept victims' reparation demands if they fit the Court's legal regime, dismissing others as 'economic' or 'political' demands, which exceed the Court's mandate.[55] But this is itself a dissimulation, because the Court's legal categories are always already infused with rather specific capitalist conceptions of ownership, market exchange and productivity. Note, for example, how the common legal representative presented victims' requests for reparations in the *Ongwen* case:

a. have access to educational programs that would allow them to strengthen their basic skills, catch-up with their lost or interrupted education and be in a better position to build a sustainable future for themselves and their families;
b. have access to vocational skills trainings with the same aims;
c. start their own income generating activities and improve their livelihood;
d. get empowered to increase their scale of production through the purchase of appropriate agricultural machinery; the rental of farmlands; the purchase of animals like oxen, dairy cows, goats, and chicken for breeding; and the purchase of seeds;

[53] I develop this concept more fully in the introduction and in ch 4. The concept of ideological labour highlights that ideology does not simply happen through discourse or argumentation but entails different types of labour by different labourers.
[54] *Prosecutor v Lubanga* (Order for Reparations amended) [2015] ICC-01/04-01/06-3129-AnxA, § 3.
[55] Zinaida Miller, 'Effects of invisibility: In search of the 'economic' in transitional justice' (2008) 2(3) International Journal of Transitional Justice 266.

e. be supported in purchasing land on which to live with their family and in building a house for the latter;
f. be able to have sufficient food and have a balanced diet;
g. be able to pay school fees for their children;
h. enable them to meet medical costs for themselves and their family members;
i. reduce their trauma and all the worries triggered by the losses during the attacks.[56]

Market forms have interspersed most requests (to buy, to pay, to purchase, to increase the scale of production). Rather than reclaiming what was taken from them, like land and animals, victims' lawyers filter their clients' reparation demands through the logic of market relations. As lawyers calculate the costs of reparations, an economic translation inhabits the legal translation of victims' demands.

In doing so, the Court's practitioners both presuppose and compound the commodification of land in Northern Uganda, where 90 per cent of land is still held either under customary tenure or as communal land.[57] Indeed, victims often ask, not to buy or to rent, but for their land to be returned, as the latter is not only a commodity but enmeshed with complex forms of belonging.[58] Generations of people are economically, spiritually and socially bound up with a particular piece of land, where they buried their ancestors and where they expect their grandchildren to live. Such land cannot easily be substituted for another piece. But demands for land to be returned can be dismissed because victims usually cannot prove ownership. As an ASF report notes:

[56] *Prosecutor v Ongwen* (Public redacted version of document No. ICC-02/04-01/15-1923-Conf With public annexes 1 to 5) [2021] ICC-02/04-01/15-1923-Red, § 72.

[57] Arthur Owor and Carolin Dieterle, 'Customary land claims are at stake in northern Uganda' *LSE Blog* (7 April 2020) https://blogs.lse.ac.uk/africaatlse/2020/04/07/customary-land-claims-reform-unrecognised-in-northern-uganda/ (accessed 18 June 2022); Carolin Dieterle, 'Global Governance Meets Local Land Tenure: International Codes of Conduct for Responsible Land Investments in Uganda' (2022) 58(3) The Journal of Development Studies 582.

[58] Lyn Ossome, 'Can the Law Secure Women's Rights to Land in Africa? Revisiting Tensions Between Culture and Land Commercialization' (2014) 20(1) Feminist Economics 155. On the complexity and variety of social and family relationships to the land in Northern Uganda see Julian Hopwood, 'An inherited animus to communal land: the mechanisms of coloniality in land reform agendas in Acholiland, Northern Uganda' (2021) 14(1) Critical African Studies 38.

> How will a clear determination of the property that they lost be carried out? Who will prove that they owned such property? Land records were often destroyed during the conflict period. In addition, for certain individuals particularly those whose elders died during the war, there may be difficulty in proving issues such as their land ownership and inheritance claims.[59]

Providing victims with access to land exceeds the ICC's reparation mandate, Ongwen's defence lawyer has argued in the reparation proceedings.[60] And while the UN in its submission did support access to land as reparation for victims of SGBV, it added that it 'could be complemented with training programmes on land productivity'.[61] Getting back their land is not a right but something victims have to first prove themselves worthy of.

Another example of a legal-economic translation in reparation proceedings is the Chambers' failure to value the subsistence and socially reproductive labour of victims. This is quite astonishing as Trial Chambers often go to great length valuing material, physical and psychological harm. In the Katanga Reparation Order, the Chamber valued everything that victims in Ituri in the DRC may have owned and lost ranging from a hen (US$8), a pair of trousers (US$10), and a goat (US$50) to the psychological harm of losing a close relative (US$8,000) and a distant relative (US$4,000).[62] Attuned to the complexity of psychological harm, the judges acknowledged 'the suffering experienced by the nearest and dearest, the impossibility of burying corpses, the indignity of burials not performed in keeping with the rites and customs of the people in question, the destruction of family roles, [and] the fragmentation of the community'.[63] Yet, while the psychological and cultural harm of losing relatives is measured, the social and material value of losing their social reproduction and subsistence work is not. By invisibilizing this work, the Chamber imprints the productivist bias of the capitalist economy onto its conception of harm and reparations: only value

[59] Avocats sans Frontières (n 48) 21.

[60] *Prosecutor v Ongwen* (Public Redacted Version of 'Corrected Version of "Defence Omnibus Response to the Submissions on Reparations", filed on 7 March 2022') [2022] ICC-02/04-01/15-1991-Red-Corr, § 22.

[61] *Prosecutor v Ongwen* (Joint Submission by the United Nations on Reparations pursuant to Rule 103 of the Rules of Procedure and Evidence) [2022] ICC-02/04-01/15-1972, § 45.

[62] *Prosecutor v Katanga* (Order for Reparations pursuant to Article 75 of the Statute) [2017] ICC-01/04-01/07-3728-tENG, § 204.

[63] ibid § 231.

that can be realized on the market counts. Katanga ends up with a whopping US$30 million reparation liability, which he cannot pay, and the victims, after all their harm was duly monetized and measured, end up with a symbolic award of US$250 each, which 'could help the victims become financially independent, by enabling them, for instance, to purchase tools or livestock, or to set up a small business'.[64] Here, the 'symbolic' reparation award is transformed into capital and the victim into a 'survivor', who is given a new lease of life, which they better use productively.

In theory, most victims' justice demands can be met through the five concepts of reparations established in the *UN Basic Principles and Guidelines on the Right to a Remedy and Reparation*: restitution, compensation, rehabilitation, satisfaction and guarantees of non-repetition.[65] The problem is that these legal categories are always already imbued with the global political economy and its social relations: you can only receive back what you can prove you owned; you can only be compensated if the perpetrator can pay for it; you can only be rehabilitated through market activities; you can only receive 'guarantees of non-repetition' from the same state, which not only failed to protect you in the first place, but which may have committed egregious crimes in its own right.

While victim participation has become a key principle in reparation processes, that does not mean victims' demands will be heeded.[66] In the *Ongwen* reparation proceedings, the Trust Fund, for instance, emphasized that victim participation in the design and implementation of reparation awards 'facilitates the sustainability and acceptance of the reparations awards, thereby ultimately aiming for a transformative effect'.[67] Yet participation does not guarantee that victims will have a real say in what reparations they receive. In the *Ongwen* case, the TFV had already noted that victims' claims for restitution (eg of their houses or land) probably fell outside the scope of the case, and has thus, against victims' strong preferences,

[64] ibid § 300.

[65] UN General Assembly, Resolution adopted by the General Assembly on 16 December 2005 (A/RES/60/147), §§ 19–23.

[66] See also Rome Statute, art 75(3). *Prosecutor v Lubanga* (Judgment on the appeals against the "Decision establishing the principles and procedures to be applied to reparations" of 7 August 2012 with AMENDED order for reparations (Annex A) and public annexes 1 and 2) [2015], ICC-01/04-01/06-3129, § 162. See *Prosecutor v Ongwen* (Amicus Curiae brief pursuant to article 75 of the Statute and Rule 103 of the Rules of Procedure and Evidence) [2022] ICC-02/04-01/15-1971, §§ 20–29.

[67] *Prosecutor v Ongwen* (Trust Fund for Victims' Final Observations on Reparations) [2022] ICC-02/04-01/15-1992, § 31.

recommended collective rather than individual reparation awards.[68] As we will see, it is precisely through the Court's participatory methodology that victims' demands are reshaped and reformed.

Misunderstanding the Court's Mandate

A more confrontational mode of ideological labour is the Court's insistence that there has been a 'misunderstanding'. The victims don't know or don't understand the Court's legal mandate, a 'cultural misunderstanding' that can be overcome through more outreach and legal knowledge transfer.[69] 'The victims still don't understand participation', one ICC judge lamented, 'in Uganda, the victims thought they would be paid for participation'.[70] Studying 622 ICC victim participants, the Berkeley Human Rights Centre, similarly, concluded that victims 'have insufficient knowledge to make informed decisions about their participation in ICC cases'[71]:

> The vast majority of Ugandan victims apply to the ICC to receive material support or reparations, not to participate in trials or seek legal convictions. While most want Joseph Kony and other LRA leaders captured and punished, Ugandan victims most often filled out ICC applications in the hopes that the court would help to pay school fees, replace livestock, or provide compensation for the death of loved ones. Many see the ICC as primarily a victims' aid organization.[72]

The problem, however, was not that victims did not understand but that they did not accept the Court's concept of participation. One victim-intermediary in Western Kenya explained:

> We know that assistance is not part of the ICC, but we have requested that if we can get a donor from anywhere. They can help us. We know that they [the ICC] know donors. We have the victims here and they are

[68] *Prosecutor v Ongwen* (Trust Fund for Victims' Final Observations on Reparations) [2022] ICC-02/04-01/15-1992, §§ 35–36: ('The Trust Fund notes that it arises already from the LRV Observations that victims refer to the houses they lost before moving in the IDP camp, i.e. these losses likely fall outside the scope of order for reparations in terms of restitution').

[69] The premise, of course, is that legal knowledge trumps other forms of knowledge.

[70] Interview with Judge, The Hague (16 January 2014).

[71] Human Rights Center, 'The Victims' Court? A Study of 622 Victim Participants at the International Criminal Court', UC Berkeley School of Law (2015) 37 https://www.law.berkeley.edu/wp-content/uploads/2015/04/VP_report_2015_final_full2.pdf (accessed 15 June 2022).

[72] ibid.

> not helped by the Kenyan government, and we are helping them with the case. You can give them something for their household or assistance.[73]

Such demands for assistance may be an expression of victims' moral economy. The latter describes how moral values and expectations form through the social relations that people enter to meet their needs.[74] The right to subsistence and the need to reciprocate guarantee people's survival in subsistence economies and shape their ideas of justice. Moral economy thus offers a different reading of victims' demands vis-à-vis the Court. The Court should compensate victims not only because the indigent perpetrator cannot pay, but because it has entered into a relationship with them. It is quid pro quo. Victims are helping the Court and should receive something in return. Victims in Lukodi, for example, demanded that those who 'help the Court' by attending its trial screenings should be paid.[75] During an ICC victims' registration meeting in Western Kenya in 2014, a woman reproached me that the transport reimbursement she received from the Court is not enough to feed her children.[76] The Court needs victim participation to legitimate its processes and victims want to be paid for their contribution.

The Court's practitioners, however, squirm when victims talk money, whether in the form of reparation, assistance, or labour compensation. For some, the Court's foot dragging is purely a question of resources. As one judge put it: '[y]ou acknowledge that you cannot give 2000 victims each US$1000. You only have US$50,000, so you build a school, and your conscience is fine.'[77] But others believe that money should not be at the centre of reparations as a matter of principle. In her separate opinion on reparations in the Lubanga case, ICC Judge Ibáñez Carranza emphasized the limitations of monetary awards:

> measures in favour of former child soldiers should guarantee the development of their personalities, talents and abilities . . . [a] monetary

[73] Interview with Intermediary, Western Kenya (22 August 2014).

[74] EP Thompson, 'The Moral Economy of the English Crowd in the Eighteenth Century' (1971) 50 Past & Present 76; James Scott, *The Moral Economy of the Peasant: Rebellion and Subsistence in Southeast Asia* (Yale UP 1976) 3.

[75] Lukodi Focus Group Discussion, Gulu (25 July 2019).

[76] Like the dynamics in the reparation proceedings, the Court reimburses victims, who attend its meetings, for transport costs, but fails to consider the non-remunerated work they lose out on by participating in the Court's processes.

[77] Interview with Judge, The Hague (19 December 2013).

> award alone is insufficient to restore these attributes, but they can be rebuilt by giving opportunities to the formerly conscripted or enlisted children, who are now adults, and by helping them improve and build capacities with a view to allowing them to deem themselves as realised, self-fulfilled individuals in their communities and in society as a whole.[78]

This chimes well with *Rwodi* Frank, a cultural chief, who was equally hesitant about the ICC simply giving money to victims. Money is bad for the poor because it will make them dependent. Rather than giving money, the *rwodi* advised giving them skills to start a business:

> I love what President Reagan once said that, you know, when it comes to Africans, if you give fish to an African, he is going to eat the fish and tomorrow he is going to ask you because he is hungry again. But if you teach the African to fish for himself, he's going to eat fish for the whole of his life . . . if you want to give them money, give them seed money to start a business. Okay? But before you do that, they have to train them to be able to sustain their lives. That, to me, is more important.[79]

The Court does not want to pay monetary reparations to victims, because it is the perpetrator, not the Court, who committed the crimes.[80] Even when the Trust Fund steps in to pay reparation awards, because the perpetrator is indigent, the monetary liability remains with the latter.[81] The Court, moreover, refuses a transactional relationship where it pays victims a wage or financial compensation for their participation. Participation is a right, not work. Money is neither good for victims nor appropriate for expressing legal relations.

[78] *Prosecutor v Lubanga* (Separate Opinion of Judge Del Carmen Ibáñez Carranza) [2019] ICC-01/04-01/06-3466-AnxII, §103. See also §§ 211, 212, 242.

[79] Interview with Cultural Leader, Gulu (20 July 2019) (not his real name).

[80] *Prosecutor v Ongwen* (Trust Fund for Victims' Final Observations on Reparations) [2022] ICC-02/04-01/15-1992, §§ 14, 17.

[81] In its first reparation decision in the Lubanga case, the Trial Chamber did not assess Lubanga's monetary liability and instead ordered the Trust Fund for Victims (TFV) to cover the costs of collective reparations due to Mr Lubanga's indigence. The Appeals Chamber overturned this decision (to much applause by legal scholars) insisting that a reparation order has to be issued against the convicted perpetrator and stipulate their monetary liability whether they are indigent or not. See 'Appeals Chamber Decision on Reparations in Lubanga' (n 66); Carsten Stahn, 'Reparative Justice after the Lubanga Appeal Judgment: New Prospects for Expressivism and Participatory Justice or "Juridified Victimhood" by Other Means?' (2015) 13(4) Journal of International Criminal Justice 801, 805.

Ultimately, the Court and victims enter into a social relationship that is rooted in different normativities which cannot be reduced to cultural differences. Differently positioned in global capitalist relations—the Court originating in the Global North where capitalist social relations are normalized, while victims in rural Uganda or Kenya operate in an environment where these relations are still contested—they have different moral economies. The Court's victims, of course, are no strangers to capitalism. Money relations have penetrated the communities for centuries, but they are not the only relationships.[82] Ongoing contestations between subsistence and capitalist relations translate into different moral claims. Depending on money to survive in a capitalist economy, where they must buy food, basic necessities, and services, victims also need land to grow subsistence crops and to reproduce people and communities. Capitalism separates the sphere of money ('the economy') from other spheres such as law, which are not about money, but about 'rights' or 'justice'. For victims in Northern Uganda or rural Kenya, on the other hand, it is normal to see money for what it is—a manifestation of a social relation rather than an objectified instrument of the 'economy'—and so it is logical to demand money both as a compensation for victimization and in exchange for their time spent with the court. By normalizing capitalist social relations and the separation of different 'spheres', the Court pushes the frontier of capitalist valorization in its victim engagement.

It is not only the Court and local leaders who perform ideological labour. Academics and experts share that labour. Scholars routinely warn that 'the expectations of victims . . . [may be] so high that they cannot possibly be met', without clarifying the economic and political premises that render victims' demands 'unrealistic'.[83] At an expert roundtable on the *Ongwen* verdict in March 2021, Grace Acan, a victim–survivor and co-founder of a local women's survivors' network in Northern Uganda, told the other 'experts' that the victims want holistic reparations from the Court, because 'if you solve one issue, the other one will still be waiting; if you solve economic

[82] See eg Jörg Wiegratz, 'Fake capitalism? The dynamics of neoliberal moral restructuring and pseudo-development: the case of Uganda' (2010) 37(124) Review of African Political Economy 123.

[83] See Marlies Glasius, '"We ourselves, we are part of the functioning": The ICC, victims, and civil society in the Central African Republic' (2009) 180(430) African Affairs 49, 66. See also Clemens N Nathan, 'Introductory remarks' in Carla Ferstman and Mariana Goetz (eds), *Reparations for Victims of Genocide, War Crimes and Crimes against Humanity* (Nijhoff 2009) 6.

challenges, health is still waiting. It is better to do everything together.'[84] The backlash was prompt. A white 'international criminal law expert' lectured the black survivor that the ICC's reparations cannot be holistic: 'It is a criminal trial that was never designed to address mass victimization. It's the nature of the system. It's not a failure of the system. It cannot do it. It's important to be honest. Unfortunately, the ICC has been creating false expectations.'[85] A court that was set up to address mass atrocities was apparently not designed to address mass victimization. The underlying message seems to be: we are rich, you are poor. We make good money as ICC experts, you do not. But that is not a failure of the system; it is how the system works. Go and read the Rome Statute and you will understand the ICC's role. The Court's practitioners do not have to perform this ideological labour by themselves: the ICC's manifold intermediaries do it for them. Case closed.

But the case was not quite closed, because Grace did come back at the end of the roundtable with an uncomfortable reminder:

> People [in Northern Uganda] are also saying that even when Ongwen is sentenced for his offences, he should be brought home to serve the punishment. Because there is a feeling that where he is right now [in ICC detention], he is actually in a better place. We don't call it punishment. He should come, stay home, actually be taken back to live a normal life he was living so that he can learn from the challenges that are coming as a result of how people are living now, the way people struggle to survive, people say that this is the greatest punishment that can be given to him. People feel that he is actually in a better position than them. He is living a better life than the punishment he deserves.[86]

Here, the system reveals its contradictions. What's the use of justice if the perpetrators live better lives in punishment than the victims in freedom?; when the 'international community' takes care of the perpetrators, but no one takes care of the victims. My interviewees in Northern Uganda often asked these questions. Rather than deterring others, they worried that Ongwen's 'lifestyle' in The Hague (wearing expensive suits, eating good

[84] PILPG, 'Expert Roundtable: The Ongwen Case' (24 March 2021) https://www.publicinternationallawandpolicygroup.org/ongwen-case-roundtable (accessed 23 January 2022).
[85] ibid.
[86] ibid.

food, enjoying media attention) may entice the youth in Uganda to join the LRA in the hope that this will eventually deliver them to the ICC.[87]

In the face of these contradictions, why don't people chase away the Court's officers? Why did Grace accept her invitation to the expert roundtable on formally equal grounds, which then allowed the legal expert to dismiss her views as ill-informed? Ideological labour occurs not only in legal filings, the courtroom, or expert roundtables. Much more direct ideological labour is expended 'in the field'. Victims' demands need to be understood in the context of the Court's active production of victims wherein victim participation takes shape not as a form of justice (eg procedural justice) but as a site of ideological intervention.

6.3 The Production Site of International Criminal Justice

Fieldwork Diary, Victims' Registration Mission, Western and Nyanza Provinces (Kenya), 21 August 2014

> We are not an NGO. We do not have a mandate to give school fees, hospital fees or land, but I know that many of you have not received any assistance or compensation by the government, so we do pressurize different groups to give assistance to victims. We have written to donors, but again, I want to emphasize that this is not our mandate. Our mandate is to defend the legal interests of the victims in the case. We seek your views on questions like 'should the trials be held in Nairobi, Arusha or The Hague? Should the accused be present at trial?' On technical issues, we just defend your interests.[88]

The victims' lawyer opens the meeting in Western Kenya with a disclaimer: 'we do not have a mandate to give school fees, hospital fees or land', a disclaimer that tries to foreclose victims' demands, demands for money

[87] Interview with Parish Chief, Lukodi (25 July 2019).

[88] Field notes taken during the registration mission in Western Kenya (Migori, Kolweny, Ahero, Vihiga) from 18 to 22 August 2014.

and land, which they express at every meeting. The disclaimer discloses that there is a struggle about what the Court can and cannot do for victims; it is a struggle between unequals, the Court versus the victims. In this struggle, victims' lawyers oscillate between flouting and reasserting the Court's legal boundaries.

To understand what is at stake in the Court's justice contestations, we need to move from the courtroom where lawyers exchange arguments as equals to the site of justice production 'in the field' where the ICC engages victims. Indeed, the relationship between the courtroom and the field works analogously to the relationship that Marx postulated between the visible marketplace and the hidden abode of production. In the former, employer and employee meet on the marketplace as commodity owners with equal rights, one buying, the other selling labour power. In the latter, we re-encounter them as capitalist and worker, tied into a profoundly unequal relationship, where surplus value is extracted by the former from the latter.[89] In the courtroom, victims' views are represented, in the field, they are manufactured. In the courtroom, legal parties make submissions as equals;[90] in the field, highly paid lawyers, with the help of barely paid intermediaries, engage victims, who are not paid for their participation labour. By treating 'The Hague' as the centre of legal production, critical scholars often reproduce the marginality of 'the field', relegating it to a secondary site in the Global South where law is applied or consumed.[91] But if we interpret international criminal justice as relations of labour, the production and consumption sites are reversed. The Global South is where international criminal justice is produced, the Global North, where it is marketed and consumed.[92]

[89] Karl Marx, *Capital Volume I: A Critique of Political Economy* (Penguin Books 1990) 279–80.

[90] The gap between formal equality and substantive inequality in the courtroom is also increasingly contested. First, victims as 'participants' are not even formally equal to other 'parties' of the proceedings. Secondly, even between defence and prosecution, the 'equality of arms' obscures how their labour is paid unequally, which also reflects the fact that the defence has much fewer material resources than the prosecution. This has been recently highlighted through the burgundy ribbon campaign at the Court. See Ciara Dinneny, 'EU dispatch: ICC legal defence staff launching historic strike over labour rights, pay disparity' *Jurist* (2 December 2022) https://www.jurist.org/news/2022/12/eu-dispatch-icc-legal-defence-staff-launching-historic-strike-over-labor-rights-pay-disparity (accessed 10 December 2022).

[91] Sara Kendall and Sarah Nouwen, 'International criminal justice and humanitarianism' in Kevin Heller and others (eds), *The Oxford Handbook of International Criminal Law* (OUP 2020) 583.

[92] Christine Schwöbel-Patel, *Marketing Global Justice: The Political Economy of International Criminal Law* (CUP 2021).

Victims' demands, in fact, are formed and shaped long before they enter the Court's legal filings. Every time the lawyers meet the victims in Northern Uganda, they clarify the preconditions for reparations: 'Whether we are repeating it or not, we always have to discuss reparations just to manage expectations', one field assistant told me.[93] As the *Ongwen* trial moved to the reparation stage, the victims' lawyers doubled down on schooling victims:

> We ask, 'what do you think would be the most appropriate thing for you as an individual, for your communities, and then, of course, you have people shouting out random numbers or figures, "I want 15 million", "I want to receive a monthly salary of this amount of money", "I want a house". We now have this discussion where we tell them, "OK, so if we try to just do basic math to see how much this money is, even 5 million or 1 million for each person, and multiply it by the number of victims . . . do you think that is reasonable?; do you think that money exists?" And then, in such discussion, you will also have someone who will say, "I don't think there's any money that will be sufficient for all of us. So, maybe we should focus on something that will help the whole community like a school or a hospital, because I have my relatives who also suffered, but they have not applied [to become victims in the ICC's cases] so we should include them" '.[94]

The victims' lawyers do 'basic maths' to demonstrate that victims' demands are unreasonable: 'I want 15 million.' It sounds a lot. But 15 million Ugandan Shillings are US$4253. Compared to what victims in the Global North receive, this is not much at all.[95] In the course of the meeting, victims' 'erroneous hopes and expectations' are transformed into more 'rational', collective reparation demands.[96]

[93] Interview with Victims' Lawyer Assistant, Kampala (9 July 2019).
[94] ibid.
[95] The 9/11 Victim Compensation Fund paid out US$7 billion to 2,700 people who suffered injuries and 2,800 families who lost a loved one in the Twin Tower attacks. That money may not exist for Ugandan victims, but it does exist in the world. Joanna Szabo, 'How much money do World Trade Center Victims Get?' *Top Class Actions* (26 May 2021) https://topclassactions.com/lawsuit-settlements/medical-problems/cancer-medical-problems/how-much-money-do-world-trade-center-victims-get/ (accessed 23 January 2022).
[96] The Office of Public Counsel for Victims, *Representing Victims before the International Criminal Court: A Manual for Legal Representatives* (2nd edn, 2012) 8. See also the TFV on the importance of expectation management; *Prosecutor v Ongwen* (Trust Fund for Victims' Final Observations on Reparations) [2022] ICC-02/04-01/15-1992, §§ 13–14.

But the meeting is a space of many happenings and the victims' lawyers are not fully in control of them. Consider, for example, how a former field assistant in Kisumu described a meeting she organized with a victims' lawyer:

> We prepared good food and I encourage people to come with plastic bags so when food remained, I would tell them, 'carry the rest home'. We have done that in all our meetings to a point where even the women that we work with know that if there is a meeting, they come prepared with a bag and they tell you, 'I have prepared today', and I said, 'well, just make sure you guys don't overeat', and they even organize themselves. When you tell them: 'Some of you people have eight children, some of you have two. And so you have to find out how you're going to do it'. And they did it very nicely without, you know, fighting or anything. And they walked away: 'look at my bag, look at this'. And I think, for me, that is really very, very important.[97]

Victims come to the meeting 'prepared', but not how the Court's representatives think they should prepare. They did not read up on the trial, but they brought plastic bags to carry food home. Complaining about an ICC lawyer who had refused to pay transport reimbursement to the companion of a female victim, the same field assistant told me: 'They [the lawyer] said, "no, no, no, we only invited one, we didn't invite two so we don't know anything about that." '[98] She sighed, 'having worked with victims, we know there are certain people who would never ever travel by themselves. If you invite her, she must come with her husband or with someone else. It's just for their protection'.[99] 'The Court doesn't understand Africa', she added, 'it's not like The Hague where you just jump on a train, and you reach the place you want to reach in seconds'.[100] Some victims travel for hours to attend the Court's meeting. That is why you should never 'make a victim come to your office at nine o'clock, knowing where they are'.[101]

The Court designates the meeting as a space for invited victims only; it is a space to discuss law and justice, but victims immediately repurpose the space. They bring bags to carry food home later; they bring people who

97 Interview with Field Assistant, Kisumu (26 August 2014).
98 ibid.
99 ibid.
100 ibid.
101 ibid.

were not invited. The victims are not just there, in one place, waiting for the Court to come. They are scattered across vast areas and need to travel, sometimes for hours, to reach the place of the meeting. They also need to feed their children and take care of the elderly. Field assistants and intermediaries understand the subsistence and social reproduction economies that sprawl in and around the meeting. The meeting cannot only be a space where lawyers and victims discuss law and justice. Or rather: there is a link between justice and social reproduction. Justice is also about reproducing people and communities.

Both the temporality and the spatiality of the meeting are contested: when it starts; who can come; who can speak; who can eat; who gets money. Victims constantly remind lawyers what really matters to them. The meeting itself has so many different sites. When I tried to go to the toilet during a break, an intermediary stopped me in my tracks, 'Don't go to these toilets. They are for the Africans here [she gestured towards the victims]. They don't know how to use the toilets', and she redirected me to other toilets that were apparently more appropriate for my use.[102] Colonial interpellation ('they are Africans'/'you are European') unfolds both inside and outside the meeting room. People are divided into different categories and directed to different toilets.

My point is not just that the Court's lawyers, intermediaries, and victims have different ideas of what the meeting is about. My point is that no one is wrong. All of these things happen at the meeting. The meeting is a space where people are interpellated as 'victims', where they learn that 'justice matters', where they ask questions about the Court, and offer their views. But it is also a space where they share food, nurse their children, and chat to friends. The meeting is a space of social reproduction: people-making, community-making, and ideology-making happen simultaneously, sometimes even within the very same act. The meeting both produces capitalist subjects and nurtures people and communities, and this tension creates a vantage point for resistance.[103]

Coming to the meeting, victims bring their social reproduction and subsistence roles along with them, sparking tensions between ideology-making and life-making. When victims say, 'they want their land back', it is easy to say, 'but can you prove you owned that land?', but when victims

[102] Field notes, Registration mission in Western Kenya (18 to 22 August 2014).
[103] Silvia Federici, *Revolution at Point Zero: Housework, Reproduction, and Feminist Struggle* (PM Press 2021) 99.

appropriate and overlay the meeting with people- and community-making, it is difficult to erase that. It is thus at the level of practices that resistance manifests most clearly: it is harder to co-opt what victims do than what they say. Lawyers helplessly watch as the meeting becomes about social reproduction and subsistence.

It is clear, then, that there is a struggle. The question is how significant that struggle is in resisting the Court's legal and capitalist interpellation. Building on the Marxist tradition, Robert Knox argues that tactics need to be framed in terms of anti-capitalist strategy.[104] Everyday struggles within the capitalist system can be strategic if they help to create the conditions that will ultimately transcend that system.[105] He gives the following example from Marx:

> The struggle for the limitation of the working day meant that the working class had to come together *as a class*, and as such recognise their common interests, as well as their opposition to the capitalist class, it also required a high degree of practical organisation and coordination. In other words, this struggle was vital to the constitution of the working class as a *political subject* . . . In this way, a tactical intervention into the conjuncture—the struggle for the limitation of the working day—is framed and directed by the strategic goal of overthrowing capitalism.[106]

Disrupting the victims' meeting with their socially reproductive labour, women not only interrupt ideology-making. Rather, they prefigure a world in which life-making trumps profit-making, which, by definition, is a world of non-capitalist relations. The problem, of course, is that few Northern Ugandans or Kenyans would interpret what they *do* at the meeting as resistance (although they may very well interpret what they *say* at the meeting as resistance). And if they do what they do without volition or knowledge, it is neither tactical nor strategic. The question, however, is whether that remains the case if we step outside the confines of the Court's meetings.

So far, we have, following in the footsteps of Marx and Fraser, descended from the visible marketplace to the hidden abodes of production

[104] Robert Knox, 'Strategy and Tactics' (2010) 21 Finnish Yearbook of International Law 193.
[105] ibid 219.
[106] ibid 218.

and reproduction.[107] Now, we will climb down even further into the hidden depths of primitive accumulation, which not only constitute capitalism's violent birthplace, long buried in the past, but remain its dirty secret in the present, concealing brutish expropriation that happens alongside more 'ordinary' forms of exploitation.[108] Such 'accumulation by dispossession' is unleashed most forcefully against gendered and racialized subjects who reside in the post-colonial periphery.[109] Far away from The Hague, but in close proximity to the ICC's meeting venue in Gulu, a battle rages between capitalist and non-capitalist ways of reproducing people and communities. What is hiding behind justice contestations is a struggle for survival, a struggle against land expropriation.[110] Tracing that struggle, the next sections will show how the reproductive symptoms of the Court's meetings transform into reproductive weapons when considered in the broader context of primitive accumulation.

Fieldwork Diary, ICC Community Outreach Event at St Monica Vocational School for Girls, Gulu, Northern Uganda, 17 July 2019, 9am

It's 9am and few people are here for the Court's outreach meeting. They are still tending their gardens. As we wait for them to arrive, I'm chatting to Joyce,[111] who sits next to me on a wooden bench just outside the vocational school. Joyce is here with Ker Kwaro Acholi, the traditional cultural institution, which claims to represent the Acholi people. She is assisting the cultural leaders. We are talking about the problems in Northern Uganda and Joyce tells me the same story that I had already heard multiple times during recent weeks in Gulu: 'The young people in Acholi don't know how to work. They depend on handouts. If they have land, they sell it and buy a *boda boda*[112] or they sell it to a big corporation and then they are forced to

[107] See also ch 4.
[108] Nancy Fraser, *Cannibal Capitalism* (Verso 2022) 14–15, 33.
[109] David Harvey, 'The New Imperialism: Accumulation By Dispossession' (2004) 40 Socialist Register 63.
[110] Sarah Jaffe and Tithi Bhattacharya, 'Social Reproduction and the Pandemic, with Tithi Bhattacharya' *Dissent* (2 April 2020) https://www.dissentmagazine.org/online_articles/social-reproduction-and-the-pandemic-with-tithi-bhattacharya (accessed 17 June 2022).
[111] Not her real name.
[112] Boda bodas are motorcycle taxis.

sell their labour.'[113] This is not a story about the LRA or the ICC; this is a story about transition, not the transition from war to peace, much less from authoritarian rule to democracy,[114] but the transition to capitalism, which is ongoing in Northern Uganda.[115] More specifically, it is a story about primitive accumulation, the appropriation of land from Northern Ugandans either directly by the government or indirectly through land sales, which are spurred by the commodification of land. Rather than merely a backdrop to the ICC's meetings, the Court is part and parcel of managing these dynamics between exploitation and expropriation that grind the surplus population, increasingly subjected as it is to both the rhythms and discipline of capitalist production, yet without earning a wage, and the violence and theft of capitalist expropriation.

Yet, Joyce, and most people I talked to, attributed these changes not to the intensification of capitalism in rural Uganda, but to the effects of the war and decades of displacement and encampment. 'We have lost our culture', Joyce sighed, 'it has been destroyed. It's all due to lives in the camps. Our cultural leaders are weak and lured by the money'.[116] By reading the victims' meeting symptomatically, we uncover not only the tensions between ideology-making and social reproduction, but also the underlying struggle between social reproduction and capitalist accumulation. That struggle centres on the land because the land is the precondition for both. To better understand that struggle, I will now turn to social reproduction theory.

[113] Field notes ICC outreach meeting, Gulu (17 July 2019).

[114] Transitional justice is ordinarily conceived as the transition from war to peace and/or the transition from military dictatorship or authoritarian rule to democracy. For a critical analysis of the field see Paige Arthur, 'How "Transitions" Reshaped Human Rights: A Conceptual History of Transitional Justice' (2009) 11 Human Rights Quarterly 321.

[115] I use capitalism rather than neoliberalism here to stress that the struggle is not only between different forms of capitalism depending on their respective articulation of state-market relations, but between capitalist life forms and relations and those that are non-capitalist in form, even though the latter are, of course, still part of the capitalist totality. See also Anne L Bartlett and James T Dhizaala, 'Post-Conflict Capitalism in Northern Uganda' (2018) 30(2) Peace Review 168; Jörg Wiegratz, Giuliano Martiniello, and Elisa Greco (eds), *Uganda: The Dynamics of Neoliberal Transformation* (Zed Books 2018).

[116] Field notes ICC outreach meeting, Gulu (17 July 2019).

6.4 Social Reproduction as Resistance

Social reproduction theory is a diverse body of Marxist-Feminist thinking.[117] Emerging from feminist political struggles in the 1960s and 1970s, it culminated in the Wages for Housework Campaign, a campaign that demanded wages for unpaid domestic labour and that gained momentum especially in Italy and the United States.[118] Mariarosa Dalla Costa, Selma James, Maria Mies, Leopoldina Fortunati and Silvia Federici were key activists and thinkers of that first generation of social reproduction theorists.[119] Their political activism went hand in hand with theoretical efforts to specify the role of unpaid domestic labour in the capitalist production of value.[120] These insights, however, had been largely forgotten by feminists until the last decade saw a revival of social reproduction theory, led by scholars such as Tithi Bhattacharya, Susan Ferguson, and Nancy Fraser, building on the work of Lise Vogel.[121] While concurring that unpaid domestic work is essential for reproducing capitalist relations, social reproduction theorists disagree on whether it directly produces surplus value or not. The first generation of social reproduction theorists tended to argue that it does, while the second generation insists that it does not, as domestic labour produces use-value (the worker) and not exchange-value (her labour power).[122]

My interest here lies less in the question of value and more in the resistive potential of that labour, which arises from the fact that women produce people, not commodities, and they do so to replenish their families

[117] For a more general overview see Eva Nanopoulos and Leila Ullrich, 'Towards Marxist-Feminist approaches to international law' in Nienke Grossman and others (eds), *Oxford Handbook on Women and International Law* (OUP forthcoming).

[118] Federici (n 103) 6; Susan Ferguson and David McNally, 'Capital, labour-power, and gender-relations: introduction to the historical materialism edition of Marxism and the oppression of women' in Vogel (n 28) xviii.

[119] Alessandra Mezzadri, for example, draws the distinction between early social reproduction analyses (ESRA) and social reproduction theory (SRT). Alessandra Mezzadri, 'Social Reproduction and Pandemic Neoliberalism: Planetary Crises and the Reorganisation of Life, Work and Death' (2022) 29(3) Organization 379.

[120] Mariarosa Dalla Costa, 'Women and the Subversion of the Community' (1971) https://la.utexas.edu/users/hcleaver/357k/357kDallaCostaSubversionTable.pdf (accessed 17 February 2022).

[121] ibid. See Vogel (n 28); Tithi Bhattacharya (ed), *Social Reproduction Theory: Remapping Class, Recentering Oppression* (Pluto Press 2017).

[122] Alessandra Mezzadri, 'On the value of social reproduction: Informal labour, the majority world and the need for inclusive theories and politics' (2019) 2.04 Radical Philosophy 33; Alessandra Mezzadri, 'A Value Theory of Inclusion: Informal Labour, the Homeworker, and the Social Reproduction of Value' (2021) 53(4) Antipode 1186, 1191.

and communities, not so that they can sell their labour power.[123] As such, a constant tension between life-making and profit-making defines that work, potentially giving rise to resistance. Caring for workers and their children is not recognized as work, because it usually happens in the home, not the market, which cheapens the reproduction of the work force. On the one hand, capitalism depends on the hidden and unpaid character of that work for cheaply maintaining and reproducing its key commodity, labour power. On the other hand, by invisibilizing that work and outsourcing it to women, capitalism also relinquishes control of the 'production process'. Women's work at home is both essential and less supervised.[124] Of course, the production process is still indirectly managed by ideological institutions (family, school, churches) and the state (police, courts), creating tensions between life-making and ideology-making. And yet, capitalism's inherent weakness is that 'labour power can only exist in the living individual', whose 'reproduction must be simultaneously a production and valorization of human qualities and capacities and an accommodation to the externally imposed standards of the labour market'.[125] These 'human qualities' are tricky for capitalism since humans can comply as well as resist, work as well as idle, reproduce as well as abort.

Yet, to understand the resistive potential of reproductive work in Northern Uganda we first need to provincialize social reproduction theory.[126] A key feature of capitalism, according to Lise Vogel, is that it 'forces a severe spatial, temporal, and institutional separation between domestic labour and the capitalist production-process'.[127] Effectively, capitalism generates a 'double separation' between the unpaid domestic worker and the means of production: first, women were separated from the means of production (a condition they share with waged labourers) and, secondly, they were separated from the sphere of production (as unwaged domestic labourers).[128] 'Confinement to a world that is walled off from capitalist production', Lise Vogel observes, 'seems to be woman's time-honoured natural setting'.[129]

[123] Federici (n 103) 99.
[124] Dalla Costa (n 120).
[125] Federici (n 103) 99; Susan Ferguson, *Women and Work Feminism, Labour, and Social Reproduction* (Pluto Press 2019) 126.
[126] Dipesh Chakrabarty, *Provincializing Europe: Postcolonial Thought and Historical Difference* (Princeton UP 2008).
[127] Vogel (n 28) 159.
[128] ibid 159, n 3.
[129] ibid 160.

Of course, this is no longer true for most women around the world and it arguably only ever described the very exceptional position of white women in Euro-America under Fordism. Largely focused on Euro-America,[130] social reproduction theorists have neglected, first, that labour exploitation is not the only source of wealth creation in the Global South and, secondly, that women often retain access to the means of production. In Uganda, primitive accumulation or, as Harvey calls it, 'accumulation by dispossession', matters at least as much as labour exploitation for the creation of wealth.[131] As Federici observes:

> Violent rivalries have exploded everywhere among different factions of the African ruling class, who, unable to enrich themselves through the exploitation of labor, are now fighting for access to state power as the key condition for the accumulation of wealth. State power, in fact, is the key to the appropriation and sale on the international market of either the national assets and resources (land, gold, diamonds, oil, timber), or the assets possessed by rival or weaker groups.[132]

In societies where capitalist accumulation relies on resource extraction more than on commodity production, social reproduction does not only matter in relation to commodity production, but also in relation to the means of production and reproduction, especially the land.[133]

In Northern Uganda, women are not doubly separated from the sphere of capitalist accumulation because they still have access to customary land, which gives rise to 'cooking pot economies'.[134] Even in urban spaces,

[130] This applies more to the second than the first generation of social reproduction theory. Silvia Federici, for example, has studied social reproduction processes in Africa, and Maria Mies's work focused on India. See Maria Mies, *The Lace Makers of Narsapur: Indian Housewives produce for the World Market* (Zed Press 1982); Maria Mies, *Patriarchy and Accumulation on a World Scale: Women in the International Division of Labour* (Zed Books 1999). See also Ossome (n 29). For the role of social reproduction under conditions of global neoliberalism see Isabella Bakker and Stephen Gill, *Power, Production and Social Reproduction: Human In/security in the Global Political Economy* (Springer 2003); Isabella Bakker and Stephen Gill, 'Rethinking power, production, and social reproduction: Toward variegated social reproduction' (2019) 43(4) Capital & Class 503.

[131] Harvey (n 109).

[132] Federici (n 103) 78.

[133] Sirisha Naidu and Lyn Ossome, 'Social Reproduction and the Agrarian Question of Women's Labour in India' (2016) 5(1) Agrarian South: Journal of Political Economy 50; Ossome (n 58); Lyn Ossome, 'The care economy and the state in Africa's Covid-19 responses' (2021) 42(1) Canadian Journal of Development Studies/Revue canadienne d'études du développement 68.

[134] Federici (n 103) 132.

women grow food on any patch of land they can access.[135] Rather than a double separation, there is a direct struggle between the social reproducers (women) and the capitalist accumulators (corporations, states) that centres on the land. What makes women in Northern Uganda resistive is that social reproduction does not only depend on commodity consumption but also on subsistence food production. As Vogel puts it, 'those who have other sources of subsistence will not easily submit to the capitalist's demands'.[136] Access to the commons also means that social reproduction and care have never been completely 'walled off' in the private sphere, but have usually been more communal and collective.[137]

6.5 The ICC and Land Struggles

6.5.1 Transitional Justice, Primitive Accumulation, and Naked Protests

> An issue that is very urgent is land wrangles because when we went to the camps, the government came out and grabbed our land. They take the land in the name of conserving vegetation like the Uganda Wildlife Authority and these people are given a lot of freedom to arrest and kill the civilians around, and then also, the community members have become greedy by selling land cheaply with the aim of acquiring motorcycles and the like.[138]

This is how victims in Lukodi described the problem of land to me. Indeed, few people talked about the LRA, the war, or the ICC. Instead, they talked about land struggles. Africa is at the heart of global land grabbing with 60 to 70 per cent of all land deals struck on the continent, selling off around

[135] ibid 134.
[136] Vogel (n 28) 170. See also Mies, *Patriarchy and Accumulation on a World Scale* (n 130) 170.
[137] Lyn Ossome, 'Land in transition: from social reproduction of labour power to social reproduction of power' (2021) 39(4) Journal of Contemporary African Studies 550.
[138] Lukodi Focus Group Discussion, Gulu (25 July 2019).

50 million hectares of land.[139] Driven by food, fuel, finance, and fun, global land deals cover around 15 per cent of total agricultural land in Uganda.[140] According to Owor and Dieterle, land acquisition in Northern Uganda has assumed two modalities.[141] In the first modality, the government has sold or leased land directly to foreign investors, claiming that it is public, not customary, land.[142] In the second modality, investors have directly negotiated sales with customary clan leaders or household heads, who had turned customary land into their private property, fuelling land conflicts as different families or different members of the same family lay claim to that land.[143] These forms of acquisition unfold amidst a more general problem of land scarcity in Acholiland, which makes it harder for families to share land, resulting in the landlessness of vulnerable groups, especially single or divorced women.[144]

Women, as a result, have been at the forefront of the struggle against land grabbing in Uganda. In April 2015, government officials received a 'strange welcome' in Apaa village, Northern Uganda: elderly women stripped naked in front of the ministers to protest land evictions. 'We were born on this land', the women sang, 'where will we, the elderly mothers, go to? Why is the government targeting our land?'[145] 'Not even the presence of their children', a TV reporter commented, 'would stop the women from shedding their clothes as others buried their heads in their palms in shame'.[146] This protest was not an isolated incident. In April 2011, 100 naked women gathered in Amuru District to prevent businessmen of the Madhvani Group from demarcating their land to build a big sugar plantation.[147] Spreading in Northern Uganda and beyond, naked protests have evolved into a global

[139] Future Agricultures, 'Land Grabbing in Africa and the New Politics of Food' Policy Brief 041 (June 2011) https://assets.publishing.service.gov.uk/media/57a08abfed915d3cfd0008fa/FAC_Policy_Brief_No41.pdf (accessed 8 August 2023). See also Ruth Hall, 'Land grabbing in Southern Africa: the many faces of the investor rush' (2011) 38(128) Review of African Political Economy 93.

[140] Giuliano Martiniello, 'Agrarian politics and land struggles in Northern Uganda' (2017) 52(3) Community Development Journal 405, 411.

[141] Owor and Dieterle (n 57).

[142] ibid.

[143] ibid.

[144] Hopwood (n 58).

[145] 'Women undress before Migereko, Gen Aronda' *Daily Monitor* (17 April 2015) https://www.monitor.co.ug/uganda/news/national/women-undress-before-migereko-gen-aronda-1607736 (accessed 30 March 2023).

[146] NTV Uganda, 'Women strip before ministers in protest over land' *YouTube* (17 April 2015) https://www.youtube.com/watch?v=F4DdYt-SnsA (accessed 30 March 2023).

[147] Martiniello (n 140) 412.

feminist strategy not only against land grabbing but also against sexual violence, police brutality, and work harassment.[148]

These protests have long roots in African history where stripping naked is a weapon of last resort against a powerful enemy.[149] 'The naked body "speaks" the language of spectacle, of rebellion, of subversion', Sylvia Tamale argues, and women have wielded it successfully against colonial administrators across Africa.[150] In Acholi culture, pointing naked female body parts against a person is a powerful curse 'as a woman's body is the source of life'.[151] As policemen fled the women and government officials reassured them that there would be no land evictions, these protests yielded interim successes against highly repressive regimes. A foreign investor, who had reportedly obtained a twenty-year concession from the Ugandan Wildlife Authority (UWA), the government designated 'owner' of the land, to turn people's land into a 'high-end trophy hunting park' for tourists, reportedly withdrew from the project 'citing poaching and land feuds with the local communities'.[152] Yet, these protests have only delayed rather than halted land expropriation in Northern Uganda as rangers of the UWA have attacked and forcibly evicted thousands of residents of Apaa since late 2017 alone.[153]

[148] Sylvia Tamale, 'Nudity, Protest and the Law in Uganda' (2019) 22 Feminist Africa 52; Rebecca Tapscott, 'Naked protest: how ordinary citizens reveal truth to repressive regimes' *The Conversation* (14 May 2020) https://theconversation.com/naked-protest-how-ordinary-citizens-reveal-truth-to-repressive-regimes-134253 (accessed 30 May 2022); NTV Uganda, 'The Naked Statement: Why is stripping in protest becoming common?' (20 May 2015) https://www.youtube.com/watch?v=Skpo6H_Oq0M (accessed 8 August 2023).

[149] Tamale (n 148); Florence Ebila and Aili Mari Tripp, 'Naked transgressions: gendered symbolism in Ugandan land protests' in Nadia E Brown and Sarah Allen Gershon (eds), *Body Politics* (Routledge 2020); see also Ossome (n 29).

[150] Tamale (n 148) 57–58.

[151] Local woman interviewed in Liam Taylor, 'Naked force meets naked resistance in northern Uganda land conflict' *Reuters* (24 November 2017) https://news.trust.org/item/20171124130614-o29zt/ (accessed 30 March 2023). See also Francis Abonga and others, 'Naked Bodies and Collective Action: Repertoires of Protest in Uganda's Militarised, Authoritarian Regime' (2020) 22(2–3) Civil Wars 198, 214.

[152] Alex Otto and Madison Stevens, 'Investor explains why he withdrew from East Madi Game Reserve Concession' *Uganda Radio Network* (15 September 2015) https://ugandaradionetwork.com/story/bruce-martin-speaks-out-on-east-madi-game-reserve- (accessed 30 March 2023).

[153] Tessa Laing and Sara Weschler, 'Displacement as resistance in Northern Uganda: How 234 rural farmers occupied a UN Compound to defend their land' *LSE Blog* (23 October 2018) https://blogs.lse.ac.uk/africaatlse/2018/10/23/displacement-as-resistance-in-northern-uganda-how-234-rural-farmers-occupied-a-un-compound-to-defend-their-land/ (accessed 18 June 2022).

Women must not only fight 'accumulation by dispossession' of the new imperialism but also 'dispossession by custom'.[154] The female body accuses not only the state and corporations but also the patriarchal family and clan as women fight to secure their and their children's reproduction also against their husbands and elders who have often facilitated land commercialization.[155] Disowning the women's naked protests, Rwot David Onen Achana II, the Paramount Chief of Acholi, condemned them as 'a strong abomination' of Acholi culture that undermines women's dignity, demanding that 'those who instigated the protests must apologise to members of the public for degrading mothers'.[156] Local women, however, disagreed. Joyce Bongomin, for example, observed that 'elderly women stripping . . . to protect what will feed their grandchildren in future, is an act that has been well thought out'.[157] We are now much more clearly in the realm of strategic tactics against capitalist dispossession.

Of course, resistance against land dispossession is not resistance against ideology but against state and corporate violence, raising the question of the relationship between ideology and violence. Similar to Fanon, Marx argued that developed capitalism operates through ideology while the transition to capitalism, primitive accumulation, must rely on violence:

> The advance of capitalist production develops a working class, which by education, tradition, and habit looks upon the requirements of that mode of production as self-evident natural laws. The organization of the capitalist process of production, once it is fully developed, breaks down all resistance . . . The silent compulsion of economic relations sets the seal on the domination of the capitalist over the worker . . . It is otherwise during the historical genesis of capitalist production [the period of primitive accumulation].[158]

[154] Harvey (n 109).

[155] Aili Mari Tripp, 'Women's Movements, Customary Law, and Land Rights in Africa: The Case of Uganda' (2004) (Spring) African Studies Quarterly 1, 15. Indeed, some cultural leaders have enriched themselves claiming 10 per cent of the sale price. Arnest Tumwesige, 'Charges on land sale illegal: Acholi prime minister' *New Vision* (4 February 208) https://www.newvision.co.ug/new_vision/news/1470415/charges-land-sale-illegal-acholi-prime-minister (accessed 14 June 2022).

[156] Peter Labeja, 'Amuru nude protests undermine women dignity: Acholi Chief' *Uganda Radio Network* (22 April 2015) https://ugandaradionetwork.com/story/amuru-nude-protests-undermine-women-dignity-acholi-chief- (accessed 30 April 2021).

[157] Monitor, 'Nude protests: the Acholi signal of distress' (29 April 2015) https://www.monitor.co.ug/artsculture/Reviews/Nude-protests--the-Acholi-signal-of-distress/691232-2701176-tcu4yv/index.html (accessed 18 June 2022).

[158] Marx (n 89) 899.

'The methods of primitive accumulation', Marx emphasizes, 'are anything but idyllic':[159] 'conquest, enslavement, robbery, murder, in short, force plays the greatest part'.[160] Primitive accumulation, in other words, describes 'the use of force and violence in separating people from a means of subsistence other than the wage', an ongoing rather than merely historical process.[161]

Yet, far from merely warping workers in developed capitalist countries, ideology also orchestrates primitive accumulation, as is already evident at the level of language. Northern Ugandans often speak not of land theft but of 'land wrangles', which suggests that there is something rather childish and irrational about them. The terminology is not surprising given that land appropriation manifests most often as conflicts within and between families about who can sell the land. The question of who buys that land and how customary land became sellable in the first place is less often asked. This is not to say that the violence of 'land wrangles' is not recognized. 'They talk about the silence of guns', a local TFV partner lamented; 'We talk about relative peace, but to me there is no peace. When people are conflicting over land within families, neighbours and clans . . . People are dying . . . There is a silent war in the communities'.[162] Around 80 to 90 per cent of cases in the local courts are about land, and even cases that, on the surface, have nothing to do with land are often rooted in land conflicts.[163] 'There are many concocted cases that are reported to the Police in the form of murder, rape and defilement', the acting Pader district police commander, Obitho Samson, noted, that 'when thoroughly investigated, [it emerges that] they emanate from land wrangles'.[164]

6.5.2 The ICC, Work Discipline, and Women's Rights

We can make at least two connections between the ICC and primitive accumulation. First, the ICC and transitional justice processes more broadly help manage the ongoing transition to capitalism. In fact, transitional

[159] ibid 874.
[160] ibid.
[161] Mark Neocleous, 'International Law as Primitive Accumulation; Or, the Secret of Systematic Colonization' (2012) 23(4) European Journal of International Law 941, 943; Harvey (n 109); Glen Sean Coulthard, *Red Skin, White Masks: Rejecting the Colonial Politics of Recognition* (Minnesota UP 2014).
[162] Interview with TFV's Local Partner, Gulu (10 July 2014).
[163] Interview with Victims' Lawyer Assistant, Kampala (9 July 2019).
[164] Tumwesige (n 155).

justice in Northern Uganda may be less about the transition from war to peace, or from authoritarian rule to democracy, and more about the accumulation of land and workers. Secondly, the ICC forms part of a broader legal articulation of land appropriation that turns women into victims. Rather than fighters for their land, women become victims of sexual and gender-based violence. Let us take these two connections in turn.

The Court does not itself take land but it interpellates people as legal subjects and consolidates a law-and-order framework that is the *sine qua non* for accumulation by dispossession. Speaking about the ICC's impact on her community, Betty, the only victim speaker at the ICC's outreach meeting in Gulu, from which this book began, said:

> Crimes have gone down in our community because people now fear accountability. Justice is an aspect of the future. We show the screenings of the ICC's trial to our children and tell them: 'if you misbehave, you will be held to account. You will be sent to the ICC'. Our children will have a better future.[165]

As the war and its atrocities have receded into the past, the ICC has been reconstructed as an educational tool: behave or you will be sent to the ICC. Local leaders have similarly embraced the ICC to discipline an 'unruly' population towards productive work. 'We survive on farming and animal production, but our farming is subsistent and cannot be a good way to generate income', the Paramount Acholi Chief Acana declared, 'people should be productive, respect their culture and change their attitude about work'.[166] It is time to stop lamenting about the war and embrace work, the prime minister of the Acholi cultural institution, Ambrose Oola, added.[167] These pronouncements echo the government's agenda. In a speech in 2019, President Museveni proclaimed, 'leaders, you have to tell people to work and get out of poverty. Everybody should engage in income generating work; we won't tolerate those that don't want to work when they have

[165] Field notes ICC outreach meeting, Gulu (17 July 2019).
[166] Parliament of the Republic of Uganda, 'Oulanyah preaches unity, productivity at Acholi cultural day' (16 December 2018) https://www.parliament.go.ug/news/3003/oulanyah-preaches-unity-productivity-acholi-cultural-day (accessed 5 June 2022).
[167] Tumwesige (n 155).

land'.[168] In October 2022, Museveni doubled down on his message: 'Uganda is so nice. Even if you are a fool, you can survive here. In other parts of the world, if you are a fool, you die and the matter is resolved'.[169] According to him, the problem in Uganda is that 39 per cent of homesteads still operate as subsistence economies ('just eating and sleeping'), surviving off their land. With the help of the army, the Ugandan government 'persuades' its citizens to join the money economy ('our answer is: produce a good or a service for sale').[170] Here, we see the contestation between capitalist and non-capitalist uses of land in full swing. It is time for people to stop living off their land and become productive.

Rather than competing or conflicting, different justice mechanisms complement each other in creating the conditions for capitalist accumulation. When we move from the courtroom in The Hague to the field, justice contestations give way to complementarity, thus further twisting the concept of complementarity as it ceases to be an admissibility rule or a discursive possibility and becomes a reality on the ground. Rwodi Frank, whom I met at an ICC 'public dialogue' in Gulu, helped me understand how capitalist complementarity is achieved in practice. He is the traditional chief of Patiko, a chiefdom that is believed to have existed for 700 years and that includes Gulu town. 'I became the chief two years ago when my brother died', he told me with a strong American accent.[171] 'Before I lived in Philadelphia for 35 years working in commercial real estate finance and management'. The *rwodi* was not particularly concerned about *mato oput* or other reconciliation rituals: 'It doesn't matter whether a person goes through the legal court system and spends 10 to 15 years [in prison] or for life. His family and his clan have to pay reparations to the deceased's clan. This is regardless of what the law says.'[172] The traditional leaders can do the reconciliation ceremonies whenever Ongwen returns to the community, whether he spent time in prison before or not. 'So, it doesn't really matter what happens in

[168] Umaru Kashaka, 'Everybody should wake up now, says Museveni' *New Vision* (20 July 2019) https://www.newvision.co.ug/new_vision/news/1503892/wake-museveni (accessed 14 June 2022); 'Wake up and work: Museveni' *Ugandan Monitor* (11 January 2019) https://www.monitor.co.ug/uganda/news/national/wake-up-and-work-museveni-1800110 (accessed 18 June 2022).
[169] *YouTube*, 'MUSEVENI says even a fool can survive in Uganda unlike other countries' https://www.youtube.com/watch?v=uJMJLzecBgQ (accessed 4 January 2023).
[170] ibid.
[171] Interview with Cultural Leader, Gulu (20 July 2019) (not his real name).
[172] ibid.

The Hague?' I asked. 'No, it doesn't', he chuckled.[173] The traditional leaders do not need the ICC's recognition of their rituals.

But the ICC is nonetheless useful as it 'restore[s] some sense of normalcy in their lives . . . It's always an experience [to attend an outreach event or trial screening]', Rwodi Frank observes, 'she [the victim] goes home with some kind of consolation that things are bad but at least I can see that somebody is making an effort somewhere . . . there is no impunity'.[174] Despite relying on more communal conceptions of harm and redress, traditional justice, as much as liberal justice, ends up stabilizing the capitalist order. The real contestation is not between different concepts of justice. As a former real estate broker, the *rwodi* himself is living proof of the capitalist complementarity between global governance and local culture.

Secondly, the ICC is also part of a broader legal articulation of land conflicts that has facilitated land commodification by turning women fighters into victims. In fact, it is not only the state and corporations that separate women from their land, women's rights lawyers have, paradoxically, further consolidated that separation. Uganda is unique in Africa for its high number of female lawyers. By tracing how these feminist legal activists responded to the 1998 Land Act, which spurred the liberalization of Uganda's land market, Manji shows how the fetishization of law enabled the commodification of land.[175] The Land Act followed in the wake of the World Bank's insistence that land, which cannot be used as a collateral for debt, is 'a dead asset' that stymies Africa's 'entrepreneurial spirit' and 'the innate ability of poor people'.[176]

These feminist lawyers recognized the danger of the Land Act to women's land rights given their inadequate protection. Despite providing 90 per

[173] ibid. Note that Ambrose Oola, the Prime Minister of Ker Kwaro Acholi, has a more critical perspective on the ICC. See Lino Owor Ogora, 'Northern Uganda is ready to accept and forgive Ongwen, says Acholi Prime Minister' *International Justice Monitor* (26 November 2019) https://www.ijmonitor.org/2019/11/northern-uganda-is-ready-to-accept-and-forgive-ongwen-says-acholi-prime-minister/ (accessed 24 April 2023). See also Refugee Law Project, 'Ongwen's Justice Dilemma Part II' (2016) 12 https://www.refugeelawproject.org/files/others/Ongwen_Justice_Dilemma_II.pdf (accessed 20 April 2022) ('Irrespective of the outcome of the Confirmation of Charges Hearing and trial if that is the case, many victims still expect that, if he is to return, Ongwen should participate in "Mato Oput" even if he is given and serves his ICC sentence').

[174] Interview with Cultural Leader, Gulu (20 July 2019).

[175] Ambreena Manji, 'Commodifying Land, Fetishising Law: Women's Struggles to Claim Land Rights in Uganda' (2003) 19 Australian Feminist Law Journal 81.

[176] ibid 83.

cent of all food producing labour in Uganda, women rarely own land.[177] Yet, rather than amplifying the moral economy of feminized workers—their understanding of the conflict and their acts of resistance—these lawyers framed the conflict in legal terms. Instead of challenging the underlying commodification of land, they tried to secure women's land rights by enshrining spousal land co-ownership in legislation.[178] Strengthening women's legal position as wives did not prevent the sale of land, not least because many couples in Northern Uganda cohabit and have children, but no longer marry since men cannot afford the high bridal price (*luk*).[179] When women tried to stop the sale of land, domestic violence was exacerbated, thus reproducing women as victims. Recalling a recent conversation with a woman who had walked into her office after her partner battered her, a women's rights lawyer in Gulu told me:

> And then she came not because she wanted to pursue that. But because the man had sold a piece of land that was the land they are living on. And she came and said, 'you know what, counsel, my husband has sold off the piece of land that we are still living on, and the buyer is currently closing in on us. But let me tell you, this man has been assaulting me, has been beating me for the past 14 years. And look at the scars that I have on my body'. And I'm like, 'Oh, this is a police case. Now let's open a case and have him answer to it', and she said 'no, I don't want to go to the police. What I want you to do, if you can speak to him, counsel him, tell him beating is bad; it is criminal, he could be charged with this'.[180]

For the women's rights lawyer the problem is domestic violence; for the woman, the problem is that her husband sold the land they live on. Domestic violence and land conflicts are the talk of the town, but the connection between them is rarely made.[181]

Women are recognized as victims of SGBV but not as defenders of their land. Their victimhood ties them back to the state and the market as solutions to their problems. 'To be a victim', Gago argues, 'requires faith in the

[177] Tripp (n 155) 6.

[178] Manji (n 175); Ambreena Manji, *The Struggle for Land & Justice in Kenya* (Boydell & Brewer 2020).

[179] Porter, *After Rape* (n 21).

[180] Interview with Women's Rights Lawyer, Gulu (24 July 2019).

[181] Interview with Cultural Leader, Gulu (22 July 2019).

state and demands redeemers'.[182] The law and order agenda swiftly hijacks the victim as reflected in the naming of punitive laws after female victims of sexual abuse or domestic violence (eg Sarah's law, Ellie's law).[183] Grief is translated into punishment and legal activism; women are politically demobilized as victims, but still put to work, economically and ideologically, as survivors.

Ultimately, the legal reading of the conflict articulates it away from the land. It becomes the problem of domestic violence, which women's rights lawyers solve through the police and the courts. Much like men and elders, women's rights lawyers are intermediaries who perform the ideological labour of policing the boundary, the boundary between women and the land, between social reproducers and the means of social reproduction. Indeed, accumulation by dispossession involves both 'violence work' and 'ideology work'.[184] By taking land, it also removes an alternative value system bound up with land that nurtures resistive subjects. As Ossome argues, 'the contemporary fetishization of land, its codification as commodity—itself an outcome of the racial capitalism of the colonial project—strips land off such symbolic, cultural significance'.[185] In short, it robs people of alternative subjectivities that are less tied to the state and the market and that can nourish counter-hegemonic practices.

Northern Ugandans themselves connect the dots between dispossession and ideology, land grabbing, and the ideological institutions. In July 2018, 234 rural farmers from Apaa travelled to Gulu to occupy the grounds of the UN OHCHR (United Nations Office of the High Commissioner for Human Rights) compound, demanding that the latter pressure the government to stop land evictions.[186] As Tessa Laing and Sara Weschler argue:

> [t]hese demonstrators essentially flipped the script on the long narrative of mass displacement in their region. By *choosing* to uproot themselves and make a nearly 100 km journey from home, they turned their own

[182] Verónica Gago, *Feminist International: How to Change Everything* (Verso 2020) 13.

[183] Sarah's law and Ellie's law are examples from the UK of punitive laws or provisions named after murdered women or children.

[184] Micol Seigel, *Violence Work: State Power and the Limits of Police* (Duke UP 2018).

[185] Ossome (n 137).

[186] They also presented a petition to the UN High Commissioner on behalf of 26,000 Apaa residents. Tessa Laing and Phil Wilmot, 'Ugandan farmers emerge victorious after month long occupation of UN office' *Waging Nonviolence: People Powered News & Analysis* (28 August 2018) https://wagingnonviolence.org/2018/08/uganda-apaa-farmers-occupy-united-nations-ohchr/ (accessed 11 January 2022).

> relocation into a means of protest. When they took up residence on the OHCHR grounds, they did so not as victims of a distant authority's policies, but rather as agents of a grassroots campaign to seek a just solution to their plight.[187]

People fight off the state and corporations while occupying and repurposing the ideological institutions. UN staff watched in disbelief as the community brought life to the idle patch of land that surrounds the UN building. They set up tents, erected an outdoor cooking area, and collectively organized care, songwriting, games, and practical tasks while supporters fetched firewood, cooking oil, food, and clothes.[188] The people, who were allegedly incapable of utilizing their land, had come to utilize the UN's land. Their occupation raised uncomfortable questions: who is occupying whom? Are they occupying the UN's land or is the UN occupying Acholi ancestral land?

The struggle forced the UN to reveal which side it *de facto* supports. UN staff explained that their 'hands were tied' because they depend on the government to operate in Uganda.[189] Refusing to communicate directly with the occupiers, the UN insisted that local elites, rather than the community itself, had masterminded the occupation. They also refused to care for the occupiers, claiming that 'its office compound is not suited to host the group and provide for their basic needs'.[190] They even prevented NGOs from entering the compound to drain the only pit latrine, causing a sanitation crisis, and intercepted the community's engagement with outside media.[191] After securing some governmental concessions and international media attention, the Apaa community ended the occupation after thirty-seven days, but vowed to continue their struggle.[192]

Let's take a moment to draw out the connections between these different struggles. The noisy naked dancing to protect land and the cooking, feeding, and chatting that disrupts victims' legal interpellation at the ICC meeting differ in their modality: the first is spectacle, and the second is

[187] Laing and Weschler (n 153).
[188] ibid.
[189] ibid.
[190] Peter Labeja, 'Displaced Apaa Residents Wait for Answers in UN' *Uganda Radio Network* (11 August 2018) https://ugandaradionetwork.com/story/a-month-later-displaced-apaa-residents-waits-for-answers-in-un-compound (accessed 18 June 2022).
[191] Laing and Wilmot (n 186).
[192] ibid.

everyday resistance. They also differ in the mode of subjection they respond to: the first is a response to violence and dispossession, and the second to ideology. Their connection is that they both assert the value of life making over profit-making. Combining these two forms of resistance, the occupation of the UN is both spectacle and everyday resistance. It turns social reproduction on its head by relocating it from Apaa to the UN compound. Social reproduction thereby transforms from invisible domestic and subsistence work into visible political work, becoming the very means of the occupation. It becomes both the means and the end, both the tactic and the strategy of resistance.

6.6 Ideologies of Resistance

Fieldwork Diary, Wednesday, 16 July 2014, Gulu, Northern Uganda

I peer suspiciously at the bus that will take me on a two-hour journey from Gulụ to Lira. It reads Gateway bus in big, colourful letters on its thin metal skin. I sigh as I recall the advice provided by my tourist guidebook considering the accident rate of this bus company: 'Personally, I would rather walk than board a Gateway bus.' But I can't walk all the way to Lira and no other bus is available, so I board. With harrowing speed and several bundles of live chickens squeezed between the passengers, we then drive on Northern Uganda's dilapidated roads. I'm sitting next to a middle-aged man who works as a clerk for the Uganda Human Rights Commission (UHRC). We talk about the UHRC's work and about the ICC.

Later, we talk about women's rights. Both he and his wife work, 'of course'. His wife sells fruits and vegetables on the market. 'Are they equal?' He laughs: 'Of course not. I don't think equality is good for relationships. Inequality between men and women, poor and rich is important for social harmony and progress'. He adds, 'and of course, it says so in the Bible. Eva was made of Adam's rib'. At this point, a woman in the row in front of us turns around and counters emphatically: 'It does not say that in the Bible.' A loud but cheerful exchange of different bible quotes follows. Many people on the bus are now showing an active interest in the argument between the two. Many root for the woman. I do too.

This little episode showcases the dance between liberalism and traditionalism. We learn that women's rights are understood first and foremost as the right to work. In addition to caring, cleaning, cultivating, and cooking at home, women participate in the informal economy, selling part of their subsistence produce on the local market.[193] That, however, does not imply that men and women are equal. Inequality is good for social harmony and progress. Here, the core values of traditionalism (social harmony) and liberalism (progress) amicably coalesce producing inequality as both a mechanism of preserving the status quo and of lubricating progress. People accept inequality and then strive to overcome it within the terms set by it. The individual perennially tries to overcome the conditions of their social group. The human rights clerk on the bus from Gulu to Lira produces a reading of women's rights in which liberalism and traditionalism, the global and the local, market and culture, work and the Bible are already enmeshed.

When the woman in the front row intervenes, she does not challenge his reading of women's rights but his reading of the Bible. Religious rather than human rights literacy gives rise to the challenge. Religious interpellation runs deep in Uganda, many say, more deeply than cultural interpellation. Rereading the scene in my field notes years later, I was reminded of what Stuart Hall said about the Rastafarians in Jamaica:

> Rasta was a funny language, borrowed from a text—the Bible—that did not belong to them; they had to turn the text upside down to get a reading which fit their experience. But in turning the text upside down they remade themselves, they positioned themselves differently as new political subjects; they reconstructed themselves as blacks in the New World. They *became* what they are.[194]

The new political movement was thus articulated through the hegemonic text, the Bible, but they had to turn it 'upside down' to remake themselves as resistive subjects.

Turning upside down is a key strategy of resistance: 'If in all ideology men and their circumstances appear upside-down as in a *camera obscura*', Marx and Engels argued, 'this phenomenon arises just as much from their historical life-process as the inversion of objects on the retina does from their

[193] Ossome, 'The care economy and the state in Africa's Covid-19 responses' (n 1082) 70.
[194] Stuart Hall, *Cultural Studies 1983: A Theoretical History* (Jennifer Daryl Slack and Lawrence Grossberg eds, Duke UP 2016) 144.

physical life-process'.[195] It is not our consciousness that is upside down; it is the world itself. Reality has been distorted through the social division of labour and the rule of the commodity form it spawned, and our consciousness is enmeshed with those distortions. Our ideas of the world are both 'false' insofar as they take capitalist social relations for granted and 'true' as these relations really do define our lives and values, and severely limit our options.[196] We cannot simply flip the image around in our head. Instead, we need to change the social reality that produces it, but we can only do so through the intellectual resources and practices that the same reality supplies. Highlighting the subversive potential of religion, Issa Shivji notes:

> Bows and arrows with a sprinkling of water to protect against the gun were part of the ideology of resistance. So were the black churches in which the statute of Jesus was painted black. Here then was an ideology of resistance reconstructed from the elements partly 'borrowed' from the ideology of domination but now turned on its head.[197]

Why is it religion and not human rights or women's rights that are turned on its head? After all, human rights as much as the Bible are what Projekt Ideologietheorie described as compromise formations, forged between the demands of the people for protection against arbitrary state violence, and the interests of the ruling class in a stable order that protects their property.[198]

Recent Afro-feminist scholarship sheds light on that question. 'Human rights is a language of struggle within class societies', Tamale observes, 'the struggle against state power that reveals the myth of the social contract. Such language would have been quite anathema to people with communal sentiments'.[199] What does that mean for the 'hustling classes'[200] in informal economies who are integrated into but not yet fully subsumed by capitalist relations? After all, the uneven development of colonial capitalism has

[195] Karl Marx and Friedrich Engels, *The German Ideology* (Lawrence & Wishart 2007) 47.
[196] Jan Rehmann, *Theories of Ideology: The Powers of Alienation and Subjection* (Brill 2013) 6, 31, 44–45. As Stuart Hall put it, drawing on Gramsci, what matters is not what is false about ideology but what 'makes good sense', which is all it really needs.
[197] Issa G. Shivji, *The Concept of Human Rights in Africa* (Codesria Book Series 1989) 1.
[198] Rehmann, *Theories of Ideology* (n 196) 256.
[199] Sylvia Tamale, *Decolonization and Afro-Feminism* (Daraja Press 2020) 203.
[200] Liam Taylor, 'The Eighteenth Brumaire of Yoweri Museveni' *Roape* (27 July 2021) https://roape.net/2021/07/27/the-eighteenth-brumaire-of-yoweri-museveni/ (accessed 27 November 2021).

sustained subsistence economies and communal values which have been eradicated in metropolitan capitalist landscapes.[201] Tamale thus proposes 'Ubuntu', rather than women's rights, as resource that African women can harness in their struggle for gender justice. 'I am because you are', forms the core principle of Ubuntu and 'sums up the reciprocity and interconnectedness that is alive in the worldview of most Africans'.[202] Oscillating between describing Ubuntu as 'culture'/'tradition', on the one hand, and as a communal residual of Africa's political economy, on the other, Tamale resolves this tension by designating 'Ubuntu' as an 'African traditional ideology of justice and fairness based on the philosophies of humanness, communitarianism, solidarity and interdependence'.[203] As ideology, Ubuntu is both a product of particular historical material conditions (the persistence of non-capitalist economic practices and values) and, potentially, a counter-hegemonic practice that turns feminized oppression under capitalism on its head and can thus be cultivated as part of Afro-feminism.

6.7 Conclusion

Peeling the different layers of resistance, this chapter began with how victims' demands for money and land pierce the Court's veil of legality and ended with how communities in Northern Uganda defend their land. While almost completely absent from the Court's discourse, land does occasionally slip in when ICC practitioners discuss the root causes of international crimes.[204] 'I mean, in Kenya', a victims' lawyer remarked, 'this is basically why we went into violence, it is a question about land ownership and land use'.[205] 'For a colonized people', Fanon argues, 'the most essential value, because the most concrete, is first and foremost the land: the land which will bring them bread and, above all, dignity'.[206] While intellectuals and national leaders get distracted by 'details' in anti-colonial struggles, the people remain focused on obtaining the land, and this is 'in the end the most

[201] See Tamale (n 199) 12. See also Walter Rodney, *How Europe underdeveloped Africa* (Verso 2018).
[202] Tamale (n 199) 221.
[203] ibid xv.
[204] Susan Marks, 'Human Rights and Root Causes' (2011) 74 The Modern Law Review 57.
[205] Interview with Victims' Lawyer, Nairobi (1 July 2014).
[206] Fanon (n 1) 34.

worthwhile and the most efficient mode of procedure'.[207] Gramsci calls this the 'good sense' of a class which spontaneously understands 'its basic conditions of life and the nature of the constraints and forms of exploitation to which it is commonly subjected'.[208] The most basic and the most revolutionary orientation is towards land and in times of climate catastrophe, this orientation does not seem traditional or backward but future-oriented, prefiguring a new world in the shell of the old.

Women are the primary defenders of land, fighting 'until the last death, because they say, where's the future of my children? It's all about this land'.[209] Viewed from the perspective of primitive accumulation, international criminal law's focus on women as victims of SGBV appears in a different light. The fact that international interventions ranging from human rights to development primarily target women may have more to do with the resistive potential of their labour than with their vulnerability. It is precisely to foreclose the possibility of resistive subjects that women are locked into the victim–survivor continuum. You are either a victim, who needs protection, or a survivor, who needs credit and skills. Resistance becomes an impossibility. Yet, subsistence, community, and caring can rewrite the Court's hegemonic script. Coming late to the meeting, arguing over transport reimbursement, forgetting or 'not understanding' the legal limitations of reparations, refusing to have their expectations managed, victims redefine the terms of the relationship making the Court's stakeholders despair as they have to reassert over and over again what the Court can and cannot do.

A social reproduction perspective makes visible all the feminized work that reproduces not only relationships and communities but also larger political and economic orders including institutions like the ICC. Of course, we should not romanticize social reproduction work. It, too, is exploited labour, the bulk of which women do under conditions not of their choosing.[210] Social reproduction and subsistence become resistance only if they are turned upside down: if people do them differently from how capitalist patriarchy wants them to be done: after work, behind closed doors, in silence and isolation, using up as little space, time and resources as possible. When women withdraw or repurpose that labour, they threaten the

[207] ibid 39.
[208] See also Stuart Hall, 'Gramsci's Relevance for the Study of Race and Ethnicity' (1986) 10(4) Journal of Communication Inquiry 5, 21.
[209] Interview with NGO worker, Gulu (18 July 2019).
[210] Marx and Engels (n 195) 52.

existing order. Once we scratch the legal surface, the struggle between social reproduction and capitalist accumulation becomes visible everywhere. Land used for subsistence cannot be used for cash crops. Time used to care for children and the elderly cannot be used to produce commodities. Mental capacity used to chat to neighbours cannot be used to listen to victims' lawyers. When people bring social reproduction and subsistence practices along with them, when they carry them from the private to the public, when they occupy the grounds of the UN and overflow the victims' meeting, social reproduction *becomes* resistance.

The ICC may seem peripheral to these issues. What does it have to do with land grabbing or social reproduction? But this is exactly what makes it effective. Its ideological role works well because it is indirect, because it flows through intermediaries and complements their local agendas.[211] Much contestation plays out between intermediaries and victims and boils down to disciplining the latter towards productive agricultural labour. As a subsidiary ideology to market ideology, law and order resonates with a war-torn population in ways that the development discourse doesn't. Resistance in times of capitalist complementarity is not straightforward. It is often neither visible nor organized. Nor does it come from the outside or top-down. By doing what matters and doing it differently people already create non-capitalist, decolonial possibilities in the interstices of the existing system.[212] Indeed, even in the absence of political organizing, the hegemonic text is constantly reworked in everyday life, including on a Gateway bus from Gulu to Lira. Turning the hegemonic text upside down may open the gateway to something else. People never stand still, and in that sense, nobody is really waiting before the law.

[211] This dynamic is theorized in chs 3 and 4 as the blame cascade.

[212] George Caffentzis and Silvia Federici, 'Commons against and beyond capitalism' (2014) 49(1) Community Development Journal 92, 100.

7
Conclusion

7.1 Three Forms of Critique

On 4 February 2021, Dominic Ongwen was convicted at the ICC for sixty-one counts of war crimes and crimes against humanity. Despite divided opinions on whether Ongwen was a victim or a perpetrator,[1] and whether international criminal justice was the most appropriate form of justice,[2] the trial did succeed, many felt, in acknowledging the plight of victims.[3] At least in Northern Uganda, the Court had eventually made good on its promise of 'local ownership'.[4] Live video and radio broadcasts brought the trial into every affected parish, exerting the same disciplinary magic in rural Uganda as in The Hague.[5] Even the Court's outreach officers were awed by the ritualistic obedience of Northern Ugandans that they themselves had created. One outreach officer reported:

[1] Mark Drumbl, '"Getting" an unforgettable gettable: The trial of Dominic Ongwen' *Justice in Conflict* (5 February 2021) https://justiceinconflict.org/2021/02/05/getting-an-unforgettable-gettable-the-trial-of-dominic-ongwen/ (accessed 30 July 2022).

[2] *Prosecutor v Ongwen* (Public Redacted Version of 'Defence Appeal Brief Against the Convictions in the Judgment of 4 February 2021', filed on 21 July 2021 as ICC-02/04-01/15-1866-Conf) [2021] ICC-02/04-01/15-1866-Red, § 430; Adina-Loredana Nistor, Andrew Merrylees, and Barbora Holá, 'Spellbound at the International Criminal Court: The intersection of spiritualism & international criminal law' in Julie Fraser and Brianne McGonigle Leyh (eds), *Intersections of Law and Culture at the International Criminal Court* (Edward Elgar Publishing 2020).

[3] Sarah Kihika Kasande, 'Beyond the Ongwen Verdict: Justice for Government Atrocities in Uganda' *Justice in Conflict* (9 February 2021) https://justiceinconflict.org/2021/02/09/beyond-the-ongwen-verdict-justice-for-government-atrocities-in-uganda/ (accessed 30 July 2022).

[4] ICC, 'Interacting with communities affected by crime' https://www.icc-cpi.int/about/interacting-with-communities (accessed 28 October 2022) ('No matter how far victims might be from the Court, the ICC endeavours to reach out and engage with them and their communities. People most affected by the crimes have the right to understand, to participate in, and to have a sense of ownership of the justice process').

[5] Maria Mabinty Kamara, 'An insider look at outreach efforts in bringing the proceedings closer to the victims and affected populations in Northern Uganda' *Justice in Conflict* (3 February 2021) https://justiceinconflict.org/2021/02/03/an-insider-look-at-outreach-efforts-in-bringing-the-proceedings-closer-to-the-victims-and-affected-populations-in-northern-uganda/ (accessed 30 July 2022).

Victims and the Labour of Justice at the International Criminal Court. Leila Ullrich, Oxford University Press.
 DOI: 10.1093/9780191915048.003.0007

> On one such live telecast of a key judicial moment, we organised a live video projection as part of our efforts to publicise the closing statements . . . The event was attended by 400 people drawn from various sections of the community . . . On the projection from the courtroom displayed on the screen, the courtroom officer from The Hague stood up to signal the arrival of the Judges.
>
> Through an interpreter she made the call 'Dano weng gu-aa malo (the Acholi translation of "All rise!")'. This announcement blared through the public address system and, to our awe, everybody in the hall stood up in conformity, in unison, fully immersed in the proceedings and experiencing the very atmosphere of the hearings in the courtroom in The Hague.
>
> Throughout the proceedings, with a pin-drop silence, everyone in the hall listened attentively to the final arguments presented by the prosecution, defence, and the lawyers of the victims. At the conclusion of the session, 'Dano weng gu-aa malo' came through the speakers again and the communities obliged to the same protocol, actualizing the sentient experience of the judicial proceedings conducted in a courtroom that is situated thousands of miles away from the victims and affected communities in Gulu.[6]

An incredible scene: 400 Northern Ugandans rise because the translator, through the loudspeakers, seemingly demands it. Now, as Chapter 6 showed, this is only one side of the story. There are many background noises that the Court tries to muffle; there is rarely 'pin-drop silence' when the Court engages victims. Yet, the scene does suggest that the ICC has been more successful in its victim engagement than is often acknowledged, although perhaps not in the way victims' advocates had hoped. As this book has argued, the Court has been very effective in producing victims as its ideological subjects. The conclusion will first place this argument in the critical literature on international criminal justice to highlight the book's contribution, before fleshing out the blame cascade, the book's key concept, and drawing out its implications for resistance and abolition in international criminal justice.

Broadly speaking, we can identify three forms of critique of international criminal justice. The first, the 'liberal' critique, finds the ICC wanting as a legal institution. It comprises critique of the Court's

[6] ibid.

selectivity, especially where its investigations and case selection imply political considerations, as well as concerns about due process and the continuing incoherence of the Court's victims' rights regime.[7] The second, the 'complexity' critique, assesses the Court as a 'transitional justice' institution, as 'one piece in a larger puzzle'.[8] There is middle ground, Mark Drumbl argues, which 'recognizes—but does not romanticize—the potential of atrocity trials; it also recognizes the limits to the criminal law's ability to rationalize complex social phenomena'.[9] Cautioning against 'overreach',[10] the complexity critique calls for more nuance in how international criminal courts narrate 'justice' for mass atrocity violence, while paying more heed to the latter's structural and colonial underpinnings,[11] and creating more space for domestic, local, victim-centred,[12] and alternative justice responses.[13]

[7] Christoph Safferling and Gurgen Petrossian, *Victims Before the International Criminal Court: Definition, Participation, Reparation* (Springer 2021); Birju Kotecha, 'The International Criminal Court's Selectivity and Procedural Justice' (2020) 18(1) Journal of International Criminal Justice 107.

[8] Nina HB Jorgensen, 'Review of Carsten Stahn, *A Critical Introduction to International Criminal Law* (CUP, 2019)' (2021) 84(6) The Modern Law Review 1447, 1456.

[9] Mark Drumbl, *Atrocity, Punishment and International Law* (CUP 2009) 10; Mark Drumbl, 'Weaving a Broader Tapestry' (2021) 15 Florida International University Law Review 27; Mark Drumbl, 'From Timbuktu to The Hague and Beyond: The War Crime of Intentionally Attacking Cultural Property' (2019) 17(1) Journal of International Criminal Justice 77. For similar lines of inquiry that focus on the selectivity and silences of transitional justice and international criminal justice narratives see Marcos Zunino, *Justice Framed A Genealogy of Transitional Justice* (CUP 2019); Barrie Sander, *Doing Justice to History: Confronting the Past in International Criminal Courts* (OUP 2021).

[10] Carsten Stahn, *A Critical Introduction to International Criminal Law* (CUP 2018) 1.

[11] Carsten Stahn, 'Confronting Colonial Amnesia: Towards New Relational Engagement with Colonial Injustice and Cultural Colonial Objects' (2020) 18(4) Journal of International Criminal Justice 793; Carsten Stahn, *Justice as Message: Expressivist Foundations of International Criminal Justice* (OUP 2020).

[12] Rianne Letschert and others (eds), *Victimological Approaches to International Crimes: Africa* (Intersentia 2011); Antony Pemberton and others, 'Coherence in International Criminal Justice: A Victimological Perspective' (2015) 15(2) International Criminal Law Review 339, 345–47.

[13] Tim Kelsall, *Culture under Cross-Examination: International Justice and the Special Court for Sierra Leone* (CUP 2009); Nicola Palmer, *Courts in Conflict: Interpreting the Layers of Justice in Post-Genocide Rwanda* (OUP 2015); Phil Clark, *Distant Justice: The Impact of the International Criminal Court on African Politics* (CUP 2018); Julie Fraser and Brianne McGonigle Leyh (eds), *Intersections of Law and Culture at the International Criminal Court* (Edward Elgar Publishing 2020); Frank Haldemann, *Transitional Justice for Foxes: Conflict, Pluralism and the Politics of Compromise* (CUP 2022); Florian Jeßberger, Leonie Steinl, and Kalika Mehta (eds), *International Criminal Law: A Counter-Hegemonic Project?* (Springer 2023).

The complexity critique falls in between what Schwöbel-Patel calls an 'effectiveness' and a 'structural' critique of international criminal law.[14] It is deeper than the former as it grapples with international criminal law's dilemmas and limitations, but more accommodating than the latter, as it finds value in international criminal trials as part of a broader ecology of justice.[15] For the structural and ideology critique, our third form of critique, the ICC, by contrast, forms part of the problem rather than part of the solution.[16] While the liberal and the complexity critique see international criminal justice, although for different reasons, as an 'incomplete project',[17] international criminal law functions almost too completely from the perspective of ideology critique.[18]

My book serves as a bridge between the complexity and the ideology critique by showing that the diagnosis of the former is not false, but represents what is on the surface, the symptoms of international criminal justice. The critique, then, needs to work through these symptoms to unravel how ideology works. The existing ideology critique, however, does not usually start with the symptoms, but with the Court's self-representation, to illustrate the gap between what the Court claims it is doing ('justice') and what it is actually doing ('ideology'). While this literature routinely acknowledges that international criminal law elides, normalizes, and entrenches the global capitalist economy that shapes atrocity violence, it rarely investigates how exactly capitalist social relations work through the quotidian practices of international criminal justice, morally and materially, in The Hague and

[14] Christine Schwöbel, 'An introduction' in Christine Schwöbel (ed), *Critical Approaches to International Criminal Law* (Routlegde 2014) 11. See also Pádraig McAuliffe and Christine Schwöbel-Patel, 'Disciplinary Matchmaking: Critics of International Criminal Law Meet Critics of Liberal Peacebuilding' (2018) 16(5) Journal of International Criminal Justice 985, where they distinguish between an 'effectiveness' and 'structural' critique of international criminal law.

[15] Laurel E Fletcher and Harvey M Weinstein, 'Violence and Social Repair: Rethinking the Contribution of Justice to Reconciliation' (2002) 24(3) Human Rights Quarterly 573; Jennifer Easterday, 'Transforming Outreach and Engagement with Local Stakeholders', International Justice Monitor (15 July 2020) https://www.ijmonitor.org/2020/07/transforming-outreach-and-engagement-with-local-stakeholders/ (accessed 12 April 2022).

[16] Baars, for example, shows how international criminal law, and the 'constructive' and 'pragmatist' critiques it allows, 'congeal capitalism'. See Grietje Baars, 'The making of an international criminal law' in Christine Schwöbel (ed), *Critical Approaches to International Criminal Law* (Routledge 2014) 196.

[17] Drumbl, 'Weaving a Broader Tapestry' (n 9) 28.

[18] Tor Krever, 'International Criminal Law: An Ideology Critique' (2013) 26 Leiden Journal of International Law 701. Not all authors who study international criminal justice as 'ideology' use the tools of Marxist ideology critique or theory so I am using 'ideology critique' here as a broader label.

in the field. This is where my book has attempted to contribute a more institutionally- and practice-grounded analysis of ideology.

7.2 Ideology, Victims, and International Criminal Justice

Critical scholars have long interrogated international criminal law as an ideological project.[19] The ICC, Schwöbel-Patel argues, was born in the 1990s, when human rights discourse and the anti-impunity agenda merged, transforming international criminal law from an aberrational legal enterprise, epitomized by the Nuremberg and Tokyo trials, into a hegemonic 'global justice project', passionately advocated for by a large coalition of non-governmental organizations (NGOs) and Western states.[20] Framing international criminal law as 'global justice' narrowed both what was legible as 'violence' and what was claimable as 'justice'. Only those acts that could be subsumed under the Court's definition of international crimes were intelligible as violence and only insofar as they were perpetrated by individuals, not states or corporations.[21] In the 'global justice' imaginary, mass atrocity violence became the doing of corrupt leaders and evil warlords in the Global South.[22] Gradually, international criminal law's solution to violence—'ending impunity'—began to occupy the meaning of 'global justice', squeezing out broader redistributive justice claims.[23]

[19] Judith N Shklar, *Legalism* (Harvard UP 1964); Elizabeth S Kopelman, 'Ideology and International Law: The Dissent of the Indian Justice at the Tokyo War Crimes Trial' (1991) 23 New York University Journal of International Law and Politics 373; Frédéric Mégret, 'Three Dangers for the International Criminal Court: A Critical Look at a Consensual Project' (2001)7 Finnish Yearbook of International Law 193, 194; Schwöbel (n 14) 11. For critical histories see Immi Tallgren and Thomas Skouteris (eds), *The New Histories of International Criminal Law: Retrials* (OUP 2019).

[20] Marlies Glasius, *The International Criminal Court: A Global Civil Society Achievement* (Routledge 2007); Karen Engle, 'Anti-impunity and the Turn to Criminal Law in Human Rights' (2015) 100 Cornell Law Review 1069; Kjersti Lohne, *Advocates of Humanity: Human Rights NGOs in International Criminal Justice* (OUP 2019); Christine Schwöbel-Patel, *Marketing Global Justice: The Political Economy of International Criminal Law* (CUP 2021) 77–78.

[21] Grietje Baars, *The Corporation, Law and Capitalism* (Brill 2019).

[22] Kamari Maxine Clarke, 'Refiguring the perpetrator: culpability, history and international criminal law's impunity gap' (2015) 19(5) The International Journal of Human Rights 592; Schwöbel-Patel (n 20) 90–91.

[23] Sarah Nouwen and Wouter Werner, 'Monopolizing Global Justice: International Criminal Law as Challenge to Human Diversity' (2015) 13 JICJ 157, 163; Samuel Moyn, 'Of deserts and promised lands: The dream of global justice' *The Nation* (29 February 2012) https://www.thenation.com/article/archive/deserts-and-promised-lands-dream-global-justice/ (accessed 9 August 2023); Samuel Moyn, *The Last Utopia: Human Rights in History* (Harvard UP

In this context, the victim emerged as a key figure, consolidating both international criminal law and the underlying neoliberal reorganization of global capitalism.[24] Launching its operations in 2002, the ICC had to vie for resources in the competitive attention economy of the Global North by selling an 'ideal' victim in the Global South, marked by weakness, vulnerability, dependency and grotesqueness.[25] 'This construction [of the victim]', Kamari Clarke observes, 'reflects the link between justice and markets in post-Cold War processes of neoliberal globalisation'.[26] In other words, a new configuration of capitalism in the economic base, neoliberal globalization, gave rise to a new construction of the victim in the ideological superstructure: a passive, helpless, innocent victim figure.[27] By portraying victims as abstract figures of suffering, whilst casting black perpetrators as containers for all evil, the spectacle of the ICC's trials has legitimated legal, military, and economic interventions in the Global South, while distracting from the structural causes of atrocity violence and the wars unleashed, funded, or condoned by the Global North.[28] For the critics, the ICC is, first

2010); Paige Arthur, 'How "Transitions" Reshaped Human Rights: A Conceptual History of Transitional Justice' (2009) 11 Human Rights Quarterly 321.

[24] Kamari Maxine Clarke, '"We ask for justice, you give us law": The rule of law, economic markets and the International Criminal Court' in Christian de Vos, Sara Kendall, and Carsten Stahn (eds), *Contested Justice: The Politics and Practice of International Criminal Court Interventions* (CUP 2015) 276.

[25] Christine Schwöbel-Patel, 'The "Ideal" Victim of International Criminal Law' (2018) 29(3) The European Journal of International Law 703; Schwöbel-Patel (n 20) 131. See also Nils Christie, 'The ideal victim' in Ezzat Fattah (ed), *From Crime Policy to Victim Policy* (Palgrave Macmillan 1986); Marian Duggan (ed), *Revisiting the 'Ideal Victim': Developments in Critical Victimology* (Bristol UP 2018).

[26] Clarke (n 24) 276.

[27] For the distinction between base and superstructure see Karl Marx, 'A Contribution to the Critique of Political Economy' [Preface] [1859] (Progress Publishers 1977) https://www.marxists.org/archive/marx/works/1859/critique-pol-economy/preface.htm (accessed 9 August 2023).

[28] Kamari Maxine Clarke, *Fictions of Justice: The International Criminal Court and the Challenge of Legal Pluralism in Sub-Saharan Africa* (CUP 2009); Christine Schwöbel-Patel, 'Spectacle in international criminal law: the fundraising image of victimhood' (2016) 4(2) London Review of International Law 247, 250 ('This type of stereo-typing and subjecting to a public gaze (spectacularising) is not only problematic for those who do not fall within the accepted image (because they may struggle for recognition of their victim status) but also for those who do fall within the accepted image (because this image is dependent on an understanding of victims as lacking agency'); Kate Leader, 'The trial's the thing: Performance and legitimacy in international criminal trials' (2020) 24(2) Theoretical Criminology 241. See also Baars (n 16) 14 ('The public become passive consumers of spectacle (cf "opium for the masses") and simultaneously producers and reproducers of commodified morality—and reproducers of international criminal law, at time baying for international criminal law blood'); Krever (n 18) 703.

and foremost, an anti-impunity project in which victims play a marginal and largely symbolic role.[29]

This account is very persuasive, but it tends to reduce the ICC's ideological function to 'distraction', which neglects its material function, its 'production' of living labour. If the whole point of capitalism is to create surplus value and if labour power, ultimately, is its source, then international criminal law should be about victims more than perpetrators. Emerging from war, newly freed of their land, victims are ripe for capitalist integration. Indeed, this book has argued that the ICC is more about victims than perpetrators, more about the Global South than the Global North, more about inclusion than exclusion, more about discipline than punishment, more about work and debt than about norms and accountability.

While 'ending impunity' discourse is prominent at the Court, very little attention has been paid to the fate of convicted perpetrators. Where will they serve their sentence, and what is the purpose of their punishment?[30] It is, therefore, only a slight exaggeration to say that victims and perpetrators have traded seats in international criminal justice: while victims used to be the 'forgotten party',[31] they are now its driving force; they are no longer international criminal law's objects, they are its subjects.[32] The perpetrator,

[29] Sara Kendall and Sarah Nouwen, 'Representational Practices at the International Criminal Court: The Gap between Juridified and Abstract Victimhood' (2014) 76 Law and Contemporary Problems 235.

[30] Drumbl (n 9); Barbora Holá and Joris Van Wijk, 'Life after Conviction at International Criminal Tribunals: An Empirical Overview' (2014) 12(1) Journal of International Criminal Justice 109.

[31] Susanne Karstedt, 'From Absence to Presence, From Silence to Voice: Victims in International and Transitional Justice Since the Nuremberg Trials' (2010) 17(1) International Review of Victimology 9; Sam Garkawe, 'Victims and the International Criminal Court: Three Major Issues' (2013) 3 International Criminal Law Review 345, 347; Conor McCarthy, 'Victim Redress and International Criminal Justice: Competing Paradigms, or Compatible Forms of Justice?' (2012) 10 Journal of International Criminal Justice 351, 354; Conor McCarthy, *Reparations and Victim Support in the International Criminal Court* (CUP 2012).

[32] They are countless statements by ICC officials highlighting that victims are at the heart of the Court's work. See ICC President's statement on the Court's 20th anniversary ('Victims are at the centre of what we do at the ICC') https://www.youtube.com/watch?v=KyZhibBjn5U (accessed 2 August 2022); International Criminal Court, 'Swearing-in ceremony: Speech of new ICC Prosecutor Karim Asad Ahmad Khan QC, 16 June 2021' https://www.youtube.com/watch?v=tDldr2ma1S0 (accessed 2 August 2022) ('The final word of course, Mr President, must be to the survivors. The survivors are the heroes of the story that we have the honour to tell. Their indefatigable energy, their stamina and persistence for justice, I have found repeatedly all over the world, stuns one into silence'); Judge Sang-Hyun Song (The 2nd President of the ICC), 'Past Achievements and Future Challenges of the ICC keynote speech for the 20th

on the other hand, increasingly looks like the forgotten party.[33] Even the anti-impunity NGOs are more interested in the types of crimes prosecuted (eg crimes against children or SGBV) than in the people charged with committing them.[34] This focus on criminalization rather than criminals also reflects the fact that those charged by the Court have either been imperfect perpetrators like Ongwen, or beyond reach like Kenyatta, Ruto, Al Bashir, and, most recently, Putin.[35] The prosecutor's recent application in the *Kony* case to hold confirmation of charges hearings without the accused 'to provide impacted communities their opportunity to engage with the Court more fully' further speaks to the Court's victim-centredness.[36]

Of course, it is widely acknowledged that victims are not only passive subjects in international criminal law. They participate in trials and express their views and concerns at most stages of the proceedings.[37] Kendall and Nouwen explain why the abstract suffering victim nonetheless remains the key figure in international criminal law. The ICC, they claim, engages in two practices of victim representation: 'the representation of victims as participants in ICC trials, and the discursive invocation of victims as the telos of the court's work'.[38] The legal regulation of victimhood, what Kendall and

Anniversary of the Rome Statute' (17 July 2018) 2 https://www.icc-cpi.int/sites/default/files/itemsDocuments/20a-ceremony/20180717-sang-speech.pdf (accessed 27 March 2023) ('As the president, I decided to lead the new institution into the future with the primary emphasis on victim protection. It was my hope that the traditional entrenchment of retributive justice could be expanded to include restorative as well as reparative justice. I felt that the victim protection was the first such experiment in human history that we could not afford to see fail'). For claims that international criminal law treats victims as objects see Liesbeth Zegveld, 'Victims as a Third Party: Empowerment of Victims?' (2019) 19(2) International Criminal Law Review 321, 330–31.

[33] On the question of how fair international criminal trials are to the accused see Sophie Rigney, *Fairness and Rights in International Criminal Procedure* (Edinburgh UP 2022).

[34] Lohne (n 20) 137.

[35] Drumbl (n 9).

[36] ICC press release, 'Statement of the Prosecutor of the International Criminal Court, Karim A.A. Khan KC: Request to hold hearing on confirmation of charges against Joseph Kony in his absence' (24 November 2022) https://www.icc-cpi.int/news/statement-prosecutor-international-criminal-court-karim-aa-khan-kc-request-hold-hearing (accessed 26 November 2022); Tom M Antkowiak, 'An Emerging Mandate for International Courts: Victim-Centered Remedies and Restorative Justice' (2011) 47 Stanford Journal of International Law 279. For a counterargument see Caleb H Wheeler, 'Justice in the Absence of the Accused: Can the Rights of Victims be Fully Vindicated without the Participation of the Accused?' (2019) 17(2) Journal of International Criminal Justice 413.

[37] Rome Statute, art 68(3).

[38] Kendall and Nouwen (n 29); Laurel E Fletcher, 'Refracted Justice: The Imagined Victim and the International Criminal Court' in Christian de Vos, Sara Kendall, and Carsten Stahn (eds), *Contested Justice: The Politics and Practice of International Criminal Court Interventions*

Nouwen call 'juridical victimhood', however, effectively filters real victims out of the legal proceedings, 'like a pyramid', leading to ever more collective and distant forms of legal representation, with one victims' lawyer in the courtroom 'giving voice' to hundreds and often thousands of victims in far-away countries.[39] While only a handful of real victims ever reach the ICC's courtroom in The Hague, the Court generously mobilizes all victims 'dead or alive, past, present, or future' through the rhetorical figure of 'the victims' on whose behalf it speaks and in whose name it renders 'justice'.[40] In other words, real victims, with the help of juridical technologies, are gradually silenced and absorbed by the abstract 'victims' figure.[41]

What this bifurcated reading[42] of real 'excluded' victims versus fictional 'included' victims overlooks are more complex inclusionary dynamics, which emerge once we shift our focus from victim *representation* in the courtroom to victim *engagement* 'in the field'.[43] Kendall and Nouwen do not ignore the field and the people who work 'there', but they see 'the field assistant . . . as another link in the chain of representation. In this sense, the victim is thus not represented but *re*-represented'.[44] The 'chain of representation' centres the courtroom with 'the field' only measured in terms of its proximity or distance to the former, and the number of representative acts and actors that connect the field to The Hague. As such, the 'chain of

(CUP 2015) 302, 322; Sofia Stolk and Wouter Werner, 'Moving images: Modes of representation and images of victimhood in audio-visual productions' in Kevin Heller and others (eds), *The Oxford Handbook of International Criminal Law* (OUP 2020) 583.

[39] Kendall and Nouwen (n 29) 241.

[40] ibid.

[41] Focusing on the Extraordinary Chambers in the Courts of Cambodia (ECCC), Rachel Killean examines 'the "gap" between the legitimising value of the 'imagined victim', and the extent to which victims are able to further their interests within the courtroom'. Rachel Killean, *Victims, Atrocity and International Criminal Justice: Lessons from Cambodia* (Routledge 2018).

[42] This bifurcated reading also maps onto the victimological literature where victims have been studied either as 'actors' or 'constituencies' by examining victims' experiences of or satisfaction with the criminal justice process, or discursively, (i) as a social construction, which is mobilized to serve political and institutional agendas, (ii) as a label that renders certain harms visible and others invisible, and (iii) as a stereotype, that creates hierarchies of more and less deserving victims. See Sandra Walklate, *Imagining the Victim of Crime* (McGraw-Hill Education 2006); James Dignan, *Understanding Victims and Restorative Justice* (Open UP 2005) 17; Carolyn Hoyle, Mary Bosworth, and Michelle Dempsey, 'Labelling the Victims of Sex Trafficking: Exploring the Borderland between Rhetoric and Reality' (2011) 20 Social & Legal Studies 313; Killean (n 41).

[43] See also Maria Elander, *Figuring Victims in International Criminal Justice* (Routledge 2018) 9–13, 32. Elander also studies the ECCC's outreach practices, but her focus is on how victims relate to and are produced through images (see ch 6).

[44] Kendall and Nouwen (n 29) 248.

representation' elides that acts of representation are forms of labour, labour that the Court outsources and thus invisibilizes, labour that is essential to the Court's functioning.

This book has argued that the field is not simply something that is represented or fictionalized in the courtroom. Rather, it supplies the material, labour, and ideological subjects out of which international criminal justice is furnished. Hidden behind the 'victim' represented in the courtroom, and 'The Victims' looming large as the moral currency of the Court, is a third victim 'in the field', who is interpellated as the Court's 'champion' and recruited as a 'working subject' in a double sense: first, working for the Court (participating in the trial, attending trial viewings and mobilizing other victims) and thus reproducing the Court as a living and working institution, and second, working for capitalism, taking up 'their position' at the bottom of the global division of labour. The field thus emerges as an important site in its own right—a site of capitalist subject production.

By shifting our focus from the courtroom to the field, we develop a different perspective on what the Court's victim engagement is about. Through outreach, participation, assistance and reparation, the ICC partially and precariously integrates victims into global capitalist social relations. It creates the ideological terms on which this integration happens. People are integrated as victim–survivors and victim–perpetrators. Victims are celebrated as survivors, but the survivor label harbours a demand: they have to move on. They can only 'move on' as capitalist subjects: take out a loan, create a business, work hard, and make money. Yet, as victims become entangled in labour and debt relationships, they become blameworthy. They fail to embody the neoliberal vision of the 'entrepreneurial poor' and sink into cycles of precarious labour and debt. They increasingly look like the perpetrator. They become victim–perpetrators. The victim–perpetrator is blameworthy, not necessarily for the crime they suffered but for their persisting condition of destitution.

While legal representation and commodification standardizes victims, they become 'the victims',[45] an undifferentiated subject of suffering, capitalist subject creation works through racialized and gendered differentiation by 'assign[ing] differential value to human life and labour'.[46] In Ruth Wilson

[45] ibid 241.

[46] Robin DG Kelley, 'Foreword: Why black Marxism, Why now?' in Cedric J Robinson, *Black Marxism: The Making of the Black Radical Tradition* (Penguin Classics 2021) xv.

Gilmore's words, 'capitalism requires inequality and racism enshrines it'.[47] Historically, as Cedric Robinson shows, capitalism 'flowered in the cultural soil of a Western civilization already thoroughly infused with racialism',[48] building the racialized and gendered differentiations of the pre-existing feudal order into its relations of production and reproduction. Rather than homogenizing the working class, 'the dialectic of proletarianization disciplined the working classes to the importance of distinctions: between ethnics and nationalities; between skilled and unskilled workers; and . . . between races'.[49] Gender works analogously. It marks some subjects ('men') as productive workers and others ('women') as reproductive workers and builds these distinctions into its forms of exploitation, for example, by undervaluing the work women do outside the house, because of their association with 'free' domestic labour, or by valorizing reproductive relationships through debt.[50] The victim that emerges from these processes is a differentiated racialized and gendered working subject.

As a working subject, the 'ideal' victim—passive, innocent, and helpless—is not so ideal. The Court needs active and blameworthy subjects in the Global South who lend their bodies and voice to international criminal justice. People in the Global South need to be productive subjects for whenever investment pours in or new forms of capitalist accumulation emerge, but they also need to reproduce the global reserve army of labour cheaply through subsistence and social reproduction work. They need to be ready to be sucked into market processes, when needed, and ready to be spit out when they become obsolete. The Court simultaneously integrates them into global capitalist relations and keeps them at their margin, cementing victims' marginality through labour and debt relationships.

Interpreting victim participation as a form of labour, on the one hand, reveals how the increasing drive to include victims as participants in legal processes has transformed them from idealized tropes or standardized

[47] Antiposeonline, 'Geographies of Racial Capitalism with Ruth Wilson Gilmore: An Antipode Foundation film' https://www.youtube.com/watch?v=2CS627aKrJI (accessed 30 July 2022); Ruth Wilson Gilmore, 'Fatal Couplings of Power and Difference: Notes on Racism and Geography' (2002) 54(1) The Professional Geographer 15; Robert Knox, 'International Law, Race, and Capitalism: A Marxist Perspective' (2023) 117 AJIL Unbound 55.

[48] Kelley (n 46) xvi.

[49] Cedric J Robinson, *Black Marxism: The Making of the Black Radical Tradition* (Penguin Classics 2021) 42. See also Stuart Hall, 'Gramsci's Relevance for the Study of Race and Ethnicity' (1986) 10(4) Journal of Communication Inquiry 5, 24–25.

[50] Silvia Federici, *Caliban and the Witch: Women, the Body and Primitive Accumulation* (Modern Classics 2004); Lucí Cavallero and Verónica Gago, *A Feminist Reading of Debt* (Liz Mason-Deese tr, Pluto Books 2021).

commodities into 'active' labourers, who produce a 'caring' international criminal justice cheaply precisely because their labour is masked as 'participation' or 'volunteering'.[51] On the other hand, such an analysis illuminates how the production of victims and the production of capitalist subjects unfolds in one and the same process. It is precisely through their interpellation as 'victims' that people in the Global South are integrated into global capitalist relations as devalued racialized and gendered workers, a process that I have tried to capture through the concept of the blame cascade.

7.3 The Blame Cascade

The blame cascade helps us place victims both in the institutional reproduction of the Court and in the broader reproduction of capitalist relations. International criminal justice works so well as initiating ritual for the victim worker, because blame is already at the heart of its operation.[52] It is the common sensibility of the international criminal law project.[53] The Court's practitioners are blamed for the ICC's narrow legal mandate and the prosecutorial selectivity created by the Court's structural dependence on powerful states, whilst the victims' lawyers and officers carry the blame for their failure to operationalize a constantly changing victims' rights regime with limited time and money, and intermediaries are 'tainted'[54] for failing to reconcile the contradictory impulses at the Court: engage as many victims as possible, but manage their expectations; make sure everyone can apply, but only admit those who apply fast enough and meet the legal criteria.

In the same way 'the most responsible' perpetrator absorbs blame for mass atrocity violence, 'victim–survivors' shoulder the responsibility for

[51] Eva Nanopoulos and Leila Ullrich, 'Toward Marxist-Feminist approaches to international law' in Nienke Grossman and others (eds), *Oxford Handbook on Women and International Law* (OUP forthcoming). I thank Eva Nanopoulos for helping me formulate my ideas here.

[52] Clarke (n 22); Chrisje Brants, 'Guilty landscapes: Collective guilt and international criminal law' in Cecilia Bailliet and Katja Frank Aas (eds), *Cosmopolitan Justice and its Discontents* (Routledge 2011) 53.

[53] I thank Richard Clements for helping me clarify my thoughts on this. For a different interpretation of the contradictions of international criminal law see Darryl Robinson, 'Inescapable Dyads: Why the International Criminal Court Cannot Win' (2015) 28(2) Leiden Journal of International Law 323.

[54] *Prosecutor v Lubanga* (Redacted Decision on Intermediaries) [2010] ICC-01/04-01/06-2434-Red2, §§ 91, 137 ('the prosecution suggests that for those intermediaries whom the Chamber has deemed "sufficiently tainted" by specific allegations, they should be brought to The Hague to appear before the Chamber as court witnesses, to be questioned by the Chamber alone (in the absence of both parties) without revealing their identities to the defence').

both capitalist profitability and social reproduction. Rather than a Fordist factory worker, the victim–survivor under neoliberal conditions in the Global South is a micro-entrepreneur who juggles between market, social reproduction, and subsistence. Victim workers are blamed when their micro-businesses fail or when they cannot repay their debt; it was their lack of skills, industriousness, market knowledge, or entrepreneurial savviness, just as they are blamed for failing to take care of their children and to keep their marriages.[55]

The logic of the blame cascade is thus not simply to 'individualize' blame, but to rope victims and victims' practitioners into hierarchical chains of differently valued labour, which simultaneously put them to work and keep them in their subordinate place. Blame isn't just flung around at the Court to diffuse responsibility, nor is it merely individualized to erase structural injustices. Blame, rather, creates working subjects and glues them together into unequal relations of production and reproduction. While the labour of judges and prosecutors is valued as 'professional' labour, the work of victims' lawyers, outreach officers, translators, intermediaries, witnesses, and victims in the Global South is devalued because 'victim engagement' and 'participation' is not really work. And yet, it is precisely that black, brown, and feminized socially reproductive labour that ultimately makes the Court an 'international' institution that works in seventeen countries across the world. What explains the devaluation of this labour and how does it operate through international criminal law?

In the long transition to capitalism from the late fifteenth to the early eighteenth centuries, criminal law played a key role in turning people into capitalist workers, a process that Marx vividly described in *Capital Volume 1*.[56] Depriving commoners of the means of production (especially the land) did not automatically produce disciplined workers for capitalist exploitation. To force people into submission and to inculcate the necessary working discipline, the law first had to criminalize any activities that could furnish means of subsistence outside of waged labour such as vagabondage

[55] Informal conversation with Cultural Leader Assistant, Gulu (17 July 2019); Interview with Cultural Leader, Gulu (19 July 2019); Interview with Teacher, Gulu (30 July 2019).

[56] See especially ch 28: 'Bloody legislation against the expropriated since the end of the fifteenth century: The forcing down of wages by Act of Parliament' in Karl Marx, *Capital Volume I: A Critique of Political Economy* (Penguin Books 1990) 896. See also Valeria Vegh Weis, *Marxism and Criminology: A History of Criminal Selectivity* (Brill 2013) ix, 24. Vegh Weis calls this initial phase of criminalization that unfolded in the historical context of primitive accumulation 'original criminal selectivity', which under-criminalized the appropriation of land from peasants and over-criminalized begging, prostitution, and vagabondage.

and begging.[57] But capitalism not only required a disciplined workforce; it also needed to reproduce that workforce, a role that it violently imposed on women by criminalizing those who had knowledge of birth control as witches in sixteenth and seventeenth century Europe. 'The persecution of witches (like the slave trade and the enclosures)', Silvia Federici argues, 'was a central aspect of the accumulation and formation of the modern proletariat in Europe as well as in the New World'.[58] This period also witnessed the professionalization of lawyers, who conducted the witch trials.[59] By vilifying women as 'witches', the witch trials cheapened their reproductive labour, gradually transforming women into reproductive machines for capital.[60]

What is ultimately characteristic of capitalism is, first, that it separated production from reproduction and attached the gendered division of labour to that key separation,[61] and, secondly, that it systematically undervalued socially reproductive work by disciplining and blaming the bodies that perform it, creating a dynamic where that work flows to the most socially devalued and precarious subjects (eg women, migrants, queer people, and people in the Global South).[62]

International criminal law underwrites both the capitalist logic of separation and of devaluation. The victim category in the current global moment arguably does similar work to the 'housewife' and the 'witches' category in invisibilizing what these people do: they work both for international institutions and for global capitalism.[63] In the same way that the housewife

[57] 'They are to be tied to the cart-tail and whipped until the blood streams from their bodies', one legislation against 'sturdy vagabonds' in Henry VIII's England (1530) stipulated, 'then they are to swear an oath to go back to their birthplace or to where they lived the last three years and to "put themselves to labour"'. Marx (n 56) 896.

[58] Federici (n 50) 116.

[59] Maria Mies, *Patriarchy and Accumulation on a World Scale: Women in the International Division of Labour* (Zed Books 1999) 84.

[60] Federici (n 50) 3–5, 77.

[61] Karl Marx and Friedrich Engels, *The German Ideology* (Lawrence & Wishart [1974] 2007) 42; Nancy Fraser, 'Contradictions of Capital and Care' (2016) 100 New Left Review 99, 102.

[62] Miriam Bak McKenna, 'Feminist materialism and the laws of social reproduction' in Paul O'Connell and Umut Özsu (eds), *Research Handbook on Law and Marxism* (Edward Elgar Publishing 2021). See also Ruth Fletcher on how the law allocates gendered obligations for social reproduction: Ruth Fletcher, 'Legal form, commodities and reproduction: Reading Pashukanis' in Maria Drakopoulou (ed), *Feminist Encounters with Legal Philosophy* (Routledge 2013) 138.

[63] Nanopoulos and Ullrich (n 51). Sara Farris makes a similar argument about how the 'victim of their culture' construction of migrant women invisibilizes their socially reproductive labour for the care economy. Sara Farris, *In the Name of Women's Rights: The Rise of Femonationalism* (Duke UP 2017) 20.

label defines women in relation to men, the victim label defines people in the Global South in relation to perpetrators, which, of course, disguises the broader relations of capitalist production in which both are enmeshed.[64] While in the case of witches, terrorizing women devalued their work, in the case of victims, it is the fusion of blame and weakness that makes the victim a loser of the global capitalist order, whose labour can be denied as acts of survival or 'income-generating activities'.[65] International criminal law, therefore, not only normalizes capitalist violence or marketizes victims, but also operates as an important medium through which the unequal productive and reproductive relations of global capitalism are constituted.[66]

While law can be used as a direct instrument of violence and persecution in the (re)making of capitalism (see enclosures, colonialism, the witch hunt, and slavery),[67] it can also work through a more subtle dynamic of blame, especially under conditions of liberal hegemony with its formal commitment to human rights and legal equality. Unlike criminal law, international criminal law creates workers in the Global South through victimization rather than criminalization. The Court first turns people who suffered harm into 'victims', who need the state and the court for protection, and, in a second step, transforms them into low-valued workers who need to bustle to survive. Of course, the production of harm usually happens before international criminal law enters the frame, which creates the impression that it has nothing to do with 'victimization'—it merely comes to save and rescue. Yet, as we saw in Chapter 6, primitive accumulation persists in the backdrop of the Court's operations while blame rationalizes and routinizes the devaluation of reproductive labour. Rather than vilified as witches, victims are blamed for failing to become productive workers, which helps to extract both productive and reproductive labour as they are intrinsically enmeshed.[68] In this way, the blame cascade seamlessly integrates both relations of production and reproduction, threaded through one subject, who

[64] Nanopoulos and Ullrich (n 51).
[65] ibid.
[66] ibid.
[67] Mark Neocleous, 'International Law as Primitive Accumulation; Or, the Secret of Systematic Colonization' (2012) 23(4) *European Journal of International Law* 941; BS Chimni, *International Law and World Order: A Critique of Contemporary Approaches* (2nd edn, CUP 2017).
[68] Alessandra Mezzadri, Susan Newman, and Sara Stevano, 'Feminist global political economies of work and social reproduction' (2022) 29(6) Review of International Political Economy 1783.

is simultaneously a capitalist subject, a bearer of labour power, and a victim subject whose labour is largely invisible, unwaged, and undervalued.[69]

In the zones of the Global South in which the Court tends to operate, like Northern Uganda, societies are often in a state of ongoing capitalist transition.[70] Women in post-colonial Africa often retain access to customary land and thus to means of subsistence outside of the wage relation. This allows capitalism to both extract surplus value and to reproduce a reserve army of labour without paying for its reproduction. But it also means that the logic of economic relations is not sufficient to manage labour between production, social reproduction, and subsistence. Capitalism thus needs intermediaries to manage this semi-free labour ideologically, and blame is a key mechanism of regulating workers, who are both squeezed by capital, and not fully subsumed under its logic. While the state is usually the producer of ideology, in peripheral zones, where colonialism and neo-colonialism constructed weak states, especially in Sub-Saharan Africa, international organizations and NGOs have proliferated to fulfil that function.[71] Indeed, the Court is most active in those zones of both food production and surplus labour, which represent key frontiers of capitalist accumulation, where raw materials can be extracted and new labourers recruited and trained.[72]

The particular forms and functions of victims in international criminal justice, however, cannot be reduced to a grand ideological conspiracy or capitalist design, but need to be read in the context of the Court's particular institutional development.[73] Victims entered international criminal law in 1998 as an uneasy hybrid between a legal form (victims' rights) and a democratic form (victim participation). As a democratic form, victim participation responded to the legitimacy crisis of 'victimless' international criminal justice in the 1990s,[74] but the democratic form also generated tensions with

[69] Nanopoulos and Ullrich (n 51); Mies (n 59) 171.

[70] Of course, the Global South is not a monolith and different peripheries play different roles in capitalist accumulation. It is noteworthy that the ICC does not operate in the industrial heartlands of the Global South (South Asia, East Asia, and South-east Asia) presumably because their states tend to be more independent and therefore did not sign up to the Rome Statute.

[71] Federici (n 50).

[72] Lyn Ossome, 'The care economy and the state in Africa's Covid-19 responses' (2021) 42(1) Canadian Journal of Development Studies/Revue canadienne d'études du développement 68.

[73] See ch 2.

[74] ibid. Mariana Goetz, 'The International Criminal Court and its relevance to affected communities' in Phil Clark and Nicholas Waddell (eds), *Courting Conflict? Justice, Peace and the ICC in Africa* (Royal African Society 2008) 65; Emily Haslam, 'Law, civil society and contested justice at the International Criminal Tribunal for Rwanda' in Marie-Bénédicte Dembour and

the legal form, and in the process evolved into something very different: victims were included not as citizen subjects but as capitalist subjects. The Court's practitioners had to reconcile the external pressure to include victims and the internal pressure to maintain the Court's legal character. In the context of managing this contradiction, a new form of justice emerged, a localized, semi-legal form of participatory justice centred on new subjects in the field who work for the Court: victims' practitioners, intermediaries, and victims. As the Court's practitioners responded to the crisis of legitimacy, they were simultaneously confronted with a new crisis, a crisis of labour. To prove its value as a new institution, the Court needed to expand, creating new situations and cases in far-away, dangerous, and hostile countries,[75] while states threatened 'zero-growth' budget conditions: precarious, local, and non-legal labour stepped in to fill the gap.[76] Victim participation thus evolved from a democratic form into a labour form; the legitimacy function of victims helped conceal their labour function, not by intentional design, but as an outcome of crisis.

Neither, however, do these particular legal and institutional dynamics exist in isolation from broader capitalist relations. Rather, they both reflect and shape them. Capitalist social relations are driven by a common logic of motion, which creates similar dynamics in very different realms, precisely because these realms are not really separate. They do not exist independently of capitalist relations of production, but instead are a particular articulation of them. It, therefore, makes perfect sense that the court's victim participation and reparation system is still so unsettled after twenty years, oscillating between inclusion and exclusion, legal consolidation, and precarity.[77] Indeed, the contradictory pressures to include and exclude

Tobias Kelly (eds), *Paths to International Justice* (CUP 2007) 68–69; Mirko Klarin, 'The Impact of the ICTY Trials on Public Opinion in the Former Yugoslavia' (2009) 7 JICJ 89.

[75] International Criminal Court, 'Strategic Plan 2019–2021' (2019) 7–8 https://www.icc-cpi.int/sites/default/files/itemsDocuments/20190717-icc-strategic-plan-eng.pdf (accessed 17 December 2022).

[76] Janet H Anderson, 'The ICC in times of budget crunch' *Justiceinfo.net* (13 December 2021) https://www.justiceinfo.net/en/85475-icc-times-budget-crunch.html (accessed 18 December 2022).

[77] Gaelle Carayon and Jonathan O'Donohue, 'The International Criminal Court's Strategies in Relation to Victims' (2017) 15(3) Journal of International Criminal Justice 567. There has been some consolidation of victim participation and reparations such as the development of a standardized application form and an application assessment process known as the A, B, C system. See *Chambers Practice Manual* (5th edition, 2021), § 96(iv). There has also been more consolidation of reparation principles through the Lubanga and the Ntaganda principles. That said, many inconsistencies remain as different chambers continue to implement different modalities for participation and reparation. See ICC, 'Independent Expert Review of

victims at the Court map onto capitalist pressures for the simultaneous inclusion and exclusion of humans as both capitalist subjects and surplus labour: everyone should be included but not on equal terms; everyone should be productive but not everyone will be paid. The contradictions of the ICC's victim engagement are thus not simply the 'teething problems' of a young court, or the irrational squabbling between different lawyers and offices; nor do they merely reflect justice contestations (eg procedural versus substantive justice, perpetrator-centred versus victim-centred justice),[78] they also mirror and help manage the contradictions of capitalism and reproduce the global division of labour.

Once we read the role of victims in a broader political economy context, victims no longer appear as mere products of international criminal justice; they are also its producers. After all, neoliberal capitalism not only needed to outsource evil; it also needed to outsource work. For that, victims in the Global South are more important than perpetrators. Rather than a failed 'white saviour' mission, the ICC, upon closer examination, looks like a relatively effective capitalist integration programme. It does not save 'innocent victims' from 'evil perpetrators' but creates 'blameworthy victims' and puts them to work. The blame cascade extracts and devalues the labour of feminized and racialized workers, which is both essential for making the Court work, and hidden as 'labour of love' by the Court's 'friends' and 'volunteers' in its African situation countries.

7.4 Resistance

By moving beyond the victim as 'courtroom actor', 'social construction', 'idealized trope' and 'standardized commodity', the book also unveiled new possibilities for resistance. 'The Victims' as a fiction 'cannot respond to claims made in its name', Kendall and Nouwen observe, but

the International Criminal Court and the Rome Statute System: Final Report' (30 September 2020) §§ 863, 865–69; FIDH, 'Whose Court is it? Judicial handbook on victims' rights at the International Criminal Court' (April 2021) 8 https://www.fidh.org/IMG/pdf/fidh_whose_court_is_it_en.pdf (accessed 10 August 2023).

[78] On the teething problems of a still young Court see Hans-Peter Kaul, 'Construction Site for More Justice: The International Criminal Court after Two Years' (2005) 99 American Journal of International Law 370, 371; Antonio Cassese, 'Is the ICC Still Having Teething Problems?' (2006) 4(3) Journal of International Criminal Justice 434; Florian Jessberger,

victim–survivors as flesh-and-blood working subjects can.[79] The example of Ni Una Menos in Argentina illuminates how productive victimhood can be as an organizing platform for anti-capitalist struggle. Ni Una Menos (Not One Woman Less), a feminist movement against gender-based violence, emerged in Argentina in 2015, and has evolved into a mass movement in Latin America and globally. Yet, in the process of organizing against victimization, Ni Una Menos also moved beyond the political and legal vocabulary of victimhood.[80] By connecting different forms of patriarchal violence and capitalist exploitation, its activists disclosed how women's positionality as victims and as precarious feminized workers is intimately entangled. The explosion of femicides in Latin America, Verónica Gago observes, were connected to the

> *maquilas*, those enormous assembly plants dotting the border between Mexico and the United States . . . It was those murdered women who made Ciudad Juarez famous as the concentration of a true 'femicide machine' . . . What mode of freedom were these young women inaugurating by migrating to these factories that became part of a gruesome sequence as well as key to global capital?[81]

Femicide, in fact, became a means of managing women's exploitation between productive work (factory) and reproductive work (family), thus revealing that work was part of the problem rather than part of the solution for women.[82]

The struggle against femicide, thus, gradually transformed into a new form of international women's strike, first called in 2017, against all work women and non-binary people do 'whether paid work in offices and factories or unpaid domestic work in homes, communities and bedrooms'.[83]

'From Rome to Reality: Introductory Observations' (2011) 22 Criminal Law Forum 171; Carsten Stahn, 'Introduction: More than a court, less than a court, several courts in one? The International Criminal Court in perspective' in Carsten Stahn (ed), *The Law and Practice of the International Criminal Court* (OUP 2016).

[79] Kendall and Nouwen (n 29) 258.

[80] Verónica Gago, *Feminist International: How to Change Everything* (Verso 2020) 6; Cavallero and Gago (n 50) xvi.

[81] Gago (n 80) 18.

[82] Susan Ferguson, *Women and Work: Feminism, Labour, and Social Reproduction* (Pluto Press 2019) 126.

[83] 'Women's Strike: About' https://womenstrike.org.uk/about/ (accessed 10 August 2023).

The strike, as Gago puts it, is 'an action that situates us as political subjects against a systematic attempt to reduce our pain to the position of a victim to be repaired (in general by the state)'.[84] Gago is especially attentive to the myriad forms of exploitation that feminized and racialized victim–workers are subjected to. By turning women into entrepreneurs, debt has become a key form of exploitation beyond the wage which accumulates both through labour exploitation (as debtors have to labour, formally or informally, legally or illegally, to repay debt and interest) and through extraction (as land and other assets can be claimed when debtors fail to repay). In Gago's words, 'the entrepreneur complements the figure of the victim: the two positions of subjectivation proposed by a pink-washing neoliberalism. The feminist response is a refusal: *we are neither victims nor entrepreneurs*'.[85]

This also suggests that ICC victimhood can become a site of struggle. At the ICC, women, too, are mainly seen as victims of sexual and gender-based violence (SGBV),[86] which is sometimes portrayed as a 'fate worse than death'.[87] Whereas victims in Northern Uganda often see losing loved ones as the worst form of victimization, the Court has foregrounded victims of SGBV, for example, through the rape, forced pregnancy, and forced

[84] Gago (n 80) 13.

[85] Cavallero and Gago (n 50) 17.

[86] Since 2012, gender has been treated as a cross-cutting issue in the Court's victims' strategy. Assembly of States Parties, 'Report of the Court on the Revised strategy in relation to Victims' (2012) ICC-ASP/11/40, §§ 5–6. The OTP furthermore has published two dedicated policy papers on gender and sexual violence: OTP, 'Policy Paper on Sexual and Gender-Based Crimes' (June 2014) https://www.icc-cpi.int/sites/default/files/iccdocs/otp/Policy_Paper_on_Sexual_and_Gender-Based_Crimes-20_June_2014-ENG.pdf (accessed 8 December 2022); OTP, 'Policy on the Crime of Gender Persecution' (December 2022) https://www.icc-cpi.int/sites/default/files/2022-12/2022-12-07-Policy-on-the-Crime-of-Gender-Persecution.pdf (accessed 8 December 2022). See also Fatou Bensouda, 'Gender crimes are prominent in our prosecutions because they are prominent in situations investigated', ICC press release (19 April 2018) https://www.icc-cpi.int/news/icc-prosecutor-fatou-bensouda-attends-international-conference-sweden-gender-equality-gender (accessed 10 August 2023). I have previously analysed the everyday refashioning of patriarchal norms at the ICC, including through the focus on SGBV: see Leila Ullrich, '"But what about men?" Gender disquiet in international criminal justice' (2021) 25(2) Theoretical Criminology 209. See also Mikkel Jarle Christensen and others, 'The International Criminal Justice Marketplace of Ideas: Setting the Agenda for Responses to Sexual Violence' (2022) 20(1) JICJ 97; Kirsten Campbell, *The Justice of Humans: Subject, Society and Sexual Violence in International Criminal Justice* (CUP 2022).

[87] See eg the Foreign and Commonwealth Office's global campaign to end sexual violence in conflict in 2014: 'Rape and sexual violence are the worst crimes you can imagine, but they are not an inevitable part of war', cited in Anette Bringedal Houge and Kjersti Lohne, 'End Impunity! Reducing Conflict-Related Sexual Violence to a Problem of Law' (2017) 51 Law & Society Review 755, 755. See also Janet Halley, 'Rape in Berlin: Reconsidering the

marriage charges in *Ongwen*,[88] and through earmarked contributions for conflict-related sexual violence in the Trust Fund's reparation and assistance programmes.[89] SGBV is the worst crime not only or primarily because of its violation of male honour or cultural norms, its centrality to white civilizational discourse ('white men saving brown women from brown men')[90] or because of the grave consequences for survivors, but also because it undermines both women's productive and reproductive functions. Unlike dead victims, victims of SGBV can be reformed and made productive.[91]

There is, however, little evidence yet that victims have used their engagement with the Court as a launching pad for political mobilization to transcend victimhood. For the most part, they remain trapped in the victim–survivor continuum. Yet, as the book has documented, there are multiple fault lines in the ideological mechanisms of international criminal justice. The first, at the level of the individual, is the contradictory

Criminalisation of Rape in the International Law of Armed Conflict' (2008) 9 Melbourne Journal of International Law 1; Janet Halley, 'Rape at Rome: Feminist interventions in the criminalization of sex-related violence in positive international criminal law' (2008) 30(1) *Michigan Journal of International Law* 1; Doris Buss, 'Rethinking "rape" as a weapon of war' (2009) 17 Feminist Legal Studies 145.

88 Women's Initiative for Gender Justice, 'Trailblazing ICC Judgment on SGBC: Ongwen verdict advances international accountability for forced marriage and forced pregnancy' (4 February 2021) https://4genderjustice.org/trailblazing-icc-judgment-on-sgbc-ongwen-verdict/ (accessed 8 December 2022).

89 Interview with Victims' Lawyer Assistant, Kampala (9 July 2019). See eg Assembly of States Parties ASP, 'Report to the Assembly of States Parties on the projects and the activities of the Board of Directors of the Trust Fund for Victims for the period 1 July 2019 to 30 June 2020' (ICC-ASP/19/14) (16 September 2020) § 15; Trust Fund for Victims, 'Trust Fund for Victims calls for contributions to provide reparations to victims of conflict-related sexual violence' (13 March 2023) https://www.trustfundforvictims.org/index.php/en/news/trust-fund-victims-calls-contributions-provide%C2%A0reparations-victims-conflict-related-sexual (accessed 14 March 2023).

90 Gayatri Chakravorty Spivak, 'Can the subaltern speak?' in Patrick Williams and Laura Chrisman (eds), *Colonial Discourse and Postcolonial Theory: A Reader* (Columbia UP 1994) 66; Ratna Kapur, 'The Tragedy of Victimization Rhetoric: Resurrecting the "Native" Subject in International/Post-Colonial Feminist Legal Politics' (2002) 15 Harvard Human Rights Journal 1; Ratna Kapur, '"The First Feminist War in All of History": Epistemic Shifts and Relinquishing the Mission to Rescue the "Other Woman"' (2022) 116 AJIL Unbound 270.

91 ASP, 'Report to the Assembly of States Parties' (n 1250) § 85 ('The majority of the project beneficiaries in Uganda are former abductees—mostly women who were raped and abused in captivity and who are now trying to balance their personal needs, including time for healing with the needs of their family and community, searching for a way to integrate those apparently diverging needs'). According to Marx, dead labour can be reanimated by living labour. James Tyner, *Dead Labor: Toward a Political Economy of Premature Death* (University of Minnesota Press 2019).

interpellation of 'victim–survivors'.[92] In the same move in which people are validated as 'victims', they are also challenged and blamed as 'survivors'. Victims need to abolish themselves ('become survivors') through capitalist integration and end up being blamed for their failure to do so. And yet, victim–survivors discover that they ultimately survive through social reproduction and subsistence labour more than through micro-entrepreneurship, making them often prioritize the former over the latter.

The second fault line, at the institutional level, is the contradictory quality of justice. The Court and victims meet in that promise of justice, but justice turns out to benefit the perpetrator (the perpetrator is fed in prison) and the lawyers (the lawyers are paid well) more than the victims. The contradiction is not so much between restorative and retributive, or cultural and legal justice, but between capitalist justice (you can only get back what you can prove you owned) and moral economy (everyone has a right to subsist and people must share resources to survive).[93] The third fault line, at the structural level, is the contradiction between life-making and profit-making; this is a deeper contradiction between relations of production and reproduction which underlies the Court's justice contestations and symptomatically expresses itself in the everyday life of international criminal justice, as Chapter 6 elucidated. These three fault lines are the 'weakest link' in the ideological project; they are possible points of rupture, where a significant number of contradictions coalesce.[94]

How can the victim subject wriggle out of her designated role as champion of international criminal justice and menial labourer for the global economy? The problem with Althusser's interpellation scene is that it slices the individual off society, which makes it difficult to conceive of collective forms of resistance.[95] Yet, as this book has shown, ideological subject formation happens through social relationships, and these relationships can be challenged and changed. Victims are not alone in interpellation, and they

[92] See also Stuart Hall on contradictory subject formation: Hall (n 49) 5, 27.

[93] As Marx put it, drawing on Hegel, 'in the midst of degradation the *revolt* against degradation, a revolt to which it [the proletariat] is forced by the contradiction between its *humanity* and its situation, which is an open, clear, and absolute negation of its humanity'. Cited from the Holy Family in 'Editor's introduction' in Karl Marx and Frederick Engels, *The German Ideology* (Lawrence & Wishart [1974] 2007) 20.

[94] Louis Althusser, *For Marx* (Verso 2005) 94–96.

[95] Louis Althusser, *On Ideology* (Verso 2020) 48; Pierre Macherey, 'Figures of interpellation in Althusser and Fanon' (2012) 173(1) Radical Philosophy 16 ('the very first effect of the call projected from offstage is to isolate the one who receives it, suspending the relations that he or she might entertain with other people').

are not a blank slate. On the contrary, they are enmeshed in pre-existing roles and relationships that sustain and reproduce communities and nourish different values and expectations. This is not something that can be overcome or superseded, nor is that necessarily the objective. Capitalism does not only want individual subjects; it wants working subjects who need to cooperate both in production and social reproduction.[96] The Court, too, needs these social networks to mobilize affected communities and transform them into the 'Court's victims', and it is these pre-existing relationships which, ultimately, give rise and shape to resistance.

Indeed, subsistence, community and caring can erode the Court's legal interpellation as victims transform the ICC's meetings into sites of community and people-making. Relations of social reproduction are a double-edged sword for capitalism as the latter needs non-commodified relations and values (trust, care, reliability, and knowledge) to reproduce itself and, at the same time, risks being undone through them. Withdrawing or reconfiguring socially reproductive labour can, therefore, destabilize 'the social relation of obedience supposed by the capitalist social relation'.[97] This, however, is difficult, political, and collective work and there is nothing natural or essentially female about it. While socially reproductive labour can help build alternative subjectivities, this is, as Kathi Weeks argues, 'a collective interpretation or reworking of a particular subject position rather than an immediate perspective automatically acquired by an individual; it is an ongoing achievement rather than a spontaneous attribute or consciousness of all women'.[98]

7.5 Abolition

'Why and whom to punish', Koskenniemi observes, 'has been a question that political communities have posed as long as they have existed, and that question has always been extended from petty crimes to civil war and large-scale "international' conflict"'.[99] As highlighted earlier, there is considerable consensus among critical scholars that the ICC embodies the rise of

[96] Marx (n 56) 447.
[97] Gago (n 80) 121.
[98] Kathi Weeks, *Constituting Feminist Subjects* (Verso 2018) 8.
[99] Martti Koskenniemi, 'Foreword' in Immi Tallgren and Thomas Skouteris (eds), *The New Histories of International Criminal Law: Retrials* (OUP 2019) vi.

the anti-impunity project in human rights and international law.[100] Karen Engle, for example, charts 'how anti-impunity and its alignment with criminal prosecutions came to be uncontested within human rights . . . relatively quickly' in the 1990s, superseding much more nuanced debates on 'truth versus justice' and 'peace versus justice' in the 1980s.[101] Of course, if we frame the ICC as an anti-impunity project, it becomes less clear what role, if any, victims play other than as staunch supporters of anti-impunity (which they rarely are). This focus on anti-impunity, perhaps, explains why scholars have been slow to revise the image of 'passive, innocent victims' as driving force of international criminal law by picking up insights from adjacent critical literatures, which have, for some time, exposed how peacebuilding and development regimes produce and responsibilize neoliberal subjects through decentralization, local ownership, and people's active participation in their own subjection.[102] Punishment, in short, continues to be seen as the key rationale of international criminal law.

Despite the growing critique of the anti-impunity project, however, there have been few attempts to subject international criminal justice to an abolitionist perspective. This is surprising, as calls to defund the police and abolish prisons have become louder in domestic criminal justice, especially since the murder of George Floyd by a police officer in Minneapolis on 25 May 2020 and the Black Lives Matter (BLM) protests that reignited in its wake.[103] Unlike domestic criminal justice systems, especially in the United States, the ICC is not an institution of mass incarceration. It lacks its own police force and depends on member states for law enforcement.[104] A dozen defendants are locked up in the ICC's detention centre, while those convicted will serve their sentences elsewhere. Whereas Marxist criminology has focused on the repressive power the criminal justice system brings to bear on 'perpetrators', this book has focused on the ideological

[100] Houge and Lohne (n 87); Schwöbel-Patel (n 20) 86–87.
[101] Engle (n 20) 1071.
[102] Bill Cooke and Uma Kothari (eds), *Participation: The New Tyranny?* (Zed Books 2001); Adam Branch and Adrian Yen, 'Neoliberal discipline and violence in northern Uganda' in Jörg Wiegratz, Giuliano Martiniello, and Elisa Greco (eds), *Uganda: The Dynamics of Neoliberal Transformation* (Zed Books 2018); Vasuki Nesiah, 'Local Ownership of Global Governance' (2016) 14(4) JICJ 985, 986; McAuliffe and Schwöbel-Patel (n 14) 985; Sara Kendall and Sarah MH Nouwen, 'International criminal justice and humanitarianism' in Kevin Heller and others (eds), *The Oxford Handbook of International Criminal Law* (OUP 2020) 719.
[103] Leila Ullrich, 'Review of Kjersti Lohne: Advocates of Humanity: Human Rights NGOs in International Criminal Justice' (2021) 29 Feminist Legal Studies 283.
[104] OTP constantly emphasizes this, for example, in its justification for using intermediaries.

power the ICC brings to bear on victims.[105] Indeed, while the Court exercises its penal power over a dozen of defendants, it exercises its ideological power over millions of victims. International criminal justice, this book has argued, works through ideology more than violence, and disciplines the victim more than the perpetrator.

Despite these differences, it is nonetheless productive to examine international criminal justice through an abolitionist lens for at least two reasons. First, abolitionists move beyond what these institutions say they do, 'punish criminals and deter crimes', to place them in a broader, historical analysis of social and political struggles. Abolitionist Ruth Wilson Gilmore, for example, has analysed the development of mass incarceration in the United States in the 1980s as a specific response of a state in crisis: when profit rates began to fall in the mid-1960s and capital started to rebel against high taxes, the Keynesian 'welfare-warfare' state transformed itself into the 'workfare-warfare' state, while absorbing the four surpluses created by capitalist crisis: (1) surplus labour (due to economic downturn and deindustrialization); (2) surplus land (idle land in rural California); (3) surplus state capacity (neoliberalism reduced the state's role in welfare, education, and health but not in law and order); and (4) surplus finance (states took out debt to build prisons).[106] Prisons, thus, became both a crisis fix and a warehouse for surplus labour at a specific conjuncture.

There are debates about the precise relationship between the labour and the racial function of carceral institutions,[107] with some arguing that the

[105] For Marxism and criminalization see Vegh Weis (n 56); Valeria Vegh Weis, 'A Marxist analysis of international criminal law and its potential as a counter-hegemonic project' in Florian Jeßberger, Leonie Steinl, and Kalika Mehta (eds), *International Criminal Law: A Counter-Hegemonic Project?* (TMC Asser Press 2023). On Marxism and Punishment more broadly see Georg Rusche and Otto Kirchheimer, *Punishment and Social Structure* (Columbia UP 1939); Alessandro De Giorgi, 'Punishment, Marxism, and Political Economy' in *Oxford Research Encyclopedia of Criminology and Criminal Justice* (OUP 2018). On punishment and racial capitalism see William Calathes, 'Racial capitalism and punishment philosophy and practices: what really stands in the way of prison abolition' (2017) 20(4) Contemporary Justice Review 442. It is also noteworthy that Marxist criminology has mainly focused on developments in the Global North.

[106] Ruth Wilson Gilmore, *Golden Gulag: Prisons, Surplus, Crisis, and Opposition in Globalizing California* (University of California Press 2007) 28, 57–86; Ruth Wilson Gilmore, *Abolition Geography: Essays towards Liberation* (Verso 2022) 119–21; Sarah Lamble, 'Practising Everyday Abolition' Abolitionist Futures https://abolitionistfutures.com/latest-news/practising-everyday-abolition (accessed 23 November 2022).

[107] Michael J Coyle and Judah Schept, 'Penal abolition and the state: colonial, racial and gender violences' (2017) 20(4) Contemporary Justice Review 399; Calathes (n 105); Michael J Coyle and Judah Schept, 'Penal Abolition Praxis' (2018) 26 Critical Criminology 319.

'prison-industrial complex'[108] is a new form of slavery, based on the hyper-exploitation, devaluation and containment of black labour, while others emphasize the role of prisons in managing racial rather than labour relations, as a 'New Jim Crow'[109] or a new form of social death.[110] Yet others highlight the more subtle, but nonetheless fatal coupling of race, class, gender, and geography as the key problematic that prisons both help create and respond to. That fatal coupling, as Ruth Wilson Gilmore argues, 'pushes disproportionately costs of participation in an increasingly monetized and profit-driven world onto those who, due to the frictions of political distance, cannot reach the variable levers of power that might relieve them of those costs'.[111] It is that fatal coupling that lies at the heart of the ICC's function at this conjuncture, as it manages surplus labour not by locking people up, but by weaving subjects in the Global South into global capitalist relations, while, at the same time, reproducing them as a global racialized underclass.[112]

It is a grim picture, but it is not the end point of abolitionist thinking, and this brings me to the second point. Abolitionist thinking, like social reproduction thinking, alerts us to how the present struggle is already pregnant with the possibilities of the future.[113] 'Abolition', Gilmore asserts, 'is about abolishing the conditions under which prison became the solution to problems, rather than abolishing the buildings we call prisons'.[114] It is a radical epistemology that detaches from 'forms of knowledge that rely on certainty', building non-carceral logics in everyday life without knowing exactly what a world without carceral institutions might look like.[115] Abolitionism is thus not simply about 'closing the ICC'; it is about working through the

[108] Angela Y Davis and Cassandra Shaylor, 'Race, Gender, and the Prison Industrial Complex: California and Beyond' (2001) 2(1) Meridians 1; Angela Y Davis, *Are Prisons Obsolete?* (Seven Stories Press 2003).

[109] Michelle Alexander, *The New Jim Crow: Mass Incarceration in the Age of Colorblindness* (The New Press 2012) 2, 4, 7.

[110] Joshua M Price, *Prison and Social Death* (Rutgers UP 2015).

[111] Gilmore (n 106) 114; Liat Ben-Moshe, 'Dis-epistemologies of Abolition' (2018) 26 Critical Criminology 341, 342–43.

[112] Alexander (n 109) 4, 7.

[113] Ruth Wilson Gilmore and Leopold Lambert, 'Making Abolition Geography in California's Central Valley with Ruth Wilson Gilmore' *The Funambulist* (20 December 2018) https://thefunambulist.net/magazine/21-space-activism/interview-making-abolition-geography-california-central-valley-ruth-wilson-gilmore (accessed 26 April 2023).

[114] Ruth Wilson Gilmore, 'Covid-19, Decarceration, and Abolition [Webinar]' https://www.haymarketbooks.org/blogs/128-ruth-wilson-gilmore-on-covid-19-decarceration-and-abolit ion (accessed 23 November 2022).

[115] Ben-Moshe (n 111) 347. See also Thomas Mathiesen, *The Politics of Abolition Revisited* (Routledge 2015).

alternatives that are created or emerge in the wake of the Court's interventions.[116] And here, a social reproduction perspective is very helpful, as it equips us with a different understanding of what international criminal justice consists of—not just courts, lawyers, statutes and codes—but social relations and forms of labour, which are gendered, racialized, and classed. We can, for example, look at the meeting between victims' lawyers and victims and see a legal site where justice is deliberated or a therapeutic site where victims share their stories and receive closure,[117] or we see all the socially reproductive labour that makes the meeting possible in the first place,[118] and that sustains international criminal law's social relations.

This also gives us a different perspective on change as it makes visible what is already emerging in the interstices of the system. If the ICC is about ideological subject production and labour subsumption, then abolition must be about creating different types of subjects and relationships. If the ICC is about what happens outside the courtroom as much as what happens inside it, then abolishing the legal institution does not capture the myriad ways in which international criminal justice binds people and their harm. Abolition, ultimately, means abolishing global capitalism and its myriad forms of exploitation and violence. Change does not only come from incremental adjustments in laws, policies, and institutions, nor does it necessarily emanate from male-dominated and organized workers' revolts, it also flows from the every-day life making practices of women in the Global South, who are in a direct struggle with colonial capitalism because they still have access to communal land, a key means of both social reproduction and capitalist accumulation.[119] Capitalist relations, ultimately, are nested in non-commodified relationships and can be resisted through them.[120]

[116] Gilmore and Lambert (n 113).

[117] Edna Erez, Michael Kilchling, and Jo-Anne Wemmers (eds), *Therapeutic Jurisprudence and Victim Participation in Justice. International Perspectives* (Carolina Academic Press 2011); Joseph A Manoba and Francisco Cox, 'Victims' participation in the Ongwen case: Strengths, weaknesses and lessons learned' in FIDH, 'Victims at the Center of Justice: From 1998 to 2018: Reflections on the Promises and the Reality of Victim Participation at the ICC' (2018) 48, 52 https://www.fidh.org/IMG/pdf/droitsdesvictimes730a_final.pdf (accessed 10 December 2022).

[118] Who organizes the meeting, who comes, who makes food, and how that food is shared.

[119] Juanita Elias and Shirin M Rai, 'Feminist everyday political economy: Space, time, and violence' (2019) 45(2) Review of International Studies 201.

[120] George Caffentzis and Silvia Federici, 'Commons against and beyond capitalism' (2014) 49(1) Community Development Journal 92, 100. See also Ferguson (n 82) 131; Nancy Fraser, 'Behind Marx's Hidden Abode: For an Expanded Conception of Capitalism' (2014) 86 New Left Review 1; Nancy Fraser, 'Crisis of care? On the social reproductive contradictions of contemporary capitalism' in Tithi Bhattacharya (ed), *Social Reproduction Theory: Remapping Class, Recentering Oppression* (Pluto Press 2017) 21.

Bibliography

Abonga F and others, 'Naked Bodies and Collective Action: Repertoires of Protest in Uganda's Militarised, Authoritarian Regime' (2020) 22(2–3) Civil Wars 198

Acharya A, 'How Ideas Spread: Whose Norms Matter? Norm Localization and Institutional Change in Asian Regionalism' (2004) 58(2) International Organization 239

Acholi Religious Leaders Peace Initiative Website, 'Women Empowerment' https://sites.google.com/a/arlpi.org/www/women-empowerment (accessed 16 April 2023)

Afako B, 'Reconciliation and Justice: 'Mato Oput' and the Amnesty Act' (2002) 11 Accord 1

Akello G, 'Reintegration of Amnestied LRA Ex-Combatants and Survivors' Resistance Acts in Acholiland, Northern Uganda' (2019) 13(2) International Journal of Transitional Justice 249

Akena W, 'From State of Hopelessness to Joy and Celebration' Diocese of Northern Uganda (29 June 2014) http://dioceseofnorthernuganda.blogspot.com/2014/06/normal-0-false-false-false-en-us-x-none.html (accessed 29 November 2021)

Alcoff L and Gray L, 'Survivor Discourse: Transgression or Recuperation?' (1993) 18(2) Signs 260

Alexander M, *The New Jim Crow: Mass Incarceration in the Age of Colorblindness* (The New Press 2012)

Allen T, 'Ritual (ab)use? Problems with traditional justice in Northern Uganda' in Phil Clark and Nicholas Waddell (eds), *Courting Conflict? Justice, Peace and the ICC in Africa* (Royal African Society 2008) 47

Allen T, Atingo J, and Parker M, 'Rejection and Resilience: Returning from the Lord's Resistance Army in Northern Uganda' (2022) 24(2–3) Civil Wars 357

Allen T and Vlassenroot K, *The Lord's Resistance Army: Myth and Reality* (Zed Books 2010)

Althusser L, 'Ideology and ideological state apparatuses (Notes towards an investigation)' in Louis Althusser, *Lenin and Philosophy and Other Essays* (NLB 1977) 121

Althusser L, *On Ideology* (Verso 2020)

Althusser L, *For Marx* (Verso 2005)

Althusser L and others, *Reading Capital: The Complete Edition* (Verso 2016)

Amnesty International, 'Crying for Justice: Victims' Perspectives on Justice for the Post-Election Violence in Kenya' (2014) https://www.amnesty.org/en/documents/afr32/001/2014/en/ (accessed 1 April 2023)

Amnesty International, 'The ICC must become a champion of justice over abuse of power' (2018) https://www.amnesty.org/en/latest/news/2018/02/the-icc-must-become-a-champion-of-justice-over-abuse-of-power/ (accessed 1 April 2023)

Amnesty International and TMC. Asser Instituut, 'The Rome Statute at 40' (May 2021) https://www.asser.nl/media/794895/report-rome-statute-at-40-final.pdf (accessed 17 December 2022)

Anand S, 'Foreclosed temporalities: Imperialism and international criminal law' *Critical Legal Thinking* (18 November 2022) https://criticallegalthinking.com/2022/11/18/foreclosed-temporalities-imperialism-and-international-criminal-law/ (accessed 2 August 2022)

Anderson J, 'The ICC in times of budget crunch' https://www.justiceinfo.net/en/85475-icc-times-budget-crunch.html (accessed 18 December 2022)

Anderson J and Duerr B, 'In a Storm of Lies and Half-truths: The Role of Media Professionals in Spreading and Combatting Misinformation about the International Criminal Court' (2022) 20(1) JICJ 191

Anghie A, *Imperialism, Sovereignty and the Making of International Law* (CUP 2005)

Antiposeonline, 'Geographies of Racial Capitalism with Ruth Wilson Gilmore: An Antipode Foundation film' https://www.youtube.com/watch?v=2CS627aKrJI (accessed 30 July 2022)

Anti-Oppression Resource and Training Alliance, 'Aorta Destabilizing Rape Culture Handout' https://www.nasco.coop/sites/default/files/srl/AORTA%20Destabilizing%20Rape%20Culture%20Handout.pdf (accessed 12 November 2021)

Antkowiak TM, 'An Emerging Mandate for International Courts: Victim-Centered Remedies and Restorative Justice' (2011) 47 Stanford Journal of International Law 279

Arbia S, 'Speech by the ICC Registrar at the Conference "Justice for all? The International Criminal Court: 10 year review of the ICC"' (14 February 2012) https://www.icc-cpi.int/NR/rdonlyres/8C6B4B5B-D854-4F18-BA76-E0F687F2D60C/284274/Speech_10anniversary_Australia.pdf (accessed 5 December 2022)

Arendt H, *Eichmann in Jerusalem: A Report on the Banality of Evil* (Penguin 2006)

Arthur P, 'How "Transitions" Reshaped Human Rights: A Conceptual History of Transitional Justice' (2009) 11 Human Rights Quarterly 321

Arruzza C, Bhattacharya T, and Fraser N, *Feminism for the 99%: A Manifesto* (Verso 2019)

Assembly of States Parties, 'Report of the Court on the Strategy in Relation to Victims' (2006) ICC-ASP/8/45

Assembly of States Parties, 'Report of the Court on the Revised strategy in relation to Victims' (2012) ICC-ASP/11/40

Assembly of States Parties, Resolution ICC-ASP/20/Res.5, 'Strengthening the International Criminal Court and the Assembly of States Parties', adopted at the 8th plenary meeting on 9 December 2021

Assembly of States Parties, Resolution ICC-ASP/21/Res.2 'Strengthening the International Criminal Court and the Assembly of States Parties', adopted at the 9th plenary meeting on 9 December 2022

Assembly of States Parties, 'Report of the Board of Directors of the Trust Fund for Victims to the Assembly of States Parties on the activities of the Trust Fund for the period 1 July 2021 to 30 June 2022' (2022) ICC-ASP/21/14

Apuuli KP, 'Peace over Justice: The Acholi Religious Leaders Peace Initiative (ARLPI) vs. the International Criminal Court (ICC) in Northern Uganda' (2011) 11(1) Studies in Ethnicity and Nationalism 116

Avocats sans Frontières, 'A Beggar has no Choice: Victims' Perspectives on a Reparations Framework for Uganda' (2017) https://www.asf.be/wp-content/uploads/2017/07/ASF_UG_ABeggarhasnoChoice_EN_201704.pdf (accessed 12 January 2022)

Ba O, 'A Truly International Criminal Court: Why the New Prosecutor should look beyond Africa' *Foreign Affairs* (18 June 2021)

Ba O, *States of Justice: The Politics of the International Criminal Court* (CUP 2020)

Baars G, 'The making of an international criminal law' in Christine Schwöbel (ed), *Critical Approaches to International Criminal Law* (Routledge 2014) 196

Baars G, *The Corporation, Law and Capitalism* (Brill 2019)

Bachvarova T, *The Standing of Victims in the Procedural Design of the International Criminal Court* (Brill 2017)

Bakker I and Gill S, Power, *Production and Social Reproduction: Human In/security in the Global Political Economy* (Springer 2003)

Bakker I and Gill S, 'Rethinking power, production, and social reproduction: Toward variegated social reproduction' (2019) 43(4) Capital & Class 503

Balta A, Bax M, and Letschert R, 'Trial and (Potential) Error: Conflicting Visions on Reparations Within the ICC System' (2019) 29(3) International Criminal Justice Review 221

Banaji J, *Theory as History: Essays on Modes of Production and Exploitation* (Brill 2020)

Banks I, 'Facilitating #dialogue or #buildingsupport? An Exploration of the International Criminal Court's Use of 280 Characters' (2022) 20(1) JICJ 55

Baines E, 'Spirits and Social Reconstruction: Rethinking Transitional Justice' (2010) 109 African Affairs 409

Baines E, 'Forced marriage as a political project: Sexual rules and relations in the Lord's Resistance Army' (2014) 51(3) Journal of Peace Research 405

Baines E, *Buried in the Heart: Women, Complex Victimhood and the War in Northern Uganda* (CUP 2017)

Balikuddembe WO, 'Access to loans for the poor: Microfinance in northern Uganda' (5 July 2022) https://ddrn.dk/3367/ (accessed 24 December 2022)

Bannerji H, *The Ideological Condition: Selected Essays on History, Race and Gender* (Brill 2020)

Barnett M and Finnemore M, 'The politics, power, and pathologies of international organizations' (1999) 53(4) International Organization 699

Bartlett AL and Dhizaala JT, 'Post-Conflict Capitalism in Northern Uganda' (2018) 30(2) Peace Review 168

Basic Principles and Guidelines on the Right to a Remedy and Reparation for Victims of Gross Violations of International Human Rights Law and Serious Violations of International Humanitarian Law, UN Doc A/RES/60/147 (21 March 2006)

Baumgartner E, 'Aspects of victim participation in the proceedings of the International Criminal Court' 90(870) International Review of the Red Cross (2008) 409

BBC News, 'African Union backs mass withdrawal from ICC' (1 February 2017) https://www.bbc.co.uk/news/world-africa-38826073 (accessed 30 September 2022)

BBC News, 'Burundi leaves International Criminal Court amid row' (27 October 2017) https://www.bbc.co.uk/news/world-africa-41775951 (accessed 30 September 2022)

BBC News, 'Coronavirus: President Trump defends tweets against US states' lockdowns' (17 April 2020) https://www.bbc.co.uk/news/world-us-canada-52330531 (accessed 12 March 2022)

Bhabha H, 'Of Mimicry and Man: The Ambivalence of Colonial Discourse' (1984) 28 Discipleship: A Special Issue on Psychoanalysis 125

Bhattacharya T (ed), *Social Reproduction Theory: Remapping Class, Recentering Oppression* (Pluto Press 2017)

Bhattacharya T, 'Introduction: Mapping social reproduction theory' in Tithi Bhattacharya (ed), *Social Reproduction Theory: Remapping Class, Recentering Oppression* (Pluto Press 2017) 1

Bhattacharya T, 'How not to skip class: Social reproduction of labor and the global working class' in Tithi Bhattacharya (ed), *Social Reproduction Theory: Remapping Class, Recentering Oppression* (Pluto Press 2017) 68

Ben-Moshe L, 'Dis-epistemologies of Abolition' (2018) 26 Critical Criminology 341

Bennett Caper I, 'Reading Back, Reading Black' (2006) 35(1) Hofstra Law Review 9

Bernstein E, 'Militarized humanitarianism meets carceral feminism: The politics of sex, rights, and freedom in contemporary antitrafficking campaigns' (2010) 36(1) Signs 45

Bensouda F, 'Gender crimes are prominent in our prosecutions because they are prominent in situations investigated' ICC press release (19 April 2018) https://www.icc-cpi.int/news/icc-prosecutor-fatou-bensouda-attends-international-conference-sweden-gender-equality-gender (accessed 8 December 2022)

Bitti G and Friman H, 'Participation of Victims in the Proceedings' in Roy S Lee and others (eds), *The International Criminal Court: Elements of Crimes and Rules of Procedure and Evidence* (Transnational Publishers 2001)

Bitti G, 'A Court for victims?' in FIDH, 'Victims at the Center of Justice: From 1998 to 2018: Reflections on the Promises and the Reality of Victim Participation at the ICC' (2018) https://www.fidh.org/IMG/pdf/droitsdesvictimes730a_final.pdf (accessed 10 December 2022)

Bodansky D, 'The Legitimacy of International Governance: A Coming Challenge for International Environmental Law?' (1999) 93(3) The American Journal of International Law 596

Boesenecker A and Vinjamuri L, 'Lost in Translation? Civil Society, Faith-Based Organizations and the Negotiation of International Norms' (2011) 5(3) The International Journal of Transitional Justice 345

Bongomin GOC, Woldie A, and Wakibi A, 'Microfinance accessibility, social cohesion and survival of women MSMEs in post-war communities in sub-Saharan

Africa: Lessons from Northern Uganda' (2020) 27(5) Journal of Small Business and Enterprise Development 749

Bosworth M and Carrabine E, 'Reassessing Resistance: Gender, Race and Sexuality in Prison' (2001) 3(4) Punishment and Society 501

Bourdieu P and Eagleton T, 'Doxa and Common Life' (1992) 191(1) New Left Review 111

Bourdieu P, 'The Force of Law: Toward a Sociology of the Juridical Field' (1987) 38 The Hastings Law Journal 814

Bradford B, 'Voice, Neutrality and Respect: Use of Victim Support Services, Procedural Fairness and Confidence in the Criminal Justice System' (2011) 11 Criminology & Criminal Justice 345

Braithwaite J, 'Restorative Justice and a Better Future' (1996) 76(1) Dalhousie Law Review 9

Branch A, 'Uganda's Civil War and the Politics of ICC Intervention' (2007) 21(2) Ethics and International Affairs 179

Branch A, 'Humanitarianism, Violence and the Camp in Northern Uganda' (2009) 11 Civil Wars 1

Branch A, *Displacing Human Rights: War and Intervention in Northern Uganda* (OUP 2011)

Branch A, 'The Violence of Peace: Ethnojustice in Northern Uganda' (2014) 45 Development and Change 608

Branch A, 'Dominic Ongwen on Trial: The ICC's African Dilemmas' (2017) 11(1) International Journal of Transitional Justice 30

Branch A and Yen A, 'Neoliberal discipline and violence in northern Uganda' in Wiegratz J, Giuliano Martiniello G, and Greco E (eds), *The Dynamics of Neoliberal Transformation* (Zed Books 2018)

Brants C, 'Guilty landscapes: Collective guilt and international criminal law' in Bailliet C and Franko Aas K (eds), *Cosmopolitan Justice and its Discontents* (Routledge 2011) 53

Brett P and Gissel LE, 'Explaining African Participation in International Courts' (2018) 117(467) African Affairs 195

Buchanan A and Keohane RO, 'The Legitimacy of Global Governance Institutions' (2006) 20 Ethics and International Affairs 405

Buckland W, 'Symptomatic reading in Althusser, Cahiers du cinéma, and Zizek' (2013) 55 Jump Cut: A Review of Contemporary Media Jump Cut https://www.ejumpcut.org/archive/jc55.2013/Buckland-Lincoln/text.html (accessed 3 December 2022)

Burgis-Kasthala M, 'Scholarship as Dialogue? TWAIL and the Politics of Methodology' (2016) 14(4) JICJ 921

Burke C and Kobusingye DN, 'Women's Land Rights in Northern Uganda' (2014) https://mokoro.co.uk/wp-content/uploads/SecuringWomenLandRightsNorthernUganda_Oxfam.pdf (accessed 2 April 2023)

Buss D, 'Performing Legal Order: Some Feminist Thoughts on International Criminal Law' (2011) 11 ICLR 409

Buss D, 'Rethinking 'rape as a weapon of war' (2009) 17 Feminist Legal Studies 145

Butler J, 'Performative Acts and Gender Constitution: An Essay in Phenomenology and Feminist Theory' (1988) 40(4) Theatre Journal 519

Butler J, *Gender Trouble* (Routledge 2007)

Butler J, 'On Cruelty' (2014) 36(14) London Review of Books https://www.lrb.co.uk/the-paper/v36/n14/judith-butler/on-cruelty (accessed 23 April 2022)

Butler J, 'When gesture becomes event' in Anna Street and others (eds), *Inter Views in Performance Philosophy: Crossings and Conversations* (Palgrave Macmillan 2017) 171

Butti E and McGonigle Leyh B, 'Intersectionality and Transformative Reparations: The Case of Colombian Marginal Youths' (2019) 19(5) International Criminal Law Review 753

Caffentzis G and Federici S, 'Commons against and beyond capitalism' (2014) 49(1) Community Development Journal 92

Calathes W, 'Racial capitalism and punishment philosophy and practices: what really stands in the way of prison abolition' (2017) 20(4) Contemporary Justice Review 442

Van Camp T and Wemmers JA, 'Victim Satisfaction with Restorative Justice: More than Simply Procedural Justice' (2013) 19 International Review of Victimology 117

Campbell K, *The Justice of Humans Subject, Society and Sexual Violence in International Criminal Justice* (CUP 2022)

Campling L, 'Debating Modes of Production and Forms of Exploitation: Introduction to the Symposium on Jahns Banaji's Theory as History' (2013) 21(4) Historical Materialism 3

Care Uganda, 'Village Saving and Loans Association' (2014) https://www.care.org.au/wp-content/uploads/2014/12/CARE-VSLA-Report-Uganda-Eco-Devel.pdf (accessed 2 May 2022)

Carlton A and others, 'Microfinance in Uganda' L and R Social Research (December 2001) https://www.oecd.org/countries/uganda/35481055.pdf (accessed 24 December 2022)

Carayon G and O'Donohue J, 'The International Criminal Court's Strategies in Relation to Victims' (2017) 15(3) JICJ 567

Catani L, 'Victims at the International Criminal Court: Some Lessons Learned from the *Lubanga* Case' (2012) 10(4) JICJ 905

Cavallero L and Gago V, *A Feminist Reading of Debt* (Liz Mason-Deese tr, Pluto Books 2021)

Chakrabarty D, *Provincializing Europe: Postcolonial Thought and Historical Difference* (Princeton UP 2008)

Chanock M, 'Neo-Traditionalism and the Customary Law in Malawi' (1978) 16 African Legal Studies 80

Chappell L, 'The gender injustice cascade: "transformative" reparations for victims of sexual and gender-based crimes in the Lubanga case at the International Criminal Court' (2017) 21(9) The International Journal of Human Rights 1223

Cheah WL, 'International criminal law and culture' in Heller K and others (eds), *The Oxford Handbook of International Criminal Law* (OUP 2020) 748

Chimni BS, 'Third World Approaches to International Law: A Manifesto' (2006) 8 International Community Law Review 3

Chimni BS, *International Law and World Order: A Critique of Contemporary Approaches* (2nd edn, CUP 2017)

Christensen MJ, 'Celebrating international criminal justice: a sociology of the twentieth anniversary of the International Criminal Court' (2021) 9(3) London Review of International Law 351

Christensen MJ, 'The Professional Market of International Criminal Justice: Divisions of Labour and Patterns of Elite Reproduction' (2021) 19(4) JICJ 783

Christensen MJ and Orina NM, 'The International Criminal Court as a Law Laboratory: Professional Battles of Control and the 'Control of the Crime' Theory' (2022) 20(3) JICJ 699

Christensen MJ and others, 'The International Criminal Justice Marketplace of Ideas: Setting the Agenda for Responses to Sexual Violence' (2022) 20(1) JICJ 97

Christie N, 'The ideal victim' in Fattah EA (ed), *From Crime Policy to Victim Policy* (Palgrave Macmillan 1986)

Chung CH, 'Victims' Participation at the International Criminal Court: Are Concessions of the Court Clouding the Promise?' (2008) 6 Northwestern Journal of International Human Rights 459

Clanchy M, 'Law and love in the Middle Ages' in John Bossy (ed), *Disputes and Settlements: Law and Human Relations in the West* (CUP 2003) 47

Clancy D, '"They told us we would be part of history": Reflections on the civil society intermediary experience in the Great Lakes region' in de Vos C, Kendall S, and Stahn C (eds), *Contested Justice: The Politics and Practice of International Criminal Court Interventions* (CUP 2015) 219

Clark P, 'Law, Politics and pragmatism: The ICC and case selection in Uganda and the Democratic Republic of Congo' in Waddell N and Clark P (eds), *Courting Conflict: Justice, Peace and the ICC in Africa* (Royal African Society 2008) 37

Clark P, 'Bringing the Peasants back in, again: State Power and Local Agency in Rwanda's Gacaca Courts' (2014) 8 Journal of Eastern African Studies 193

Clark P, *Distant Justice: The Impact of the International Criminal Court on African Politics* (CUP 2018)

Clark P and Nicola Palmer P, 'Challenging transitional justice' in Palmer N, Clark P, and Granville D (eds), *Critical Perspectives in Transitional Justice* (Intersentia 2012)

Clark J, 'The impact question: The ICTY and the restoration and maintenance of peace' in Swart B, Zahar A, and Sluiter G (eds), *The Legacy of the International Criminal Tribunal for the Former Yugoslavia* (OUP 2011)

Clark J, 'International Criminal Courts and Normative Legitimacy: An Achievable Goal?' (2015) 15(4) International Criminal Law Review 763

Clark J, *International Trials and Reconciliation: Assessing the Impact of the International Criminal Tribunal for the Former Yugoslavia* (Routledge 2014)

Clarke KM, *Fictions of Justice: The International Criminal Court and the challenge of legal pluralism in Sub-Saharan Africa* (CUP 2009)

Clarke KM, 'We ask for justice, you give us law': The rule of law, economic markets and the International Criminal Court' in de Vos C, Kendall S, and Stahn C (eds), *Contested Justice: The Politics and Practice of International Criminal Court Interventions* (CUP 2015)
Clarke KM, 'Refiguring the perpetrator: culpability, history and international criminal law's impunity gap' (2015) 19(5) The International Journal of Human Rights 592
Clarke KM, 'Why Africa?' in Steinberg RH (ed), *Contemporary Issues Facing the International Criminal Court* (Brill | Nijhoff 2016) 326
Clarke KM, 'Affective Justice: The Racialized Imaginaries of International Justice' (2019) 42 (2) PoLAR 244
Clarke KM, *Affective Justice: The International Criminal Court and the Pan-Africanist Pushback* (Duke UP 2022)
Clarke KM, Knottnerus AS, and de Volder E (eds), *Africa and the ICC: Perceptions of Justice* (CUP 2016)
Clarno A and Vally S, 'The context of struggle: racial capitalism and political praxis in South Africa' (2022) 46 Ethnic and Racial Studies 3425
Clements R, '*Re*Visiting the ICC Registry's *Re*Vision Project' (2019) 17 JICJ 259
Clements R, 'From bureaucracy to management: The International Criminal Court's internal progress narrative' (2019) 32(1) Leiden Journal of International Law 149
Clements R, 'Near, Far, Wherever You Are: Distance and Proximity in International Criminal Law' (2021) 32(1) European Journal of International Law 327
Close J, 'The ICC refrains from affirming a general ban on amnesties in the Gaddafi admissibility appeal decision' *International Law Blog* (20 April 2020) https://internationallaw.blog/2020/04/20/the-icc-refrains-from-affirming-a-general-ban-on-amnesties-in-the-gaddafi-admissibility-appeal-decision/ (accessed 14 June 2022)
Coalition for the International Criminal Court (CICC), 'Comments and Recommendations to the 11th Session of the Assembly of States Parties' (9 November 2012) https://iccforum.com/media/background/outreach/2012-11-09_CICC_Communications_Team_Comments_and_Recommendations_to_the_Eleventh_Session_of_the_ASP.pdf (accessed 6 August 2023)
Coalition for the International Criminal Court (CICC), 'Victims could lose out with states' double-standard on International Criminal Court resources' (30 March 2022 https://www.coalitionfortheicc.org/news/20220330/OpenLetter_ICCresources (accessed 15 July 2022)
Coalition for the International Criminal Court (CICC), 'A sufficient budget' https://www.coalitionfortheicc.org/fight/state-support/sufficient-budget (accessed 15 July 2022)
Cockburn C, 'Don't talk to me about war: My life's a battlefield' *Open Democracy* (25 November 2012) https://www.opendemocracy.net/5050/cynthia-cockburn/%E2%80%9Cdon%E2%80%99t-talk-to-me-about-war-my-life%E2%80%99s-battlefield%E2%80%9D (accessed 16 April 2023)
Cohen M, *Realizing Reparative Justice for International Crimes: From Theory to Practice* (CUP 2020)

Cohen HG and others, 'Legitimacy and International Courts - A Framework' (2017) 17(3) PluriCourts Research Paper 1
Coker D, 'Transformative Justice: Anti-Subordination Processes in Cases of Domestic Violence' in Strang H and Braithwaite J (eds), *Restorative Justice and Family Violence* (CUP 2002) 128
Confortini C, 'Galtung, Violence, and Gender: The Case for a Peace Studies/ Feminism Alliance' (2006) 31 Peace & Change 333
Connell R, 'Using Southern Theory: Decolonizing Social Thought in Theory, Research and Application' (2014) 13(2) Planning Theory 210
Cooke B and Kothari U (eds), *Participation: The New Tyranny?* (Zed Books 2001)
Cooper M, *Family Values: Between Neoliberalism and the New Social Conservatism* (Princeton UP 2017)
Cooper V and Whyte D, 'Grenfell, Austerity, and Institutional Violence' (2022) 27(1) Sociological Research Online 207
Corsi M and de Angelis M, 'Gender Discrimination in Microfinance? Some Evidence from Uganda' (2017) 53(5) The Journal of Development Studies 723
Couillard V, 'The Nairobi Declaration: Redefining Reparation for Women Victims of Sexual Violence' (2007) 1 IJTJ 444
Coulthard GS, *Red Skin, White Masks Rejecting the Colonial Politics of Recognition* (Minnesota UP 2014)
Coyle MJ and Schept J, 'Penal abolition and the state: colonial, racial and gender violences' (2017) 20(4) Contemporary Justice Review 399
Coyle MJ and Schept J, 'Penal Abolition Praxis' (2018) 26 Critical Criminology 319
Dalla Costa M, 'Women and the Subversion of the Community' (1971) https://la.utexas.edu/users/hcleaver/357k/357kDallaCostaSubversionTable.pdf (accessed 17 February 2022)
Daly E, 'Transformative Justice: Charting a Path to Reconciliation' (2002) 12(1–2) International Legal Perspectives 73
Damaska M, 'What Is the Point of International Criminal Justice?' (2008) 83 Chicago-Kent Law Review 329
Davis AY and Shaylor C, 'Race, Gender, and the Prison Industrial Complex: California and Beyond' (2001) 2(1) Meridians 1
Davis AY, *Are Prisons Obsolete?* (Seven Stories Press 2003)
DeFalco RC and Mégret F, 'The invisibility of race at the ICC: lessons from the US criminal justice system' (2019) 7(1) London Review of International Law 55
De Giorgi A, 'Punishment, Marxism, and Political Economy' *Oxford Research Encyclopedia of Criminology and Criminal Justice* (OUP 2018)
De Gurmendi F, 'Remarks to the United Nations General Assembly delivering the Court's annual report' (30 October 2017)
Delker BC, Salton R, and McLean KC, 'Giving Voice to Silence: Empowerment and Disempowerment in the Developmental Shift from Trauma "Victim" to "Survivor-Advocate"' (2020) 21(2) Journal of Trauma & Dissociation 242
Derrida J, 'Before the law' in Derek Attridge (ed), *Acts of Literature* (Routledge 1992) 181

De Silva N, 'Intermediary Complexity in Regulatory Governance: The International Criminal Court's Use of NGOs in Regulating International Crimes' (2017) 670(1) The ANNALS of the American Academy of Political and Social Science 170

Dezalay S, 'Book Review: Distant Justice: The Impact of the International Criminal Court on African Politics by Phil Clark (Cambridge: Cambridge University Press, 2018, 379 pp., £26.99 (pbk))' (2020) 47 Journal of the Law Society 175

Dieckmann J, 'The Participation of Victims in Proceedings of the International Criminal Court: Observations from a Counsel's Perspective' Speech at the University of Oxford (2 March 2015)

Dieterle C, 'Global Governance Meets Local Land Tenure: International Codes of Conduct for Responsible Land Investments in Uganda' (2022) 58(3) The Journal of Development Studies 582

Dignan J, *Understanding Victims and Restorative Justice* (Open UP 2005)

Dinneny C, 'EU dispatch: ICC legal defence staff launching historic strike over labour rights, pay disparity' *Jurist* (2 December 2022) https://www.jurist.org/news/2022/12/eu-dispatch-icc-legal-defence-staff-launching-historic-strike-over-labor-rights-pay-disparity/ (accessed 10 December 2022)

Dixon P and Tenove C, 'International Criminal Justice as a Transnational Field: Rules, Authority and Victims' (2013) 7(3) *International Journal of Transitional Justice* 393

Dixon P, 'Reparations, Assistance and the Experience of Justice: Lessons from Colombia and the Democratic Republic of Congo (DRC)' (2016) 10 International Journal of Transitional Justice 88

Dranginis H, 'The Middle Man: Intermediaries of International Criminal Justice' *Justice in Conflict* (21 August 2011) http://justiceinconflict.org/2011/08/21/the-middle-man-the-intermediaries-of-international-criminal-justice/ (accessed 10 April 2023)

Drumbl M, Atrocity, *Punishment and International Law* (CUP 2009)

Drumbl M, *Reimagining Child Soldiers in International Law and Policy* (OUP 2012)

Drumbl M, 'Victims who victimise' (2016) 4(2) London Review of International Law 217

Drumbl M, 'From Timbuktu to The Hague and Beyond: The War Crime of Intentionally Attacking Cultural Property' (2019) 17(1) Journal of International Criminal Justice 77

Drumbl M, '"Getting" an unforgettable gettable: The trial of Dominic Ongwen' *Justice in Conflict* (5 February 2021) https://justiceinconflict.org/2021/02/05/getting-an-unforgettable-gettable-the-trial-of-dominic-ongwen/ (accessed 30 July 2022)

Drumbl M, 'Weaving a Broader Tapestry' (2021) 15 Florida International University Law Review 27

Duggan C and Abusharaf A, 'Reparation of Sexual Violence in Democratic Transitions: The Search for Gender Justice' in de Greiff P (ed), *The Handbook of Reparations* (OUP 2006)

Duggan M (ed), *Revisiting the 'Ideal Victim': Developments in Critical Victimology* (Bristol UP 2018)

Dunn JL, '"Victims" and "Survivors": Emerging Vocabularies of Motive for "Battered Women Who Stay"' (2005) 75 Sociological Inquiry 1

Dutton A and Ní Aoláin F, 'Between Reparations and Repair: Assessing the Work of the ICC Trust Fund for Victims Under Its Assistance Mandate' (2019) 19(2) Chicago Journal of International Law 490

Eagleton T, *Ideology: An Introduction* (Verso 1991)

Easterday J, 'It's complicated: The ICC Prosecutor's Office and the need for reform' *International Justice Monitor* (18 May 2020) https://www.ijmonitor.org/2020/05/its-complicated-the-icc-prosecutors-office-and-the-need-for-reform/ (accessed 31 March 2023)

Easterday J, 'Transforming Outreach and Engagement with Local Stakeholders' *International Justice Monitor* (15 July 2020) https://www.ijmonitor.org/2020/07/transforming-outreach-and-engagement-with-local-stakeholders/ (accessed 12 April 2022)

Ebila F and Tripp AM, 'Naked transgressions: gendered symbolism in Ugandan land protests' in Brown NE and Gershon SA (eds), *Body Politics* (Routledge 2020)

Edelbi S, Making Race Speakable in International Criminal Law: Review of Lingaas' The Concept of Race in International Criminal Law' (2020) TWAILR: Reflections #16/2020

Edwards I, 'An Ambiguous Participant: The Crime Victim and Criminal Justice Decision-Making' (2004) 44 British Journal of Criminology 867

Ehrenreich B and Ehrenreich J, 'Professional-Managerial Class' (1977) 11(2) Radical America 1

Elander M, *Figuring Victims in International Criminal Justice: The Case of the Khmer Rouge Tribunal* (Routledge 2018)

Elias J and Rai SM, 'Feminist everyday political economy: Space, time, and violence' (2019) 45(2) Review of International Studies 201

Engle K, 'Anti-impunity and the Turn to Criminal Law in Human Rights' (2015) 100 Cornell Law Review 1069

Eslava L, 'TWAIL Coordinates' *Critical Legal Thinking* (2 April 2019) https://criticallegalthinking.com/2019/04/02/twail-coordinates/ (accessed 29 June 2022)

Eslava L and Pahuja S, 'The State and International Law: A Reading from the Global South' (2020) 11(1) Humanity: An International Journal of Human Rights, Humanitarianism, and Development 118

Evans C, *The Right to Reparation in International Law for Victims of Armed Conflict* (CUP 2012)

Evans M, 'Structural Violence, Socioeconomic Rights, and Transformative Justice' (2016) 15(1) Journal of Human Rights 1

Evans M (ed), *Beyond Transitional Justice: Transformative Justice and the State of the Field (or Non-field): Directions and Developments in Criminal Justice and Law* (Routledge 2022)

Erez E, Kilchling M, and Wemmers JA (eds), *Therapeutic Jurisprudence and Victim Participation in Justice. International Perspectives* (Carolina Academic Press 2011)

Factory at Chorzów (Germany v Poland) (Judgment) (1928) PCIJ Series A No 13 (September 1928)

Fanon F, *The Wretched of the Earth* (Penguin Classics 2001)

Farris S, 'Femonationalism and the "Regular" Army of Labor Called Migrant Women' (2012) 2(2) History of the Present 184
Farris S, *In the Name of Women's Rights: The Rise of Femonationalism* (Duke UP 2017)
Fattah E, 'Victimology: Past, Present and Future' (2000) 33 Criminologie 17
Fattah E, 'The evolution of a young and promising discipline: sixty years of victimology, a retrospective and prospective look' in Shoham SG, Knepper P, and Kett M (eds), *International Handbook of Victimology* (1st edn, CRC Press 2010) 43
Federici S, *Caliban and the Witch: Women, the Body and Primitive Accumulation* (Modern Classics 2004)
Federici S, 'From Commoning to Debt: Financialization, Microcredit, and the Changing Architecture of Capital Accumulation' (2014) 113(2) The South Atlantic Quarterly 231
Federici S, *Re-enchanting the World: Feminism and the Politics of the Commons* (PM Press 2018)
Federici S, *Revolution at Point Zero: Housework, Reproduction, and Feminist Struggle* (PM Press 2021)
Feldman G, 'If ethnography is more than participant-observation, then relations are more than connections: The case for nonlocal ethnography in a world of apparatuses' (2011) 11 Anthropological Theory 375
Feldman G, 'Illuminating thė Apparatus: Steps toward a Nonlocal Ethnography of Global Governance' in Shore C, Wright S, and Peró D (eds), *Policy Worlds: Anthropology and the Analysis of Contemporary Power* (Berghahn 2011)
Ferguson S, *Women and Work Feminism, Labour, and Social Reproduction* (Pluto Press 2019)
Ferguson S, 'Social Reproduction: What's the Big Idea?' https://www.plutobooks.com/blog/social-reproduction-theory-ferguson/ (accessed 28 January 2022)
Ferguson S and McNally D, 'Capital, labour-power, and gender-relations: Introduction to the historical materialism edition of Marxism and the oppression of women' in Vogel L, *Marxism and the Oppression of Women: Toward a Unitary Theory* (2nd edn, Brill 2013)
Ferstman C and Lawry-White M, 'Participation, Reparation, and Redress: Draft Article 12 of the ILC's Draft Articles on Crimes Against Humanity at the Intersection of International Criminal Law and Human Rights Law' (2018) 16(4) Journal of International Criminal Justice 813
Fichtelberg A, 'Democratic Legitimacy and the International Criminal Court: A Liberal Defence' (2006) 4(4) JICJ 765
FIDH, Five Myths about Victim Participation in ICC Proceedings (December 2014) https://www.fidh.org/IMG/pdf/cpi649a.pdf (accessed 12 December 2022)
FIDH, 'Whose Court is it?: Judicial handbook on victims' rights at the International Criminal Court' https://www.fidh.org/IMG/pdf/fidh_whose_court_is_it_en.pdf (accessed 9 April 2023)
Findlay M and Henham R, *Transforming International Criminal Justice: Retributive and Restorative Justice in the Trial Process* (Routledge 2012)
Finnström S, *Living with Bad Surroundings: War, History, and Everyday Moments in Northern Uganda* (Duke UP 2008)

Fletcher LE and Weinstein HM, 'Violence and Social Repair: Rethinking the Contribution of Justice to Reconciliation' (2002) 24(3) Human Rights Quarterly 573

Fletcher LE, 'Refracted justice: The imagined victim and the International Criminal Court' in Christian de Vos, Sara Kendall, and Carsten Stahn (eds), *Contested Justice: The Politics and Practice of International Criminal Court Interventions* (CUP 2015)

Fletcher R, 'Legal form, commodities and reproduction: Reading Pashukanis' in Maria Drakopoulou (ed), *Feminist Encounters with Legal Philosophy* (Routledge 2013) 138

Foucault M and Deleuze G, 'Intellectuals and power: A conversation between Michel Foucault and Gilles Deleuze' Transcript from 1972 https://libcom.org/library/intellectuals-power-a-conversation-between-michel-foucault-and-gilles-deleuze (accessed 15 February 2022)

Ford S, 'Funding the ICC for its third decade' in Stahn C (ed), *The International Criminal Court in its Third Decade: Reflecting on Law and Practice* (Brill 2023)

Fraser J and McGonigle Leyh B (eds), *Intersections of Law and Culture at the International Criminal Court* (Edward Elgar Publishing 2020)

Fraser N, 'Behind Marx's Hidden Abode: For an Expanded Conception of Capitalism' (2014) 86 New Left Review 1

Fraser N, 'Crisis of care? On the social reproductive contradictions of contemporary capitalism' in Bhattacharya T (ed), *Social Reproduction Theory: Remapping Class, Recentering Oppression* (Pluto Press 2017) 21

Fraser N, 'Contradictions of Capital and Care' (2016) 100 New Left Review 99

Fraser, N *Cannibal Capitalism* (Verso 2022)

Fuchs C and Sevignani S, 'What Is Digital Labour? What Is Digital Work? What's their Difference? And Why Do These Questions Matter for Understanding Social Media?' (2013) 11(2) tripleC 237

Fulford A, 'The Reflections of a Trial Judge' (2011) 22 Criminal Law Forum 215

Future Agricultures, 'Land Grabbing in Africa and the New Politics of Food' *Policy Brief 041* (June 2011) https://assets.publishing.service.gov.uk/media/57a08abfed915d3cfd0008fa/FAC_Policy_Brief_No41.pdf (accessed 12 August 2023)

Gago V, *Feminist International: How to Change Everything* (Verso 2020)

Galtung J, 'Violence, Peace and Peace Research' (1969) 6(3) Journal of Peace Research 167

Garbett C, 'The International Criminal Court and restorative justice: victims, participation and the processes of justice' (2017) 5(2) Restorative Justice 198

Garikipati S, Johnson S, Guérin I and Szafarz A, 'Microfinance and Gender: Issues, Challenges and The Road Ahead' (2017) 53(5) The Journal of Development Studies 641

Garkawe S, 'Victims and the International Criminal Court: Three Major Issues' (2013) 3 International Criminal Law Review 345

Gaynor F, 'Letter to the Special Rapporteur on the Human Rights of IDPs Dr. Chaloka Beyani' (22 May 2014) (on file with the author)'

Gaynor F, 'Letter to the Security Council' (3 November 2013) (on file with the author)

Gevers C, 'The 'Africa Blue Books' at Versailles: The First World War, narrative, and unthinkable histories of international criminal law' in Tallgren I and Skouteris T (eds), *The New Histories of International Criminal Law: Retrials* (OUP 2019) 145

Gevers C, 'Africa and International Criminal Law' in Heller K and others (eds), *The Oxford Handbook of International Criminal Law* (OUP 2020)

Gilmore RW, 'Fatal Couplings of Power and Difference: Notes on Racism and Geography' (2002) 54(1) The Professional Geographer 15

Gilmore RW, *Golden Gulag: Prisons, Surplus, Crisis, and Opposition in Globalizing California* (University of California Press 2007)

Gilmore RW, 'Covid-19, Decarceration, and Abolition [Webinar]' https://www.haymarketbooks.org/blogs/128-ruth-wilson-gilmore-on-covid-19-decarceration-and-abolition (accessed 23 November 2022)

Gilmore RW, *Abolition Geography: Essays towards Liberation* (Verso 2022)

Gilmore RW, *Change Everything: Racial Capitalism and the Case for Abolition* (Haymarket Books 2023)

Gilmore RW and Lambert L, 'Making Abolition Geography in California's Central Valley with Ruth Wilson Gilmore' *The Funambulist* (20 December 2018) https://thefunambulist.net/magazine/21-space-activism/interview-making-abolition-geography-california-central-valley-ruth-wilson-gilmore (accessed 26 April 2023)

Gill S, 'Globalisation, Market Civilisation, and Disciplinary Neoliberalism' (1995) 24(3) Millennium 399

Glasius M, '"We ourselves, we are part of the functioning": The ICC, victims, and civil society in the Central African Republic' (2009) 180(430) African Affairs 49

Glasius M, 'Do International Criminal Courts Require Democratic Legitimacy' (2012) 23 The European Journal of International Law 43

Glasius M, *The International Criminal Court: A Global Civil Society Achievement* (Routledge 2007)

Gondi J, 'Victim participation in ICC case is crucial' *The Star* (15 October 2012) https://allafrica.com/stories/201210161157.html (accessed 30 March 2023)

Goetz M, 'The International Criminal Court and its relevance to affected communities' in Clark P and Waddell N (eds), *Courting Conflict? Justice, Peace and the ICC in Africa* (Royal African Society 2008) 65

Goldstone R, 'The International Criminal Court deserves the continued support of South Africa and all other peace-loving nations' *Wayamo Foundation* (19 August 2020) https://www.wayamo.com/archives/goldstoneiccoped/ (accessed 5 January 2023)

Gonzalez and Others ('Cotton Field') v Mexico, Inter-American. Court of Human Rights (series C) No 205 (16 November 2009)

Gotby, A, *They Call It Love: The Politics of Emotional Life* (Verso 2023)

Government of Uganda, 'Uganda Vision 2040' http://www.npa.go.ug/wp-content/uploads/2021/02/VISION-2040.pdf (accessed 12 August 2023)

Goodale M, 'Locating rights, envisioning law between the global and the local' in Goodale M and Merry SE (eds), *The Practice of Human Rights: Tracking Law between the Global and the Local* (CUP 2007)

Graeber D, *Debt: The First 5000 Years* (Melvin House Publishing 2011)

Graeber D, 'Dead zones of the imagination: On violence, bureaucracy, and interpretive labor' (2012) 2(2) Journal of Ethnographic Theory 105

Gready S, 'The Case for Transformative Reparations: In Pursuit of Structural Socio-Economic Reform in Post-Conflict Societies' (2022) 16(2) Journal of Intervention and Statebuilding 182

Gready P and Robins S, 'From Transitional to Transformative Justice: A New Agenda for Practice' (2014) 8(3) IJTJ 339

Gready P and Robins S, 'Transitional Justice and Theories of Change: Towards evaluation as understanding' (2020) 14(2) International Journal of Transitional Justice 280

de Greiff P, 'Deliberative Democracy and Punishment' (2002) 5 Buffalo Criminal Law Review 373

de Greiff P, 'Justice and Reparations' in de Greiff P (ed), *The Handbook of Reparations* (OUP 2006) 451

Gupta R, '"Victim" vs "survivor": Feminism and language' *Open Democracy* (16 June 2014) https://www.opendemocracy.net/en/5050/victim-vs-survivor-feminism-and-language/ (accessed 22 January 2023)

Haldemann F, *Transitional Justice for Foxes: Conflict, Pluralism and the Politics of Compromise* (CUP 2022)

Hall R, 'Land grabbing in Southern Africa: the many faces of the investor rush' (2011) 38(128) Review of African Political Economy 93

Hall S, *Cultural Studies 1983: A Theoretical History* (Jennifer Daryl Slack and Lawrence Grossberg eds, Duke UP 2016)

Hall S, 'Gramsci's Relevance for the Study of Race and Ethnicity' (1986) 10(4) Journal of Communication Inquiry 5

Hall C, 'Racial Capitalism: What's in a Name?' (2022) 94 History Workshop Journal 5

Halley J, 'Rape in Berlin: Reconsidering the Criminalisation of Rape in the International Law of Armed Conflict' (2008) 9 *Melbourne Journal of International Law* 78

Halley J, 'Rape at Rome: Feminist interventions in the criminalization of sex-related violence in positive international criminal law' (2008) 30(1) *Michigan Journal of International Law* 1

Hammett D and Sporton D, 'Paying for interviews? Negotiating ethics, power and expectation' (2012) 44(4) Area 496

Haraway D, 'Situated Knowledges: The Science Question in Feminism and the Privilege of Partial Perspective' (1998) 14(3) Feminist Studies 575

Harney S and Moten F, *The Undercommons: Fugitive Planning & Black Study* (Minor Compositions 2013)

Harvey D, 'The New Imperialism: Accumulation By Dispossession' (2004) 40 Socialist Register 63

Harvey D, *Seventeen Contradictions and the End of Capitalism* (Profile Books 2014)

Haslam E, 'Law, civil society and contested justice at the International Criminal Tribunal for Rwanda' in Dembour MB and Kelly T (eds), *Paths to International Justice* (CUP 2007)

Haslam E, *The Slave Trade, Abolition and the Long History of International Criminal Law: The Recaptive and the Victim* (Routledge 2019)
Haslam E and Edmunds R, 'Common Legal Representation at the International Criminal Court: More Symbolic than Real?' (2012) 12(5) International Criminal Law Review 871
Haslam E and Edmunds R, 'Managing a New Partnership: Professionalization, Intermediaries and the International Criminal Court' (2013) 24 Criminal Law Forum 49
Haslam E and Edmunds R, 'Victim Participation, Politics and the Construction of Victims at the International Criminal Court: Reflections on Proceedings in Banda and Jerbo' (2014) 14 Melbourne Journal of International Law 727
Haslam E and Edmunds R, 'Whose Number is it Anyway? Common Legal Representation, Consultations and the "Statistical Victim"' (2017) 15(5) *Journal of International Criminal Justice* 931
Hayden S, 'Lukodi massacre: "They should pay us because we lost so many people"' *The Irish Times* (5 February 2021) https://www.irishtimes.com/news/world/africa/lukodi-massacre-they-should-pay-us-because-we-lost-so-many-people-1.4477432 (accessed 12 January 2022)
Hellman M, 'Challenges and limitations of outreach' in de Vos C, Kendall S, and Stahn C (eds), *Contested Justice: The Politics and Practice of International Criminal Court Interventions* (CUP 2015) 251
Hill Collins P, *Black Feminist Thought Knowledge, Consciousness, and the Politics of Empowerment* (2nd edn, Routledge 2000)
Hirst M and Sahyouni S, 'Effective legal representation for participating victims: principles, challenges and some solutions' in Jasini R and Townsend G, *Advancing the Impact of Victim Participation at the International Criminal Court: Bridging the Gap Between Research and Practice* (ESRC, OUP 2020) https://www.law.ox.ac.uk/sites/files/oxlaw/iccba_-_oxford_publication_30_november_2020_.pdf (accessed 11 March 2022)
Holá B and Van Wijk J, 'Life after Conviction at International Criminal Tribunals: An Empirical Overview' (2014) 12(1) JICJ 109
Hopwood J, 'An inherited animus to communal land: the mechanisms of coloniality in land reform agendas in Acholiland, Northern Uganda' (2021) 14(1) Critical African Studies 38
Hooks b, 'Homeplace: A site of resistance' in bell hooks, *Yearning: Race, Gender, and Cultural Politics* (South End Press 1990)
Houge AB and Lohne K, 'End Impunity! Reducing Conflict-Related Sexual Violence to a Problem of Law' (2017) 51 Law & Society Review 755
Hoven E, 'Civil Party Participation in Trials of Mass Crimes: A Qualitative Study at the Extraordinary Chambers in the Courts of Cambodia' (2014) 12 JICJ 81
Hoyle C and Young R (eds), *New Visions of Crime Victims* (Hart Publishing 2004)
Hoyle C, Bosworth M and Dempsey M, 'Labelling the Victims of Sex Trafficking: Exploring the Borderland between Rhetoric and Reality' (2011) 20 Social & Legal Studies 313

Hoyle C, 'Can international justice be restorative justice? The role of reparations' in Palmer N, Clark P, and Granville D (eds), *Critical Perspectives in Transitional Justice* (Intersentia 2012) 189

Hoyle C and Ullrich L, 'New Court, New Justice? The Evolution of 'Justice for Victims' at Domestic Courts and at the International Criminal Court' (2014) 12(4) JICJ 681

Human Rights Center, UC Berkeley School of Law, 'The Victims' Court?: A Study of 622 Victim Participants at the International Criminal Court' (2015) https://humanrights.berkeley.edu/sites/default/files/publications/vp_report_2015_full_rev_b-4.pdf (accessed 9 March 2022)

Human Rights Watch, 'The Lack of Accountability' (2005) http://www.hrw.org/reports/2005/uganda0905/6.htm (accessed 16 April 2023)

Human Rights Watch, 'Courting History: The Landmark International Criminal Court's First Years' (2008) 200 https://www.hrw.org/reports/2008/icc0708/icc0708web.pdf (accessed 29 November 2021)

Human Rights Watch, 'Who will stand for us?: Victims' Legal Representation at the ICC in the Ongwen Case and Beyond' (2017) https://www.hrw.org/sites/default/files/report_pdf/ijongwen0817_web.pdf (accessed 31 October 2021)

Human Rights Watch, 'First ICC Trial on Darfur Crimes: Ali Mohammed Ali, Known as Ali Kosheib or Kushayb, Janjaweed Leader Questions and Answers' (22 March 2022) https://www.hrw.org/news/2022/03/29/first-icc-trial-darfur-crimes-ali-mohammed-ali-known-ali-kosheib-or-kushayb (accessed 12 December 2022)

Human Rights Watch, 'Kenya: ICC Defendant Found Dead Tried on Alleged Witness Tampering in Case Involving Kenyan President Ruto' (2 November 2022) https://www.hrw.org/news/2022/11/02/kenya-icc-defendant-found-dead (accessed 11 March 2023)

Human Rights Watch, 'Uganda's Parliament Threatens to Criminalize Homosexuality Protect, Don't Punish Vulnerable Minorities' (6 March 2023) https://www.hrw.org/news/2023/03/06/ugandas-parliament-threatens-criminalize-homosexuality (accessed 30 March 2023)

Hunter R, 'Critical Legal Studies and Marx's Critique: A Reappraisal' (2021) 31(2) Yale Journal of Law & the Humanities 389

Hurd I, 'Legitimacy and Authority in International Politics' (1999) 53(2) International Organization 379

International Center for Research on Women, 'External Evaluation of the Trust Fund for Victims Programmes in Northern Uganda and the Democratic Republic of Congo: Towards a Perspective of Upcoming Interventions' (2013) https://www.icrw.org/wp-content/uploads/2016/10/ICRW-TFV--Evaluation-Report.pdf (accessed 4 March 2022)

ICC, 'Access to justice: watching the ICC Ongwen trial' https://www.icc-cpi.int/get-involved/pages/aj-story/from-courtroom-to-communities (accessed 21 April 2022)

ICC, 'Cases' https://www.icc-cpi.int/Pages/cases.aspx (accessed 29 March 2022)

ICC, *Chambers Practice Manual* (5th edn, 2021)

ICC, 'Code of Conduct for Intermediaries' (March 2014) https://www.icc-cpi.int/sites/default/files/CCI-Eng.pdf (accessed 17 December 2022)

ICC, 'Guidelines Governing the Relations between the Court and Intermediaries for the Organs and Units of the Court and Counsel working with intermediaries' (March 2014) https://www.icc-cpi.int/iccdocs/lt/GRCI-eng.pdf (accessed 16 November 2021)

ICC, 'ICC marks opening of the Judicial Year 2022' https://www.youtube.com/watch?v=lyTRSzYhUk4 (accessed 4 December 2022)

ICC, 'ICC Outreach: Building bonds every day' https://www.icc-cpi.int/sites/default/files/Publications/outreachENG.pdf (accessed 22 April 2022)

ICC, 'Independent Expert Review of the International Criminal Court and the Rome Statute System: Final Report' (30 September 2020)

ICC, 'Integrated Strategy for External Relations, Public Information and Outreach' http://www.icc-cpi.int/NR/rdonlyres/425E80BA-1EBC-4423-85C6-D4F2B93C7506/185049/ICCPIDSWBOR0307070402_IS_En.pdf (accessed 10 April 2023)

ICC, 'Interacting with Communities' (2014) https://iccforum.com/media/background/outreach/2014-07-08_Interacting_with_Communities-ICC-PIDS.pdf (accessed 16 February 2022)

ICC, 'Interacting with communities affected by crime' https://www.icc-cpi.int/about/interacting-with-communities (accessed 28 October 2022)

ICC, 'Understanding the International Criminal Court' https://www.icc-cpi.int/resource-library/documents/uicceng.pdf (accessed 4 March 2022)

ICC, 'Humanity against Crimes' https://www.icc-cpi.int/humanity-against-crimes (accessed 4 March 2022)

ICC, 'Justice Matters' https://www.icc-cpi.int/get-involved (accessed 4 March 2022)

ICC, 'Justice at Work' https://www.icc-cpi.int/get-involved/justice-at-work (accessed 10 April 2023)

ICC, 'Making justice happen: Stories from ICC staff' https://www.icc-cpi.int/get-involved/staff-stories (accessed 21 January 2032)

ICC, 'Ongwen case: summary of the verdict' (4 February 2021)

ICC, 'Outreach Report' (2010) https://www.icc-cpi.int/iccdocs/PIDS/publications/OUR2010Eng.pdf (accessed 4 March 2022)

ICC, Press Release, 'Following Mr Bemba's acquittal, Trust Fund for Victims at the ICC decides to accelerate launch of assistance programme in Central African Republic' (13 June 2018) https://www.icc-cpi.int/news/following-mr-bembas-acquittal-trust-fund-victims-icc-decides-accelerate-launch-assistance (accessed 27 November 2022)

ICC, Press Release, 'The Embassy of Ireland and the Trust Fund for Victims conclude a joint monitoring visit to northern Uganda between 13–17 September 2022' https://www.icc-cpi.int/news/embassy-ireland-and-trust-fund-victims-conclude-joint-monitoring-visit-northern-uganda-between (accessed 30 September 2022)

ICC, Press Release, 'ICC President and Acting Executive Director of the Trust Fund for Victims visit Central African Republic to witness Court's work on the ground' (28 November 2022) https://www.icc-cpi.int/news/icc-president-and-act

ing-executive-director-trust-fund-victims-visit-central-african-republic (accessed 9 December 2022)

ICC, Press Release, 'Danish Ambassador and ICC Registrar Launch "Access To Justice" Project in Uganda and mark International Criminal Justice Day' (17 July 2017) https://www.icc-cpi.int/news/danish-ambassador-and-icc-registrar-launch-access-justice-project-uganda-and-mark (accessed 9 December 2022)

ICC, Press Release, 'ICC judges in Ongwen case visit northern Uganda' (11 June 2018) https://www.icc-cpi.int/news/icc-judges-ongwen-case-visit-northern-uganda (accessed 3 December 2022)

ICC, Press Release, 'Statement of the Prosecutor of the International Criminal Court, Karim A.A. Khan KC: Request to hold hearing on confirmation of charges against Joseph Kony in his absence' (24 November 2022) https://www.icc-cpi.int/news/statement-prosecutor-international-criminal-court-karim-aa-khan-kc-request-hold-hearing accessed 26 November 2022

ICC, Press Release, 'Trust Fund for Victims calls for contributions to provide reparations to victims of conflict-related sexual violence' (13 March 2023) https://www.icc-cpi.int/news/trust-fund-victims-calls-contributions-provide-reparations-victims-conflict-related-sexual accessed 19 March 2023

ICC, 'ICC President's statement on the Court's 20th anniversary' https://www.youtube.com/watch?v=KyZhibBjn5U (accessed 2 August 2022)

ICC, 'Promoting Access to Justice' https://www.icc-cpi.int/get-involved/access-to-justice (accessed 21 April 2022)

ICC, 'Prosecutor Karim Khan's speech for the opening of the judicial year 2022' https://www.youtube.com/watch?v=lyTRSzYhUk4 (accessed 26 November 2022)

ICC, 'Registry Strategic Plan 2023–2025' https://www.icc-cpi.int/sites/default/files/2023-08/2023-strategic-plan-registry-v.2.pdf (accessed 20 February 2024)

ICC, 'Regulations of the Court' (2018) ICC-BD/01-05-16

ICC, 'Regulations of the Registry' (2018) ICC-BD/03-03-13

ICC, 'Republic of the Philippines' https://www.icc-cpi.int/philippines#:~:text=While%20the%20Philippines'%20withdrawal%20from,and%20including%2016%20March%202019 (accessed 30 September 2022)

ICC, 'Report of the Court on the Public Information Strategy 2011–2013' (22 November 2010) ICC-ASP/9/29

ICC, 'Report of the Bureau on Victims and Affected Communities and the Trust Fund for Victims and Reparations' (23 October 2012) ICC-ASP/11/32

ICC, 'Report to the Assembly of States Parties on the projects and the activities of the Board of Directors of the Trust Fund for Victims for the period 1 July 2017 to 30 June 2018' (23 July 2018) ICC-ASP/17/14

ICC, 'Report on activities and programme performance of the International Criminal Court for the year 2020' (2021) ICC-ASP/20/7

ICC, 'Proposed Programme Budget for 2023 of the International Criminal Court: Executive Summary' Assembly of States Parties 21 July 2022, ICC-ASP/21/INF.2

ICC, Rome Statute https://www.icc-cpi.int/sites/default/files/RS-Eng.pdf (accessed 11 April 2023)

ICC, 'Rome Statute: 25 years' https://www.youtube.com/watch?v=URKsOqo0GYE (accessed 10 August 2023)

ICC, Rules of Procedure and Evidence https://www.icc-cpi.int/sites/default/files/RulesProcedureEvidenceEng.pdf accessed 11 April 2023

ICC, 'Second Report of the Court on the financial implications of the draft Guidelines governing the relations between the Court and Intermediaries' Assembly of States Parties (30 October 2013) ICC-ASP/12/53

ICC, 'Strategic Plan for Outreach of the International Criminal Court' (2006) ICC-ASP/5/12 https://www.icc-cpi.int/sites/default/files/ICCASP512_English1.pdf (accessed 10 April 2023)

ICC, 'Strategic Plan 2019–2021' (2019) https://www.icc-cpi.int/sites/default/files/itemsDocuments/20190717-icc-strategic-plan-eng.pdf (accessed 17 December 2022)

ICC, 'Swearing-in ceremony: Speech of new ICC Prosecutor Karim Asad Ahmad Khan QC, 16 June 2021' https://www.youtube.com/watch?v=tDldr2ma1S0 (accessed 2 August 2022)

ICC, 'The speech of the Registrar on the launching of the 4th Outreach Report' New York (7 December 2010) https://www.icc-cpi.int/sites/default/files/NR/rdonlyres/F3BAEC29-4029-4829-8637-3A2314D59F36/0/RegSpeech.pdf (accessed 22 April 2022)

ICC, '30 billboards in #CentralAfricanRepublic announce the #ICC #Said trial opening on 26/9' https://twitter.com/IntlCrimCourt/status/1572585259564421122 (accessed 12 August 2023)

ICC, 'The Trauma Expert' https://www.icc-cpi.int/get-involved/justice-at-work/story/the-trauma-expert accessed 10 April 2023

ICC, 'Trauma, healing and hope in northern Uganda' https://www.icc-cpi.int/get-involved/pages/aj-story/trauma-healing-and-hope-in-northern-uganda (accessed 21 April 2022)

ICC, 'Ugandans say: "This is the writing of history . . . about us"' https://www.icc-cpi.int/get-involved/pages/aj-story/this-is-the-writing-of-history accessed 24 April 2022

ICC, 'Victims' https://www.icc-cpi.int/about/victims (accessed 31 March 2023)

ICC, 'Victims' participation before the International Criminal Court' *YouTube* (23 April 2013) https://www.youtube.com/watch?v=chymGL8teX4 (accessed 21 April 2022)

ICC, 'Questions and Answers: The Court's Engagement with Intermediaries' https://www.icc-cpi.int/iccdocs/lt/QA-ICC-intermediariesEng.pdf (accessed 27 November 2021)

ICC Weekly Update #135 (9 July 2012) https://www.icc-cpi.int/sites/default/files/NR/rdonlyres/E6D289BC-9672-4304-BC32-79BD024D1E07/284716/ED135_ENG.pdf accessed 28 January 2023

ICC Forum, 'Africa question: Is the International Criminal Court (ICC) targeting Africa inappropriately?' https://iccforum.com/africa (accessed 30 September 2022)

ICCBA and Oxford Workshop on Victim Participation (31 May–1 June 2018) https://www.law.ox.ac.uk/centres-institutes/centre-criminology/advancing-impact-victim-participation-international-criminal (accessed 31 March 2023)
ICC Twitter Account, 'Chair of @TFV_FPV Board of Directors at #ASP21' (5 December 2022) https://twitter.com/IntlCrimCourt/status/1599756626373726208 (accessed 5 December 2022)
ICC Twitter account (5 December 2022) https://twitter.com/IntlCrimCourt/status/1599754055341199361 (accessed 9 December 2022)
ICC Women, 'ICC Judges uphold conviction of Lubanga: *The Prosecutor v. Thomas Lubanga Dyilo*' http://www.iccwomen.org/documents/First-conviction-and-sentence-upheld-on-appeal-at-the-ICC-REVISED-April-2015.pdf (accessed 31 March 2023)
Ince OU, *Colonial Capitalism and the Dilemmas of Liberalism* (OUP 2018)
Institute for War & Peace Reporting, 'ICC Intermediaries Allegedly Concocted Evidence' (12 February 2010) https://iwpr.net/global-voices/icc-intermediaries-allegedly-concocted-evidence (accessed 10 April 2023)
International Justice Monitor, 'Lubanga Witness Says He Was Paid US$200 To Tell Lies' (8 February 2010) https://www.ijmonitor.org/2010/02/lubanga-witness-says-he-was-paid-us200-to-tell-lies/ (accessed 17 December 2022)
International Refugee Rights Initiative and Open Society Initiative, 'Commentary on the ICC Draft Guidelines on Intermediaries'(18 August 2011) https://www.justiceinitiative.org/uploads/020e3651-cbf2-4fe7-8ab4-a9ef4e64a5ed/icc-intermediaries-commentary-20110818.pdf (accessed 17 December 2022)
IRIN, 'Uganda: Land Disputes threaten Northern Peace' (19 April 2012) https://www.refworld.org/docid/4f990e032.html (accessed 16 April 2023)
Jaffe S and Bhattacharya T, 'Social Reproduction and the Pandemic, with Tithi Bhattacharya' *Dissent* (2 April 2020) https://www.dissentmagazine.org/online_articles/social-reproduction-and-the-pandemic-with-tithi-bhattacharya (accessed 17 June 2022)
Jameson F, *The Political Unconscious: Narrative as a Socially Symbolic Act* (Cornell UP 1981)
Jasini R and Townsend G, *Advancing the Impact of Victim Participation at the International Criminal Court: Bridging the Gap Between Research and Practice* (ESRC, OUP 2020) https://www.law.ox.ac.uk/sites/files/oxlaw/iccba_-_oxford_publication_30_november_2020_.pdf (accessed 11 March 2022)
Jeßberger F and Geneuss J, 'Down the Drain or Down to Earth? International Criminal Justice under Pressure' (2013) 11 JICJ 501
Jeßberger F and Geneuss J (eds), *Why Punish Perpetrators of Mass Atrocities?* (CUP 2020)
Jeßberger F, Steinl L, and Mehta K (eds), *International Criminal Law: A Counter-Hegemonic Project?* (Springer 2023)
Jiwa J, 'Trial of LRA commander Ongwen still divides northern Uganda' *The New Humanitarian* (30 June 2021) https://www.thenewhumanitarian.org/news-feature/2021/6/30/trial-of-LRA-commander-ongwen-still-divides-northern-uganda (accessed 8 August 2023)

Jones B and Brudholm T, 'Introduction: Rethinking Resistance to Transitional Justice' (2016) 2 Conflict and Society 68

Jorda C and de Hemptinne J, 'The status and role of the victim' in Cassese A, Gaeta P, and Jones J (eds), *The Rome Statute of the International Criminal Court: A Commentary* (OUP 2002)

Jordash W, 'The Practice of "Witness Proofing" in International Criminal Tribunals: Why the International Criminal Court Should Prohibit the Practice' (2009) 22(3) Leiden Journal of International Law 501

Jorgensen NHB, 'Review of Carsten Stahn, *A Critical Introduction to International Criminal Law* (CUP 2019)' (2021) 84 (6) The Modern Law Review 1447

Jouet M, 'Reconciling the Conflicting Rights of Victims and Defendants at the International Criminal Court' (2007) 26 Saint Louis University Public Law Review 249

Jung CG and Jaffé A, *Memories, Dreams, Reflections* (Vantage Books 1989)

Justice Hub, 'My Justice: Mariana Pena' (27 February 2015) https://justicehub.org/article/mariana-pena-of-osji-bridging-the-gap-between-the-courts-and-the-victims/ (accessed 10 April 2022)

Justice and Reconciliation Project, 'Gender and Generation in Acholi Traditional Justice Mechanisms' (2012) http://justiceandreconciliation.com/wp-content/uploads/2012/11/Gender-and-Generations-in-Acholi-Traditional-Mechanisms-Web.pdf (accessed 16 April 2023)

Justice and Reconciliation Project, 'Establishing the Extent of SGBV Revictimisation among Female Survivors of Conflict SGBV in Northern Uganda' (2014) http://justiceandreconciliation.com/wp-content/uploads/2014/11/SGBV-Baseline-Report-Summary-WEB.pdf (accessed 16 April 2023)

Justice and Reconciliation Project (JRP) and the University of British Columbia, 'After the Verdict: Dominic Ongwen & the Many Sides of Justice' (7 May 2021) https://sppga.ubc.ca/events/event/after-the-verdict-dominic-ongwen-the-many-sides-of-justice/ (accessed 14 June 2022)

Kafka F, 'Before the Law' (Franz Kafka Online, Ian Johnston tr) https://www.kafka-online.info/before-the-law.html (accessed 4 January 2024)

Kafka F, *The Trial* (David Wyllie tr, Dover Publications 2012)

Kamara MM, 'An insider look at outreach efforts in bringing the proceedings closer to the victims and affected populations in Northern Uganda' *Justice in Conflict* (3 February 2021) https://justiceinconflict.org/2021/02/03/an-insider-look-at-outreach-efforts-in-bringing-the-proceedings-closer-to-the-victims-and-affected-populations-in-northern-uganda/ (accessed 4 March 2022)

Kapur R, 'The Tragedy of Victimization Rhetoric: Resurrecting the "Native" Subject in International/Post-Colonial Feminist Legal Politics' (2002) 15 Harvard Human Rights Journal 1

Kapur R, *Erotic Justice: Law and the New Politics of Postcolonialism* (Routledge 2005)

Kapur R, '"The First Feminist War in All of History": Epistemic Shifts and Relinquishing the Mission to Rescue the "Other Woman"' (2022) 116 AJIL Unbound 270

Karim L, *Microfinance and its Discontents: Women in Debt in Bangladesh* (University of Minnesota Press 2011)

Karstedt S, 'From Absence to Presence, From Silence to Voice: Victims in International and Transitional Justice Since the Nuremberg Trials' (2010) 17(1) International Review of Victimology 9

Kasande SK, 'Beyond the Ongwen Verdict: Justice for Government Atrocities in Uganda' *Justice in Conflict* (9 February 2021) https://justiceinconflict.org/2021/02/09/beyond-the-ongwen-verdict-justice-for-government-atrocities-in-uganda/ (accessed 30 July 2022)

Kashaka U, 'Everybody should wake up now, says Museveni' *New Vision* (20 July 2019) https://www.newvision.co.ug/new_vision/news/1503892/wake-museveni (accessed 29 November 2021)

Kaul HP, 'Victims' rights and peace' in Bonacker T and Safferling C (eds), *Victims of International Crimes: An Interdisciplinary Discourse* (TMC Asser Press 2013)

Kearon T and Godfrey BS, 'Setting the scene: a question of history' in Walklate S (ed), *Handbook of Victims and Victimology* (Routledge 2007)

Kelsall T, *Culture under Cross-Examination: International Justice and the Special Court for Sierra Leone* (CUP 2009)

Kendall S and Sarah Nouwen, 'Representational Practices at the International Criminal Court: The Gap between Juridified and Abstract Victimhood' (2014) 76 Law and Contemporary Problems 235

Kendall S, 'UhuRuto' and Other Leviathans: The International Criminal Court and the Kenyan Political Order' (2014) 7(3) African Journal of Legal Studies 399

Kendall S, 'Beyond the restorative turn: The limits of legal humanitarianism' in de Vos C, Kendall S, and Stahn C (eds), *Contested Justice: The Politics and Practice of International Criminal Court Interventions* (CUP 2015) 352

Kendall S, 'Commodifying Global Justice: Economies of Accountability at the International Criminal Court' (2015) 13 Journal of International Criminal Justice 113

Kendall S and Nouwen SMH, 'International criminal justice and humanitarianism' in Heller K and others (eds), *The Oxford Handbook of International Criminal Law* (OUP 2020) 719

Kersten M, 'Whither the aspirational ICC, Welcome the "practical" court?' *EJIL:Talk!* (22 May 2019) https://www.ejiltalk.org/whither-the-aspirational-icc-welcome-the-practical-court/ (accessed 1 April 2023)

Kim ME, 'Transformative justice and restorative justice: Gender-based violence and alternative visions of justice in the United States' (2021) 27(2) International Review of Victimology 162

Kim ME, 'From carceral feminism to transformative justice: Women-of-color feminism and alternatives to incarceration' (2018) 27(3) Journal of Ethnic & Cultural Diversity in Social Work 219

Killean R, *Victims, Atrocity and International Criminal Justice: Lessons from Cambodia* (Routledge 2018)

Killean R, 'From ecocide to eco-sensitivity: 'greening' reparations at the International Criminal Court' (2021) 25(2) The International Journal of Human Rights 323

Kirabira TR, 'NGOs and the Legitimacy of International Criminal Justice: The Case of Uganda' in Florian Jeßberger F, Steinl L, and Mehta K (eds), *International Criminal Law: A Counter-Hegemonic Project?* (TMC Asser Press 2023) 153

Kiyani A, Reynolds J, and Xavier S, 'Foreword' (2016) 14 (4) JICJ 915

Klarin M, 'The Impact of the ICTY Trials on Public Opinion in the Former Yugoslavia' (2009) 7 JICJ 89

Knox R, 'Strategy and Tactics' (2010) 21 Finnish Yearbook of International Law 193

Knox R, 'Valuing race? Stretched Marxism and the logic of imperialism' (2016) 4(1) London Review of International Law 81

Knox R, 'Marxist approaches to international law' in Anne Orford and Florian Hoffman (eds), *The Oxford Handbook of the Theory of International Law* (OUP 2018)

Knox R, 'Haiti at the League of Nations: Racialisation, Accumulation and Representation' (2020) 21(2) Melbourne Journal of International Law 245

Knox R, 'Taking Capital's Laws of Motion Seriously: Marxism, Law and Capitalism' (2023) https://www.youtube.com/watch?v=3CtlnO1pvhk&t=3156s (accessed 13 March 2023)

Knox R, 'International Law, Race, and Capitalism: A Marxist Perspective' (2023) 117 AJIL Unbound 55

Kelley RDG, 'Foreword: Why black Marxism, why now?' in Robinson CJ, *Black Marxism: The Making of the Black Radical Tradition* (Penguin Classics 2021)

Koller DS, 'The Faith of the International Criminal Lawyer' (2008) 40 International Law and Politics 1019

Kopelman ES, 'Ideology and International Law: The Dissent of the Indian Justice at the Tokyo War Crimes Trial' (1991) 23 New York University Journal of International Law and Politics 373

Koskenniemi M, *From Apology to Utopia: The Structure of International Legal Argument* (CUP 2006)

Koskenniemi M, 'Foreword' in Tallgren I and Skouteris T (eds), *The New Histories of International Criminal Law: Retrials* (OUP 2019)

Kotecha B, 'The International Criminal Court's Selectivity and Procedural Justice' (2020) 18(1) Journal of International Criminal Justice 107

Krever T, 'International Criminal Law: An Ideology Critique' (2013) 26 Leiden Journal of International Law 701

Kristjánsdóttir E, 'International mass claims processes and the ICC Trust Fund For Victims' in Ferstman C, Goetz M, and Stephens A (eds), *Reparations for Victims of Genocide, War Crimes and Crimes Against Humanity: Systems in Place and Systems in the Making* (Martinus Nijhoff 2009) 167

Kundani A, 'What is racial capitalism?' (23 October 2020) https://www.kundnani.org/what-is-racial-capitalism/ (accessed 1 December 2021)

Labeja P, 'Amuru nude protests undermine women dignity: Acholi Chief' *Uganda Radio Network* (22 April 2015) https://ugandaradionetwork.com/story/amuru-nude-protests-undermine-women-dignity-acholi-chief- (accessed 30 April 2021)

Labeja R, 'Displaced Apaa residents wait for answers in UN' *Uganda Radio Network* (11 August 2018) https://ugandaradionetwork.com/story/a-month-later-displaced-apaa-residents-waits-for-answers-in-un-compound (accessed 18 June 2022)

Labuda, P, *International Criminal Tribunals and Domestic Accountability: In the Court's Shadow* (OUP 2023)

Laing T and Weschler S, 'Displacement as resistance in Northern Uganda: How 234 rural farmers occupied a UN compound to defend their land' https://blogs.lse.ac.uk/africaatlse/2018/10/23/displacement-as-resistance-in-northern-uganda-how-234-rural-farmers-occupied-a-un-compound-to-defend-their-land/ (accessed 18 June 2022)

Laing T and Wilmot P, 'Ugandan farmers emerge victorious after month long occupation of UN office' *Waging Nonviolence: People Powered News & Analysis* (28 August 2018) https://wagingnonviolence.org/2018/08/uganda-apaa-farmers-occupy-united-nations-ohchr/ (accessed 11 January 2022)

Lambourne W, 'Transitional Justice and Peacebuilding after Mass Violence' (2009) 3 The International Journal of Transitional Justice 28

Lamble S, 'Practising Everyday Abolition' (2021) https://abolitionistfutures.com/latest-news/practising-everyday-abolition (accessed 23 November 2022)

Laruni E, 'From the Village to Entebbe: The Acholi of Northern Uganda and the Politics of Identity, 1950–1985' PhD thesis, University of Exeter (2014) https://core.ac.uk/reader/43093940 (accessed 13 August 2023)

Lazzarato M, *The Making of the Indebted Man* (Semiotext(e) 2012)

Leader K, 'The trial's the thing: Performance and legitimacy in international criminal trials' (2020) 24(2) Theoretical Criminology 241

Legal Representatives for Darfur Victims Division, 'Legal Representatives for Darfur Victims, Attorneys Raymond M. Brown and Wanda M. Akin, Urge United Nations Security Council Not To Defer Indictment of Omar Hassan Ahmad al-Bashir' https://brownakin.com/wpbrownakin/wp-content/themes/brownakin/pdf/IJP-DVP_Press_Release_Bashir_Indictment.pdf (accessed 31 March 2023)

Lekalake R and Buchanan-Clarke S, 'Support for the International Criminal Court in Africa Evidence from Kenya' (2015) 23 Afrobarometer Policy Paper https://www.afrobarometer.org/wp-content/uploads/migrated/files/publications/Policy papers/ab_r6_policypaperno23_kenya_anti_corruption.pdf (accessed 1 April 2023)

Lemay-Hébert N and Freedman R, 'Appraising the Socio-Economic Turn in Reparations: Transitional Justice for Cholera Victims in Haiti' (2021) 15(3) International Journal of Transitional Justice 533

Letschert R, Haveman R, De Brouwer AM, and Pemberton A (eds), *Victimological Approaches to International Crimes: Africa* (Intersentia 2011)

Levi-Strauss C, *Tristes Tropiques* (Penguin Classics 2011)

Lexico Dictionary https://www.lexico.com/definition/comprador (accessed 27 November 2021)

Linehan S, 'International Criminal Courts: Progress Made, Progress Needed' *iLawyer* (1 November 2014) http://ilawyerblog.com/international-criminal-courts-progress-made-progress-needed/ (accessed 30 March 2022)

Loader I and Sparks R, 'Ideologies and crime: political ideas and the dynamics of crime control' (2016) 17(3) Global Crime 314

Lockard C, 'Unhappy confessions: The temptation of admitting to white privilege' (2016) 2(2) Feminist Philosophy Quarterly 1

Lohne K, *Advocates of Humanity: Human Rights NGOs in International Criminal Justice* (OUP 2019)

Los Angeles Review of Books, 'Critical Intimacy: An Interview with Gayatri Chakravorty Spivak' (29 June 2016) https://www.lareviewofbooks.org/article/critical-intimacy-interview-gayatri-chakravorty-spivak/ (accessed 15 July 2022)

Lugano G, 'Counter-Shaming the International Criminal Court's Intervention as Neocolonial: Lessons from Kenya' (2017) 11 International Journal of Transitional Justice 9

López R, 'Black Guilt, White Guilt at the International Criminal Court' in Matiangai Sirleaf (ed), *Race and National Security* (OUP 2023)

Lostal M, 'The Ntaganda Reparations Order: a marked step towards a victims-centred reparations legal framework at the ICC' *EJIL:Talk!* (24 May 2021) https://www.ejiltalk.org/the-ntaganda-reparations-order-a-marked-step-towards-a-victim-centred-reparations-legal-framework-at-the-icc/ (accessed 22 January 2023)

Lostal M, 'Implementing Reparations in the Al Mahdi Case: A Story of Monumental Challenges in Timbuktu' (2021) 19(4) Journal of International Criminal Justice 831

Luxemburg R, *The Accumulation of Capital* (1913) https://www.marxists.org/archive/luxemburg/1913/accumulation-capital/ch31.htm (accessed 1 December 2021)

Luban D, 'After the Honeymoon: Reflections on the Current State of International Criminal Justice' (2013) 11 JICJ 505

Lukács G, *History and Class Consciousness: Studies in Marxist Dialectics* (The Merlin Press 2010)

Lynch G, 'Electing the 'alliance of the accused': the success of the Jubilee Alliance in Kenya's Rift Valley' (2014) 8(1) Journal of Eastern African Studies 93

Lyons B, 'The Intermediary Industry and the ICC' *INTLAWGRRLS* (6 June 2014) https://ilg2.org/2014/06/06/the-intermediary-industry-and-the-icc/ (accessed 17 December 2022)

Macaulay S, 'Non-Contractual Relations in Business: A Preliminary Study' (1963) 28(1) American Sociological Review 55

Macherey P, 'Figures of interpellation in Althusser and Fanon' (2012) 173(1) Radical Philosophy 9

Macdonald A and Allen T, 'Post-Conflict Traditional Justice: A Critical Overview' (2013) 3 Justice and Security Research Programme Working Paper https://assets.publishing.service.gov.uk/media/57a08a34ed915d3cfd000642/JSRP3-AllenMacdonald.pdf (accessed 16 April 2023)

Macdonald A and Porter H, 'The Trial of Thomas Kwoyelo: Opportunity or Spectre? Reflections from the ground on the first LRA prosecution' (2016) 86 Africa 698

Madlingozi T, 'On Transitional Justice Entrepreneurs and the Production of Victims' (2010) 2(2) Journal of Human Rights Practice 208

Makinda SM, 'Kenya, Uhuru Kenyatta and politicising the International Criminal Court' *The Conversation* (30 May 2013) https://theconversation.com/kenya-uhuru-kenyatta-and-politicising-the-international-criminal-court-14583 (accessed 1 April 2023)

Maliti T, 'Away from Courtroom, Ongwen Plays Football, Does Light Cleaning at Detention Center' *International Justice Monitor* (12 August 2019) https://www.ijmonitor.org/2019/08/away-from-courtroom-ongwen-plays-football-does-light-cleaning-at-detention-center/ (accessed 16 July 2022)

Mamdani M, 'Beyond Nuremberg: The Historical Significance of the Post-apartheid Transition in South Africa' (2015) 43(1) Politics & Society 61

Mamdani M, *Citizen and Subject: Contemporary Africa and the Legacy of Late Colonialism* (2nd edn, Princeton UP 2018)

Mani R, 'Dilemmas of Expanding Transitional Justice, or Forging the Nexus between Transitional Justice and Development' (2008) 2(3) International Journal of Transitional Justice 253

Manikis M, 'Conceptualising the Victim in England and Wales and the United States within a Spectrum of Public and Private Interests' (2021) 41(1) Oxford Journal of Legal Studies 219

Manji A, 'Commodifying Land, Fetishising Law: Women's Struggles to Claim Land Rights in Uganda' (2003) 19 Australian Feminist Law Journal 81

Manji A, *The Struggle for Land & Justice in Kenya* (Boydell & Brewer 2020)

Manjoo R, 'Introduction: reflections on the concept and implementation of transformative reparations' (2017) 21(9) The International Journal of Human Rights 1193

Manoba JA and Cox F, 'Victims' participation in the Ongwen case: Strengths, weaknesses and lessons learned' in FIDH, 'Victims at the Center of Justice: From 1998 to 2018: Reflections on the Promises and the Reality of Victim Participation at the ICC' (2018) https://www.fidh.org/IMG/pdf/droitsdesvictimes730a_final.pdf (accessed 10 December 2022) 48

Marcus GE, 'Ethnography in/of the World System: The Emergence of Multi-Sited Ethnography' (1995) 24 Annual Review of Anthropology 95

Marks S, 'Big Brother Is Bleeping Us: With the Message that Ideology Doesn't Matter' (2001) 12(1) European Journal of International Law 109

Marks S, *The Riddle of All Constitutions: International Law, Democracy, and the Critique of Ideology* (OUP 2003)

Marks S, 'Human Rights and Root Causes' (2011) 74 The Modern Law Review 57

Martiniello G, 'Agrarian politics and land struggles in Northern Uganda' (2017) 52(3) Community Development Journal 405

Mathiesen T, *The Politics of Abolition Revisited* (Routledge 2015)

Marx K and Engels F, *The German Ideology* (Lawrence & Wishart 2007)

Marx K and Engels F, *The Communist Manifesto* (OUP 2008)

Marx K, *Capital Volume I: A Critique of Political Economy* (Penguin Books 1990)

Marx K, 'The Introduction to Contribution to the Critique of Hegel's Philosophy of Right' (1844) https://www.marxists.org/archive/marx/works/1844/df-jahrbucher/law-abs.htm (accessed 14 November 2021)

Marx K, *A Contribution to the Critique of Political Economy* Preface 1859 (Progress Publishers 1977) https://www.marxists.org/archive/marx/works/1859/critique-pol-economy/preface.htm (accessed 24 April 2023)
McAuliffe P and Schwöbel-Patel C, 'Disciplinary Matchmaking: Critics of International Criminal Law Meet Critics of Liberal Peacebuilding' (2018) 16(5) Journal of International Criminal Justice 985
McCarthy C, 'Victim Redress and International Criminal Justice: Competing Paradigms, or Compatible Forms of Justice?' (2012) 10 Journal of International Criminal Justice 351
McCarthy C, *Reparations and Victim Support in the International Criminal Court* (CUP 2012)
McEvoy K and McGregor L, *Transitional justice from Below: Grassroots Activism and the Struggle for Change* (Hart Publishing 2008)
McEvoy K and McConnachie K, 'Victims and Transitional Justice: Voice, Agency and Blame' (2013) 22(4) Social & Legal Studies 489
McEvoy K, 'Beyond Legalism: Towards a Thicker Understanding of Transitional Justice' (2007) 34 Journal of Law and Society 411
McGonigle Leyh B, *Procedural Justice? Victim Participation in International Criminal Proceedings* (Intersentia 2011)
McGonigle Leyh B, 'Victim-Oriented Measures at International Criminal Institutions: Participation and its Pitfalls' (2012) 12 International Criminal Law Review 375
McGonigle Leyh B and Fraser J, 'Transformative Reparations: Changing the Game Or More of the Same' (2019) 8(1) Cambridge International Law Journal 39
McKay F, 'Victim Participation in Proceedings before the International Criminal Court' (2008) 15 Human Rights Brief 2
Bak McKenna M, 'Feminist materialism and the laws of social reproduction' in O'Connell P and Özsu U (eds), *Research Handbook on Law and Marxism* (Edward Elgar Publishing 2021)
Mégret F, 'Three Dangers for the International Criminal Court: A Critical Look at a Consensual Project' (2001) 7 Finnish Yearbook of International Law 193
Mégret F, 'Justifying Compensation by the International Criminal Court's Victims Trust Fund: Lessons From Domestic Compensation Schemes' (2010–2011) 36 Brooklyn Journal of International Law 124
Mégret F, 'International Criminal Justice as a Juridical Field' (2016) 8 Champ pénal/Penal field 1
Meierhenrich J, 'Foreword: The Practices of the International Criminal Court' (2013) 76(3–4) Law and Contemporary Problems i
Meierhenrich J, 'The Practice of International Law: A Theoretical Analysis' (2014) 76 Law and Contemporary Problems 1
Meijers T and Glasius M, 'Trials as Messages of Justice: What Should Be Expected of International Criminal Courts?' (2016) 30(4) Ethics and International Affairs 429
Merry SE, 'Transnational Human Rights and Local Activism: Mapping the Middle' (2006) 108(1) American Anthropologist 38

Mezzadri A, 'On the value of social reproduction: Informal labour, the majority world and the need for inclusive theories and politics' (2019) 2.04 Radical Philosophy 33

Mezzadri A, 'A Value Theory of Inclusion: Informal Labour, the Homeworker, and the Social Reproduction of Value' (2021) 53(4) Antipode 1186

Mezzadri A, 'Social Reproduction and Pandemic Neoliberalism: Planetary Crises and the Reorganisation of Life, Work and Death' (2022) 29(3) Organization 379

Mezzadri A, Newman S and Stevano S, 'Feminist global political economies of work and social reproduction' (2022) 29(6) Review of International Political Economy 1783

Miéville C, *Between Equal Rights: A Marxist Theory of International Law* (Brill 2005)

Mies M, *The Lace Makers of Narsapur: Indian Housewives produce for the World Market* (Zed Press 1982)

Mies M, *Patriarchy and Accumulation on a World Scale: Women in the International Division of Labour* (Zed Books 1999)

Mignolo W, *The Darker Side of Western Modernity: Global Futures, Decolonial Options* (Duke UP 2011)

Miller Z, 'Effects of invisibility: In search of the 'economic' in transitional justice' (2008) 2(3) *International Journal of Transitional Justice* 266

Minha D, 'The Proposed Definition of the Crime of Ecocide: An Important Step Forward, but Can Our Planet Wait?' *EJIL:Talk!* (1 July 2021) https://www.ejiltalk.org/the-proposed-definition-of-the-crime-of-ecocide-an-important-step-forward-but can-our-planet-wait/ (accessed 14 November 2021)

Minow M, 'Do alternative justice mechanisms deserve recognition in international criminal law: Truth commissions, amnesties, and complementarity at the international criminal court' (2019) 60(1) Harvard International Law Journal 1

Moffett L, *Justice for Victims before the International Criminal Court* (Routledge 2014)

Moffett L, 'Elaborating Justice for Victims at the International Criminal Court: Beyond Rhetoric and The Hague' (2015) 13 Journal of International Criminal Justice 281

Moffett L, 'Meaningful and Effective? Considering Victims' Interests Through Participation at the International Criminal Court' (2015) 26 Criminal Law Forum 255

Moffett L, 'Reparations for victims at the International Criminal Court: a new way forward?' (2017) 21(9) The International Journal of Human Rights 1204

Moffett L, *Reparations and War: Finding Balance in Repairing the Past* (OUP 2022)

Moffett L and Sandoval C, 'Tilting at windmills: Reparations and the International Criminal Court' (2021) 34(3) Leiden Journal of International Law 749

Daily Monitor, 'Women undress before Migereko, Gen Aronda' (17 April 2015) https://www.monitor.co.ug/uganda/news/national/women-undress-before-migereko-gen-aronda-1607736 (accessed 30 March 2023)

Monitor, 'Nude protests: the Acholi signal of distress' (29 April 2015) https://www.monitor.co.ug/artsculture/Reviews/Nude-protests--the-Acholi-signal-of-distress/691232-2701176-tcu4yv/index.html (accessed 18 June 2022)

Moore SF, 'Law and Social Change: The Semi-Autonomous Social Field as an Appropriate Subject of Study' (1973) 7 Law & Society Review 719

Moosavi L, 'A Friendly Critique of "Asian Criminology" and "Southern Criminology" ' (2019) 59(2) The British Journal of Criminology 257

Morris R, *Stories of Transformative Justice* (Canadian Scholars Press 2000)

Moyn S, 'Of deserts and promised lands: The dream of global justice' *The Nation* (29 February 2012) https://www.thenation.com/article/deserts-and-promised-lands-dream-global-justice/ (accessed 23 August 2016)

Moyn S, *The Last Utopia: Human Rights in History* (Harvard UP 2010)

Mudukuti A, 'Gender imbalance at the ICC: The continued hegemonic entrenchment of male privilege' in Jeßberger F, Steinl L, and Mehta K (eds), *International Criminal Law: A Counter-Hegemonic Project?* (TMC Asser Press 2023)

Ndahinda FM, Mosley J, Palmer N, Clark P and Shenge S, 'Rwandan researchers are finally being centred in scholarship about their own country' *The Conversation* (25 May 2022) https://theconversation.com/rwandan-researchers-are-finally-being-centred-in-scholarship-about-their-own-country-183142 (accessed 3 December 2022)

Muttukumaru C, 'Reparations to victims' in Lee RS (ed), *The International Criminal Court: The Making of the Rome Statute: Issues, Negotiations, Results* (Kluwer Law International 1999)

Mutua M, 'Savages, Victims and Saviors: The Metaphor of Human Rights' (2001) 42 Harvard International Law Journal 201

Mutua M and Anghie A, 'What is TWAIL?' (2000) 94 Proceedings of the Annual Meeting (American Society of International Law) 31

Nader L, *Harmony Ideology: Justice and Control in a Zapotec Mountain Village* (Stanford UP 1990)

Naidu S and Ossome L, 'Social Reproduction and the Agrarian Question of Women's Labour in India' (2016) 5(1) Agrarian South: Journal of Political Economy 50

Nairobi Declaration on Women's and Girls' Right to a Remedy and Reparation (2007) http://www.fidh.org/IMG/pdf/NAIROBI_DECLARATIONeng.pdf (accessed 22 January 2023)

Namayengo F, van Ophem J and Antonides G, 'Women and microcredit in rural agrarian households of Uganda: Match or mismatch between lender and borrower?' (2016) 10(2–3) Applied Studies in Agribusiness and Commerce 77

Namayengo F, Antonides G, and Cecchi F, 'Microcredit and Food Security: Evidence from Rural Households in Uganda' (2018) 27(4) Journal of African Economies 457

Nanopoulos E, *The Juridification of Individual Sanctions and the Politics of EU Law* (Hart Publishing 2021)

Nanopoulos E and Ullrich L, 'Towards Marxist-Feminist approaches to international law' in Grossman N and others (eds), *Oxford Handbook on Women and International Law* (OUP forthcoming)

Nathan CN, 'Introductory remarks' in Ferstman C and Goetz M (eds), *Reparations for Victims of Genocide, War Crimes and Crimes against Humanity* (Nijhoff 2009)

National Planning Authority, 'Third National Development Plan (NDPIII) 2020/21: 2024/25' (July 2020) http://www.npa.go.ug/wp-content/uploads/2020/08/NDPIII-Finale_Compressed.pdf (accessed 24 December 2022)

NBS Television, 'Museveni's Wealth Creation Tour' (18 July 2019) https://www.facebook.com/nbstelevision/photos/president-museveni-ugand

ans-are-rich-look-at-all-of-you-youre-all-dressed-in-clo/2404837896273828/ (accessed 22 December 2022)

Neocleous M, 'International Law as Primitive Accumulation; Or, the Secret of Systematic Colonization' (2012) 23(4) EJIL 941

Nesiah V, 'The Ground beneath her Feet: "Third World" Feminisms' (2003) 4(3) Journal of International Women's Studies 30

Nesiah V, 'Local Ownership of Global Governance' (2016) 14(4) Journal of International Criminal Justice 985

Nesiah V, 'Indebted: The cruel optimism of leaning into empowerment' in Halley J, Kotiswaran P, Rebouché R, and Shamir H (eds), *Governance Feminism: Notes from the Field* (Minnesota UP 2019)

Ní Aoláin F, O'Rourke C, and Swaine A, 'Transforming Reparations for Conflict-Related Sexual Violence: Principles and Practice' (2015) 28 Harvard Human Rights Journal 97

Nichols L, *The International Criminal Court and the End of Impunity in Kenya* (Springer 2015)

Nistor AL, Merrylees A, and Holá B, 'Spellbound at the International Criminal Court: The intersection of spiritualism & international criminal law' in Fraser J and McGonigle Leyh B (eds), *Intersections of Law and Culture at the International Criminal Court* (Edward Elgar Publishing 2020)

Nocella AJ II, 'An Overview of the History and Theory of Transformative Justice' (2011) 6(1) Peace & Conflict Review 1

Nouwen S, *Complementarity in the Line of Fire: The Catalysing Effect of the International Criminal Court in Uganda and Sudan* (CUP 2013)

Nouwen S, '"*As You Set out for Ithaka*": Practical, Epistemological, Ethical, and Existential Questions about Socio-Legal Research in Conflict' (2014) 27 Leiden Journal of International Law 227

Nouwen S and Werner W, 'Monopolizing Global Justice: International Criminal Law as Challenge to Human Diversity' (2015) 13 JICJ 157

NTV Uganda, 'Women strip before ministers in protest over land' *YouTube* (17 April 2015) https://www.youtube.com/watch?v=F4DdYt-SnsA (accessed 30 March 2023)

NTV Uganda, 'The Naked Statement: Why is stripping in protest becoming common?' *YouTube* (20 May 2015) https://www.youtube.com/watch?v=Skpo6H_Oq0M accessed 26 August 2015)

Nyanzi S, 'Dismantling Reified African Culture through Localised Homosexualities in Uganda' (2013) 15(7–8) Culture, Health & Sexuality 952

Okafor OC and Ngwaba U, 'The International Criminal Court as a "Transitional Justice" Mechanism in Africa: Some Critical Reflections' (2015) 9(1) International Journal of Transitional Justice 90

Ochola II MB, 'Where is Justice in the case of Dominic Ongwen, who is being tried by the ICC in The Hague' (28 March 2016) (on file with the author)

O'Connor J, 'On the two contradictions of capitalism' (1991) 2(3) Capitalism Nature Socialism 107

Okello MC and Hovil L, 'Confronting the Reality of Gender-Based Violence in Northern Uganda' (2007) 1 IJTJ 433

Open Society Justice Initiative, 'Intermediaries and the International Criminal Court: A Role for the Assembly of States Parties' (2011) http://www.opensocietyfoundations.org/sites/default/files/intermediaries-20111212.pdf (accessed 10 April 2023)

Ossome L, 'Can the Law Secure Women's Rights to Land in Africa? Revisiting Tensions Between Culture and Land Commercialization' (2018) 20(1) Feminist Economics 155

Ossome L, 'Land in transition: from social reproduction of labour power to social reproduction of power' (2021) 39(4) Journal of Contemporary African Studies 550

Ossome L, 'The care economy and the state in Africa's Covid-19 responses' (2021) 42 (1) Canadian Journal of Development Studies/Revue canadienne d'études du développement 68

Ossome L, 'Pedagogies of Feminist Resistance: Agrarian Movements in Africa' (2021) 10(1) Agrarian South: Journal of Political Economy 41

OTP, 'Policy Paper on Victims' Participation' (2010) https://www.icc-cpi.int/iccdocs/otp/Policy_Paper_on_Victims_Participation_April_2010.pdf (accessed 4 March 2022)

OTP, 'Policy Paper on Sexual and Gender-Based Crimes' (June 2014) https://www.icc-cpi.int/sites/default/files/iccdocs/otp/Policy_Paper_on_Sexual_and_Gender-Based_Crimes-20_June_2014-ENG.pdf (accessed 8 December 2022)

OTP, 'Policy on the Crime of Gender Persecution' (December 2022) https://www.icc-cpi.int/sites/default/files/2022-12/2022-12-07-Policy-on-the-Crime-of-Gender-Persecution.pdf (accessed 8 December 2022)

OTP, 'Strategic Plan 2023–2025' https://www.icc-cpi.int/sites/default/files/2023-06/OTP-Strategic-Plan_2023-2025.pdf (accessed 10 July 2023)

Otto A and Stevens M, 'Investor explains why he withdrew from East Madi Game Reserve Concession' *Uganda Radio Network* (15 September 2015) https://ugandaradionetwork.com/story/bruce-martin-speaks-out-on-east-madi-game-reserve- (accessed 30 March 2023)

Owiso O, 'Remuneration Debacle at the International Criminal Court: Should ICC Judges Get a Pay Rise?' *OpinioJuris* (23 November 2020) http://opiniojuris.org/2020/12/23/remuneration-debacle-at-the-international-criminal-court-should-icc-judges-get-a-pay-rise-part-i/ (accessed 29 November 2021)

Owor Ogora L, 'Ongwen trial screenings in Uganda: Lessons in making justice visible?' *Coalition for the International Criminal Court* (2017) http://www.coalitionfortheicc.org/news/20170119/ongwen-trial-screenings-uganda-lessons-making-justice-visible (accessed 9 March 2022)

Owor Ogora L, 'Victims of sexual and gender based violence crimes need special reparations' *International Justice Monitor* (3 July 2017) https://www.ijmonitor.org/2017/07/victims-of-sexual-and-gender-based-violence-crimes-need-special-reparations/ (accessed 10 March 2022)

Owor Ogora L, 'Northern Uganda is ready to accept and forgive Ongwen, says Acholi Prime Minister' *International Justice Monitor* (26 November 2019) https://www.ijmonitor.org/2019/11/northern-uganda-is-ready-to-accept-and-forgive-ongwen-says-acholi-prime-minister/ (accessed 24 April 2023)

Owor Ogora L, 'Communities in Northern Uganda optimistic for a timely judgment in Ongwen's case' *International Justice Monitor* (16 June 2020) https://www.ijmonitor.org/2020/06/communities-in-northern-uganda-optimistic-for-a-timely-judgment-in-ongwens-case/ (accessed 21 April 2022)

Owor Ogora L, 'Mixed reactions from Northern Uganda as ICC delivers judgment in Ongwen's case: Community members call for light sentence' *International Justice Monitor* (5 February 2021) https://www.ijmonitor.org/2021/02/mixed-reactions-from-northern-uganda-as-icc-delivers-judgment-in-ongwens-case-community-members-call-for-light-sentence/ (accessed 13 August 2023)

Owor A and Dieterle C, 'Customary land claims are at stake in northern Uganda' *LSE Blog* (7 April 2020) https://blogs.lse.ac.uk/africaatlse/2020/04/07/customary-land-claims-reform-unrecognised-in-northern-uganda/ (accessed 18 June 2022)

Oxford References, 'Political Unconscious' https://www.oxfordreference.com/display/10.1093/oi/authority.20110803100334787;jsessionid=41AE0DA5E0EB98A308E220BE30FC2FDD (accessed 2 April 2023)

Palmer N, 'Re-examining resistance in post-genocide Rwanda' (2014) 8(2) Journal of Eastern African Studies 231

Palmer N, *Courts in Conflict: Interpreting the Layers of Justice in Post-Genocide Rwanda* (OUP 2015)

Palmer N and Hamilton T, 'Legal Humility and Perceptions of Power in International Criminal Justice' (2022) 23(3) International Criminal Law Review 416

Pankhurst D, 'Introduction: Gendered war and peace' in Donna Pankhurst (ed), *Gendered Peace: Women's Struggles for Reconciliation and Justice* (Routledge 2008)

Parfitt R, *The Process of International Legal Reproduction: Inequality, Historiography, Resistance* (CUP 2019)

Parliament of the Republic of Uganda, 'Oulanyah preaches unity, productivity at Acholi cultural day' (16 December 2018) https://www.parliament.go.ug/news/3003/oulanyah-preaches-unity-productivity-acholi-cultural-day (accessed 5 June 2022)

Pemberton A and others, 'Coherence in International Criminal Justice: A Victimological Perspective' (2015) 15(2) International Criminal Law Review 339

Pena M, 'Victim Participation at the International Criminal Court: Achievements Made and Challenges Lying Ahead' (2009) 16 ILSA Journal of International and Comparative Law 497

Pena M, 'The role of intermediaries and third parties in victim participation' in Tibori-Szabo K and Hirst M (eds), *Victim Participation in International Criminal Justice: Practitioners' Guide* (TMC Asser Press 2017) 81

Pena M and Gaelle Carayon G, 'Is the ICC Making the Most of Victim Participation?' (2013) 7(3) International Journal of Transitional Justice 518

Perez-Leon-Acevedo JP, 'Victims and appeals at the International Criminal Court (ICC): evaluation under international human rights standards' (2021) 25(9) The International Journal of Human Rights 1598

Peskin V, 'Courting Rwanda: The Promises and Pitfalls of the ICTR Outreach Programme' (2005) 3 Journal of International Criminal Justice 950

PILPG, 'Expert Roundtable: The Ongwen Case' (24 March 2021) https://www.publicinternationallawandpolicygroup.org/ongwen-case-roundtable (accessed 23 January 2022)

Po-Keung H, 'Comprador politics and middleman capitalism' in Ngo TW (ed), *Hong Kong's History: State and Society under Colonial Rule* (Routledge 1999) 30

Porter H, 'Justice and Rape on the Periphery: The Supremacy of Social Harmony in the Space between Local Solutions and Formal Judicial Systems in Northern Uganda' (2012) 6 Journal of Eastern African Studies 81

Porter H, *After Rape: Violence, Justice and Social Harmony in Uganda* (CUP 2016)

Poulantzas N, *Classes in Contemporary Capitalism* (Verso 1978)

Price JM, *Prison and Social Death* (Rutgers UP 2015)

Profitt NJ, '"Battered Women" as "Victims" and "Survivors": Creating Space for Resistance' (1996) 13(1) Canadian Social Work Review/Revue Canadienne de Service Social 23

Prosecutor v Al-Basir (Request to the Republic of Belarus for Cooperation in the Arrest and Surrender of Omar Hassan Ahmad Al-Bashir') [2018] ICC-02/05-01/09-395

Prosecutor v Banda and Jerbo (Defence Application to restrain legal representatives for the victims a/1646/10 & a/1647/10 from acting in proceedings and for an order excluding the involvement of specified intermediaries) 2010 ICC-02/05-03/09-113

Prosecutor v Bemba (Decision on Sentence pursuant to Article 76 of the Statute) [2016] ICC-01/05-01/08-3399

Prosecutor v Katanga (Queen's University Belfast's Human Rights Centre (HRC) and University of Ulster's Transitional Justice Institute (TJI) Submission on Reparations Issues pursuant to Article 75 of the Statute) [2015] ICC-01/04-01/07-3551

Prosecutor v Katanga (United Nations Joint Submission on Reparations) 2015 ICC-01/04-01/07-3550

Prosecutor v Katanga (Order for Reparations pursuant to Article 75 of the Statute) [2017] ICC-01/04-01/07-3728-tENG

Prosecutor v Lubanga (Judgment on victim participation in the investigation stage of the proceedings in the appeal of the OPCD against the decision of Pre-Trial Chamber I of 7 December 2007 and in the appeals of the OPCD and the Prosecutor against the decision of Pre-Trial Chamber I of 24 December 2007) [2008] ICC-01/04-556

Prosecutor v Lubanga (Transcript) [2010] ICC-01/04-01/06-T-236-Red2-ENG

Prosecutor v Lubanga (Prosecution's Submissions in Response to Trial Chamber's Oral Request of 10 February 2010) [2010] ICC-01/04-01/06-2310-Red

Prosecutor v Lubanga (Redacted Decision on Intermediaries) 2010 ICC-01/04-01/06-2434-Red2

Prosecutor v Lubanga (Redacted Decision on the 'Defence Application Seeking a Permanent Stay of the Proceedings') [2011] ICC-01/04-01/06-2690-Red2

Prosecutor v Lubanga (Second Report of the Registry on Reparations) [2011] ICC-01/04-01/06-2806

Prosecutor v Lubanga (Trust Fund for Victims' First Report on Reparations) 2011 ICC-01/04-01/06-2803-Red

Prosecutor v Lubanga (Observations on Reparations in Response to the Scheduling Order of 14 March 2012) [2012] ICC-01/04-01/06-2872

Prosecutor v Lubanga (Consultant's report on reparations in the Inter-American Human Rights System, Annex to the Second Report of the Registry on Reparations) [2012] ICC-01/04-01/06-2806-Anx

Prosecutor v Lubanga (Observations of the Women's Initiatives for Gender Justice on Reparations) [2012] ICC-01/04-01/06-2876

Prosecutor v Lubanga (Decision establishing the principles and procedures to be applied to reparations) [2012] ICC-01/04-01/06-2904

Prosecutor v Lubanga (Judgment pursuant to Article 74 of the Statute) [2012] ICC-01/04-01/06-2842

Prosecutor v Lubanga (Judgment on the appeals against the 'Decision establishing the principles and procedures to be applied to reparations' of 7 August 2012 with AMENDED order for reparations (Annex A) and public annexes 1 and 2) [2015] ICC-01/04-01/06-3129

Prosecutor v Lubanga (Order for Reparations amended) [2015] (ICC-01/04-01/06-3129-AnxA)

Prosecutor v Lubanga (Draft Implementation Plan for collective reparations to victims Submitted to the Amended Reparations Order of 3 March 2015 in the case against Thomas Lubanga Dyilo) [2015] ICC-01/04-01/06-3177-AnxA

Prosecutor v Lubanga (Annex A: Collective Reparations projects in relation to the conviction of Thomas Lubanga Dyilo before the International Criminal Court) [2017] ICC-01/04-01/06-3273-AnxA

Prosecutor v Lubanga (Separate Opinion of Judge Del Carmen Ibáñez Carranza) [2019] ICC-01/04-01/06-3466-AnxII

Prosecutor v Ntaganda (Registry Observations in compliance with the Decision ICC-01/04-02/06-54-Conf) [2013] ICC-01/04-02/06-57

Prosecutor v Ntaganda (Decision Establishing Principles on the Victims' Application Process) [2013] ICC-01/04-02/06-67

Prosecutor v Ntaganda (Reparations Order) [2021] ICC-01/04-02/06-2659

Prosecutor v Ntaganda (Judgment on the appeals against the decision of Trial Chamber VI of 8 March 2021 entitled 'Reparations Order') [2022] ICC-01/04-02/06-2782

Prosecutor v Ongwen (Annex I Public Registry Report on the Mapping Exercise) 2012 ICC-02/04-01/15-1919-AnxI

Prosecutor v Ongwen (Public redacted version of 'Report of the Registry on the outreach mission' (9 April 2015) ICC-02/04-01/15-218-Conf-Exp) [2015] ICC-02/04-01/15-218-Red

Prosecutor v Ongwen (First Report on Applications to Participate in the Proceedings ICC) [2015] ICC-02/04-01/15-303

Prosecutor v Ongwen (Decision on contested victims' applications for participation, legal representation of victims and their procedural rights) [2015] ICC-02/04-01/15-350

Prosecutor v Ongwen ('Public Redacted Version of 'Defence Appeal Brief Against the Convictions in the Judgment of 4 February 2021', filed on 21 July 2021 as ICC-02/04-01/15-1866-Conf) [2021] ICC-02/04-01/15-1866-Red

Prosecutor v Ongwen (Registry Submission on Reparations in the *Ongwen* Case) [2021] ICC-02/04-01/15-1919-AnxII

Prosecutor v Ongwen (Trust Fund for Victims' Observations relevant to Reparations) [2021] ICC-02/04-01/15-1920

Prosecutor v Ongwen (Victims' Preliminary Submissions on Reparations) 2021 ICC-02/04-01/15-1921

Prosecutor v Ongwen (Public redacted version of document No. ICC-02/04-01/15-1923-Conf with public annexes 1 to 5) [2021] ICC-02/04-01/15-1923-Red

Prosecutor v Ongwen (Amicus Curiae brief pursuant to article 75 of the Statute and Rule 103 of the Rules of Procedure and Evidence) [2022] ICC-02/04-01/15-1971

Prosecutor v Ongwen (Trust Fund for Victims' Final Observations on Reparations) [2022] ICC-02/04-01/15-1992

Prosecutor v Ruto and Sang (Amicus Curiae Observations of Kituo Cha Sheria pursuant to Rule 103 of the Rules of Procedure and Evidence) [2012] ICC-01/09-01/11-478

Prosecutor v Ruto and Sang (Decision on victims' representation and participation) [2012] ICC-01/09-01/11-460

Prosecutor v Ruto and Sang (Common Legal Representative for Victims' Comprehensive Report on the Withdrawal of Victims from the Turbo area by Letter dated 5 June 2013) 2013 ICC-01/09-01/11-896-Corr-Red

Prosecutor v Ruto and Sang (Public redacted version of 'Ruto defence request to appoint an amicus prosecutor') [2016] ICC-01/09-01/11-2028-Red

Prosecutor v Muthaura and Kenyatta (Decision on victims' representation and participation) [2012] ICC-01/09-02/11-498

Prosecutor v Kenyatta (Dissenting Opinion of Judge Eboe-Osuji) [2016 ICC-01/09-01/11-2038-Anx

'Raising Voices: Preventing Violence against Women & Children' https://raisingvoices.org/women/sasa-approach/ (accessed 14 November 2021)

Ranger T, 'The invention of tradition in colonial Africa' in Hobsbawm E and Ranger T (eds), *The Invention of Tradition* (CUP 1983) 211

Rao R, 'Global homocapitalism' (2015) 194 Radical Philosophy 38

Rauschenbach M and Scalia D, 'Victims and International Criminal Justice: A Vexed Question?' (2008) 90 International Review of the Red Cross 441

Regina Rauxloh, 'Good intentions and bad consequences: The general assistance mandate of the Trust Fund for Victims of the ICC' (2021) 34 (1) Leiden Journal of International Law 203

Redress, 'The Participation of Victims in International Criminal Court Proceedings' (2012) https://redress.org/wp-content/uploads/2017/12/121030participation_report.pdf (accessed 9 April 2023)

Redress, 'Independent Panel of experts report on victim participation at the International Criminal Court' (2013) https://redress.org/wp-content/uploads/2017/12/July-Independent-Panel-of-experts-report-on-victim-participation-at-the.pdf (accessed 11 April 2023)

Redress, 'Comments to the Trust Fund for Victims on its Draft Strategic Plan 2014–17' (2014) https://redress.org/wp-content/uploads/2017/12/May-14-REDRESS-Comments-on-the-draft-strategic-plan-of-the-ICC-Trust-Fund-for-Victims.pdf (accessed 16 April 2023)

Redress, 'Webinar: Victim Participation and Reparations at the ICC: Assessing the Impact of the IER' (*YouTube* (8 December 2020) https://www.youtube.com/watch?v=kcbYcmMe-T4 (accessed 25 October 2021)

Redress, 'At Long Last: Reparations for Victims can now proceed in the ICC's first case' (3 March 2015) http://www.redress.org/downloads/pr-lubanga-reparations-appeals-decision030315.pdf (accessed 31 March 2023)

Redress, 'No Time to Wait: Realising Reparations for Victims before the International Criminal Court' (2019) https://redress.org/publication/no-time-to-wait-realising-reparations-for-victims-before-the-international-criminal-court/#:~:text=Landmarks%20Half%20Marathon-,No%20Time%20to%20Wait%3A%20Realising%20Reparations%20for%20Victims%20before%20the,enshrined%20in%20its%20legal%20texts (accessed 12 January 2022)

Refugee Law Project, 'Gender against men' (2009) https://www.youtube.com/watch?v=mJSl99HQYXc (accessed 16 April 2023)

Refugee Law Project, 'Shoot us all Down: The Lakang & Apaa Land Conflict' https://www.youtube.com/watch?v=2IJUP4xuHp8 (accessed 16 April 2023)

Refugee Law Project, 'Ongwen's Justice Dilemma Part II' (2016) https://www.refugeelawproject.org/files/others/Ongwen_Justice_Dilemma_II.pdf (accessed 20 April 2022)

Regulations of the Trust Fund for Victims, Resolution ICC-ASP/4/Res.3 (3 December 2005)

Rehmann J, *Theories of Ideology: The Powers of Alienation and Subjection* (Brill 2013)

Reisman T, 'Q & A with International Criminal Court Registrar Herman von Hebel: Part I' *International Justice Monitor* (21 August 2013) https://www.ijmonitor.org/2013/08/q-a-with-international-criminal-court-registrar-herman-von-hebel-part-i/ (accessed 30 March 2023)

'Report of the Special Rapporteur on Violence against Women, its Causes and Consequences, Rashida Manjoo', A/HRC/14/22 (19 April 2010)

Republic of Uganda, 'National Financial Inclusion Strategy 2017–2022' (October 2017) https://www.bou.or.ug/bou/bouwebsite/bouwebsitecontent/publications/special_pubs/2017/National-Financial-Inclusion-Strategy.pdf (accessed 24 December 2022)

—— 'The Peace Recovery Development Plan 3 for Northern Uganda July 2015: June 2021' (August 2015)

Reynolds J and Xavier S, '"The Dark Corners of the World": TWAIL and International Criminal Justice' (2016) 14(4) JICJ 959

Ring KL, 'The Evolution of the Procedure for Reviewing Victim Applications at the International Criminal Court' (2023) 21(1) JICJ 29

Risse T, '"Let's Argue!": Communicative Action in World Politics' (2000) 54(1) International Organization 1

Richie BE, *Arrested Justice: Black Women, Violence, and America's Prison Nation* (New York UP 2012)

Robinson CJ, *Black Marxism: The Making of the Black Radical Tradition* (Penguin 2020)

Robinson D, 'Serving the Interests of Justice: Amnesties, Truth Commissions and the International Criminal Court' (2003) 14 EJIL 481

Robinson D, 'The Identity Crisis of International Criminal Law' (2008) 21 Leiden Journal of International Law 925

Robinson D, 'Inescapable Dyads: Why the International Criminal Court Cannot Win' (2015) 28(2) Leiden Journal of International Law 323

Rock P, *Constructing Victims' Rights* (OUP 2004)

Rock P, 'Theoretical perspectives on victimisation' in Sandra Walklate (ed), *Handbook of Victims and Victimology* (1st edn, Routledge 2007)

Rodney W, *How Europe underdeveloped Africa* (Verso 2018)

Rogers RJ, 'Assessment of the ICC's Legal Aid System' *Global Diligence* (5 January 2017)

Rojas C, Kim M, and Bierria A, 'Community Accountability: Emerging Movements to Transform Violence' (2012) 37(4) Social Justice 1

Rose J, *Mothers: An Essay on Love and Cruelty* (Faber & Faber 2018)

Rubio-Marín R and Sandoval C, 'Engendering the Reparations Jurisprudence of the Inter-American Court of Human Rights: The Promise of the Cotton Field Judgment' (2011) 33 Human Rights Quarterly 1062

Rusche G and Kirchheimer O, *Punishment and Social Structure* (Columbia UP 1939)

Saferworld, 'Promoting Conflict-Sensitive Approaches in Amuru District, Northern Uganda' (2015) https://www.saferworld.org.uk/resources/publications/896-promoting-conflict-sensitive-development-in-northern-uganda (accessed 16 April 2023)

Safferling C and Petrossian G, *Victims Before the International Criminal Court: Definition, Participation, Reparation* (Springer 2021)

Salehi M, 'Trying Just Enough or Promising Too Much? The Problem-Capacity-Nexus in Tunisia's Transitional Justice Process' (2022) 16 (1) Journal of Intervention and Statebuilding 98

Salih, Zeinab Mohammed and Oliver Holmes, 'Sudan's ex-leader Omar al-Bashir being held in military hospital, says army' *The Guardian* (26 April 2023) https://www.theguardian.com/world/2023/apr/26/sudan-former-president-accused-of-genocide-may-be-free-after-prison-attack (accessed 6 August 2023)

Salmon P, *An Event Perhaps: A Biography of Jacques Derrida* (Verso 2020)

Sander B, 'We Need to Talk About Ongwen: The Plight of Victim-Perpetrators at the ICC' *Justice in Conflict* (19 April 2016) https://justiceinconflict.org/2016/04/19/we-need-to-talk-about-ongwen-the-plight-of-victim-perpetrators-at-the-icc/ (accessed 20 April 2022)

Sander B, *Doing Justice to History: Confronting the Past in International Criminal Courts* (OUP 2021)

Schomerus M, *The Lord's Resistance Army: Violence and Peacemaking in Africa* (CUP 2021)

Schulz P, 'Discussing community-based outreach activities by the International Criminal Tribunal for Rwanda' (2017) 11(2) Journal of Eastern African Studies 347

Schulz P, 'Research, relationships and reciprocity in Northern Uganda' *Open Democracy* (25 June 2019) https://www.opendemocracy.net/en/beyond-trafficking-and-slavery/research-relationships-and-reciprocity-northern-uganda/ (accessed 16 July 2022)

Schwöbel C, 'An Introduction' in Schwöbel C (ed), *Critical Approaches to International Criminal Law* (Routlegde 2014)

Schwöbel-Patel C, 'Spectacle in international criminal law: the fundraising image of victimhood' (2016) 4(2) London Review of International Law 247

Schwöbel-Patel C, The 'Ideal' Victim of International Criminal Law' (2018) 29(3) EJIL 703

Schwöbel-Patel C, 'Figuring Victims in International Criminal Justice: The Case of the Khmer Rouge Tribunal' (2020) 31(4) European Journal of International Law 1597

Schwöbel-Patel C, *Marketing Global Justice: The Political Economy of International Criminal Law* (CUP 2021)

Schwöbel-Patel C, 'A Brand New Justice' in Schwöbel-Patel C, *Marketing Global Justice: The Political Economy of International Criminal Law* (CUP 2021)

Schwöbel-Patel C, 'Symposium on 'Marketing Global Justice': A Letter on Kafka, Coca-Cola, and Vergès' *OpinioJuris* (11 May 2023) http://opiniojuris.org/2023/05/11/symposium-on-marketing-global-justice-a-letter-on-kafka-coca-cola-and-verges/ (accessed 24 July 2023)

Scott J, *The Moral Economy of the Peasant: Rebellion and Subsistence in Southeast Asia* (Yale UP 1976)

Scott J, *Weapons of the Weak: Everyday Forms of Peasant Resistance* (Yale UP 1985)

Shivji IG, *The Concept of Human Rights in Africa* (Codesria Book Series 1989)

Shivji IG, 'The Concept of "Working People"' (2017) 6(1) Agrarian South: Journal of Political Economy 1

Shklar JN, *Legalism* (Harvard UP 1964)

Sehmi A, 'Now that we have no voice, what will happen to us?': Experiences of Victim Participation in the Kenyatta Case' (2018) 16(3) JICJ 571

Seibel HD with Armstrong A, 'Reparations and Microfinance Schemes' in de Greiff P (ed), *The Handbook of Reparations* (OUP 2006)

Seigel M, *Violence Work: State Power and the Limits of Police* (Duke UP 2018)

Sesay M, 'Decolonization of Postcolonial Africa: A Structural Justice Project More Radical than Transitional Justice' (2022) 16(2) *International Journal of Transitional Justice* 254

Sexual Assault Centre of Edmonton (SACE), 'Understanding Transformative Justice and Restorative Justice' https://www.sace.ca/learn/transformative-restorative-justice/ (accessed 12 November 2021)

Sharp DN, 'What Would Satisfy Us? Taking Stock of Critical Approaches to Transitional Justice' (2019) 13(3) International Journal of Transitional Justice 570

Shaw R, Waldorf L, and Hazan P (eds), *Localizing Transitional Justice: Interventions and Priorities after Mass Violence* (Stanford UP 2010)

Sikkink K, *The Justice Cascade: How Human Rights Prosecutions are Changing World Politics* (WW Norton & Co 2011)

Simion K, *Rule of Law Intermediaries: Building Influence in Myanmar* (CUP 2021)

Simons M, 'In The Hague's lofty judicial halls, judges wrangle over pay' *The New York Times* (20 January 2019) https://www.nytimes.com/2019/01/20/world/europe/hague-judges-pay.html (accessed 21 April 2022)

Situation in the State of Palestine (Decision on Information and Outreach for the Victims of the Situation) [2018] ICC-01/18-2

Situation in the People's Republic of Bangladesh/Republic of the Union of Myanmar (Order on Information and Outreach for the Victims of the Situation) [2020] ICC-01/19-28

Situation in Afghanistan (Dissenting Opinion of Judge Luz del Carmen Ibáñez Carranza to the Majority's decision dismissing as inadmissible the victims' appeals against the decision rejecting the authorisation of an investigation into the situation in Afghanistan) [2020], ICC-02/17-137-Anx

Situation in the People's Republic of Bangladesh/Republic of the Union of Myanmar (Victims' joint request concerning hearings outside the host State) [2020] ICC-01/19-34

Smith A, 'The Color of Violence: Violence against Women of Color' (2001) 1(2) Meridians 65

Soederberg S, *Debtfare States and the Poverty Industry Money, Discipline and the Surplus Population* (Routledge 2014)

Sang-Hyun S, 'Speech: From Punishment to Prevention on the Future of International Criminal Justice' Wallace Wurth Memorial Lecture (14 February 2012) https://www.icc-cpi.int/Pages/item.aspx?name=14022012lecture (accessed 4 March 2022)

Sang-Hyun S, (The 2nd President of the ICC), 'Past Achievements and Future Challenges of the ICC keynote speech for the 20th Anniversary of the Rome Statute' (17 July 2018) https://www.icc-cpi.int/sites/default/files/itemsDocuments/20a-ceremony/20180717-sang-speech.pdf (accessed 27 March 2023)

Spencer ME, 'Weber on Legitimate Norms and Authority' (1970) 21(2) The British Journal of Sociology 123

Sperfeldt C, *Practices of Reparations in International Criminal Justice* (CUP 2022)

Spiga V, 'Indirect Victims' Participation in the *Lubanga* Trial' (2010) 8(1) JICJ 1

Spivak GC, 'Can the subaltern speak?' in Patrick Williams and Laura Chrisman (eds), *Colonial Discourse and Postcolonial Theory: A Reader* (Columbia UP 1994)

Srinivasan A, *The Right to Sex* (Bloomsbury Publishing PLC 2021)

Stahn C, 'Between 'Faith' and 'Facts': By What Standards Should We Assess International Criminal Justice?' (2012) 25(2) Leiden Journal of International Law 251

Stahn C, 'Justice civilisatrice? The ICC, post-colonial theory, and faces of "the local"' in de Vos C, Kendall S, and Stahn C (eds), *Contested Justice: The Politics and Practice of International Criminal Court Interventions* (CUP 2015) 46

Stahn C, *A Critical Introduction to International Criminal Law* (CUP 2018)

Stahn C, 'Reparative Justice after the Lubanga Appeal Judgment: New Prospects for Expressivism and Participatory Justice or 'Juridified Victimhood' by Other Means?' (2015) 13(4) JICJ 801

Stahn C, 'Confronting Colonial Amnesia: Towards New Relational Engagement with Colonial Injustice and Cultural Colonial Objects' (2020) 18(4) JICJ 793

Stahn C, *Justice as Message: Expressivist Foundations of International Criminal Justice* (OUP 2020)

Stevens B, *The Prosecutor* (Movie) (2011)

Stolk S and Werner W, 'Moving images: Modes of representation and images of victimhood in audio-visual productions' in Heller K and others (eds), *The Oxford Handbook of International Criminal Law* (OUP 2020) 583

'Stop Ecocide Campaign' https://www.stopecocide.earth (accessed 2 April 2023)

Strang H and Sherman L, 'Repairing the Harm: Victims and Restorative Justice' (2003) 15 Utah Law Review 15

Suchman MC, 'Managing Legitimacy: Strategic and Institutional Approaches' (1995) 20 The Academy of Management Review 571

Sukarieh M and Tannock S, 'Subcontracting Academia: Alienation, Exploitation and Disillusionment in the UK Overseas Syrian Refugee Research Industry' (2019) 51(2) Antipode 664

Szabo J, 'How much money do World Trade Center victims get?' *Top Class Actions* (26 May 2021) https://topclassactions.com/lawsuit-settlements/medical-problems/cancer-medical-problems/how-much-money-do-world-trade-center-victims-get/ (accessed 23 January 2022)

Tallgren I, 'The Sensibility and Sense of International Criminal Law' (2002) 13 EJIL 561

Tallgren I, 'The Voice of the International: Who is Speaking?' (2015) 13(1) JICJ 135

Tallgren I and Skouteris T, 'Editors' Introduction' in Tallgren I and Skouteris T (eds), *The New Histories of International Criminal Law: Retrials* (OUP 2019)

Tamale S, 'Nudity, Protest and the Law in Uganda' (2019) 22 Feminist Africa 52

Tamale S, *Decolonization and Afro-Feminism* (Daraja Press 2020)

Tapscott R, 'Naked protest: how ordinary citizens reveal truth to repressive regimes' *The Conversation* (14 May 2020) https://theconversation.com/naked-protest-how-ordinary-citizens-reveal-truth-to-repressive-regimes-134253 (accessed 30 May 2022)

Taylor L, 'Naked force meets naked resistance in northern Uganda land conflict' *Reuters* (24 November 2017) https://news.trust.org/item/20171124130614-o29zt/ (accessed 30 March 2023)

Taylor L, 'The Eighteenth Brumaire of Yoweri Museveni' *Roape* (27 July 2021) https://roape.net/2021/07/27/the-eighteenth-brumaire-of-yoweri-museveni/ (accessed 27 November 2021)

Thambinathan V and Kinsella EA, 'Decolonizing Methodologies in Qualitative Research: Creating Spaces for Transformative Praxis' (2021) 20 International Journal of Qualitative Methods 1

The Office of Public Counsel for Victims, *Representing Victims before the International Criminal Court: A Manual for Legal Representatives* (2nd edn, 2012)

The UK Supreme Court, 'Moving Education and Outreach Online' https://www.supremecourt.uk/news/moving-education-and-outreach-online.html (accessed 2 January 2023)

Teitel R, *Transitional Justice* (OUP 2000)

Teitel R, 'Transitional Justice Genealogy' (2003) 16 Harvard Humanitarian Rights Journal 69

Tenove C, 'International Justice for Victims? Assessing the International Criminal Court from the Perspective of Victims in Kenya and Uganda' Africa Portal (September 2013) https://www.researchgate.net/publication/320386086_International_Justice_for_Victims_Assessing_the_International_Criminal_Court_from_Victims%27_Perspectives_in_Kenya_and_Uganda (accessed 16 April 2023)

Terdiman R, 'Translator's introduction' in Bourdieu P, 'The Force of Law: Toward a Sociology of the Juridical Field' (1987) 38 The Hastings Law Journal 805

Terwiel A, 'What Is Carceral Feminism?' (2020) 48(4) Political Theory 421

Therborn G, *The Ideology of Power and the Power of Ideology* (Verso 1980)

Thompson EP, *The Making of the English Working Class* (Pelican Books 1968)

Thompson EP, 'The Moral Economy of the English Crowd in the Eighteenth Century' (1971) 50 Past & Present 76

TFV, 'Background Summary' (2008) https://www.icc-cpi.int/sites/default/files/NR/rdonlyres/E582AE21-D718-4798-97ED-C6C9F0D9B42D/0/TFV_Background_Summary_Eng.pdf (accessed 2 January 2023)

TFV, 'Decisions taken by the Board of Directors of the Trust Fund for Victims, January to July 2021' (5 October 2021) https://www.trustfundforvictims.org/en/news/decisions-taken-board-directors-trust-fund-victims-january-july-2021 (accessed 12 November 2021)

TFV, 'Highlights of Trust Fund for Victims Activities, Q3 2022 (1 July–30 September 2022)' https://www.trustfundforvictims.org/sites/default/files/reports/Highlights%20of%20Trust%20Fund%20for%20Victims%20Activities%2C%20Q3%202022%20%2801%20July%20-%2030%20September%202022%29.pdf (accessed 15 March 2023)

TFV, 'Management Brief Q3/2021 (1 July–30 September 2021)' https://www.trustfundforvictims.org/sites/default/files/reports/TFV%20Management%20Brief%20Q3_2021_ENG.pdf (accessed 13 August 2023)

TFV, Management Brief Q2/2021 (1 April–30 June 2021) https://www.trustfundforvictims.org/sites/default/files/reports/TFV%20Management%20Brief%20Q2%202021_0.pdf (accessed 15 March 2023)

TFV, 'Material Support' https://www.trustfundforvictims.org/en/what-we-do/assistance-programmes/material-support (accessed 13 March 2022)

TFV, 'Mobilising Resources and Supporting the Most Vulnerable Victims through Earmarked Funding, Programme Progress Report Winter' (2012) https://www.trustfundforvictims.org/sites/default/files/reports/TFV%20Programme%20Progress%20Report%20-%20Winter%202012.pdf (accessed 11 April 2023)

TFV, 'Empowering Victims and Communities towards Social Change' (2012) http://www.trustfundforvictims.org/sites/default/files/imce/TFV%20PPR%20Summer%202012%20ENG%20Final_.pdf (accessed 16 April 2023)

TFV, 'A Road to Recovery: Healing, Empowerment and Reconciliation' (2014) https://www.trustfundforvictims.org/sites/default/files/reports/TFV%20Programme%20Progress%20Report%20%20-%20Winter%202014.pdf accessed 13 March 2020

TFV, 'Programme Progress Report Summer' (2014) https://www.trustfundforvictims.org/sites/default/files/reports/TFV%20Programme%20Progress%20Report%20-%20Summer%202014.pdf (accessed 16 April 2023)

TFV, 'Assistance & Reparations Achievements, Lessons Learned, and Transitioning' (2015) https://www.trustfundforvictims.org/sites/default/files/reports/TFV%20Programme%20Progress%20Report%202015.pdf (accessed 16 April 2023)

TFV, 'Press Release: On International Women's Day 2021 the TFV calls for renewed commitment to the most vulnerable women and girls' (8 March 2021) https://www.trustfundforvictims.org/en/news/international-women%E2%80%99s-day-2021-tfv-calls-renewed-commitment-most-vulnerable-women-and-girls (accessed 2 January 2023)

TFV, 'Trust Fund for Victims calls for contributions to provide reparations to victims of conflict-related sexual violence' (13 March 2023) https://www.trustfundforvictims.org/index.php/en/news/trust-fund-victims-calls-contributions-provide%C2%A0reparations-victims-conflict-related-sexual (accessed 14 March 2023)

TFV, 'Promoting income generating activities', https://www.trustfundforvictims.org/en/about/our-impact/income-generating-activities (accessed 23 April 2022)

TFV, 'Victims Voices' https://www.trustfundforvictims.org/en/victims-voices (accessed 30 March 2022)

TFV, 'Mary (Northern Uganda)' https://www.trustfundforvictims.org/en/stories/mary-northern-uganda (accessed 30 March 2022)

TFV, 'Marie (Democratic Republic of Congo)' https://www.trustfundforvictims.org/en/stories/marie-democratic-republic-of-congo (accessed 30 March 2022)

TFV, 'Salima (Democratic Republic of Congo)' https://www.trustfundforvictims.org/en/stories/salima-democratic-republic-of-congo (accessed 30 March 2022)

TFV, 'Cissy (Democratic Republic of Congo)' https://www.trustfundforvictims.org/en/stories/cissy-democratic-republic-of-congo (accessed 30 March 2022)

TFV Global Strategic Plan 2009–2012 (2008)

TFV Strategic Plan 2014–2017 https://www.trustfundforvictims.org/sites/default/files/imce/1408%20TFV%20Strategic%20Plan%202014-2017%20Final%20ENG.pdf (accessed 16 April 2023)

TFV Strategic Plan 2020–2021 https://www.trustfundforvictims.org/sites/default/files/reports/TFV%20Strategic%20Plan%202020-2021.pdf (accessed 15 March 2023)

TFV Strategic Plan 2023–2025 https://www.trustfundforvictims.org/sites/default/files/reports/Draft%20TFV%20Strategic%20Plan%202023-2025.pdf (accessed 15 March 2023)

TFV Website https://www.icc-cpi.int/tfv (accessed 13 March 2022)

The Independent, 'Speaker urges finance minister to resolve challenges slowing saving groups' (1 December 2022) https://www.independent.co.ug/speaker-urges-finance-minister-to-resolve-challenges-slowing-saving-groups/ (accessed 24 December 2022)

Thomson S, 'Whispering truth to power: The everyday resistance of Rwandan peasants to post-genocide reconciliation' (2011) 110(40) African Affairs 439

Transnational Justice Project, 'After the verdict: Dominic Ongwen & the many sides of justice' *YouTube* (8 June 2021) https://www.youtube.com/watch?v=y9biRu5YHCs (accessed 12 January 2022)

Tripp AM, 'Women's Movements, Customary Law, and Land Rights in Africa: The Case of Uganda' (2004) (Spring) African Studies Quarterly 1

Trumbull CP, 'The Victims of Victim Participation in International Criminal Proceedings' (2007) 29 Michigan Journal of International Law 777

Tuck E and Wayne Yang K, 'Decolonization is not a metaphor' (2012) 1(1) Decolonization: Indigeneity, Education & Society 1

Tuhiwai Smith L, *Decolonizing Methodologies: Research and Indigenous Peoples* (Zed Books 2012)

Tumwesige A, 'Charges on land sale illegal: Acholi prime minister' *New Vision* (4 February 2018) https://www.newvision.co.ug/new_vision/news/1470415/charges-land-sale-illegal-acholi-prime-minister (accessed 14 June 2022)

Tyler TT, 'Social Justice: Outcome and Procedure' (2000) 35 International Journal of Psychology 117

Tyner J, *Dead Labor: Toward a Political Economy of Premature Death* (University of Minnesota Press 2019)

Tzouvala N, *Capitalism as Civilisation: A History of International Law* (CUP 2020)

Ugandan Monitor, 'Wake up and work: Museveni' (11 January 2019) https://www.monitor.co.ug/uganda/news/national/wake-up-and-work-museveni-1800110 (accessed 18 June 2022)

Ullrich L, 'Schizophrenic Justice: Exploring 'Justice for Victims' at the International Criminal Court (ICC)' (2016) University of Oxford https://ora.ox.ac.uk/objects/uuid:8d73d52b-9cd6-4d06-b613-69b0827aa03e (accessed 16 July 2022)

Ullrich L, 'Doing gender justice in northern Uganda' *Open Democracy* (23 July 2015) https://www.opendemocracy.net/en/author/leila-ullrich/ (accessed 16 March 2023)

Ullrich L, 'Beyond the 'Global–Local Divide': Local Intermediaries, Victims and the Justice Contestations of the International Criminal Court' (2016) 14(3) Journal of International Criminal Justice 543

Ullrich L, ' "But what about men?" Gender disquiet in international criminal justice' (2021) 25(2) Theoretical Criminology 209

Ullrich L, 'Review of Kjersti Lohne: Advocates of Humanity: Human Rights NGOs in International Criminal Justice' (2021) 29 Feminist Legal Studies 283

UN General Assembly, 'Declaration of Basic Principles of Justice for Victims of Crime and Abuse of Power', UN Doc A/Res/40/34 (29 November 1985)

UN General Assembly, Resolution adopted by the General Assembly on 16 December 2005 (A/RES/60/147)

UN General Assembly, 'Basic Principles and Guidelines on the Right to a Remedy and Reparation for Victims of Gross Violations of International Human Rights Law and Serious Violations of International Humanitarian Law', UN Doc A/RES/60/147 (21 March 2006)

UN Women, 'Progress of the World's Women: In Pursuit of Justice' (2011) https://www.unwomen.org/en/digital-library/publications/2011/7/progress-of-the-world-s-women-in-pursuit-of-justice (accessed 14 April 2023)

Urban Walker M, 'Transformative Reparations? A Critical Look at a Current Trend in Thinking about Gender-Just Reparations' (2016) 10 IJTJ 108

USAID, 'Microfinance, Youth and Conflict: Central Uganda Case Study' (February 2006) https://www.marketlinks.org/sites/default/files/resource/files/ML3488_mr_38_mf__youth___conflict_central_uganda_case_study.pdf (accessed 24 December 2022)

Vasiliev S, 'Victim Participation Revisited: What the ICC is Learning about Itself' in Carsten Stahn (ed), *The Law and Practice of the International Criminal Court* (OUP 2016)

Vasiliev S, 'The crises and critiques of international criminal justice' in Heller K and others (eds), *The Oxford Handbook of International Criminal Law* (OUP 2020) 626

Vice News, 'Is the International Criminal Court racist?' *YouTube* (15 March 2021)

Victims' Rights Working Group, 'Speech by Fiona McKay on behalf of the Victims' Rights Working Group' (1998) http://www.vrwg.org/VRWG_DOC/1998_Flyer_speech.pdf accessed 10 August 2016

Victims' Rights Working Group, 'Comments on the Role and Relationship of 'Intermediaries' with the International Criminal Court' (2009) https://www.fidh.org/IMG/pdf/VRWG_Role_of_intermediaries_ICC_-_February_2009_En_.pdf (accessed 12 December 2022)

Victims' Rights Working Group, 'Recommendations to the 14th Session of the Assembly of States Parties' (2015) http://www.vrwg.org/downloads/2015asp14vrwgfinal.pdf (accessed 14 August 2016)

Vinck P and Pham PN, 'Transitioning to Peace: A Population-Based Survey on Attitudes about Social Reconstruction and Justice in Northern Uganda' (December 2010) https://www.law.berkeley.edu/files/HRC/Publications_Transitioning-to-Peace_12-2010.pdf (accessed 16 April 2023)

Vogel L, *Marxism and the Oppression of Women: Toward a Unitary Theory* (2nd edn, Brill 2013)

Vorhölter J, 'Youth as "identity entrepreneurs": emerging neoliberal subjectivities in Uganda' in Wiegratz J, Martiniello G, and Greco E (eds), *Uganda: The Dynamics of Neoliberal Transformation* (Zed Books 2018)

De Vos C, Kendall S, and Stahn C, 'Introduction' in de Vos C, Kendall S, and Stahn C (eds), *Contested Justice: The Politics and Practice of International Criminal Court Interventions* (CUP 2015)

De Vos C, *Complementarity, Catalysts, Compliance: The International Criminal Court in Uganda, Kenya, and the Democratic Republic of Congo* (CUP 2020)

VPRS, 'Victim's Booklet: Victims before the International Criminal Court: A guide for the participation of victims in the proceedings of the ICC' https://www.icc-cpi.int/sites/default/files/itemsDocuments/vprs/abd-al-rahman/VPRS-Victims-booklet_ENG.pdf (accessed 17 December 2022)

Van Wijk J, 'Who is the 'little old lady' of international crimes? Nils Christie's concept of the ideal victim reinterpreted' (2013) 19(2) International Review of Victimology 159

Vegh Weis V, *Marxism and Criminology: A History of Criminal Selectivity* (Brill 2013)

Vegh Weis V, 'A Marxist analysis of international criminal law and its potential as a counter-hegemonic project' in Jeßberger F, Steinl L, and Mehta K (eds), *International Criminal Law: A Counter-Hegemonic Project?* (TMC Asser Press 2023)

Walklate S, *Imagining the Victim of Crime* (McGraw-Hill Education 2006)

Walleyn L, 'The Participation of Victims in the Process of Collective Reparations at the ICC' in Jasini R and Townsend G, *Advancing the Impact of Victim Participation at the International Criminal Court: Bridging the Gap Between Research and Practice* (ESRC, OUP2020) https://www.law.ox.ac.uk/sites/files/oxlaw/iccba_-_oxford_publication_30_november_2020_.pdf (accessed 11 March 2022)

Weber M, *Law in Economy and Society* (Simon and Schuster [1954] 1967)

Weeks K, *Constituting Feminist Subjects* (Verso 2018)

weinformers1, 'Mato Oput Acholi Traditional Justice System' *YouTube* (17 April 2010) https://www.youtube.com/watch?v=eb2hnrkvRXA (accessed 30 July 2023)

Wemmers JA, Van der Leeden R, and Steensma H, 'What Is Procedural Justice: Criteria used by Dutch Victims to Assess the Fairness of Criminal Justice Procedures' (1995) 8 Social Justice Research 329

Wemmers JA, 'Victims' Rights and the International Criminal Court: Perceptions within the Court Regarding the Victims' Right to Participate' (2010) 23(3) Leiden Journal of International Law 629

Wheeler CH, 'Justice in the Absence of the Accused: Can the Rights of Victims be Fully Vindicated without the Participation of the Accused?' (2019) 17(2) JICJ 413

Whitman J, 'At the Origins of Law and the State: Monopolization of Violence, Mutilation of Bodies, or Fixing of Prices?' (1996) 71 Chicago-Kent Law Review 41

Wiegratz J, 'Fake capitalism? The dynamics of neoliberal moral restructuring and pseudo-development: the case of Uganda' (2010) 37(124) Review of African Political Economy 123

Wiegratz J, Martiniello G, and Greco E (eds), *Uganda: The Dynamics of Neoliberal Transformation* (Zed Books 2018)

Women's Initiative for Gender Justice, 'Trailblazing ICC Judgment on SGBC: Ongwen verdict advances international accountability for forced marriage and forced pregnancy' (4 February 2021) https://4genderjustice.org/trailblazing-icc-judgment-on-sgbc-ongwen-verdict/ (accessed 8 December 2022)

'Women's Strike: About' https://womenstrike.org.uk/about/ (accessed 13 August 2023)

Van den Wyngaert C, 'Victims Before International Criminal Courts: Some Views and Concerns of an ICC Trial Judge' (2012) 44 Case Western Reserve Journal of International Law 475

YouTube, 'MUSEVENI says even a fool can survive in Uganda unlike other countries' (2022) https://www.youtube.com/watch?v=uJMJLzecBgQ (accessed 4 January 2023)

Ypi L, 'Why the right's new strongmen are winning everywhere' *The Guardian* (16 March 2020) https://www.theguardian.com/commentisfree/2020/mar/16/right-new-strongmen-winning-everywhere-brazil-hungary-rightwing (accessed 23 October 2021)

Zappalà S, 'The Rights of Victims v. the Rights of the Accused' (2010) 8(1) JICJ 137
Zedner L, 'Reparation and Retribution: Are They Reconcilable?' (1994) 57 The Modern Law Review 228
Zegveld L, 'Victims as a Third Party: Empowerment of Victims?' (2019) 19(2) International Criminal Law Review 321
Zunino M, *Justice Framed: A Genealogy of Transitional Justice* (CUP 2019)

Interviews

Interviews and Informal Conversations at ICC, The Hague (2013–2014)

Interview with Legal Adviser, Trust Fund for Victims (23 October 2013)
Interview with Kenyan Lawyer, The Hague (28 October 2013)
Informal conversation with Senior Programme Manager, Trust Fund for Victims (31 October 2013)
Interview with Legal Officer, Registry (12 November 2013)
Interview with Appeals Counsel, Office of the Prosecutor (OTP) (13 November 2013)
Interview with Senior Official, Registry (18 November 2013)
Interview with Senior Official Registry (19 November 2013)
Interview with Senior Official, Trust Fund for Victims (22 November 2013)
Interview with Legal Representative for Victims (LRV) (24 November 2013)
Interview with Senior Official, OTP (29 November 2013)
Interview with Defence Counsel (4 December 2013)
Interview with Defence Counsel (4 December 2013)
Informal conversation with Victims' Lawyer (12 December 2013)
Interview with Senior Official, Registry (16 December 2013)
Interview with Judge (17 December 2013)
Interview with Judge (19 December 2013)
Interview with Legal Adviser, Presidency (8 January 2014)
Interview with Senior Legal Adviser, Chambers (8 January 2014)
Interview with Senior Official, Registry (10 January 2014)
Interview with Legal Adviser, Chambers (10 January 2014)
Interview with Judge (16 January 2014)
Interview with Legal Officer, Registry (21 January 2014)
Interview with Psychologist, OTP (22 January 2014)
Interview with Judge (30 January 2014)
Informal conversation with Legal Adviser, Presidency (31 January 2014)
Interview with Legal Officer, Registry (4 February 2014)
Interview with Judge (13 February 2014)

Interviews in Kenya (2014)

Interview with Civil Society Representative, Nairobi (19 June 2014)
Interview with ICC Outreach Coordinator, Nairobi (23 June 2014)
Interview with LRV Assistant, Nairobi (25 June (2014)
Interview with Civil Society Representative, Nairobi (25 June 2014)
Interview with LRV Assistant, Nairobi (30 June 2014)

Interview with LRV, Nairobi (1 July 2014)
Interview with Civil Society Representative, Nairobi (1 July 2014)
Interview with Civil Society Representative, Nairobi (2 July 2014)
Interview with Civil Society Representative, Nairobi (2 July 2014)
Interview with LRV Assistant, Nairobi (3 July 2014)
Interview with Consultant, Nairobi (4 July 2014)
Interview with Officer, Registry, Nairobi (12 August 2014)
Interview with Civil Society Representative, Nairobi (14 August 2014)
Interview with Victim-Intermediary, Migori (Western Kenya) (18 August 2014)
Interview with Victim-Intermediary, Kolweny (Western Kenya) (19 August 2014)
Interview with LRV Intermediary, Ahero (Western Kenya) (20 August 2014)
Interview with Civil Society Representative, Kisumu (21 August 2014)
Interview with Civil Society Representative, Kisumu (21 August 2014)
Interview with ICC Intermediary, Kisumu (21 August 2014)
Interview with LRV Intermediary, Vehica (Western Kenya) (22 August 2014)
Interview with LRV Intermediary, Vehica (Western Kenya) (22 August 2014)
Interview with ICC Intermediary, Kisumu (23 August 2014)
Interview with IDP Leader, Kisumu (25 August 2014)
Interview with ICC Intermediary, Kisumu (26 August 2014)
Interview with Outreach Intermediary, Kisumu (28 August 2014)
Interview with Civil Society Representative (30 August 2014)

Interviews in Uganda (2014)

Interview with TFV Officer, Kampala (7 July 2014)
Interview with former TFV Partner, Kampala (7 July 2014)
Informal conversation with TFV Partner, Kampala (9 July 2014)
Interview with TFV Partner, Gulu (9 July 2014)
Interview with TFV Partner, Gulu (10 July 2014)
Interview with former TFV Partner, Gulu (10 July 2014)
Interview with TFV Partner, Gulu (11 July 2014)
Interview with Religious Representative, Gulu (13 July 2014)
Interview with Civil Society Representative, Gulu (15 July 2014)
Interview with ICC Outreach Intermediary, Gulu (15 July 2014)
Interview with TFV Partner, Lira (16 July 2014)
Interview with TFV Partner, Lira (17 July 2014)
Interview with TFV Partner, Lira (17 July 2014)
Interview with TFV Partner, Lira (18 July 2014)
Interview with ICC Victim Intermediary, Lira (18 July 2014)
Informal conversation with TFV Partner Assistant, Lira, Northern Uganda (19 July 2014)
Interview with TFV Partner, Lira (20 July 2014)
Interview with Civil Society Representative, Kampala (22 July 2014)
Interview with ICC Registry Officer, Kampala (22 July 2014)
Interview with Civil Society Representative, Kampala (23 July 2014)
Interview with former ICC Intermediary, Kampala (28 July 2014)
Interview with Civil Society Representative, Kampala (29 July 2014)

Interview with Women's Rights Activist, Kampala (30 July 2014)
Interview with Civil Society Representative, Kampala (7 August 2014)

Telephone Interviews

Telephone Interview with Civil Society Representative (Uganda) (29 February 2012)
Telephone Interview with Civil Society Representative (Central African Republic) (10 March 2012)
Telephone Interview with Civil Society Representative (The Hague) (21 March 2013)
Telephone Interview with Civil Society Representative (Brussels) 30 March 2012)
Telephone Interview with Civil Society Representative (The Hague) 8 March 2013)
Telephone Interview with Civil Society Representative (The Hague) 27 March 2013)
Telephone Interview with Civil Society Representative (Uganda) (26 April 2013)
Telephone Interview with Civil Society Representative (The Hague) 3 July 2013)
Telephone Interview with Civil Society Officer (19 July 2013)
Telephone Interview with Legal Representative of Victims (4 November 2013)
Telephone Interview with Trust Fund for Victims (TFV) Evaluator (3 January 2014)
Telephone Interview with Legal Representative of Victims (15 January 2014)

Supportive Interviews for Contextualizing the Research

Email communication, 'Research Request' (4 December 2013)
Email communication with Head of Outreach Unit (1 May 2012)
Informal conversation with a Legal Officer who works at the ICTY, Oxford (1 December 2014)
Informal conversation with Legal Advisor, Presidency (31 January 2014)
Informal conversation with Study Investigator, Berkeley (August 2015)

Interviews in The Hague and London (2018)

Interview with Victims' Lawyer, London (10 September 2018)
Interview with OTP Representative (31 May 2018)
Interview with Legal Advisor, The Hague (1 June 2018)
Interview with Victims' Lawyer, The Hague (1 June 2018)
Interview with Victims' Lawyer, The Hague (1 June 2018)
Interview with Legal Officer, Registry, The Hague (1 June 2018)

Interviews Uganda (2019)

Interview with Victims' Lawyer Assistant, Kampala (9 July 2019)
Interview with Victims' Officer, Kampala (9 July 2019)
Interview with TFV Officer, Kampala (9 July 2019)
Interview with Victims' Lawyer, Kampala (10 July 2019)
Interview with NGO worker, Kampala (11 July 2019)
Interview with Former Intermediary, Kampala (11 July 2019)
Interview with NGO worker, Kampala (12 July 2019)
Interview with NGO representative, Gulu (16 July 2019)

Field Notes, ICC Community Outreach Event at St Monica Vocational School for Girls, Gulu, Northern Uganda (17 July 2019)
Informal conversation with Cultural Leader Assistant, Gulu (17 July 2019)
Interview with Field Assistant, Gulu (17 July 2019)
Interview with Outreach Officer, Gulu (17 July 2019)
Interview with NGO Worker, Gulu (18 July 2019)
Interview with NGO Representative, Gulu (18 July 2019)
Interview with Victims' Lawyer (18 July 2019)
Interview with Victims' Representative (19 July 2019)
Interview with Outreach Attendee (19 July 2019)
Interview with Cultural Leader, Gulu (20 July 2019)
Interview with Cultural Leader, Gulu (22 July 2019)
Interview with Religious Leader (22 July 2019)
Field notes, Gulu, Uganda (23 July 2019)
Interview with NGO worker (23 July 2019)
Interview with Women's Rights Lawyer, Gulu (24 July 2019)
Interview with Victim-Intermediary, Gulu (24 July 2019)
Teacher, Focus Group Discussion, Lukodi (25 July 2019)
Lukodi Focus Group Discussion, Gulu (25 July 2019)
Interview with Parish Chief, Lukodi (25 July 2019)
Interview with Victims' Representative (26 July 2019)
Interview with Survivor, Gulu (27 July 2019)
Interview with Healer, Gulu (29 July 2019)
Interview with Local TFV Partner (29 July 2019)
Interview with Local TFV Partner (30 July 2019)
Interview with Teacher, Gulu (30 July 2019)
Interview with Politician (1 August 2019)
Interview with NGO Representative, Kampala (1 August 2019)
Interview with ICC Outreach Staff, Kampala (2 August 2019)

Index

For the benefit of digital users, indexed terms that span two pages (e.g., 52–53) may, on occasion, appear on only one of those pages.

Figures and boxes are indicated by *t* and *b* following the page number